The publisher gratefully acknowledges the generous support of the Ahmanson Foundation Humanities Endowment Fund of the University of California Press Foundation.

Treatise on Musical Objects

CALIFORNIA STUDIES IN 20TH-CENTURY MUSIC

Richard Taruskin, General Editor

Treatise on Musical Objects

An Essay across Disciplines

Pierre Schaeffer

Translated by Christine North and John Dack

UNIVERSITY OF CALIFORNIA PRESS

University of California Press, one of the most distinguished university presses in the United States, enriches lives around the world by advancing scholarship in the humanities, social sciences, and natural sciences. Its activities are supported by the UC Press Foundation and by philanthropic contributions from individuals and institutions. For more information, visit www.ucpress.edu.

University of California Press
Oakland, California

A translation commissioned by the Groupe de recherches musicales of the National Audiovisual Institute of France (Ina-GRM) with an editorial team formed by: Marc Battier, Leigh Landy, Daniel Teruggi, and Valerie Vivancos.

Library of Congress Cataloging-in-Publication Data

Names: Schaeffer, Pierre, 1910–1995, author. | North, Christine, translator. | Dack, John, translator.
Title: Treatise on musical objects : an essay across disciplines / Pierre Schaeffer ; translated by Christine North and John Dack.
Other titles: Traité des objets musicaux. English
Description: Oakland, California : University of California Press, [2017] | Series: California studies in 20th-century music ; 20 | Includes bibliographical references and index.
Identifiers: LCCN 2016052008 (print) | LCCN 2016055109 (ebook) | ISBN 9780520294295 (cloth : alk. paper) | ISBN 9780520294301 (pbk. : alk. paper) | ISBN 9780520967465 (ebook)
Subjects: LCSH: Music—Philosophy and aesthetics.
Classification: LCC ML3800.S252 T713 (print) | LCC ML3800.S252 (ebook) | DDC 781.1—dc23
LC record available at https://lccn.loc.gov/2016052008

Manufactured in the United States of America

26 25 24 23 22 21 20 19 18 17
10 9 8 7 6 5 4 3 2 1

In memory of my violinist father,

whose precept was:

"Work at your instrument."

CONTENTS

THE *TREATISE ON MUSICAL OBJECTS* AND THE GRM

The *Traité des objets musicaux* was first published in 1966. It was the result of twenty years of experimentation and research by Pierre Schaeffer on sound and its relation to and impact on music. The inventor of *musique concrète*, Schaeffer pursued the quest of understanding how we listen and how our perception of sound determines what music is and how we listen to and enjoy it.

Schaeffer considered this book "untranslatable" owing to the complexity and novelty of the concepts, as well as to his understanding of the translation difficulties of the French language. Several attempts were made, in Portuguese (from Brazil),[1] Spanish,[2] and Dutch,[3] always based on an abridged version; however, the task of bringing it to English was still to be undertaken, even though musicians and musicologists around the world currently use many of his concepts. The *Traité*, or TOM as it is called in French, was written as a consequence of his work and discoveries while he was leader of the GRMC (Groupe de recherche en musique concrète), which he created in 1951, and the GRM (Groupe de recherches musicales), into which he transformed the initial group in 1958 in order to give to it a broader outreach than musique concrète. Since the GRM still exists today as a department of the French National Audiovisual Institute (Ina) and continues to promote and foster Schaeffer's ideas on sound and sound creation, it seemed appropriate for the GRM to undertake the translation of the *Treatise on Musical Objects*.

---

1. *Tratado dos objetos musicais*, trans. Ivo Martinazzo (Brasília: Edunb Editora Universidade de Brasília, 1993).

2. *Tratado de los objetos musicales*, trans. Araceli Cabezón de Diego (Madrid: Alianza Música, 1998).

3. *Traktaat van de muzikale objecten*, trans. by Konrad Boehmer (Beek Ubbergen: Tandem Felix, 2006).

The works and thoughts of Pierre Schaeffer have had a strong influence on musicians and musicologists, as well as on scientists; he challenged many preexisting concepts in the long tradition of musical craftsmanship and practice, and he challenged the way we listen and how our brain makes sense of audio phenomena. The reason for this radical change in the way of understanding musical phenomena was not based on science but on Schaeffer's experience with radio technology, when he studied how radio as a medium brought new ways of using the voice and the dramatic influence of recorded sounds on our perception. It was through experimentation that Pierre Schaeffer slowly built up a new understanding of how the listening process works and how sounds have the extraordinary capacity to create meaning for our minds through listening.

His main question was, What intrinsic difference is there between listening to an event happening in front of us and listening only to the sound produced by the same event? There was, indeed, a difference, but what was it, and how could it be analyzed? The initial point for Schaeffer was radio production, and particularly radio drama, a domain in which he started working in the early 1940s. Using recorded sounds to enhance the dramatic effects of voices, he slowly progressed toward a point where he started considering recorded sound as a musical element. Music has always been based on performance, which is the act by an individual of producing a specific sound with a musical function; this, however, limits the number of possible sounds for music since the sound produced has to be controllable and produced at a specific moment of the performance. The fact of using prerecorded sounds enlarges the sound possibilities for the orchestra and brings a new range of potential sounds into music. To prove the potential of recorded sounds, he started combining and assembling them in sound structures, which he called "études" or experiments on different types of sound sources and combinations. The result of these experiments he called *musique concrète*, defining through this expression the situation where, through concrete listening to sound material, the composer creates the musical structure, in opposition to traditional musical writing, in which the abstract creation of the composer on the score leads to the concrete listening situation of the performance.

While working on his musical *études*, Schaeffer started to understand the properties of sounds and the ease or difficulty of combining them depending on their spectral nature or their behavior through time; most of all, he understood the musical difficulty of dealing with sounds that strongly refer to their causal origin, for example the fact that a barking dog will be listened to with regard to its origin and behavior before being listened to as a potential musical source. This understanding brought two immediate conclusions: the first was that a conceptual framework was needed to deal with the complexity and diversity of sound; the second was that specific technological tools were needed to modify the physical structure or the behavior of sounds. One of Schaeffer's important contributions concerns his concept of typomorphology, indicating that a twofold approach should be taken in analyzing sounds: their "type," or spectral distribution, and their "morphology," or behavior through time. These ideas underlie the concept of spectromorphology, which was developed years later and became a powerful tool for sound analysis.[4]

This could have remained as the experimental approach of a musician-scientist, who then publishes his results and makes them available to the scientific community. But Pierre Schaeffer was both a radio and communications person, as well as a musician. He worked hard on the diffusion of his discoveries through writings, conferences, and his main medium: radio programs. He understood the need for an interdisciplinary approach to understand the phenomena and to push his ambition even further by creating structures within institutions that would deal with musique concrète, with research on perception and analysis of musical structures, and build tools for sound creation and transformation. Thus began one of the most unusual experiments of forming the Musical Research Group, which through different technological and institutional developments and modifications still exists. In 1960, based on the experience of the GRM and wishing to expand the experiment to the audiovisual domain, he created the Service de la Recherche (Research Department), bringing together the GRM, a newly created Group for Image Research (the GRI), the Technical Research Group (GRT), and the Critical Studies Group (GEC).[5] In 1975, when the National Radio and Television Office (ORTF) was split into different institutions and companies, he created the National Audiovisual Institute, which brought together archives, training, research, and the GRM. Pierre Schaeffer had the capacity to imagine and build original institutions with all the complexity this means in terms of convincing authorities and regulatory bodies, but most of all he had the incredible gift of bringing people from different domains to work together and collaborate toward a common aim. He once said that the GRM was an "impossible and necessary institution"; this probably sums up the whole of his vision and the strength of his action.

Today, sixty years after the first edition of the *Traité des objets musicaux* and almost seventy years after the first works of musique concrète, the GRM has not only continued the tradition of promoting the creation of new music based on recorded sounds or other technologies but has continuously put Schaeffer's ideas into practice, adapting them to new technological environments. Pierre Schaeffer was born in 1910 and died in 1995; his work has interested several generations of researchers and musicians and they concern all those who wish to understand music differently.

4. See Denis Smalley, "Spectromorphology: Explaining Sound-Shapes," *Organised Sound* 2, no. 2 (1997): 107–26.

5. Readers interested in the history of the GRM should see Évelyne Gayou, *Le groupe de recherches musicales: Cinquante ans d'histoire* (Paris: Fayard, 2007).

THE TRANSLATION OF THE *TRAITÉ DES OBJETS MUSICAUX*

Over the last twenty years, the GRM has felt the need for an English version of the *Traité des objets musicaux*. Schaeffer's ideas keep spreading, and scholars often work on his writings in French or mostly quote sentences and concepts from his work. It was clear from the beginning of the project in 2005 that this task was too long and complex for a single person. This is why, knowing their excellent work in translating Schaeffer's first book on musique concrète,[6] I contacted and met Christine North, former senior lecturer, Middlesex Polytechnic/University, and John Dack, musician and senior lecturer at Middlesex University, to talk about the project and a possible method of work. Furthermore, Christine and John had translated the *Guide des objets sonores*, a wonderful reference book written by Michel Chion in 1977 explaining Schaeffer's concepts and terms.[7] The idea was that they would take on the huge task of making the first translation of the book, and then a group of selected readers concerned with electroacoustic music, and familiar with Schaeffer's ideas, would read the book and comment on the English terms and sentences and propose a common approach and style to be used throughout the book. The GRM would finance the translation and costs of traveling for the meetings that would be necessary in the process.

The difficulty with the translation of the *Treatise* is the complexity of the language associated with new concepts and terms that already exist in French but that are not used in a musical context. Thus, a reading group was formed including both translators along with Marc Battier, a French composer and professor at the Paris Sorbonne University; Leigh Landy, an American composer and professor at the De Montfort University in Leicester; and myself, a composer and the director of the GRM. A sixth person was added on the second round of amendments: Valérie Vivancos, a musician and English translator who had some previous knowledge about Schaeffer and read the English version of the *Treatise*.

After the reading group had read the first translation, we held a three-day meeting in Paris, in September 2013, where we went through the terms, the style, and the meaning of a number of sentences. I have no hesitation in saying it was a tremendous meeting; we had so much to say and discuss, so many equivalent terms to find, so many sentences to discuss and understand. Without the initial translation process it would have been chaos! We left with agreements on terms, uses, and sentences that would need to be updated and amended.

6. Pierre Schaeffer, *A la recherche d'une musique concrète* (Paris: Seuil, 1952); Pierre Schaeffer, *In Search of a Concrete Music*, trans. Christine North and John Dack (Berkeley: University of California Press, 2012).

7. The English translation can be downloaded at www.iremus.cnrs.fr/fr/projets-de-recherche /electroacoustic-resource-site-ears.

We met again in September the following year, after Christine North and John Dack had incorporated many of the committee's suggestions, for a final reading of the book over three days, the committee this time including Valérie Vivancos. It proved to be a highly profitable meeting in which most issues were cleared, and by the end of the meeting we had produced a highly polished version, coherent in language and with an established vocabulary. We also decided to include a series of footnotes, which were needed to explain the origin of some words, to give details on events, or to explain who people named in the book are. Also the English references for the books mentioned by Schaeffer were added. After all our meetings and interesting discussions, one of the words that kept ringing in our ears as we searched for an English equivalent was *trame*, describing a continuous sound with some kind of permanent spectral structure. We translated it as *weft*, conscious that the English word *drone* used today in music also describes this kind of sound, however with a more harmonic perspective. The concept of *trame*, however, is closer to that of *weft* and retains the all-important imagery. We also took into account the language of the day, when these concepts were only beginning to take root.

The *Treatise* often speaks about technology in a period when computers were a distant dream in sound processing; often technological concepts are used that have to be understood within the technology of that period. There are some images in the book that are sound representations made with the technology of the 1960s; actually, they were very fine images and some of the first successful attempts to visualize sound. Many new ideas and concepts brought much novelty to musical thought and established musical research as a complex technical, philosophic, and semiotic action. The *Treatise on Musical Objects* explores all these domains and creates a coherent framework where disciplines collaborate and blend to propose a new understanding of music and humankind.

My special thanks to all the team who participated in this important work and to all those colleagues who worked with Schaeffer and contributed to the production of his unique work.

Daniel Teruggi

TRANSLATORS' INTRODUCTION

Theoretical works in French are notoriously difficult to translate into English, and Schaeffer's *Treatise on Musical Objects* is no exception. In fact, the six hundred pages of this book present more than the usual problems, as Schaeffer was attempting to outline a whole new theory of music and had to find the terminology to articulate the concepts and describe the phenomena on which it was based. He himself considered his work untranslatable; indeed, the task of producing the first translation into English was at first quite daunting.

We should say immediately that this is not intended to be a critical edition of the *Treatise*. Our aim is to give as accurate a translation of the original as possible in good academic English to be used as a foundation text by musicologists, students, and anyone interested in the history of music. One problem for a modern reader is that Schaeffer, in both editions of the *Traité*,[1] tended to give rather incomplete bibliographical references, rarely supplying page numbers for his quotations and often omitting details of publication. We have added what supplementary bibliographical information we have for some of these quotations, but where sources are extensive, obscure, or out of print, we have simply given the bibliographical details that appear in Schaeffer's original text.

A consequence of this is that, especially after such a lapse of time, it is difficult, even in the case of a French source, to know the full details of quotations and almost impossible, in the case of a work translated into French, to know which translation Schaeffer used. The difficulty is compounded by the fact that many of

---

1. Pierre Schaeffer, *Traité des objets musicaux: Essai interdisciplines* (1966; repr., with an additional chapter, Paris: Seuil, 1977).

the sources from which he quotes have not been translated into English. We therefore decided to translate all direct quotations in the text ourselves. The reader
should therefore be aware that where details of an English translation of a book or
review are given in the footnotes, the English will not be exactly the same as the
translation in the *Treatise*.

We also thought it important to give something of the flavor of this pioneering
period in musicology by trying, as far as possible, to reproduce the terminology of
the 1950s and 1960s. We have therefore used terms such as *wireless, gramophone,*
and *record* in an attempt to reproduce something of the flavor of this period and
have tried to avoid words and expressions that came into English at a later date. In
some places, where Schaeffer is making a joke or launching one of his tirades
against contemporary life or theoreticians of music, which he does quite often, we
have used a more relaxed, colloquial register, but generally the style is quite formal.
We do not, especially where academic works are concerned, subscribe to the
school of thinking that holds that the task of the translator is to produce a "recast-
ing" of the original in an accessible, modern idiom, clearly stamped with the translator's identity. The *Treatise* is a difficult and complex book, and any attempt to
"simplify " or "modernize" it would do it a great disservice and color the reader's
interpretation to an unacceptable degree. Although, of course, it is impossible for
translators not to imprint something of themselves on a text, we have endeavored
to keep this to a minimum in order to give the reader, as nearly as we can, the
impression of actually reading the original.

One problem linked with such an approach is the noninclusive nature of
Schaeffer's language, which, of course, was quite standard in his day. As in our
translation of *In Search of a Concrete Music*, we decided not to change this, and we
hope our female readers will accept male-centered language as giving a sense of
period to the text. We have, however, changed some of the expressions that are
now considered politically incorrect—for example, "le tam-tam nègre," "l'Indien,"
and "les Hindous," which we felt might give racial offense. We have translated
these expressions as "native tom-tom," "Native American," and "Indians," which
we hope will be more acceptable to a modern readership.

Many of the difficulties facing the English translator of any French academic
work arise from differences apparently inherent in the two languages and in the
way of thinking of the two cultures, which, it may be argued, are to a greater or
lesser extent interlinked. French, since the time of Descartes, has been much happier to deal in abstractions and general notions than English, with the result that
many French sentences translated literally appear hopelessly stilted and pompous
in English. This is often true of everyday as well as academic language; there is, or
was, a public notice on French trains and the métro: "Le signal sonore annonce la
fermeture imminente des portières," which translates literally as "The sonorous
signal announces the imminent closure of the doors." An English translation

would probably be something along the lines of "When the signal sounds, the doors will close," but it is a good illustration of the differences between the two languages—French with its abstract nouns and adjectives, English with its preference for more down-to-earth verbs and clauses.

Schaeffer, despite the fact that "musique concrète" focuses on examining the musical potential of real sound of any sort, and despite his criticism of the headled a priori music of the serialists, writes firmly within the French academic tradition. In fact, he constantly refers to Descartes when outlining his method, and the *Treatise* concludes with a quotation from the *Discourse on Method*. His work is full of long, abstract sentences and complex syntax, which sometimes must be analyzed much as a Latin expression before being transcribed into acceptable English. To give an example: a characteristic sentence, if translated literally, would read: "Comparable in originality to the ostinato of cells of which the elements, taken in isolation, are totally unforeseeable, but of which the repetition, considered globally, is of no information, the mixed weft, making a complex content and a not necessarily regular facture slowly evolve, is relatively foreseeable, although of not negligible information."[2] More than seven hundred pages of this may well decide the reader to abandon the text altogether. The Schaefferian sentence constantly raises the question, familiar to translators but here particularly challenging, of how far to deviate from a literal translation for the sake of writing comprehensible English. Sometimes it was as if we were creating something along the lines of a parallel, though we hope still accurate, text, where syntax was loosened, nouns changed into verbs, adjectives changed into adverbs, Anglo-Saxon words replaced Latinate words, and word order was drastically altered. We have not, however, altered the length of sentences or the ordering of paragraphs as these do not affect the quality of the English and can shed light on the structure of Schaeffer's thought.

Schaeffer shares with French tradition a desire for generalization and the creation of universally applicable rules, such as his breakdown of Jakobson's comments on language into "general rules" (299), or the definition of the "laws of the piano" (234), which may sometimes seem overly schematic to Anglophone readers. In addition, as can be seen from the second example, the language used in these contexts does not always sit very easily in English. One expression, "the most general instrument possible," caused some debate; we considered translating it as "the most universal instrument possible" but finally for the sake of accuracy stayed with the literal translation, as indeed we have done with the whole vocabulary of generalization and laws. This aspect of the treatise is important to the understanding of Schaeffer's thought, and to modify it would be to fail in our aim to be as

2. Schaeffer, *Traité des objets musicaux*, 457. All pagination refers to the 1977 edition; subsequent citations are given parenthetically in the text.

faithful as possible to the text. It also gives a fascinating insight into a different mode of thought.

Coupled with this, and still broadly in the French tradition, Schaeffer's way of thinking about the new music is highly schematic. He sees it almost diagrammatically, as a sequence of vertical or horizontal levels going, for example, from the most complex to the most simple or from the most specific to the most general. The whole music theory is based on a series of abstract and opposing dualisms, or "pairs" as he calls them—for example, natural/cultural and ordinary/specialized, for different ways of listening, or the "four musical axioms" depending on the pairs form/matter, articulation/stress, criterion/dimension, and value/characteristic. Two key dualisms, which are introduced at the very beginning of the treatise, are abstract/concrete and objective/subjective.

The terminology used here is immediately problematic. The adjective *concrete* and even more the noun in "the concrete" are not used readily in English; indeed, the immediate connotation of *concrete* in English is the building material. We considered using the expression *real-world* but decided to stay with *concrete* as we felt that *real-world* did not have the breadth of meaning to cover the whole range of Schaeffer's usage of the term, which goes beyond everyday reality to encompass the concrete in the philosophical sense. This was amply illustrated when we realized that for the sake of consistency *musique concrète* would have to be translated as "real-world music," which does not at all convey the full implications of *musique concrete*. *Concrete*, in Schaeffer's sense, refers to the listener's perception of every feature that constitutes the sound, whether the sound is real-world, electronic, instrumental, or virtually any other manifestation. In contexts in which the word *concrete* sounds particularly odd, as in "concrete composer," we have used expressions such as "composer of concrete music."

"Subject/subjective" and "object/objective" present similar difficulties. In French, *subject* is used to denote the perceiving individual and *subjective* everything that pertains to that individual, whereas *object* and *objective* refer to everything that belongs to the world external to the subject. In English the distinction is not as strict; English speakers do not refer to an individual as a subject but, for example, talk about the "subject" of a thesis, while in French it is the "object." In general we have used the word *individual* for "subject" when it refers to a person, with the occasional exception when the argument requires the contrast "object/subject" to be absolutely clear, and we have changed *object* to *subject* when it refers to the theme of research or of books.

Another key term is *sonore*, used as both an adjective and a noun "le sonore," and here we believe the translations we finally adopted are something of a compromise. In French, *le sonore* is "sound" in its most general sense; to translate it as "the sonorous" would be both clumsy and inaccurate, as *sonorous* refers only to a particular type of deep, resonant sound in English. We considered using the relatively new term *sonoric* but finally decided quite simply on *sound*, partly because "objet sonore" is already widely translated as "sound object." We are still not entirely happy with this solution, however, particularly as a translation of *le sonore* as "sound" does not quite have the generality of meaning to convey Schaeffer's thought in every context.

Other French terms that can cause confusion, but that are used constantly in the treatise, are the verb *faire* and the noun *expérience*. Schaeffer's aim was to encourage musicians to "faire de la musique" based on concrete sounds. The problem is that *faire* means both "to make" and "to do" in English. The composer François Bayle, who knew Schaeffer personally, told us in conversation that Schaeffer's emphasis would have been on "doing" rather than "making," but after much thought we decided to stick to the conventional expression "to make" rather than "to do" music. Similarly, *expérience* has two meanings in English: "experience" and "experiment." Here it is often much more difficult to decide which meaning Schaeffer intended, since, indeed, the whole of "musique concrète" was both an experiment and an experience. The subject matter of chapter 28, for example, could just as well be "the musical experiment" as "musical experience," and the reference to electronic music as an "experience" (520) could carry both meanings. It may be useful for the reader to keep these ambiguities in mind.

Apart from these general difficulties, there is a whole group of specialist terms devised or adopted by Schaeffer as he tried to hammer out a vocabulary that would adequately articulate the theory of "musique concrète." Finding an English equivalent, or deciding to leave these terms in French, taking into account that many of them have been taken into the English vocabulary of musicology, was one of our most difficult tasks, particularly as they are vital to the understanding of Schaeffer's *Treatise*. Often they are words current in the French language but with an extended or modified meaning, such as *allure, trame, lutherie,* or *contexture,* but Schaeffer also coins new terms, such as *grosse note* or *acoulogie*. Most of these key words are dealt with in the footnotes as they occur in the text and therefore need no further comment here, but *allure* caused particular problems. As mentioned in the footnotes, *allure* has a number of widely different meanings in French, its basic meaning being "way of going." Schaeffer defines *allure* in music as " 'revealing' the energetic agent's way of being and, very broadly, whether this agent is living or not" (550). The English word nearest in meaning is probably *gait*, but after much consideration we decided that the homonym *gate* was too intrusive and despite the rather unfortunate English meaning of *allure* decided to keep the French term.

Schaeffer uses the accepted term *solfège* to describe both music theory in general and his own new theory. Where he is clearly alluding to his own theory, we have translated *solfège* as "the music theory" as opposed to "music theory" when the term is used in its general sense. As is mentioned in the notes, *solfège* also has wider connotations than "music theory" and where appropriate is translated as "musicianship."

Given the above remarks, the reader may expect to find a rather dry manual of music theory, of interest only to the most committed musicologist. This is, in fact, far from the case. As well as fulfilling its serious musicological purpose, the *Treatise* is an entertaining and often amusing read. Schaeffer was a highly educated polymath, who had studied at the École Polytechnique in Paris, one of the most prestigious universities in France. He was widely read, cultured, and, at least as a young man, a devout Catholic, and he brought all these factors to bear in his writing. In fact, he initially considered himself a writer, publishing not only articles and essays but also works of fiction, of which the best known is probably the novel *Clotaire Nicole* (1938). He has a novelist's gift for storytelling, an essayist's ready wit and cutting sarcasm, and a religious person's awareness of what might be called the mystic or spiritual dimension of music and the arts. The *Treatise* is, indeed, a theoretical work, but it sparkles with wit, energy, and humor, some of the latter quite risqué, as when he plays on the two meanings of *consommation* in French, "consumption" and "consummation" in the sexual sense (649). References to the Bible and to the Mass abound, often used wittily to ridicule his contemporaries, as in his diatribe against modern composers who are carried away by their "digital Catechism" and the "electronic laying on of hands" (657), but also to articulate his firm belief in the profound philosophical significance of music. The text is studded with literary allusions to, for example, Molière (55), Boileau (686), and Queneau (365), as well as to French fairy tales and Greek mythology. Schaeffer's "most general instrument possible" is implicitly compared to the comic fairy-tale figure of "Mère Gigogne" (12), while the computer is personified as "the beloved Ogre" with his aficionados following the "Cartesian pebbles of total reduction to numbers" like the Babes in the Wood, into the trap of worthless music (128). Perhaps the most important of these allusions, however, are the references to Orpheus, which run throughout the book, and to which we shall return later. Schaeffer had a lifelong fascination with this myth and, indeed, believed he had much in common with its tragic hero. *Orphée* was the title of his first "concrete opera," performed in 1951.[3]

Perhaps, however, what most contributes to the *Treatise*'s literary as well as musicological merit is the abundance of entertaining stories, parables, parodies, conceits, and metaphors, often based on details as banal as hotel plumbing, a doctor's surgery, or sheaves of corn, which are used by Schaeffer to illustrate and explain many of his more abstruse ideas. The difficulty of finding typological criteria is exemplified in the parable of the attic (429), the anatomy of musicianship in the vignette of the child and the grass (339), a method of analyzing those sounds usually called noises in the description of a farmyard scene involving a toad, a paddle wheel, and a waterfall (394). The critique of traditional music theory is couched

---

3. For a discussion of this work see Pierre Schaeffer, *In Search of a Concrete Music*, trans. Christine North and John Dack (Berkeley: University of California Press, 2012), chaps. 9 and 10.

in terms of its elements being presented at Customs and being treated with great suspicion and bafflement by the customs officers (315), while the pianoforte is presented as a bulldozer, "steel-clad and rosewood finished," crushing the fragile structures of other musics (603). Apart from their explanatory function, these and the many similar tropes that occur throughout the book are often extremely amusing. They are also great fun for the translator as Schaeffer moves from register to register, ironical, narrative, literary, poetic, using puns and double entendres that require an exercise in ingenuity to render in English.

Yet beneath all the wit there is a deeply spiritual man, angry about what he considers the commodification and trivialization of contemporary music and anxious to see it restored to its proper status. It is through the myth of Orpheus that Schaeffer explains his ideas about the deeper significance and purpose of music. He sees the musician-god's descent into the Underworld as an exploration of the depths of the unconscious, which only art makes possible, a test of the courage and faith required to challenge human limitations, even if this ultimately means failure. This is where human beings reach the ultimate goal, "to understand what we are" (661), and hence Schaeffer's well-known definition of music as "man described to man in the language of things" (662). Even if a modern reader finds it hard to sympathize with these aspects of the *Treatise* that verge on the mystic, they add another, poetic, dimension to the writing and even today give food for reflection.

We are very pleased to have had the opportunity to translate the complete text of Pierre Schaeffer's *Treatise on Musical Objects* rather than the shorter version that he himself prepared for translation purposes. The shorter version omits these nontheoretical aspects of his writing, which are, we believe, what make the *Treatise* such an approachable and engaging text, as well as a key theoretical work. We hope the reader will agree.

Christine North

PIERRE SCHAEFFER'S *TREATISE ON MUSICAL OBJECTS* AND MUSIC THEORY

"The main fault of this book is in fact that it is still the only one. More than six hundred pages devoted to objects weigh down one pan of the scale. To counterbalance it, the author should also have produced a *Treatise on Musical Organization* of equal weight."[1] This statement appears on the first page of the "Penultimate Chapter" of the *Treatise*. It could be construed as a mitigating disclaimer, although this would be a grave mistake. But we should not forget that the *Treatise* is a work by Pierre Schaeffer; his prose style, along with the scrupulous care with which he used the French language, is part and parcel of his message. Consequently, the passage must be read within the context of the book and its overall formal plan. I could have begun with another apparently alarming sentence written some eleven years earlier: "It is possible to devote six hundred pages to not saying what one had to say" (659). But neither of these passages is an admission of failure or regret. On the contrary, they represent a deliberate rhetorical strategy. In addition to closely argued sections on linguistics, acoustics, classification, and description, Schaeffer's writing contains many self-effacing remarks and wry comments on contemporary music (these are often directed to "a priori" methods of composition). His language is, therefore, integral to the book's subject matter and its methodology. With commendable honesty Schaeffer acknowledged there are areas where more still needs to be done, but rather than suppressing such sentiments, he identifies them and invites readers to acknowledge that as far as music is concerned, "making" and "doing" are ongoing processes.

---

1. Pierre Schaeffer, *Traité des objets musicaux: Essai interdisciplines* (Paris: Seuil, 1977), 663. Subsequent citations of this edition are given parenthetically in the text.

How, then, can we situate this unique and, I would argue, indispensable book within the broad field of music theory? There can be little doubt that the *Treatise* deserves respect, owing not only to its considerable length but also to the formidable range of disciplines to which Schaeffer referred. To make a claim for its status as music theory, albeit a distinctive type of contemporary music theory, we must turn to Schaeffer's writing. A good starting point is to examine the work's structure: seven books each drawing on subjects such as making, hearing, acoustics, linguistics, physics, physiology, and even philosophy. The books are divided into chapters (plus three appendices) that deal systematically with the specific topic under consideration. Moreover, each of the thirty-six chapters contains several subsections (nineteen in the case of chapter 35). The aforementioned "Penultimate Chapter" is, in fact, the book's final section. As a result, the adjective *penultimate* immediately presents the reader with a conundrum challenging traditional notions about how authors bring their books to a satisfactory conclusion. This "Penultimate Chapter" was added in 1977 as an addendum to the original 1966 publication and demonstrates Schaeffer's methodology, which is simultaneously playful and serious. Despite the passage of eleven years between the two editions the aims of Schaeffer's book remained consistent: research into the *sound object* and the importance of this research for music in general. The final pages from the first edition are rather lyrical in tone. Schaeffer referred to the special status of music and claimed that sound objects and musical structures "are man described to man, in the language of things" (662). This style is maintained throughout much of the "Penultimate Chapter," where it becomes obvious that the real conclusion, if indeed *conclusion* is the correct term, will be the body of musical compositions resulting from the research conducted by Schaeffer and his colleagues (Schaeffer always acknowledged his research was a "group" project). If, therefore, a final chapter in the conventional sense was problematic in 1966, it was, without a doubt, impossible in 1977. The practical work of composition would be informed by the research presented in the *Treatise*, and practice would in turn elaborate a new music theory. The activities of *homo faber* would exist in mutual cooperation with those of *homo sapiens*.

Schaeffer was no doubt fully aware of the implications of calling his book a *Treatise*. A long and distinguished tradition can be identified of theoretical treatises in French. For example, Jean-Philippe Rameau (1683–1764) wrote his *Traité de l'harmonie réduite à ses principes naturels* in 1722, and François-Joseph Fétis (1784–1871) produced his *Traité complet de la théorie et de la pratique de l'harmonie* in 1844. These are just two of the many important *Traités* written in French since the Middle Ages. But neither of these provides a satisfactory model for Schaeffer's *Treatise*. Fétis assumed that his work was, in effect, an exhaustive summary of a deterministic, historical development. Chords were evaluated as part of an evolutionary process culminating in tonality as defined by Fétis himself. Rameau's *Treatise* convincingly demonstrated the natural foundations of harmony, which was in turn based on physical phenomena observable in acoustical studies. Rameau's theories of chord generation and fundamental bass are still recognized as crucial stages in our understanding of tonality. Scholars continue to contextualize both of these works as major contributions to the development of musical thought. Self-evidently, Schaeffer's *Treatise* is too recent for such a historically based comparison.

In his introduction Schaeffer writes that the book is not a "theory of music" (11) (the quote marks are Schaeffer's) constituting a manual for composers. The *Treatise* is "the summation of a body of research presented as it developed, rather than a logical presentation of results and possible applications" (665). In yet another self-deprecating statement Schaeffer refers to a "zigzag run-through" (11). Despite this apparent repudiation of systematic thinking, however, there are features in common between the *Treatise on Musical Objects* and earlier works. Many treatises draw on contemporary studies in acoustics. There are references to tuning systems investigated via monochords and Pythagorean ratios. Classification of chords and the systematization of mensural notation as promulgated by Philippe de Vitry (1291–1361) (with whom Schaeffer has been compared) are also common. Schaeffer was aware of these and certainly made use of contemporary findings in physics, for which his technical training makes him particularly suited. There are many references to scientists such as Helmholtz, Fourier, and Fletcher. But Schaeffer remained skeptical of an excessive reliance on scientific positivism and constantly reminded the reader that musicians hear not only with their ears but also with their brains. It is the interaction between cognitive capacities and sound (or the "sonorous") from which music will emerge—man described to man. Similarly, he identified potential similarities in how language systems operate and investigated theoretical paradigms such as structuralism in order to discover the possibility of fundamental, perhaps even permanent, ways in which humans structure their materials, be they sounds, words, or myths. He quoted scholars such as Lévi-Strauss, Malmberg, and Jakobson. Research in the *Treatise* clearly benefited from the dual nature of music as both an art and a science. This is clearly one of its great strengths, and in Schaeffer's opinion music became the supreme example of interdisciplinary research. But here another linguistic conceit demands attention (and Schaeffer must accept full responsibility for it!). The book's subtitle is *Essai interdisciplines*.[2] Schaeffer's research does indeed draw on various fields of study. For example, in his discussion on transients there are references to the acoustics of instruments and how stretched strings behave when struck or plucked. With the support of images, Schaeffer investigated the effects of such events on the processes of hearing. Such wide-ranging references to physics and human physiology

---

2. "Across disciplines": here Schaeffer uses the word *interdiscipline*, which he apparently coined, rather than *interdisciplinaire*, the more usual term.

are by definition interdisciplinary in that two independent fields of study are used to corroborate the results of a specific experiment. But the term *interdisciplines*, coined by Schaeffer, implies an intellectual area *across* the disciplines, one that demands to be studied on its own terms and might even emerge as a research field in its own right. Consequently, measurable physical data and physiological predispositions still cannot tell us what these transients *mean* in a musical sense. Science can be enlisted for factual information, but it cannot provide a satisfactory solution to the mystery of music. We are, once again, left with man confronting himself.

The value of the *Treatise* for musicians lies in Schaeffer's insistence on asking fundamental questions relevant to all aspects of music. He adopted a position of Cartesian doubt, where everything had to be interrogated and reevaluated. The starting point for this project was the sound object. But this object is not merely something in the world that is separate from us and that demands our attention. As suggested in the previous comments on transients, the sound object is both an acoustic event and the listening intention of the musician. It is a correlation between the outer world of objective physical occurrences and the inner world of subjective human experience. Two consequences stem from this. The first is that musicians can reassess the communicative potential of all sound material. Careful experimentation will go beyond a simplistic assumption that all perceptible characteristics are equivalent and that spectral detail and dynamic level can be used in the same way as pitch. By repeated, focused listening, previously disregarded features move to the fore and suggest themselves as candidates for new musical structures. Second, the whole enterprise might appear to be fixated on the single sound object. But the book's title is *Treatise on Musical Objects*. A sound object in isolation cannot create relationships; it can only be examined for its form-creating potential. The individual sound object must be placed within a structure that encourages perception and comparison of its features between other objects. It is precisely here that values and characteristics are identified and differentiated and that the transformation into a *musical* object occurs. Schaeffer even suggested that a single musical object does not exist (670): its musical status is conditioned on the creation of relationships with other objects. At this point we come full circle to the missing second volume. The next stage, that of musical organization at all levels of structure, can only really be undertaken by composers.

The central aim of the *Treatise*, the investigation of the sound object, is not compromised by this deferral of compositional practice. Instead, it asserts the role of music theory as an active aural procedure. What Schaeffer provides for the contemporary musician is a range of methods for investigating the materials of music and how they might ultimately be formed into structures. Naturally, there is some urgency to this endeavor given the vast repository of sounds that modern composers have at their disposal. This highlights the role technology can play in revealing new musical languages. Indeed, the origins of Schaeffer's entire research project can be traced to the technology of musique concrète, though with great foresight he rapidly realized that his theories could be generalized to music as a whole. The recording process is of particular significance and can be compared to other technological methods that fix temporal events. In a sense a recording, like a photograph or a film clip, provides too much sensory information. The natural tendency when hearing a sound, even one that is unfamiliar, is to associate it with a known one. A sound object with an abrupt attack followed by a gradual decay in dynamic level and spectral content might simply be classed as one more member of the "percussion-resonance" family. But recording technology and the new conditions of acousmatic listening can also defamiliarize our presuppositions and provide the conditions for perceiving details of shape and color that can be exploited in music. Thus, the classification and description of sound objects by means of typology and morphology provide examples of how all sound material—the "sonorous"—has potential for use in music. Furthermore, typology in particular also shows how sound objects of long duration and unpredictable dynamic and spectral behavior can lead to entirely new, previously "unheard," musical languages. Sounds that are common in contemporary music (both electroacoustic and orchestral), but that theory often consigns to the periphery of music, can now be rehabilitated. In conjunction with the four listening modes we see yet again the sound object as the conjunction between a given sonic event and human perception. Schaeffer proposed that if the *Treatise* were to be renamed, it should be called a *Treatise on Listening*. I can think of no better legacy for musicians, whether they are composers, performers, or analysts seeking to learn about their art, than Schaeffer's discussions on the listening modes.

The *Treatise on Musical Objects*, therefore, remains relevant despite its origins in research initiated in the immediate postwar years. If Schaeffer's suspicions about received wisdom forced a reconsideration of musical materials, the inevitable corollary was to revisit that most basic tool of music making: the instrument. By means of "characterology," as outlined in the *Treatise*, musicians' attention is now shifted to how sound objects are grouped in families according to their inherent characteristics, as well as the listener's perceptual predispositions. The physical sound source, whether a traditional instrument or a new interface, is not repudiated. Instruments can now celebrate a "virtual" status and take an active role in creating musical languages where source recognition fluctuates between the real and the imaginary, between unambiguous recognition of causality and the unknowable and mysterious.

If readers are willing to accept Schaeffer's research program, there is much in the *Treatise* that will encourage them to consider many musical practices and theories in an entirely new light. But no book is perfect. Doubtless, our respect for Schaeffer's intellect and integrity is obvious. We hope we are able to exercise sufficient self-restraint to remain objective. Proselytizing is seldom appropriate in any introduction. If readers seek a broad sweep of contemporary music theory (which is, in any case, not the book's subject), I must confess they will have to accommodate Schaeffer's prejudices. His suspicions about "a priori" methods were touched on in the opening paragraph. The writing of complex scores without aural verification, algorithmic procedures, the use of chance, and, in particular, serial techniques were targets of his disapproval. Many will agree with such comments, of course. Moreover, his remarks were entirely consistent. Schaeffer recommended that musicians work directly with sound, and as a result, any excessive reliance on notation methods (necessary though they often are) before hearing the result can be misleading. But this would imply that serial composers disregard the listening process, and this is manifestly untrue. Schaeffer failed to recognize that serialism is a collection of different techniques. There is no one type of serial thought. It is a way of thinking about materials and their organization that must be reconsidered and modified for each new composition. It developed constantly, and its effects are still in evidence today (*Formel-Komposition* is one example). When used by composers such as Karlheinz Stockhausen, Pierre Boulez, and Henri Pousseur (none of whom, it must be admitted, were particularly complimentary to Schaeffer's research), there are moments of real, even transcendental, beauty. But Schaeffer's comments are not gratuitous; they always support his arguments and illustrate the consistent nature of his viewpoints. And this must be borne in mind while reading this book. Schaeffer starts the *Treatise* with a lengthy quotation from E. T. A. Hoffmann. This romantic text seemed to encapsulate for Schaeffer the "dialogue . . . between spirit and Nature" (11). Sounds are all around us in Nature. But it is human beings who make them into music. Schaeffer wanted to alert us to the risk posed by "a priori" thinking in this vital relationship. On the last page of the *Treatise* Schaeffer uses the image of an archer whose real target is within himself. The *Treatise on Musical Objects*, therefore, is not a work that sets out a single music theory. It investigates what Schaeffer called the "phenomenon of music," the art that is both scientific and sensory. The contemporary musician needs to understand both.

John Dack

ACKNOWLEDGMENTS

Our sincerest thanks go to Daniel Teruggi (director of the Groupe de recherches musicales, Paris) for commissioning this translation and for entrusting such a major undertaking to us. We are also most grateful to the GRM committee formed by Daniel for their friendly assistance and helpful recommendations in bringing it to fruition. Madame Jacqueline Schaeffer has, as always, given us her unfailing support and encouragement, and we thank her most warmly for her active interest throughout. Furthermore, we are extremely grateful to Professor Martin Laliberté (University Paris–Est Marne-la-Vallée) and Professor Emeritus Denis Smalley (City University, London) for their perceptive comments, as well as to the readers appointed by the University of California Press for their invaluable advice and positive feedback. A final word of thanks is due the editorial staff of the University of California Press for their patient guidance through the complexities of publication.

PREFACE

"Our kingdom is not of this world," say musicians,

> for where do we find in nature, like the painter and the sculptor, the prototype for our art? . . . Sound inhabits everything; but sounds, I mean melodies that speak the higher language of the kingdom of the spirit, dwell only in the breast of man. However, does not the spirit of music, like the spirit of sound, embrace the whole of nature? The sound body, touched mechanically, awakens into life, makes manifest its existence or rather its structure, and thus comes to our consciousness. And what if the spirit of music, similarly aroused by the initiate, were to express itself, harmoniously and melodically in mysterious chords, intelligible to him alone?
>
> Thus, the musician's sudden inspirations, the birth of melodies within him, would be the perception, the unconscious, or rather ineffable, conception of the secret music of nature, considered as the principle of life or of all vital activity. Hence, must the musician not stand in the same relationship with nature as the hypnotist with the sleepwalker?
>
> . . . Hearing is seeing from within . . ."[1]

Hoffmann's text carries, as lightly as *Kreisleriana*'s 150 years of age, the problem of today and always. But romanticism has lordly posturings that we have had to shed: they were naive and generous; we are competent and reserved. Which one of us, even in other terms, would dare to interrogate Music in this way?

---

1. E. T. A. Hoffmann, *E. T. A Hoffmann's Musical Writings: "Kreisleriana," "The Poet and the Composer," Music Criticism*, ed. David Charlton, trans. Martyn Clarke (Cambridge: Cambridge University Press, 1989), 74, 163–64.

Such boldness, however, inspires us. Even if we no longer invoke Nature by its stage name since it is now Science, and even if the spirit, called up without a capital letter, is examined in all its mechanisms for the phenomenon of knowledge of which it is the instrument, we are hardly any clearer. Knowledge increases; experiments grow ever more numerous; the field of investigation becomes larger and fragments. It is only on the face of it that relationships are set up between different fields now marked out by technique and technology, instrumentarium[2] and acoustics, music theory[3] and composition, psychology and musicology, the history of musical civilizations and our own. The rifts in a land now so vast are perhaps deeper for being less apparent, better camouflaged.

The challenge of synthesis is always tempting but divides two sorts of minds: those who think that the accumulation of knowledge provides the solution, and that eventually music will be put into an equation, and those who know that well-conducted thought leads back to simple questions on which rest both the equations of science and the intuitions of art.

There is scarcely a philosopher or a true scholar, whatever his discipline, who has not at some time or other formulated a thought like this, such as this from Claude Lévi-Strauss: "Perhaps one day we shall discover that the same logic is at work in mythical and scientific thought, and that man has always thought in the same way. Progress—if indeed the word still applies—would not have had consciousness as its domain, but the world, where a humanity endowed with unchanging faculties would, in the course of its long history, have been continuously grappling with new objects."[4]

Seen in this way, music would have provided a highly original opportunity for research and scrutiny. Indeed, in no field, just as in no other language, do the objects seem so precisely given while the ways of choosing and assembling them seem so free. So in its development music could be seen as being linked to scientific progress—insofar as it takes its means from acoustics, and now from electronics and electroacoustics—but it should be possible, with so many new sound objects, to discern the permanent structures of human thought and sensibility. We should then see, in this complementariness of naturally given means and cultural

2. The word used in French is *lutherie*, which means the craftsmanship of instrument making but which Schaeffer used in a broader connotation to refer to virtual instruments as well. *Instrumentarium*, we hope, captures this double meaning, although where the context is appropriate, *lutherie* is translated simply as "instrument making."—Trans.

3. The word used in French is *solfège*, a word occurring in romance languages but that does not have an English equivalent. *Sol-fa* is sometimes used in the United Kingdom or *Ear-training* in the United States. *Music theory* is mainly used when referring to *solfège*, although occasionally, where the context demands this, it is translated as "musicianship."—Trans.

4. Claude Lévi-Strauss, *Anthropologie structurale* (Paris: Plon, 1958), 254. Published in English as *Structural Anthropology* (New York: Basic Books, 1963).—Trans.

structures, the resolution of numerous superficial contradistinctions, between the ancients and the moderns, the arts and sciences, sound and the musical. This is the dialogue, dreamed of by Hoffmann, between the spirit and Nature.

The whole plan of this book is inspired by this dualism. It aims to cover the ever-increasing domain of sound objects and to see how musical structures derive from phenomena whose more general laws they simply verify in one highly important particular case. Thus, from one discipline to another it should be possible to find the missing link—not based on physical content or literary analogy, those crude or fragile linkages, but on a transverse relationship whose original mechanism we hope to discover.

Even, however, with these twin objectives in mind, it is not so easy to split up our thought processes, and our account is limited to a run-through; all the more so as, even if it aims to bring together various categories of minds and abilities, it hopes to attract each of these with what is most familiar, unless our reader, through a spirit of inquiry that we would also like him to have, turns to the discipline that is the least familiar to him. Thus, this zigzag run-through, in seven leaps called "books," aims to move from current information on *making* and *hearing* (books 1 and 2) to two meditations more specifically inspired, one (book 3) by physics, and the other (book 4) by philosophy. Scarcely have these words been written than we must think again. These two books do, in effect, touch on subjects from the discipline in question, but our main aim is to catch a glimpse, on the frontiers of these disciplines, of the little-explored zones of the domain of music. So we would suggest, to everyone, to give priority to the account that is not written in their language.

Last but not least, the musician should be reassured, since the entire work is addressed primarily to him. But he should not expect a "theory of music" here: it merely concerns the practice of the musical object. Even if music theory is essential for expressing the problem of musical composition conveniently, we must allow that it does not remotely claim to tackle the art of composition itself. The musician reading this book, if eager to get to the morphology of sound and the theory of the musical, can certainly run more rapidly through books 3 and 4, if only to be sure of the rudiments he will find applied in the final books. Perhaps then he will think that these deserve revisiting. The effort demanded of him in these philosophical and scientific fields is justified; contemporary music often strays too naively on to one or the other for us to be able to find satisfaction in such a superficial approach.

As for the last book, it is not written with the same pen as the earlier ones. The author admits that he allowed himself to speak more personally here. He would not therefore blame the reader for not following him right to the end of his conclusions. But he asks him not to be offended by them and to study the earlier books dispassionately: they are the fruit of almost twenty years of experimental work carried out with the intention of bringing disciplines face-to-face.

When, for years and years, one pursues a fundamental piece of research like this, which in many ways also appears to be an original discipline itself, the right moment to present it to the public never seems to come. Even if the starting point is full of promise, and the method coherent, what one learns above all, from stage to stage, is how little one knows and how vast the whole research undertaking is. But then there would be no reason ever to publish, and we would find ourselves in a position entirely contrary to our method, which presupposes group research.

We are well aware that this way of proceeding is quite at odds with contemporary practice: no one should publish without great care, in a very narrowly defined area of his expertise! Where we find all these areas of expertise together, we are disarmed indeed. Unraveling the knots of the most diverse, and often the most divergent, disciplines, we are stuck with them all. An unfair fight: all these Curiatii[5] assail us at once, each in perfect health, while we will soon be showing signs of exhaustion. If only we were bearing the olive branch! But it is to be feared that the author, through temperament even more than necessity, has armed himself with some sort of powder to make the specialists sneeze.

Another reason compels us. This book, the fruit of teamwork, is a source of information now indispensable for those who wish to use our work and for those who wish to pursue it. The work of synthesis it represents is naturally the responsibility of the author, but it also rests on much related work and the cooperation of a whole group. This was the case from the very beginnings of this original research in 1950. Technical imagination came from Jacques Poullin and Francis Coupigny,[6] while musical experimentation was a "chain reaction" in which Pierre Henry, Luc Ferrari, and François Bayle[7] were the most essential links. More recently, Guy Reibel and Enrico Chiarucci[8] have made documentary and experimental contributions in the field of acoustics. Finally, editorial tasks have been shared with Pierre Janin and Sophie Brunet,[9] which, in the case of the latter, does not say nearly enough. My heartfelt thanks to all of them.

5. According to the Roman historian Livy (50 BCE–CE 17). The Curiatii and the Horatii were male triplets from Alba Longa and Rome, who fought to settle the war between the two cities during the reign of Tullus Hostilius (672–642 BCE). The Horatii finally overcame the Curiatii.—Trans.

6. Jacques Poullin and Francis Coupigny were Schaeffer's chief engineers from 1950 to 1975. They contributed significantly to the invention and development of new tools for sound processing.—Trans.

7. Pierre Henry was Schaeffer's first collaborator in his "musique concrète" compositions and later became one of the great figures of electroacoustic music; Luc Ferrari and François Bayle are two major composers who worked at the Groupe de recherches musicales founded by Schaeffer in 1958. Bayle became director of the group in 1966.—Trans.

8. Guy Reibel and Enrico Chiarucci, both composers working at the GRM in the 1960s, wrote and developed a book of sound examples, the *Solfège de l'objet sonore*, in 1967, which is a guide for the understanding of the *Treatise on Musical Objects*. In 1998 the *Solfège de l'objet sonore* was reissued by the Ina/GRM as a booklet with 3 CDs.—Trans.

9. Two close collaborators of Pierre Schaeffer.—Trans.

Moreover, the same team is tackling a complementary task, the results of which will be published in the form of several gramophone records at the same time as this work: it is the sound counterpart of the text, the indispensable *listening material* that alone can give the reader the means to move on from concepts to perceptions.

It would be most ungrateful, finally, to pass over the constant support of the Office de radiodiffusion-télévision française (ORTF), which, from the first words of encouragement from Wladimir Porché, in 1948, to those of Jacques-Bernard Dupont,[10] has generously supported this strange research.

Paris, August 14, 1966

10. Wladimir Porché was the head of the RTF (Radiodiffusion-télévision française) in 1951 when Pierre Schaeffer, after starting his experiments on "musique concrète," created the Groupe de recherche de musique concrète (GRMC); Porché supported this experimental approach and provided the infrastructure for Schaeffer's work. Jacques-Bernard Dupont was the head of the ORTF (Office de radiodiffusion-télévision française) when Schaeffer published the Treatise on Musical Objects in 1966.—Trans.

Introductory Remarks

The Historical Situation of Music

Although the taste for controversy is widespread in some quarters, it is, we believe, unheard of for a radical revision of accepted ideas to be undertaken lightheartedly or through the arbitrary decision of an adventurous mind.

Discoverers themselves, when they first start, fail to recognize their discoveries, making every effort to force them to fit into the thought systems they have learned to use; new methods are rarely grasped in their own originality, for what they enable us to do, but only as so many means of building on what we already know; new facts are perceived as the continuation of the past or, when this becomes impossible, as anomalies, something supplementary, an exception—until the moment when the real is decisively transformed, before the concepts that would allow us to account for it are changed.

Suddenly these concepts, which appeared both obvious and exhaustive, turn out to be challengeable and outmoded, inappropriate for a comprehensive understanding of phenomena. What, in relation to the inventory drawn up by our predecessors, appeared eccentric now becomes the chance to reexamine everything that was most universally accepted. This is when every serious researcher should adopt Cartesian asceticism for himself: "to rid (himself) of every opinion which (he) had until then accepted as true, and start all over again from the basics."[1]

Music today is in the same historical situation. Over the last decades, the contemporary musician, whether he wants to or not, and sometimes despite himself,

---

1. Renée Descartes, "Remarques sur septièmes objections, Méditations métaphysiques" (1641).—Trans.

1

has seen his horizon expand. The new phenomena that have appeared are less well known to the public, more misunderstood by music lovers than are, in painting for example, surrealism, cubism, abstract art, or, in every imaginary museum, the growing influence of primitive arts. They are no less capable of revolutionizing music, not only in all its manifestations but also in its principles.

THREE NEW PHENOMENA

We will quote them in the order of the importance that is generally given to them, while, for our part, being of the opinion that this importance should be in reverse order.

The first is *aesthetic* in nature. Greater and greater freedom in the way works are put together has, in half a century, allowed a rapid development in Western music. In return this void demands its rules. The analysis for this has been done so fully that we do not need to go over it again. We should, however, note that it was not really done in depth, being more a working model than an explanation.

Above all, we should note that this marks not only a gradual break with the rules of counterpoint and harmony taught in the conservatories but a reappraisal of musical structures. Speaking of dissonance and polytonality in relation to that well-defined structure that is the Western scale is one thing. It is quite another to attack the structure itself, be it—as Debussy had already done—by using a six-tone scale, or—as Schoenberg has done—a scale of twelve semitones, in which the canonical arrangements of dodecaphony aim to eliminate all tonality. Finally, from now on, certain concepts, even tentative, like *Klangfarbenmelodie*,[2] indicate an interest in using specific structures other than pitch.

The second phenomenon is the appearance of new *techniques*. For musical ideas are, and more than you would think, the prisoners of the whole baggage of music, just as scientific ideas are of their experimental equipment. Indeed, two unusual modes of sound production, known as *musique concrète* and *electronic music*, came into being at about the same time, about fifteen years ago. These developments were in opposition for more than twelve years, before several complementary aspects were revealed.

Musique concrète claimed to compose works with sounds taken from anywhere—in particular those we call noises—judiciously chosen and then assembled through the electroacoustic techniques of editing and mixing recordings.

---

2. Literally "timbre melody," consisting of a succession of sounds of the same pitch but different timbres. [The word-for-word translation is, in fact, "Sound-Color-Melody"; it implies splitting a melody among different instruments. Sounds may or may not have the same pitch but are often within a narrow pitch range.—Trans.]

Conversely, electronic music claimed to synthesize any sound at all, without going through the acoustic phase, by electronically combining its analytical components, which, according to physicists, could be reduced to pure frequencies, each one given a measure of intensity and developing through time. This strongly reinforced the idea that every sound could be reduced to three physical parameters[3] and that synthesizing these, which was now possible, could make all other instrumental devices, traditional or "concrete," unnecessary, at least in the long term.

In both cases, the works created using the new means made available by electroacoustic or purely electronic techniques had, in some strange fashion, their own style, an aesthetic peculiar to them, so peculiar, in fact, that they were often refused the name of music. Instead of extending the creative range, as might have been expected, modern equipment seemed to give rise to idiosyncrasies, eccentricities even, at the margins of music properly speaking.

In addition, all aesthetics apart, these two types of music—if we may provisionally call them this—displayed worrying anomalies: the former was not written down; the latter was written in numbers. By going too far or not far enough, they did more than challenge traditional notation: they did without it altogether. The former was to abandon it when faced with a sound material whose variety and complexity eluded all attempts to transcribe it. The latter made it anachronistic through a rigor so absolute that the approximations of traditional scores paled before such precision.

The third phenomenon involves a reality that is very ancient and is also gradually disappearing. It concerns *vestiges of civilizations* and *musical geographies* other than Western. For our contemporaries this phenomenon does not yet seem to have taken on all the importance it deserves.

Traditional musicians, as their name suggests and also as their interests incline them, are very curious about the historical sources of music and a musical ethnology that would not be very different from the ethnology of languages. But, a relative latecomer into this field, ethnology initially concentrated on and referred back to its own object of study rather than the musical phenomenon its discoveries could have explained. And musicologists, with few exceptions, do not really seem ready to decipher these other languages, which, however, should give us the keys to a true musical universalism.

How could they be? Music, for Westerners, is inseparable from a "theory of music," which in turn, if we believe the manuals, rests on a scientific basis: acoustics. University teaching backs up teaching at the conservatories, which starts from a number of definitions: musical note, scale, chord, and so forth, which are seen as principles laid down once and for all, under the discreet guardianship of specialists,

---

3. Frequency, measured in hertz (Hz); intensity, measured in decibels (dB); and time, measured in seconds (s) or milliseconds (ms).

physicists and musicians who trust each other or, as the case may be, declare themselves incompetent in a field that is not theirs.

Under these conditions it is understandable that musicologists, confident in their own system, should quite naturally strive to reduce primitive or non-Western languages to the concepts and terms of Western music. And it is not surprising that the need to go back to authentic sources should have been argued precisely by the most modernist musicians, of musique concrète in particular, who found themselves obliged, through their own experience, to question seriously the universal value of this system.

THE THREE DEAD ENDS OF MUSICOLOGY

Thus the musical interpretation of sound phenomena as it is generally practiced these days has come up against three main dead ends.

One of these dead ends is *musical concepts*. It is now not only the scale and tonality that have come to be rejected by the most adventurous, as by the most primitive, musics of our time, but the very first of these concepts: the musical note, the archetype of the musical object, the basis of all notation, an element of every structure, melodic or rhythmic. No music theory, no harmony, even atonal, can take into account a certain general type of musical objects, and in particular those used in most African or Asian musics.

The second dead end is *instrumental sources*. Whatever the tendency of musicologists to reduce exotic or archaic instruments to our norms, they suddenly found themselves disarmed when faced with the new sources of electronic or "concrete" sounds, which—surprise, surprise!—sometimes got on famously with African or Asian instruments. More worrying still was the possible disappearance of the concept of the instrument. Universal[4] or synthetic instruments, these were going to be the ornaments of our concert halls, or maybe they were going to be stripped of any instruments at all. Were we going to witness the disappearance of the orchestra and the conductor, apparently threatened by the disappearance of musical scores, and about to be replaced with magnetic tapes played by loudspeakers?

The third dead end is *aesthetic commentary*. Taken as a whole, the copious literature devoted to sonatas, quartets, and symphonies rings hollow. Habit alone can hide from us the poverty and the disparate nature of these analyses. When we put aside the smug comments on the composer's or the performer's state of mind that litter the work, we are left with the most tedious list, in the language of musical technology, of his methods of production or, at the very best, a study of his syntax.

4. The French term is *instruments gigognes*, a reference to the figure from children's stories, Mère Gigogne, who produced hordes of children from beneath her voluminous skirts. Here the expression implies "the instrument that contains all instruments."—Trans.

But there is no real critical appraisal. Should we perhaps not be surprised? Perhaps, as good music is itself a language, and a specific one, it completely eludes any description or explanation in words? Whatever the case, we simply acknowledge that the problem is important enough not to be whitewashed over and that the difficulty has been neither resolutely faced nor clearly addressed.

The analysis is doubtless severe, but we must one day realize that the musicology it criticizes is running out of steam. If no explanation is forthcoming—conceptual, instrumental, or aesthetic—it would be better to admit that, after all, *we do not know very much about music*. And worse still, what we do know is more likely to lead us astray than to guide us.

A PRIORI MUSIC

So unless musicians resign themselves to stagnation, where will they find principles that will enable them to understand and direct their own activity?

In a time of crisis, when we are inclined to doubt both received ideas and ourselves for having previously accepted them, it is a natural reaction to turn to science and, in particular, the most prestigious of our time: mathematics and the physical sciences. This would explain historically the importance of the tendency toward doctrine that for some years now has sought to find a model and a medium in these disciplines.

Starting from serial music, the rules of which were already being formulated like some sort of algebra, "*a priori* musics" have evolved, their main preoccupation seeming to be intellectual rigor and the total ascendancy of abstract intelligence over both the composers' subjectivity and the sound material. The idea of sensitive and intuitive music, which seems unable to free itself from dull repetitiveness, is being challenged by a desire for austerity, indeed aridity: let us rather make musical constructions that are perhaps arbitrary but clearly conceived, obeying precise and precisely formulated rules that will guarantee their coherence at the most objective level. The stricter the rules and the more meticulous the calculations, the more the composer will be shielded from his own whims, his subconscious preferences, which might mask his enslavement to automatic habits of composition.

And besides, the arbitrary itself must be codified. What else does the traditional composer do than simultaneously use and break certain rules? Whoever wants to do this scientifically must do it consciously. The use of calculating machines, by making him formulate the rules that determine what he does, will be a salutary exercise for him. Chance, which has its own laws that can be counted on, will provide the succession of notes and sequences. From the rules of the series, which automatically excluded any tonal allusion, it is a completely logical step to the calculation of probabilities. The paradoxical result of a composition such as this is that it will prove to be completely conscious, perfectly willed, as soon as the hateful self of the composer is totally eliminated from it.

Moreover, it is science, acoustics as it happens, that guarantees the rigorous correspondence between the sound structure and the intellectual construct. Since—and no one doubts this—musical concepts can be reduced to the definitions of acoustics, we will prefer the latter, more precise and reliable, to the former, contingent and approximate. As we have seen, electronic equipment has allowed the composer to familiarize himself with the concept of parameters and with calculating the variation of every sound phenomenon in relation to these.

There remain these two contingent elements, which are not readily reducible: the human performer, if the orchestra is being used, and the consumer, if we are thinking about the audience. The least that can be said is that the attitude toward these is resolutely authoritarian. The orchestra must follow and mold itself to the austere purposes imposed on it. The audience as well. A new music is not made to please, or move, or be immediately understood. It will be understood little by little, through people learning the language it forges. It will give pleasure to those who have themselves taken the trouble to understand it.

Thus we have witnessed the birth of works that are undeniably new, and doubtless interesting in this respect, but also very disappointing on other levels, and not necessarily assured of survival.

We are scarcely in a position to criticize them for this: if we accept their intention, which has its logic, nothing, as far as our sensibility is concerned, would allow us to say whether they are good or bad. In fact, either our ear will get used to them—and we know about the amazing power of adaptation of the musical ear—or it won't, and all these works, despite their intrinsic qualities, will never amount to an intelligible language.

So must we leave it to posterity to decide for a whole generation what its life and work will be? The risk is worthy of respect, but the stakes are huge. Perhaps we could shed more light on this by analyzing the two premises on which the whole meaning of the undertaking rests.

The first is not the worst: a rigorously constructed music *must* be intelligible. The only things against it are our habits and our determination to reduce it to a traditional language. Deconditioning or education should be enough, once our attention has been steered in the right direction, for us to hear it as it was made.

But to what do all these calculations, intended to guarantee rigorous coherence of construction, apply? As we have seen, to sound, as defined and measured by acousticians. Is this the sound that we really hear?

Clearly the value of the first premise depends on this second one: if our ear functions effectively as an acoustic receptor, there is a possibility that a music devised *a priori* in keeping with these parameters may one day become accessible. But what if this is not the case? If these works, intellectually and acoustically impeccable, speak in reality only to a theoretical ear, which ours will never be, then surely the wager becomes absurd.

We should state here and now what we intend to demonstrate fully in this work: the wager is lost; the correspondence between music and acoustics is remote; experiments show that it is not an easy task to reduce the facts of human perception to the parameters measured by machines.

But for those experiments to take place, research must take a new and quite different path and define another method.

MUSIQUE CONCRÈTE

First, we should clear up a misunderstanding. It is true that the electronic mode of composition can, more than any other, satisfy a systematic mind and, reciprocally, that the use of electronic equipment has certainly strengthened this tendency. It is true also that the problems of composition in musique concrète have, historically, given rise to a different type of musical research, which lays claim to the experimental method and, reciprocally, that the choice of a living and complex material, resistant to analysis, and a mode of composition that can only be carried out empirically and through a series of approximations may be characteristic of another type of mind. But we must not go any further and fall into two all-too-common misunderstandings: the first is confusing two different ways of tackling the problem of music, by using particular instrumental means; the second is believing that *a priori* and experimental music stand face-to-face, opposing each other like two schools of aesthetics.

A point of terminology, which will necessitate a personal parenthesis, will help to clarify these perhaps-too-abstract comments. When in 1948 I suggested the term *musique concrète*, I intended, by this adjective, to express a *reversal* of the way musical work is done. Instead of notating musical ideas using the symbols of music theory, and leaving it to known instruments to realize them, the aim was to gather concrete sound, wherever it came from, and to abstract the musical values it potentially contained. This "wait and see" attitude justified the choice of the term and opened the door to very varied lines of thought and action. I first had to pay the price of the discovery. It was still the age of gramophones, and only by means of the closed groove[5] could we make cuts in sounds that would lead to collages. So we thought about precedents in painting, and the parallel with a nonfigurative type of painting called "abstract" led immediately to the antipodes of the *concrete*: in any case we were not going to give the name *abstract* to a music that did without the symbols of music theory and was carved out of living sound! From here to imagining a reciprocity between painting and music was only a short step, quickly

---

5. This is a groove closed in on itself, thereby isolating a fragment of recording, which can be listened to indefinitely.

taken by people in love with symmetry: they said figurative painting takes its models from the *external world*, from what can be seen, whereas nonfigurative painting relies on necessarily abstract pictorial *values;*[6] conversely, music at first grew up without an external model, having reference only to abstract musical "values," and it becomes "concrete," one might say "figurative," when it uses "sound objects"[7] taken directly from the "external world" of natural sounds and given noises.

This way of seeing things, however, failed to take into account the potential of our discovery. This book contains a critique of a too naive faith in the so-called external world and in the distinction, no less so, between a concrete and an abstract, dissociated in this way. For us, who have long been convinced that these two aspects are "isotopes" of the real, the choice of one of these adjectives aims only to mark a new starting point in music and, it must also be said, a tendency to oppose the bias toward abstraction that had invaded contemporary music. As for shutting ourselves up in a music whose objects referred to the "external world" (or, more precisely, whose objects had a double meaning, relating to sound, by reminding us of the source they came from, and musical, through being organized), there were either wrong interpretations or the choice of lines of approach other than ours. Works like this are possible and interesting (the *Symphonie pour un homme seul* was a good illustration of this), but they do more than choose a so-called expressionist or surrealist aesthetic; they explore a particular type of art, halfway between music and poetry. I would not reject this particular type of art, scarcely explored and so often parodied, but I think I have also quite clearly indicated another option, which is to carry out musical research starting from the concrete, certainly, but wholly dedicated to reclaiming the indispensable musical abstract.

I therefore abandoned the name *musique concrète* in 1958, not without congratulating myself on this initial stage, to which I still owe everything I have done. But it was necessary to avoid misunderstandings, tenacious as are all misunderstandings when they are both aesthetic and technical. If these first experiments had any consequences beyond particular procedures and the inspiration of a few, it is because it became possible to conceive of an experimental music that made every experimental process its own and preceded all aesthetics.

EXPERIMENTAL MUSIC

The two opposing musics of 1950 to 1955, concrete and electronic, had ended their match in a draw, both of them too ambitious—one to conquer sound in one fell

6. In contrast with the *natural* external world, values are norms established within a determined *cultural* group.

7. By "sound object" we mean sound itself, considered as *sound*, and not the material object (instrument or some sort of device) that produces it.

swoop, the other to try and produce the whole of the musical by synthesis. The traces of both, which reveal the joint temptation of the possible and the impossible, mark out what is now a historical fact: that it was possible, in two ways, to make music without performers, or instruments, or music theory. It was the first of these that was remembered by public opinion, always very keen on these performances, fascinated by music machines and thinking of them rather as the cinema was thought of in the age of the Lumière brothers. In effect, the tape recorder had practically replaced the closed grooves of the former and mingled the concrete with the electronic sounds of the latter. The most remarkable so-called electronic works—Luciano Berio's *Omaggio a Joyce* and Karlheinz Stockhausen's *Gesang der Jünglinge*—use every sound source and allow two types of freedom: one of procedure and the other of the aesthetic that flows from it. No matter that the term *electronic* is still attached to such musics, which are in reality electroacoustic. I should, for my part, have preferred the term *experimental*, inasmuch as no one putting together on the tape recorder instrumental and vocal sounds, and those that come from acoustic sound bodies as well as electronic generators, can deny that he is in full experimental mode. Besides, this term had triggered the first serious international debate on this subject, in Venice in 1961. In fact, the best-known contemporary experimental composers have by and large gone back to the orchestra, fortified by the instruction received from the studio.

Is this return to the orchestra a sign that so-called experimental music procedures have failed? How is it that most of the composers who first took up arms for this cause turned away from it more or less of their own accord, just when they were being crowned with success? Moreover, how can we explain the worldwide increase in studios that mix the concrete and the electronic (and now also aim to use the "computer"),[8] with several dozens at least per continent?

It seems quite easy to unravel this knot, provided we hold some of the threads. If the talented composer turns to the orchestra as soon as he can, it is out of an all-too-natural impulse, and maybe also, talent for talent, it is the composer trained in the disciplines of the experimental studio who is best placed to do this, through the advantage he has gained in musical knowledge of a type that is neither practiced nor taught anywhere else. His desires urge him to develop what he has acquired and to apply it to the living reality of the orchestra and the concert hall, infinitely more pleasing than the austere solitude of the studio.

The fact that new studios are opening, however, is due to an automatic reflex of our time, which strives to occupy all available spaces for what is possible or doable, even if we don't know what is possible or what to do. In any case electronic music, in the strict sense of the term, cannot but tempt the young composer emerging

---

8. A very powerful calculating machine. [In the early 1960s, when the *Treatise* was written, computers were quite unknown devices.—Trans.]

from a classical, then serial, training: he finds reassurance in notation in numbers, and to him this seems like progress itself—that is, a far better continuation of what he has been taught. Others, captivated by a different scientific mode, are fascinated by the aleatoric, the combinatorial, either machines for "making music," as formerly, or for "inventing music," as never before. Only a minority follows the advice that we have always given to many foreign correspondents: that a good broadcasting studio, even a small facility with no sound or recording equipment, is enough to provide years of fruitful experimental work. The lack of appetite with regard to technical tools arouses suspicion. And when we add that the revolution is still to take place in the field of musical ideas, and that we must agree to some years of *aural retraining*, which can be done without complicated equipment and which no device can do for us, there is disappointment among the proselytes.

The fact is that, ultimately, experimental music for most of its followers has meant only a number of technical procedures and specific musics composed outside the norms of score and orchestra.

If, indeed, there are many devotees among musicians, they are convinced that, ultimately, it is all to do with a new instrument or instruments. While there are also many talented technicians among them, inventive and motivated by music, there are scarcely any who feel inspired to take it as their subject. Between musicians who are still primarily composers and researchers who are primarily technicians, there are no candidates, practically speaking, for *fundamental musical research*.

NO-MAN'S-LAND

So we are obliged to acknowledge an almost total deficiency in this field, which is all the more surprising as this deficiency is felt daily. Those musicians captivated by science are more empirical than ever: their borrowings from formulae or devices are almost like pilfering, rapidly transformed into trade secrets, and sometimes decked out with a few romantic theories, except that their dreams are put into equations. As for serious scientists, they are busy elsewhere, music not yet being considered a major objective for the cosmos or the bomb. Those among them who are interested in music seek in it, as in art in general, a just compensation for other more austere disciplines. They expect perceptible pleasures, and they respect all the more the heritage that provides this. In the arts, scholars are not progressives.

So it seems that in no other of the innumerable areas where so many new questions are raised, where ideas have to be rethought in the light of recent events, where specialists (who until now had no reason to collaborate) are obliged to come together is there such neglect of the essential, such a conspiracy of silence. Can it really be that we have just discovered all manner of ways to create and assemble previously unheard sounds, and nothing in music has changed, that we merely work on what we already know, what we already do? For fifteen years we have had a sound film that allows us to slow down, speed up, expand, contract, and, above all, fix sound, which until then was ephemeral, and there is nothing to be drawn from this except a few strange works of secondary importance? These same recordings, coming from all points of the compass, give rise to extraordinary comparisons among different human ways of perceiving, and there is not one new thought to be had about the problem of musical languages?

We often think we can find answers to this sort of research by using two types of approximations: the philosophical and the scientific. A physicist accustomed to dealing with and measuring facts, who transfers his habits of mind and his experience to music, is doubly threatened by the trap of words and things. Musical words have a double meaning: they designate magnitudes as well as phenomena. It is possible to measure parameters but rarely perceptions. And we can always go and look for the phenomenon in the "external world," without necessarily encountering, in the slightest, the phenomenon of music, which is within human consciousness, even though, paradoxically, it is materialized by the instruments and notations of the past, as well as by the tools and calculations of the present.

This is the justification for the double unlinking that we have attempted to bring about in both the meaning and the name of this activity, which has gone from concrete to experimental and is now focusing unreservedly on musical research. The word *concrete* had attached itself spontaneously to the result, the aesthetic form of the products; the word *experimental* had come to designate only devices, procedures, and methods; the word *research* assumed reflection that would bring everything into question, and this everything dared to speak its name, without any particular qualifier: *music.*

DIVERGENCE OF DISCIPLINES

What ultimately seems to us so essential and so linked to the conclusion of a particular process still appears incomplete and incidental to specialists of our time. If scarcely anyone can deny the importance of an in-depth reflection on music and a fundamental research approach with regard to the phenomenon of music, it is difficult to see the means, the circumstances, or who is competent to do this. It could also be objected that those who feel responsible for music are already engaged in it: musicians have rethought their traditional activities over the last decades; acoustic physicists have accumulated works on hearing that bring them very close to experimental psychology; electronic and cybernetic engineers are continually making technological contributions and developing not only a new *instrumentarium* but *composing machines* in unforeseen and radical ways. So our criticisms seem unfounded and unfair in the face of so many researchers who are preoccupied in various capacities with the musical.

Far from denying this fact and refusing the contributions of all these people, we point out that they all only labor so well because implicitly they accept that several arguments are won and that there is a common basis, indeed, even a language precise enough for people to be able to understand each other when music is discussed. But quite a few eminent people are working like this in good faith on principles that, to our mind, are only assumptions and words with double meanings.

The purpose of the whole beginning of this work is to identify these assumptions and expose these terms that are not the common fund but a common misunderstanding. This brings us to a second intention: to explore relationships among various disciplines as far as music is concerned. Indeed, it cannot be denied that the musical—and this is at one and the same time its interest and its difficulty—is a frontier land where the Arts, like the Sciences, have to be involved. As happens among neighbors in a disputed territory, relations are not particularly easy: too much courtesy, consisting of stepping out of each other's way and in effect leaving the territory underdeveloped, can be followed by a will to annexation pure and simple. Besides, the real has too many disparate aspects not to let everyone seize something that properly belongs to his specialty, but what specialist will come forward to link these particular disciplines together?

In truth, instead of parallels, serious examination is far from revealing any clear correlations, a preestablished harmony between music and mathematics, or an easy one between psychology and acoustics; we are obliged to acknowledge the disparate and the dispersed: music is a mountain with everyone tunneling into it, and the tunnels cross each other without ever meeting.

Rather than being upset, or underplaying the difficulty, it is better to take it on board and, as a strategist said, make this difficulty into "a springboard" for action. If the disciplines fail to meet in music, which nevertheless is a favored place for them to come together, it is not because they have something wrong with them or because their coming together is badly organized; it is because they are each pursuing their own goal, without the essential objective being addressed by any of them. In effect, the musical enigma contains its converse. It offers to any mind, from the layman to the professional, from the ordinary to the superior, the strangeness of being both the most material manifestation of mechanical vibrations (and their physiological deciphering) and the most spiritual (indeed the most esoteric) means of communication between one person and another. This well-known fact does not stop people applying to music, with scholarly stubbornness, the iron rule of our Culture, which carefully separates the Arts from the Sciences. Perhaps this separation of powers does not suit it?

MUSIC AS INTERDISCIPLINE

It would be as unwise to reject this division of work wholesale as to adopt it respectfully by virtue of established rights. Music, in particular, brings a discordant note into the concert of knowledge.[9] It jars with one of our favorite scruples: to separate as clearly as possible facts from ideas, the sensory from the intellect, or, in other words, objects and language. So music must be treated as scholars have learned to treat a fact that refuses to fit in with the system of explanations intended for it: it is not the fact that is wrong or that they deny; rather, they review the system.

First, we notice that the most common terms—pitch and duration, sensation and perception, objects and structures—which are used daily by everyone, do not have the same content, or they designate different circuits of experience or use. As can be seen, this is not yet about questions of principle: distinguishing pure sound from the sound called noise; basing a musical system on tonality or series (on a calibration of six, seven, twelve, or thirty sounds) or even on pitch rather than timbre. Over and above terminology it is a question of concepts themselves and, over and above concepts, of attitudes toward the musical. Thus, as soon as we move beyond the first premises of the two approaches—the musical arts and those sciences that touch on music (acoustics, physiology, experimental psychology, electronics, cybernetics, etc.)—we discover a problem of pure method, of how to define objects of thought or elucidate processes of reflection, which is properly the realm of the philosophical.

Can we find in philosophy the solution, the term or the means for a newly efficient way of thinking? To turn so soon to philosophy to find a way out of our uncertainties would doubtless be to prejudge it as well as to run it down. What we can ask of it is to contextualize them, and in particular, to spring the trap of words.

Once we are better prepared by considerations such as these, and, above all, better situated among the body of approaches that have put the same sort of question to philosophy, it would seem possible to define a type of research directed, this time in essence, toward the musical. Does this mean putting forward a new discipline, which would take over from or supplement the earlier ones? It is doubtless too early to say or to choose between two equally presumptuous options. Let us at the very least point out that there is a void between musical acoustics and music properly speaking, and that it must be filled by a science that would describe sounds, together with an art of hearing them, and that such a hybrid discipline is clearly at the basis of the music of musical works. A more ambitious approach is to put forward music, above all others, as a "universalizing" activity, a true *interdiscipline*, an activity that, taking from many specific disciplines, validates their partial contributions through synthesis, as much on the level of facts as ideas, and presents

9. The same remark can be found in Saussure with reference to language; see Ferdinand de Saussure, *Cours de linguistique générale* (Paris: Payot, 1916). [Translated by Roy Harris into English as *Course in General Linguistics*, ed. Charles Bally and Albert Sechehaye (La Salle, IL: Open Court, 1983).—Trans.]

itself on an equal footing with them, as an activity of discovery, aiming just as much, if not more, to establish a branch of knowledge as to create works.

RESOURCES FOR MUSICAL EXPERIMENTATION

Such high ambitions may seem desirable but lack their most elementary means. After all, they were there before, in musical literature, and are in keeping with the noblest, yet also the emptiest, of themes since time began. What new element would open up the harmony of the spheres to us?

Without aspiring so soon to that harmony, let us say that this figure of speech makes a mockery of it. We only speak so well, in such pompous terms, about a dream that we do not believe in. The way music is spoken about, vapid and prosaic by turns, going straight from the sublime meditations of the inspired to the laborious vaticinations of the inspirers, scarcely gives us confidence in a genuine approach to music.

We think new facts could bring about a radical rethinking of musical attitudes—facts that allow us, for the first time in history, to put together *musical facts* and *musical experimentation* worthy of that name.

These new facts are, after all, very modest in comparison to those to which they are added. Even if, by and large, there is already wide musical experimentation in the music of all times and all places, it does not obey the norms of the *experimental*. It is the discovery of *recording* (over the last twenty years since the preliminary problem of *fidelity* was resolved) that creates new conditions for traditional musical experimentation. These have not been clearly recognized. Once again, we have not seen the wood for the trees. The experimental music of these last years, in accumulating devices and increasing the number of sources, has inadvertently hidden from us the main means of experimentation in music: the ability to preserve, repeat, and examine at leisure sounds that until now were fleeting, tied to the playing of instrumentalists and the actual presence of the audience.

Does this amount to saying that the same thing is happening in music as probably happened in biology, when the photograph, aided by the microscope, prolonged by the camera, allowed the observer to hold between two slides what had been hidden from him and to fix this spectacle in time and space? The idea is fair enough but would not reveal the extent of the observable phenomenon and the construction we can put on it. Putting slivers of sound between slides, "observing" it through the microphone, or fixing it with the tape recorder would be yet again to consider sound as an object that is inert, essentially physical, physiological at a pinch. Fixing a sound on film is consistent with the first goal, to subject it to detailed and completely new observation. But to limit the field of inquiry in this way would be to forget both the listener altogether and music altogether. Sound cuttings are made in two worlds: they are a slice of the listener's time, and they are an extract from the message of the person expressing himself.

It could then be pointed out, as far as these two worlds of listening and musical creation are concerned, that the fact of recording adds nothing. It fixes sounds in its own way, repeating earlier, different, and differently developed fixations of the musical: precisely, the musical scores of works and the symbols of music theory, which enabled them to be translated. That the fact of recording only gives one particular packaging of the sound, only allows one phase of examination, without touching on the essence of the problem, does not lessen the significance of the means of observation. It is by noting the apparently slight differences between notated and recorded sound, between sound as *live listening* and sound as *acousmatic listening*,[10] that a whole process of revision and discovery seems to us to have taken off.

THE AIMS OF MUSICAL EXPERIMENTATION: OBJECTS, STRUCTURES, LANGUAGES

Initially we were, we admit, fascinated by this particular phenomenon. One needs to have gone through these moments, which any interested person can experience personally, when sound, the captive of the tape recorder, repeats itself indefinitely the same, cuts itself off from contexts, reveals itself in other perceptual perspectives, to rediscover that fervor of listening, that fever of discovering. It is very much like the feeling that takes hold of cinematographers when through the camera, its slow motion and close-ups, they discover faces, objects, movements that their eyes could see only rarely and indistinctly. So, for several years, the discovery of *sound objects* grabbed our attention, mobilized our research.

Limiting musical investigation like this would be to forget that "objects are made to serve" and the basic paradox about using them: that, once they are grouped in *structures*, they are forgotten as *objects*, and each simply brings a value to the group.[11] In any case this is a naive thought, which is expressed in ordinary language thus: objects, in our normal experience, seem to us to be "given." In reality we do not perceive the objects but the structures that allow us to identify them. These structures do not themselves take us by surprise in an original listening experience. We have never stopped hearing sounds since the awakening of our sense of hearing, and it did not awaken in just any period or just any civilization.

So from objects to structures and from structures to language there is an unbroken chain, all the more indiscernible as it is absolutely familiar to us, spontaneous, and we are completely conditioned to it. And here we have the second aspect of the tape recorder, which initially we had taken to be a machine for making sounds,

10. These terms will be clarified later in the work, in particular in chapter 4.
11. The problem of the relationship between objects and structures will be discussed at a deeper level in the philosophical book (book 4).

putting them together, creating new objects, indeed, new musics. It is also, first and foremost (for research purposes), a machine for observing sounds, for "decontextualizing" them, for rediscovering traditional objects, listening again to traditional music with a different ear, an ear that, if not new, is at least as deconditioned as possible.

Here we must understand the dissymmetry of its use. In the sense of *making* or even analyzing sound, the tape recorder is a laboratory or instrument-making tool. It works at the basic level, let us say the level of objects. In the sense of *hearing*, the tape recorder becomes a tool to prepare the ear, to provide a screen for it, to shock it, to remove masks from it. The tape recorder, but no more than any other acoustic device, cannot exempt us from a thorough study of listening, but it prepares the way for this through new contexts. Because of it, we can ask why, and how, and with reference to what context (ancestral, traditional, conventional, natural, etc.) we hear.

People may find these thoughts surprising, and wonder about the meaning of this sybilline suggestion that the tape recorder can place the ear outside its usual contexts. Surely it faithfully gives back what has been recorded on it? This phenomenon, astonishing in its simplicity, has nothing properly technical about it; to understand it, we have to look elsewhere for a precedent in the use of phonetics for the study of language.

The tape recorder allows us to focus our attention on sound itself, its matter and form, through cuts and comparisons that, apart from the technique, are very much like work done on the materials of language. Taking language only in context, it is difficult, if not impossible, to arrive at this kind of knowledge. The flow of meaning and the functions of the various elements are far too determinant for the infrastructure to be revealed. Patient reconstitution of the objects of phonation was needed to arrive at this surprising discovery: that some phonetically different sounds are heard as the same in one language system, whereas they are heard as very different—or, as they say, significant—in another. It has even been said that at a pinch phonology could do without phonetics. We would agree with Robert Francès that "musical perception has little in common with hearing" (physicists' hearing).[12] We cannot be content with such a dichotomy, even while using it to justify the necessary separation of sound and the musical, just like the distinction between phonetics and phonology.

General linguistics has been reflecting on language systems in this way for several decades. It was no longer content to explain language systems through one or several reference languages, as traditional linguists had done. From phonetic material to phonological functional units there are correlations that explain each other. Of course, doubt can be cast on any close parallelism between language

---

12. Robert Francès, *La perception de la musique* (Paris: Vrin, 1958). [Published in English as *The Perception of Music* (Mahwah, NJ: Lawrence Erlbaum, 1988).—Trans.]

systems and music because of the arbitrariness attached to the choice of meaning and the free relationship between signifier and signified, which makes the word into a sign, whereas the musical note has always appeared to impose itself independently of any arbitrariness, like a given from the physical world to which we seem to respond. This statement contradicts the previous one: that the musical is deduced from sound. This debate will have repercussions throughout this work and lead to the conclusion that there is a fundamental dualism in music, which gives it all its interest and also conjures up its mystery. We do indeed find in musical objects an objective basis related to the physical world, but we have also chosen a meaning for it within a far broader framework than people seem to realize at present. Hence, the symbols of music theory do not simply represent physical sounds but are relatively arbitrary signs, musical "ideas."

MUSICAL RESEARCH

Suggesting a new approach to music in this way means daring to envisage generations of researchers working over a very long time. Sketching out the program and the method for this, making a start on it, is already highly ambitious. This means, as well, that our first concern will be to limit it, to outline a program of approaches rather than a list of results.

We could say, in the most everyday language, that we could tackle the investigation of the musical from both ends—material and works—and *that we have exclusively chosen material.* But to put forward such a clear separation would be to forget the essential connectedness that articulates structures from the simple to the composite and that does not necessarily start with the simple: we enter into such relationships at any level, so we gain access as much to the higher as to the lower levels. In other words we perpetually keep in our minds and ears the part played in every work by *objects* (sound building blocks) that we can isolate and compare with each other independently of the context from which they come. Therefore, the reader will not be surprised to see throughout this work references to traditional, primitive, non-Western, and contemporary musics. There will be, however, no reference to any of these at the level of language, as this is beyond our remit.

There should be no misunderstanding about this attitude. Not only does it presuppose what is constantly present and accompanies the most general musical experience (i.e., works, civilizations, composers, audiences), but it allows, of course, for further or simultaneous stages of investigation into objects still more decisive than what we have attempted here.

Now it remains for us to say in what ways such a limited stage is possible and indispensable. We can see several reasons.

(a) One of them comes from the fact that, in linguistics, where the objects are much more involved at the higher levels, it seems possible to arrange the subdivision

of disciplines into hierarchies, each of which has a different "degree of freedom." And so, Jakobson writes:

> There is a rising scale of freedom in the combinations of linguistic units. When distinctive characteristics are combined into phonemes, the individual speaker has no freedom at all; the code has already fixed all the possibilities that can be used in the language system in question. The freedom to combine phonemes is circumscribed; it is limited to the fringe situation of creating words. When sentences are formed from words, the speaker is less constrained. Finally, when sentences are combined into utterances, the action of the constricting rules of syntax ceases and the freedom of each particular speaker is substantially increased, although the number of clichéd utterances should not be underestimated.[13]

It is quite easy to draw a parallel with traditional music. There is no more freedom to combine phonemes than the composer has using an instrumental "language": the orchestral sounds are given in the same way as the sounds of the vocal apparatus. The "words" of the orchestra are the notes, and the only new ones that can be expected are in a zone of "neologisms": those gongs, those cinceros, even those *ondes martenot* that are coming into the orchestra with the boldness and toughness typical of innovations. Musical "sentences" are clearly the dependence on scales, modes, rules of harmony, and so forth, with the same situation of semifreedom as the linguistic sentence in relation to syntax. Finally, musical "utterances" come under the final remark: there are many clichés: cadences, responses, accompaniment, resolutions, while contemporary music puts forward new stereotypes.

An initial comment must be made here: every new music, whether concrete or electronic, or quite simply contemporary, that tries to destroy all or part of such a robustly constituted system cannot claim either to be particularly logically based or to be easy to hear or immediately understood. Everything has to go right back to basics, and it is better to acknowledge its discontinuities than to plead development, or progress.

(b) If the argument for such a parallel were to be repudiated, we could point out that practical music teaching has also traditionally made a distinction between the theory of music and composition. In putting aside any preoccupations that may justify traditional rules of composition, or contradict or replace them, we are doing no more than returning to a time-honored musical custom. Besides, our theory of music will be less theoretical than the theory taught in musicianship classes, which rapidly turns to the uses of the scale, intervals, tonalities, and so forth. Our standpoint still falls short of this mark, and we are much closer to whatever concerns the instrument, determined never to separate *hearing* from *making*.

13. Roman Jakobson, *Essais de linguistique générale*, vol. 1, *Les fondations du langage* (Paris: Minuit, 1963). [The *Essais* are a collection of lectures by Jakobson; a second volume appeared in 1973.—Trans.]

(c) And this brings us to a third reason for a preliminary examination such as this. Inasmuch as the musical appears so bound up with physical sound, it is important to look at this first of all. Just as it would be difficult to imagine the linguist not being interested in the speech organs and the various "phonic objects" it is capable of delivering, it would be hard to see a fundamental investigation of music fail to reexamine sound such as we are able to make it. Now, unlike speech organs, which have not changed since Neanderthal times, the means of making musical sound have not ceased to vary from one age, one civilization, to another. We must make the prosaic, but often forgotten, remark that the musical thus singularly depends on the means of making music. This does not at all detract from the importance of hearing it, or from the fact that, in music as in phonetics, civilizations have made an instinctive and everyday choice of what they have retained as *significant.*

Even within these limits, our investigation should not be presented as the first stage of a journey that is concerned first and foremost with the instrumental and the ear in the context of the laboratory, and which would keep complementary matters until later, in particular the impact of this research on composition, its relationship with audiences, and its interaction with the material of other civilizations. In the same way as limiting it to elementary objects and structures involves constant reference to higher levels and the implicit presence of the end results they suggest, reflecting on making and hearing is inseparable from group research and the social and cultural context of which it is part. We are not talking here of castles in the air and good intentions. It will be seen how much the research we are suggesting is directed toward not an object *in itself* but an object *for an act of communication* and of group communication.

BOOK ONE

Making Music

1

The Instrumental Prerequisite

As will be seen, this work has no other purpose than to encourage *listening to sounds*, a traditional function of musicianship as opposed to performance classes. Given this, it is surely illogical to start by talking about instruments?

Certainly. But, before any logical considerations, there is our reader. We presume he is a musician; we know he is conditioned not only by acquired notions but through experience that probably preceded, and even formed, his musical consciousness. If we invite him to listen, to analyze his listening, he will refer back to that particular training in a way that is all the more impossible to resist as it is implicit. From the educational point of view the direct approach proves immediately to be no good.

If there were any doubt about what we have just suggested, the hermeticism of musical civilizations in relation to one another should give us pause: throughout Africa it is possible to experience fascinated crowds listening for hours on end to tom-tom music that at best inspires bored admiration in the Western listener, rather like the response he deigns to give to a concert of contemporary works. There are only two explanations for this boredom: either the language is intrinsically incoherent, or it is incomprehensible to those who are listening. And the fervor of the African crowds shows that the language of tom-toms, at least, is not inaccessible to everyone.

To understand this fact, we have to place ourselves upstream from these civilizations and try to see how they have arrived at this point, how, little by little, they were able to form and establish themselves. Beyond historical circumstances, and without making any claims to prehistoric truth, we must go back to the crude experience, directly linked to instinctive practice, of a *homo faber*, who probably, in everything and always, precedes *homo sapiens*.

1.2. NEANDERTHAL MUSIC

As we were not there, and as our man has left no other evidence but his bones, we must fall back on suppositions.

Did he meet his muse while listening to the belling of the stag or the roaring of the bison? Probably not. It is easier to imagine him on the alert, calculating distance, direction, the chances of a successful hunt. Not for one second does he linger or show interest in sound itself, which is immediately subordinated to the event it indicates and the plans it suggests to him.

But, in addition to a group of activities that are directly connected with his own survival, and are never dissociated from his perceptions, he has others, this time disinterested, taken from the example of young animals themselves: running, stretching, mock fighting, trying things out, exercising muscles for no particular reason; these activities, even if they have a use, as they contribute to furthering nature's plan, also have a margin of gratuitousness. Hence, prehistoric man must surely be familiar with two ways of using the voice: to call out, to give cries of warning or anger, or else to try out what specialists pompously call his speech organs, the pleasure of shouting at the top of his voice, and the pleasure also of hitting things, without there being necessarily any dissociation between the gesture and its effect, the satisfaction of exercising his muscles and "making a noise." Ought we to seek in games like these, later perfected as their meaning developed, the simultaneous origins of dance, song, and music?

We will not take this unverifiable hypothesis any further but make the limits of our investigations clear: we simply wish to point out the presence, from the very beginning, of these two tendencies: actions in response to external requirements; disinterested activities in response to autonomous inspiration. Essentially different, these types of activity constantly interact in reality, of course, and we have separated them here only for the purposes of exposition.

Although they became more and more different, the utensil and the musical instrument were in essence probably related and contemporary in just the same way. We are equally willing to wager that there was no distinction between them in reality, either, and that the same calabash did equally well for soup and music.

1.3. THE INSTRUMENTAL PARADOX:
THE BIRTH OF MUSIC

Doubtless a single calabash would not have been enough. But two, three calabashes? The signal, which referred to the utensil, becomes a pleonasm and cancels itself out through repetition. All that is left is the "sound object," perceived completely disinterestedly, which "strikes the ear" as something that has absolutely no use but imposes its presence and is enough to transform the cook into an experimental musician.

Connected to his own activity and the sound body, but also, paradoxically, independent of these, he has just discovered *Music*—because that is already what it is—and, along with this, the possibility of *playing* what will later be called an *instrument*.

Let us make ourselves clear. Instrumental activity, the first and visible cause of every musical phenomenon, has the peculiarity that above all else it tends to cancel itself out as material cause. And this in two ways:

The *repetition* of the same causal phenomenon, through saturation of the signal, removes its practical significance (for example, a particular object strikes another in a particular way) and suggests a disinterested activity: this is how the utensil becomes the instrument.

The *variation* of *something perceptible* within the causal repetition accentuates the disinterested nature of the activity in relation to the instrument itself and gives it a new interest by creating a different kind of event, an event that we have to call musical. This is the simplest, the most general, and the least preconceived definition of music. Even if the calabash player does not yet know how to play it, expresses nothing or does not make himself understood, he "is making music." What else would he be doing?

1.4. FROM THE INSTRUMENT TO THE WORK

The three calabashes make up a given, imposed vocabulary, allowing ways of playing that are impoverished, certainly, but already numerous and unconstrained. And our improvised musician improvises. The variation the instrument permits gives rise to *variations*, that is, "pieces of music." As soon as one of these is recognized, distinguished from the others, deliberately repeated, we can say that we have, if not a language, at least a work. Leaving aside any aesthetic judgment, the work is a fact, almost as clear as the fact of the instrument and undeniably connected to it.

Thus, we would be happy to argue, it precedes even what it postulates—a language and what this is made of: objects. If there are rules for playing an instrument, registers, and concepts, it will require thousands of years and a long period of learning by musical civilizations to develop and formulate them.

Spontaneous starting points such as these even explain the diversity of these languages: they come from material circumstances, historical tendencies that are infinitely varied but also very specific, each responsible for a particular *musical experience*, each opening up a *field of music*.

1.5. FROM THE INSTRUMENT TO THE MUSICAL
DOMAIN: MUSICAL CIVILIZATIONS

So we return to our calabashes and suppose that they have been refined by being covered with a skin. Clearly, what is given is the device. What is to come is the broadening of experience, depending on the various ways of behaving in relation to the device. The behavior that dominates will determine one kind of music—that is, one musical field—rather than another: our primitive man, by dint of playing his calabashes, arrives at a particular form of virtuosity that will *condition* his music. He may play them in several ways: on the one hand, with a stick or the tips of his fingers he will obtain sounds of greater or lesser intensity but, above all, in a given order, which will produce a language of rhythms; on the other hand, if, independently of the percussive movement of his fingers, he learns to control the pressure of his palm on the skin, each of these sounds will be modulated in pitch and will involve an additional value in which these pitches, even ill-defined, will play a part.[1]

Prior to any rhythmic or melodic codification, we can see four *dimensions* in this instinctive activity: two of these, rhythm and pitch, are relatively explicit; the other two, timbre and intensity, are implicit. Finally, we can classify these four planes where music operates according to their dominance.

For example, the rhythmic plane will dominate if the melodic modulation is only an ornament. The other two will be integrated into the preceding ones: nuance will merge with the rhythmic structure, and timbre will differentiate one calabash from another. But, more often, the primitive musician playing two or three tom-toms or joining other tom-tom players will keep rhythm dominant, "ornamented" with the other values. Conversely, if he invents the lithophone,[2] the melodic will dominate in his music.

What might be a Western musician's attitude toward these phenomena? He would begin by reducing them either to "percussion rhythm" motifs or to a study in scales of pitch, thus moving rapidly from instrumental technique to the structures it delivers. He will not notice that even though, generally speaking, rhythmical structures predominate in primitive musics, they always coexist with the other three types of modulation. He will tend to notate in eighth notes and sixteenth notes something that cannot of course be reduced in this way, even on the rhythmic level; he will certainly not adopt a holistic approach, through *musical objects*, that is, the *given components* of other types of musical expression different from his own. And so he will find himself engaged in an undertaking as meaningless as deciphering hieroglyphics with a two-foot ruler or the Greek alphabet. This

---

1. One of the two instruments of the Indian *tabla* is played according to the technique described here.

2. A primitive instrument composed of resonant stones of different sizes, giving a number of sounds of different pitches.

explains why musical civilizations are sealed off from each other; to overcome this, we must go back to the beginning to take into account a fact that could be described as a miracle of virtuosity. The discovery of registers is no more than the art of using the instrumental material that a particular civilization has to hand. The concrete precedes the abstract.

1.6. CONCRETE AND ABSTRACT IN MUSIC

So the phenomenon of music has two related aspects: a tendency toward abstraction, inasmuch as performing draws out structures, and an involvement with the concrete,[3] inasmuch as it remains tied to the potential of the instrument. It is worth noting here that, depending on what the instrumental and cultural context is, the music produced will be mainly concrete, mainly abstract, or more or less a balance of the two.

In light of this we should note the constant interdependence of abstract and concrete in the interplay of *pitches* in most musics. Even if the Sicilian scarcely manages to get A E I O U colored with harmonics from his *Jew's harp*, if the tom-tom is still on the threshold of a perfect chord, and if the *reita*, the Arab violin, happily lingers on notes that we find out of tune, the Indian *baladar* plays a more and more refined calibration of pitches and, in the course of interminable *ragas*, never tires of perfecting unisons and octaves. Indian music, like Chinese music, achieves an amazing synthesis of the two tendencies: it uses the calibration of pitches, not only pentatonic, as is conventionally taught, but often diatonic, along with sliding sounds, greatly extended in the pitch register, between perfectly defined intervals where it is delightful to fill in the gaps, particularly if the dynamic profile of these sounds is expertly gauged. Here we are anticipating notions of calibration from which this book ascetically turns away but which could shed light on it. . . . Where, indeed, could we find the origin of the use, both so free and so complex, of everything that is capable of *making music* except in the instrument pushed to its limit?

Clearly, as far as pitch is concerned, an instrument can be used in all sorts of different ways, from the crudest to the most subtle. The African *balaphone*, for example, can be calibrated according to a completely arbitrary local tradition, whereas the *baladar*, it seems, was intended for a most scholarly marking off into sections, allowing for division into microintervals, as well as continuous passages. The Hawaiian guitar gives only a crude, almost automatic wailing, whereas Indian or Japanese instruments, like the *hsiennfou* or the *kunanoto*, can produce an attack

---

3. Schaeffer explains here that music leads to abstraction while remaining grounded in physical experience. He uses the expression "adhérence au concret" to explain the tendency of all perceived sounds to refer to their physical cause.—Trans.

within an interval of pitches that are precise, contained, and carved out in time in all freedom and originality. And when we come to the voice, how can we ignore the richness of uses like these, from the cry, almost detached from any calibration, right down to vocalized sound in a well-defined interval, or Tibetan murmuring, where melody is simply a background for the spoken word?

Do people think that, even in the West, we are insensitive to this interplay of approximate pitches, which we scarcely dare acknowledge? Does a good voice, in a Lied that particularly highlights this, express itself only through the pitch indicated on the score? Is there not, in genuinely subtle interpretations, an almost Asian vocal latitude[4] and an interplay of timbres even in the course of the sounds? This is even clearer in jazz.

So from now on no instruments, even and above all Western ones, should be reduced to the stereotyped registration that governs the way they are played. We must recognize their *concrete* aspect and appreciate the "rules for playing" that mark the extent and the limits, the degree of freedom they allow the performer. It is absurd to criticize, as do too many contemporary musicians, the so-called imprecision of instrumental playing, which would necessitate the technical perfection expected of machines, under the pretext that the best music is the most precise.[5]

In truth it is neither pitches nor timbres nor intensities nor durations that need to be accurate or strictly obedient to a notation. It is the presence of a composer's or a performer's intention, superimposed on these very approximate or too-abstract reference points, that ultimately calibrates every sound entity and gives it its form, its two-, three-, or fourfold originality: the specific originality of a particular violin, the contingent, or varying, but keenly recognized as "successful" or "failed," originality of the performance of a particular musical object that is, however, attributed to the style of a particular performer. And this by virtue of a truly wonderful ambivalence in every sound entity that must necessarily be heard as responsive to fixed values, and yet, from one note to another, from one performance to another, as infinitely varied.

1.7. REGISTERS AND MUSICAL DOMAINS

Whether we are dealing with strings, membranes, strips of wood, or metal pipes, simple or complex instruments, it is nonetheless apparent that musical experimentation has centered almost exclusively on variations of pitch. Indeed, it seems

4. This statement is eloquently corroborated by acoustic enhancements, where huge differences in pitch can be seen between various transmissions of the same note, all of which, however, are heard as in tune by a Western ear.

5. This paragraph is a criticism of the preconceived methods of electronic and serial music, where pitch, intensity, or duration are more important than the sound itself and are often precalculated.—Trans.

that pitch is the key to the liberating gesture and the power of abstraction that give rise to music and to musical potential, as well as instrumental music-making.

But whether it is pentatonic, dodecaphonic, thirty-one-isonic, accurate, approximate, lacunary, tempered, or incongruous, we will not dwell exclusively on the pitch register of a balaphone, an electric organ, or a Pleyel here. Not that we also do not give it pride of place, but as almost all musical literature is devoted to it, our aim, faced with the general neglect, is to give the same importance to everything else as well. We will not return to the concept of pitch until later to show that, far from existing in the abstract, it also is conditioned by the other registers.

Incidentally, it is worth observing that the registration of pitches has not always dominated with such pride and such claim to exclusivity. In African music, as we have said, pitch more often qualifies rhythms than being a modulation sought after for its own sake, whereas Asian music seeks a balance between dynamic and melodic modulation.

Now all we need to do is to open our ears to the third register, timbres, even though the Western musician will find himself yet again quite ill-prepared for this.

If there are a few cases where the instrument has a practically dominant register of timbres, these are, we must admit, the exception. The Sicilian Jew's harp is not representative of a very highly evolved musical civilization. But it exists, and it demonstrates that, failing all else, or perhaps from deliberate choice, the Sicilian porter prefers the *Klangfarbenmelodie* to the panpipes, just like the Khmer shepherd who fashions his Asiatic instrumental counterpart from bamboo. At the two ends of the earth, these solitary people charm away their boredom with this melody of vowels, these ambivalent modulations, at the margins of music and language, the primitive models for modern synthetic musics.

Another example is the organ, that universal instrument that "summarizes" history and geography and would seem, like the great dinosaurs, destined to be replaced by those better adapted than it. In truth it is the only one that explicitly possesses all four registers: pitch, timbres (you can see the keyboards and the stops), durations, and intensities (strongly emphasized by the mechanical context). How can the most abstract of instruments, since it has these four registers, be spontaneously concrete as well, linking together the most primitive musical instinct and the most up-to-date musical developments? We will reflect on this originality later.

In the context of the three dominant types of instruments and the way they are used, we may be tempted to distinguish a mainly melodic or harmonic musical field, a mainly rhythmic field and a timbre field—that is, three great musical families. But though this classification takes into account *grosso modo* the three main continents of musical geography—Europe, Africa, and Asia—we need to take many more factors into account for it to be complete. The modern musician, as well, is all too inclined to simplify not thousands of years of development but his own short experience in this field. The success of *Modes de valeurs et d'intensités* by Messiaen, and of the concept of *Klangfarbenmelodie*, is characteristic of this tendency: a curiosity about areas of music that are less hackneyed than the register of pitch but also a naive haste to take hold of them, with the help of a notation that is itself dubious and whose abstract nature is ill-adapted to the concrete content.

1.8. LIMITATIONS OF "MUSICAL CATECHISMS"

It has long been the experience in instrumental playing that the performers' virtuosity has adapted to a very crude type of instrument making or has demanded an ever better means of shaping sound, and this has led musical civilizations to take over areas specific to them. Before obeying "laws of music," these areas are first and foremost historical, characterized by habit and custom: habits of playing and listening, and customs that set arbitrary limits within which musical objects are made to vary by means of a given way of making instruments that are used in accordance with a traditional virtuosity and appreciated by educated audiences.

Thus, the present Western musical catechism hands down to us as incontrovertible knowledge a notional system in which the musical note, easily identifiable through criteria of pitch, duration, and intensity, is the archetype. By means of these concepts, considered as universal, and an adequate system of notation, musicians compose: that is to say, they anticipate, through the symbolism of a form of writing, what the work ought to be (and it therefore coincides with his score). Then the score, entrusted to instruments and instrumentalists, is performed, and the work, already implicit, and which a professional can read from the symbols in the text, becomes explicit, that is to say, audible, perceptible to the uninitiated.

Every type of approach to music in the West is so impregnated with these premises that it is impervious in advance to any generalization, any universalism, any curiosity about the phenomenon itself and the puzzles it contains.

If, however, the reader is willing to follow us in our analysis, he will admit that music was not born out of the reflections of Pythagoras or the science of vibrating strings. Only elementary manuals present the origins of these notions "back to front" like this, as if they emerged fully armed, like Minerva, from Jupiter's thigh. Here and there they are the culmination of specific musics, the crowning achievement of a great number of experiments: they each form a musical civilization.

So we should not be surprised if other instruments, other experiments have upset the established order in the instrumental field and have led to a rethinking of its norms. The aim of this first book is to illustrate this.

First of all, in the next chapter we must look more closely at the concept of the instrument.

Playing an Instrument

2.1. DEFINITION OF AN INSTRUMENT

An instrument does not conform to any theoretical definition, except permanence-variation, which we have mentioned above (section 1.3), a concept that dominates all musical phenomena. Every device that makes it possible to obtain a varied collection of sound objects—or of varying sound objects—while keeping us aware of the permanence of a cause, is a musical instrument, in the traditional sense of an experience common to all civilizations.

If the description "musical" is attached mainly to the variety and the arrangement of the collection of objects, the instrument will reveal registers and will give rise to a domain of music dominated by the resultant structures. If the description is applied mainly to the objects themselves, which are interesting in their form or matter but isolated and disparate enough not to have registers, and not leading to any structures, we discover a type of instrument some examples of which can be found in the tradition but which have always been placed, by Westerners at least, on the fringes of music: for example, gongs, cymbals, cowbells, and other bits and pieces. These instruments do not, it is true, give a collection of distinct objects with an abstract quality that could allow them to be graded, but stereotypical objects, although in a variety of examples, differentiated only by concrete characteristics. Thus instrumental practice already reveals the alternation between a sound *structure* and the *characteristics* of a structured sound.

2.2. COMPOSITION OF INSTRUMENTS

Concentrating exclusively on the abstract in music leads, of course, to a system of classification that depends on this: instruments with fixed or melodic sounds, instruments with indeterminate sounds (percussion) for rhythmical use, interplay of timbres. But, since pitch dominates, the greatest emphasis will be placed on instruments that have a register of predetermined pitches (temperaments, keyboards) and allow the use of continuous pitches (stringed instruments or instruments with slides, for example).

There could also be a system of classification based on a "major feature" of the materials of the sound bodies (strings, wood, wind) or, again, from a prominent aspect of their technology (keyboards, percussion, bows . . .).

Now, both systems of classification are defective for similar reasons: the first involves referring the instrument back to an established musical system and the second to the details of a given instrumentarium. For the resources of an instrument go far beyond the registration intended for it. Nor do they depend as closely as people think on its technology or a system of classification by families; based on the procedures, a particular instrumentarium is not necessarily a good system of musical classification—that is, one based on effects.

Neither of these classification systems properly highlights the potential inherent in the sound sources themselves, particularly the variety and freedom of ways of playing. This latter notion is the most important: not just the instrument in itself but also the relationship it allows with the instrumentalist. But this relationship and its twofold potential, abstract and concrete, cannot be understood without a universal concept of the musical instrument, and in practice the musician hardly ever reflects on this.

We would say that a musical instrument has three components, the first two being essential. They are the vibrating mechanism, which starts to vibrate, and the stimulating mechanism, which starts the vibration off or, in the case of sustained sounds, prolongs it; the third component, which is secondary but almost always present, is the resonator—that is, a device that adds its effects to those of the vibrating body to amplify, prolong, or modify them in some way.[1]

We can therefore easily compare a violin, a piano, a gong, or a pipe. They all have a vibrating component: strings for the violin and the piano, a membrane or a column of air for the gong and the pipe. The stimulating component, for the piano or the gong, is short-lived, a hammer or bass drumstick; for the violin or the pipe we have a sustaining stimulator, a bow or the breath. Finally, the first two

1. The Baschet brothers quite rightly use the term *adaptors* rather than *resonators:* this is the device that couples the vibrating element to the air, taking into account any acoustic impedance. [Bernard and François Baschet were two well-known instrument makers and artists who created totally original instruments, among them the Baschet Crystal, which was used for music and sculptures or in education. The Baschet brothers worked closely with Schaeffer from the end of the 1950s and during the 1960s.—Trans.]

instruments have such clearly visible resonators that they hide the whole instrument all by themselves: the encasement of the violin, and the soundboard of the piano, while the last two have no resonators at all.

As soon as a system of classification such as this is sketched out, it sheds much light, as we will see, on the approach to another system of classification, much more difficult this time: the classification of sound *objects* themselves, obtained from sources, or sound *bodies* (this distinction, which we have already used previously, is fundamental). A pizzicato on the violin is infinitely nearer to a note on the piano than a sustained violin sound, which in its turn can be compared to a sustained sound on the pipe.

Besides, for as long as he sees the instrument at the same time as he hears it, the listener is psychologically conditioned and takes note of differences that seem huge to him. But if the instrument is hidden, or if the recording, without being in any way rigged, plays back only some moments of unevenness in intensity, extraordinary confusions become possible, which demonstrate the similarity between sounds or, more precisely, *sound objects*, perceived musically, from sources that are radically different either because of the principle of the instrument (bowed or wind instruments; tempered instruments or instruments with indeterminate sounds) or their historic or ethnological construction.

2.3. SIMPLE OR MULTIPLE INSTRUMENTS

Once a sound source has been discovered, the instrument maker has two choices: to repeat the same source and extend it into various sizes or, conversely, to stay with the same source and try to vary it in itself. The second procedure is not the simplest, as it will inextricably link together the three components: vibrating, stimulating, and resonating. It is likely that circumstances will oblige the instrumentalist not to use these variations independently of each other but to use them together in keeping with the aesthetics of the object. Thus, a violinist can only use high notes with care, within a limited and precarious register of intensities and timbre.

This is true above all of the voice, which cannot be compared to any precisely and suitably calibrated instrument. Any analysis of the voice that does not, from the outset, accept that there is a close relationship between timbre, pitch, and intensity, not to mention duration and dynamics,[2] will probably not be very true to life.

If, however, we move on to multiple instruments composed of a number of vibrating bodies, we can see immediately that each of these vibrating bodies repeats the combination of all three components. The piano, which seems to be one of the simplest, required a long and difficult process of development, precisely because it

2. The *dynamic* of a sound is the variation in intensity of this sound in the course of its duration. (The expressiveness, the life of vocal sounds, for example, is closely linked to their dynamic.)

involved varying the collection of vibrating elements, while at the same time keeping the percussive elements and the resonator unchanged as far as possible. Even so, we should point out the crudeness of the procedures that were used, since the strings must be doubled or tripled depending on the register; if we listen carefully, when it goes from high to low, there is hardly any similarity between the various performances of the same percussion-resonance device. This does not stop the musician from speaking of the "timbre" of the piano as if it were a single entity. The timbre of the piano is recognizable, it is true, and the most out-of-tune piano can be identified by the most inexpert listener. But it is surprising that acousticians have been taken in for so long by such an obvious booby trap. So let us say, *a priori*, that it is highly likely that the piano does not have *a* timbre but *several*, as many timbres as notes.

2.4. INSTRUMENTAL ANALYSIS

Although indispensable for giving an account of different types of instrumentarium, the above analyses do not tell us anything about what a musical instrument essentially is. We must look elsewhere, to the relationship of the instrument with the sound families it produces. So what, without going into details, is both essential and enough to say to give a full account of its musical functions?

If the definition we gave at the beginning of this chapter is right, this should emerge from the definition itself. On the one hand, what is the permanent element, common to all the sound objects that come from one instrument? And, on the other hand, what are its capacities for variation?

(a) *"Timbre," a permanent quality of the instrument*

In response to the first question, all we will give is a tautology, as at the moment we know of no other acceptable definition of *timbre* than this: "that by which we can recognize that various sounds come from the same instrument." At least in this way we avoid long explanations, like the doctors in Molière, of "why your daughter is dumb."[3] We will hope to do better later on.[4]

---

3. Schaeffer refers here to Molière's 1666 play *Le médecin malgré lui* (act 2, scene 6). In English the title is *The Doctor in Spite of Himself*. The answer to the question, after lengthy disquisitions, is that she is dumb because she's lost the power of speech.—Trans.

4. We would ask the reader not to be offended here by the apparent lightheartedness of the analysis and to keep in mind, on the one hand, that in this treatise we deliberately start from hackneyed definitions in order to distance ourselves from the technical meanings that these key terms often take on in specific disciplines and, on the other hand, that in this particular case the origin of the word *timbre* justifies our attitude: in effect, it initially designated a sort of drum made with a series of strings under tension that gave the sound a characteristic color; in practice, therefore, the word *timbre* and the thing itself as musical instrument were one and the same; again, when we consider the ancient meaning of *timbre* as a "stamp of origin" attached to a particular object to indicate where it came from, it is clear that we could hardly, initially, think of timbre as anything else but a reference to the instrument, a trademark.

(b) *Instrumental registers, sources of "abstract" variations*

Quite independently of what type of instrument it is, we discover a registration for it—not, as we may be prematurely tempted to say, a *sound* structure that can be detected in the series of objects it delivers but *what produces* the variation of these objects, not exactly the effects but the totality of causes involved in producing them. This distinction, subtle for those who have not yet noticed it (and this is generally the case with traditional musicians), is nevertheless essential. It is one thing to notice that the violin string is shortened, quite another to hear that its notes are more, or less, high; one thing to observe the register of the piano keyboard, quite another to analyze the nature of the notes it produces.

Of course, there are multiple registers in any instrument: a main register that, in advanced instruments, in theory controls the pitch, and secondary registers that, to employ the usual terms, act on intensity or timbre.[5] The distinction between causes and effects we have just made immediately demonstrates its usefulness: since the variations produced by these different registers are, as we have seen, perceived at the level of effects, it would be wise to study these effects in themselves, causally, taking care not to make any hasty inferences concerning *structures* as they are perceived in the musical mind: even if there is correlation, there is not necessarily coincidence.

(c) *Instrumental play, the source of "concrete" variations*

Until now the instrument has been a given. Although made, and calibrated in accordance with certain more or less precise rules, it is inert; it is played only in the mind. It is quite another thing to place it in the hands of an instrumentalist, a *particular* instrumentalist. We will not consider here the situation, perfectly possible however, in which, like John Cage, the instrumentalist plays the instrument in registers and for uses for which it was not intended. Even observing the rules of play, he can deliver varieties of objects that bring out his own *shaping of sound*. In the most stereotyped of instruments, the piano, it is accepted that there is a "touch" specific to the pianist, in the same way that people speak of a rider's "style," however mediocre the horse. A fortiori, a violinist or a flautist is capable of drawing from the instrument a variety of objects that are, however, within the same registers and have the same form: slurred or staccato objects, pizzicato, vibrato, and so forth, but where their personality, their "sound" as people say, dominates, for it would not be enough to use the word *timbre* here either.

2.5. TRIPLE NATURE OF THE INSTRUMENT

Thus we find ourselves faced with a trinity of factors that from now on will pervade nearly all our analyses. Sound, drawn from the physical world, requires first

5. In another meaning of the word, clearly different from the one above, and which is defined below.

and foremost care in the making. The instrument is therefore studied in itself, as a physical device. At the other extreme this device only has meaning through its aesthetic purposes, which are completely dominated by "musical ideas." Finally, the traditional instrument is traditionally activated by an artist, the performer, who brings with him a certain degree of originality: the score indicates how he should use the instrument for both abstract and concrete effects and leaves him a margin of freedom to demonstrate both his virtuosity and his sensibility.

When a new way of making instruments comes to light, we instinctively approach it in these three ways. When we want to construct an instrument, we endeavor to imagine one with registers that are as rich and abundant as possible, producing the most complex and delicate structures, and, finally, giving the instrumentalist opportunities for extended and subtle ways of playing. Such was the list of specifications with which every new instrument, and particularly the electronic instrument, had to comply, even before it came into being.

2.6. THE ELECTRONIC INSTRUMENT

First we will briefly summarize the doctrines of the electronic instrument's protagonists. Musical pitch corresponds to the number of oscillations per second of an electronic circuit, played back by an electroacoustic "engine" (a loudspeaker). A pitch comes either from a pure frequency, calculated in numbers of hertz, or a combination of frequencies, the proportions of which determine the timbre[6]—harmonic timbre, in the case of a harmonic sound reconstituted by the basic sound and its harmonic partials; color, when arbitrary frequencies are put together, creating a complex sensation of pitch and timbre mingled together.

So, compared with the crude way the piano functions, with its scales or temperaments, infinite possibilities are opened up for experimentation on "bundles of frequencies," from *white noise* (a random accumulation of components whose frequencies fill the whole of the spectrum) to *complex* sound,[7] calculated in advance from the number and intensity of its frequencies. Similarly, the interplay of levels of intensity can be accurately calibrated for each bundle of frequencies. Finally, the profiles,[8] that is, the way the intensities, overall or partial, develop in relation to time, can be predetermined.

6. Here, of course, we are referring to the "coloration" particular to each sound and not to the instrumental timbre defined in section 2.4.

7. By *complex sound* we mean all sounds of undefined pitch, and therefore containing a fairly large number of components with nonharmonic frequencies.

8. *Profile* is a technical term referring to what in sound synthesis is called the envelope found in early analog synthesizers. The envelope, or overall dynamic shape of the sound, is often structured in four sections: Attack, Decay, Sustain, and Release (called ADSR).—Trans.

The score now becomes a blueprint, as we are able to give a precise description of every sound through a reference trihedron, where the axes time, frequency, and dynamic level correspond respectively to sensations of duration, pitch, and intensity. As for the immediate timbre, this is the overall coloration of the sound matter, that is, of the bundle of frequencies, each with its own intensity, presented to the ear at a given moment.

It is not surprising that a whole generation of composers, instantly seduced by correlations such as these, should immediately have embarked on constructions in which everything could be calculated in advance . . . except the effect. For, by rushing headlong like this into systems of composition, they sidestepped the phase of authentic experimentation: the phase that would have been about the *correlations* between our *musical perceptions* and such abundantly available *stimuli*. As for physicists, they could consider their work finished, since they had developed instruments, truly perfect from the physical point of view, that allowed the most extensive use of the three acoustic parameters.

The quite unexpected consequences might have provided food for thought; even if the scores were perfectly intelligible, the resultant sounds were surprising. Not because of their complexity but because a number of rapidly recognizable effects clearly revealed their "electronic" origins.

If we had managed to produce anything like a real reconstruction of traditional sounds by means of synthesis, this technique might have been perceptible like a fault in production; thus, in a bad recording of a symphony, we recognize both the orchestral instruments and the faults in the recording. But the phenomenon was quite different: the electronic source appeared as one of the instruments. While it claimed either to recreate preexisting timbres or to create appropriately varied "previously unheard" ones, it branded both with its own "timbre," in the pragmatic definition we have given this term. As for the various modes of playing, they also seemed to become contained within their own particular qualities—not at all for want of originality, even less for lack of virtuosity, but again by accentuating an electronic character that was already perceptible in the sound materials.

Without being a failure in itself, electronic music therefore failed as far as its initial claims were concerned: to replace instruments and performers in one fell swoop, by giving composers a universal palette of sounds, together with an objective musical way of using them, and so to open up infinite possibilities while ensuring total virtuosity of performance. We could catch glimpses of such potential and such virtuosity but enclosed in a far too recognizable instrumental field and a form of aesthetic expression that depended on this.

Let us be quite clear: we are not saying that it could not, at a stretch, be different. But musicians fascinated by electronics must agree to revise their principles, to direct their aims accordingly, and above all, initially, to carry out methodical experiments with the registers and types of play at their disposal.

2.7. MUSIQUE CONCRÈTE

Musique concrète had followed a similar, and equally surprising, path: starting from the same sort of claim to universality, it also became enclosed in its own particular limitations. Without wishing either to go over or enlarge on what has been said elsewhere,[9] we will restrict ourselves to what is directly relevant to our discussion.

The "concrete faction," apparently, behaved differently from its electronic contemporaries. Having made a fresh start with registers and values, these musicians took their sounds from anywhere but preferably from acoustic reality: noises, traditional instruments (Western or exotic), voices, languages, and some synthetic sounds, to be sure that the panoply was complete. Then, by means of various electroacoustic manipulations, these recorded sounds were transformed and assembled. We will not for the moment place too much emphasis on the final processing of these musics, which were on magnetic tape and were developed by listening to several tracks simultaneously (stereophony) so that we could spend more time on the business of making them.

The speeding up and slowing down provided by the turntable in 1948, and soon after by the tape recorder, had initially been used in a chaotic fashion. But, if they were used along with splitting up sounds in time—by cutting the tape—and on the level of timbre—by filtering—we could assume with certainty that every sound could be decomposed and could then, through the techniques of editing and mixing, be recomposed with other sounds.

Thus, musique concrète definitely had the same pretensions as electronic music, which believed that it could produce any preexisting sound by synthesis. Only it went through a preliminary stage of analysis. It also used the name *reference trihedron*, to the invention and success of which the author is unfortunately no stranger.[10]

By cutting up sound according to the three axes of the trihedron—time, frequency, and dynamic level (by editing, filtering, and copying at different sound levels)—it was possible to isolate a "slab of sensation," which, compared with synthetic sound, had the advantage of retaining the complex characteristics of the natural sound. Of course, it was just as possible to do the reverse: raise or lower these "slabs" in pitch, by slowing down or speeding up, only taking care to

9. See Pierre Schaeffer, *A la recherche d'une musique concrète* (Paris: Seuil, 1952), translated into English by Christine North and John Dack as *In Search of a Concrete Music* (Berkeley: University of California Press, 2012).—Trans.

10. And which our friend Abraham Moles then very unwisely helped to circulate, in the same way as the theory of the "slab of sensation," in his various works. [Abraham Moles was a French engineer and philosopher working on aesthetics and information theory. He collaborated with Schaeffer at the end of the 1940s and beginning of the 1950s.—Trans.]

compensate for the simultaneous effect on time (this can be done automatically with the "universal phonogène"), recompose the spectra by mixing, and join up the elements again by collage.[11]

As can be seen, the thinking in both musics was centered on the same error: faith in the trihedron and the decomposing of sound, for one group into the Fourier series, for the other into "slabs of sensation." At that time we were working, the former to construct robots, the latter to dissect corpses. Living music was elsewhere and would only give itself to those who knew how to escape from these simplistic models.

Furthermore, oddly, the works ended up resembling each other. Meanwhile, the pioneers had watered their wine. Whereas members of the "concrete faction" were gradually freeing themselves from the trap of their turntables, which in truth remained very crude, the "electronic faction" was making borrowings from musique concrète that were both unacknowledged and clearly apparent: voices, manipulated instruments, anything would do for a music where only the label of origin was purely electronic; and this label would eventually prevail, setting the initial misunderstanding in stone, doubtless for a long time to come.

2.8. CONFUSION OVER INSTRUMENTS

A second error, common to the two systems and doubtless compounding the first, was the confusion, over quite a long period, between studio instruments and musical instruments.

The synthetic instruments of electronic music did indeed present a very subtle trap: they were wonderfully calibrated to create registers of sound and lent themselves to fascinatingly virtuoso uses. The same could not be said of turntables and tape recorders, which, in fact, were only recording devices, really intended for radio broadcasting, and which musicians had gradually infiltrated, not without conflicts or feelings of guilt. They nevertheless got results; amid so many formless and facilely surrealist works, so many failed experiments, an unexpected musical landscape was revealed to them, surprising, incongruous sound entities, where the most difficult question was what to do with them.

The first of these musics seemed to offer everything, in particular magnificent scores docilely obedient to any preconceived ways of organizing them. The other gave crude and explosive combinations of sound, ill-assorted objects that eluded any notation.

It was not obvious to "concrete" musicians that they should give up all electroacoustic manipulation, when they seemed to be there precisely for this, and the studio hung over them with all its working potential for new procedures. If,

11. The reader will find a fuller account in chapter 23 of what is only briefly summarized here.

however, we compared a tape recorder with a traditional instrument, we could not deny a feeling of unease: manipulating even a well-chosen component on the tape recorder, by speeding it up or slowing it down, made it appear like a "special effect," "rigged,"[12] even more obviously than in electronic music.

Even so, every time we took the trouble to record with care, to choose sound entities judiciously, to vary what we did with them, through recording or purely acoustic devices, we obtained sound samples that were hugely varied and interesting.

Toward 1958, ten years after we began, metal sheets and rods appeared on the scene, and little by little our work moved from the electronic booth to the acoustic studio. Several provisional rules for using it were circulated: these allowed only a very small margin of intervention in recorded sound, forbidding practically all manipulation other than dissecting it in time, by editing it. But they lent themselves to a very considerable degree of initiative in the creation of acoustic sounds. Through prolonging traditional sounds, we rediscovered the concept of the instrument and the instrumentalist, as well as of performance that is sometimes spontaneous or chance rather than willed.

After this, with its name changed to *experimental music*, musique concrète, although continuing to use natural sound sources, abandoned overhasty manipulations; it endeavored to assemble sounds with as little distortion as possible. This change in behavior was accompanied by a radical change of attitude; we no longer considered sound in relation to the three acoustic parameters: we were dealing with perceived "sound objects" and with a new music theory to study them.

What had become of machines in all this? After being led into the temptation of considering them as musical instruments, we no longer attributed anything to them except the strange power to explain the phenomenon of sound. For a time there was no question of using them to make music but for *musicianship*—that is, for practicing better hearing.

2.9. CRITIQUE OF THE ELECTRONIC INSTRUMENT

After these historical sections, we will now endeavor to dispel any misunderstandings. And in the first place, by applying the criteria set out above (in sections 2.1 to 2.5) to the electronic instrument, we will gain a better understanding of the deception it caused.

In its basic workings it did not obey the definition of an instrument (section 2.1). Since it aimed to be the sum of all instruments at once, this meant that it had not only registers, in the sense that we defined this term, but a super-register: the register that would have allowed it to move from one instrument to another. In fact, the concept of instrument was downplayed. We thought we could go beyond

12. Criticized, not without reason, by John Cage, who did not understand our viewpoint.

it by means of structures; we were confused about the concept of timbre: we prematurely extrapolated the second meaning of the word, and timbre became simply a characteristic of the musical object, and no longer the perception of a common cause for a family of objects.

In truth, the same sort of thing had been done with the organ: this instrument does indeed remind us, quite naively, of different instrumental sources (these are the "stops," in the precise organological sense), while, to all intents and purposes, the timbre remains that of the organ. But the electronic instrument failed through an excess of originality. Without being what it claimed to be—a universal instrument—it was undoubtedly a new instrument, a generator of original sounds, often never previously heard, with varied registers, and yet possessing what, in keeping with our own definition, we are obliged to call a characteristic *timbre*. But, paradoxically, at the two extremes the balance between permanence and variation were so completely upset that the instrument turned out to be almost too much for our customary musical ways.

To understand this more fully, we will apply the three criteria of our instrumental analysis to it (section 2.4).

It conforms well to the second of these, *registers*, where indeed it has remarkable richness. We cannot say the same about the other two.

First of all, it is clear that its *stops* give little room for interpretation. The objects, because they are all predetermined, give variety only in one sphere: abstract values, and not in the concrete sphere of live performance. It has no human presence, as a plastic object has no vegetable or mineral textures of wood or stone.

As for *timbre*, our contention from now on is that in traditional instruments it appears to result from subtle, and in general appropriately and cleverly applied, laws of association between the components of the objects in relation to their position in the register.[13] In the electronic instrument these laws do not exist. All the variables can be used independently. So timbre is reduced to what the ear reveals of the causal identity of all these sounds: synthetic, predetermined, without any of those accidents, fluctuations, or imprecisions that an age-old musical conditioning has made indispensable for us and also without that indispensable continuity evenly spread over the whole register.

As can be seen, our criticism is based not on principles but rather on the contingencies of the way we are conditioned. It can therefore be either accepted or rejected. We are perfectly willing to accept that new ways of listening may be possible after a period of training. We find it difficult to believe, however, that our ear, and our entire sense of music, should willingly adjust to all and any disruptions of their usual practices: the presence of something living, something sensory behind the craftsman's mark, seems inseparable from aesthetic appreciation and, similarly,

13. Cf. book 3.

the appreciation of instrumental identity. Once this identity is lost, what is there to hold on to when, in fatal disequilibrium, variation prevails over permanence?

2.10. CRITIQUE OF "MUSIQUE CONCRÈTE"

In reality, if we ask ourselves what the instrument in "musique concrète" is, we find ourselves in a very awkward position. Is it the gathering of sounds in the studio and the intention to gather them from anywhere? The practice of recording and working with sounds that are preferably recorded? The use of special equipment for manipulating these sounds, changing their speed, filtering, mixing them?

None of this, in truth, answers our definition of the instrument, yet so constraining are musical practices that at the beginning of this research we instinctively made every effort to find, at any price, something that might fit in with them. Thus in 1948 I had imagined a "turntable piano" linking twelve gramophones to a controlling device that enabled them to be "played." We will pause for a while over this ridiculous attempt. At least it has the merit of revealing something.

I did indeed have what appeared to be a musical instrument, which I had even dared to call "the most universal possible." Suppose, in fact, that, with the help of the "closed groove" technique, the sound of musical instruments were engraved on the twelve records. On each record was a different pitch—chromatic, for example. The keyboard enabled the pitches to be played. A device would just about have allowed the gramophones to change groove and, as in the case of the organ, create registers for the instruments themselves. In fact, Dereux thought up a "recording organ" along the same lines: "sound synthesis," which is not synthetic but depends on the phonographic reproduction of natural sounds.

But—we will not spend time on Dereux's organ,[14] which was judiciously restricted to the reproduction of some of the most illustrious organ sounds—my "most universal instrument possible," if it could have been made, would only have given a crude combination of sounds, equivalent to the orchestra. At best, a sort of organ capable of giving continuity even to short-lived, and thus self-contained, sounds. Except, and this is important, for the fact that it could use the permanent character of sounds, the only innovation it would have contributed would have been a barbaric reduction, for a single player, of the performers in the orchestra.

We shall now move on to the opposite type of experience, since, by 1950, those attempts were to be abandoned in favor of magnetic recording and editing.

Do sounds, however they are processed later, always stand in relation to an instrumental device? In other words, where, between our filters and our transposers, will we rediscover our criteria?

14. Electronic organ, based on electrostatic generators technology, developed by Jean-Adolphe Dereux between 1950 and 1955.—Trans.

Contrary to what was possible with the electronic instrument, there was no leeway in *register* but, in contrast, extraordinary potential for *performance* both in the invention of sound entities captured by the microphone and in the interventions after recording. Finally, if all electronic effects were avoided, there was, of course, no instrumental *timbre*, every sound object clearly proclaiming its own origin.

We can see how both developments ended, in quite different ways, in the negation of the instrument as the instrument of a specifically musical expression. One of the musics was the by-product of a juggling of parameters, the other a simple juxtaposition of objects.

2.11. FAULTS COMMON TO BOTH MUSICS

Both musics are affected by opposing types of imbalance in relation to normal instrumental structure. They meet at extremes, where they share the fact that they have severely strained our usual practice in relation to one or another of our three norms. Thus we can see—and this is still odd—that the ear perceives indiscriminately, as one and the same fault, the errors that arise from music that is too concrete or too abstract. Having already briefly mentioned the second, we will concentrate mainly on the first.

(a) *Excess of timbre*

Sounds that are speeded up or slowed down without proper care show a variation so bound up with their cause that the two are no longer dissociated; thus, properly speaking, there is no longer any balance between permanence and variation. This goes against the very definition of the instrument. It is no longer forgotten; it makes its presence felt as an event. We have gone beyond the blueprint of music. And this is why anything that suggests the melodic wailing of sirens without careful handling will always seem to be alien to musical discourse, even though it may be perfectly justified as a structure.

If speeding up and slowing down affect both the rhythm and the tessitura of the object, the permanence-variation relationship will seem so rigid that the event, with or without the siren effect, will appear like a sound effect—that is, totally bound to its causality, without the freedom necessary for music.

The reader will see how much we need to extend the meaning of the word in our definition of *timbre*, or instrumental permanence. By way of amusement let us compare it to its traditional definition, using what, for us, is called "the speeding up timbre." If we accelerate a vocal or piano sound, taking care to eliminate the parallel rhythmic effect, nothing, according to acousticians, will change: the whole spectrum of frequencies is simply transferred. The timbre of the sound under consideration, for them characterized by this spectrum, should therefore remain exactly the same, and only the tessitura should change. This would be the ideal musical instrument from the point of view of consistency of timbre in the objects it provides.

But what do we find? The piano becomes shrill, the voice begins to waver and bleat. . . . This is because, precisely, the speeding up does not affect the "spectral" timbre of objects, whereas a real musical instrument combines its effects in relation to the tessitura, so that the composition of the objects varies according to precise and precious laws. Acousticians, while defining *timbre* as a quality peculiar to each sound, also habitually speak of the timbre of an instrument, implicitly assuming that this quality has a certain consistency. In truth, if the timbre of an instrument is recognizable, in the original meaning we gave in section 2.4, this is because the objects that this instrument delivers each have a timbre in the scientific sense and, above all, because there are laws relating to the instrument that link these timbres together. On the contrary, when an object is accelerated, its physical timbre is an invariable, and the different examples of it in the tessitura clearly show this invariance as a *specific timbre* of speeding up. We could therefore say that speeding up, insofar as it is an instrument, is recognized by its "nil" timbre.

(b) *Excess of register*

A consequence of the above comment: a registration that reveals the instrument rather than fashioning the object will also be heard as a mechanical effect (another timbre if you will).

A filtering process, for example, can be presented as the use of a registration. By synthesis, we combine a particular group of frequencies with a view to obtaining an object. By analysis, applied to an earlier object, we extract a particular group of frequencies by filtering. The result? Occasionally identical, if the filtering has been done crudely or intensively, it is the filtering that is heard. The causality of the process is more noticeable than the variety of the objects made in this way. It is enough for now to draw attention to this strange phenomenon, without explaining it. The procedure obliterates the object, defaces it, marks it with its timbre, in the pejorative sense of this term.

(c) *Excess of play*

The above analyses already give an account of certain similarities, which were not slow to emerge over the first years of parallel experimentation, between electronic sounds and the manipulated sounds of musique concrète. They do not explain everything, in particular certain resemblances, generally in the type of faults, between the two musics at the level of languages. So we should seek the explanation in the excess of play (we are using the word *play* in its broadest sense, attributing to the composer a traditional function of the interpreter, whom this composer claimed to replace). An accumulation loaded with synthetic sounds and a crude analysis of a natural material both lead to a lack of economy of means. Too many intentions wear the object out or make it formless or unreadable.

2.12. CONCEPT OF THE PSEUDO-INSTRUMENT

It sometimes happened, however, in electronic music, as in musique concrète, that a series of well-formed and appropriately recorded objects showed relationships of permanence such that they *seemed* to come from the same instrument.

And this is very fortunate, for, otherwise, what could we have relied on to give a measure of coherence to the series of sounds spread over all the tessituras and in the most disparate durations and intensities? Therefore, without necessarily being aware of it, the contemporary musician often sought to link together a particular sequence of sounds with "something" that, pragmatically speaking, is the same as an instrumental timbre.

But then the foundation of this definition itself disappears; the ground gives way beneath our feet. In any work in which the composer, of concrete or electronic music, is incapable of naming the causal process that gave rise to a series of sounds, everything takes place as if these sounds came from a particular instrument. What is the timbre of an *instrument that does not exist?*

So here we are, at the end of our instrumental analysis, obliged to look elsewhere for this link, stronger even than structures and more mysterious: timbre, the definition of which, far too pragmatic, is crying out to be superseded. This will only happen after a long digression.

Capturing Sounds

3.1. THE PARADOX OF DISCOVERY

While the publications of the last decades have drawn attention to the new instruments that have come from the electron—from the theremin to the mixturtrautonium by way of the ondes martenot—I really know of hardly any texts that highlight the amazing revolution brought about by *recording* sounds.

As so often happens in the sort of adventure where, both suddenly and gradually, the machine gives new potential to human activity, we did not have time to be amazed by the discovery, so busy were we trying to improve it. From the cylinder to wax, the bell to the baffle, the gramophone to the record player, 78s to LPs, ebonite to vinyl, the phonograph to the tape recorder, mono to stereo, it was, from Edison and Charles Cros, a long journey, with its halts, surprises, and moments when we surpassed our expectations. Progress was so conspicuous that the phenomenon itself got away. Besides, at the beginning the discovery was so crude, apparently so far from fulfilling its promise, that we needed a robust faith, a lively imagination, to anticipate developments that—so it seems today—anyone could have foreseen.

So this is the paradox: when a new discovery is made and at first does not live up to expectation, contemporaries, in their initial amazement, catch a glimpse of its astonishing implications; but they immediately turn away, postponing testing it to see if it can be generalized until later and concentrating on the evidence, the immediate results. Then, once the technical process is involved, they pay attention only to the area of development they have under their noses. As the discovery fulfills its promises, it recedes and becomes part of acquired knowledge. Any reflection on it seems anachronistic, whereas no one has ever really stopped to consider it. The mists of initial investigation may have prevented our predecessors from seeing clearly, but we, too, lack the time for discovery, the shock of the unexpected find, to fill us with wonder and make us relearn what we think we already know.

3.2. MYSTERY OF THE CYLINDER
AND POWERS OF THE EAR

What was already surprising about Edison's cylinder was that a three-dimensional acoustic field, carrying various messages, could be transformed into a one-dimensional mechanical signal[1] and that playing it back, even crudely, as we know, delivers "something" of the messages stored in this way.

What precisely? The answer is fairly clear. Edison's phonograph gave back, as best it could, the semantic content of the messages. Across a dreadful distortion of the signal, a brutal defacing of the sound elements, and in an acoustic field that had only one dimension, it remained possible for the listener to recognize what had been recorded: not only the meaning of the message—words or sentences, refrains or harmonies—but also some aspects of its origin. Thus Dranem or Cécile Sorel, the violin or the clarinet, could just about be identified.

This is the mystery that we no longer perceive, blinded as we are by false appearances: how can we account for the fact that certain natural sound structures, completely familiar to us, appear indestructible, recognizable against all odds, through the crudest distortions and dislocations? Will it do to give purely electroacoustic explanations here? Did Edison's phonograph allow us to recognize timbres? Well, what, then, is a timbre, for even the cylinder to retain traces of it? A spectrum of frequencies? But this was played back in a piteous state. Only the most empirical definition of timbre survives: Dranem could be recognized because he was Dranem, that's all. The origin of vocal sounds remained perceptible. Something of the Dranem-timbre, a causal continuity called Dranem, was still identifiable.

The phenomenon of recording and reproduction would, therefore, even in its earliest days, call for a strange comment: if the cylinder was a primitive wonder, our ear, not at all primitive, was another. In fact, even if, today, advanced equipment gives us a signal that is reputed to be accurate, Edison's experiment remains: the ear, despite a distorted signal, gets the essential of the message. This essential, then, shows its strange independence from response curves.

1. In the first chapter we used, and we will use again, the word *signal*, which refers back to the event, in contrast to the sound or musical *object* perceived for itself. We will use *signal* here (in contrast to the sign, a component of musical language) in the sense used by physicists: they use the term to designate the physical components they manage to extract from a complex phenomenon, which they have grasped.

Yet later, how particular we have become about those same response curves, high fidelity, respect for timbres! The advances in recording machines have all been about fidelity to the signal and have revealed nothing about the powers of the *ear*. And as music is made of perceptions, not physical signals, it is to be expected that, over such a long period, we have not known how to use the tape recorder and the microphone to do properly musical research and elucidate traditional musical values in all their profundity.

3.3. THE HISTORICAL CONTRIBUTION OF RADIO BROADCASTING

Recording alone would doubtless not have been enough to cause the present explosion of activity in the field of sound, any more than photography, in her black veil, would have led to what is called "the civilization of the image." But once the means of mass broadcasting joined forces with phonography and photography, these discoveries were the beginning of a huge blossoming of original techniques. Certainly, the cylinder contained in embryo all the mysteries of capturing sound, fixing it as a "fact" and, hence, the possibility of taking hold of it as an *object* for experimentation. And it was the same for the image with the Lumière brothers' invention. But, as always, we have to go a long way down the path of tangible achievements before we can retrace our own footsteps and interpret them. In order to see the almost insidious flowering of a new way of looking at music, broadcasting had to go beyond its own capacities. It had the historic circumstances for this: studios, money, and, above all, people quite different from traditional musicians yet sound specialists also. Omitting to examine this historic situation would be to deprive ourselves of a powerful source of illumination in this study.

So what has happened since sound capture, together with recording and broadcasting equipment made the whole planet echo with the sound of the violinist or the voice of the singer in the studio?

We have seen two equally modern and equally anachronistic trends in practical research: modern because they used and continuously improved on new inventions, anachronistic because they allowed scarcely any time to reflect on their basic principles, neglecting fundamental research for a hasty technology in pursuit of applications.

One of these pieces of research attempted to reproduce the entire acoustic field in three dimensions: it led to stereophony. The other, on recording, which came first, was to overcome extraordinary difficulties in the narrow context of monophony. It gradually demonstrated the skill required by those who practiced this new art. How can we explain why these two pieces of research neither brought about the rethinking of musical ideas that, after the event, we consider they could have achieved, nor shed adequate light on the very nature of their own undertaking? It is rather as if someone had thought of developing the magnifying-glass into a microscope without thinking about the particular way in which this extension of sight brought us close to the infinitely small, which raises the problems of preparations (dishes, special lighting) and the requirements and tolerance of the eye (resolving power, maximum magnification, etc.). This work attempts to remedy this important omission.

3.4. THE MYTH OF SOUND REPRODUCTION

A whole trend in electroacoustics therefore tends toward the integral reproduction of sound, especially stereophonic sound reproduction. What could be more tempting for the engineer than to place the listener in front of an imaginary orchestra, where he can situate the first violins on his left and the seconds on the right? But here a comment is called for, which does not condemn the attempt but reduces its significance: if integral reproduction were so important, going from monophony to stereophony would have a radical effect. The engineer would have to have a thorough control over the phenomena he is dealing with, and the listener would have to be highly sensitive to this. Now, experience shows that it is all quite vague; it really seems that these refinements are secondary phenomena, quite unstable, and marred, on the practitioner's part, by some degree of insecurity and, on the listener's part, by great uncertainty. In fact, improving a monophonic system is more worthwhile, in terms of the musical result, than setting up a hasty stereophonic system. Our engineer, like our listener, comes up against complex problems here, and it is not absolutely clear that improvements in techniques are suited to the properties of the ear.

If, for example, we recall the subterfuge of "false stereophony," we will greatly embarrass the specialists. Without going into details, the reader will remember that this procedure quite simply placed the bass instruments on one side, the high ones on the other. Now, in these circumstances we still situate the instruments to some extent. So how is it that, when the orchestra goes from low to high, the whole orchestra does not shift from left to right? Or how is it that the piano keyboard does not occupy the whole stage?[2]

As a consequence, tackling the practical problem of sound *reproduction* must mean bringing into play a series of transformations leading from the "live" sound event to its imitation using electroacoustic means, transformations that we are far from knowing how to control with the refinement and sureness that can be imagined in theory. We will therefore look more closely at some aspects of this type of reproduction.

2. See, e.g., Robert Kolben, "The Stereophoner," *Gravesaner Blätter*, no. 13 (1959). Kolben reports on the disquieting experiments in pseudo-stereophony carried out by Hermann Scherchen based on monophonic recordings.

3.5. FROM ONE SOUND FIELD TO ANOTHER

An orchestra plays in a concert hall. Later, elsewhere, this same orchestra, engraved on a record, plays for a listener in his house. As everything, from technique to marketing, is geared to making the listener believe that he practically possesses this orchestra at home, it is not surprising that, by a sort of social convention, the whole emphasis is placed on *fidelity* and that nothing very clear has been said about the *transformation* involved in substituting one sound field for another.

Let us add that the secret is so well kept only because of the complicity of our ear: this amazing organ is equally capable of letting us perceive nuances with great sophistication and of covering up evidence: this substitution of one sound universe for another, this upheaval of the rules of unity of time and place, must have importance. How is it, then, that the magic trick seems so perfect, that the orchestra comes to play in our house as if nothing had happened?

Reflection on this subject, if it is to be thorough, must, from the outset, take into account physical as well as psychological data. The change of field does indeed impinge on both levels. Let us not forget that listening cannot take place without a listener; he, too, is elsewhere and afterward, like the reproduced sound. We will see that, with what appear to be the most objective phenomena at the time of recording, psychological factors come into play much more decisively than hertz or decibels.

So how will we go about it if we must tackle everything at once, a psychological inquiry and certain physical descriptions of the phenomena? While referring to book 4 for the concept of object, we will for the moment limit ourselves to a description in everyday language of the psychoacoustic transformation brought about by the recording of sounds. Sound practitioners will have no problem with this. We are simply recapitulating facts that they know perfectly well. If they have nothing to learn, they will forgive us in the knowledge that many readers know almost nothing about this recent and major experiment of transforming one sound field into another.

Here, a warning about terminology. We must avoid confusing different concepts that are described in the same words—on the one hand by physicists, on the other by psychologists: in the pair *object-image*, in fact, the word *object* has one current physical meaning (in optics, for example); in psychology it has another. Initially, we will stay on the side of physicists, researching the physical magnitude that is more or less retained after electroacoustic procedures and that allows us properly to speak of sound *reproduction*.

3.6. THE PHYSICAL OBJECT IN THE
TRANSFORMATION

There are two big differences between experiencing light and sound phenomena. The first of these differences comes from the fact that most visual objects are not light sources but simply objects, in the usual sense of the word, with light shining on them. Physicists are therefore quite accustomed to distinguishing the latter from the objects that reflect it. If the object itself gives out light, then we say it is a light "source."

With sound there is nothing like this. In the overwhelming majority of the sounds we are dealing with, the whole emphasis is on sound insofar as it comes from "sources." The distinction, classic in optics, between sources and objects has therefore not been necessary in acoustics. All our attention has been taken by *sound* (just as we say *light*) considered as emanating from a source, with its trajectories, its modifications, and so forth, without the "contours" of a specific sound, its form, being appreciated for its own sake, without reference to its source.

This attitude has been reinforced by the fact that sound (until recording was created) has always been linked in time to the energetic source that gave rise to it, to the point of being conflated with it in practice. Moreover, this fleeting sound is only accessible to one sense and remains under its sole control: the sense of hearing. A visual object, in contrast—and this is the second difference—has something stable about it. Not only is it not confused with the light that illuminates it, not only does it appear with contours that are permanent in various lights, but it is also accessible to other senses: it can be felt, touched, smelt; it has a form our hands can embrace, a surface that touch can explore, a weight, a smell.

So it can be understood that the concept of *sound object* had scarcely any claim to attract the physicist's attention. Besides, as his natural tendency was to trace facts back to their cause, this was largely satisfied by the energetic evidence of the sound source: there was no reason why the ear, once mechanical radiations had spread out an elastic medium (air) should perceive anything other than the sound source itself.

There is, in truth, nothing wrong with this reasoning. Let us simply say that if it is valid for a physicist or a maker of electroacoustic machines, it will not do for a musician or even for an acoustician of the ear. After all, the latter do not have to account for how the sound arises, then is propagated, but only the way it is heard. Now, what the ear hears is neither the source nor the "sound" but, truly, *sound objects*,[3] just as what the eye sees is not directly the source, or even its "light," but illuminated objects.

The "materialization" of sound in the form of a recording—a fragment of tape, the groove of a record—should have drawn particular attention to the sound object. Indeed, in these experiments sound was apparently no longer evanescent, and it kept its distance from its cause: it acquired stability; we could manipulate it, copy it, vary its energetic dimensions, without being bound by its initial contingencies. A dualism like the dualism between illuminated objects and light sources

---

3. Here, in the psychological sense.

emerged; the separation between a medium that is inert, but has all the "information," and the energy necessary to make this information perceptible, should have been enough to make acousticians change their terminology and explain more clearly the distinction between the energy source, the sound, and finally the sound object. Nothing of the sort happened. They simply note an implicit distinction between *sound* and *sounds* or between *sound* and *a sound*. The link that, for the physicist, binds the cause to the effect is so strong that, even as a recording or a modulation of an electrical current, the "information" received by the ear never seems to have been clearly differentiated from its material medium (record, tape, etc.) nor from its temporary form of energy (electric current, mechanical vibration). The term *signal* still seems best to shed light on the content of *what* sound conveys. The real physical object revealing itself to the ear is therefore, ultimately, a signal, and it is this signal that is involved in the transformation of sound produced by recording and reproducing sounds.

3.7. TRANSFORMATIONS IN THE SOUND FIELD

Intense commercialization of electroacoustic equipment has greatly muddied the waters for fundamental research. Fidelity, response curves, tone, spatial effect, and so forth have been pushed to the foreground; no one, it seems, has mentioned the essential; a given number of sound sources are in a studio, a concert hall, anywhere; sound is captured, recorded, "read," listened to. . . . What is going on? What, in short, are we listening to that is different from what we would have heard live?

(a) *Transformation of the acoustic space*

From a four-dimensional[4] acoustic space we take a one-dimensional space in monophony, or a two-dimensional space in stereo. We will concentrate on monophony, the more significant. The microphone or microphones, wherever they are placed or however balanced, ultimately deliver *one* modulation, that is, an electric current that represents the sum total of the different acoustic vibrations captured by each of them. Let us suppose, for the sake of simplicity, that there is just one microphone: it is the convergence point of all the "beams" coming from the sound points in the surrounding space. After the various electroacoustic transformations, all the sound points in the initial space will be condensed in the membrane of the loudspeaker: this space is replaced by one sound point, which will bring about a new distribution of sound in the new space of the place where it is listened to. In any case the staging of the sources in the initial space is only perceptible in the "sound point" of the loudspeaker in the form of differences in intensity: through the loudspeaker sound is not more or less distant; it is more or less faint, depending on the length of the beam that linked it to the microphone.

4. Three spatial dimensions plus intensity.

(b) *Transformation of the surroundings, or intelligent listening*

We cannot think about the phenomenon above, which is purely physical, without closely linking it to the subjective listening space: it would be difficult to understand the profound transformation of sound without taking into account the transformation of the "nonlive" listener's perception compared to the "live" listener. The latter, who is present at the sound event, listens to it with both ears, in the original acoustic surroundings, at the moment when it happens, and his listening is accompanied by vision and other attendant perceptions. The "nonlive" listener also, of course, listens with both ears but from the sound point of the loudspeaker, in different surroundings, far from the moment, the circumstances, and the place where the original event took place. He does not have the help either of the spectacle or any other direct experience of the environment.

Although so many truisms, these comments are nevertheless heavy with often ill-perceived consequences, which have two aspects:

(1) a mainly physical aspect: the appearance of a *noticeable reverberation*, imperceptible in live listening,

(2) and a mainly psychological aspect: on the one hand, the highlighting of sounds in nonlive listening that would not have been heard live and, on the other hand, the blurring of sounds that live listening would certainly have had no trouble in discerning—this being partly due to the lack of audio-visual balance, which would have been present in live listening.

Let us return to these two points.

(1) Change of surroundings or noticeable echo

We know that the ear is directional or, more precisely, that binaural listening has the power of localization. In live listening we hear the sound sources in two ways: live sound locates them, whereas the sound reverberating round the concert hall, coming from all directions (except in a straightforward echo, which would be located), does not. Our listening mediates between live sound, which is localized, and reverberated sound, which is not. If our two ears are replaced by a microphone, it will capture both live and reverberated sound, conflate them and thus ultimately convey to the loudspeaker a product that has not been selected as would have been the case with our two ears in live listening. This is why the concert halls that appear suitable for live listening seem, for nonlive listening, to possess a noticeable reverberation, which can make them inappropriate for recording sound. Hence the precautions taken in broadcasting studios. We can experience something of this noticeable echo and nonlocalization by covering one ear and noting the resultant confusion.

The term *intelligent listening* is used by practitioners to describe the sum total of those activities of the ear in live listening discovered with such amazement by beginners in sound recording. While other perceptions, particularly visual, are involved in the apprehension of sound *content*, the eye unquestionably plays no part in that selective listening to live and reverberated sound, which makes our hearing so clear even in very echoing concert halls. Paradox would have us say that such halls have "good acoustics" precisely because they amplify the singers' voices, which proves that the ear is also aided by reverberated sounds.

In any case, whatever physicists' interpretation, the facts are there before us: in live listening, with two ears, concert halls have less noticeable echo than when listening to the sound played back on an electroacoustic music system. The observation is very simple, but it is not so easy to unravel its mystery.

(2) Transformation of the content

It is perhaps more surprising, but doubtless less embarrassing, to observe that in a recording we begin to hear all sorts of things that we did not hear in live listening: background noise, interference, our neighbor's coughing, orchestral events, mistakes or overeagerness on the performer's part.

This is because when he listens live, the listener is wholly present with all his senses. People have sought in vain, and very stupidly, to explain the superiority of live listening by some shortcomings in sound recording machines. Machines are inanimate: it is we who have nerves, senses, consciousness, who make choices from the thousands of disparate pieces of information that come our way, even in the calmest of concert halls. In nonlive listening, the act of listening takes place in a quite different context. It is not surprising that there is a transformation in the psychological field, even more radical than in the field of acoustics.

3.8. PROPERTIES OF RECORDED SOUND

Centering (planes) and enlargement (details)

Centering and enlargement are both consequences of these two aspects of transformation: in the acoustic and psychological fields we will indicate some of the properties of recorded sound, which now appear as objective.

Three-dimensional space becomes one-dimensional, but if something has been lost (localized intelligent listening), something has also been gained: on the one hand, amplification, which consists in hearing sound "larger than life," and on the other hand, centering, which consists of "cutting out" a particular segment from the auditory field.

Of course, since photography, such experiments are already known and understood in the visual field. We know that, even if photography deprives us of the fluidity that vision possesses, it gives us, within a frame (which fortunately hides the rest from us), a concentration on the object, or on a detail of the object, and in addition it enlarges their dimensions as much as we desire. However linked together in practice, these two properties are quite distinct: enlargement, a positive factor, "enables us to see" what we could not see before: the texture of the skin, the detail of an eyebrow. Centering exempts us from seeing the rest; our attention is concentrated on what we need to see.

It will be the same with sound. But how? On the one hand, the *dimensions* of sound will change, with a simple adjustment of the potentiometer, and with this same adjustment the source will be far away, in the middle distance, or nearby. On the other hand, what will *centering* be? In the first place it will consist in foregrounding one source, near at hand, rather than the others, in the distance: this is the most elementary process. But there are subtler ones to come: in live listening we never have our ear inside the soundboard of the piano or pushed up against the sound-post of the violin or the singer's glottis; now, the microphone can take the liberty of such indiscretions and not only give intensity close-ups but be positioned in such a way that the inner proportions of sound will be redefined. This is where the microphone takes its revenge: even if we can say that it has not, like the ear, the intelligence to differentiate live and reverberated sound, we cannot deny that it is capable of capturing a whole world of details that as a rule elude our listening. The sensitivity of the microphone when it captures nearby sounds contributes a number of sound components that are usually ignored. Certainly, the microphone adds nothing to the sound, but it captures it as would an unusual act of listening, in which the normal balance between what accompanies the musical sound (noises, shushings, people leaving, irregularities, etc.) and the value of the sound itself, indicated on the score, can be radically changed. In extreme cases there is "contact" microphone sound-capture, which, with no movement through air, consists in pushing our ear straight up against wood or metal. This could be the beginnings of a new generation of instruments and a listening process unavailable to live listening, representing, generally speaking, an important break with the latter, and illustrating the transformative power of the microphone.

3.9. FIDELITY

We have left this quality until last, a major one for enthusiasts, convinced that in any case the salesman will guarantee it. As for us, it remains surprising that people manage to provide customers with a sound signal illusory enough to allow the gramophone to take the place of the orchestra so easily. After everything we have just said about the radical changes to the acoustic and psychological field, it really makes one think. How can our ear, which is so exacting, be so tolerant here? The fact is clear. Moreover, people have tried to demonstrate it, usually for reasons of publicity. This is why an orchestra has been asked to play some sequences from a program onstage, alternating with other prerecorded sequences, in which the musicians pretend to play. Experts—without mentioning the uninitiated—were occasionally taken in, maintains the *Revue du son*.[5] They could, however, have been given a clue by the imperfections of the miming, as well as, or more easily than, a particular quality of the sound reproduction.

A more rigorous experiment could be done by giving a listener a series of sounds recorded by a pianist or a violinist, alternating with sounds played live by the same instrumentalist. Could the listener, blindfolded, distinguish one from the other? We do not think so, provided, of course, the necessary precautions had been taken to prevent the sounds from being different for reasons external to the recording itself (different surroundings, for example; or reverberation, if the loudspeaker has been positioned in the same place as the instrumentalist).

If we are even more demanding and would wish to compare the *same* recorded or live musical object, we would come across an additional difficulty. As two instrumental sounds are never identical, we will always have to have the instrumentalist play first, and the listener will consequently have no problem in getting it right. This is true of the violin, for example, the object being so closely linked to the way the sound is shaped that the violinist will find it very difficult to imitate himself. But we have to acknowledge that with more stereotyped instruments we could, at a pinch, reverse the order of events: could a recording of a piano note be confused with the same note on the same piano played a second time? . . . We believe it could.

As far as we know, however, very few experiments such as this have been done. We may ask why, when the mania for experimentation is rife. Is it only because performing them raises awkward technological and practical problems? Or is it because as high fidelity is for the most part presented as a value in itself, bound up with the electronic definition of the equipment, guaranteed by response curves, distortion coefficients, protected by a whole vocabulary, the experimenter is intimidated from the start?

This latter reason is doubtless the best explanation for the uncertainty or lack of interest in possible proofs of the existence of fidelity. This is because, when the recorded orchestra plays through the sound system as if it were in the room, *we don't really know* what is involved in our appreciation of it, and we should probably find it very difficult if we had to commit ourselves to an explanation of the electroacoustic or psychological cause of a particular impression. The experiments we have mentioned—and this is why we find them interesting—show that, in fact, fidelity is *just about* possible, that it is possible for there to be no appreciable difference to the ear between live and recorded sound; but this is an extreme experi-

---

5. *Revue du son et de la radiodiffusion-télévision*, no. 90 (Oct. 1960).

ment; in practice, an experiment in perfect reproduction would require infinite precautionary measures.[6]

3.10. TIMBRE OF THE EQUIPMENT

Above a certain level of fidelity, therefore, the question of quality has more and more to do with the ear and less and less with the equipment. Nevertheless, we can see that, even when this is the case, the system itself gives the reproduction its own "sound shaping." Several systems, reputedly with equal fidelity, will each possess a characteristic "sonority," which, even when all precautions have been taken, will ultimately influence the sounds. The latter factor, doubtless difficult to perceive when dealing with only one sound system, becomes clear when we start to make comparisons: people will say that one system is better for voices, strings, or percussion instruments. So to the four aspects of sound transformation already mentioned we must add a "signature" attributable to everything played on the particular system being used.

To summarize: reverberation, surroundings, centering, enlargement, and "nuanced" fidelity, in total, therefore, five variation dimensions in the reproduction of a given sound event, or rather in the transformation of the sound object into which this event is translated, fixed, and available to be heard again, such as the sound engineer and the transmitting equipment, have changed it into itself.

3.11. THE SOUND RECORDIST AS INTERPRETER

The above analysis leads us to inquire into the role of the sound recordist, his true nature and his importance.

As long as we think only in terms of reproduction and transmission, it seems that he needs only to be a more or less competent technician. Now in professional circles the distinction between a good, bad, or mediocre sound engineer does not depend solely on this one criterion but also, even principally, on talent. In fact, as we have just seen, fidelity is not simply reproducing but reconstituting; in reality it is the result of a series of choices and interpretations that the recording device makes both possible and necessary. So we must allow that the sound engineer—or the chief sound operator—must ask himself questions that are no longer purely technical but are ultimately answerable to sensitive listening and musical judgment.

6. Conversely, it may be that a reproduction is "better" than direct listening because of the highlighting of the properties described in sections 3.7 and 3.8.

How, in fact, can we judge a reverberation time without evaluating its aesthetic character? How can we measure high fidelity in bands of frequencies without subjectively assessing how far timbre has been preserved? How can we reproduce levels in decibels without discovering, further to the concept of intensity, the concepts of plane, distance, and salience? These concepts have only very gradually been discovered; it has taken a long time for their originality to appear.

In this context we should like to refer to a professional situation so paradoxical that nowhere, it seems, has it been honestly described.

3.12. MUSICIANS HAVE NO EAR

It might be thought that, when judging the quality of a musical recording or a radio broadcast, the musician would have an incomparable advantage over the technician. We very quickly perceive that this is wrong. If the equipment "distorts," the music is ruined, but the musician can do nothing about it. The technician, *even if he has little ear for music*, will very quickly know if there is a hole in the loudspeaker, a poor contact, or a worn-out valve.

Yes, but, people will say, that's more to do with repairing than musical criticism. Indeed. Only, apart from the above faults, which are obvious, more difficult problems can arise when, for example, a microphone is placed too near or too far from a soloist, in a concert hall that has more or less reverberation.

What will happen then? An excellent engineer will be as embarrassed as a brilliant musician. Or, on the contrary, a moderately good engineer, like a moderately good instrumentalist, will be particularly clever at discerning the main errors in sound capture.

We should explain this. The pure technician's ear is a car mechanic's, an airplane engineer's ear: it looks through the music for causes, with the aim of finding material solutions. The pure musician, for his part, is trained only in music. Accustomed though he is to judge the work and the performers, he will find himself almost as unprepared as the pure technician in the art of recording, when it is a question not so much of a repair job as of musical value, properly speaking: the proportionality of sound planes, the overall blending, the reverberation in the concert hall.... It may even be that, carried away by his personal tastes, he makes great mistakes. Knowing the score too well, he will not notice that the sound is fuzzy, the singer too near or too far away, or at least he will be "biased" in his listening. And if he nevertheless realizes that "something is not quite right"? Because of his conditioning, he is disposed to turn to the instrumentalist, to ask him to put to rights the magic trick of which he is the victim. This is why we have come to talk about voices, works, instruments that are more or less "radiogenic," depending on how well they "come across" on the radio.

As for the engineer, it is quite clear that the most extensive and profound technical knowledge will be of no use if he is incapable of appreciating the musical outcome, and the mastery of technical resources will be pointless without an instinctive understanding of the purpose for which they might best be used.

We have said that a moderately good musician or technician could do equally well, or, if he is gifted and trained, even better than pure specialists, in music as well as acoustics. When we say "moderately good," we mean in the sense in which, traditionally, these skills are understood. A person with a polytechnic[7] education, like someone who has won the Prix de Rome,[8] could practice recording for years without success. A technician who is not very good at integrals, or a not particularly original composer, may, however, be in a better position to approach it, away from preconceived ideas and the false assurance that an entirely theoretical ability in music or acoustics would give him.

What will not be mediocre with these two specialists in new listening, what they will have in common, which can be developed by both a technical and a musical training, is, quite simply, an ear: an instrumentalists' ear, *whose instrument is the microphone*. Their listening will be neither technical nor musical in the classical sense of these two terms: watchful and matter-of-fact, completely free of *a priori* thinking, it will be wholly concentrated on the success of sound transformation itself. The emphasis will no longer be on the workings of machines, the quality of the score or the performance, but the "rendering" based on a model. It is "practitioner" listening, both technical and musicianly.

It will doubtless be clearer now that innate tastes and gifts, and a certain freshness of judgment, seem to us preferable to preconceived ideas and postgraduate confidence for this type of work. If we had to underpin these surprising assertions with hard facts, we would say that in our experience of "sound mixing" musicians, their talent as sound engineers was not always in keeping with their talent and originality for composing. To say that it was in inverse proportion would be far too mathematical and not at all charitable.

3.13. PROSE COMPOSITION AND TRANSLATION

The reason for our trying to give an account of these apparent peculiarities is so that we can return to our central theme: the phenomenon of music.[9]

7. Schaeffer refers here to the École polytechnique, a French public institution of higher education and research, renowned for its ingénieur polytechnicien degree in science and engineering. This is one of the institutions where Schaeffer studied.—Trans.

8. This French scholarship for arts students, dating back to 1662, includes a two-year stay in Rome.—Trans.

9. The notion of "thème et version," the French terms used here, is central to Schaeffer's concept of "la musique concrète." These are the academic exercises of translation into and translation from the target language. We decided to adopt the university terms "prose composition" and "translation" as being less cumbersome than "translation into" and "translation from."—Trans.

How is it, then, that the musician, short of submitting to a learning process that in fact requires a veritable readaptation, is so bad at hearing? It is because he has not been prepared for it. So what has he been prepared for? *Making* music, which is a very different thing.

A glance through musical literature is enough to enlighten us in this respect. Among so many volumes on instrumental and compositional techniques, will we find merely a handful of articles dealing with the art of hearing and analyzing what we hear?

Everything the composer does conforms strictly to the musical catechism that we mentioned in section 1.8. He starts from notions and signs familiar to him and, having gone through the stage of performance, finishes up with a sound-translation that will be comprehensible to others. This approach is like *prose composition*. If he listens, it is *upstream* of his musical activity; he sings in sol-fa in his head, plays in his mind and, if he is a very good musician, reads a score mentally, without any help from instruments; he composes in the same way. He does not hear; he reads—he "prehears."

The sound engineer, in contrast, makes it his duty to listen *downstream* from the sound phenomenon. The details of a score, which he does not even need to be able to read, are of little importance to him. What he is continually comparing, from his own listening, is the sound image provided by the electroacoustic system and the original sound phenomenon, which he is endeavoring to reconstitute— that is, the sound that comes from real instruments and takes its place in the acoustic field with true grandeur. What he does is *translation*.

3.14. "RADIOGENICITY"

The reader may well wonder, on reading this chapter, if the author has indulged in a number of professional confidences that are irrelevant to his subject. Professional confidences, certainly; irrelevant, no, for if the reader accepts that the microphone and the tape recorder give him a new way of grasping sounds, as film and the cinema camera do for images, he will understand that he must more or less familiarize himself with a professional field where amateurism is to be avoided. If, moreover, he wishes to adopt this approach himself and, if not dedicate himself to experimental music, at least work with and for the microphone and the cinema camera, as the immense majority of musicians of our time are called on to do, he must recognize that he must master these basics.

This is all the more essential as amateurs, who have not analyzed this very deeply, are strongly tempted to use the far-too-widespread language that reveals a naive anthropomorphism where machines are concerned. We mean the quasi-primitive attitude of a large number of nontechnicians: musicians, actors, authors, and composers, who, for want of anything better, display a completely subjective relationship with machines; they say that they "favor" or do not favor, "improve" or distort a sound, a voice, a work or a "presence." So there are, they say, voices, works, temperaments suited to radio, "radiogenic" (as we say photogenic for faces and images). There is some truth in this: for in practice they are right that certain voices, works, and performances "come across" better than others. What is wrong is the vague, sentimental, in short superstitious, interpretation of this, which boils down to a lack of explanation and justifies laziness.

Since transformation, transposition, and change of physical medium occur anyhow, we cannot say to what extent this is fidelity, trickery, or distortion. Every work, every voice, every performance undergoes manipulation, filtering, amplification, centering. The listener, for his part, is placed in conditions that, by and large, increase his demands. With these two things in mind it is hardly surprising if one thing "comes over" better than another. The mystery does not lie either in the equipment, as such, or in the sound content as it is heard live. There is no microphone or work that is "good" in itself nor any voice that is "better" for the microphone. There may be a surprising or predictable "suitability." It all becomes clear if we relate the object to be transmitted with the conditions of the transmission, if we consider every aspect of the transformation it undergoes, both obvious and subtle.

3.15. ADVICE FROM AN ELDER

As early as 1943, Jacques Copeau, with great lucidity, was becoming aware of these realities in the fields of speech, the text, and voices.[10] Contrary to those who maintained that the radio called into question the traditional criteria for the quality of works and performers, he implied that the texts "best suited to take to the airwaves" were still without doubt and quite simply the best, provided that a new art of acting for the new modes of communication was developed. Certainly, what was asked of them was not a momentary adaptation but fundamental progress:

The microphone, like the microscope and the cine-camera, enlarges, emphasizes, exaggerates everything it lights upon.

... In front of the microphone, the usual practices of stage acting must be dropped: gesticulation—which can be sensed—sudden attacks (which give rise to insecurity), rapid changes of tone (which hinder clarity of perception).

Across all pitches, voice production must be supported because neither facial nor gestural mime are there to complement meaning, or to make clear through action what is not clearly audible through diction.

10. Jacques Copeau (1879–1949) was an influential theater director who left his mark on twentieth-century French theater. Schaeffer contacted him in 1942 to organize a radiophonic art workshop.—Trans.

. . . Performance for the microphone is an act of reading.

. . . Posture for the microphone is purely mental.

That measured tone, discreet and intimate, which communicates the slightest inflexions of the voice, the slightest nuances of a sensibility right down to the slightest mannerisms of a person, so that, after a while, the listener will think he knows the character who speaks to him better than if he had seen his face, that tone alone opens up a vast domain to the microphone, a domain that is its own, that is exclusive to it.

. . . Faceless, without the authority of the gaze, without hands or body, the speaker's voice is not disembodied. On the contrary. It conveys the person with utter faithfulness. It even conveys it indiscreetly.

. . . The voice with nothing in its heart and nothing in its head cannot really have anything to do with the microphone.

. . . Radio could therefore be a school for sincerity.[11]

Is it necessary to add that the same applies, even more subtly, to music and musicians?

3.16. NOTHING NEW UNDER THE SUN

Now, in total confusion, we tend to superimpose two types of phenomena: one modern and technical, the other classical and psychological. On the one hand, telecommunications (magically making the message ubiquitous and its range vast); on the other, the mode of perception, which seems new because of the technical relaying between the transmitting source and the receiving subject. Many interpretations of the radiophonic phenomenon have vainly sought explanations from both the studio and the transmitter, explanations that in reality came only from perception itself, the most traditional.

Copeau was not mistaken. It is because of this new type of listening—we will examine its norms in the next chapter—that the actor had to undergo a new learning process. But what did he learn from this new medium—neither more nor less specific and contingent than are reading, concertgoing, dramatic or lyrical productions—other than to go beyond, to surpass, earlier techniques for one that was purer? Far from being the acquisition of a specialist technique, this school of the microphone, as we know, influenced theatrical diction in return, not without destroying some stereotypes of dramatic performance. For his part, far from being frustrated or perceiving only what was distorted in these phenomena, the listener was invited to experience something new, a different approach to texts, speech, musics.

---

11. Jacques Copeau, in *Dix ans d'essais radiophoniques*, an album of recordings edited by the research services of the ORTF. [A CD edition was produced in 1989 by Phonurgia Nova and Ina. Reference PN 0461/5.—Trans.]

With this experience now so commonplace, it is odd that there is no ordinary word for it. We have to search through the dictionary to dig up a very old neologism: *acousmatic*. This term has so little to do with our techniques that it comes to us from way back down the centuries. Long before Jacques Copeau, someone else had experienced the powers of a faceless voice, had identified the phenomenon: Pythagoras.

4

Acousmatics

4.1. RELEVANCE OF AN ANCIENT EXPERIMENT

Acousmatic, says the *Larousse* dictionary: *Name given to the disciples of Pythagoras who, for five years, listened to his lessons hidden behind a curtain, without seeing him, and observing the strictest silence.*[1] Only the voice of their master, hidden from their eyes, reached the disciples.

From this initiatory experience we will take the concept of acousmatic in the sense we wish to use it. The *Larousse* continues: *Acousmatic, adjective: a noise that is heard without the causes from which it comes being seen.* As we briefly mentioned at the end of the last chapter, this term, in fact, emphasizes the perceptual reality of sound, as such, by distinguishing it from its methods of production and transmission: the new phenomenon of telecommunications and mass broadcasting of messages can only take place *with reference to* and *in accordance with* a fact that has been rooted in human experience forever: natural sound communication. This is why, without being anachronistic, we can go back to an ancient tradition that, no differently and no less than radio and recording today, gave back to the ear alone the entire responsibility for a mode of perception normally backed up by other sensory evidence. In former times the device was a curtain; today, the radio and sound reproduction systems, using all forms of electroacoustic transformations, place us, modern listeners to an invisible voice, once more under the conditions of a similar experiment.

1. As Jérôme Peignot also remarked. [A French writer and poet who collaborated with Schaeffer in the 1950s, Peignot suggested the word *acousmatic* to Schaeffer to describe the listening situation of musique concrète.—Trans.]

4.2. ACOUSTIC AND ACOUSMATIC

It would be a wrong use of this experiment if we submitted it to a Cartesian analysis by differentiating the "objective"—what is behind the curtain—from the "subjective"—the listener's reaction to these stimuli. From this viewpoint it is the so-called objective factors that contain the references for the sought-after elucidation: frequencies, durations, amplitudes . . . ; the curiosity aroused is an acoustic curiosity. Compared to this approach, the acousmatic is a reversal of the pathway. It asks parallel questions: the question now is not how subjective listening interprets or distorts "reality" or of studying reactions to stimuli; listening itself becomes the phenomenon under study. The concealment of causes is not the result of technical imperfection, nor is it an occasional variation: it becomes a prerequisite, a deliberate conditioning of the individual. Now the question: "What can I hear? . . . What exactly can you hear?" is turned back *on him* in the sense that he is being asked to describe not the external references of the sound he perceives but his perception itself.

But *acoustic* and *acousmatic* are not opposites like *objective* and *subjective*. While the former approach, starting from physics, may go as far as the "individual's reactions" and therefore, at a pinch, include psychological factors, the latter should in effect ignore measurements and experiments that apply only to the physical object, the acousticians' "signal." But although this type of research concentrates on the individual, it cannot, for all that, abandon its ambition to have *an objectivity of its own:* if what it studies were to be no more than the changing impressions of each listener, all communication would become impossible; Pythagoras's disciples would have had to give up *a shared* way of naming, describing, and understanding what they heard; an individual listener would even have to give up trying to understand himself from one moment to another. The question here is how, through comparing subjective reactions, we might find something on which several experimenters can agree.

4.3. THE ACOUSMATIC FIELD

In acoustics we started from the physical signal and studied its transformations through electroacoustic processes, with tacit reference to the norms of a supposedly familiar mode of listening—one that could hear frequencies, durations, and so forth. On the contrary, the acousmatic system, generally speaking, symbolically forbids any relationship with the visible, touchable, measurable. In other respects the differences between Pythagoras's experiment and the experiment that radio and recording make us part of, between live listening (through a curtain) and non-live listening (through a loudspeaker) become, ultimately, negligible. Under these conditions, what are the characteristics of the present-day acousmatic situation?

(a) *Pure listening*

For the traditional musician and the acoustician one important aspect of sound recognition is the identification of sound sources. When this takes place without the help of sight, musical conditioning is thrown into disarray. Often taken by surprise, sometimes uncertain, we discover that much of what we thought we could hear was in reality merely seen, and explained, by the context. This is why it is just about possible to confuse some sounds produced by instruments as different as strings and woodwind.

(b) *Listening to effects*

Through listening to sound objects with their instrumental causes hidden, we come to forget about the latter and attend to the objects in their own right. The dissociation of sight and hearing encourages another way of listening: listening to sound forms, without any other aim than to hear them better, so that we can describe them through analyzing the content of our perceptions.

In reality, Pythagoras's curtain is not enough to discourage a curiosity about causes to which we are instinctively, almost irresistibly, inclined. But the repetition of the physical symbol made possible by recording helps us in two ways: by exhausting this curiosity, it gradually imposes the sound object as a concept worth studying in its own right; furthermore, with the help of more attentive and accurate acts of listening, it reveals to us little by little all the richness of this mode of perception.

(c) *Variations in listening*

In addition, as these repetitions take place under physically identical conditions, we become aware of the variations in our listening and can better understand what is generally called its "subjectivity." This is by no means, as we may perhaps be inclined to think, an imperfection, for example some "blurriness" scrambling the physical signal, but different perspectives or ways of hearing that are accurate every time, and every time reveal a new aspect of the object, which engages our deliberate or unconscious attention.

(d) *Variations in the signal*

Finally, we should mention the special ways open to us to operate on sound, which when implemented intensify the characteristics of the acousmatic situation described above. In effect, we are in control of the physical signal fixed on the record or the tape; we can also make different recordings of one sound event or approach it from different angles when capturing sound, as we would, say, when capturing images. Assuming that we keep to one recording, we can play it back more or less fast or more or less loud or even cut it into pieces, thus giving the listener several versions of what, in the beginning, was a single event. What, from the point of view of the acousmatic experiment, are the implications of drawing these divergent sound effects from one material cause? Can we still talk of one single sound object? What correlation can we expect between the modifications made to what is recorded on the tape and the variations in what we hear?

4.4. ON THE SOUND OBJECT: WHAT IT IS NOT

We have spoken several times about the sound object, using a concept that has already been introduced but not explained. The reader will see, in the light of this chapter, that we could only put forward this concept because implicitly we were referring to the acousmatic situation we have just described; the sound object exists only insofar as there is blind listening to the effects and content of sound: the sound object is nowhere so much in evidence as in the acousmatic experience.

Once this has been made clear, it is easy for us to avoid wrong answers to the question raised at the end of the section above.

(a) *The sound object is not the instrument that played*

It is obvious that in saying "that's a violin" or "that's a creaking door" we are alluding to the *sound* produced by the violin, the *creak* of the door. But the distinction we wish to make between instrument and sound object is even more radical: if we are given a tape with a recording of a sound whose origin we are incapable of identifying, what do we hear? Precisely what we call a sound object, independent of any causal reference covered by the terms *sound body, sound source,* or *instrument*.

(b) *The sound object is not the tape*

Although materialized by the tape, the object, in our definition, is not on the tape either. There is only the magnetic trace of a signal on the tape: a *sound medium* or an *acoustic signal*. Listened to by a dog, a child, a Martian, or a citizen of another musical civilization, this signal takes on different meanings. The object is the object of our listening *alone*, and it is relative to it. We can physically act on the tape, cut into it, change its speed. Only a given listener's act of listening can give us an account of the perceptible result of these manipulations. Coming from a world in which we can intervene, the sound object is nonetheless *entirely contained within our perceptual consciousness.*

(c) *The same few centimeters of tape can contain a number of different sound objects*

This remark flows from the previous one. The manipulations we have just mentioned did not change *a* sound object with its own intrinsic existence. They *created others*. There is, of course, a *correlation* between the manipulations applied to a tape or the various ways of playing it back, the listening conditions, and the object perceived.

A simple correlation? Not at all. We have to look for it. Suppose, for example, that we were listening to a sound recorded at normal speed, then slowed down, then played again at its normal speed. The slowing down, acting on the temporal structure of the sound like a magnifying glass, will have allowed us to distinguish certain details, of grain, for example, which our ear, alerted, informed, will also find in the second playing at normal speed. Here we must let ourselves be guided by the evidence, and the very manner in which we had to formulate our assumption provides the answer: it is indeed the *same* sound object observed in different ways that we are comparing with itself, the original and the transposed version. But what makes it the same object is, precisely, our will to compare (and also the fact that the way we have manipulated it, with this same intention to compare it to itself, has changed it without making it unrecognizable).

Now give this slowed-down sound to a nonspecialist listener. Two things can happen. Either the listener still recognizes its instrumental origin and, with it, the manipulation. For him there is *an original sound source that he cannot hear* properly but to which, nevertheless, he refers his act of listening: what he hears is, in fact, a *transposed version*. Or else he will not identify the real origin, will not suspect the transposition, and he will hear *an original sound object*, which is so *in its own right*. (It cannot be a case of illusion or lack of information, since in the acousmatic state our perceptions cannot rely on anything external.) Conversely, for us who have just carried out one or more transpositions of the sound object, it is likely that there will be a single object and its various transposed versions. It is also possible, however, that, abandoning any intention to make comparisons, we attach ourselves to one or other of these versions in order to use them, for example, in a composition; they will then become for us so many original sound objects, entirely independent of their common origin.

We could make similar analyses using different sorts of manipulations (or variations in sound capture) that, depending on our intention, our knowledge, and our previous training, will result in either variations of one sound object or the creation of several sound objects. In the slowed-down example we deliberately chose a modification that lends itself to ambiguity. Other manipulations can transform an object in such a way that it becomes impossible to discern any perceptible relationship between the two versions. In this case we cannot talk about the permanence of a single sound object, if identifying it depends only on remembering the various operations performed on "something that was on the tape." If, even when guided by memories and a desire to find comparisons, it is impossible to detect any similarity between the various results by listening, we can say that, whatever our intentions, the manipulations of one signal have given rise to several sound objects.

(d) *But the sound object is not a state of mind*

To avoid its being confused with its physical cause or a "stimulus," we seem to have based the sound object on our own subjectivity. But—our preceding remarks already indicate this—it does not, for all that, change either with the variations in individual listening or the incessant fluctuations of our attention and our sensibility. Far from being subjective, in the sense of individual, incommunicable, and practically ungraspable, sound objects, as we will see, can be described and analyzed quite easily. We can gain knowledge of them. We can, we hope, transmit this knowledge.

The ambiguity revealed by our brief consideration of the sound object—objectivity bound to subjectivity—will surprise us only if we persist in seeing "the workings of the mind" and "external realities" as opposites. Theories of knowledge have not needed the sound object to perceive the contradiction to which we refer, and which does not derive from the acousmatic situation as such. This debate will be the subject of the whole of book 4.

4.5. ORIGINALITY OF THE ACOUSMATIC APPROACH

Our approach is therefore different from spontaneous instrumental practice, where, as we saw in the first chapter, everything is given at once: the instrument, the first principle and vehicle of a musical civilization, and the virtuosity that goes with it, and therefore a certain structuring of the music played on it. Nor have we in mind "the most general instrument possible"; what we are aiming for, in fact, and what follows from the above remarks, is the most general musical situation possible. We can now describe this explicitly. We possess nearly all sounds—at least in theory—without having to produce them; we only have to press the tape recorder button. Deliberately ignoring any reference to instrumental causes or preexisting musical meanings, we seek to give ourselves over entirely and exclusively to *listening*, and so to come upon those instinctive pathways that lead from pure "sound" to pure "music." That is what acousmatics proposes: turning our backs on the instrument and musical conditioning, and *placing sound and its musical "potential" squarely before us.*

One more remark before ending this first book which still only deals with "making." In the course of this chapter we have already begun to *listen* with a new ear. It may perhaps have seemed more logical to start the next book precisely with this chapter. That is of little consequence. The interest of this remark is not purely formal: it lies in the observation that technology has itself created the conditions for a new mode of listening. Let us render unto audiovisual techniques that which is their due: we expect previously unheard sounds, new timbres, dizzying modes of playing, in a word, instrumental progress from them. They do indeed contribute all of this, but very soon we do not know what to do with them; these new instruments cannot so easily be integrated with the existing ones, and the questions they raise fundamentally challenge received ideas. First of all, the tape recorder has the virtues of Pythagoras's curtain: it may create new phenomena to be observed, but above all it creates new conditions for observation.

And so we move on from "making" to "hearing" through a redefinition of "hearing" through "making." It is in this sense that the next book will deal with both the most ancient definitions of hearing and the newest ways of making us hear.

BOOK TWO

Hearing

5

___

"What Can Be Heard"

5.1. TO HEAR (ENTENDRE) ACCORDING TO LITTRÉ

First, we must consult the *Littré* dictionary under the word *to hear* (entendre),[1] restricting ourselves to establishing a little order in its entries:

To hear (entendre): to direct the ear toward, in order to receive sound impressions. To hear noise. I hear someone talking in the next room; I hear that you are giving me some news.

1. *To hear–to listen* (entendre-écouter): to hear is to be struck by sounds; to listen is to lend the ear to hear them. Sometimes we do not hear even though we are listening, and often we hear without listening.

2. *To hear–to perceive aurally* (entendre-ouïr): these two words, originally very different, are completely synonymous today. *Ouïr* was the correct word, gradually replaced by *entendre*, which is the figurative word. *Ouïr* is to perceive aurally; *entendre* is, properly speaking, to pay attention. Usage alone has given it the distorted meaning of *ouïr*. The only difference is that *ouïr* has become a defective verb with restricted usage. When the meaning may be doubtful, *ouïr* must definitely be used. Hence the saying of Pacuvius on astrologers: "It's better to let what they say fall on your ears (ouïr) than to listen (écouter) to them." To hear (entendre) would be wrong.

3. *Etymologically*: to hold out toward, hence to have an intention, a plan: "What's your take on it?"

---

1. Schaeffer uses four different words in French to describe the listening modes: *écouter, ouïr, entendre,* and *comprendre.* Since there are no perfect equivalents in English, the decision has been made to include the French original word in brackets throughout this chapter.—Trans.

4. *To hear–to conceive of–to understand* (entendre-concevoir-comprendre): *entendre* and *comprendre* both mean to know the meaning of. This distinguishes them from *concevoir*, which means to comprehend by way of the mind. I know the meaning of (j'entends) or I understand (je comprends) that sentence, not I conceive of it (je la conçois). On the other hand, in Boileau's line "What is clearly conceived of (se conçoit) is clearly expressed," to know the meaning of (entendre) or to understand (comprendre) would not do. The distinction between to know the meaning of (entendre) and to understand (comprendre) is different; the idea behind to know the meaning of (entendre) is to pay attention to, to be skilled in, whereas for to understand (comprendre) it is: to take in. I know the meaning of (j'entends) German, I know it, I am skilled in it. "I understand (je comprends) German" would be to say less. However, I say I understand (je comprends) a proof.

Based on this initial description, and taking the liberty of stretching the sense of the terms a little in order to make their specialized meanings clearer, we would suggest four definitions:

1. *To listen* (écouter) is to lend the ear, be interested in. I move actively toward someone or something that describes or signals its presence through a sound.

2. *To perceive aurally* (ouïr) is in contrast to listening (écouter), which describes the more active attitude; what I perceive aurally is what is given to my perception.

3. With *to hear* (entendre), we will retain the etymological sense: "to have an intention." What I hear, what is manifest to me, is a function of that intention.

4. *To understand* (comprendre), to take in, has a double relationship with listening (écouter) and hearing (entendre). I understand (je comprends) what I was aiming to listen to (mon écoute), thanks to what I chose to hear (entendre). But, reciprocally, what I have already understood (j'ai compris) directs my listening (mon écoute) and informs what I hear (j'entends).

We will look at this more closely.

5.2. TO PERCEIVE AURALLY (OUÏR)

Properly speaking, I never stop perceiving aurally. I live in a world that is always present to me, and this world is a world of sound, as well as of touch and of sight. I move in an "ambience" as in a landscape. The most profound silence is still a sound background like any other, and against it, the noise of my breathing and my heart stand out with unexpected solemnity.[2] We can glimpse how strange a world suddenly deprived of this dimension would be when there is a technical hitch, when the sound tape of a film suddenly stops or in some of our dreams. It is like Baudelaire's dream and its "moving marvels" over which "hovered—dreadful novelty—everything for the eye, nothing for the ear—a silence as of eternity." As if

2. Cf. cosmonauts' stories about "space silence."

the continuous hum that inhabits even our dreams were mingled with the sense of our own duration.

But for all that, to perceive aurally is not "to be struck by sounds" coming to my ear without reaching my consciousness. Rather it is because of my consciousness that the backdrop of sound has reality. I adapt to it instinctively, raising my voice without even thinking when its level increases. It is associated for me with the sight, the thoughts, the actions that went along with it without my knowing, and sometimes it alone is enough to recall these to my mind. The music of a film, to which, completely absorbed by the dramatic events, I had paid not the slightest attention, will, when I hear it on the radio, reawaken the emotions the film had aroused, even before I have properly identified it. Finally, I instantly notice any sudden or unusual change in this backdrop of sound that I was not even aware of: the example is well known of people living near a station who wake up when the train does not go by on time.

But it is true that I can only ever become aware of the backdrop of sound indirectly, by reflection or memory. I hear the clock strike. I know it has struck already. I hastily reconstruct in my mind the first two strokes, which *I had perceived aurally*, establish which one I heard as the third, even before the fourth strikes. If I had not wanted to know the time, I would not, in fact, have known that the first two strokes had reached my consciousness. . . . Someone speaks to me, I am thinking about something else. The person I was speaking to, annoyed, stops talking. I hear this ill-omened silence. I manage to dig the second half of his sentence out of the backdrop of sound before it is irretrievably swallowed up in it, and this, with a little luck, will allow me to answer him and persuade him that my loss of attention was only apparent.

5.3. TO LISTEN (ÉCOUTER)

But now suppose I listen to this person. This means, by the same token, that I do not listen to the sound of his voice. I turn toward him, obedient to his intention to communicate something to me, ready to hear, from all that is offered to my aural perception, only what has value as a semantic indicator. Perhaps he has a southern accent that amused me when I first met him, that I still notice when I meet him again after a long absence, that distracted me then from even his most serious conversations, but that at present I ignore. (However, when I think back to this conversation, not intellectually, to go over the remarks we exchanged or to draw conclusions from them, but spontaneously, for example on going back later to the place where they occurred, I remember not only what we said but that accent from a part of the South, that particular turn of phrase, that voice I can immediately distinguish from so many others by a number of characteristics I had not, after all, ceased to perceive aurally even if I am quite incapable of analyzing them.)

To listen, as we have just seen, is not necessarily to be interested in a sound. It is even only rarely to be interested in it but rather, through it, to focus on something else.

At a pinch we may even forget that it has passed through our hearing. Then, listening to someone becomes practically synonymous with obeying ("Listen to your father!") or giving credence (thus Pacuvius advises never to listen to astrologers, even if we cannot prevent perceiving aurally what they say). Listening to what is said to me, I strive, through the words, but also beyond a formulation that may be flawed, toward ideas that I endeavor to understand.

I listen to a car. I locate it, estimate how far away it is, even possibly recognize its make. What do I know of the noise that gave me all this information? The more quickly and reliably it gave me information, the more impoverished would be the description I would give of it if anyone asked me.

Conversely, it is precisely the noise of the car I focus on if the car is mine and if it seems the engine is "making a funny noise." But my listening is still utilitarian, for I am seeking to infer information about the state of my engine from it: in my uncertainty about causes, I am constrained first and foremost to analyze the effects.

Finally I can listen, as I had initially promised myself, with no other goal than to *hear better*. That analysis, which a moment ago was a necessary stage, becomes its own purpose. Concentrating on the event, I relied on my perception. I used it unawares. Now, I have taken a step back from my perception. I am no longer making use of it; I am *disinterested*. It can finally reveal itself to me, *become an object*. Here to listen is still to focus, beyond the immediate sound itself, on something else than it: a kind of "sound character," which becomes present to the whole of my perception.

5.4. TO HEAR (*ENTENDRE*)

We can now better define *to hear* (entendre) in relation to the other two verbs.

(a) *To perceive aurally–to hear* (ouïr-entendre)

We will start by observing that it is practically impossible for me not to select from what I perceive aurally. Background noise is not the most important; this is only so in an organized structure where it actually has this function. As long as I am occupied with what I am watching, thinking, or doing, I am in fact living in undifferentiated surroundings, perceiving scarcely anything but general impressions. But if I stay still, with my eyes closed and my mind empty, it is highly probable that I will not continue to listen impartially for more than an instant. I locate noises; I separate them, for example, into close or distant noises, coming from outside or in the room, and, inevitably, I begin to prefer some to others. The ticking of the clock asserts itself, obsesses me, wipes out all the rest. In spite of myself, I impose a rhythm on it: stressed beat, unstressed beat. Powerless to destroy this rhythm, I try at least to substitute another. I am at the point of wondering how I could ever have slept in the same room as this infuriating clock . . . and yet it only needs a car in the road to brake sharply for me to forget it. Now, for all I know, the room I am in could be an oasis of calm, battered by noises from outside. But I hear someone knocking at the door; and all these changing structures instantly sink back into the background noise, while I open my eyes and get up to go and open the door.

At least, thanks to those changes, I have been able to make an inventory, little by little and, as it were, by surprise, of the backdrop against which they occurred and to realize that I was responsible for those endless variations. When my intention is firmer, the corresponding structure will be stronger, and it is then, paradoxically, that I will have the impression that it is imposed on me from outside. Thus it is that, joining in a familiar conversation with several people, I will go from one subject and from one person to another, without having the slightest inkling of the huge confusion of voices, noises, laughter, from which I am making an original composition, different from any that each of my companions is making on his own account. I need a sound recording to reveal it to me, but, as the tape recorder will have not selected anything, it will often be indecipherable.

(b) *To listen–to hear* (écouter-entendre)

What will happen if, on the contrary, I listen in order to hear, either because I do not know where the sound object is coming from, in which case I am obliged to go through the process of describing it, or because I want to ignore where it is coming from and concentrate exclusively on the object? It would be a great mistake to think that the object would reveal itself to me, with all its qualities, just because I have taken it out of the background into which I relegated it: I will continue to make a series of choices, consider various aspects of it, one after the other.

In the same way, when I look at a house, I locate it in the landscape. But if my interest in it continues, I will examine the color of the stone, its material, or the architecture, or the detail of a carving over the door; then I will go back to the landscape, in relation to the house, to observe that it has a "lovely view," and I will once more see it as a whole, as I had done at first, but my perception will be enriched by my previous investigations. Moreover, it is almost impossible for me to see it in the same way as if it were a rock or a cloud. It is a house, a piece of human handiwork, made to shelter human beings. I see it and appreciate it in relation to this meaning. And my inquiry, like my appreciation, will also be different depending on whether I am looking at it through the eyes of a future owner, an archaeologist, someone walking by, or an Inuit expert in igloos.

In the next chapter we will find a more detailed approach to the process of *qualified listening*, the diversity of which arises from this fundamental law of perception, which is to proceed "by a series of sketches," without ever exhausting the object, to all our knowledge and former experiences (which give the overall appearance of the object different meanings or significations), and to the variety of our listening intentions, toward what we are looking for. Here we will simply give a typical example taken from Max Frisch's novel *Homo Faber*:

> Every day, in the morning, I was awoken by a weird noise, half-industrial, half-musical, a hubbub that I could not explain, not at all loud, but frenetic like crickets, metallic, monotonous, it must be a piece of machinery, but I couldn't tell which, and afterward, when we went to have breakfast in the village, it had stopped, nothing could be seen.
>   . . . We packed our bags on Sunday. . . . And the strange noise that had awoken me every morning turned out to be music, the din of an ancient marimba, a clattering noise devoid of timbre, a hideous music, absolutely chaotic. It was for some festival to do with the full moon. Every morning before going to work in the fields they had been practicing to accompany the dance, five Native South Americans beating furiously with little hammers on their instrument, a sort of xylophone as long as a table.[3]

The two descriptions are clearly related: frenzy, monotony and clattering, hubbub and absence of timbre, metallic noise and hammer blows on a xylophone. Every morning from his bed, then outside, as he was leaving, Walter Faber *perceived*, more or less, *the same thing aurally* (il a ouï).

We cannot say the same about what he *heard*. On the first occasion he heard a *noise* and tried to *explain* its cause; on the second, aware of the causes, he *is judging* a *music*. Immediately, what was only "weird" becomes "hideous." The "frenzy" that at first appeared as a simple descriptive analogy (our hero not dreaming of blaming it literally on crickets) is more strongly perceived when it is shown to be the result of furious instrumental activity, and then it becomes "absolutely chaotic." At the same time, however, the monotony of the clattering, which might have suggested a machine, became less noticeable. Having managed to *describe* what he was listening to, Walter Faber began to *hear* (entendre), then to *understand* (comprendre), by virtue of a precise signification.

5.5. TO UNDERSTAND (*COMPRENDRE*)

In effect, informed, not directly by the sound object, which remained unclear, "half-industrial half-musical," but with the help of sight, he *understood* that he was dealing with music.

Like Max Frisch's hero, I can understand the exact cause of what I have heard by connecting it with other perceptions or by means of a more or less complex series of deductions. Or again, through what I am listening to, I can understand something that has only an indirect link with what I hear: I note simultaneously

---

3. Max Frisch, *Homo Faber* (Paris: Gallimard, 1961). [Frisch's novel was first published in German in 1957 (Frankfurt am Main: Suhrkamp), then, in English as *Homo Faber* in 1959 (London: Abelard-Schuman).—Trans.]

that the birds are silent, the sky is lowering, the heat is oppressive, and I understand that there will be a thunderstorm.

I understand as a result of brainwork, a conscious activity of the mind that is no longer happy just to accept a signification but abstracts, compares, deduces, links information from different sources and of different types; I clarify the initial meaning or work out an additional one.

That noise that came from the next room and made her jump is pregnant with meaning for the mistress of the house: it is the noise of something falling or breaking. She hears it as such. Furthermore, she notices that her son is no longer there, remembers that the Chinese vase has very unwisely been left on a table within his reach, and very quickly understands that the child has just broken the Chinese vase.

I listen to (j'écoute) and hear (j'entends) what people say to me, but picking up contradictions in what is said, and linking them with certain facts that I already knew, I also understand (je comprends) that the person I am talking to is lying. Immediately, the mistrust this arouses in me changes the focus of my listening, and I also understand hesitations, certain cracks in the voice, and "even looks that you would think were dumb."

As this last example suggests, sometimes *entendre* (to listen) and *comprendre* (to understand) are used interchangeably, in the sense in which they are synonyms: to grasp the meaning of. This is the case, for example, when we say either "I understand you" (using *comprendre*) or "I understand you" (using *entendre*), or when we complain that we do not understand (*comprendre* or *entendre*) modern music. In both cases, in fact, the act of understanding precisely coincides with the activity of listening: the whole work of deduction, comparison, and abstraction is part of the process and goes far beyond the immediate content, "what can be heard."

6

The Four Listening Modes

Although this treatise is about the musical object, we should acknowledge that what is obvious to musical experience in every age is not, as we have seen, the musical object but instrumental activity, which gives rise to musical languages. Nor, as far as musical consciousness is concerned, is the mechanism of the ear, so eagerly analyzed in the manuals, of the first importance. Nor is the daily activity of hearing (entendre) itself, which appears elementary.

If the object chimes with our way of *making* and *hearing*, we must, to get near to it, apply simple common sense in these two fields of our most ordinary everyday activity. The first book gave an overview of the various activities linked with musical *making*. This second book concentrates on *hearing* (entendre), and the last chapter contains an initial description of the possible usages of this word, based on its current meanings.

In this chapter we will methodically delve more deeply into these meanings, while trying to attach them to typical attitudes and characteristic, although in practice almost indissociable, behaviors. In fact, rather than tackle the simple adjective *musical* directly, to see what is behind it, it seems to us better to start from the usual meanings of "to hear" (entendre) and, with reference to these meanings, highlight the listening *functions* that correspond to them.

To give a quite empirical description of "what happens" when we listen, we will make a sort of summary of the various forms of activity of the ear. Indeed, from the most to the least complex, *to perceive aurally* (ouïr), *to hear* (entendre) and *to understand* (comprendre) suggest a perceptual itinerary going from one stage to the next. Our intention here is not to break down listening into a chronological sequence of events proceeding one from the other as effects flow from causes but, for methodo-logical reasons, to describe the objectives of specific listening functions. As these functions are involved in the sound "communication circuit" that goes from produc-tion to reception, and inasmuch as they have complementary characteristics, we thought that placing them on a symmetrical, perhaps rather too systematic, diagram might be of help to some of our readers. This is an initial plan of the diagram:

4 to understand (comprendre)	1 to listen (écouter)
3 to hear (entendre)	2 to perceive aurally (ouïr)

6.2. *LITTRÉ* (CONT.): THE COMMUNICATION CIRCUIT

We will start from the findings in the last chapter and examine them more closely.

1. I listen (j'écoute) to what interests me.

2. Provided I am not deaf, I perceive aurally (j'ouïs) the sounds that go on around me, and this whatever my activities and interests are.

3. I hear (j'entends) in relation to what interests me, what I already know, and what I seek to understand (comprendre).

4. After hearing (entendre), I understand (je comprends) what I was trying to understand, what I was listening for (j'écoutais).

This analysis could probably be applied to any perceptual activity. We would find similarities between *to look at* (regarder) and *to listen* (écouter), *to perceive aurally* (ouïr) and *to see* (voir), *to hear* (entendre) and *to notice* (apercevoir). The difference is less marked, it is true, the etymology closer between *to see* (voir) and *to notice* (apercevoir) than between *to perceive aurally* (ouïr) and *to hear* (enten-dre). Doubtless because we more often experience a mechanically perceived back-ground noise than a mechanically perceived sight. Whatever may be the case, we can easily imagine all this being transposed into the visual domain.

We will now return to each of these points:

1. Silence, thought to be universal, is broken by a sound *event*. It may be a natu-ral event (a stone rolling, a weathervane creaking) or the willed production of a sound (by an instrument, for example). In any case, what we spontaneously listen to at this level is the energetic anecdote communicated by the sound.

2. Corresponding to the objective event, we find the subjective event in the lis-tener, the *raw perception* of the sound, which is linked, on the one hand, to the

physical nature of the sound and, on the other hand, to general laws of perception that we are justified in assuming are *grosso modo* the same for all human beings (as, for example, the gestaltists do in their descriptions).

3. This perception, which is then related to past experiences, to dominant, current, interests, brings about a *choice* and a *judgment*. We would say the perception is *qualified*.

4. Qualified perceptions are directed toward a particular form of knowledge, and ultimately what the perceiving individual finally achieves is *abstract significations* rather than the concrete sound itself. Generally speaking, at this level the individual understands a particular sound *language*.

6.3. THE INDIVIDUAL AND OBJECTS: PERCEPTUAL INTENTIONS

We must first clarify this communications terminology. In what ways can a sound present itself to me?

1. I listen to the *event*, and I try to identify the sound source: "What's that? What's happened?" So I do not stop at what I perceive; I use it without realizing. I treat the sound as an *indicator* that tells me something. This is doubtless what happens most commonly, because it tallies with our most spontaneous attitude, the most primitive role of perception: to warn of danger, to guide an action. Generally, identifying the sound event with its causal context in this way is instantaneous. But it may also be that, when the indicators are ambiguous, it happens only after various comparisons and deductions. Scientific curiosity, although using highly developed knowledge, pursues a basically similar goal to spontaneous perception of the event.

2. I may, on the contrary, return to the type of perception I was using a moment ago, and the question "What's that?" will apply to the sound itself. That is, I am treating it as an object in itself. This is what we call *the raw sound object*. (This topic will be treated at length in book 4.) It is what remains the same throughout the "flood" of successive and various impressions I have of it, as well as in the face of my various intentions regarding it. The second essential characteristic of a perceived object is to reveal itself piecemeal: in the sound object I am listening to, there is always *more* to be heard; it is a wellspring of potentialities that never runs dry. Thus, every time a recorded sound is repeated, I listen to the same object: although I never hear it in the same way, although from being unknown it becomes familiar, although I perceive different aspects in succession, and it is therefore never the same, I still identify it as that clearly defined object.

3. Similarly, different listeners gathered round a tape recorder are listening to the same sound object. They do not, however, all hear the same thing; they do not choose and evaluate in the same way, and insofar as their mode of listening inclines them toward different aspects of the sound, it gives rise to different *descriptions* of

the object. These descriptions vary, as does the hearing, according to the previous experience and the interests of each person. Nevertheless, the single sound object, which makes possible these many descriptions of it, persists in the form of a halo of perceptions, as it were, and the explicit descriptions implicitly refer back to it. So, when I focus my qualified perception on the details of a house—window, carving over the door—the house is not any the less there, and I see that window or that carving as belonging to it.

4. Finally, I may treat sound as an *indicator* that brings me into a particular domain of values and focus on its *meaning*. The most typical example is, of course, the word. Here we have a semantic listening mode, revolving around semantic signs. Among the various possible "signifier" listening modes, we are naturally most particularly interested in musical listening, referring to musical values and giving access to a musical meaning. We would point out that the values in question here could, just about, be detached from their sound context, which is then reduced to the role of medium. It is generally believed that communication effects a coming together of minds; hence, it is natural that at the two extremities of the circuit, and particularly here, at the receptive stage, we should abandon the contingency of the sound vehicle for its signifying content. Traditional musical values are no exception, inasmuch as musical symbols preexist performance: we strive to improve the latter in relation to the former, not vice versa. This is why, at point 4, we could talk about abstract meanings; the abstract at this level is the opposite of the tangible of level 1:

4. TO UNDERSTAND (comprendre)
- for me: signs
- in front of me: values
  (meaning-language)
 	
Emergence of a sound content and *reference to*, *encounters with*, extra-sonorous concepts.
	1. TO LISTEN (écouter)
	- for me: indicators
	- in front of me: external events
	  (agent-instrument)
	
	Sound *production*
		1 & 4:
		objective

3. TO HEAR (entendre)
 	
- for me: qualified perceptions
 	
- in front of me: qualified sound
  object
 	
Selection of certain specific aspects of the sound
	2. TO PERCEIVE AURALLY
	  (ouïr)
	- for me: raw perceptions,
	  vague idea of the object
	- in front of me: raw sound
	  object
	
	Reception of the sound
		2 & 3:
		subjective

3 & 4: abstract	1 & 2: concrete	

Listening functions.

6.4. STAGES AND OUTCOMES OF LISTENING:
DIVERSITY AND COMPLEMENTARITY

We can now put together everything we have discovered in the diagram above.[1] Of course—we must emphasize this—*we must not* infer from our compartmentalizations and numberings a chronology or a logic that our perceptual mechanism obeys. If we find this diagram useful in highlighting a number of processes that are not normally analyzed, that does not mean it is a working diagram. Therefore:

· The need to move from one sector to another in order to give a logical description of a particular perceptual process is simply an expository device and does not imply any time sequence in the perceptual experience itself. Perceptual deciphering happens instantaneously, even when all four sectors are involved.

· Even if we have isolated what we call qualified perceptions in sector 3, we must not forget that these are refined and enriched by the tacit references made by the listener to the events in sector 1, the values in sector 4, and the sound detail of the raw object in sector 2.

· The listener has direct access to objective results, both when he is looking for the meaning in a series of sound signs or wishes to decipher the sound signals in terms of events (physicists, acousticians, often instrumentalists). In the first case, however, the signs he obtains in 4 emerge from qualified listening in 3: in the second, it is listening to the raw sound object (in 2) that brings about its organization into indicators in 1. Naturally, the listener will not be aware in either situation that he is practicing two kinds of listening in parallel, he will only feel involved in the last aspect of his perceptual activity, which gives him what he is looking for, and he will have difficulty imagining that it is only one of many other possible aspects, as well as that he is implicitly dependent on them. This spontaneous listening for signs or indicators can be represented in two "short-circuits":

---

1. The pictures on the cover of this work have been chosen to illustrate this diagram. Here is how the visual metaphor they contain should be interpreted: the two ways of playing an instrument such as the violin suggest two "events" in sector 1; the half-profile of a listening woman highlights the ear but also all the surrounding activity that goes with it; in sector 3 there are various qualified sound objects (both the musicianly perception of "pizzicato" and "swelled sound" and the acoustician's depiction of different dynamic profiles); finally, these two sounds emerge as "signs" and acquire their "meaning" in sector 4. Although there are five pictures for reasons of format, it can be seen that the two "violins" could just as well be in sector 1 as sector 3, if the metaphor is interpreted in different ways: the first interpretation suggests the "prior" event; the second, musicianly perception, a quality of the listening individual.

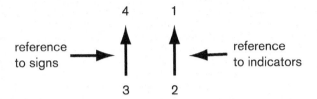

- As long as there remains perceptual uncertainty in relation to the object being listened to, whatever the sector in which this occurs, the investigation will consist in highlighting and cross-referencing the "partial" objects obtained in the auditory activity as a whole; this is why listening several times and going more deeply into the phenomenon will clarify the results in all four directions at once.
- Group listening to new objects will probably reveal great divergences among different listeners from the outset. It will only be after listening many times, facilitating an in-depth exploration of both group and individual perceptual experience at every level, that the listeners will be able to reach a consensus on results. This will lead to a sort of paring down that would just about exhaust the potential of sector 2 (the raw sound object): a degree of objectivity, or at least a number of intersubjective agreements, will then emerge from comparing observations.

6.5. TWO PAIRS: SUBJECTIVE-OBJECTIVE AND CONCRETE-ABSTRACT

The top and bottom parts of our diagram, that is sectors 2 and 3, on the one hand, and 4 and 1, on the other, are a good illustration of the pair subjective and objective, or, rather, subjective and intersubjective. Everyone hears what he can in sector 3, knowing that the possibility of hearing something comes before sector 2. Moreover, there are (sound, musical) reference signs (sector 4) and techniques for sound production (sector 1) specific to a given civilization, and these are, therefore, objectively present in a particular sociological and cultural context. Similarly, in scientific experiments we will find, at sectors 2 and 3, observations that depend quite specifically on the observers, and, for the purposes of explaining or determining the event (1), go against the body of knowledge to which these observations are linked (4).

The vertical line in the middle of the diagram contrasts the two abstract sectors (3 and 4) on the left and the two concrete sectors (1 and 2) on the right. For both qualified listening at the subjective level and the values and knowledge that emerge collectively, the whole effort in 3 and 4 is toward stripping down and consists in retaining only *qualities* of the object that enable it to be linked with others or to be referred to signifying systems. In 1 and 2, on the contrary, whether we are dealing with all the perceptual possibilities contained in the sound object or all the causal references contained in the event, listening focuses on a concrete given, which as such is inexhaustible, although specific.

So in every mode of listening there is, on the one hand, a confrontation between an *individual*, who is receptive within certain limits, and an *objective reality*; on the other hand, *abstract value judgments* and logical descriptions detach themselves from the *concrete given*, which tends to organize itself around these without ever being reduced to them. Of course, different listeners will place a different emphasis on each of the four poles that result from this two-way tension and will favor only the one that pertains to the explicit aim of his listening; there will therefore be specialists in each listening function. But we should not make the mistake of thinking that one of them (for example, the listening musician) only brings into play the function that pertains to the obvious aim of his listening (here listening for musical meaning). To express what we are describing in appropriate language, we should say that no specialist could, in fact, dispense with "running through" the whole cycle of sectors several times; for none of them can escape either from his own subjectivity when faced with a meaning or an event that is presumed to be objective, or from logically deciphering a concrete phenomenon inexplicable in itself, hence from the uncertainties and gradual learning processes of perception. So even within a given discipline, one single diagram is not enough to give an account of all our listeners' approaches. We would come quite near to a figurative representation of the complexity of the auditory process if, on the one hand, we balanced out the emphasis placed on each section in a given "run-through" of the cycle and, on the other hand, superimposed such "run-throughs" one on top of the other in a vertical third dimension, as it were. The overall result would then give a picture of the type of discipline, the personality of the experimenter, and the successive stages of its development.

6.6. TWO PAIRS OF LISTENING MODES: NATURAL AND CULTURAL, ORDINARY AND SPECIALIZED

Given that, with the help of our theoretical "summary," we managed to define the two contrasting pairs in the last section, we can find the same pattern in ordinary or spontaneous approaches to listening. This analysis will help to define a terminology that we will use constantly from now on.

So we will examine two pairs of characteristic tendencies in listening: first, we will contrast *natural* and *cultural* listening; then we will compare *ordinary* and expert or *specialized* listening.

(a) By *natural* listening we mean the primary and primitive tendency to use sound for information about the event. This approach we will (as is generally

accepted) call *natural*, because it seems to us to be common not only to all people whatever their civilization but also to man and certain animals. Some animals have more acute hearing than humans. This not only means that they can hear better "physically" but that they can more easily infer from such signals the circumstances that have caused or are revealed by the sound event. Here the ultimate aim is clearly at sector 1, and we assume that there is a particularly acute *aural perception* (ouïe) at sector 2. It is the *concrete*, the right-hand part of the diagram, that we find used spontaneously, and universally, almost as a priority. In contrast, giving priority to sector 4 can be a result of explicit conventions (codes such as language systems, Morse code, warning bells, or horns). If there is no explicit code, there are forms of *conditioning* to musical sounds, for example, in a community in a clear historical or geographical context. Here (without ceasing to hear it), the sound event and the circumstances it reveals are deliberately ignored in favor of the message, the meaning, the *values* it conveys. This listening mode—less universal than the previous one in the sense that it varies from one community to another and that the most intelligent animals can only master a few pitiful elements of it, and only after training that goes against their nature—could be called *cultural*. It sums up the left-hand side of the diagram: the two *abstract* quadrants.

(b) In the same way we could contrast *ordinary* and *specialized* listening—not simply in order to complete the pair natural-cultural (in sectors 1 and 4) with another (in sectors 2 and 3) but to illustrate the difference in listening skill, quality of attention, and the confusion of intentions in ordinary listening, whereas specialized listening deliberately chooses from the mass of things to be listened to only what it wants to hear and elucidate.

Furthermore, the confusion between these two levels of listening explains many misunderstandings. Because in *ordinary* listening, even if our ear is untrained, we are always free to attend to some *dominant* perception, natural or cultural, we forget that *specialized* listening, precisely because of the intention to hear this and not that, precisely because it is trained and skilled, loses this character of universality and overall intuition, which is one of the advantages of ordinary listening.

Certainly, ordinary listening pays little attention to sectors 2 and 3: it goes immediately to the event and its cultural significance but remains relatively superficial. I hear a violin playing in the high register. But I do not know that, were I more of a musician, I should hear many details about the quality of the violin or the violinist, the accuracy of the note he is playing and so forth, which I cannot access because of my lack of specialized training. I therefore have a "subjective" mode of listening, not because I hear anything and everything but because I have refined neither my aural perception (ouïe) nor my ear. The ordinary ear, however untrained it is, has, however, the merit of being able to be *open* to all sorts of things that would be closed to it by later *specialization*.

Take, on the contrary, an acoustician, a musician, and . . . a Native American from the Wild West. The same galloping horse will be heard by them in very different ways. Immediately, the acoustician will have an idea of how the physical signal is made up (frequency band, fading due to transmission, etc.); the musician will go spontaneously to the rhythmic groups; the Native American will immediately conclude that he is in danger of being attacked, by how many, and how far away. So these types of listening will tend to be thought of as more objective. Yes, insofar as, not being concerned with the same objects (the sound is merely the medium), they explain and relate these objects to sector 1 and sector 4. But at the same time we can see that this can only be achieved through enhanced subjective input, because, in each of these different listeners' consciousness, the raw or qualified sound object is perceived or analyzed quite differently on each occasion. So it is not surprising that misunderstandings tend to arise among such skilled people. This all the more as they are not talking about the same thing. But don't they hear the same sound? Certainly, it cannot be denied that the same physical signal reaches ears that we suppose to be identically human, potentially alike, but their perceptual activity, from the sensory to the mental, certainly does not function in the same way.

So we can see how far we need to be wary of the terms *objectivity* and *subjectivity* if we wish to apply them to listening—the former to specialized, the latter to ordinary. For we could just as well argue the contrary: that ordinary listening is more open to the objective (even though the individual is not skilled), whereas specialized listening is profoundly affected by the individual's intention (even though his attention is focused on objects that are precise in a different way).

This section will, we hope, help the reader to understand the last section better: that a *specialized use* of a certain listening mode has only very little to do with the use by another expert: each has made a choice from the potential for interest of ordinary listening and has developed its aims and also the training it requires.

We will now look more closely at the specialization of listening modes.

6.7. EXCLUSIVES OF SPECIALIZED LISTENING

In ordinary listening, the listening done by everyone, the listener has no particular curiosity or reference point; he simply, as we all do daily, locates what he hears in the multitude of sound entities that make up his usual sound world—a sound world that, being common to a whole community, has no *a priori content* as far as meanings are concerned. I hear and understand that someone is speaking, a car is going by, a child is playing the piano: nothing, in short, that anyone else would not hear as I do, at my level of attention.

The specialist is initially an ordinary listener. Like everyone else, he first orients himself in relation to everyday sound data. But, in addition, he approaches the object through a well-determined system of sound significations, thus with the deliberate intention to hear only what his attention is specifically focused on. The hallmark of specialized listening is precisely that ordinary meaning gives way to the aims of a particular activity. Thus, the phonetician ignores the meanings of words and hears only their phonetic elements; the doctor only uses "99, 99 . . ." to deduce the state of his patient's lungs; the musician shows no interest in the equation of the vibrating strings but thinks only about the quality and accuracy of his notes. The acoustician, in his turn, armed with his *Sonagraph*,[2] is busy with the sound, ignoring, like everyone else, what does not concern him: the meaning of a word, intonation, instrumental sophistication; he attends only to the specific aim of his work as a physicist: the measurable characteristics of sound (frequencies, amplitudes, transients, etc.).

These few examples show in different ways how ordinary listening takes second place to specialized listening, once the ordinary man takes on his specialized functions. When the patient says "99, 99 . . .," the repetition of the signal itself, demonstrating the semantic irrelevance of the words, shows clearly that the doctor's interest is in something other than their usual meaning; similarly, the same series of 99s will enable the phonetician to recognize a certain accent or particularity of speech; however, neither the doctor nor the phonetician will be tempted to believe that the signs and indicators they finally deduce have anything to do with the meaning or musicality of the sound object they are using.

Awareness of the limitation of his skills is less clear in the case of the acoustician. He, for whom the spirit of the times has made a modest demeanor difficult, perceives with difficulty, or not at all, that he has chosen to abandon the world of ordinary listening to enter one in which everything that is heard is referred back to certain supposedly simple perceptions that can be shown as marks on dials or points on graphs. The example of the analysis of the spoken voice on the *Sonagraph* demonstrates this professional blindness particularly well: thinking that the meaning of the word or sentence under analysis is part and parcel of the overview of its acoustic characteristics, the acoustician really thinks he will find its material trace there. He can only make elementary reconstructions, however, and only very approximately recognize phonemes or syllables.

The musician also often does not know to what extent his specialized listening involves shifting and choosing significations when creating a field reserved for so-called musical objects. Outside this field nonvalues are discarded and called noises. Prone, like the physicist, to link his activity to some abstract and absolute target, the musician will easily ignore mechanical contingencies, the energetic origins of objects, and his cultural practices, and he will lose sight of the fact that there were

2. An American device that gives a sound diagram, which for the sake of convenience is called a "sonogram."

vibrating and resonant bodies, familiar to ordinary listening, long before the first instrument came into being. Hence the great difficulties the boldest musicians had in getting the musical establishment to accept new objects, which were still as yet only "sound" and were always rejected precisely under the same pretext: that they were not "music."

Here again the specialist's conditioning dismisses and discredits ordinary meanings.

There is more. Although the acoustician abandons speech for phonemes or sonograms, and music conceals energetic events from the musician, we should acknowledge that neither is retreating to a desert island; on the contrary, each belongs to a community that is very much alive, within which specialized listening, which a moment ago seemed likely to turn them into loners, soon appears as normal and as open to potential description as the ordinary listening of the uninitiated was in the everyday sound world. Not stopping at the limited problem of the correlations between his own results and everyday sound significations, the acoustician pursues his specifically physics-based investigation, defines magnitudes, establishes links, sets up experiments, extensively compares his activities with those of his colleagues, in short sets about inhabiting the world that his specialized listening opens up to him. Similarly, the musician, soon tiring of the ordinary mechanical significations of sounds, moves into musical listening and practice, makes objects, seeks an expressive language, writes, sings, plays, listens, innovates.

So group practices take shape, based on communities that listen in the same way. We saw in the last section that we cannot understand these practices by situating them in one single sector of our diagram. In fact, we must take the view that when we move from ordinary to specialized listening, the circuit of communication belonging to ordinary significations is replaced by a new circuit linked to a different emphasis on descriptions and values. An emphasis that ordinary listening did no more than make possible: I heard music was being played or someone was speaking with a southern accent; as a musician or phonetician I attach myself exclusively to one or other of these particular approaches to my ordinary listening, and from this I define a general field of activity in which the two opposed pairs, *abstract-concrete* and *subjective-objective*, come into play all over again, in an original manner, and related to different aims.

These reflections enable us to go back and correct our initial idea of a dualism between ordinary and specialized listening within a broader context. The specialist cuts himself off from the world of ordinary significations in sector 3; but in so doing he sets up a new world of significations that, in turn, brings subtleties of perception into play in a new sector 3—subtleties soon made ordinary through habit—which perhaps subsequently sow the seed for the development of other auditory practices. Thus the increase in the number of approaches seems limitless.

In other words, every specialized mode of listening suggests specialized types of attention that will make it ordinary.

The implications of these few findings are wide-ranging. We will retain only what is relevant to our discussion: if the auditory activity of the specialist is destined to supersede itself in this way through a perpetual renewal of listening, we can see that it would be at the very least problematic to attempt to define the general nature of the *musical* in terms of conventional musical practice; rather, not wishing to limit ourselves in any way to already established musics, we will have to ask the listener about his general approach to the music he chooses to hear, whatever his level. We will therefore conclude this book with an investigation into *hearing intentions*, in chapter 8.

6.8. COMPARISON BETWEEN SPECIALIZED MODES OF LISTENING

First, we must examine what happens when we attempt to compare the findings of one or two specialized modes of listening. In practice there are many cases where we try, or even where it is necessary, to establish correlations: for example, the physicist studying the sounds of words or music will express semantic or musical values in terms of pure acoustics; the concert hall builder has to perfect an acoustic area in accordance with requirements that are strictly musical; similarly, in another field, the linguist may be tempted to link the phonetic or grammatical structuring of speech with its semantic content (a problem that comes up in automatic translation).

As we have seen, every specialized mode of listening has a relatively independent specialized circuit of communication; we are therefore entitled to ask to what extent such comparisons are justified—that is, how far it is legitimate to use the findings of one specific practice in relation to another.

We will go back to what we consider the typical example, the acoustician who embarks on "an acoustic analysis of the phenomenon of speech." Once, with the aid of that sophisticated instrument the *Sonagraph*, he has obtained the printout of all the acoustic components of the word as it is being said, the researcher tries to find the word on his printout; that is, he hopes to discover a constellation of points or curves (for frequencies, amplitudes, time) characteristic of that word. His aim in this is to define a method that would allow semantic values to be linked to physical structures and, later, perhaps, a general law setting out the *acoustic nature* of spoken language.

Now, we believe that such preoccupations are doomed to failure because they arise from a fundamental misunderstanding. Besides, at least until now, the acoustic recognition of words, whether by sight on a sonogram or automatically with equipment working along the same general lines as the *Sonagraph*, can only proceed by reconstituting syllables (from elements that in themselves are not semantic), which is all the more difficult as the word can, in fact, be pronounced in very many different ways. So we are nowhere near a synthetic printout that alone would reveal if there is a direct relationship between the word and an acoustic medium: such a reduction could not naturally correlate with a semantic content. The fact is that in reality language cannot have an acoustic identity, for the very general reason that language responds to semantic imperatives, which, as such, do not signify anything in relation to the particular concerns of acoustic investigation.

Even if it is still permissible to make comparisons, it is therefore unthinkable to hope for more than similarities, correlations, between spoken language and acoustics—the specialized "pathways" of oral communication and physics. Besides, no one has raised the question—the opposite of the question about the acoustic nature of spoken language—of the *semantic nature* of the physical components of sounds. An absurd question? Indeed. For the scientist, however, no more so than the first question. Obsessed with unity, the typical scientist can imagine no objectivity other than physical; his recognition of significations that are not those of physics is for him only the stage preceding their annexation. He does not see that all specialist auditory activity establishes a field of entirely original objective practices where one practice cannot use the findings of another unless it discounts the significations belonging to that practice.

This is why several modern musicians—discouraged by the prevailing disorder in musical values, and turning to one of the many forms of composition justified, according to their promoters, by their rational or scientific basis—have in effect lost sight of the musical essence of music and no longer compose anything but sound encodings of scientific notions, as it were.

We do not expect so easily to overcome the reticence of those among our readers who are most convinced of the validity of physical or mathematical explanations. They bank on these to get them out of dead ends, in particular the present musical dead end; they are too involved to take on the discussion at this resolutely theoretical level. In truth it is probably beyond us to persuade them; this is why, in writing all this, we are thinking mainly of a number of younger researchers—musicians, of course, but also artists in general, all the future creators of forms and languages who are to a greater or lesser extent mesmerized by the idol of science. These Tom Thumbs think themselves modern when they count off the Cartesian pebbles of "total reduction to numbers," which today lead to the beloved Ogre: the electronic computer.

We do not despise this tool; we simply refuse to use it as inexperienced amateurs. Indeed, like any other tool, it functions in accordance with the principles imposed on it: so, no computer music without *a priori* reflection on the musical and deliberate choice about principles on the part of the user.

This basic consideration is precisely the subject of this treatise. However convinced we may be that in order to persuade the reader to make the effort, which is not slight and is very likely to disconcert him in both his artistic and scientific habits, we must patiently show him that there is no other way. We will therefore, in all honesty, attempt the physicist's approach, in order to demonstrate that ultimately it leads nowhere. There is, however, no question of killing off acoustics for the sake of music; in accordance with our reflections on the previous pages, we believe that it is only when we have defined both the objects and the specific methods of each discipline that we can establish true correlations between them. And thus, even if the next chapter deals with giving proofs through the absurd, the whole of book 3 will give a summary of the reasonable and reasoned correlations between physics and music.

7

Scientific Prejudice

7.1. THE PRESTIGE OF LOGIC

Even before we are blinded by the brilliance of science, we are tempted by the logic that facilitates it. Faced with the phenomenon of music, our first reaction, in the spirit of Descartes, will be to analyze it in our minds, to "break it down into as many small parts as will be needed . . . the better to resolve" the problem it presents to us. And the logical analysis that seems to impose itself unbidden is what makes it appear as a chain of successive events.

(a) At the top of the list we will put the visible origin of sounds, the instrumental gesture: first comes the *performer*, his physiology, his technique, his art.

(b) Then comes instrumental vibration itself, strings and membranes, which spreads at the speed of sound right to our ears: this is the purely *acoustic result* of the player's activity.

(c) This traditional trajectory, these ancestral acoustics are becoming more complicated nowadays: the *electroacoustic music system*, microphones and tape recorders, amplifiers and loudspeakers, stereophonic or otherwise, broadcast on the wireless or not, are now, in a great number of cases, coming between player and listener.

(d) At the entrance to the ear the *physiology* and the acoustics of sensations await us. The union between watts and the organ of Corti, the labyrinth and frequencies, is fragile, it is true, but no one will dispute that we must resign ourselves to it.

(e) Then *musical impressions* occur in the listener, by means of what Henri Piéron goes so far as to call aesthesio-neurones or, more simply, aesthesiones.[1] This is *psychophysiology*.

---

1. Professor Henri Louis Charles Piéron (1881–1964) was a French psychologist and one of the founders of scientific psychology.—Trans.

(f) And the listener recognizes the *work* the composer intended him to hear, which is truly a stroke of good fortune. This is pure *psychology, aesthetics* even.

(g) We could, in fact, have started with the composer and his intentions, which are recorded on the score by the musical signs that, according to the good Danhauser,[2] enable us "to read and write music as easily as a book," with the result that all the performer has to do is follow them. We are at the level of *pure music, Art*.

This is the canonical breakdown, coach by coach, of the train that runs through that fertile land from aesthetics to symbolism, from symbol to the mechanism of the muscles, from muscles to frequencies, from frequencies to the auditory nerves, and from the auditory nerves to you know what.

7.2. PRACTICE: MUSICAL COMMUNICATION

We could, however, look at this chain from two different points of view: it represents either a series of *artistic activities* transmitted from a more or less gifted composer to a more or less sensitive and informed listener, by means of the virtuoso and the sound recordist, or a succession of *results* (score, physical phenomenon, physiological stimulus, musical perception), in which the problem of music is raised only at the two extremities: the imagined and the perceived work. The first point of view immediately brings with it observations that cast doubt on the order we have just neatly established.

First, none of our characters keeps to the limited role that the event assigns to him within the chain. Take, for example, the performer. If the performer really followed after the composer, and came before the listener, simply as an intermediary, instrumental education would be like training a horse, associating a reflex gesture with the sight of the sign written on the score. In reality, we know it is nothing of the sort and that a good teacher bases his instrumental teaching on an analysis of the circuit of communication. The formation of a violin note is not worked on like a reflex but as an intention: the intention of forming a clean sound that "carries"—giving it, of course, the qualities required by the sign (accuracy, duration, nuance) and the intention also of affecting the listener emotionally, through a particular quality (vibrato, holding the sound). Not only does the instrumentalist hear what he is doing, but he hears it as the listener in the concert hall would hear it, like a painter who can paint in close-up what has to be seen from a distance.

We could do this sort of analysis for each of our characters, whose activity, including the sound engineer's, linked to or anticipating what the others are doing,

2. Adolphe Danhauser, *Théorie de la musique*, reviewed and corrected by Henri Rabaud (Paris: Lemoine, 1929).

does indeed go round the entire circuit of communication, from intention to reception. We need only repeat what is common knowledge: from the listener's point of view an instrumental experience, even by an amateur, can help to guide his listening; as for the composer, he prehears as he composes, anticipating what will finally be perceived, and sometimes he even writes for a particular virtuoso.

This sort of complicity, which allows each activity to be carried out in relation to the others, apparently depends on shared experience. On the one hand, this can operate within any given culture, language, or musical field. On the other hand, in relation to this shared conditioning, it highlights the freedom for personal expression left to each individual talent.

7.3. AN OPTION FOR MUSIC: A LANGUAGE IN ITSELF

The second point of view, in contrast, which gives us a succession of "things in themselves," which can be studied for themselves, seems likely to lead us to "objective" knowledge and scientific, universally valid, types of truths.

This movement into science can take place in two different ways, depending on whether more or less emphasis is placed on the abstract aspect of music as a language or on its realization in sound. We will consider the first point now and deal with the second in the next section.

A skilled musician can analyze a work, not as communication from one mind to another but for its own structure, its intrinsic proportions. At a pinch, that is, at the level of abstraction of a perfect score, this analysis has absolutely nothing to do with performance. Appalling instrumentalists or disastrous transmission can indeed "massacre" a classical work; but "massacred," it nonetheless remains what it is, just as a mutilated body is still a body.

Insofar as it is language, music has, in fact, all the right properties—those, as Husserl would say, of a "spiritual objectivity," distinct from the ways it can be reproduced or realized:

> In the same way we can distinguish the engraving itself from the thousands of reproductions of it ... present, in each reproduction, like an identical ideal entity. ... The same is true when we speak of the Kreutzer Sonata, as opposed to particular performances of it. It may very well itself be made of sounds, but it is nevertheless an ideal unit, and its sounds are just as much ideal units. Its sounds are not at all the sounds of auditory perception, sounds as a perceptible thing, which, precisely, exist in reality only in an actual reproduction and in the perception of this. ... Like the whole, the part is an ideal entity that becomes real *hic et nunc* only in the shape of individualization in the real world.[3]

3. Edmund Husserl, *Logique formelle et logique transcendantale*, translated from the German by Suzanne Bachelard (Paris: PUF, 1957). [Translated into English by Dorion Cairns as *Formal and Transcendental Logic* (The Hague: Martinus Nijhoff, 1969).—Trans.]

We are not talking about disembodied music but about some highly developed forms of music, based on objects that are so perfectly understood, or at least so exclusively used as *signs*, that their realization in sound is, as it were, immaterial or at least secondary. Such is Bach's *The Art of the Fugue*, where the composer's genius actually allows any instrumental arrangement of the voices.

It often seems premature for contemporary music to aspire immediately to these lofty heights; besides, for our part, without precluding any reference to a possible musical language at the level of objects, we will endeavor to examine which objects, or better, which type of objects, could be made into the most universal music possible: we will limit our excursions into the abstract side of music to this; in addition, in this quest we will not lose sight of the postulate, for us fundamental, that *all music is made to be heard*. So we will link any possible musical language to values established at the *perceptual* level.

Here we should note that the analysis of music into abstract structures—that is, into terms that are meaningful to the intellect and not to perception—has tempted many a mind. Contemporary experiments show that it is possible to go a long way down that road, to the point of looking to mathematical functions or chance theories for the organizational rules of musical language. These attempts are scientific only *a posteriori*: insofar as they are "experiments just to hear." It is clear, however, that they are not of the first importance for us, since we wish to hear *before* understanding and *in order to understand*. We take it as read that, even if the *Art of the Fugue* can be completely reduced to a numbers game, the meaning of this game is in its manifestation in sound, because ultimately it is entirely based on criteria of *musical perception*, which arithmetic may represent but certainly does not determine.

7.4. ANOTHER OPTION: SYNTHETIC MUSIC

The tendency toward the work-in-itself, which must not only have a totally internal organization and rigorous figuring, but in which the sound components themselves, thoroughly familiar, can all be expressed in abstract terms, "parameters," is emerging today as the most powerful myth in contemporary music. It seems to tie in with a scientific approach to music based on the elements that allow it to be played.

If this were really how it is, these musical elements would be given simultaneously as *signs*, and our whole approach through *perceived* objects would become otiose. We could doubtless experiment on the relationships between these signs, which now correlate to a physical signal, and our musical sensibility, but that would be secondary research and would avoid the arduous task that for us, as will be seen throughout this work, consists in selecting the object insofar as it is meaningful material for a possible music.

So it is worth examining this to see if it is a necessary evil or if there is a more direct way, which would make the construction of a piece of music flow from the immediate use of sound materials that come from a physical synthesis of simple elements.

This seductive hypothesis has not only been advanced but enthusiastically and persistently applied by the electronic school of Cologne, whose theoretician was the distinguished Werner Meyer-Eppler, a physicist from Bonn University, taken from us too soon to pursue its validity and measure its consequences. He would doubtless have moved on from a position that is already out of date. We, however, with the aim of highlighting this point of view, will take the liberty of quoting some of this physicist's words from a lecture given in 1951:

> Because we can now produce sounds electronically, the modern composer is no longer tied to sounds made in advance, which can only be modified within very narrow limits, depending on the directions for performance: he can create his sound material himself. So the initial product he uses no longer has to be identified, as tradition dictated, by its instrumental timbre (for example, oboe or harpsichord sound, etc.).
>
> The terminology of *acoustics* must be revised, and sounds and noises must be named, not according to their *origin* but their physical *composition*. However, in the process, the capacity of the human ear must be taken into account. Since Helmholtz, its ability to analyze acoustic phenomena "from their spectrum" has been acknowledged; and, consequently, given the current development in our understanding of the way the sense of hearing works, it would be appropriate to represent the structure of the causes of our auditory sensations on a *time and frequency diagram*. The usual notation can also be considered as an approximation of a diagram such as this.

7.5. FROM PHYSICS TO MUSIC

These assertions merit closer inspection.

First, Meyer-Eppler takes the possibility of synthesizing sounds for granted. This has yet to be tested both in practice and in theory.

In practice we will have to show that every sound used in music can be reproduced synthetically with all its musical characteristics and qualities. Thus, electronic technology would be able to explain systematically what traditional technology, empirical and traditional, has been unable to deliver. Since 1951, this has not been the case, rather the opposite (see section 2.9).

Moreover, Meyer-Eppler's theory is not based on any tests, which he did not have time to carry out, but on a proposition: the "time and frequency" sound diagram would account for the whole phenomenon of sound. For the acoustician, this is quite true. Is it the same for the musician?

Meyer-Eppler does mention the need to "take the capacity of the human ear into account" before identifying spectral and musical sound. But this vague statement scarcely tells us whether he has in mind a study of sensations—thresholds, sensitivity curves—or the perceptions that surface in the musical consciousness. It seems, however, that once the physical makeup of sounds and the workings of that more or less imperfect device, the ear, are understood, there is nothing else really important for him to learn. He does not even claim to give an account of our auditory sensations (as for the concept of perception, this is totally absent from his thinking) but explains them in terms of their material *causes*, having taken into account the transformations they undergo on the way. More precisely, he considers this explanation as a foregone conclusion and the chain of causes as obvious enough for it to be already possible to preplan music on the basis of physics.

Doubtless not every specialist will go with him all the way. But doubtless none of them would reject his attempt at explanation itself, considered as the height of the scientific mode of discovery. And so we come back to that project, vigorously laid claim to by Fritz Winckel, to whom, incidentally, we owe so many subtle observations and useful cautions:

> If we wish to go more deeply into the phenomena we have hinted at, we must above all study the natural laws that govern the production of sounds, and examine their physical or physiological action on the sense of hearing and the brain. Perhaps these factors will enable us to shed light on the way music influences man. Some may bridle at too scientific an approach to these problems and will content themselves with groundless impressions and metaphysical explanations rather than embarking on a systematic study of the secrets of a natural phenomenon. Of course, sounds can be neither touched nor seen; they nonetheless have a physical reality, since they reveal themselves by a variation in air pressure, mechanical vibrations in the middle ear, oscillations in the fluid of the inner ear, and finally electrical impulses conducted by the nerve fibers to the brain. Sound phenomena are, after all, produced by the vibration of material bodies.[4]

7.6. THE SYSTEM

The findings of Winckel's research could indeed lead to responses of a very different hue. But we must keep to the text. We find statements of varying significance:

- The production and transmission of sounds, from the vibration of material bodies right to the brain, take place by means of mechanisms arising from natural laws. We have absolutely no reason to doubt this, any more than the importance a study of this may have.

---

4. Fritz Winckel, *Vues nouvelles sur le monde des sons*, trans. Abraham Moles (Paris: Dunod, 1960). [Published in English as *Music, Sound and Sensation*, trans. Thomas Binkley (New York: Dover, 1967).—Trans.]

- This research, physical or physiological, must be undertaken *before anything else* if we wish to "go right into" the phenomena of perception and aesthetic evaluation mentioned earlier by Winckel.
- Its ultimate aim would be to explain how music influences man. That is to say, music, itself arising from physical and physiological processes, is presented as an objective reality and, in relation to the listener, as a cause producing certain effects.

Whereas the first statement is simply an observation and working hypothesis, the other two constitute a stance that must have a motive. We are therefore, in return, entitled to ask two kinds of questions.

1. What conditions must be obeyed for the system of explanation outlined here to be valid within its premises?

2. Since it claims an almost exclusive validity, we would take the liberty of wondering on what he bases this claim and, if it cannot be justified, whether there is another, more justified, approach.

7.7. AMBITIONS AND INADEQUACIES OF PHYSICS

In the Cartesian breakdown in section 5.2. we are, as has been seen, obliged to embrace a whole raft of different disciplines.

So, as far as music is concerned, each of these disciplines should contribute a huge amount of information, and we must, moreover, take particular care to check the "continuity" across disciplines, so that our logical progress is not weakened.

The perilous nature of the undertaking can be seen at once, as can its probably utopian goals, masquerading as logic. We can also see what preconditions it implies, since it claims to trace out a chronological investigatory pathway. How and when will we tackle the phenomenon of music if we must first of all understand the secrets of the workings of the inner ear and also establish a flawless connection between the elementary levels of sensation and the higher levels of perception? What experimental psychologist, what brain surgeon, will come forward to give reliable answers to these questions?

In response to this scientific dream we must bring in other realities that have been the subject of psychological research rather too often neglected by our physicists. Indeed, we can see that they merely refer to "musical sensations," as if sensations were the prime factor of musical consciousness. Now, sensation is not instantly there in our consciousness; it comes, in general, only from a selection process on the part of perception. There is therefore a "break" in the apparently logical circuit championed by our scientists. We should send them off to read the whole library of research, spanning almost fifty years, by other specialists, just as worthy of respect, on this point.

Even before referring to the work of gestaltists and phenomenologists, we should point out to our physicists that there is a serious risk of error in their seemingly rigorous approach: it is the discontinuity of specialist knowledge that most often rears its ugly head at each new intersection between one discipline and another. We will simply point out, in musical acoustics alone, the ambiguity of the terms used, according to circumstances, to designate both a physical phenomenon and its musical effect.

In fact it must be either one thing or the other: either the science enthusiast that the contemporary musician is must accept the correlations between frequency and pitch, level and intensity, time and duration, spectrum and timbre, and so forth, as established fact, or else, better informed, he must be aware of the care that physicists themselves take to suggest two calibrations, one physical, the other sensory. This could serve as a warning. But doubtless he sees in it further reasons to trust the experts, who, for their part, maintaining out of principle that they are incompetent in music, trust him. So what happens next?

What happens is that extremely rigorous research on the physical level leads to results that cannot be used for music, unless they are inappropriately extended into a field to which they do not apply. This is why most of the response curves of the ear, set up for elementary stimuli, do not apply to complex signals or simultaneous sounds in the context of strictly musical listening, which has nothing in common with the quasi-surgical conditioning of a well-conducted sensory experiment.

We will see below an attempt to explain the more absurd misunderstandings. But since it does not seem possible to fulfill the conditions for an objective scientific approach, we will have to find another way.

7.8. POSSIBLE MUSICAL EXPERIMENTATION

In rejecting the above approach to the phenomenon of music, which claims to be scientific because it is based on the physics of sounds, are we rejecting a scientific approach to music?

On the contrary. We are saying that a scientific approach is defined by a method that is adequate for its subject. Suppose we reconsider the "chain" of the phenomena that form a circuit of communication from man to things, and vice versa, in music. At either end we find, on the one hand, the physical universe and, on the other hand, the world of consciousness. There is nothing to say we should not pursue our investigation along parallel lines, using a "pincer movement" and preferably attacking the weakest fronts, which afford the most effective way in. The most modern cybernetic practice teaches us to put all the links in the chain, which form, as it were, a "black box," "in parentheses," and to concentrate only on what is going on at the two ends.

If we put stimuli at only one of these ends, there is little chance of our experimenting on music at the other—just as, if we present symphonies only to the ear, there is little chance of our finding the truly experimental level of a psychology of music, at least at the initial stage.

These are, however, the two most common mistakes—the first the prerogative of physicists, the second of some psychologists. If we have clearly understood the error of the former, who impoverish their experimental material too much, we can also begin to see the error of the latter, who take their experimental material from too high a level (melodies, modes, etc.) and thus, despite encouraging statistics, obtain only vague results about aesthetic emotion.

Between these two types of mistake, excess and insufficiency, there should be room for a reasonable experimental program, concerning the object itself. What elementary factors are we listening to in all music? How do we listen? Between sensations, which are only an "unstable," artificial state of consciousness, and aesthetic emotions, already inaccessible and too complicated, surely there is an experimental field for specifically musical perception, where the stimulus of an external signal and the awareness of a musical signification could be adequately explored?

The Hearing Intention

8.1. PLEONASM

That the title of this chapter should be possible without shocking people as an obvious pleonasm is already an indication of the fact that the word *to hear* (entendre) has lost its meaning. Etymologically, it expresses tending toward, therefore intention. The fact that we have to reinforce it with a synonym to give it back its strength of meaning shows how listening has become automatic. It is the same with every human achievement. Only the incompetent or beginners are aware of how they go about it: later, they will have "reflexes."

The accomplished musician or the skilled physicist will perhaps accept the diagrams in chapter 6 as, in effect, an account of the activities or education that led to their specialty. But it is unlikely that they will go further and admit so easily what we have finally implied: that every specialized act of listening comes not only from a system of training but from a property of perception itself. In short, we are saying that we only hear what we intend to hear, with each practitioner focusing on something different. It must be understood, moreover, that we are not thereby laying the emphasis on the subjectivity of the individual (which is apparent at the time of the training needed for effective practice) but on the objectivity of the objects scrutinized by particular experts.

At this point we must take the probable diversity of our readers into account, their education and habits of thought. If they are unwilling to accept that the objects of listening are different for each category of ear (musicians, acousticians, linguists, etc.), there is no point in repeating this statement. They will all want to be convinced through their own particular access route. Hence the need to create a sort of crossroads at this stage of the book, where there will be a parting of the ways.

8.2. THE TWO PATHWAYS

"The middle way," Schoenberg writes somewhere, "is the only one that does not lead to Rome." We must accept that this is the one we have taken until now, as long as it suited everyone, and that, under the guidance of the *Littré* dictionary and in the name of common sense and the sense of words, we led down it every specialist, who must have an "ordinary ear" to start with and with which initially he hears like everybody else.

For some people, despite our warnings, the scientific approach wins out and will always do so. The universe, including the mental universe of music, does not elude the chain of causalities. Human effectiveness demonstrates this. We make rockets; we split the atom; and so forth. Thus our mind proves its objectivity. In the same way, we make violins and tape recorders, and our signs, even if they do not exhaust musical reality, give an often unhoped-for account of it. For those readers with a "scientific turn of mind," what we demonstrated in the last chapter is not convincing. Clever, perhaps, but it must be hiding a sophism somewhere.

For philosophical minds it is, on the contrary, likely that our warnings are unnecessary. For professional psychologists these are no more than rehashed college questions: after the gestaltists' rather perfunctory clearing of the decks, fifty years ago, everyone knows that "sensation" does not come first, is not *prior* to perception, that *perceptual structures* inform our entire sensory stock. Merleau-Ponty considers that the *classical antinomies*—soul-body, external-internal, mentalism-materialism—are out of date in modern philosophy.[1]

And our musicians are suspicious. They, like everyone else, are convinced that complete scientific explanation is possible, and in comparison philosophy seems superfluous to them. If by chance they have to choose, they will instinctively incline toward mathematics. They have done this since Pythagoras and do it all the more readily since electronics took over the baton from instrument makers, worthy craftsmen but overtaken by technology; association in the studio and then of minds brings them much closer to the engineer than to the philosopher.

The contemporary musician who wishes to be progressive has therefore little hesitation in joining the friendly camp. He definitely has something in common with the scientist, handling instruments like him, learning how to use them, and perhaps how to construct new ones; what does he do but relate causes and effects? As for his scores, are they not also blueprints? Do not the structures they contain come, in their own way, from quantifiable formulae?

It is, in the first instance, with the aim of taking into account this instinctive tendency to go back to the schema of experimental "causality," that we are writing

1. Maurice Merleau-Ponty (1908–61) was a French phenomenological philosopher.—Trans.

book 3, showing the potential and the limitations of the scientific approach in music. Only then, once we have explored this, do we hope to engage our reader in a phenomenological approach in book 4.

First, in this final chapter on "hearing" (entendre) we must attempt to sketch out these two pathways and to see how they begin, though in divergent ways, from the diagram analyzing the "four listening modes."

One of the pathways consists in taking "experimental" routes, linking cause and effect, but based on *two separate copies* of the diagram, with two parallel, nonoverlapping routes. We will give an outline of this first approach, the subject of book 3, in the sections below. The other pathway consists in drawing out the philosophy of this diagram and seeing that it conceals *two sets of quadrants:* one for verbs and one for nouns, in other words activities and objects of perception. We will give a short account of this at the end of this chapter as an introduction to book 4.

We will thus have attempted to address what we suppose to be the wishes of the reader: to be able to use the commonsense data of both approaches seamlessly and in the order that he finds the most natural or the most up-to-date.

8.3. THE HEARING INTENTION FROM A SCIENTIFIC POINT OF VIEW

For now we will leave aside our synthetic approach to the diagram in four quadrants and argue for the *scientific* side: we will give up trying to understand the mechanisms of listening immediately and instead experiment in the same way as physicists, linking causes and effects.

And so we are modifying the original meaning of a diagram that is too literary, too "psychological," by explicitly making it into a circuit of causality. But we should not lose sight of the fact that there are *two circuits*, two ways round, and that what unites or links them is precisely *not* a relationship of cause and effect but a *correlation*. We will give illustrations of this.

First we will let the physicist take the initiative, then the musician.

First example. The acoustician has a *stimulus generator*—that is, an instrument known in physics that can deliver simple, measurable signals that are linked to a system of "understanding" based in scientific thought. The circuit is described as follows: the cause of the event (the device) (sector 1) delivers a signal that is its effect (2) qualified by measurements (3) based in scientific concepts (4).

At the same time that it is being measured by instruments (imperceptible to human beings but scientifically very clever), this signal falls on the musician's ear. The stimulus generator is still the cause (1) of the sound object perceived by the musician (2′) musically described by him (3′) and referred to a system of traditional musical values (4′) (see fig. 1).

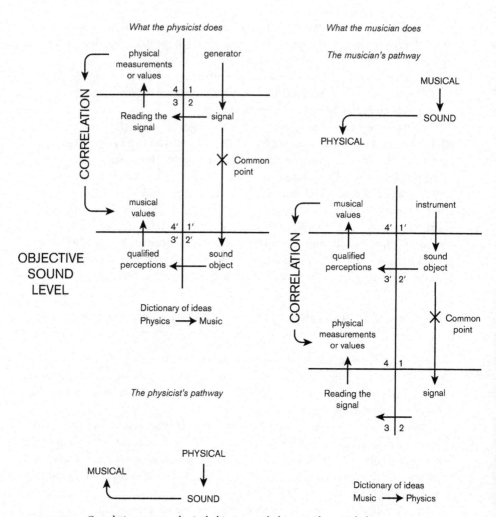

FIGURE 1. Correlation among physical object, sound object, and musical object.

Second example. The initiative is given to the musician, as we intend to do in experimental music. The musician's preferred choice will be an ordinary *musical instrument*, delivering not stimuli but normal (musical) sounds. The two circuits are clearly of the same type, although "what can be heard," like "what can be measured," are different in nature. The musician will listen to a musical object produced by the instrument (a relationship of cause and effect), will describe it, and relate it to his traditional value system. The acoustician will consider this effect as a signal; that is, he will try to measure it and relate it to a system of physical values.

What would happen in the best of worlds? Made aware of the necessity of working together, musician and physicist would meet on "common ground," around exhibit A, now tangible in the shape of the tape recorder, receptor of the "physical signal," as well as potential memory, after playback, for the "musical object." The physicist will say to his colleague: what can you hear? And the musician would say to the physicist: what are you measuring? In this way the correlations we have mentioned would appear.

In fact, it does not really happen like this. Usually the physicist has the advantage over the musician as far as the initiative is concerned, since he chooses the stimuli to be listened to. Then, the physicist naively plays the musician, whereas the musician has only been thinking of playing the physicist for a few years. What is more, each risks behaving like an amateur in the other's field. Our physicist, who suspects and dreads this, surrounds himself with safeguards: he chooses simple phenomena (the simplest, he thinks) and summons listeners, to create more ears, so that their statistics make an "average ear."

8.4. THE STUMBLING BLOCK

So he seems to have taken all necessary precautions. In actual fact, the stumbling block in his thinking about these questions, and the way of representing them that seems to go right to the heart of the matter, is the logical linking: instrumental cause (1) → hearing (2) → perceptions (3) → musical values (4): if we accept this schema, how can we doubt that the acoustician is really dealing with the musical?

Although they have magnetic tape in common, we can easily understand how fundamentally different the two pathways described in the last section are.

That tape, in fact, is a matter for study for physicists independently of any listening. Although "sound," it is identical to numerous other magnetic tapes, with other signals on them too slow to be audible (seismograms, encephalograms, etc.) or too fast to be heard (e.g., ultrasound). All these tapes are studied in the same way, by measuring devices. What do they measure? Frequencies, intensities, different systems of combined waves—that is, spectra. Surely these are the dimensions of sound? Absolutely not. They are the dimensions of vibrating phenomena, material particles moving in an elastic medium *independently of any ear.*

The circuit of these phenomena only involves the ear as an *add-on* and for a *tiny fraction* of their field. Measuring devices, in any case, do without the ear and function on their own account. A tuning fork vibrates; its vibrations are transmitted through the air; and the to-and-fro motion of its prongs creates pressures from a distance on the membrane of the microphone, which act on the needle of a voltmeter. To explain sound (i.e., what we hear) by readings on a voltmeter is a fatal mistake. We can see this clearly since, at any one time when the frequency increases, the ear can no longer hear; there is no audible sound any more, yet the apparatus continues to indicate something. That something, obviously independent of what we can hear, since we can't hear anything, is still what it has never ceased to be: the phenomenon of the elastic vibrations of the tuning fork, studied for itself, in an electroacoustic measuring system.

Now the tape is played. It creates a signal that, as we have just seen, goes toward the measuring devices. But through the loudspeaker it also provides a sound object for the ear. Consequently, what is on tape (A) produces a physical effect (B), as well as a sound or musical effect (C): at best we could say that the musical effect C *correlates with* the physical effect B, since they both have the same origin A. Perception and measurement are on the same level; one is not subordinate to the other: we cannot say that B explains C; at the very most it accompanies it. In terms of sound or musicality, the values in B have no significance: the musical pathway completes the circuit without them. We have to accept that, even if the two approaches do indeed have magnetic tape in common, they are completely different in principle.

8.5. CORRELATIONS

Even if we overcome this difficulty, by the same token we move on to the concept of *correlation* between the two experimental circuits that have magnetic tape in common. A series of experiments has led to the establishment of two types of correlations depending on whether the physicist or the musician was in charge. In the first case the physicist used stimuli, expressed in physical magnitudes, and he asked the musicians or his guinea pigs in (musical) listening to formulate responses. So we obtain a sort of physics-music dictionary. In the other case the musician used sounds, and the physicist measured what he could: so we get the other half of the dictionary, music-physics.

But surely this is what happened in the past?

Yes, to the extent that physicists have worked very hard at the first part of the dictionary.

No, to the extent that the others have not.

Hence, we have an imbalance that tends to see music only from the angle of "prose composition," not as "translation." But much more serious is the misunderstanding arising from this unilateral language system: an attempt at synthesis has implicitly taken the place of experimenting on correlations. By combining stimuli, and thus starting from physically defined sound "models," people thought they could infer combinations of musical impressions, *thus inappropriately using for perception a law of accumulation that is only valid for physical measurements*, and thereby reintroducing a cause-effect relationship by the back door, in the shape of a parallelism between combinations. It should be noted that the solution to the "stumbling block" does not safeguard us against this latter snare in particular.

8.6. THE HEARING INTENTION FROM A
PHILOSOPHICAL POINT OF VIEW

Just as rational as the physicist's attitude, or more precisely the only scientific one from a musical research point of view, is the attitude that consists in exploring the listening consciousness.

We have already seen, with the help of the *Littré* dictionary, that we listen to many different things as soon as we listen to something. And we have learned to appreciate the shades of meaning in a sentence such as this: "I unintentionally perceived (j'ai ouï) what you were saying, without listening (écouter) at the door, but I didn't understand (je n'ai pas compris) what I heard (j'ai entendu)."

The four listening functions appeared to summarize the complex situation defined by the four verbs: to listen (écouter), to perceive aurally (ouïr), to hear (entendre), and to understand (comprendre). But there are no verbs without an object. We thought it appropriate to give each one a complement, as in this list: I listen to (j'écoute) an engine; I perceive (j'ouïs) a noise; I hear (j'entends) a bassoon; I "understand" (je comprends) a common chord. Thus, these four activities seemed to have four counterparts: the cause, the thing, the description, the meaning. But if I were to say, I listen to (j'écoute) a chord, I hear (j'entends) an engine, I perceive (j'ouïs) a bassoon aurally, I understand (je comprends) that noise, would I be using French incorrectly? Would I be going against the rules of meaning? Surely not. On the contrary, I can see variations of meaning, but these are, in fact, quite vague and imply much more than they express.

So this leads us to divide the summary of the listening modes into two—not, as in the context of physics, in order to describe two parallel experiences in independent fields of causality but, by separating auditory intentions from objects of audition, to show the complexity of perceptual phenomena. In a sound that is presented to me, I notice that passive listening makes me hear what "dominates" at that moment; but active, willed listening allows me to hear what I want to hear, what I am "targeting." In an orchestral fragment my aim can be to recognize a certain instrument or, again, to pick out the theme, name the notes, or finally enjoy the solo violinist's vibrato. With each act of listening, my perceptions are different, and in the first place the result of the choice of my object of listening. It goes without saying that my other activities contribute to this. Once I have chosen the preferred object, I listen (j'écoute), I perceive with my ear (j'ouïs), I assess what I hear, and I refer back to what I already know I understand (je comprends). But all this applies just as much to the bassoon as to the chord, to the engine as to the noise. Will we ultimately discover the sixteen combinations of the four verbs and four objects?

To pursue this analysis within the framework of our research, we must ask ourselves what the intentions of hearing musically are. Here we will see that music, far from appearing as the result of a simple activity, gives an endless number, an infinite variety of objects of listening.

8.7. ON SOME MUSICAL HEARING INTENTIONS

We cannot deny that a concertgoer, a virtuoso, a theory or violin teacher, their respective pupils, a music critic, an orchestral conductor, a piano tuner, and finally, the latest arrival, the sound engineer, intend to listen musically. We will see that they do not hear the same objects and that they are in very different musical situations:

The musicianship situation:

The teacher makes the pupil turn his back and plays various notes on the piano. Or else he plays notes on different instruments. The pupil has to identify a "value" or recognize a "timbre."

The instrumentalist's situation:

The young violinist is asked to make sure he plays in tune and to avoid making too much of a scraping sound. The situation is much more complicated.

The listener's situation:

The listener can simply say, That's a violin, or, That's a high note. If the listener is a musician or, again, if he is the violin teacher, he compares the result with others. He says: It's better, or, It's not as good. He can be indulgent or severe, proving that he is judging not only the result but also the intention. He will say, That's fine, to a (wrong or bad) note from a beginner and, That's no good, to the same note played by an advanced pupil. A critic would say the same about a virtuoso: He's on form, or, He's got the jitters.

All this implies that the hearing intention has many different objects and many listening mechanisms for the most traditional, simple violin note. What will we say about listening to an incongruous sound, where a large number of different elements can be discerned: that it is unlike anything else, that it reveals an unknown value, that it reveals an intention or not?

What is the difference between a pianist and a violinist? Surely the pianist has more or less prefabricated sound objects, which the violinist must create? And the singer, who is both ear and instrument? Surely the instrumentalist is in a very different situation depending on the instrument he plays? And surely these instrumentalists are in a different situation again from the listener, generally speaking? In addition, one listener is surely fundamentally different from another, depending on his culture and education? As for the piano tuner, whose ear is considered to be so musical, does he behave like a musician or a physicist? Surely the violinist tuning his instrument is different from the violinist playing? Finally, if we forget all these musical craftsmen or artists, and keep in mind only the circuit of communication from the composer to the listener, surely this also has a specific object, the aim of one or other of the protagonists? Take the conductor in particular, the one (together, these days, with the sound engineer) mainly responsible for this communication; how does he hear, and what does he attempt to put across?

8.8. MUSICAL LISTENING MODES

We can see that a detailed analysis of each of these examples would need pages and pages of descriptions. Furthermore, the aim of this work is not to complete a particular piece of research but to give an overall response to the question, What is the musical? We will nevertheless try to shed some light on this question, which is never altogether pointless in a discussion with so many repercussions. We will identify:

(a) *Three musical situations*

The first is purely passive. We are placed in front of given sound objects, simple ones, such as violin notes, or complex ones, such as new or previously unheard sounds. We make the pupil turn his back, just as when a tape is played to us: *an acousmatic situation* that in the first place means disconnection from the audiovisual context, but above all makes it possible—but not compulsory—to explore the sound itself, its properties that refer only to sound, unconnected to its mechanical origin or the intentions of others. We must emphasize the fact that this type of interest does not follow automatically from simply being disconnected from the audiovisual complex but from a specific intention on the part of the listener, as we have already suggested in chapter 4 and as we will see later.

The second is *the instrumentalist's situation*, which is essentially active: he makes what he hears. In a way it is still an acousmatic situation: this sound tells us nothing about the external world, or at least there is no other person, unless the instrumentalist splits himself in two: one doing, the other hearing and judging the first on the success of his intentions.

The third is *the normal listening situation*, by far the most complicated. We can see that it combines something of the first two. It is passive but not acousmatic, because of the associated perceptions motivated by a curiosity that turns spontaneously toward what is emitting the sound, and that, this time, is a true other. But then, it cannot understand this other except by implicitly "simulating" his activity, as far as possible taking his place.

(b) *Three more or less musical groups of objects of auditory attention*

- I may essentially be drawn toward what is going on with the emitter of the sound: pupil, virtuoso, non-Western instrument, amplifier, conductor, and so forth, or a quality of the piano. We will not go on enumerating so many points of interest and different levels of complexity but will keep in mind what they have in common: we are looking for *indicators* in the sound, to tell us about the people or things from which they originate.

- I may be drawn exclusively to the *effects:* accuracy of the note or the instrument, too rapid a tempo, precise nuance; or again, over and above these details, *to the music itself*, as I speak its language: theme, reprise of the theme, counterpoint, and so on. I may also stop listening to the musical language and wonder what, objectively speaking, is characteristic of the conductor's style.
- Finally, but in rather exceptional circumstances that are scarcely those of the concert hall, I may ponder *the sound itself*, suddenly *detached from the two poles of musicianly production and musical value:* an unknown sound strikes my ear, and its strangeness makes me hear it apart from any indicator as to what is producing it, or any referential value. We should nevertheless point out that, as an instrumentalist, this is very often how I hear my own sound or work at my voice, for example. After many years of practice, what do I hear that I do not already know, coming from my instrument or my score, except the way I am shaping a particular swelled note at this moment, or a particular timbre of my voice?

On the one hand, only the natural ease with which I can move among these various perceptions and the virtuosity of my musical listening conceal from me the complexity of my "pathways" from one to another and the diversity of my aims. But, on the other hand, it would be wrong to describe these different types of listening as subjective: there is nothing subjective in all these "aims" that can be shared, defined, and studied in agreement with other people.

(c) *Four listening approaches or behaviors*

We have already mentioned them: they are the two pairs of listening modes *ordinary-specialized* and *natural-cultural.* We might expect to see these four approaches reduced to two where music is concerned: specialized and cultural then. Not so.

Listen to an out-of-tune piano or, more precisely, a note on this piano, where the strings are not at the same pitch. Here already we can see the distance between "ordinary musical" listening (the piano is out of tune) and specialized listening: the tuner's diagnosis (the three strings are not at the same pitch). We can see that these two listening modes have in common that they link the left and right of the diagram, the abstract and the concrete. *Ordinary listening* is not totally unaware of either the piano or its accuracy, elements of a situation in civilization that is both natural and cultural, but it does not pay particular attention to the sound object; it gives an "automatic response" and cannot really target the object itself. *Specialized listening* is more skilled and better informed.

Now let us take the pair *natural-cultural.* The tuner's listening seems eminently "natural": the tuner acts like a physicist responsible for tuning the note to a tuning fork, acting purely on physical causes to obtain a result that can be measured on an interferometer. We cannot hold him responsible for either the tuning fork or the structure of the scale. The violinist tuning his instrument is in the same situation, totally concentrated on causalities. But neither of them stops there: they will not be playing their instrument later to try out causalities but for cultural purposes: making or striking out sounds for their sonority, nuance, and so forth. So here again, we have to identify a dualism in musical activity. We are indeed in the presence of four typical auditory approaches.

8.9. FINAL SUMMARY OF INTENTIONS

The polyvalence of musical listening invites the following summary:

(a) We have had to abandon grouping verbs and substantives, activities and objects of listening too closely together, as we did in chapter 4.

(b) We have identified three typical situations: (1) the *ordinary* listener, in general drawn toward musical meaning and at the same time responsive to the conditions in which the sound is made; this first situation, in fact, relates to the other two: (2) the *acousmatic* listener, and (3) the *instrumentalist* who makes the sound.

(c) We have seen, in relation to the acousmatic situation, that it did not predetermine the listening intention of the listener in that situation. The acousmatic listener is, in fact, free to focus through the sound on anything he was entitled to see, infer, understand about the origin of the sound, as well as the sound itself in the normal situation. More precisely, the acousmatic situation can intensify *two complementary types of interest:* (1) the *ordinary* intention to trace causes or decode meanings in which we are deprived of the sight of the instrument or the operator, are given no explanation from outside, are cut off from the context: we are all the more curious to know who is playing and what is being played, where this odd sound is coming from, what causes it, or what it means. If Pythagoras has his disciples listen to him through a curtain in this way, it is because he hopes they will hear and understand better both what he is and what he is saying. (2) The other type of interest, the converse of the previous one, is rarer. It is the tuner's interest, "tasting" the sound as one tastes a wine, not to tell the vintage but to identify its virtues. It is also the instrumentalist's way of listening, confident in his accuracy and his violin but endlessly shaping the same sound until he is satisfied with it. He does find indicators and values in this type of listening, but that is not enough for him: he nourishes the sound with them himself.

(d) Finally, in all the above examples, we can see the variety of contexts arising from the two pairs of listening modes described above: ordinary-specialized and natural-cultural.

To sum up these ideas, we have produced a figure (see fig. 2) showing the new point of view at which we have arrived and which replaces the diagram in section 6.3: on the line down the middle, we have put the, as it were, "average" activity of a

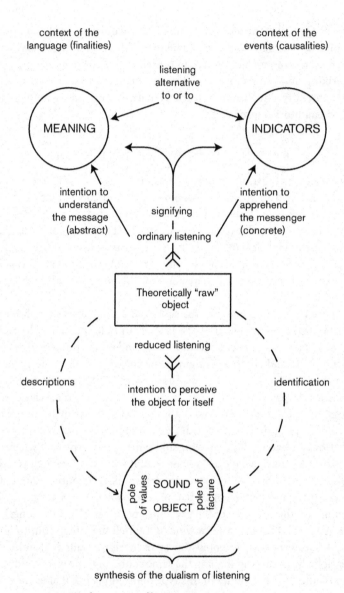

FIGURE 2. Final summary of listening intentions.

normal listener's listening, where sound is described in all sorts of ways, polarized both in the concrete sense (indicators concerning the origin of the sound) and in the abstract sense (sound value on the horizon of a particular group of musical significations). It should be noted that a mixture of perceptions such as this, called the "raw object" on our illustration, is not a well-defined whole but only an unstable collection thrown together, of hardly any use except to demonstrate our conclusions, in much the same way as those bodies that cannot really be isolated but that chemists sometimes postulate in their chemical reactions in order to describe them better.

So we must reorganize the pictures on the cover in another, seemingly less clear but more authentic, way. First of all, we should abandon the "picture of the two violins," an audiovisual complex from which we must now extract an acousmatic type of perception, without a visual backup. These two images of the instrumental gesture will therefore be removed, and the memory of them in watermark representing the "raw object" suggests, in fact, a "deletion," a theoretical concept that ultimately corresponds to nothing real. We must seek reality in two ways: either in the emergence of signifieds (the bathygrams then moving up to sector 1, as indicators of the physical phenomenon, of interest to the physicist; the score remaining in sector 4), or in a different kind of attention, a new type of interest directed toward perception itself, represented by the listening woman. This questioning ear will of course be "polarized" by two sorts of information: from the event itself (factures)[2] and from information that already indicates a meaning (values).

From this central point, listening will turn toward a particular external perception: the perception of the origin of the sound, the *indicators* revealing the circumstances of the event, or the perception of its meaning—its *values* in relation to an established sound language. Finally, in a third scenario, if the listening intention is directed toward *the sound itself*, as with the instrumentalist—or the acousmatic listener, indifferent to conventional language and the anecdotal origin—indicators and values are surpassed, forgotten, redefined, for a unique, unusual, but nevertheless irrefutable, perception: *having ignored the source and the meaning, we perceive the sound object.*

How did we manage to get there? By making an unexpected diversion in listening or, more prosaically, by reversing the pathways, reorganizing what at the outset seemed to lead inevitably both to the concrete origins of sounds and to their abstract meaning; by refusing to put listening on the rack between this event and that meaning, we apply ourselves more and more to perceiving what their original unit is—that is, the sound object. The sound object is therefore the synthesis of

---

2. The word *facture* refers to how something is made; it is used in this sense when speaking of literary productions, music, or painting.—Trans.

perceptions that are usually dissociated. We cannot, in fact, deny, or break, their connections with signification and anecdote, but we can reverse their aims in order to grasp their shared origin. We will return to this sound object, the aim of the activity we will call *reduced listening*, with philosophers in book 4, and musicians in books 5 and 6.

BOOK THREE

Correlations between the Physical Signal and the Musical Object

9

Ambiguities in Musical Acoustics

9.1. AN AMBIGUOUS CONCEPT

In this book we hope to deal with two concerns: to settle the argument over the relationship between music and acoustics and then to suggest a method of approaching a music that is experimental, at least in one of its main activities: the comparison of physical sound with the objects of musical experience.

Our intention is not to cast doubt on the validity of the work of the many researchers who have dedicated themselves to the acoustics of music, but we should be more comfortable if they had not come together under such an ambiguous name. Associating a noun that belongs to the physical sciences with another that belongs to an art is enough to make us quake with fear at the danger of being dragged into the worst misunderstandings by the formal power of a somewhat irresponsibly used word. Conversely, we could equally hope that a truly providential discipline might suddenly make the two extremes meet and bridge the gap between science and art. No one has really examined the question closely.

9.2. SIGHT AND HEARING

We saw in chapter 3 that beneath an apparent similarity, optics being concerned with light and acoustics with sound, there is a very instructive, profound dissimilarity between the contents of the two disciplines. Etymology conceals this from us: optics comes from "to see," and acoustics comes from "to hear." But, without going right back to the beginning, we can observe that there is no danger in optics of confusing areas as distinct as the study of light, light sources, illuminated bodies, sight, perspective, and so forth. Who makes such distinctions in acoustics?

We should set up a sort of embryology of these sciences that are thought to be rigid, fixed in absolutes, based on commonsense data. In ordinary experience, as we have already said, the visual object is armed, surrounded by a panoply of other perceptions; it does more and better than meet the definition of the object: it makes it available to ordinary language. Generally speaking, we can explore with our fingers, feel the weight of, smell the objects of our sight. Who would think of reducing a vase, a rose, to a system of dots in a spatial reference trihedron, with, at each point, as a fourth dimension, the wavelength in angstroms, depending on whether the light is diffused or reflected? The fact is that the visual object is very different from a volume of light.

Any confusions or superimpositions of various orders of phenomena were very quickly avoided: in particular, without coming to any premature conclusions about their material nature, a geometry of objects was isolated, in which light is only an element that "plots out" contours, whether from a light "source" or an illuminated object. Moreover, it seems that the eye, considered as an "optical" instrument, can to a certain extent be separated from sight itself: the system of sight starts, supposedly, at the retina. In fact, the laws of perspective, in human sight, seem to come *grosso modo* from a geometry external to our sensations, similar to the devices of physicists.

Consequently, when physicists, physiologists, and psychologists focus on the organ of sight, they have no reason to confuse the objects of sight with the functions of that organ, since Nature, as if to facilitate their task, seems itself to have made a distinction between the optical organ and the psychological process. We can therefore deal with the physiology and physics of the eye under one heading and the physiology and psychology of light sensations—that is, the eye's (or rather the brain's) "responses" to these simple stimuli—under another.

Finally, no school of painting claims there is a close correspondence between the plastic arts and optical science. Not that people deny the existence of clear correlations between the geometry and photometry involved in the mechanics of sight and the arts that use them as vehicles or structures, but the simplistic idea of explaining painting, sculpture, or architecture in terms of the laws of optics has never occurred to anyone.

Now, this type of confusion does exist between acoustics and music, and its domineering presence hangs over many a contemporary development. Rather than being disturbed by this, it is interesting to look into the causes.

The fact is that Nature, contrary to what went on with the eye and light, seems, where sound and the ear are concerned, to have telescoped everything together, in the physical as well as the physiological and psychological world. The concept of object, unnoticed until now, is revealed only through truly mental, or at least sensory, exercises: this is because the sound object comes under only one sense. We may well see a string vibrate, but the connection is not very apparent between this arc, analyzed for the eye by the stroboscope, and the sound unit that brings it so convincingly to our ear. We cannot see anything where a gong or a trumpet is concerned. Only the violinist's bow has some connection in its movements with the sound it forms. But, as we have seen, we are then distracted by causality, and the object, as such, is only of secondary importance. As for a possible "geometry" of sound, which could have helped us to "perceive" sound objects, this comes up against a double problem. Such a geometry is relatively formless because of the poor directional ability of the ear, and above all, as the essence of sound is to be ephemeral, it is, by its very nature, never attached to an object fixed in time: every sound is born, lives, and dies. So the unit of perception that comes to our hearing is an event with all its phases. We could say, by way of illustration, that the world of sound would be comparable to the world of sight only if, in the latter, the eye perceived nothing but the—variable and temporary—flames from more or less short-lived fires, which would then necessarily consume the very thing that is burning. And does sound, in fact, tell us about the world? Hardly. In former times the prehistoric hunter or the Native American perhaps used his ear more than his eye to decipher the world, but his was a world of events and not of concerns about the nature of the universe. Even if the way the coins ring gives forgers away, and if the famous calm before the storm warns the farmer or the mariner, these are feeble resources for the exact sciences that metallurgy and meteorology now are. Only the doctor retains his stethoscope and even then, does he not prefer a good X-ray?

But acoustic research, rapidly exhausted as far as physical phenomena are concerned, comes into its own as soon as we start to break down the process of listening, to analyze the phenomenon of audition. Here we discover a fundamental correlation between numbers, fractions, and our sensibility: octaves, fifths, and fourths are simple relationships, and so the ear appears to be a natural calculator. Consequently, since music itself is a hybrid language, a suspension bridge between matter and our sensibility, responsive to the same vibrations, musical acoustics perhaps offers the mind an unhoped-for pathway between the inner and the outer, the cosmos and man.

Far from rejecting these insights, we will, on the contrary, ultimately return to them for a natural justification of what is truly musical, together with a philosophical and physical investigation. It is precisely for the sake of such a project, such high ambition, that we must challenge the shortcuts (or labyrinths) that are suggested to us today.

9.3. THE "THEORY OF THEORIES"

We could further reproach acousticians for lack of discernment in their intrusion into music, if musicians themselves had not lent their hand to this, indeed since time immemorial, thus betraying their own discipline at the deepest level; the scientific confusion and misunderstandings that are rife today, in fact, have famous precedents.[1] Without embarking here on a chapter on the psychology of musicians, we will simply say that the musician throughout the ages has always been in the situation, paradoxically, of serving the music of the spheres, provided he has resolved a number of trivial problems: skins and strings to be stretched, drumsticks to be covered in felt, fingers to be "accommodated," voices to be "placed" here or there. How should this person, condemned to craftsmanship, clearly neither angel nor beast, not have sought some support in a rather more sophisticated thought process, a little surer of its principles than even the best method of learning music—and this *a fortiori* today, in the context of a triumphant industrial age?

This is indeed what he has done since the time of Pythagoras and several others, the last of whom, although little known to the public, is nevertheless presented to conservatory students, at least in the traditional school, as the master thinker, the priest and guardian of the treasure. This is what the venerable Augustus says:

> Music is the art of sounds.
>
> It can be written and read as easily as the words we say are read and written.
>
> To read music and understand what it says, it is necessary to know the signs in which it is written and the laws that organize them.
>
> The study of these signs and these laws is the aim of the Theory of Music.

Thus spake the honorable Adolphe Danhauser in 1872, corroborated by honorable members of the Institute, including Charles Gounod, Victor Masse, and Henri Riber, in his *Théorie de la musique*, the last edition of which (1929) is still in use in conservatories.

The *Théorie* starts with an initial section: the signs that deal with the concept of duration: "the whole note has the longest duration, and each of the other notes is half the length of the one before it, and, consequently, double the length of the one after it." In other words, a half note is worth two quarter notes, and so forth.

The second part deals with scales and intervals, after defining the musical scale as "the collection of all sounds perceptible to the ear, from the lowest to the highest, and that can be performed by voices or instruments."

Finally, a third part on tonality sanctions the creation of the diatonic scale as the reduction to the common chord *(do-mi-sol)* of harmonics three and five of a tonic taken as the fundamental, and the addition of two other common chords, one with this tonic as the dominant *(fa-la-do)*, the other with a new tonic as the dominant *(sol-ti-re)*, which causes the good Danhauser to say that this arrangement "is not the result of chance or fancy, but of the natural resonance of sound bodies." (But this section, considered as a digression, is already in small letters.)

---

1. This is the title of the elementary manual familiar to beginners. [The title that Schaeffer references in this section's heading is Danhauser's *Solfège des solfèges.*—Trans.]

But a reference attached to the opening sentence, "Music is the art of sounds," directs us to a note at the end of the book, which we will also quote. Then we will be in possession of all the background knowledge the musician has, up to and including the Prix de Rome, on musical genetics. Here it is.

9.4. TRADITIONAL DOCTRINE:
ACOUSTIC BASIS OF MUSIC

Sound is a sensation effected on the organ of hearing by the vibrating movement of sound bodies.

Musical sound is distinct from noise in that its pitch can be precisely measured, whereas the musical value of a noise cannot be assessed.

Musical sound possesses three special qualities: pitch, intensity, and timbre.

Pitch is the result of the greater or lesser number of vibrations produced in a given time: the more vibrations there are, the higher the sound.

The intensity, or loudness, of the sound depends on the amplitude of the vibrations.

Timbre is that particular quality of sound that makes it impossible to confuse one instrument with another, even when they are playing a note of the same pitch and intensity. The least expert ear can easily distinguish the timbre of a violin from a trumpet or an oboe.[2]

As for the treatises on harmony by Savart (1851) and Théodore Dubois (1901), they may be happy to hold forth on the origins of the diatonic scale and the notorious comma for adjusting temperament, but they are even less forthcoming about the rudiments than Danhauser, to whom we ought to be grateful for pinning down the doctrine, albeit briefly.

Our reasons for quoting this text, for us fundamental, even though printed in small letters in the manual, are that we are pleased to find a reference to what we know so well that it seems superfluous to write it down. We should consequently take note that the musician, like the acoustician, is nourished from the breast on this guaranteed and homogenized milk:

1. The way into music is through the signs of notation.

2. There are two definitions, both pragmatic, of pitch and timbre: pitch, which can be sung or played, timbre, which can be recognized. In addition, we are given:

3. A metrical definition of durations.

4. An acoustic basis for the sounds of the scale.

5. A scientific basis for all this in three assertions:

2. Adolphe-Leopold Danhauser, *Théorie de la musique*, reviewed and corrected by Henri Rabaud (Paris: Lemoine, 1929), 119, note a.

· musical sound is (essentially) a sensation of pitch;
· this pitch depends on the frequency of vibrations;
· its intensity depends on amplitude.

Paradoxically, contemporary music, so attached to scientific proofs, is turning its back on explaining the scale through the resonance of sound bodies and breaking with this objective fact, which Danhauser quite rightly said showed that the aforementioned scale was not the result of fancy.

But, setting apart this display of independence, there has not been one line, in the course of a century, to question these bold premises, as limited as they are categorical:

(a)   a wholly notated music from the very beginning,
(b)   a music limited to musical sounds defined by pitch,
(c)   the three assertions that pitch, duration, and intensity are linked to the physical values of a frequency, a time, and an amplitude (or level) that coincide with the acoustic phenomenon.

To this scientists have added what musicians have, however, never said until very recently: that timbre coincides with the spectrum of frequencies.

We cannot blame the theoreticians of 1870 for reducing music to the abstract, which is excusable in its extreme simplicity, nor even for limiting it to sounds of given pitch. We see all too often how the abstract, in the last century as in this, has tempted many other types of thinking, as well as that of musicians. But where, without even leaving the field of the most traditional music, we really must raise the standard of revolt is against the assertion, never challenged, and today commonly accepted, shared, and disseminated, that musical values are measurable and identifiable within three acoustic parameters: frequency, time and level, plus, why not, spectrum.

For these assertions are so many mistakes. Experimentation only confirms them in very specific cases, set up in acousticians' laboratories, and hardly ever in the music we make or hear every day.

This book, dealing with musical values, should put an end once and for all to such a well- and long-maintained confusion.

9.5. THE ACOUSTICS OF MUSIC

We have reached a better understanding nowadays of the plan for an acoustics of music. Proposed by musicians themselves, and focused entirely on the mystery of hearing, rather than on uninteresting "sound bodies," it will heroically strive to make both ends meet, objective data and perceptions, and in this, we admit, it is not very different from our own aim; indeed, do we not also wish to present "sound objects" to the ear, and through in-depth listening describe and assess how they are perceived?

Without denying that both approaches share a common type of interest, we should take note of the way in which they differ in both their methods and their aims.

The method in so-called musical acoustics is to progress systematically from one domain to the other. It could perhaps be summed up as follows:

1. Following Western musical tradition in this respect (cf. Danhauser's definitions), it considers that the domain of music is, above all, harmonic sounds, as provided in a variety of forms by the Western orchestra. It therefore implicitly eliminates everything that is "noise."

2. It believes these harmonic sounds can be broken down into constituent elements: roughly, the *permanent* part, which generally speaking forms the matter of sounds, and the *transients*, which give rise to their attack, an aspect that is particularly in evidence in the percussion family.

3. In the domain of permanent sounds it identifies "pure" sounds in particular—that is, sounds with an acoustic composition of only one frequency—called the fundamental. By making a close study of audible pure sounds, it can "map" them according to the pitch and intensity responses to the type of stimuli calibrated in frequencies and decibels, undeniably the simplest from the physicist's point of view.

4. Slight variations of these "simple" stimuli will lead to the study of the differential sensitivity thresholds of the ear in frequency and level.

5. Returning to the time factor, it will also be possible to highlight temporal thresholds: the minimum duration for the recognition of permanent pitches or timbres, or the limit below which the ear can no longer distinguish between two successive sounds (the resolving power of the ear).

6. Thus the zone of audibility will be cut up into infinitesimal particles, the dimensions of which are precisely the differential thresholds and the resolving power. These particles appear as "units of sensation," the "smallest discernible elements" in pitch, level, and duration. These "microsounds" have even been given names: "phonon" (Matras)[3] or "slab of sensation" (Moles).

7. Finally, we will study the perception of simultaneous sounds: masking effects, for example, where the presence of one sound modifies the perception of another, or the effects of combination, where the presence of two sounds gives rise to the perception of additional (or differential) sounds that are not physically there.

Once these different points have been explored, we will see that acoustics can now aspire to account for the perception of any "musical" sound (as in 1) by

3. Jean-Jacques Matras (1909–92) was an acoustician and engineer who wrote several books and essays on acoustics; on Moles see chap. 2n10.—Trans.

recombining the elementary data provided in steps 3, 4, and 5 and the laws established in step 7, along the lines of the basic principles outlined in step 6.

9.6. PSYCHOACOUSTICS AND EXPERIMENTAL MUSIC

All the experimental part of the work done by physicists based on the above principles is irrefutable and of great general interest. On the one hand, we cannot but be grateful to Helmholtz, Fletcher, and their followers for having created a systematic approach to auditory phenomena by applying the experimental method to purely sensory relationships—that is, bringing together physical and perceptual phenomena.

On the other hand, all the hypotheses either limiting the domain of music, analyzing perceived sounds into simple elements, or recombining them lead to approximations, contradictions, and uncertainties. More seriously, they raise numerous scientific, psychological, and musical objections. Finally, the approach to musical phenomena seems to have been forgotten in the meantime. Not that earlier research does not appreciably "take the edge off" many questions of a musical nature. But the emphasis on elementary analyses, of the sort we mentioned in the section above, has caused other opportunities for experimentation more directly linked to music to be ignored. Moreover, the boldness of the syntheses being attempted at present calls for vigilance and requires at least some simple checks.

The controversy would be reduced to a minimum, it seems to us, if we agreed not to use the ambiguous phrase the *acoustics of music* and to use two others instead, reflecting two very different aspects of these experimental concerns: *psychoacoustics* would be used for all the studies we have just mentioned, and *experimental music* or *musical experimentation* would clear the way specifically for research that directly concerns musical perceptions, without being cluttered *a priori* with any tendency to systematization arising from the findings of psychoacoustics.

The latter, in fact, although involved at the level of perception, consists merely of giving people physically defined stimuli and observing the psychophysiological consequences. Experimental music, however, does not at all seek to elucidate psychoacoustic phenomena and is particularly uninterested in elementary stimuli. It starts from the experiential fact of the existence of music as a universally practiced type of communication, the structures and specific objects of which we are obliged to accept exactly as they are actively brought into play. Or again, we can submit the physical signal to musical perception, which incidentally does not necessarily give results that are much more inaccessible when the objects are acoustically complex. It seems therefore possible to establish experimental links between the physical signal (sound, defined by acoustic parameters) and the musical object (perceived within a musical listening intention): this is precisely what musical experimentation sets out to do.

9.7. INVESTIGATE OR USE THE "BLACK BOX"

To define the originality of the experimental musician's approach more clearly, we will first give a typical example of the physicist's approach, for instance in defining the network of Fletcher's curves. This involves studying the sensation of the intensity of a sound in relation to the frequency (hertz) and level (decibels) of the sound. On the one hand, we have pure frequencies shown as numbers on a dial, that is, representing an acoustic magnitude; the same goes for levels in decibels. On the other hand, one or several listeners are asked to compare the corresponding sensations—in our particular example, to locate sensations of equal intensity at different pitches (and this across the whole tessitura).

The physicist calls sounds of pure frequency and of known fixed level *elementary stimuli*. And so, after the experiments described here, his results consist of a network of correlations between elementary stimuli and perception that he tends to interpret as "elementary sensations," since they correspond to physically simple objects. But there is nothing to tell the inexperienced listener that, for example, the sensation from a sound of pure frequency is particularly "elementary," and the schema of the physicist's investigation remains as follows:

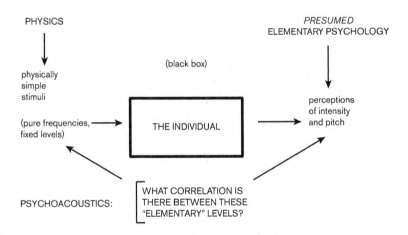

Thus Fletcher's curves provide the explanation for a certain degree of correlation between the physical world and the perceiving individual.

Just like the physicist, the experimental musician, as we have seen, makes use of physically locatable sound objects and investigates perception. Like the physicist, he acts on sounds by manipulating them with great precision. His approach, however, is different and specific: he does not seek to establish a system of correlations between the variations in an elementary physical dimension of the object and the variations in a sensory value; rather, he attempts to determine to what extent the combination of the physical characteristics of the object correlates with *the perception of simple structural relationships* among the various objects provided for musical listening in this way. This type of evaluation is not a measurement but the perception of an order (borne out by a certain similarity in the descriptions given by different individuals or by the same individual on several occasions). In fact, we are content with a *description* of musical phenomena, unconnected to any physical or psychological phenomena, a description that will find its reference point and its criterion in a collection of *control objects*, whose determining physical features we will endeavor to elucidate at the same time.

With this approach, the experimental musician will have no particular predilection for physically simple stimuli. What interests him are dominant, clearly perceived musical perceptions that may perfectly well come from physically very complex sounds. As we have already pointed out several times, the musician's ultimate reference point is the ear. For him, the physical dimensions of sound objects are a convenient means of stimulating characteristic *perceptions* for their own sake, where simplicity and complexity in particular are not necessarily linked with the acoustic composition of what is perceived. The definitive representation of musical research would thus be:

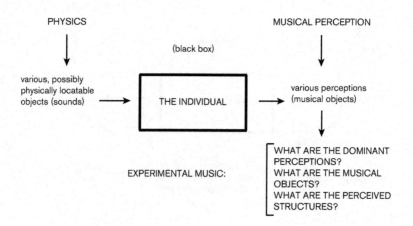

Thus, comparing the physicist's and the musician's schemas, we could say that basically the physicist tends to explain the "black box," to link physics and psychology together as rigorously as possible, which is why ultimately his approach, becoming more and more precise physically, will more and more tend to raise physiological, then psychological, questions—and this is certainly the way present-day experimentation is going. On the contrary, the musician, thrust into an original world that he studies for its own sake, the world of musical perceptions, seeks to discover, inhabit, understand this world, which he can do all the more easily as present-day sound production and manipulation techniques allow him to become a "crafter of sounds" with almost limitless resources.

10

Correlation between
Spectra and Pitches

10.1. THE TRADITIONAL DOCTRINE

We are all guilty of old habits: hearing with our eyes and wanting to understand before perceiving with our ears.

If we attach both ends of a string to a Greek zither or the soundboard of a Pleyel piano, we know perfectly well that these two points will in future remain fixed and that the string cannot vibrate without one, two, three antinodes, thus tracing out either the half-wave of the fundamental, the full wave of harmonic 2, or the three half-waves of harmonic 3, and so forth. These vibration shapes taken on by the string and corresponding to a given sound, compared with the shapes of other strings of a half, a third, and so forth of the length and giving precisely the same harmonics 2, 3, etcetera, clearly lead to these basic acoustic-musical observations: a sound "contains" other sounds, and these sounds are in simple (harmonic) relationship with each other. By adding strings to each other or piercing holes in vibrating pipes, we repeat the phenomenon of the antinodes, and the whole of traditional music appears as the interaction of various possible and intertwined multiplication tables.

If our musician tends so easily to forget his ear in favor of arithmetic, it is doubtless because his ear has perceived so logically that his eye alone is enough: all these strings—two, three, four times the length of each other—cause us to hear sounds that are so alike, except in the tessitura, that they are notated by the same name: they are all *dos* or *res* and so forth, the repetition of the initial sound one, two, three octaves higher. . . .

Moreover, the third harmonic (three antinodes of the string) forms a particularly striking interval with the second (two antinodes), noticed by all musical civilizations, which is in the fraction 3/2 and can be read either as "three antinodes over two" (in terms of string length) or "three vibrations over two vibrations," if we take the vibration of the fundamental as the unit.

Is it our aim to work from the opposite direction? Coming to the rescue of those of us who have complained that we have not seen prose composition and translation brought together, Helmholtz brings the intuition of his genius, the inventiveness of his famous experiments and, what is often forgotten, an exceptional "ear." We will go back to those sources, for they are well worth the trouble.

10.2. HELMHOLTZ'S RESONATORS

Helmholtz has a series of resonators, each one tuned to one of the harmonics of the fundamental to be analyzed. They are a series of spheres, with two holes in each one. The first receives the sound and conveys it into the sphere, where only some frequencies can be propagated; if one of these was present in the initial sound, it will be selected to come out of the sphere (second hole); otherwise, the acoustic energy will be dissipated as heat. The resonance frequencies are determined by the geometrical and physical characteristics of the resonator, such as the volume, the diameter of the holes, the temperature, and so forth. Provided these are known, we can of course construct a whole "harmonic" series of spheres.

Stimulated by a rich sound of clear pitch adjusted for sphere no. 1, each of these spheres selectively takes up one of the harmonics of the sound. If you put your ear next to the hole, you will clearly perceive the selected harmonic. Play another sound, of the same pitch, but on another instrument—that is, with a different timbre—and the resonators make a similar selection but with a different proportion of harmonics. Besides, Helmholtz will say, apply yourself, work hard at listening to a sound, and you may manage to perceive its harmonics directly: with a little practice. . . .

Several generations of musicians have accepted not only Helmholtz's theory but his advice as a teacher of music theory: they have "heard the harmonics." I rest my case. . . .

Moreover, Helmholtz builds on his advantage. The same property of the ear to distinguish harmonics explains, according to him, the ability to listen to simultaneous sounds. We quote:

> The movement of air in the auditory canal has no property whereby composite musical sound (coming from several vibrating bodies) can be distinguished from simple musical sound (coming from one vibrating body). Unless the ear is guided by some accidental circumstance, for example one tuning fork beginning to vibrate before the other, so that we can hear them being struck, or perhaps the sound of air against the embouchure of a flute or the slit in the organ pipe, it has no means of deciding whether the musical sound is simple or composite.

Now, how does the ear behave in relation to this movement of air? Does it analyze it or not? Experiments show that when two tuning forks with pitches an octave or a twelfth apart are set in motion together, the ear is entirely capable of distinguishing each simple sound, although it is a little more difficult with these intervals than others. But if the ear is capable of analyzing a composite musical sound produced by two tuning forks, there is no reason why it cannot operate in the same way when the same movement of air is produced by a single flute, or a single organ pipe. And this is indeed what happens. The single musical sound from such instruments, coming from a single source is, as we have already pointed out, analyzed into partial simple sounds, that is, in every case a fundamental sound and a higher partial, the latter different each time.

The analysis of a single musical sound into a series of partials consequently depends on the same property of the ear that enables it to distinguish different musical sounds from each other, and it must necessarily carry out both analyses in accordance with a rule that is independent of whether the sound wave is coming from one or several instruments.

The rule that governs the ear in its analysis was first formulated as a general rule by G. S. Ohm: only the particular movement of air that we called *simple vibration*, in which the particles move backward and forward according to the law of pendular movement is capable of giving the ear the sensation of a single simple sound. Therefore, all movement of air arising from a composite group of musical sounds can, according to Ohm's law, be analyzed into a number of simple pendular vibrations, and each of these simple vibrations is associated with a simple sound, locatable by the ear, and with its pitch determined by the duration of the associated movement of air.[1]

Helmholtz, however, modifies such categorical assertions. So his words are those of a physicist rather than a psychologist: "The question is very different," he says,

if we set out to analyze less common examples of perception, and to understand more fully the conditions under which the above distinction can or cannot be made, as we do with the physiology of sounds. We observe then that there are two pathways or levels when we become aware of a sensation. The lower level of this awareness is when the influence of the sensation in question is only felt through the concept of external things or processes we create for ourselves, and that help us to identify them. This can happen without our needing to or even being capable of recognizing which element of our sensations a particular link between our perceptions relates to. In this case, we would say that the expression of the sensation in question is *perceived synthetically*. The higher level is where we immediately identify the sensation in question as a real part of the sum of the sensations within us. In this case we would say

1. Herman von Helmholtz, *Die Lehre von den Tonempfindungen als physiologische Grundlage für die Theorie der Musik* (Braunschweig: Vieweg, 1877). [Translated into English by A.J. Ellis as *On the Sensations of Tone as a Physiological Basis for the Theory of Music* (London: Longmans, 1895).—Trans.]

that the sensation is *perceived analytically*. The two situations must be carefully distinguished from each other.

Serbeck and Ohm agree that the higher partials of a musical sound are perceived synthetically.[2]

We can see that a physicist of genius, even in acoustics, is not so easily misled. This text already sketches out the fundamental difference between the physicist's and the musician's mode of listening. It is to be expected that Helmholtz's "higher" level should belong to the former and not the latter. But we should pay tribute to Helmholtz's reservations, which foreshadow the reversal of positions we are advocating:

> What is more, the sound of most instruments is usually accompanied by characteristic irregular noises, like the scraping or rubbing of the bow on the violin, the flow of air in the flute and organ-pipes, the vibration of reeds, and so forth. These noises, already familiar to us insofar as they characterize the instrument, physically facilitate our ability to identify them in a composite mass of sounds. Partial sounds in a compound sound do not, of course, have the same characteristic features.
>
> We therefore have no reason to be surprised that the resolution of a compound sound into its partials is not as easy for the ear as is the resolution of a composite mass of musical sounds from many instruments into its immediate constituents, and that even a practiced musical ear needs to apply itself carefully when it is trying to resolve the first of these problems.
>
> It can easily be seen that the secondary circumstances we have mentioned do not always lead to musical sounds being correctly separated. In uniformly sustained sounds, one can be considered as the higher partial of another, and our judgment may very well be led astray.[3]

10.3. FOURIER'S SERIES

The physicist having harmoniously taken over the baton from the musician, we could expect the mathematician, in his turn, to take over from the physicist.

We may indeed easily "explain" the quivering of strings, despite the extreme complexity of the patterns they make all the time, but we have more difficulty in explaining what happens with the eardrum: it deals only with the air pressure that carries the energy from the "acoustic field" created by the movement of strings or reeds. We know, for example, that if we replace the eardrum with a microphone connected to a cathode ray tube, which displays the pressures on the membrane, we can see a spot of light moving around in an apparently highly disordered way. When recorded, this movement creates an absolutely incomprehensible

2. Ibid.
3. Ibid.

oscillograph line on the time axis: it is indeed the outline of the sound, but it is illegible.

With Fourier, everything becomes easy again. Fourier showed us how to "analyze into series" the most complicated function, even the one that gives as the only value for *t* the pressure or elongation of the eardrum.[4]

The different terms of Fourier's series are sinusoidal, "pendular" vibrations, that is, functions that accurately represent the sounds detected by Helmholtz's resonators. So now, to perfect the scientific explanation, we only have to imagine an internal ear mechanism that behaves like a series of resonators to reach the conclusion that the ear hears sounds by analyzing them into Fourier series. This is effectively what Helmholtz thought and what he tried to prove, though he surrounded himself with many caveats. It is regrettable that some hasty readers have forgotten his warnings and built a general theory of musical listening that, in addition to gross errors and unwarranted simplifications, contains even more serious methodological errors. These are Helmholtz's wise words:

> Fourier's theorem, shown here, demonstrates first that it is mathematically possible to consider a musical sound as a sum of simple sounds, in the sense we have given to these words, and, indeed, mathematicians have found it convenient to base their acoustical research on this way of analyzing vibrations. But it certainly does not follow from this that we are obliged to look at things in this way. Rather we should be asking: do these partial components of musical sound, demonstrated by mathematical theory and perceived by the ear, really exist in the mass of air outside the ear? Surely this method of analyzing vibrations, stipulated and made possible by Fourier's theorem, is simply a mathematical fiction, good for helping with calculations, but not necessarily having any real meaning for things themselves? Why do we find that pendular vibrations, and not others, are the simplest elements of all sound-producing movements?

4. Fourier's theorem: every periodic and continuous function $f(t)$, of period T, can be represented by a series in the following form:

$$f(t) = \frac{a_0}{2} + \sum_{n \geq 1} (a_n \cos n\omega t + b_n \sin n\omega t), \qquad \left(\omega = \frac{2\pi}{T}\right)$$

where

$$a_n = 2 \int_T \frac{d\tau}{T} \, f(\tau) \cos n\omega t, \text{ and } b_n = 2 \int_T \frac{d\tau}{T} \, f(\tau) \sin n\omega \tau.$$

We could also write:

$$f(t) = \sum_n c_n \cos (n\omega t - \varphi_n).$$

Moreover, this series is unique (i.e., the a_n and b_n, or the c_n are determined unequivocally).

In "musical" terms, we could say this: every regular periodic vibration can be obtained by a sum of simple vibrations, each with a frequency that is a whole multiple of the fundamental frequency $f_0 \left(f_0 = \frac{1}{T}\right)$ and a determined amplitude.

A whole can be divided into parts in all sorts of very different and arbitrary ways. Thus, it may be convenient for a particular calculation to think of the number 12 as the sum of 4 and 8, because the 8, for example is relevant elsewhere, but it does not follow that 12 must always and necessarily be thought of as the sum of 4 and 8. In a different situation, it may be more convenient to think of 12 as being 7+5. The mathematical possibility of breaking down all periodic vibrations into simple vibrations as demonstrated by Fourier does not further authorize us to conclude that this is the only permissible form of analysis, if we cannot also establish that it has an essential significance in nature as well. That this is in fact the case (that this form of analysis has meaning in nature independently of theory) is made probable by the fact that the ear carries out precisely the same analysis, and also because it happens that, as we have already mentioned, this sort of analysis has more advantages for mathematical investigation than any other. The approaches to phenomena that are closest to the innermost composition of the matter under consideration are of course those that also lead to the fullest and clearest theoretical presentation. But it is not appropriate to begin the investigation with the functions of the ear, given their great complexity, and the explanations they themselves require. This is why we shall try to find out if the analysis of complex into simple vibrations has any real perceptible significance, independently of the action of the ear, in the external world, and then we shall be fully in a position to show that certain mechanical effects depend on the presence or absence of a particular partial sound in a composite mass of musical sounds. The existence of partial sounds will find a meaning in nature, and in return the understanding of their mechanical effects will shed a new light on their relationships with the human ear.[5]

10.4. THE PERCEPTION OF PITCHES

Going back to the sources, while giving us the opportunity to pay well-deserved tribute to a great physicist without entering into disagreement with him, also shows us the research pathway that has been discontinued since he passed away, at least as he apparently envisaged it: two ways of hearing, on two distinct levels, and in different ways. In one of them the ear is conditioned as much as "the objects are prepared." This is experimentation in sensory physics, in "analytical" audition. The other is a total act of listening with those "auxiliary circumstances," as Helmholtz says, that make it easier for the musician to identify sounds (we would say sound objects).

Keeping our thoughts away from Helmholtzian caveats, what could we say today about the perception of pitch? Even before we turn to the most recent acoustic theories, we should start with some commonsense observations:

1. There is no doubt that the "structure of the signal" is harmonic and can be broken down into the Fourier series, and there is even a probability that in the first stage the physiological ear behaves like an analyzer.

5. Ibid.

2. Between this and saying that we hear distinct "harmonics," there is something of a difference. That the observer, his ear glued to Helmholtz resonators, hears them, there is no doubt. And it has been seen that he then rehears the sound, convincing himself that he is separating the harmonics out one from another. It is already more likely that he "separates out" the harmonics of a sound as they are dying away, as harmonics are formed in the course of the duration of the sound. Nothing is very certain in these rather convoluted musicianship exercises. And this is fortunate: if a practiced ear managed to distinguish all the harmonics in this way, we should point out that its musical listening would very rapidly be seriously disturbed. It would no longer separate the clarinet from the oboe, or the violin from the cello . . . or again, in a piano, string, or woodwind chord, especially a consonant chord, it would no longer identify the notes, which have so many harmonics in common. None of this has been borne out; quite the contrary: the whole package of harmonics seems to be fully merged with the sound.

3. When, as (musicians' and acousticians') "common sense" suggests, we link the sensation of pitch to the number of vibrations, we forget the object—that is, what actually comes to the ear—and focus entirely on the visible signal, whether on the zither, the oscillograph, or the mathematical expression in the Fourier series. There is, on the zither, one string that is longer than the others, which of course vibrates less rapidly, and which in Fourier's series is a first term designating the fundamental. But what is going on in the ear? Doubtless, we are tempted to say, the analysis of a group of harmonic frequencies, each one allocated a coefficient. But if, for example, the zither "hardly" vibrates in the fundamental, that is, if the first term of the Fourier series has a very small coefficient, will my ear continue reacting quantitatively to that first term, that fundamental? If this were the case, depending on whether a string is attacked with timbre or not, we should have different perceptions of pitch depending on whether the first, second, or third harmonic dominated. Now, we observe that the ear nearly always assesses pitch in relation to the fundamental, whether this is physically strong or weak, as if it were going back to a sort of "first reason" for spectral data.

We should therefore conclude that the ear does not hear the fundamental but *infers the fundamental* by perceiving the *harmonic network*—that is, its internal correlations.

It is time to take a closer look, using two essential experiments.

10.5. EXPERIMENTS ON RESIDUALS

This is the reverse of Helmholtz's experiment. His experiment untangled the partials by analyzing "a rich sound." If we take several partials, will we be able to recompose a fundamental?

Schouten's experiments throw into confusion any idea of a simple relationship between perceived pitch and the physical presence of fundamentals. In fact, if we listen to three or four equally distributed frequencies in the high register, we perceive, in general, a low pitch. For example, the group 1800, 2020, 2240 Hz will have the pitch of a fundamental sound 220 Hz (A^3), called the "residual sound" of the three initial frequencies: so we have a complex of sounds in the high register with a (perceived) low pitch. If we now observe that this low pitch is sometimes very obvious, sometimes unclear, and that this depends on the phase relationship between the three high-register harmonics, and also the distance between them and their intensity; and if we add that the residual sound is not a phenomenon arising from the nonlinearity of the ear and that, putting aside the questions of phase, it appears in a very specific area in the field of audibility that depends on intensity and frequency; and if we notice, finally, that it sometimes gives rise to the perception of several low pitches—then we believe we have given some idea of the number of problems that must still be resolved before we arrive at a simple theory of the perception of pitch, or even simply of residual sound. We should keep this in mind: our present understanding of psychoacoustics rejects any direct link between frequency and pitch, even if this is often a useful way of presenting them. Rather, we are inclined to see pitch as a perception that depends on both the *frequency* and the *periodicity* of a sound. (It is understood that here the *frequency* of a sound is the frequency of the lowest harmonic of the sound that actually contains energy; the *periodicity*, on the contrary, is determined by the frequency of the *theoretical fundamental* harmonic of the sound, independently of questions of energy.) For example: a sound complex formed by the superimposition of two sinusoidal sounds of 200 and 250 Hz will have a frequency of 200 Hz and a periodicity of 50 Hz. The periodicity is therefore determined by the greatest common divisor of the harmonics of a sound; normally, of course, the two concepts coincide, for in sounds there is nearly always energy at the frequency of the fundamental harmonic.

Equally, there seem to be two mechanisms in the ear: one peripheral (the internal ear), which analyzes from the frequency, activating a *spatial* analysis of the sound vibration in the cochlea, where the different frequencies are perceived in relation to their own energy; the other central (nervous), which seems to be linked to the periodicity and not the energy of the sound vibration. These two mechanisms coexist and are interpreted by means of schemas that are not yet entirely clear. We do not have unanimous agreement on this model, however, and, besides, it does not explain every phenomenon. . . . Furthermore, the rules that claim to "find out" the perceived pitch of a sound from the physical knowledge of the signal are complex, often vary from one person to another, and, in a universe of nonharmonic sounds, are nearly always unknown.

10.6. EXPERIMENT ON UNISONS

For our part we wanted to do a similar experiment on the relationship between pitches and frequencies, taking the perception of unison as our assessment criterion. Our approach is broadly as follows:

The mathematical analysis of a sound A shows that it can be broken down into a number of sinusoidal vibrations with frequencies f, $2f$, $3f$, and so forth. If, furthermore, we consider the sound A′, containing all the components of A except the first, f, which is taken out by filtering, A′ will have the structure $2f$, $3f$, ... The fundamental of A′ is $2f$, whereas the fundamental of A is f; but the periodicity is still f, the same as the periodicity of A. If the (perceived) pitch depended only on periodicity, A and A′ would be permanently in unison. In fact, the findings are as follows:

(a)   There is indeed unison between A and A′ for low sounds.

(b)   But as we go up the register of pitches, the filtered sounds (A′) are more and more perceived as an octave higher than the original sounds (A).

But we were able to go further and carry out a second group of observations using the particular methods we had introduced for the previous experiment: for practical reasons we had, in fact, decided to compare orchestral instrument sounds (sounds A, unfiltered) and sinusoidal sounds S of the same frequency f. The results were quite unexpected:

(a)   There is indeed unison, as may be expected, between the sounds A and the sounds S, in the medium and high registers; but,

(b)   as we go further down the register, the listener tends more and more to perceive unison between an orchestral instrumental sound A with a frequency f and a sinusoidal sound S with a frequency not of f but of $2f$. In other words, unfiltered instrumental bass sounds are perceived an octave higher in relation to the sinusoidal sound that has the same frequency as their fundamental.

We should note, however, that the respective calibrations of the orchestral instrumental sounds and the sinusoidal sounds are coherent in themselves, which means, on the one hand, that a bassoon C^1 will not be confused with a C^2 nor, on the other hand, will a 50 Hz and a 100 Hz sinusoidal. So we must allow that there are several calibrations for the perception of pitches, which coincide in the medium and high registers but diverge in the low register, although each is perfectly coherent in itself.

Here again we could refer to the two mechanisms mentioned at the end of the last section to explain these results. Whatever the explanation may ultimately be, the phenomena observed seem to us to amount to a serious warning not to be too eager to transfer from one field to another concepts that have the same name but

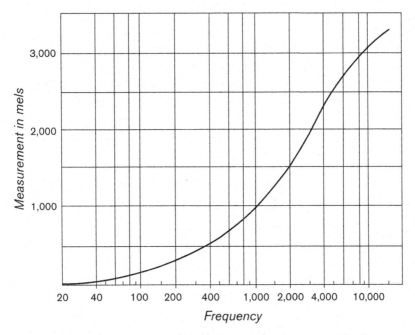

FIGURE 3. Scale for assessment of melodic pitches according to Stevens and Volkman.

turn out to refer to different realities (for more detailed information on these experiments see the appendix at the end of the chapter).

10.7. MUSICAL AND PSYCHOACOUSTIC CALIBRATIONS

Our normal "musical values," the foundation of our musical intervals, operate within the framework of a tonal music or at least a music with highly defined degrees, ultimately almost conventions, or at least the result of "specialized" training. The situation is quite different for the experimental psychologist, for whom "interval" designates a *perception* of "a space" between two pitches, which is conveniently represented by the psychoacoustic unit called a *mel*. So, from the experimental psychologist's point of view, a fifth or a third in the bass register is much tighter than in the middle register: it has a smaller number of mels. The reader will perhaps then ask how it is that musically all fifths are identical, since from a subjective point of view they are not. Without claiming to answer this question, we will, in order to make things clearer, simply illustrate how the calibration in mels was constructed by Stevens, based on sinusoidal sounds (fig. 3).

A sound is presented to a listener periodically; during the periods of silence he has to tune an oscillator to a frequency such that the pitch of the sound it gives is in a certain relationship (1/2, 2, or 4, 10, or 1/3, etc.) with the test sound. This process is repeated many times: for different values in the relationships, for different initial test sounds, then closer and closer together to get a succession of responses, and finally, of course, with different participants. Then all the results are statistically analyzed, and the most probable values are used to construct the mels curve (subjective units of pitch obtained from judgments about relationships) in relation to frequency. So mels are based on at least three working hypotheses, the validity of which is demonstrated only by the consistency of the final results:

Hypothesis 1: the concept of pitch always relates to some subjective magnitude of the perceived sound: it is not necessarily the same from one person to another, but everyone has at least one criterion, a sort of unique perception, which for a certain class of stimuli he links to the word *pitch*.

Hypothesis 2: the expression "half" or "double" or "one-third" pitch, even if it refers to a mathematical relational concept, which is a nonintuitive abstract concept, is a judgment criterion for everyone that has proved to be stable through time and consistent, whatever the initial sound.

Hypothesis 3: so there is for everyone, even if the reason for it is not understood, an idea, quite subjective it is true, of a yardstick for pitch, in relation to which judgments of half, a third, and so forth can be made.

We could question these hypotheses. In any case it has been possible to set up an experimental scale of mels, which coincides with the harmonic scale only in a limited portion of the register. Does this amount to proof of a divergence between the objects of scientific and artistic study, or are we dealing with two distinct phenomena, equally important for music, depending on the experimental conditions and the way the objects for listening are used? We will return to this enigma.[6]

10.8. PITCH DIFFERENTIATION THRESHOLDS: IMPORTANCE OF CONTEXT

Some composers, a little too naively smitten with the acoustics of music, are tempted to use uncritically all research that comes from science and, in particular, acousticians' work on *thresholds*. This makes them think that the area of audibility is broken up into as many intervals as differential listening to pure frequencies by the ear will allow (cf. Moles's "slabs of sensation"). We will attempt to clarify the concept of differentiation threshold and to highlight the wrong use of it that is likely to be made in music.

6. See chap. 30.

These thresholds have been accurately measured by audiometry, under carefully controlled conditions: a slight change in frequency at a certain level, without any other sound or masking. As soon as a musician uses a natural or a synthetic sound, he must know, as we have seen, that he is mobilizing not only the nominal frequencies on his score. On the one hand, he is providing an object that is already frequency-rich, affecting a whole zone of differentiation thresholds. On the other hand, this sound is with other sounds, which produce a masking effect, and consequently tend to disrupt any predictions that might be made from a simple mathematical hypothesis. But in the calculations on noise, based on elementary stimulus curves, Fletcher and other researchers have had remarkable results; selecting their field of reference on each occasion, they studied the effect of raising or lowering the thresholds when the sound is continuous or discontinuous. The musician, quite overwhelmed by such calculations, is advised to turn to the nearest and also the most accurate electronic machine in music: his ear.

Then he will observe this: if we must take the concept of threshold into account in music, we will probably have to look for it at the two extremities of a "polarization" of the ear induced by the context. Indeed, disrupt the ear with huge gaps in pitch and intensity or the effects of large numbers of objects: perceptions of slight differences in pitch will blur. Train it to perceive more and more subtly, during a pianissimo, with a huge reduction of objects: it will then perceive tiny variations.

Moreover, learning to listen can teach us to hear objects or nuances within objects better. It is with this in mind that another experimenter, Heinz Werner, has attracted our attention. He has his listeners listen five consecutive times to a group of two tonic sounds (i.e., with highly defined pitch) that are very close together in pitch.[7] The interval formed by these sounds is markedly smaller than the minimum interval normally perceived by the ear (estimated as a twentieth of a tone in the register under study); so it is not perceived on the first time of listening. But repetition makes it become more and more apparent, until it appears as a well-defined interval. Not only is this experiment simple and convincing, but it is also of fundamental importance, for it gives the lie to theories that fix the norms of listening as an absolute, without taking into account either context or training.

More generally, we should observe that, when the physicist habituates his ear to perceive a stimulus, he behaves no differently from the musician seeking to make a subtle structure perceptible: he must lead his ear to it and not violate it by imagining that, like a printing machine, it will regurgitate a whole network of curves or pour out its "slabs of sensation" with no problem. . . . So perception depends on context. Hence an instrumentalist will instinctively remember Pythagoras's scale to add an accidental to a note, but also, above and beyond this, the intervals will be

7. The term *tonic sound* is used to describe a continuous pitched sound with a clearly recognizable main frequency.—Trans.

more or less "right" in relation to the "vectors" of the music that contains them, as Robert Francès has so clearly demonstrated:

> If we take as our base line the tempered accuracy of a piano and lower the pitch of two of its notes, we can predict that this change will be felt less by the listener when these notes form part of a structure in which, as with the tendency described above, they have descending vectors, than the converse. So, for example, if the note is in both a descending and an ascending appoggiatura phrase, the lowering of the note objectively will be better tolerated (i.e., less noticed) in the first than in the second; in the former the lowering is in keeping with the harmonic vector of the note, but in the latter it runs contrary to it.[8]

Furthermore, we wonder whether the tuning of the piano, in the high and bass registers of this instrument, is not done tendentiously to satisfy musical imperatives, as if to force the ear to perceive as lower or higher sounds whose pitch is in truth very confused at the outer zones. R. W. Young gives a much more scholarly explanation of this fact.[9]

We could also think of dodgy horn notes, this time beyond the limits of tolerance, but whose charm induces smiles and indulgence in the listener. We should note that this is nothing to do with the dialectic of the musical discourse but the difficulties of the instrument maker.

10.9. CONCLUSIONS: THE VARIOUS PITCH STRUCTURES

After these various experiments and observations, a conclusion is called for: the concept of pitch, far from being obvious and linked, as people say, to the frequency of the fundamental, is complex and plural.

It is time to sum up what we have learned, going from the most complex to the most elementary,[10] from the musical to physics.

(a) *Instrumental calibrations* (register of given instrumental sounds)

Here we mean the musician's sound, and not the heterodyne sound of the acoustician. Musicians have keyboards, valves, fingering, and so forth, which produce notes that are fixed or at least agreed on in advance. These registers, tuned as well as possible to a "temperament," are used, in the case of the piano and keyboard instruments, melodically and harmonically. The instrument lends itself just as well to either use, although the ear makes a fundamental distinction between

---

8. Robert Francès, *La perception de la musique* (Paris: Vrin, 1958). [Published in English as *The Perception of Music*, trans. W. Jay Dowling (Hillsdale, NJ: Lawrence Erlbaum, 1988).—Trans.]

9. See Colloque d'acoustique de Marseille (Paris: Éditions C.N.R.S., 1959), 169–84.

10. In Helmholtz's terminology. A musician is, conversely, justified in saying: from the most "natural" to the most "artificial," moving in the same way from music to physics.

them: for the ear it is not at all the same thing to hear two pitches together (chord) or one after the other (melody). It is to be noted, as we have seen, that the confusion that occurs over a bass *A* on the piano, when heard an octave higher than a pure frequency nominally of the same value, is not likely to be repeated when the piano is being played or when the piano plays with the orchestra. Experience, just as much as Western orchestral convention, assures the ear that the bass A is indeed a bass A and not the octave above.

The fact that the acoustician can find no acoustic energy in the reference frequency makes no difference. It is a musical fact, distinct from an acoustic fact. So, written in the same place on the musical staff, there are Cs and As that are acoustically different depending on the instrument on which they are played: each one has a particular spectrum, a particular localization of energy, which is "somewhere" in the tessitura, more or less high or low. So we can see to what extent a score can mislead about the "acoustic" content of the work and, reciprocally, how little chance a score that aims to be acoustically accurate has of recording what the ear will really perceive of those spectra that are so accurately defined. The champions of the electronic score would do well to think about this.

(b) *Calibration of intervals*

A calibration of intervals can only be correctly assessed if instrumental registers are available: in the absence of these, the ear—the musical ear, of course—tends nevertheless to retain a certain number of "relationships" from this group of instrumental pitches. Here again we find the concept of pitch as *structural* value, as independent as it can be of any characteristics or the nature of the objects that produce it.

When we come to evaluating, describing, or justifying such a calibration of intervals, attitudes vary considerably: will it be harmonic or melodic, depending on whether the ear hears simultaneous or successive sounds? Will the perception of intervals be based on consonance? Or (as the capricious tuning of the African *balaphone* might suggest) on custom?

This type of question seems to us to be a waste of time for the researcher, and we would suggest, rather, that he should consider these two pieces of information based on musical experience:

1. The perception of intervals is a cultural fact, conditioned by a specific practice and a specific number of conventions about the use of pitches, which provide waymarks for perception. The diatonic scale, a horrible arithmetical compromise between a number of simple relationships, is perfectly well tolerated by us. For an Indian it is only a crude calibration, and he, for his part, places other scalar degrees between the existing ones.

2. This perception of intervals will still be closely linked to the instrumental context: far from being better with pure sounds, the ear will clamor for sounds full of substance, demonstrating to the acoustician that it prefers to compare spectra

rather than waves. In addition, the ear will judge performances by intentions: depending on context, a singer will appear to be singing on the right note, whereas she is a semitone out, but, on other occasions, the ear will not forgive her for being a few commas wrong.

(c) *Functional and experimental calibrations*

In the two previous examples the ear situates pitches within a context that is instrumental (registers) or structural (intervals).

But—as in Helmholtz's experiment with resonators—it is equally prepared to free itself from these contexts and even, when the occasion arises, to break down into harmonics the instrumental unity in which these harmonics "merge."

Thus, in a rich harmonic sound heard several times, we will initially hear only a pitch taken to be a tonic, crowned with a harmonic timbre. Then we will more clearly identify various "components," which seem to create points of "condensation" in this sound; then, listening to those resonances, we will perceive that one resonance stands out more than another. Better still, if we compare this sound (which we suppose to be harmonically very ambiguous by now) with a "resolution into a chord" that the piano, or any other registered instrument, suggests, experience shows that there will be attraction or repulsion, and in response we will not always hear the sound at the same pitch: it will be heard in relation to the pattern the piano suggests. And so we observe that a given object, which has certain harmonic characteristics, can assume various values depending on the environment.

Is it legitimate to call such possible calibrations of evaluation by pitch "subjective"? No, if we think that they arise from a relationship between objects that is itself a function of group conditioning and individual training.

(d) *Calibration of "gaps" in the tessitura*

This is a psychophysical calibration of mels, very strange for a musician. The word *mel* seems very ill chosen if it suggests a *melody* of degrees, where all the ears in the world agree in their judgment that a third or a fifth are similar in the high or low register. So we must point out the risk of confusion this terminology may cause. It describes certain particular conditions for the perception of pitch relationships on the part of the experimenter and a particular listening approach on the part of the participants, who must use a type of evaluation quite uncommon in music. Our aim is not to criticize the objectivity of these evaluations but to draw attention to the experimental context that justifies them and, hence, to the potential interpretations. We will make ourselves clear at the end of this work.

10.10. SOUND MASS AND FILTERING

Since the concept of musical pitch is dependent, on the one hand, on instrumental registers and, on the other hand, on a particular cultural conditioning, there is nothing to stop us extending the perception of pitch by including in it sounds that are chosen differently or listened to in a new way.

Here we must distinguish between the concept of pitch linked to instrumental registers and the concept of pitch linked to the perception of intervals: register obviously comes from instrument making, intervals from music theory. If we are hoping to make a general statement about the way pitch is perceived, we must of course start with the ear. The very concept of register in the traditional sense loses its meaning as soon as we leave the field of classical instruments: a scale played on the phonogène using any concrete sound no longer has any meaning. But if we listen carefully to this random concrete sound (for example, it may come from a membrane, a metal sheet, a rod . . .), we notice that, without having a clearly locatable pitch like traditional sounds, it nevertheless presents a sound "mass" situated somewhere in the tessitura and is more or less characterized by occupying fairly decipherable intervals. It includes, for example, several sounds of gradually evolving pitch, crowned or surrounded with a conglomeration of partials that also evolve, all of this more or less locatable in a certain pitch zone. The ear soon manages to locate the most prominent components and aspects of these, provided it is trained to do so; such sounds can then become as familiar to it as traditional harmonic sounds: they have a characteristic *mass*.

If we applied the same criteria to these sounds as to harmonic sounds, we should expect that filtering them would limit them to slices of pitch strictly determined by the frequencies at which the filters cut off. We have already seen, with traditional sounds, that filtering a bass piano note has some surprises in store for experimenters: when it is done in the frequency zone that contains the fundamental, it does not change the perceived pitch of the note. On the contrary, in the high register it changes the piano-like character of the sound but without modifying the perception of pitch. Generally speaking, a symphony can still be recognized on the telephone: this shows us that structural pitch relationships remain indestructible, despite the system's weak pass band. Similarly, on a small transistor the bass notes are reduced to practically 100 or 200 Hz (because of the smallness of the loudspeaker)—that is, only one or two octaves below the A on the tuning fork: musical works nevertheless continue to be "played" with physically nonexistent bass fundamentals.

These first experimental observations on filtering enable us to see that, even for harmonic sounds, which are in theory very localized in the tessitura, the concept of the "mass" of a sound is based in a concrete reality resistant to a number of manipulations that are, nevertheless, theoretically capable of modifying it considerably (proportionately with the changes in the spectrum of frequencies). Nontraditional sounds present the researcher with a permanence that is just as, if not more, obstinate where their occupation of the pitch field is concerned. So we can see that the beginner in experimental music, desperate to filter sounds, is in fact performing very minor surgery. From one incision to another, the sound is indeed transformed, painted in different "colors," from dark to light; but through all these transformations it is nevertheless the same sound, with a *mass* that is still identifiable.

So this leads us to a very general conclusion about the correlation between pitch or mass, on the one hand, and the spectrum of frequency, on the other: the apparent bulk or mass of a sound, or its precise location in pitch *are not* in direct correlation with the physical bulk of the spectrum and its fragmentation, or the localization of a fundamental.

Very limited fragments of this type of spectrum will, in fact, retain the subjective characteristics of the mass, or localization, or harmonic makeup of the original sound, albeit with "colors" that depend on the filtering: the ear, while recognizing an impoverishment or distortion of this original sound, will tend to reconstruct it with its characteristic individuality. In practice, anyone wishing to make experimental music is advised not to try to give the sound material he uses, concrete or synthetic, any pitch or mass values that are very closely related to the portions of spectrum determined by filtering.

Appendix

(Cf. section 10.6)

EXPERIMENT ON UNISONS

Our aim initially is to find out whether the perception of the pitch of a musical sound depends exclusively on the frequency of its fundamental harmonic.

We know that the pitch of a (harmonic) musical sound is a well-defined value on which practically all Western music has come to depend. But the perceived pitch of a sound is not always determined by its fundamental. Although the fundamental alone sometimes does account for the greater part of the energy of the note, in other cases its energetic importance is, on the contrary, negligible. Thus it would appear that we cannot properly account for the perception of pitch solely by the presence of the fundamental.

To clarify the situation, we devised the following experiment: we played normal musical sounds, then the same sounds after filtering out their fundamental (using an electronic device), and compared the (perceived) pitch of these sounds with the pitch of those pure (sinusoidal) sounds that have a frequency related to the frequency of the fundamentals in question.

1. The sound material used in our experiment consisted of sixty-four instrumental sounds, with pitch varying between Eb_1 ($f = 38.9$ Hz) and Gb_7 ($f = 2960$ Hz).

These sounds came from:

Piano	9 sounds	Viola	4 sounds
Xylophone	3 —	Piccolo	3 —
Vibraphone	3 —	Violin	5 —
Oboe	5 —	Cello	4 —
Clarinet	3 —	Double Bass	4 —
Flute	6 —	Bassoon	4 —
Trumpet	3 —	Electronic source	5 —
Trombone	3 —		

Except for the percussion instruments, these sounds were presented as swelled notes, without vibrato, with a duration of 3–5 s, played mf, and then heard at a similar intensity (80–90 dB, i.e., 0.0002 bars). The five electronic sounds, produced by an appropriately distorted sinusoidal wave, were given a fairly slow attack and a gradual decay: their timbre was somewhat like a violin, and in general their electronic origin was not noticed by the participants. Each sound was listened to twice during the test: once as it had been recorded and once after the fundamental had been filtered out; in total, therefore, $2 \times 64 = 128$ sounds were played.

2. In practice, these 128 sounds were divided over six tapes, each lasting approximately twenty minutes; there was a break between tapes. The six tapes were played in two separate sessions: three tapes per session.

Each of the 128 sounds whose pitch was being evaluated appeared in a sequence arranged as follows:

Sound played;
1s silence, then reference no. 1.
2s silence.
Sound played;
1s silence, then reference no. 2.
2s silence.
Sound played;
1s silence, then reference no. 3.
(30s silence before the next sequence).

The three reference sounds consisting of sinusoidal sounds of frequency f, $2f$, and $f/2$ or $4f$, in any order—where f denotes the frequency of the fundamental of the sound under consideration (filtered or unfiltered).

The sounds were played randomly; in particular, unfiltered and filtered sounds followed each other in no fixed order.

3. The participants, mainly final-year students from the Paris conservatory, or composers at the Groupe de recherches musicales, had been instructed in the aims of the experiment and introduced to the way it would be run by means of a preliminary training tape. We asked them to indicate, in a given sequence, which of

the three reference sounds was in unison with the sound, which was played three times. Twenty-two people agreed to take the test; some of the responses, however, were discarded for reasons that will be explained later.

4. Eliminating the fundamental, in theory easy at the time of recording, had in practice to be done live—that is, by means of an adequate filter that could be inserted into the listening circuit. The intermodulation coefficient of magnetic tape does not, in fact, allow effective filtering out of the fundamental in a recorded sound above 40 dB, whereas we wanted to go to 50 dB. The efficiency of our device was monitored by a reference microphone positioned in front of the loudspeakers, in the premises where the listening was taking place.

5. *Findings*. The question may be asked why we did not make a direct comparison between the pitch of the filtered and the homologous unfiltered sounds: the reason is that actual experiments of this type gave only very varied results, which were difficult to interpret. This may be because the change of timbre that accompanies the elimination of the fundamental, and varies according to the instrumental origin of the sound, disrupts the perception of pitch in an unpredictable manner. Whatever the case may be, the use of sinusoidal reference sounds seemed to us to resolve the difficulty by giving the ear a fixed reference point valid as much for unfiltered as for filtered sounds. It should be noted that the choice of sinusoidal sounds as "benchmarks" is not obligatory but for convenience. We intend, moreover, to go back over all our experiments later on with reference sounds that will themselves be instrumental.[11]

Under these conditions we should expect to obtain two categories of findings:

1. The breakdown of the answers for the sixty-four "unfiltered" sounds in effect gives us an insight into the question: "To what extent is the (perceived) pitch of a harmonic sound (such as is found in traditional music) linked to the pitch of a sinusoidal sound with a frequency that is in simple relationship with the fundamental?"

2. Comparing these answers with the answers for the corresponding filtered sounds gives us an insight, although indirectly, into the question: "Do an unfiltered and a filtered sound have the same pitch?"

To ensure maximum reliability in the interpretation of the results, we took the following precautions:

(*a*) Seventeen of the twenty-two people tested linked musical unison (even perceived pitch) with physical "unison" (equality of frequency) in more than 90 percent of cases, which is in conformity with the most general hypothesis. The other five people were not considered to have had the usual conditioning, and their answers were disregarded.

11. See "Rapport entre la hauteur et le fondamental d'un son musical," a paper by the GRM delivered at the Cinquième congrès international d'acoustique, Liège, Sept. 1965.

(b) As the listening sessions were relatively long and, most important, boring, we wanted to be sure that the quality of the answers was not affected by tiredness: we could detect no variation in fatigue levels between the beginning and the end of the sessions.

(c) Finally, we checked that the position of the participant in the listening room did not affect the perception of pitch of filtered sounds (we feared phenomena such as intermodulation, which are liable to "restore" the fundamental artificially) by comparing the answers of a control person who moved from place to place during one sequence, repeated several times.

The findings shown in section 10.6 are from the experiment carried out and interpreted in accordance with the directions above.

11

Thresholds and Transients

11.1. TRANSIENT PHENOMENA

Physicists simplify the field of operation as much as possible by limiting themselves to harmonic sounds, like Helmholtz, or by using pure sounds, like Stevens. But what they also and most importantly assume is that these sounds are of infinite duration or, at the very least, that they are long enough to achieve a "steady state" between them and the ear, after the decay of the phenomena that established them, which are called "transient" phenomena. "Transient" regimes generally arise from the inertia that all physical systems initially have in reaction to an external stimulus. They are found just as much in sound bodies (physical signal transients) as in the ear (the problem of the time constant and the ear's powers of integration).

It is important first of all to study the transient regimes of the ear in order to assess more accurately the possible impact of signal transients on hearing.

The study of these can be perfectly well carried out without the help of the ear. It consists in establishing the energetic history of a string, a membrane, or a rod from the moment of zero vibration, taking into account all the initial conditions. This rapidly gives rise to very complicated problems if the sound body and the initial conditions are only a little out of the ordinary.

But acousticians consider such studies to be very important, and this not with a view to technical applications, such as, for example, the building of concert halls, but with the aim of helping music to understand itself better. . . . How valid is an ambition such as this?

We should let some acousticians speak for themselves so that we can get a clearer grasp of their intentions.

11.2. PHYSICISTS' MUSICAL POSTULATES

First, we quote Léonid Pimonow, drawing attention to several expressions as we go:

> We may wonder how it is that, throughout its history, the science and technology of music has been almost exclusively concerned with periodic sounds, although, compared with transients, they only occupy a small portion of time.
>
> It seems to us that the main reasons are these. First, it is theoretically and experimentally easier to work with periodic rather than transient phenomena. In particular we should take note of the fact that music is an ancient art and that in the course of its development it has not had equipment capable of *measuring transient spectra*.
>
> In addition, as we have already pointed out, the appearance of a sustained sound after a transient is a sort of *concession to what will be done* by the organ of hearing, which generally speaking evaluates sounds before they are fully stabilized. The ear behaves like this because, and let us emphasize this once more, it is *an information receptor before being a harmonic analyzer*. Finally, the aim of music is not only to supply the ear with one or several sustained sounds, but mainly to give it *sounds that are pleasant;* as Helmholtz recognized, it is particularly necessary that these sounds do not create a discord because they clash; in other words, they *must not be dissonant*. Music, precisely because it is trying to fulfill this condition, has thus concentrated almost exclusively on combining continuous sounds.
>
> So we have settled for establishing a measure of order represented by the scale, which has further developed into the tempered chromatic scale, and we have left *the freedom to use transients*, which are bound to appear with each variation or combination of sounds, to creators of musical instruments, composers, and interpreters. An isolated note from a melody, or an isolated chord, thus has an acoustic, but not a musical, value. What gives them a musical value is their succession, their sequencing, and this succession, this sequencing, has indeed the characteristics of a transient.
>
> Therefore, the freedom to work with transients cannot possibly be seen as something inferior: *music is not a trade but an art.*
>
> But in some cases it is essential to clarify the sensations caused by transient phenomena in music scientifically in relation to their spectral development, for sometimes they can be extremely unpleasant. So we have reason to think that *the analysis of transients will be able*, very soon, *to improve the conditions for music* and even, perhaps, open up new technical possibilities for it.[1]

For his part, Professor Winckel writes:

> Musical timbre is determined not only by the spectrum of partials in the stationary state (formant structure), but the attack and decay transient processes of sound vibrations play an extremely important role. Unfortunately this latter point seems to

---

1. Léonid Pimonow, *Vibrations en régime transitoire* (Paris: Dunod, 1962).

have been ignored in recent works on musical aesthetics, which have largely been concerned only with the distribution of partials in permanently stable sound.[2]

We feel somewhat guilty for presenting these two quotations without more circumspection. It is always a delicate matter to separate affirmations like these from their context, and, like every other author, we ourselves would dread one particular page, which could appear very dubious, being taken in isolation from this treatise. Moreover, not only do we consider these two scholars to be distinguished scientists, but we also recognize that they are themselves reacting against the simplifications of some of their colleagues. This makes these quotations all the more important. Our critique affects neither our respect for their person nor our consideration for their competence as physicists.

11.3. CRITIQUE OF THE APPROACH TO MUSIC THROUGH TRANSIENTS

To start with, we agree on the essential point: the acoustics of permanent sounds have come nowhere near to resolving the infinitely opaque problem of the perception of musical objects. But it is to be feared that, while continuing with and improving the acoustic approach itself, we may be perpetuating a fundamental methodological error. The problem is only so opaque because it is presented in the context of highly debatable premises; we have pointed out their various manifestations in Pimonow's text, and Winckel's text agrees with his on the particular point he is discussing. We will look at the first of these texts.

Pimonow distinguishes between ways of ordering sounds that have a historical origin, such as the scale, and the freedom to use sounds within these structures: "freedom to use transients," are his exact words; and, going from a precise meaning to a broad acceptance of the term, he locates the musical in the changes and succession of sounds in general. Of course, it is tempting to concede that an isolated note or chord "has no musical value": in any case it is clear they have less value than the work of which they are a part. But surely every isolated note becomes stable after a transient period? And, consequently, surely it conveys a certain musical content? And if music resides in the art of using transients, how is it that *The Art of the Fugue* played on the harmonium, an instrument that gives no choice of transients—as all of them are based on existing models—is still *The Art of the Fugue*? We can see that the text we are discussing, by playing on the two possible meanings, attempts to conflate the "transient" in the sense of the physical establishment of the sound and the "transient" in the sense of the sequencing of notes that constitutes music.

2. Fritz Winckel, *Vues nouvelles sur le monde des sons*, trans. Abraham Moles (Paris: Dunod, 1960). [Published in English as *Music, Sound and Sensation*, trans. Thomas Binkley (New York: Dover, 1967).—Trans.]

Moreover, Pimonow links "musical progress" to the study of transients—with no further explanation of the ambiguity criticized above—a study that would involve relating spectra of frequencies and sensations. If, as we have every right to expect, musical progress involves musicians, would they therefore be invited to use transients freely and simultaneously to subordinate their use of them to the findings of psychoacoustic experimentation? An unexpected combination, to say the least. But suppose that it is necessary. According to what norms will the promised improvement take place? The author tells us explicitly: the aim of music is "to provide pleasant sounds," that is, sounds "that are not dissonant." This is a stance already suggested by Helmholtz.

Here we should clarify the ordinary thinking of acousticians about dissonance. When we listen simultaneously to pure frequencies of adjacent values, there is no doubt that the differential and additional frequencies arising from their proximity are occasionally very unpleasant to the ear. With no overall aesthetic meaning, this sensation relates only to the appearance of parasitic sounds in a defined sound context. In any case, seeing the door open to a rationalization of music that identifies the dissonant with the disagreeable, the logical mind immediately thinks up the following procedure: as every natural sound is the sum of a certain number of pure frequencies, we can calculate in advance all the clashes that arise from bringing two natural sounds close together and consequently, *a priori*, all the dissonances; hence, we have the possibility of systematically eliminating them and giving consonance—that is, music—an objective basis.

In addition to this concept of dissonance, which is firmly contradicted by most known music, we must also refute the hypothesis that considers a combination of sounds in the ear to be analogous to the mathematical composition of frequencies. We should note that Helmholtz, to whom Pimonow nevertheless refers, had seen that this was only a hypothesis and had warned against the potential errors of the interpretation it implies (see section 10. 3). Besides, the simplest experiment, done with *instrumental* sounds where some harmonics at least "should" produce unpleasant clashes, shows that in reality nothing unpleasant is perceived. At the very most we may attribute the particular "color" of the sound to the said clashes.

Here, as can be seen, we come back to the basic position (which is ours) and to our most radical criticism of acousticians: the simplest road leading to music sets out neither from physics nor from abstract considerations but quite simply from musical experience, as provided by all existing music. It is this experience that we use to confirm the absence, from the musician's point of view, of the parasitic sounds expected by the physicist and the positive role of dissonance in music. We are not, of course, rejecting consonance, but we are observing that it appears in an essentially historical context and not as an absolute. How, for example, can we speak of consonances—with absolute accuracy at least—where the sounds of the tempered scale are concerned, when, in fact, they are adjusted away from the precise relationships of the harmonic series? How, for example, can we disown so many musical civilizations, very different from our own, in which consonance does not at all play the important part it has for us?

Finally, we take from Pimonow's text the suggestion that the ear is an "information receptor" and not a simple "harmonic analyzer"; we are sorry that the author is not more precise on this subject. Is this "information" simply measured in physical magnitudes? Or is it a waymark toward an awareness of the existence of musical objects? Pimonow's text does not give enough information for us to make up our minds on this point.

11.4. THE EAR AS A DEVICE

So, quite simply, we blame physicists for wanting to achieve music without making any or, more precisely, for considering the ear and its physiology as the key to an explanation of *music seen as a particular physical phenomenon*. We have already pointed out this mistake in several places (in particular in chapter 9). We will now go back to the diagrams in section 9.7 to clarify how some physical knowledge of the ear can help the experimental musician. As we have said, he examines the "black box," the individual, to find out the general norms governing the way he functions in the context of a musical activity: having almost limitless sound-producing technical resources, he seeks to discover the conditions at the "outer limits" of the ear's musical "potential," conditions that are themselves written into basic principles such as frequencies situated in the zone of perceptible pitch, a minimum level below which nothing can be heard, and so forth. After this, it is in the general context defined by this elementary knowledge that the musician will embark on the "long learning process" that will lead to the development of a new musicality. The musician's, and therefore music's, limitations have indeed long been with musical *making*: the limitations of instrument making, of virtuosity. By getting rid of or reformulating these, present-day electroacoustic techniques have unmasked the limitations of musical *hearing*: suddenly, our ear appeared as the first cause of all musical appreciation and at the same time as a *listening device* subject to precise physical norms. So now our understanding of the musical in general cannot do without knowledge of the ear as a device. This is what we might say about it:

(*a*) As an inert sound body, the ear is an acoustic link just as the eye is an optical intermediary. Therefore, properly speaking, it has the physical characteristics of any acoustic device—for example, band-pass, mechanical inertia, and so forth.

(*b*) As a physiological organ, perfused and innervated, it must, in common with all the other organs, also have characteristics arising from general laws of physiology—for example, sensibility thresholds, physiological inertia, and so forth.

(c) When studied, it gives perceptions that are described in relation to the stimuli, the complex objects, or the particular types of attention it is given. Here we can identify:

1. Experiments in which the ear (or any other sensory organ) is asked to compare two objects or stimuli, that is, to *describe* two perceptions *comparatively*. As it is difficult to measure perception, the physicist, in the majority of cases, experiments only on identical or very closely related perceptions, as was the case with Fletcher's curves, where people were asked to detect the (perceived) equal intensity of two pure frequencies with very similar values. We can imagine that the conditions in experiments such as these are rarely the same as in musical practice. They are mainly of interest to the physicist.

2. Experiments to find out not the comparative quality of perceptions but whether they exist or not: we can or cannot hear them. Generally speaking, the aim is to determine:

·   zones of sensitivity: ultraviolet light cannot be seen, ultrasounds cannot be heard, and so forth.
·   resolving powers: whether we can or cannot distinguish two sound impulses so many tenths of a second apart or two points of light so many tenths of a millimeter apart.
·   thresholds of sensitivity to a particular perceptual quality: too short a signal will be heard only as a click: a little longer, and we perceive a pitch; longer still, and we can discern a timbre.

This second type of study is less ambiguous than the first. The former, in effect, was to do with evaluating objects perceived in relation to each other simply on the basis of their physical proximity, thus giving rise to problematic comparisons; here, conversely, we simply locate characteristic perceptions physically, thereby clarifying useful norms for manipulating sounds for specific perceptual effects; and so we come back, albeit in a very crude way, to the experimental musician's field of interest.

11.5. TEMPORAL THRESHOLDS

We must therefore pay attention to the study of temporal thresholds made by acousticians. Indeed, just as experiments on differential perceptions (in frequency or intensity) of pure sounds of unlimited length are laboratory curios, so experiments on short sounds, whatever they may be, reconnect us with everyday musical practice.

Beats at intervals place us in the domain of rhythms. We can distinguish them further if they become closer together, then, roughly beyond the sixty-fourth note, everything becomes confused. Say a quarter note is one second, then these sixty-fourth notes last 1/16 of a second: this is the moment when we begin to hear a very low pitch, yet without ceasing to perceive a very rapid succession of beats that give the note a characteristic rough consistency. Thus, the bassoon bass register allows us to hear simultaneously both a low tonic note and what we call the "grain," which is precisely this perception of distinct beats. As they get closer together, these beats can no longer be perceived as such, and the grain that comes from them becomes secondary perceptual information, in relation to the pitch of the note.

Thus, a phenomenon of a physically discontinuous nature (repeated beats), when one of its physical dimensions (here, time) varies continually, is perceived in three *distinct* registers: rhythm, grain, and pitch. These perceptions are all suggestions for music: so we can see how knowledge of the physical thresholds of the ear directly concerns the experimental musician. We will now summarize some findings on temporal thresholds following the plan indicated in the last section: the time constants of the ear as an acoustic, then a physiological, device, then as an instrument for making qualified perceptions, with reference to the work of Haas, Winckel, and others.

11.6. MECHANICAL TIME CONSTANT OF THE EAR

After many controversies it seems now to be recognized that an initial analysis of sound vibration occurs in the inner ear in the form of spectral analysis. This, as we have said, is the mechanism suggested by Helmholtz, but whereas the German physicist thought it was the solution to the mechanism of hearing, today we have to admit that the ear's "resonators" form only a first stage of analysis, which gives only very fragmentary information about what the ear is capable of drawing out from sound.

Thus the cochlea, which carries out this initial process, is apparently a whole series of filters connected to each other in parallel; these filters, which are not very selective at all, only allow a rough determination of the frequency of the sound (in the form of spatial location of a vibrating zone). Once we have accepted a mechanism like this in principle, we can deduce two important consequences:

(*a*) One, to do with the ear, is the existence of an initial time constant; indeed, selectivity and speed of analysis are closely linked in a device of this type, and their variations are inversely proportional:

$$(\text{selectivity}) \times (\text{speed}) = \text{constant}$$

In practice, equivalent resonators in the ear have a band-pass of around 400 Hz, which fixes their time constant at 5 ms (milliseconds); they are therefore rapid and not very selective.

(*b*) The other, to do with stimuli, explains the fact that a very short sound (for example, an impulse) has no characteristic of pitch but is perceived as a noise (a click). We know that the spectrum (i.e., what comes out of the analyzing system) of a pure sinusoidal vibration is reduced to one single frequency only if the vibration has infinite duration: a sinusoidal with limited duration presents a broader spectrum (a continuous zone of frequencies) with a spread inversely proportional to its duration. A very short sound will therefore have a very broad spectrum; that is, in the cochlea a whole series of contiguous filters will be affected, so this will give rise to a perception with a pitch that remains indeterminate.

It is important to understand that *(a)* and *(b)* are two ways of looking at the analysis of the same phenomenon and that each is implied by the other; thus, the time constant of 5 ms is, for an isolated sound, precisely the outer limit of the duration below which any pitch characteristic is lost.

11.7. TIME CONSTANT OF THE EAR'S PHYSIOLOGICAL POWER OF INTEGRATION

After being analyzed in this way by the cochlear filters, the sound vibration is turned into a nervous impulse. It may be that only a few questions still have to be resolved about the mechanical stage of hearing, but we still have almost everything to discover about the neural stage; here we will simply point out that there is a second time constant, which could be called "the integration constant": lasting around 50 ms, this operates at the level of time discrimination between two successive events. It is the ear's "resolving power" (or "thickness of the present" according to composers): two consecutive sound events within a time frame of 50 ms cannot generally be distinguished from each other, at least if they are not too dissimilar.

Further than this, it would be the task of the physicist to explain how, with not very selective cochlear filters, and a resolving power of about 50 ms, the ear can:

(a)   find its way around language (some consonants are very short, 5–6 ms; the timbre of a vowel varies from one voice to another through slight differences in the formant zones, etc.);

(b)   have a very high differentiating power, in both pitch and intensity (i.e., perceive very slight differences in pitch and intensity);

(c)   identify temporal differences as slight as 20 microseconds in stereophonic hearing,

but these are precisely the answers that we expect from a general theory of hearing. . . . The reader wishing to know more will find a very fine example of such a theory in Pimonow's book, which we have already quoted.

As for us, who are less concerned with acoustic theories, we will simply give a few more experimental results, this time directly touching on musical practice— that is, describing the ear insofar as it is a particular kind of perceptual instrument.

11.8. PITCH, ARTICULATION, AND TIMBRE
RECOGNITION THRESHOLDS

We have just seen how, when we wish to consider it as a detecting device, the ear is subject to constraints that follow elementary laws of physics. The main effect of these is a certain lack of clarity in the acoustic analysis of sound vibration, which can only become worse as we go further into the different sensory stages, and which we will therefore approach at the level of perception.

When we try to explain the acoustic nature of music, or attempt to compose experimental musics, the ear's time constants and the lack of clarity at the level of perception arising from this become important; on the one hand, they can help in the understanding of certain musical rules that span the ages, and on the other hand, they provide acoustic limits for the composer (accuracy of frequencies, durations, etc.). So, for example, it is pointless to think up on paper, then play electronically, melodic microstructures of fiftieths of a tone, or subtle interplays of intensity of a quarter of a decibel.

Here we will concern ourselves only with temporal thresholds for the recognition of the different characteristics of a sound: to this end, we would ask the reader to follow us in a short experiment, which will give interesting orders of magnitude, and which he can easily do himself, if he wishes.

First, let us take a familiar, traditional sound, a sustained trumpet note, for example, recorded on magnetic tape. The tape is the meeting point between our perceptions and physical magnitudes (here time, represented by a certain number of millimeters of tape). Armed with scissors, let us cut out a whole series of sound fragments of different durations from several copies of the trumpet sound. With a bit of skill, we can manage to cut out a 1 mm fragment, which, at a speed of 38 cm/s is a little less than 3 ms of sound. When we mount it between two pieces of blank tape and play it on the tape recorder, we find that our trumpet fragment is totally unrecognizable: we hear a "blip" with no timbre, pitch, or even duration; in short, we only just notice that it is there at all. This is because, with such a short sound, we are below all thresholds; we can hear something, but we cannot recognize any characteristics other than a "blip." We can, still with this first fragment, lower the listening level until we no longer hear anything; the whole original sound, however, played back at the same volume, would still be clearly audible. So in addition we have charted our perception's absolute threshold for short sounds; in any case this is intuitive and can, in fact, be easily explained by energetic factors. We have seen that the ear's time integration constant is of the order of 50 ms; among other things this means that the perceived intensity of a sound increases with its duration, then stabilizes at a fixed value once the duration reaches more than 100–150 ms (i.e., two or three times the physiological time-constant).

Let us now take other, longer and longer, fragments of the trumpet-sound: gradually, the "blip" will disappear (and this all the more if care is taken as soon as possible to bevel the tape slightly to avoid an artificial blip), and be replaced by a musical note, where at first only the approximate register is clear, the nominal pitch only becoming so later, with longer durations.

Now let us make the following edit: splicing together two 20 ms fragments, not side by side, but almost—that is, separating them by no more than a few millimeters of leader tape—and listening to the result: instead of two short "almost tonic" impulses one after the other, we will hear *one single* sound: we are still below the resolution time threshold of events. If we vary the editing a little, this time inserting our 20 ms fragment right in the middle of any sound, then the short tonic impulse will appear as an "accident" within the surrounding sound, but we notice that it has lost its tonic note characteristic.

These last experiments can also be explained through calculations using the 50 ms time constant, and now we can begin to see the implications of this in practice:

(a) On the one hand, it plays a part in the perception of intensity; it integrates energy. As long as the sound phenomenon is no longer than two or three times the value of this time constant, it will not reach the intensity of its stationary state.

(b) On the other hand, it fixes a time resolution limit. This is why it has been called "thickness of the present."

(c) Yet this certainly does not imply we cannot hear sounds shorter than 50 ms, and in particular it does not mean we are insensitive to the originality of the attack of a particular sound, which sometimes lasts for only a few milliseconds.

(d) These rapid transients will not be perceived in themselves with all the details of their development, but they will merge into what will appear as the initial moment of the sound, giving it an often quite distinctive character.

This point provides the answer to a dilemma that phoneticians have been up against for some time. With the appearance of the *Sonagraph* in about 1945, phonetics found its most valuable tool and could move on from a qualitative empirical stage to using quantitative and incontrovertible concepts. The idea that certain consonants were very short was confirmed: it could be demonstrated that sometimes they lasted only 20 ms or even 10 ms. According to the classical theory of 50 ms—thickness of the present—and considering that, in general, consonants are surrounded not by silences but by other unambiguously perceived sounds, they would have had to come to the conclusion that consonants are inaudible. This was all the more absurd as consonants, in fact, appear to transmit the major part of language information, as can easily be seen: a text with all the vowels removed is still, generally speaking, comprehensible, whereas this is not the case if, conversely, all the consonants are removed.

In reality the contradiction only arose because the problem was badly stated. Familiarized with writing from primary school, we are highly conditioned, to the point where we often visualize words as a series of letters. But, in fact, the basic elements of language, those which carry the information, are neither the consonants nor the vowels but the syllables, even though in practice each of these is represented by several letters of the alphabet (with at least one vowel). Now, we observe that syllables last more than 50 ms: two linked syllables will therefore always be distinguished from one another, which accounts for the intelligibility of language. Seen in this light, consonants are simply useful names for the transients that give a distinctive color to the vowel in each syllable.

Let us return for one last time to our fragments of trumpet-sound, this time to discover the perception threshold for timbre. The experimenter who has been careful to cut the fragments while retaining the beginning of the sound will probably very quickly recognize the instrument from a 50 ms fragment; the others, who have cut rather randomly, will, even after a second or more of sound, be able only to recognize the instrumental family (wind instruments).

Yet others may find themselves in the presence of strange instrumental transmutations and will think, for example, that they have spotted the resonance of a stringed instrument. . . . This is because instrumental timbre is an ambiguous concept arising from very complex perception; we will return to this delicate question in a later chapter.

11.9. COMPARISON BETWEEN TIME THRESHOLDS AND DURATION OF TRANSIENTS

It is certainly wise to use time constants, as do acousticians, to explain the effects of concert hall reverberation, the perceptual limit for too rapidly repeated notes, or the blending of a tutti: these phenomena do, in fact, arise from time lags in the sound reaching the ear, which are of the order of magnitude of the physiological integration constant. What is the situation when we have to explain how timbres are recognized from instrumental "transients"? (20 ms for the trumpet, a particularly "clean" instrument; the clarinet needs 50–70 ms, the saxophone 36–40 ms; the flute requires 200–300 ms. We should note in passing that, in effect, only the flute seems to the ear to struggle to reach its timbre.)

On these questions we quote Winckel:

> If the two sounds follow each other with an interval of less than 50 ms, they seem to the ear to be only one sound: the "blurring threshold" is near to the ear's own time constant, and, like it, is probably determined by the physiological properties of the organs of hearing. When the secondary wave caused by its bouncing off the walls reaches the listener less than 50 ms after the direct wave, it can be considered useful as it reinforces the sound pressure of the primary wave. In truth, no one has ever very clearly explained the fact that the time lag between these two sounds is imperceptible when it is less than 0.05 s; perhaps the ear has the ability to screen out the echo

THRESHOLDS AND TRANSIENTS   161

within this time limit; this fact would also explain why the small time lags in attack between instruments of the same group—strings, for example—are not perceived, and why their overall sound establishes itself in time gradually, which apparently makes the character and timbre of the sound objects more vivid. It is doubtless for this reason that the timbre of a group of instruments in the orchestra is brighter than the timbre of just one instrument. We can also imagine that the listener's attention will be drawn toward the first sounds that come to him directly, and is sustained by reverberated sounds that follow less than 0.05 s later: we may try to deduce some of the orchestra's spatial properties, particularly its directional effects, from this.[3]

The important thing is to note that there is no contradiction between our remarks and the experiments reported by Winckel. These experiments involve the ear's time-resolving power, which "blurs" sound objects occurring within a time interval of less than a twentieth of a second (either in a "tutti," where the attacks always have a slight time lag, or when there is a lot of rebound from the walls of the concert hall).

Now, our earlier remarks highlight the perception of phonemes or dynamic details with a duration of fewer than 50 ms; this can be explained as follows: in the first case we are dealing with "separating" two events where the time lag is enough for them to be perceived *one after the other* and to be easily identifiable. In the other case we perceive *as a whole* two sound elements, which certainly cannot be dissociated but whose respective qualities are still noticeable when they are fused together.

We will be in a position to go into more detail on this second point in the next chapter, in the study of edited attack, and we will see then that the ear is capable of describing the steepness of attacks accurately to the point where it takes only a duration of 5 ms for the sound energy to appear.

11.10. SPATIALIZATION

It is interesting, from our point of view, to make a digression here into spatialization. It introduces a new differentiating power that has nothing to do with the earlier ones. Why, in fact, do we have spatial listening with the naked ear? The simplest explanation is that the sound waves reaching the two ears are "out of step." At 300 meters per second, and in the most favorable circumstances however, as the distance between our two ears in profile is only about 20 cm, this difference (20/30,000) is less than a thousandth of a second. Surely such a negligible time lag would be imperceptible? Now, an inexperienced listener can easily locate with his eyes closed, therefore by using only his hearing; the opposite experiment, listening with one ear and with the eyes closed, gives hearing with vague or nonexistent three-dimensionality, in which all direction and all distance are confused. So perhaps we should

3. Ibid.

allow that there is a particular differentiating power not just for the ear but also for hearing in general.

But some experiments show that, despite the above observations, spatialization is not a simple phenomenon. As an example, we quote an experiment by M. Haas, which specifically highlights the part played by sight in orientating listening. A live speaker is placed beside a loudspeaker, which "dubs" him. The listener does not notice the loudspeaker, even when it is turned up to 10 dB above the level of the live speech. When, later, the loudspeaker is gradually moved away from the speaker, the listener still does not notice anything, until the time lag between the two reaches the threshold of 1/20 of a second. Until this point the retransmitted sounds from the loudspeaker had merely "fed" listening, which, guided by the eye, was entirely centered on the live speaker.

We know, furthermore, that radio broadcasting studios are specially "sound-proofed," so an excellent recording studio does not necessarily make a good concert hall (see section 3.7). This is because we had to recognize that the same orchestra, heard live, then as a microphone recording, sounded different: the recorded sound is more fuzzy, less clear, than the live sound. Here, it is binaural listening alone, much more than the "audiovisual complex," that seems to be the problem. In the concert hall the listener heard both live sounds from the instrumental source and their reverberation, which, reflected by the concert hall, came from all directions. He could locate the former, distinguishing between the two "images" from each ear; as for the reverberated sounds, they "fed" his listening through a phenomenon rather like the one we described in the experiment above. On the radio, however, he hears only an indistinguishable mixture of live and reflected sounds; as these can no longer be localized or ordered, reverberation immediately becomes more significant.

11.11. MECHANISM AND FUNCTION

We hope we have given the reader some understanding that, insofar as it is an instrument of perception, the ear marks out a specific domain of perceptible data where correlations with scientific grandeurs are demonstrable but not predictable. The experimental musician, who manipulates this instrument (in practice, he "plays" with sounds), therefore owes it to himself to understand its elementary physical characteristics, of which temporal thresholds are an important part. But consequently, instead of leading us to explain the nature of the ear in *physical* terms through more and more subtle experiments, our study of thresholds opens on to the more general study of the temporal aspects of auditory *perception*: instead of laying siege to the *mechanism*, we will endeavor to understand listening as a procedure for grasping duration, and consequently we will be concentrating on *its original temporal functions*.

12

Temporal Anamorphoses I

Timbres and Dynamics

12.1. TIME LOCALIZATION

Sound information does indeed pass through the ear inasmuch as it is a mechanical organ. But the processes that prepare this information and continue it at a higher level elude our reconstructions and models. So only by observing and impartially describing the raw results of perception can we hope to reach a more accurate understanding of hearing phenomena. One of these, practically unnoticed until now, directly questions our sense of time: what comes before or after. In this chapter our approach will be through these "temporal localizations," building on our first experiments in 1957,[1] and so identifying an initial category of *temporal anamorphoses.*[2]

So here we are no longer concerned with determining time thresholds. A threshold, of course, has no sense of duration: it is a "speck of time," the smallest perceptible, more or less describable, temporal event. On the contrary, evaluation in duration involves going in a more or less conscious, controlled, or instinctive way through these "slices of present," which are no longer thresholds, since they blend and become a whole in the short-term memory, and so give that real-world

---

1. The first account of these, by Hermann Scherchen, appeared in *Gravesaner Blätter*, no. 17 (1960).

2. Properly speaking, the term *anamorphosis* refers to the distortion of the image of an object in a curved mirror compared with the object itself. We are using it here in a figurative sense, to designate certain noticeable "irregularities" when the *physical* vibration becomes *perceived* sound, suggesting a sort of psychological distortion of physical "reality," and which, as we will see, simply shows that perception cannot be reduced to physical measurements. *Temporal anamorphosis* is by and large the anamorphosis that appears in the perception of time.

163

grasp of the object that we call its *temporal form*, already in the past although almost present. Between thresholds without duration and those durations not formed of successive points, might we find some distinctive feature of time perception?

We must confess we had hardly ever thought about this. If it were the case, surely our many predecessors would have told us about it? We would still be just as innocent were it not for a decisive experiment that, as sometimes happens, we did by chance. We will give an account of it before moving on to a more systematic analysis, and we would invite the reader to imagine himself at our own stage of work, ignorance, and even ready-made ideas.

Musical listening, as well as practice, lays the emphasis mainly on sound attacks. The contributions of physicists are along similar lines, as we have seen again and again, with "transient phenomena," which supposedly give the beginnings of sounds both their richness and their mystery. But even if our listening exercises prompted us to question the way duration is evaluated, and led us from a linear concept of the way time is distributed to the idea that not all the moments of sound are equivalent in duration, nothing made us abandon the very Cartesian schema of a succession of moments: the first before the second, the second before the third. Consequently nothing suggested that we should look for a sound's attack anywhere else but . . . at the beginning. So this is where, in the wake of so many others, we looked for it.

12.2. BEGINNINGS OF SOUNDS

So, convinced that, linked to the famous transients, the first moments of sound held the secret of attacks, and thus also of timbre, and, with the piano, of the "touch" specific to instruments or virtuosi, we started to observe the beginnings of sound with the oscillograph. And so we compared the initial phases of different types of sound: piano, and later wind or bowed instrument sounds. We expected to find not a characteristic vibration line but at least an overall curve that would, for example, have explained the steepness of attack sensed musically. The experimentation was carried out on the first 50 milliseconds of sounds, this length of time being empirically accepted as long enough for all transient phenomena arising from the establishment of the sound to be over.

Our first finding was that the documents we obtained seemed to defy investigation. For example, two open Es on the violin, with attacks identical to the ear, played by the same instrumentalist, gave atypical oscillograms (fig. 4a); the same thing happened for two As played under the same conditions (fig. 4b). A more spectacular experiment involved asking a very good trumpet player to play a staccato with an accuracy appreciable to the ear: none of this sound's eight impulses gave an oscillogram similar to the others (fig. 5).

What do we understand by a "typical oscillogram"? An oscillogram that would be obtained under the following conditions:

(a) the samples from the same musical object (two As on the violin, for example) would give images with at least some features in common;

(b) two musical objects with different (musical) attacks would generate images that differed in a similarly characteristic way.

In fact, the oscillogram may have given an account of some aspects of the sounds under study, but it remained silent on the main point. What were we to conclude from these astonishing findings?

First, it is important to know what we are looking for and what we hope to understand: is it the transient electroacoustic workings of the complex chain sound object–microphone–tape recorder–oscillograph or the musical perception of attack? But above all, why should we want to explore the first 50 milliseconds and endeavor to find characteristic elements there, when the events that take place in that sliver of time are precisely not isolated by the ear, because of its poor resolving power?

We were not alone in such difficulties. Many other researchers were earnestly working away with infinitely more care and expertise than we—too many, perhaps, for they restricted themselves, it seems, to the comfort zone of their experimentation. Dayton Miller, says Fritz Winckel, was analyzing the first ten harmonics of a piano note (well beyond the first moments), played piano, mezzo forte or forte, and of course did not find the same spectrum; he therefore concluded that . . . timbres are variable, still, of course, in relation to spectra. Winckel continues:

> On the other hand, we still have not managed to find a satisfactory explanation for the influence on the sound object of the individual player's attack on the piano key. We are not unaware, of course, that timbre changes with the strength of the attack, as is shown by the spectra. . . . A medium attack makes the sound harsher, while a powerful attack gives a bright timbre not unlike a wind instrument. This is not enough to account for the various shades of sonority that the pianist can produce through secondary variations of touch; researchers at the University of Pennsylvania (U.S.A.) compared the sound spectra produced on the same piano by a famous pianist's touch and by a weight dropped on to the note: the oscillograms showed no difference.[3]

Here we can see the weakness of musical acoustics: problematic measurements and hypotheses, as well as a lack of specific observations. We are failing to see the wood for the trees. We will soldier on.

3. See p. 152n2.

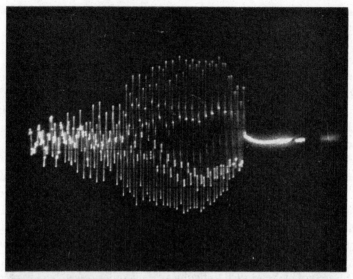

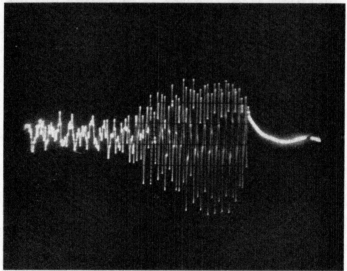

FIGURE 4a. Oscillograms of the first 50 milliseconds of two open Es on the violin.

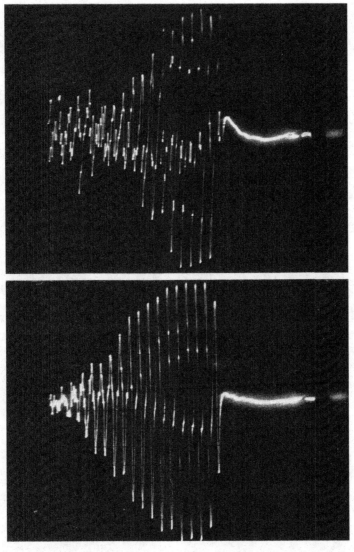

FIGURE 4b. Oscillograms of the first 50 milliseconds of two As on the violin.

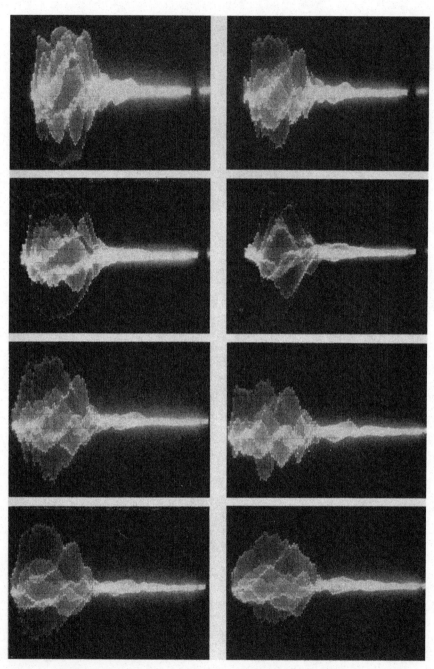

FIGURE 5. Oscillograms of eight successive staccato impulses on the trumpet.

12.3. THE SPLICED PIANO

Poor laboratories have at least one advantage; they make the researcher go back to simple experiments. Keeping to the experimental method we will describe more fully in chapter 13, we had just the tape recorder and scissors. How was it that we had not thought of this earlier, before embarking on a whole battery of delicate operations on the beginnings of sounds? Because, to our minds, the attack was so bound up with TEMPORAL LOCALIZATION that if we cut off the beginnings of sounds, we were certain to eliminate it from our listening. So it was without any preliminary conviction, and as one might carry out a somewhat absurd check to set one's mind at rest, that we recorded a bass piano note and, by cutting somewhere after several tenths of a second, eliminated what was certain to be the attack. When we replayed the tape, we expected to hear a sound with its characteristic beginning decapitated. Now, this bass sound, with several tenths of a second, then half a second, indeed one second cut off, *reproduced the whole* of the piano note, *with all its characteristics of timbre and attack.*

So, after this first experiment, we could already conclude that, for bass piano sounds, the perception of attack is not linked to the phase when the sound is being physically established, since the beginning can be removed without changing the attack. Hence, our initial approach, which was based on the study of transient regimes, became null and void *at least* in the bass piano register and was likely to be so in other cases. It should be noted that this strange finding, once we have got over our initial surprise, can be quite easily explained if we consider that the transients at the beginning of a sound occur precisely within a space of time below or, at most, equal to the resolving power of the ear. We have already pointed out this contradiction in the previous chapter. This proof allows us finally to put aside a persistent misunderstanding. We perhaps had no greater understanding of the attack itself, but since it was clear which way we should go, we repeated this experiment first of all with the various piano registers, then with sounds from various other instruments. We will try to give more details about these experiments.

First, with the piano we found that the perception of the *steepness* of attack varied according to where the cut was made: the steepness was greater if the cut was made in a portion with a steeper descending dynamic. With bass piano notes the dynamic line is perceptibly linear, and, in fact, these cuts can be made a long way beyond the initial moments of the sound without the character of the attack (or indeed the timbre) changing perceptibly: in practice we can cut up to a second into the beginning of the sound (fig. 6). If we go any further, the artificial attack seems less powerful than the original attack. If, however, we cut an A4 on the piano at 1/2 a second, or 1 sec., the sound becomes unrecognizable; it is more like a flute than a piano. In keeping with the general rule given above, we also note that

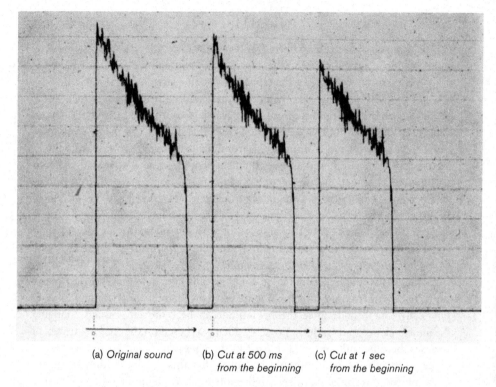

(a) *Original sound*   (b) *Cut at 500 ms*   (c) *Cut at 1 sec*
                            from the beginning   *from the beginning*

FIGURE 6. Bathygrams of an A1 on the piano with the attacks cut out: (a) the average slope of
the decreasing dynamic is constant; (b) and (c) the cut sounds are heard with approximately the
same attack as the original sound.

the dynamic of this A4, which is fairly steep immediately after the beginning of the
sound, is almost flat at the end (fig. 7).

Cuts that do not change the attack are difficult to make in the high register of
the piano, since the dynamic gap is very tight because of the brevity of the sounds,
and unless we cut very near to the beginning of the sound (barely 50 ms), the slope
after the cut is not as strong as it is at the very beginning of the original sound,
which explains why we obtain gentler attacks then.

It is tempting to extend this experimentation to all instruments that give the
same type of objects as the piano: attack-resonance. Say, for example, that we cut
into a vibraphone sound. Now, even when the cut is quite near the beginning of
the sound, we have to admit that the attack (as well as the timbre) is clearly different. This countercheck makes us clarify our vocabulary, on the one hand, and the
limits of our investigation, on the other. In fact, with the bass piano, we were in the
straightforward situation of experimenting on a sound with a stable harmonic

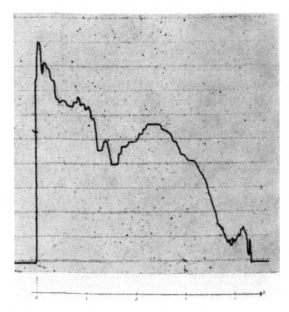

FIGURE 7. Bathygram of an A4 on the piano.

content: the cuts therefore only affected the steepness of the attack (the dynamic aspect) but had no effect on the harmonic content, since this was constant. It is not the same with the vibraphone: this instrument—as, in fact, we noted in most percussion instruments—gives a double attack, where the vibration of the metal strip, which seemingly constitutes the main part of the sound, is superimposed on the initial sound of the stick, which rapidly disappears. The experiment in deleting this double attack shows that this short sound is nevertheless part of what characterizes the vibraphone perceptually, and this is why, although the cut does not change the *steepness* of the attack (the vibraphone's dynamic is remarkably linear), it changes its *timbre*. This analysis implies a new type of ear training. Aided by the experiment in cutting, the ear learns to identify both a *steepness* and a *color* in an attack.

12.4. SCISSOR ATTACK

At this point, after these various trials, we must make an important comment: in practice, all we have done with our cuts is eliminate the natural beginning of the sound and in each case replaced it with an artificial beginning using scissors: the sound must indeed start somewhere, and we can only replace one beginning with another. To what extent is this "scissor attack" parasitic?

First we must settle a question of terminology. We will use the phrase "the beginning of the sound" for the beginning of the *signal*, materialized by the tape, and the term *attack* for the *perception* localized at the initial moment. Now, to return to our bass piano note: in our first experiment we made straight cuts in the tape. Now we make a 45 degree cut in the same place: the attack is slightly gentler. If we repeat the experiment with different piano notes, we observe that in every case the sloping cuts give gentler attacks than the straight cuts; the latter are therefore the only ones able to reproduce the piano's percussive attack in the right circumstances (a suitable dynamic slope).

We should note, further, that, for the piano as for the vibraphone, whether the cut is more or less angled seems less of a determining factor in the perception of attack than the dynamic slope of the sound at the place where the cut is made: we would say that the effect of the angle of the cut is secondary to the dynamic slope of the sound.

To summarize what we have learned from this first series of experiments:

· With the bass piano the attacks obtained by straight cuts are identical to the original attack (as, in fact, is the timbre).
· With the midregister piano these cuts give attacks that are more or less steep, depending on whether the slope of the decreasing dynamic of the sound is itself steep at the point where the cut is made; if it is made very near to the beginning of the sound, where the slope is the same as at the very beginning, we obtain the whole original note in both steepness of attack and timbre.
· If the cut is angled, the attack seems slightly gentler, but this effect is secondary to the one above.
· For percussion instruments, such as the vibraphone, or the high notes of the piano, in which there is a marked change in harmonic content in the course of the sound (the disappearance of noise because of the very short initial shock), such cuts give sounds with a different timbre, but the above rules remain valid for the quality now perceived, after ear training, as the *steepness* of attack.

We will now test these experiments on the "scissor attack" against the comments we made on the integration threshold of the ear (50 ms): it is easy to calculate that the 45 degree cut, which we have just said produces a gentler attack than the straight cut, gives a time for the sound energy to appear of about only 20 ms. We may wonder how far below its integration threshold the ear is still sensitive to the time it takes for the sound to appear: we observe by way of experiment that, from 0 to 5 milliseconds, the attack obtained from the straight or slightly angled cut retains the *same* character of steepness and gives rise to a slight sensation of shock (a phenomenon due to the ear's mechanical inertia; see section 11.6). When it takes more than 5 ms for the sound to appear, the attack becomes progressively gentler.

12.5. CUTTING SOUNDS OTHER THAN PERCUSSIVE

Now we will attempt to make cuts in sustained sounds and to assess their importance in the perception of these sounds.

We observe, for example, that with a swelled flute sound a straight cut distorts the timbre, giving an explosive attack that has nothing in common with the original attack, whereas a steeply angled (60 degree) cut reproduces the original attack. But this sort of manipulation on an expressive flute sound (with vibrato) gives an appreciably less strange sound. With a very short note, on the contrary, it makes the sound unrecognizable.

Conversely, a straight cut in a trumpet sound restores the tonguing sensation characteristic of this instrument's attacks on sound reasonably well; this finding is hardly surprising, for we know that the time for a trumpet sound to appear is very short; however, an angled cut gives a gentle attack that, in some cases (e.g., a swelled piano type sound) can cast doubt on the source of the sound and indeed even bring about veritable instrumental mutations. And so we manage practically to "transform" a middle-register trumpet sound into a flute sound.

The importance of the attack as an element in identifying sound with its timbre is therefore very variable depending on the nature of the objects delivered by the instrument:

- With very short sounds the attack plays a decisive role; it is characteristic of the timbre, as in percussive instruments (e.g., the piano).
- With swelled sounds of medium duration the importance of the attack diminishes; attention starts to be directed toward the evolving sound.
- With sustained sounds with vibrato (this is the norm) the role of the attack becomes almost negligible, and we may think that in these cases the ear is mainly directed toward the development of the sound, which constantly fixes its attention.

Cuts in violin or oboe sounds confirm the above findings: to study the influence of cuts, it would be worthwhile to work with fairly short swelled sounds: cuts to reproduce the original attack should be more or less angled in keeping with the steepness of the attacks themselves.

If, finally, we make cuts in rich, fluctuating sounds, such as a gong sound, the new objects obtained in this way may be very different from the initial objects: the cut, in fact, brings out a part of the object that was masked by an initial harmonic content, which was particularly overwhelming for the ear. Nevertheless, the steepness of the scissor attacks obeys the general rule that emerged from the above experiments. And the ear "learns" similarly to distinguish between two qualities: the *timbre of the attack*, a function of the harmonic content "discovered" at the moment of cutting, and the *steepness of the attack*, always linked to the dynamic slope.

12.6. GENERAL INTERPRETATION OF THESE FINDINGS

We have discovered through making cuts in the magnetic tape that the musical perception of attack correlates, on the one hand, with the *general dynamic of the sound*— that is, its *energetic development*—and, on the other hand, with the *harmonic content*.

So we have reached a first milestone, since these correlations account for all first-order phenomena at least.

Here is an overall review of these results:

In general every sound has three temporal phases (fig. 8):

- an establishment phase A
- a sustainment phase B
- a decay phase C

We should note that these three phases are often so bound together that we have some difficulty separating them. With percussion sounds followed by resonance there is no phase B; A is directly linked to C, which is of variable length (fig. 9).

We have seen that the musical perception of attack correlated in two ways with the physical structure of the sound signal, involving, on the one hand, the general dynamic of the sound, linked to its energetic history, and, on the other hand, its harmonic content.

1. The *general dynamic* comes into play through the speed of establishment of the sound (phase A), which brings us to suggest three orders of magnitude:

- very rapid establishment (lasting fewer than 5 to 10 ms), where the ear cannot "follow" the too rapid variations;
- medium duration establishment (about 50 ms);
- and finally very slow establishment.

The general dynamic also comes into play in percussive sounds followed by resonance through its downward slope after the beginning of the sound.

2. On the physical level harmonic content is commonly described in terms of spectrum, using a Fourier series analysis. The ear perceives the greater or lesser richness of sound, the distribution of partials and their development.

We find two different types of perceptions to characterize the attack, corresponding to two sorts of physical variables:

- the first we call the *steepness* of the attack, related to the dynamic phenomena;
- the second we call the *color* of the attack, related to the harmonic phenomena.

These two types of perception are in theory independent. Nevertheless, it often happens that an attack is both steep and rich (a sudden shock giving rise to an increased number of partials) or else gentle and poor.

The laws that follow apply first to sustained sounds, then to percussive sounds followed by resonance. In both cases they deal first with the perception of the

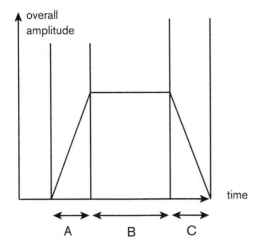

FIGURE 8. Dynamic phases of sustained sounds.

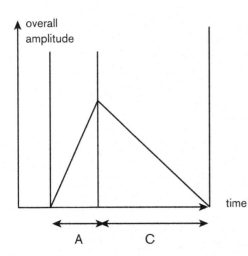

FIGURE 9. Dynamic phases of resonance-percussion.

steepness of attack alone, without taking its color into account. Then we will discuss the overall perception of attacks: steepness + color.

12.7. LAWS OF PERCEPTION OF ATTACK

First law: *To describe its perception of the steepness of attack with sustained sounds, the ear, as a general rule, is sensitive to the way in which sound energy appears in time* (phase A).

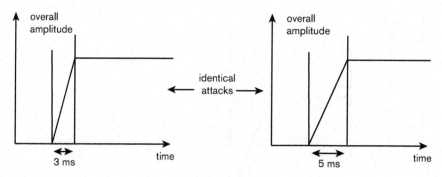

FIGURE 10. The energy appears in a time less than or equal to 5 ms: all the attacks are perceived as having the same steepness.

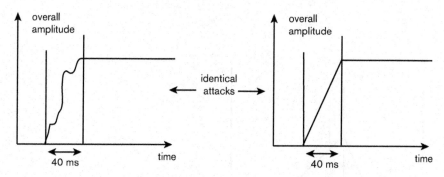

FIGURE 11. The energy appears in a period of time between 10 and 50 ms. To describe its perception of the steepness of attack, the ear is sensitive to the time it takes for the energy to appear but not to the various fluctuations that accompany this.

It should be noted that by this we mean the total energy and not the energy of a particular isolated harmonic component of the sound.

There are several possibilities:

1. *The energy appears in roughly 3 to 10 ms* (see fig. 10). In this case, whatever the sound, the sensation of steepness of attack is always the same: the ear is not capable of following such steep ascents, which then give a sort of attack noise (a result of the spectrum spreading out in the ear): this is a short click, which may disappear if it is masked by a large harmonic content (for example, in an attack with a rosined bow). This clicking sound is more apparent in relatively poor sounds (trumpet). It is the rule in all artificial (straight) tape cuts (see fig. 7).

2. *The sound energy appears in roughly 10 to 50 ms* (see fig. 11). Here it seems that the perceived steepness of attack is linked only to this appearance time and not to

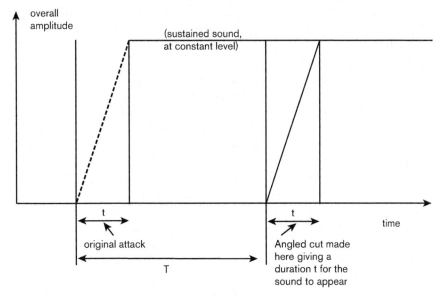

FIGURE 12. The harmonic content is stable; in this example, whatever T is, and if t remains the same, the cut will reproduce an attack *identical* to the original in steepness and color.

its fluctuations in detail. Take, for example, a sustained flute sound with an establishment duration of about 40 ms: we observe that a 60 degree or 70 degree cut in the tape quite perceptibly reproduces the flute's attack; now, with a "scissors" beginning, the attack appears in a strictly linear way, which is not the case with the natural beginning; the ear is therefore not sensitive to the detail but only to the overall duration of establishment of the energy (see fig. 8).

Experiments such as these can be repeated with violin or clarinet sounds, as well as others.

Moreover, *in the two examples 1 and 2, if the harmonic content of the sound is constant throughout their duration, a cut made at a suitable angle reproduces the original attack in its entirety, with its degree of steepness and its color.*

Indeed, in both cases the original steepness can be reproduced by making the cut at the appropriate angle, and in theory the same harmonic content would be found at any point in the sound. This rule can be verified with very consistent flute or violin sounds (see fig. 12).

However, as it is practically impossible, even with sounds such as the flute, which can easily be sustained, to obtain rigorous consistency of harmonic content, because a performer always allows tiny fluctuations to form, the cuts always give slight differences of color compared with the original attack. In addition, it is very rare for the beginning of a sound, particularly if it is rapid (example 1), not to contain some parasitic sound (the noise of a peg, tonguing); these noises, although in general not very noticeable, are nevertheless an integral part of the characteristic timbre of instruments, so it is only very rarely that we are really in the situation presumed by these hypotheses.

3. *The sound energy takes much longer than 50 ms to appear.* In this case the ear is able to follow the dynamic and harmonic developments when the sound appears; this finding logically rounds off our previous conclusions. It should be noted that here the term *attack* is only used by extrapolation from the earlier examples, for it is difficult to say where the attack finishes and where the *continuation* of the sound, properly speaking, begins; the concept of steepness of attack no longer has much meaning, since the sound emerges progressively out of silence. On the one hand, the technique of cutting will not now help us to study the beginnings of sounds; on the other hand, it may shed light on our perception of particular moments of the sound, which may be masked by the moments immediately before, by eliminating these.

Second law: *To describe its perception of steepness of attack with sounds that have a percussive or plucked attack followed by resonance, the ear is sensitive to the way the energy disappears even more than to the way it appears.* As we have seen, the steepness of attack is linked in the first place to the slope of the decreasing dynamic immediately after the beginning of the (natural or artificial) sound and only in second place to the upward slope as the sound appears.

Here, in theory, we should come back to the three processes described in 1, 2, and 3 on sustained sounds; in practice, when a string is struck or plucked, the energy moves in very quickly, about 5 to 10 ms; so the original attack can be reproduced by a straight cut, provided that it is made at a point where the descending dynamic has the same slope as immediately after the beginning of the original sound. At a point where the slope is less steep, cutting produces a gentler attack; similarly, an angled cut softens the attack, but this effect is secondary.

In addition, and as above, *if the harmonic content is constant (as in the bass register of the piano), a straight cut in a part of the sound where the dynamic has the same slope as at the beginning reproduces the original attack in its entirety, with its steepness and color.*

We may wonder why, with attack-resonance sounds, the ear is more sensitive to the descending dynamic than the ascending slope; it may be that, as the energy appears quite abruptly in both cases, the most perceptible difference between the sounds is where they decrease; the ear limits itself to accepting delivery, insofar as it is able, of an energy that establishes itself quite suddenly but disappears more or less quickly. The oscillations of the energy are all the more significant in their decay phase if they are still apparently the same in their appearance phase.

Other researchers had preceded us in this line of thought. "Karl Stumpf," says Winckel, "showed that a sound with a timbre and intensity that are constant in time loses its character to some extent if the characteristic attack is eliminated by any sort of procedure (cutting with scissors). Then, after an abrupt attack, the influence of which can be evaluated, there remains the sound object's *continuation itself*, with characteristics that no longer vary in time."[4]

We would have to consult Stumpf's original work to verify the quotation. Oddly, if it is based on experimentation similar to our own, it shows how far, in the view of the person quoting it, the attack is linked to the beginning of the sound.

12.8. EFFECT OF DYNAMIC ON THE PERCEPTION OF TIMBRES

The above experiments have helped us to reach a better understanding of the importance of attack as an element in the identification of instrumental timbre. Although we have been careful to note our findings, we should like at this point to summarize our conclusions. We observed, for example, that it was possible, by means of an exaggeratedly toned-down attack, to transform a piano sound (in the midregister) into a flute sound and that a vibraphone sound, with its natural beginning cut off, becomes unrecognizable.... In other words, at least for a certain type of sound, the ear deduces the elements necessary for identifying the instrument from the attack. We have seen that the same is almost true of "swelled" sustained sounds that are short or do not develop; conversely, the attack becomes secondary as an element in the identification of timbre when the sounds have dynamic or harmonic variations in the course of their duration (vibrato, for example), and this all the more so if these variations are numerous and unpredictable. We could, therefore, as a general rule, say that:

1. Every percussion-resonance type of sound has its characteristic timbre immediately from the moment of attack.

2. The timbre of every sustained sound with dynamic or harmonic variations will only be identified secondarily by its attack; the timbre will be the result of a perception that evolves throughout the duration of the sound.

We could also conflate these two statements into one: perceived timbre is a synthesis of the variations in harmonic content and dynamic development; in particular, it exists immediately from the first moment of the attack whenever the rest of the sound flows directly from this.

4. Ibid.

Temporal Anamorphoses II

Timbre and Instrument

13.1. TIMBRE OF AN INSTRUMENT AND OF AN OBJECT

Until now we have been maintaining a truism, the concept of "instrumental tim-bre," in keeping with the quite empirical definition in chapter 2: the sum of the characteristics that refer the sound to a given instrument.

In the last chapter, however, we alluded on several occasions to the *timbre of a sound* without clearly referring it to a specific instrument but rather considering it as a characteristic belonging to the sound, perceived in itself. It is high time to point out that, when the musician keeps on saying "a very rich note," "a good, or bad, timbre," and so on, it is because he does not confuse two concepts of timbre: one relative to the instrument, an indication of source in ordinary listening, which we spoke about in chapter 2, and the other relating to *every object* produced by the instrument, an appreciation of the musical effects contained in the objects them-selves, effects that are desired by both musical listening and musicianly activity. We even went further, attaching the word *timbre* to a part of the object: the timbre of attack, as opposed to its steepness.

But, defined in this way, the timbre of an object is nothing other than its sound form and matter, a complete description of it, within the limits of the sounds that a given instrument can produce, when all the variations in facture it may have are taken into account. The word *timbre* with reference to the object is therefore of no further help to us in the description of the object in itself, since it merely involves us in a reanalysis of the most subtle of the informed perceptions we have of it. If we happen to mention the *timbre* of an object, it will therefore be by virtue of musical habit and for the sake of using an expression familiar to musicians who understand

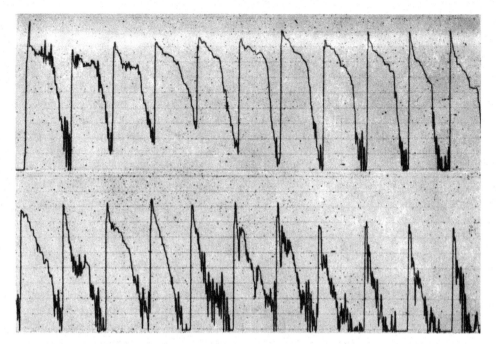

FIGURE 13. Bathygrams of piano notes going from bass to high register (arpeggio C, E, G-sharp, C), over seven octaves, twenty-two notes.

by implication that it belongs to a well-defined collection of objects. We still need, however, to reach a better understanding of this latter use of the term, by shedding light on the paradox that makes out that instruments have *a* timbre and, at the same time, that every sound object obtained from them still has *its own* particular timbre.

13.2. TIMBRE OF PIANO NOTES

If we strike various notes on the piano and examine both their dynamics (fig. 13) and their harmonic content, we discover several things:

1. A general law of dynamics: they are steeper and steeper as we move higher in the tessitura. The bathygrams of the six open strings of a guitar would show a similar progression.

2. More precisely, dynamic registers, shown in regular lines in the bass, and fluctuating lines in the mid- and high registers (these fluctuations can be revealed by cutting: in fact, if a cut is made in a dynamically steeper or less steep place, the ear immediately senses a harder, or softer, and even, if the cut is in a fairly pronounced dip, a progressive, attack).

3. Harmonic developments in the course of the resonance, also revealed by cuts, which reproduce sounds of various timbres, and can go as far as resembling a flute.

What conclusions can be drawn from these experiments on the timbre of piano notes? Since this instrument (like all other instruments, we may suppose) seems to produce notes with physical characteristics that vary according to the register, how can we explain the fact that it nevertheless possesses a characteristic overall sonority, in short, a *timbre* that is so clearly identifiable?

Is it the cultural conditioning of the ear to specific instruments? Or are there objective reasons, "laws of the piano," which adequately account for the perception of a consistent instrumental timbre, or at least explain and justify such effective cultural conditioning?

13.3. CONCEPT OF A MUSICAL INSTRUMENT: LAW OF THE PIANO

Looking simultaneously at the harmonic content and the dynamic profile of each note puts us on the right track. In fact, the higher the tessitura, the steeper the dynamic; and the lower the tessitura, the richer the harmonic complexity. We can illustrate these contrasting variations in the following way: a melody played in the midregister of the piano is recorded on magnetic tape, then transposed two octaves higher by speeding it up, and two octaves lower by slowing it down. In doing so, the natural dynamic steepness is changed by a constant factor (here equal to 4 or 1/4), while the relative harmonic composition of each note remains unaltered (since the entire spectrum is transposed with the fundamental).

Now we obtain a sound that is completely different from the sound of the natural piano at the same pitches: a melody played *on the piano* two octaves higher or two octaves lower; yet it is a completely unrecognizable sound, as if in some way it were coming from a new instrument, which is simply the "transposed piano." If we compare the "transposed piano" with the natural piano, we observe, on the one hand, that the natural bass is both dynamically steeper and harmonically richer than the bass obtained by slowing down; on the other hand, the natural high register is both softer and poorer than the high register obtained by speeding up. Finally, we notice that the transposed piano, which keeps the properties of the notes constant, is unbearable and "random." Its registers seem to clash, whereas in the natural piano they balance and complement each other. We can therefore say that an instrument such as the piano, which generates a whole family of musical objects that are different but undeniably belong to the same type, comes, as an instrument, from a characteristic correlation between the following factors:

· the dynamics (therefore the steepness of attack) vary in direct ratio to the tessitura;

· the harmonic complexity varies in inverse ratio to the tessitura. We could therefore write, entirely in symbols (since no quantitative law can express perceptions such as these):

Dynamic steepness × Harmonic richness = a constant, a formula that represents the "law of the piano" we were looking for to explain the "musical suitability" characteristic of the objects this instrument presents to the ear.

13.4. EXPERIMENTS ON THE TIMBRE OF THE PIANO: TRANSMUTATIONS AND FILTERING

We can verify these findings in a rather amusing way:

(a) *Transmutations:*

Imagine that we can obtain a sound from the midregister of the piano that is both richer and steeper than the usual attack: if it is transposed by slowing down into the bass register, its harmonic richness may then be exactly the same as the richness of the bass register, and its dynamic, similarly flattened out by the transposition, may also be the same as the dynamic of the bass notes. A sound like this can actually be obtained by striking a medium piano string with a plectrum, which of course gives a different musical object from the usual object when the string is played. But when totally transposed into the bass register, it is very close to a note played on the keyboard in this register. This plectrum piano resembles a guitar as well. When a slowed-down guitar sound is used, it also is like the bass register of the piano.

(b) *Filtering:*

1. If we take a bass piano sound (A1, 55 Hz) and, with the aid of a low-pass filter, eliminate the high register zone, the sound rapidly becomes strange or even unrecognizable: the ear is therefore sensitive to the slightest reduction in the high register.[1] More precisely, if we filter above 400 Hz, the piano, mutilated in this way, cannot be recognized. It is only recognizable if it is left intact up to about 1,000 Hz.

If we carry out the reverse manipulation, and this time without touching the high notes, eliminate part of the bass, we observe that we can remove much more than we might have supposed a priori, without the ear's having any trouble recognizing the sound; in practice, eliminating bass frequencies up to 200 Hz (which amounts to removing the fundamental and the first two harmonics) leaves the perception of both the instrumental origin and the initial pitch intact (see fig. 14).

---

1. In the French text Schaeffer refers to a high-pass filter; however, it is obvious from his explanation and figure 14 that as the high frequencies are suppressed, he is in fact referring to a low-pass filter.—Trans.

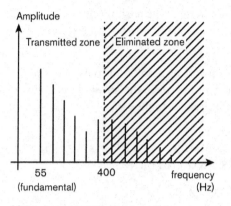

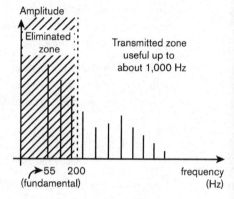

(a) Filtering in the high register: pitch unchanged, but timbre unrecognizable

(b) Filtering in the bass register: perception unchanged

FIGURE 14. Filtering a bass note (55 Hz).

2. If, on the one hand, we take a very high note (C7, 2,092 Hz), we observe that the ear is hardly disturbed by filtering in the frequencies above the note, on condition, however, that it does not descend into the frequency of the fundamental; on the other hand, filtering in the bass (just below the frequency of the fundamental) profoundly impairs the perception of timbre; in practice we observe that a zone of about three octaves must be left below the sound if we want to avoid changing it (see fig. 15).

What conclusions can we draw from these experiments on filtering? We have mentioned the harmonic content of natural or transposed piano notes. Here we discover that there is, in fact, much more to this content than a simple harmonic coloring added on to the fundamental. In effect, sounds with bass fundamentals have their energy in the high register more than at the pitch of the fundamental, and the opposite is also true: the high notes on the piano make use of bass resonances much lower than the frequency of the fundamental; perhaps it is the muffled thump of the hammer that is eliminated in this case by the high-pass filter: the note, deprived of its "punch," reduced to its harmonic vibration, would become unrecognizable through this alone.

Whatever the case may be, we can see that in reality every piano note has a whole range of pitches extending into the high and bass registers, where resonances that do not seem to be connected to the frequency of the fundamental, and a harmonic cluster belonging to the string or strings that are struck, operate simultaneously. The timbre of the piano is therefore based on a second correlation, a second law, a second invariant, which could be formulated symbolically, and with the same reservations as above: Localization in degree × situation of the energy in the tessitura = constant or: nominal pitch × "timbre" of the corresponding note = constant.

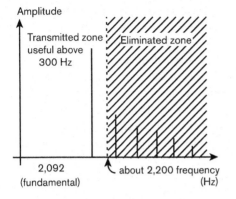

(a) Filtering in the high register: perception unchanged

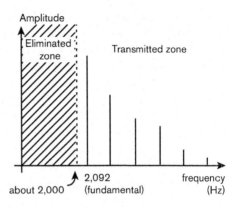

(b) Filtering in the bass register, pitch unchanged, but timbre unrecognizable

FIGURE 15. Filtering a high note (2,092 Hz).

13.5. TIMBRES AND CAUSALITIES

It may be surprising that justifying the perception of an instrumental timbre—that is, an apparently simply caused permanent feature, as we were saying in the last chapter—should occasion such detailed discussions. In effect, the *ordinary* ear, accustomed to discern and describe the energetic history of sounds, will never confuse an organ with a piano sound, or a kettledrum with an oboe. So what more is there to the concept of instrumental timbre? The question, as we have already suggested, is not in simply distinguishing a pipe from a string or a membrane; indeed, we should not lose sight of the fact that we are talking about musical instruments and that, consequently, it is ultimately the *musical* ear that is involved. Moreover, this of course is what has guided instrument makers throughout their long history. Returning to our earlier experiments and reflections, we notice, in fact, that even if the perception of an instrumental timbre is based on a causal permanence (a series of metallic strings, all made to vibrate by one percussive procedure), it owes its description as specifically musical to a certain relationship between the objects given by the various strings that is by nature *musical* and allows us not only to recognize, but also to evaluate and describe, one or other particular timbre. To the causal permanence (struck string) is added a certain variation of musical effects, desired by the instrument maker, proportionate to artistic requirements, and obtained mechanically in a variety of ways: doubling or tripling the strings in the high register, winding the strings in the bass register, coupling and resonance from the soundboard, different thicknesses of felt on the hammers, and so forth. The high notes, in particular, are certainly the hardest to "get hold of," and we could say that with these there is a sort of "wheeling and dealing": the impact is there to attract attention and make the note in question stand out dynamically, while its pitch value is weak, barely adequate.

So through the piano we gain a general idea of the concept of instrumental timbre: a musical variation "counterbalancing" a causal permanence and making it more flexible. From these findings we can now shed light on the discussion we started in chapter 2 on the timbres of electronic and concrete sounds. We had come to the conclusion that these timbres are situated on both sides of the balance that traditional instruments achieve. In fact, electronic sounds, calibrated in acoustic parameters, present registers that have no connection with ancestral contiguities: what irritates us the most about them? That we cannot understand how they are made? On the contrary. We soon get used to this: the ear is quite happy to classify and name them as "electronic sounds." But what it cannot cope with is failing to find the interplay of balance between causal permanence and musical variation, safeguarded by a law of compensation across the register, which traditional instrument makers had so much difficulty in achieving, and which modern instrument makers could no doubt manage to rediscover if they paid more attention to it. Meanwhile, electronic sounds announce their presence by an, as it were, "nonexistent" instrumental timbre. Thus the permanence-variation theory proposed in a very general way in chapter 2 finds a more precise explanation here.

In relation to the concept of instrumental timbre, concrete sounds, for their part, have the two characteristics of coming mainly from disparate causes and of not having qualities as familiar to the musical ear as, for example, a piano note: dynamic form and harmonic content. It therefore seems difficult at first to find a point where a musical element could possibly "counterbalance" the causal element and, consequently, to define clearly identifiable registers of concrete sounds; we come back to the same difficulty as for electronic sounds: the timbre eludes us.

In both cases there is nothing but timbres of objects, strung together in the electronic world but disparate in the real world.

Now, the reflections in this and the last chapter, dealing mostly with the piano, help us to identify two factors in the perception of instrumental timbre: the dynamic form, which is recognized in ordinary listening and sensitive to causations (the energetic anecdote of the sound), and the harmonic content and development, which are more specifically musical perceptions. This would lead us to a method for "discovering" timbres, especially in concrete sounds. We will illustrate this natural distinction between causalities and structures by means of an experiment to see how, by removing causalities that are too intrusive and specific to each object, it is possible to get nearer to the perception of musical structures.

13.6. CAUSALITIES AND HARMONIC STRUCTURES:
FUNCTIONAL ANAMORPHOSES

If we play a sound heavily loaded with harmonics, such as a metal rod played with a bow, then a piano chord that endeavors, as far as it can, to give an imitation of the complex harmonies of the rod, it is most unlikely that a traditional musician would hear in the latter sound anything but a crude subterfuge, a " putting into music" of the former.

But what happens if we get rid of the perception of causality, eliminating the attack by cutting? Clean cuts in objects, and the new relationships that develop because of these cuts, cannot be understood in the context of the localization anamorphoses examined in the last chapter. These are not anatomical cuts, at the level of an individual component, but macroscopic cuts, which separate "articulations of sound." But in both of these cases, by cutting objects out of time, we create other objects, and their content, as well as their relationship to each other, may be fundamentally changed. Thus we can compare a piano chord and a rod rubbed with a bow and find certain relationships between them, and then we can compare fragments of these same objects and discover surprising relationships between these also: it is this phenomenon that we call *functional anamorphosis.* In the example we chose, the sound of the rod is what we will call a complex "large note," the causal unity of which is indisputable, whereas its reduction to the piano is a little piece of music: we cannot compare a raw object and a fragment of language without bias. But by cutting, and retaining only the final resonance of the "piano piece," we will see not only that the functional relationships of objects fragmented like this are changed but that a real similarity of structure is revealed in the place of the earlier crude, anecdotal imitation.

Let us call the rod-object A and its piano "reduction" a. To avoid being satisfied with one single experiment, we will also compare a bow striking a piece of sheet metal, sound B and its piano reduction b. Let us cut these sounds into two pieces: $A = A_1 + A_2$ and $a = a_1 + a_2$, etc. (fig. 16).

It is of course understood that the experiment in question should take place acousmatically, with listeners who are more or less musical but less informed than the reader may be.

First experiment; final portions: structural relationships; sound A_2 will be played followed by a_2, then sound B_2 followed by b_2. We observe what follows:

1. Causality (anecdotal listening): the ear senses that A_2 and B_2 definitely come from analogous acoustic (and sound) phenomena but is not able to tell which and, in the same way, that sounds a_2 and b_2 also come from one instrument (which is quickly identified by the practiced ear as a piano).

2. Musical character: but we also observe that the ear can detect another similarity between these sounds, which is musically more interesting than the quest for causes, that is to say, a certain likeness of harmonic character. This is only a very

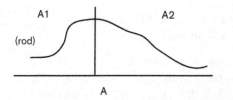
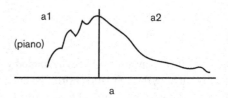

FIGURE 16. Functional anamorphoses.

crude comparison, where we need simply to observe that the listener clearly perceives the intention we had to compare A_2 with a_2, and B_2 with b_2: musically there is a greater resemblance between sounds a_2 and A_2, and sounds b_2 and B_2 (although their origins are different), than there is between sounds A_2 and B_2 or sounds a_2 and b_2 (with the same origin but with different harmonic characteristics).

Second experiment; initial portions: masking of structures by causality; the above observations are corroborated by what follows. Now we will play the initial portion of these four sounds, which clearly indicate their instrumental origins, and we will have to agree that here there can be no possible musical comparison between the harmonic contents. All the musical attention is now absorbed by the phenomenon of causality: the difference between the causal origins is so intrusive (a rod being rubbed and the percussion of a piano hammer) that the ear ignores any relationship between the harmonic characteristics. Here we must emphasize the psychological nature of the "masking" that causality imposes on the ear. We could say that when instrumental causalities are very dissimilar, the musical ear is blinded and becomes incapable of musical analysis.

Third experiment; illustration of functional anamorphosis: musical attraction and continuity; insofar as all the musical effort is directed toward a type of listening that is to some extent purified of causality, where the ear is placed in the best possible conditions to establish relationships not between events but structures, the importance of the following exercise will be understood, despite its crudeness. We will use the opportunity afforded by the tape recorder to play sounds "backward" and then listen to:

> A_2 played backward, followed by a_2 the right way round
> a_2 played backward, followed by A_2 the right way round

then

> B_2 played backward, followed by b_2 the right way round
> b_2 played backward followed by B_2 the right way round.

We observe that these permutations amount to varieties or variations in the musical meaning of the term. They are all musically interesting and different, which shows that ordering the components, reversing them, and comparing them provide new musical information, through a sort of attraction that demonstrates that the observed structural similarity is effective.

What can we conclude from these experiments? What we see is that the perception of a functional relationship is not necessarily linked to a causal factor: we establish musical correlations between sounds simply on the basis of their harmonic content, by giving them the same "neutral" attack (cutting with scissors).

Once the anecdotal attack is masked or eliminated, a new type of musical relationships appears, dependent only on the qualities of the contents, so that we can hope to find similarities between sounds with disparate origins and so establish registers of *concrete* sound objects. Is this enough to restore a timbre? Surely this is going back to electronic fusion? Not anymore. To find a timbre, we will have to establish a new balance involving an invariant suggesting a "likeness." Concrete materials, because of their disparity and the number of their characteristic sources, allow us, better than electronic sounds, to shape this type of timbre and thus to create a "pseudo-instrument," from which collections of objects appear to come.

13.7. CAUSALITY AND MUSIC

So, having drawn out the idea of the *timbre of a series of objects* from the idea of instrumental timbre, we are now in a position to make a few remarks about the perception of causalities in music.

Inasmuch as the perception of causality is directed toward the perception of an instrumental timbre, and is consequently at the basis of the *structures* perceived among musical objects, we can see that it is impossible to overemphasize its fundamental role in traditional music. Even if we think the composer uses sounds that are abstract enough to remove any anecdotal element, the fact remains that the mode of sustainment, for example, imposes its logical, predictable, functional nature on the ear. We fly in the face of the evidence if we believe that pure music exempts the ear from its most essential function: to inform the individual about events that are taking place. We are talking here about *classical* sounds—that is, clearly defined causalities, with an aural understanding (a particular type of instrument conditions a particular musical civilization) and occurring in registers characterized by specific instrumental timbres.

But the concept of the *timbre of a series of sounds* allows us to extend these conditions to any type of sound (concrete, in particular): to ensure that his work is well structured, the experimental composer will, in fact, use *cleverly unusual* sounds, such that the newly conditioned ear will no longer insist on knowing their instrumental cause but will persist in seeking out their *logical nature*.

14

Time and Duration

14.1. A LONG DIGRESSION

Sound objects, unlike visual objects, exist in duration, not space: their physical medium is essentially an energetic event occurring in time. We should perhaps have begun our reflections on the links between the musical and the physical object with this statement of the obvious; but, for greater simplicity, we preferred to adopt the classical acoustic approach, where the perception of duration as a specific phenomenon only appeared gradually.

And we began, just like acousticians, by eliminating time, a troublesome problem, and concentrating on permanent sounds—that is, pitches and spectra. Then we went on from permanent sounds to consider the most obvious psychological limitations: perceptual thresholds (which incidentally physicists analyze as physical data of the auditory system, not as interfaces between different perceptual domains). And finally we arrived at those apparent "anomalies" in the movement from the physical to the perceptual we call *anamorphoses*.

Now, what happens in the course of these experiments is a sort of psychological modification of physical time, as we will see in more detail in this chapter. We have made a long detour, it seems, to arrive at observations that can be discovered without the need of any particular laboratory and that anyone can make through a careful comparison of how the duration of various sounds is perceived and the corresponding physical time. The fact is that nothing and no one, in music or present-day physics, suggests that we do this; in fact, there is a deeply rooted belief, on both sides, that there is only one sort of time. For the physicist this is perfectly clear: time is a divisible, additive magnitude that can be measured with the chronometer. For the musician it is almost the same: a quarter note is worth two eighth notes and can be measured by the metronome, the musical chronometer. And so some composers today construct their scores with their rulers calibrated into seconds permanently to hand.

To demonstrate the naivety or the bias of these convictions, and following the method we have adopted in this third book (which will perhaps be contradicted, or at least refined, in the next), we will once again draw attention to the physical object materialized on magnetic tape and our perceptions. We could, while continuing to compare them closely, begin our investigation from either pole of this relationship. We could compare sound objects measured in a certain number of centimeters and listen to the resultant temporal structures they make. Conversely, this time starting with the ear, we could gather together all our musical experiments on listening to durations and strive for a better understanding of what "hearing time" really is.

14.2. RHYTHMS AND DURATIONS

This historical discrepancy and experimental lacuna, which we aim to remedy, can be quite easily explained when we see that music, like physics, has directed its whole cultural endeavor toward "normalizing" what was by nature not normal. It was part of our civilization, the vocation of which is to establish a commonality of practices, to domesticate a virgin natural world of sound by creating objects that can be compared. Instruments were devised for this purpose, as was traditional music theory. So little by little two concepts were conflated, which is incidentally a success for *homo faber*: the inner durations of objects apparently obey the same chronometer as the duration between them. This cannot be denied, certainly, in sustained sounds: so we can speak of eighth notes and sixteenth notes with a fair chance of not straying too far from perceptual reality. We only need to hear a virtuoso passage on the flute or the violin, an arpeggio in the medium register of the piano, and we are attentive to the slightest mistake in rhythm, the slightest shortcoming of the artist in this respect: if he hurries or slows down, if he is nervous, or if his playing is not "polished," we notice it immediately.

If that were the end of the story, we should be quick to declare that rhythm is king; we should reduce it, as we did with consonances, to a question of simple arithmetical relationships, which would easily account for the binary or ternary combinations of traditional music. But there is every reason to challenge the equivalence of duration and spacing when we are dealing with objects less easily comparable than those ordinarily used for rhythm. If, instead of similar objects, made to mark out positions in time, we gather together or compare objects that are variously loaded with information, metrical time fades away, as we will see, giving way to a perception of durations clearly related to the content of the objects. We might have foreseen this phenomenon but hardly its extent: truly surprising, it makes reliance on metrical time in music almost pointless as soon as the objects are vigorously "formed" or organized into highly differentiated temporal structures.

So we are going to suggest to the reader a series of experiments that highlight the discrepancy between perceived durations and physical time when the sound contents of an object (or a structure of objects, which, from our present point of view, amounts to the same thing) are very dissimilar.

14.3. EXPERIMENT ON THE "SEVEN DISSYMMETRICAL SOUNDS"

The experiment on the "seven dissymmetrical sounds" is the experiment carried out in 1959 that we reported in issue 17 of the *Gravesaner Blätter*. The sound examples we used would, it is true, have been better had they been simpler and more likely to lend themselves to more systematic observation; but this first experiment has the merit, in our eyes, of being historical and sufficiently important. It remains for our readers to follow it up.

As traditional musical sounds almost always come from two quite distinct temporal types—sustained sound and percussion-resonance—we endeavored, in order to remain on familiar ground, to create "composite" sounds, with a percussion phase, which continued right up to the sustainment, and a more or less prolonged resonance phase. These two parts of the sound can be clearly distinguished from each other, both by their different qualities and by the obviousness of two different factures. So there can be no possible doubt about discerning the respective durations of the sustainment and the resonance. The former, for example, came from a metal sheet being rubbed with a metal beater, the latter from the resonance of the same metal sheet once this stimulus had stopped.

Then we said to the listeners: compare the duration of the two phases of this phenomenon. Try to assess the length of their duration in relation to each other. This, of course, in acousmatic conditions: listening to the recorded tape, with no other information, and independently of any chronometric or bathygraphic measurement. Our reader can refer to figure 17 for the resultant bathygrams.

The seven sounds we had selected fall into three groups:

· Sounds 1 and 2 are percussion sounds followed by resonance.
· Sounds 3, 4, and 5 are (more and more progressively, but briefly) sustained creaking noises, followed by resonances.
· Sounds 6 and 7 have, as it were, permanent periods of sustainment, continuous for sound 6, iterative for sound 7, and all followed by resonance-silence.

What do the participants hear?

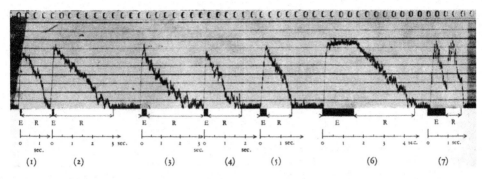

E: *sustainment phase*
R: *resonance phase*

FIGURE 17. Bathygrams of the dissymmetrical "seven sounds."

1. For the first two sounds it turns out to be difficult to make a judgment: the attack certainly seems important and of a shorter duration than the resonance, but no shared tempo is felt.

2. For sounds 3, 4, and 5, however, we can detect shared tempo: the durations of the sustainment phases are more or less equivalent, it seems, to the durations of the resonance phases.

3. For sounds 6 and 7 the durations of the (continuous or iterative) sustainment phases seem distinctly longer than the resonance phases that follow them.

Compared with these perceptual evaluations, what, in fact, are the various lengths of these phases in physical time?

1. For the first two sounds the attack is more or less instantaneous in sound 1 (simple attack) and sound 2 (double attack with an interval of about 40 ms). These sounds last about 1.5 and 3 seconds respectively, until the decay of the resonances.

2. For sounds 3, 4, and 5 the sustainment phase lasts 250 ms, 200 ms, and 300 ms respectively, whereas the durations of the whole sounds are between 1.5 and 3 seconds.

3. For sound 6 the duration of the sustainment is roughly a third of the duration of the resonance; for sound 7 the duration of the sustainment pulsation is slightly longer than the duration of the resonance.

This experiment demonstrates the following results:

1. The resonance duration of a (double or single) attack below the threshold of 50 ms is not really perceptible.

2. As soon as events that continue beyond the perceptual threshold appear, the ear can discern durations, but it does so in relation to the energetic events much more than their metrical duration. This is why in sound 3 it happily considers as equivalent phases that, metrically, are in the ratio 1/4 second and 3 seconds—that is, 1 to 12.

3. *A fortiori*, it is not therefore surprising that, in examples 6 and 7, where the two phases are in the ratio 1/3 and 1, the ear thinks the sustainment phase is much longer than the resonance phase.

It is this discrepancy between perceived duration and physical time that we call *time-duration anamorphosis*.

14.4. DURATION AND "INFORMATION"

All these results could be summed up in this statement:

Musical duration is a direct function of density of information.

It should be noted that we cannot, nor in any case do we want to, define these last two terms with any particular precision. What is the point of talking about "quantity of information" in relation to a musical activity that eludes all measurement, or of trying to divide it into problematic time units? We will settle for the words "density of information" in a figurative sense, which simply suggests a relatively greater or lesser quantity of differentiated (and differentiable) energetic events in a given phase of a given musical object.

This concept will be somewhat further explained in the chapters on typology, together, of course, with the variations of the qualities perceived in the object.

How should such results be interpreted? The short moments of attack or sustainment focus the attention in two ways: by the presence of a causation in action (facture) and by the significance of the developments centered on the sound (variation). The ear is thus harnessed just as much to the analysis of causes as effects. As soon as this first event is over, the ear senses, or presumes, that all the characteristics that develop through resonance were already there in the sustainment phase. In the first phase the effort of attention increases the sense of the duration of the event, and, it seems, the memory retains a major impression of this; the second phase only requires vague attention; curiosity diminishes: the impression left by this is less important.

To corroborate the above findings, we decided to include, in addition to the initial series of 7 sounds, the following:

1. A version of the first five played at quarter speed;
2. The beginnings of these sounds, isolated from their resonances.

The record of sound examples, kindly edited by Hermann Scherchen to accompany our paper,[1] played the first five slowed-down sounds, then the beginnings of the same sounds cut to 250 ms for the first 4, 300 ms for the fifth, about 500 ms for the sixth, and 500 and 250 ms for the last. This is what we observed:

1. *Slowed-down sounds:* the ear, clearly more at ease with deciphering sounds that in any case it already knows, can make precise judgments (all the more so as

---

1. We should also mention the support and advice unstintingly given by this expert and incomparable presenter of contemporary music.

this time there is a smaller gap between the active and passive phase in the density of information). So we see a very important phenomenon. Yet again it depends on the ear's "musical education" and, using the experimental method, on the participant's adapting to what is being observed.

2. *Fragmented sounds:* it is very interesting that to the ear, despite these significant mutilations, the "decapitated heads" of these sounds retain musical characteristics almost like the original sounds. With fragments 4, 5, and 6 the ear can clearly perceive that they are now without prolongation or resonance; yet, as the most typical phase has been retained, it quite quickly makes up its mind, perhaps remembering all by itself the effect of an almost nonexistent resonance. Only the sixth and seventh sounds lost their meaning in 250 ms. They need the first 500 ms to retain their characteristic rhythm.

So we can see to what extent the ear's judgments depend on a particular quality of events that is not necessarily part of physical duration: it makes short shrift of this type of duration, provided that it has just enough of it to recognize the objects under consideration.

14.5. SOUND PLAYED BACKWARD

The impact of density of information on the perception of duration would suggest that a sound played "the right" or "the wrong" way round may be perceived very differently where its temporal dimensions are concerned. Indeed, in the first case, after a beginning in which all the information seems to have been provided, the ear loses interest and "gets bored," whereas when the same sound is reversed (and begins with the resonance), it gradually wakes up and awaits the ending in a sort of "state of suspense."

Sounds played backward have two or three noteworthy characteristics arising from the fact that, in these sounds, not everything is given at once as in a direct attack; in a way, the effects come before the causes. Consequently:

1. *The density of information is better distributed.* Our attention can be more sustained and more gradual. Furthermore, the object is shown from a better angle (from this particular point of view, which has nothing to do with pleasure).

2. *Listening is more abstract.* The musical characteristics of the sound, in both the resonance and the attack or sustainment phase, are more clearly perceived, as our attention is better maintained because it is unable to identify the sound (by its facture): we have a sort of "disguise," an acousmatic veil over the sounds: the wrong way round tends to mask the right way round.

3. But, unfortunately, sounds such as this are *strange and illogical.* Not only does the instrumental causation of sounds played backward generally elude the ear, but it immediately recognizes the procedure: unless it is specially trained, it is difficult for it to refer such sounds to the causations with which it is familiar, and furthermore, it

is upset, indeed shocked, by the use of "unnatural" sounds. (By *shock* we do not mean an aesthetic reaction but a natural repugnance of the ear to accept an energetic phenomenon that does not fade away or in which the sustainment regularly "explodes" after a certain time.)

This strangeness is of very great importance in experimental music. It could be said that it is both the spice and the danger of a new musicality. We have just seen how, on the sensory level, it can refine listening, but this is at the price of a sensation that offends the ear.

14.6. TEMPORAL SYMMETRY AND DISSYMMETRY: ASPECTS OF TEMPORAL ANAMORPHOSIS

This experiment draws our attention to three sorts of correlations:

(a) Let us first go back to the question of the discernment of durations: will a sound played backward be longer or shorter than the same sound the right way round? We can find out through three sound examples. First, sound 1, then sound 2, from the first series will be heard both forward and backward. The participants can make the same comments on these sounds as before: however strange the sound, attention is better distributed, and the ear feels more able to identify the attack when it occurs at the end. In particular, the ear perceives better, if not the attack itself, at least what the attack was masking when it came first—that is, the harmonic content. As for the question of whether the sound played backward appears longer or shorter, this produces very varied, and sometimes contradictory, answers. For some the "suspense" makes the time feel long; for others it fills and shortens it. The important thing is the observation that the listening *journey* is neither of the same length nor of the same type in sound played backward or forward. By *journey* we mean the amount of consciousness it takes to cover the duration of the sound in the usual way.

The third sound example from this series is even more interesting: when played forward, two distinct phases (sustainment-resonance) are heard; when played backward, sustainment and resonance appear continuous. The two phases can no longer be differentiated. Playing the composite object backward transforms it into an object that is more fused together.

(b) Continuity and discontinuity of a group of objects by inversion: the phenomenon discussed in the above example emerges with remarkable clarity when the seven objects are played backward one after the other: here the three comments made earlier apply to the group. Indeed, whatever the unfortunately odd nature of the seven sounds played backward may be, it is clear that our attention is more sustained and that, in particular, as it is no longer disrupted by the masking effect of the attack, and the relatively slight interest of the resonance, it is distributed not only over each object but across the entire series: instead of a succession

of seven discontinuous objects separated by silences, we now hear a *sequence* of seven interlinked musical objects. We had already noticed that listening was more subtle and in a way more abstract when each object was played backward than when they were the right way round; moreover, the harmonic contents of the objects, better perceived in themselves, bring each other into prominence. At the same time, these seven objects appear to be connected to each other, with what happens between them no longer being felt as silences but as links.

(c) Finding symmetrical objects: The above experiments were done with highly dissymmetrical sound material. If, on the contrary, we try to construct sounds that are symmetrical in musical duration, we should not be surprised if we have to look for this musical symmetry independently of any metrical regularity, while taking into account the various phenomena mentioned above, where an important part is played by the density and distribution of information, or, in other words, the balance between causation and strangeness, information, and redundancy.

14.7. HEARING TIME

We will now gather together the various experiments we have described so far, in this and earlier chapters, to give a general outline of the question of perception of durations.

1. In the experiment on time thresholds, we saw that the ear cannot grasp in detail anything given to it in too short a time: it perceives only one single event. If the duration of the sound object is increased, and a period of silence is left for the ear (to reflect, one might say), it absorbs, recalls, understands what it had been too startled to analyze. From a musical point of view this is a commonsense measure: not to give the ear a lot of information without time to "digest" it. So we come to the idea of broken time, successive "bursts of duration"—in short, discontinuous listening time.

2. The experiment on anamorphoses reinforces the above suggestion: the ear's attention appears to concentrate on the instants when the energetic explanation, and in general the characteristic variations of the object, occur in a group: for example, if this is at the beginning of the sound, as with the piano, the attack mobilizes the ear at the expense of the resonance, which looks after itself. . . . The experiment with sounds played backward corroborates these findings. In both cases we can see to what extent the ear, when given or deprived of causal information about the object it is listening to, or distracted by or attentive to properly musical structures, can place itself in different durations, each of them original, without any direct link to physical time.

Until now, however, we have only listened to short objects of medium duration. Is there no moment when the ear lets go of time, when no fragmentation articulates its own naturally discontinuous activity, and will it not then begin to listen differently?

Put in this way, the question encourages us to reorganize what we know within a broader context:

(a) There is a medium temporal zone that varies with the nature of the object, in which it can be listened to in the optimum way. The musician's informed listening is at its best here. The ear is sensitive to the overall form of the object, which it perceives as a whole, without necessarily having to make an effort to discern its duration; it also grasps its internal proportions, its significant details. If an object such as this, independent in some way of duration, since this does not appear as a fundamental perceptual value, is speeded up on the tape recorder, it will give the impression of greater density, but listening will be more uncomfortable as there is no time for a detailed analysis of the object. In contrast, when it is slowed down, the object appears as if through a magnifying glass, and we lose the "overall view," which, as it were, eludes the temporal sound screen, like a light projection that is larger than the screen.

To sum up, within certain time limits the ear is spontaneously sensitive to a more or less balanced form and a more or less clear content when they are conveniently contained in an easily memorable zone, which, of course, depends on the nature of the objects. Within this zone the ear is not distracted by discerning the duration of the object.

(b) Conversely, disproportionately long objects, even when they are well formed, cannot be grasped in their entirety by the ear, which will only have the ability to follow them point by point in the course of their duration, just as the eye follows a moving object; or again, just as a screen isolates a part of the projection that is too big for it, a sort of auditory screen cuts the sound into "slices," easily assimilated pieces.

From the point of view of perceived duration, long sounds are distributed between two extremes: either they are too unvaried and fatigue the ear, which, quickly realizing that it has nothing more to learn from them, and since time takes on the nature of an endless wait, stops attending. Or else, too loaded with information, they force the ear into constant activity, leaving it no time to absorb, rest, recapitulate: perceived duration is then as if the attention ran out of breath at regular intervals: it is noise.

In any case, in neither situation does a disproportionately long sound display any characteristic form. We can see that classical music simultaneously uses objects that are within the ear's time frame (notes that are clearly delineated as defined sound entities) and long objects, "held notes." These held notes, which evolve hardly at all, are followed less attentively or with less accuracy, without any evaluation of their form; they serve as a medium or link between other, formed, objects.

(c) At the other extreme we find short sounds localized at their beginning through the temporal anamorphosis that is natural to us. The ear already cannot grasp their form, which is too rapidly delineated to be perceived, unless their general content is typical, determined, in fact, by the initial conditions. It is these conditions (dynamic slopes) that are retained by the ear, and it ignores the rest.

(d) It should be noted that the short objects we are speaking of are well outside the ear's temporal differentiation thresholds. With extremely short, staccato sounds there is no appreciable duration for perception compared to the duration of formed long and even short objects.

To sum up, "hearing time" has three typical aspects (not including thresholds, which are of little interest in music). One consists in following the object over its duration without losing the perception of the passage of time, like a moving object whose position is constantly being evaluated. Another consists in perceiving the general form of the object within an optimal time frame for memorization. The third consists in referring the form back to the initial moment through an informed perception of the attack.

The ear is thus like a device for incorporating time in three different ways around the optimal duration for memorization, which, of course, depends to a great extent on the form of the object itself, the nature of the information it gives, and the conditioning of the ear.

A mind given to symbolism or mathematical analogies could sum up this triple function of the ear by saying that, depending on the circumstances, the ear incorporates the energetic function $f(t)$, goes all the way through it, or, finally, retains only its initial information.

14.8. MUSICAL DURATIONS

Now that we are better informed about the relationship between physical time and perceived duration, we will take a look at classical musical usage and the potential of experimental music.

We will see how traditional music has sometimes managed to confuse duration and the spacing of objects. Conversely, we will see to what extent contemporary music cannot do this.

It could, in fact, be said that traditional music prefers to use:

1. Well-sustained sounds, with flat or highly profiled dynamics;
2. "Rich" percussive sounds that have had to be balanced by using soundboards to bring the values of the decay "slopes" of the vibrations somewhat closer together (the development of the piano, harp, etc.).

So we are between two extremes: held sounds perceived at every stage and percussive sounds referred back to their beginnings and their "slopes."

With sustained sounds, by definition, the temporal values of the sustainment can be brought into line with the spacing (the value of a violin half note is equal to the value of the corresponding silence).

With percussive sounds, if we allow that the slopes are more or less parallel in any part of the register, only the values of the spacing count; we become accustomed, however, to objects having durations that vary from one register to another and are ready to use dampers to suppress resonances that are too long.

And so, through many tricks of instrument making, we have managed to adapt psychological duration to an almost metrical time.

What happens in a "generalized," or experimental, music, which endeavors to use objects with very different forms and development? Tempos can be masked by very variable perceived durations, for which no trick of instrument making or performance can compensate. Compositions will, therefore, escape metrical time—except when this is desired by the composer, who in any case is the only person responsible for the way his objects are organized in time. In general, it could be said that he will use his instinctive judgment to contrast or mutually enhance the three types of objects corresponding to the ear's three "listening times":

(a) sounds with marked development, where the ear is required to listen in a linear fashion, with regular progress through time in accordance with the limited musical information it is given;

(b) "well-formed" sounds, where maximum emphasis is placed on the balancing of duration across the various phases of the object; these relationships, defying all metrical time measurement, will depend particularly on the dynamic dissymmetry of the objects, especially contrasts or similarities between modes of sustainment;

(c) and, finally, short percussive sounds, or artificial, as it were, isolated impulses, where the "impact" is highlighted by their strange nature rather than their dynamic slope. Such impulses will force the ear to "integrate" them into the moments that follow them, and it is therefore likely that they will psychologically mask, or, according to circumstances, be masked by, sounds that follow them too soon.

14.9. DURATION AND INFORMATION

If we really wanted to establish a way of measuring musical information, how should it be linked to the perception of duration? By approaching it through the variations in value that indeed seem to constitute the specifically "musical" in every deployment of sound? Or through causality, which is not specific to music but determines the evaluation of durations through the vigilance of the ear, which is always trying to explain what it has heard or predict what it is going to hear? The example of the seven sounds heard the right way round as a succession and backward as a continuity gave us a striking illustration of this alternative.

So it would not be enough to conclude this chapter with the idea that the duration of objects is linked to their form within a structured act of perception. We must add that as the ordinary ear remains vigilant in the midst of the most abstract composition, the ear will experience the length of the work in terms of "suspensions" or resolutions of mysteries or facts. It never pays attention to sounds impartially because it is never passive: it does not take in something measured out by the meter or the second but a variety of events presented to it. If the event happens as its energetic experience expects, it is only interested in the prologue, and this information dominates the whole of the duration. If it happens in a disconcerting way, as is the case with sounds played backward, it will recoil from taking in the absurd. So the secret is to keep it constantly attentive, without offending it, all the way to the epilogue.

BOOK FOUR

Objects and Structures

Reduction to the Object

15.1. FROM EXPERIMENT TO EXPLANATION

From the very beginning of this work, we have imposed on our reader a learning process not unlike learning a foreign language: we have employed key terms such as *sound object, musical object, structure,* and so forth, without a precise definition of their meaning, leaving it to the reader gradually to make some sort of sense out of them from the various contexts in which these terms were used.

At the very most we have defined them in terms of what they are not: the sound object as distinct from signals and signs; the musical object as distinct from the sound object, at least for now (although it is impossible to draw a line between sounds that are supposedly musical and those that are not, based on their origins and intrinsic properties).

This information could be enough to avoid the worst misunderstandings, which otherwise are almost inevitable. But, at the stage where we now are, it has become necessary to know, positively this time, what we are talking about. We will spend seven chapters on this attempt to explain, to define our domain and our method, beginning in this chapter by clarifying what reduction to the sound object is.

We must confess that after fifteen years of research, we are scarcely able to do this. This will doubtless come as a shock. Yet if we had not all been under the iron fist of an education that starts with the lesson, an exposition of principles and laws, and then moves on to the exercises that are the application of these, there would be nothing to be surprised about. From chance discovery to experiment, from experiment to explanation, we have followed the normal path of all experimental research.

Furthermore, as Kierkegaard says: "Thought progresses backwards." As soon as we arrived at the problem we had set out to resolve, we noticed that it depended on another, and so on, to infinity. The concept of the sound object, apparently so simple, quite soon obliges us to refer to the theory of knowledge, and the relationships between man and the world.

This is no laughing matter except to someone who has never himself experienced that inexorable movement from one question to another, which only intellectual honesty holds us to. Now, the philosophical questioning that then proves to be necessary by its own dynamic fatally distances us from our initial intention. So we will strive not to lose ourselves in a centuries-long debate and, at least when we find them formulated by philosophers, to recognize those principles that are in accordance with our implicit experience. We will choose, from the intellectual tools others have spent their lives forging, those best adapted to our needs.

15.2. TRANSCENDENCE OF THE OBJECT

So, for years, we have time and again been doing phenomenology without realizing it, which is better, all things considered, than talking about phenomenology without doing it. It was only after the event that we recognized the concept of the object postulated by our research in the definition given by Edmund Husserl, with an admirable insistence on precision to which we are far from aspiring. We will summarize here, and briefly, only what seems necessary to contextualize what, in a more restricted sense, we mean by *sound object*.

We will begin with the observation that classical, if not current, language considers the object as "the opposite, generally speaking, of the subject": the object of my concern, my hatred, my study . . ., in short, any point of interaction with the world, any activity of consciousness; and not only in the world even: there are also *ideal objects* (a logical proposition, an abstract category, language, even music, independently of the way it is played, as we have already pointed out in section 7.4), which do not present themselves as existing anywhere but within our consciousness.

What are the characteristics that enable us to recognize the *objectivity* of all of these? Husserl tells us, somewhat summarily. The object is "the pole of identity immanent in particular personal experiences, and yet transcendental through the identity that goes beyond these particular experiences."[1]

What does this mean?

Those particular personal experiences are the many visual, auditory, tactile impressions that follow each other in a never-ending flux, through which I aim for,

1. Edmund Husserl, *Logique formelle et logique transcendantale*, translated from the German by Suzanne Bachelard (Paris: PUF, 1957). [Translated into English as *Formal and Transcendental Logic* (The Hague: Martinus Nijhoff, 1969).—Trans.]

I "target," a particular object and the various modes through which I relate to this object: perception, memory, desire, imagination, and so forth.

In what way is the object *immanent* in these? Because it constitutes an *intentional unit*, involving *acts of synthesis*. These many experiences are directed toward it, and they organize themselves around it so well that I cannot account for the structure of my consciousness except by perpetually recognizing it as "consciousness of something." To this extent the object is contained in it.

But it does not any the less present itself as *transcendental*, inasmuch as it remains *the same*, throughout the flux of impressions and the diversity of modes. For example, the perceived object never merges with the perception I have of it. On this point we will quote a well-known passage from *Idées directrices pour une phénoménologie:*

> Let us begin with an example. I continually see that table; I go round it and as always change my position in space; I am still aware of the corporeal existence of the one identical table, the same table that remains unchanged in itself. Now, the perception of the table constantly varies; it is a continuous series of changing perceptions. I shut my eyes. I have no relationship with the table through my other senses. I no longer have any perception of it. I open my eyes and the perception reappears. *The* perception? Let us be more precise. When it reappears, it is never the same twice. Only the table is the same: I become aware of its identity through the synthesizing awareness that attaches the new perception to my memory. The thing perceived may exist, without being perceived, without my even having this purely potential awareness of it. . . . It may exist without changing. As for perception itself, it is what it is, carried along in the incessant flux of consciousness and itself constantly in flux: the now of perception is ceaselessly converted into a new consciousness that connects with the preceding one, the consciousness of the has-just-been . . . at the same time a new now lights up. Not only the thing perceived in general, but every part, every phase, every moment happening to the thing, are, for exactly the same reasons, necessarily transcendent to perception, whether they are primary or secondary qualities. The color of the thing seen cannot as a matter of principle be a real moment in the awareness of color; it appears; but while it appears, it is possible and *necessary* that throughout the experience that legitimizes it, its appearance ceaselessly changes. The *same* color appears *in* an uninterrupted miscellany of *rough sketches* of color. . . . The same analysis applies to every sensory quality and every spatial form. One single form (presented corporeally *as* identical) ceaselessly reappears to me *in a different way* in rough sketches of form that are always other.[2]

As for the *ideal object*, a mathematical theorem, for example, this is also transcendental in the most general sense—that is, distinct from the operations of

2. Edmund Husserl, *Idées directrices pour une phénoménologie* (Paris: Gallimard, 1950). [Translated into English as *Ideas Pertaining to a Pure Phenomenology and to a Phenomenological Philosophy—First Book: General Introduction to a Pure Phenomenology* (The Hague: Martinus Nijhoff, 1982).—Trans.]

consciousness by means of which I manage to formulate or understand it. When I *think about it again* after an interval of a few months, it appears as *the same* theorem that I *identify* once more. But, unlike the real object, perceived as external, *it is not individualized in time and space*, so the relationship between perception and recall is not the same. "Every clear, explicit memory concerning an ideal *species* is transformed by a simple and theoretically possible change of attitude into a perception"[3] (the word is used here in its broadest sense, the perception referred to being in actuality an intellectual fact). But even the very clear memory of a table obviously does not change into a perception of that table according to my will, "by a simple change of attitude."

Finally, for the sake of completeness we should add that the object transcends not only the various moments of my individual experience but the totality of that individual experience: it is situated in a world I recognize as existing for all. If I go toward a mountain, it appears the same as I approach it, whatever my viewpoint; but I also acknowledge that my companion walking beside me is going toward the same mountain as I, although I have reason to think his vision of it is different from mine. The consciousness of the *objective world* passes through the consciousness of others as subjective individuals and supposes it to be preexisting. In the same way, the evidence for a scientific truth supposes that it will be recognized by a scientific community for which it is valid.

15.3. THE NAIVE THEORY OF THE WORLD: *ÉPOCHÉ*

Why are we laying such emphasis on the transcendence of the object? Because the most common reaction, as soon as it is distinguished from its *physical reality* and said to be relative to the individual, as we have just done, is to confuse it with perception and maintain that it is totally *subjective*. So, then, it is difficult to understand how knowledge could have any effect on constantly changing images, points of view that are always partial, incommunicable impressions.

Beyond these two both complementary and contradictory approaches, the realism of the thing in itself and "psychologism," Husserl suggests a challenging equilibrium. Both, he says, arise from a "naive" faith in the external world. The mental process that would allow us to progress beyond them consists, precisely, in putting this faith "in parentheses."

What in fact happens in everyday, unreflecting experience? Busy perceiving, I am unaware of my perception. I cannot yet describe it in two ways, as in our quotation in the last section. All I am aware of is the perceived object: there is a table, with such and such a quality, about which I constantly notice new details, which were there "before" but which I had not yet perceived. I unquestioningly accept two certainties: it is the thing itself I see; that thing is external to me.

3. Husserl, *Logique formelle et logique transcendantale*.

The difficulty begins as soon as I decide to think about it: if I accept that this table is external to me, that it exists independently of the experience I may have of it, it necessarily follows that I do not see it "itself." There will be, on the one hand, "something" in the absolute and, on the other, the vision I have of it. As has already been observed, this perception is imperfect, since it always grasps only one aspect of the object at a time; it is changing, subject to illusion, and so forth. In short, I am "subjective." As for the object "in itself," it is unknowable.

I will try to explain my perception starting with the world. The external object will appear to me as the cause, or at least the source, of my subjective impressions. As I have a body, a nervous system, and so forth, I also am part of the world. My perception becomes the result of a series of psychophysiological processes (in which the "coach by coach" analysis described in section 7.1 will be recognized).

> I suppress the consciousness I had of my gaze as a means of knowing, and I consider my eyes to be fragments of matter. Now they take their place in the same objective space in which I am trying to situate the external object and I think I am creating the sight perceived by the projection of objects on to the retina. In the same way, I consider my own perceptual history to be a result of my relationships with the objective world; my present, which is my viewpoint on time, becomes one instant in time among all the others; my duration, a reflection of or an abstract space in universal time, like my body, a mode of objective space. . . . In this way an "objective" thought (in Kierkegaard's sense) is formed—belonging to common sense, to science—which ultimately makes us lose contact with the perceptual experience of which it is nevertheless the result and the natural continuation.[4]

What has happened?

Wishing to be lucid, I endeavored to submit ordinary evidence to criticism. I thought I had distanced myself from perception: "What I see as red is, in itself, neither red, nor blue, nor green. Red, blue, green result from the action on my retina, and from there right to my brain, of luminous vibrations of different frequencies." I may even add: "This explanation makes no claim to absolute truth. It is only valid within the present state of my knowledge, relative to my thought system, as just now the perception of colors was relative to my senses." I will then think I have reached the height of scientific cautiousness.

In fact, I am still being naive. I have cast doubt on the whole of my experience, which I challenge as imperfect, except the main thing. From my experience I have uncritically accepted *precisely my belief in the external world*. The highly developed discourse of science is based on this initial act of faith. The object I set in contrast as an *in itself*, ultimately unknowable to perception, is the perceptual experience that began by telling me the object existed.

---

4. Maurice Merleau-Ponty, *Phénoménologie de la perception* (Paris: Gallimard, 1945). [Published in English as *Phenomenology of Perception* (London: Routledge and Kegan Paul, 1965).—Trans.]

How can we escape from this naivety? By returning to perception, not to reject it, not to criticize it, but to become aware of it, which implies that we stop being immediately interested in its results: the information it gives us about the perceived object.

In other words, I must *disengage myself* from the world.

Époché, putting into parentheses, amazement, how can I describe this transformation of my gaze? We can only get there indirectly, by describing the transformation of what we are looking at.

To help us to understand the *époché,* Husserl compares it to and distinguishes it from Cartesian doubt. Putting the existence of the external world in doubt is still taking up a position in relation to it, substituting another theory for the theory of its existence. The *époché* means abstaining from any theory. But in order to move from naive faith to doubt, I have had to detach myself from that faith, to stop being its captive. The whole question is to keep oneself in this state of freedom.

The "switching off" of any judgment about the world does not shake my faith in the world. We know, in any case, that it is unshakeable and that the most hardened skeptic would stop at the edge of a precipice. But I am aware of it as of a faith: I see it instead of being led by it.

If I stop blindly identifying with my perceptual experience, which presents me with a transcendental object, I then become capable of grasping this experience along with the object it gives me. And then I notice that it is *in my experience* that this transcendence is *formed:* in other words, the *style* of perception itself, the fact that it never uses up its object, proceeds by rough sketches and always refers to other experiences that may contradict the previous ones and make them appear illusory, is not the sign of an accidental and regrettable imperfection that prevents me from knowing the external world "as it is." This style is, in fact, the mode in which the world is given to me as distinct from me. It is a particular style that allows me to distinguish the perceived object from the products of my mind or imagination that have other structures of consciousness. *So every domain of objects has its type of "intentionality." Each of their properties refers back to the activities of the consciousness that are "constitutive" of it: and the perceived object is no longer the cause of my perception. It is its "correlate."*

15.4. THE SOUND OBJECT

We now know enough to explain clearly what we mean by our concept of the sound object.

When I listen to a galloping noise on the gramophone, the object I target, in the very general sense we have given the term, is the horse galloping, just as the South American Indian in the Pampas does.[5] It is in relation to this that I hear the sound

5. The horse is no less present in the recording (without sight) than in the photo (without hearing). Acousmatics does not ipso facto create the sound object.

as an *indicator*[6] and around that intentional unity that my various auditory impressions organize themselves.

When I listen to speech, I target concepts, which are transmitted to me by this medium. In relation to these concepts, *signifieds*, the sounds I hear are *signifiers*.

In both cases there is no sound object: there is a perception, an auditory experience, through which I target *another object*.

There is a sound object when I have achieved, both materially and mentally, an even more rigorous reduction than the acousmatic reduction: not only do I keep to the information given by my ear (physically, Pythagoras's veil would be enough to force me to do this); but this information now only concerns the sound event itself: I no longer try, through it, to get information about something else (the speaker or his thought). It is the sound itself I target and identify.[7]

Of course, this sound object possesses the essential properties of the other perceived objects. Why, indeed, should the sound produced by a galloping horse be more subjective than the horse? At the most we must recognize that, with sound, it is easier to confuse *the perceived object* with *the perception I have of it*: the horse appears to me in a series of different and similar experiences, first auditory, then audiovisual, and possibly tactile; if I have only the sound, I am deprived of these cross-checks; furthermore, the sound object occurs within a time I am all too prone to confuse with the time of my perception, without realizing that the object's time is *constructed* by an act of synthesis, without which there would be no sound object but a flux of auditory impressions; finally, as it is ephemeral, the experience I have of it is unique, without sequel. Or so it remained until sound recording. When recorded, the sound object will be identical across all the different perceptions I have of it every time I listen; it will be *the same*, transcending all individual experiences, and we have emphasized how much several listeners with different specialties, gathered round a tape recorder, will differ about it.

So how is it distinct, then, from the physical signal? Surely, in fact, the concern of the acoustician is sound itself, independently of the information it might give about something else?

The fact is that in reality the physical signal is not *sound*, if by this we understand that it is taken up by the ear. It belongs to the physics of elastic media. It is defined in relation to the norms and frame of reference of this; this science itself, like all physics, being based on the perception of certain orders of magnitude; here, displacements, speeds, pressures.

As we saw in chapter 8, the acoustician, in fact, focuses on two objects: the sound object, which he listens to, and the signal, which he measures. A victim of

6. We have abandoned the terms *signal* and even more *sign* to refer to this.

7. This intention to listen *only* to the sound object we call *reduced listening*. It was introduced at the end of chapter 8, and it will be described in more detail in the next section.

the error of perspective criticized in the last section, which sees the origin of our perceptions in the external world, he simply has to present the physical signal at the outset, consider listening as its outcome, and the sound object as a subjective by-product. This is, indeed, the schema that he implicitly accepts when he applies the information received from the former directly to the latter, thinking that in this way he is getting nearer to reality.

He is forgetting that *it is the sound object, given during perception, that indicates the signal to be studied* and that there cannot be any question of reconstructing it from the signal. The proof of this is that there is no principle of physics that would enable him not only to identify but to have any idea of, the three sounds, C, E, G, contained (and blended together) in a few centimeters of magnetic tape.

The fact remains that the decision to listen to a sound object with no other intention than to hear better, and more, every time we listen is more easily said than done.

Most of the time, as we have seen, my listening targets *something else*, and I hear only indicators or signs. Even if I attend to the sound object, my listening will for an initial period be *referential listening*. In other words, there will be no point in being interested in the sound itself; at first I will still be incapable of saying anything else about the sound than "it's a galloping horse," "it's a creaking door," "it's a G-flat on the clarinet," "it's 920 periods per second," it's "Hello, hello." The cleverer I have become at interpreting these sound indicators, the more difficult it will be for me to hear the objects. The better I understand a language, the more difficult it will be to *perceive it with my ear*.

Compared with these referential listening modes, therefore, listening to the sound object necessitates a new awareness: "What are the perceptions from which I derived these indicators? How did I recognize that voice? How, purely in terms of sound, can I describe galloping? What precisely did I hear?" I have to go back to the auditory experience, take hold of my impressions again, to discover, through them, information about the sound object and not the horse. This is what could give the impression that music theory inclines to subjectivity. In reality it is a "going back to the beginnings"—to the "founding experience" as Husserl would say—which is made necessary by a *change of object*. Until a new type of training becomes possible, and another frame of reference (this time appropriate for the sound object) is devised, I must *free myself from the conditioning* created by my former habits and run the gauntlet of the *épaché*. This has nothing to do with a return to nature. Nothing is more natural to us than to go along with our conditioning. We are talking about an *antinatural* effort to see what, previously, determined our consciousness without our knowing.

15.5. REDUCED LISTENING

We saw in chapter 8 that ordinary listening refers back indiscriminately to the event or the meaning, without our ever being particularly aware of where we have come from or where we want to go. Do we want to listen to the accuracy of this note, that violinist's vibrato, the quality of this violin? Are we starting out from professional experience, superficial amateurism, or the shores of the Danube? So whether we are listening to a discourse in words or music, in familiar or unknown language systems, everyone's aim will appear specific to him (people say, wrongly, subjective), not because the objects of listening tend to be confused with "states of mind" but because each individual will target different objects, or perhaps change objects from one moment to another. They will, however, be precise objects, magnetized by a whole "field" of consciousness, where both the *natural* and the *cultural* come into play.

If we vigorously push all that aside—and what diligence, what repeated exercises, what patience, and what new rigor we will need!—could we, by freeing ourselves from the ordinary, "throwing out the natural" as well as the cultural, find an authentic *sound object*, the offspring of the *époché*, that, if possible, would be accessible to every listener? We have already outlined this listening discipline, and its corresponding schema, in section 8.9 at the end of book 2. We should say straightaway that it is not so easy to empty our minds quickly or completely of its usual contents, its automatic references to indicators or values that will always guide everyone's perceptions. But it is possible that little by little these differences will become blurred, and everyone will hear the sound object, if not like his neighbor, at least in much the same way, with the same aim. For we can *direct our interest elsewhere* without fundamentally disrupting the "constitutive" intention that governs the structure: *ceasing to listen to an event through the intermediary of sound, we will still be listening to sound as a sound event.* This means that the identification criteria will remain the same. The objects we then discover coincide exactly in time with the structure and unity of events. Listening to the sound object given by a creaking door, we can very easily detach our interest from the door and focus on the creaking alone. But the history of the door and the creaking coincide precisely in time: the sound object's coherence is the same as the coherence of the energetic event. In speech this unity would be the unity of respiration or articulation, in music of the instrumental gesture. *The sound object is the coming together of an acoustic action and a listening intention.*

Take the example of the arpeggio: musical listening, analogous to linguistic listening, will recognize a pitch structure, which can be broken down *into several musical objects* coinciding with the notes. Natural listening will recognize the unity of the instrumental gesture and, following the same criteria, musicianly listening, concentrating on the energetic, will discern *one single sound object.*

Now take another example: if we listen to a not-too-rapid drumroll, we may hesitate about the definition of the object. Will we include the whole of the drumroll in it, or will we hear it as a succession of percussive sounds, each of which should count as an object? We can see straightaway that the reasons for hesitation are not the same. In the case of the arpeggio, going from note objects to bow-stroke objects amounts to a *change of intention*. With the drumroll we are only dealing with the choice of level of complexity, depending on whether our attention is more or less stimulated. It is rather like examining a visual object with a magnifying glass and finding it more complex than it appeared to the naked eye. But we are still on the same level of sound objects and structures. In the case of the arpeggio, musical objects heard through musical references become a sound object, defined by its belonging to sound-event structures. The two are not the same, any more than semantic units are the same as phonetic units.

15.6. GESTALTTHEORIE

Although the concept of musical object has until now scarcely been mentioned except by ourselves, it tallies with many other experiences. For almost fifty years now there has been a new awareness, expressed in various and more or less radical terms, that links what we see or hear with what we are. It is expressed in two words, which have taken on an increasing, one might say a tyrannical, importance: *form* and *structure*, between which, for the time being, we will make no distinction.

For Koehler, Wertheimer, or Koffka, *Gestalt* was a new descriptive principle for perception, behavior, intellectual procedures, standing in opposition to the concepts of simple element, measurement, and summation that prevailed in physics.

From a phenomenological point of view, *psychologists of form*[8] could be criticized for their "amphibious" stance: they refuse to reconstruct perception artificially from simple sensations, which respond immediately to stimuli, and immediately rebuild a physical world parallel to the perceived world, but independent of it, which, though it may no longer be the cause of the perceived world, remains its condition. The ambiguity is particularly noticeable in Wertheimer's concept of *good form*, or *isomorphism*, dear to Koehler. We will simply refer our reader to Merleau-Ponty's appraisal, which, already penetrating in *Phénoménologie de la perception*, becomes severe criticism in *Le visible et l'invisible*.[9]

For his part, Paul Fraisse, in his *Manuel pratique de psychologie expérimentale*,[10] informs us that *Gestalttheorie* is both accepted and outdated. It is, in short, a classic of a historical stage in psychology, which only the self-taught such as ourselves would spend any time discussing. We could immediately reply to this that this is not our impression: even if the word *form* is widespread, it does not follow that the

8. Adherents of *Gestalttheorie*, also called gestaltists.

9. Maurice Merleau-Ponty, *Le visible et l'invisible* (Paris: Gallimard, 1964). Published in English as *The Visible and the Invisible*, trans. Alphonso Lingis (Evanston, IL: Northwestern University Press, 1968).—Trans.

10. Paul Fraisse, *Manuel pratique de psychologie expérimentale* (Paris: PUF, 1956).—Trans.

change of mind-set implicit in *Gestalttheorie*, the break with positivist or mechanistic thought systems, is a fait accompli in every field. And particularly not in musical acoustics.

Moreover, despite—or perhaps because of—the lack of rigor in their philosophical stance, the gestaltists have carried out a series of experiments that no one thinks of challenging, even if it means interpreting them differently. We cannot, at the very least, deny that the concept of form has been useful here. What exactly is it?

If we believe Lalande's philosophical dictionary, *forms* are "wholes, constituting autonomous units, showing internal cohesiveness and having their own laws. It follows that each component's way of being depends on the structure of the whole and the laws that govern it. Neither psychologically nor physiologically does the component pre-exist the whole. . . . Knowledge about the whole and its laws cannot be deduced from separate knowledge about the parts that are found in it."[11]

The classic example of form—historically the first definition ever given—is the melody that cannot be reduced to the series of notes of which it is composed. It remains recognizable in transposition, where the pitches of all the notes are changed but where the relationships between the pitches are preserved.

Conversely, altering these relationships by changing one single note turns it into a different melody.

But one isolated note, against a background of silence, is also a form. It appears as a *figure* standing out against a *background*. It is similar, in the visual domain, to a spot of color on a sheet of white paper.

We never perceive anything as a single element, or, at least, the element never presents itself as anything other than a unit detached from a complex whole. The more robust the form of the whole, the more stable, robustly individualized, will its elements seem to us, and, paradoxically, the less conditioned by that form will we believe them to be.

Therefore, most of the gestaltists' experiments will consist in disconcerting our perceptual system, shaking up the solidity of the world to take it by surprise in the process of formation: studying pathological cases and optical illusions; presenting ambiguous forms where the figure and the background can subvert each other: at one time a black vase on a white background, at another two white profiles on a black background; disrupting our frame of reference: total darkness with a moving point of light, mirrors at an angle, spectacles to invert images on the retina, and so on.

Through such slippages a problem comes to light: the demarcation of the object, which was masked by being too obvious. The fact is that the units that appear to us

11. Variant, with exactly the same meaning: "A part of a whole is entirely different from the same part in isolation or as part of another whole." [Schaeffer refers here to André Lalande, *Vocabulaire technique et critique de la philosophie* (Paris: Alcan, 1926).—Trans.]

are not only likely to be different once they are part of another whole. They are likely not even to appear as units. The trick pictures where we are invited to find Napoleon in what seems at first sight to be a woodland scene are a good example: a line, which represented the outline of a branch standing out against the sky, suddenly changes its function, to become the outline of a profile against the amorphous background that the branch of a moment ago has become. Certain features, a moment ago independent of each other, have reorganized themselves into a new figure. A detail, essential just now, fades into the background, another heaves into the foreground, and yet another is omitted altogether because it does not cohere with the main form.

15.7. GESTALT, FORM, STRUCTURE

How are we going to use this concept for our own purposes? We must first clarify an initial point. This is the term *structure*, which we will use in the sense of *organized entity* instead of *form*, the equivalent of *Gestalt*. We will, in fact, need the latter term for a very precise meaning: the *temporal form* of the object, as opposed to its *matter*.

Later, we will also have to talk about *structure* in the restricted sense of Lalande's definition: the term will no longer refer to the *organized whole* (perceived structures) but the activities that tend to organize wholes (perceptual structures). Whether we call it *form* or *structure*, the organized whole can be an *activity* as well as its *correlate, perception* as well as the *perceived*, the action as well as the observable behavior through which this action is externally expressed, or the coherent changes it introduces into the world.

If the categories subjective and objective are in constant correlation, it is inevitable that the same concept, and therefore the same word, will apply to them.

Now we will return to the example of the melody we quoted a while ago:

1. This melody forms a whole—*a structure*, therefore—of which the notes are the parts. Within this whole they are perceived as simple units, constituent elements.

But each one of these notes, if I consider it carefully, may appear *as a structure in itself*, with an internal organization.

So up to this point there is no more than a difference in complexity between the whole and its components. Choosing to consider the note as a part of a whole, or as an organized whole, is choosing a level of complexity. A question of attentiveness. But things are not so simple. When I break down the melody into notes, and when I break down a note into its constituent elements, *I am not following the same criteria*. It is not only that I am more or less attentive that makes what a moment ago seemed simple appear complex. *With the change of level comes a change of intention*. We will return to this problem. We needed to point it out at this stage to avoid any ambiguity.

2. Whether I listen to a note or a melody, it is against a background. We have already spoken about this relationship in chapters 5 and 6. It is the relationship between what I hear—which I identify as a figure—and what I perceive with my ear: a background of sound (silence, which in any case is always relative, also being a background of sound, comparable to the blank page).

The figure-background whole is also a structure in which the two components are indissolubly linked (we only ever perceive a figure against a background, and the background is only perceived as such in relation to the figure). At the same time, they are at war. I can choose to hear either a conversation against a background of music or a piece of music against a background of conversation but never both structures simultaneously: if I want to hear the background of sound, it immediately becomes a heard figure, at one and the same time destroying the preceding figure, which becomes the background.

When we look more closely, we find the same antagonism between the parts and the whole. Listening to each note as an "autonomous unit" destroys the melody. (Thus, certain drugs, changing the perception of the duration in which the melody would normally take place, transform the latter into a succession of isolated sound events.)

3. Finally, we may suppose that this melody is a scale. If so, this scale will be an efficiently perceived structure, in sense 1. Nonetheless, every melody, with its possible "wrong notes," will be heard with reference to the scale to which we are accustomed.

What is this Western scale that conditions our whole perception without itself being perceived? It is a structure as well, obviously, but *a reference structure*, at the moment implicitly suggested in the abstract. It is an integral part of a *musical system*, which is to the melody I hear as the code of etiquette to the conduct of the visitor who, at this very moment, is sitting in my armchair.

15.8. THE OBJECT-STRUCTURE PAIR

How is it that the concept of the object, which is the central topic of this treatise, should be so novel and surprising in music, whereas the term *structure* is all the rage? Did we not say that they were synonymous or, at least, embedded in each other?

It is because, in fact, the term *structure*, which is used all the time and with absolutely any meaning, ultimately means nothing at all and throws us off the scent.

We have just mentioned three "levels," *each one coming under* the pair object-structure but only on condition that they are clearly distinguished from each other.

1. The most accessible, let us say *ordinary*, level in the sense of the listening mode of the same name, is a *group of notes*. Here the object-structure relationship

is immediately obvious. The notes are the component objects of this structure. This little statement, despite appearing all too obvious, is nevertheless already misleading. I notice, as did the first gestaltists, that this melody appears to me to be identical through different transpositions and orchestrations: so I focus on it more as an object *(identified in various contexts)*; and then I explain its permanence by its *structure*, which *describes* it.

2. If, however, I focus on each note in isolation, I am forced to acknowledge that when they were heard in the melody, I remembered only their pitch and that to hear them as objects in their turn, I have to separate them out from each other. Perhaps if I listen more carefully to each one, this will reveal their internal complexity: I will hear unnoticed qualities, and perhaps, like Helmholtz, a "melody" of harmonics, relating their pitches to my earlier experience of "melodies." . . . So I now go on to scrutinize the *note*, no longer as the *object* revealed to me in the earlier melodic structure but as a structure in itself, which is not necessarily simple. The last section in fact stated that this object could not necessarily be resolved using the same structural schemas that explain or resolve the level above. This is well known in physics: the structure of the atom does not in any way indicate the structure of its nucleus.

3. Finally, the melody we assumed was formed of *the notes of the temperament—* and why should we not assume this, at least in the West?—could just as well have been an Indian, Chinese, or quarter-tone *motif*. The laws of *Gestalt* would apply just as well. Even better, instead of being scalar[12] this melody could be a continuous glissando, an arabesque of pitches, or finally a concrete *motif*: dynamic profile, variation of mass. This fragment is still recognizable and relatively transposable. It is still a form that lends itself to the same type of analysis. So we must look elsewhere for both what is common to and what is distinctive in experiences such as the *melodic phrase*, which is canonical and which, in addition, has a *reference structure* appropriate to a *system*.

A question now arises that is likely to dominate all research of this type: are we dealing with a problem specific to music, concerning the perception of our *auditory structures*, or a more general one, to do with *perceptual structures* themselves, whatever the sense involved?

In the first case, music, as a closed domain, will only have to look to the empiricism of its own experiments to gradually differentiate its objects, its structures, and its systems.

In the second, music would be one of the training grounds for more general, interdisciplinary research, which often comes under the aegis of *structuralism*.

Saussure for one, and above all Troubetzkoi and Jakobson, with the Prague School, were the promoters of a development so terrifyingly full of prestige today

---

12. By *scalar* we mean using the different degrees of a discontinuous *calibration*.

that the term *naturalism*, with which it is contrasted, is considered a real insult, a little like the term *bumpkin* applied to an amateur by an ace at the wheel. Although we are no more than an amateur in this field, we will nevertheless venture into it with interest and not without respect: musical research cannot be left abandoned in such isolation. It is to be hoped that comparisons with linguistics can enlighten us about *modes of structuring*, which are, in fact, general. But we will also have to return to our specific territory and, in addition, retain some bumpkin's mistrust of this far-too-universal panacea.

16

Perceptual Structures

16.1. THE TWO INFINITIES

What would establish a general basis for the rules of perception, applicable to music as well as languages—and, why not, to the image as well as to sound—is not a miraculous affinity between things but, of course, a similar mental activity when dealing with them. This promising point also promises many difficulties.

Since the perceived object (as an intentional unit) corresponds to a structure (of perceptual experience), we always tend to separate these two aspects: the object, which we think is on one side, and the experience, which we think is on the other; or again, the perceived structure and the constituent activity. We know that this is, in fact, tantamount to ruining the object, forgetting the authenticity of perception. But becoming aware of this experience involves giving ourselves a new object for thought, using a certain distancing from perception in order to examine its mechanism more fully—no longer hearing, but hearing oneself hear. If, in turn, I examine this mechanism, it is by virtue of a structure of reflective consciousness that in turn remains hidden from me . . . and so on, to infinity.

In the same way, at the end of the last chapter we spoke of the embedding of levels of structuring, which form an endless double-linked chain. As soon as I investigate the mechanisms of a perception, I am obliged to refer it to a higher level, in which it appeared to me as an object in a structure, and if I then investigate it in itself, isolated from this structure, it will present itself again as a structure and enable me to identify the objects on the level below. So there is something annoying about the choice of words, since in present-day language it is the word *object* that seems best suited to describe the grasping of something quite distinct that can be examined at leisure. By a reversal of meaning, this type of object is indeed provided by the structure above it, which allows us to identify it, but its properties, as we have said, are still concealed from us. If we take this object out of the structure to which it belongs, it immediately becomes a structure in itself, and it can only really be evaluated through being resolved into objects belonging to the level below.

If we use two letters to symbolize this double object-structure interplay, we could represent the chain of levels symbolically as follows:

$$(SO)\,1 \text{——} (SO)\,2 \text{——} (SO)\,3 \text{——}$$

This schema summarizes what we have just been saying: (SO) 2 has been identified as an object in S 3, and it forms the structure for identifying objects at level O 1.

We should add that a perpendicular chain of *mutual reflection* (complexity of perceptual structures) may branch off from any level.

(PA)*a*   P*a* representing any of the perceptions represented by one of the pairs SO, A*a* the activity giving rise to this perception,

(PA)*b*   which becomes the object of the perception P*b* in response to a new activity forming A*b*,

(PA)*c*   which in turn becomes, etc.

Is there any need to say that it is easier to get lost in this dimension than in the previous one?

16.2. AMBITION FOR THE ELEMENTARY

This treatise set out to discover the elementary. Nothing is more ambitious than aiming for this, nothing less certain, these days, than reaching it. At best we can see that levels are embedded and things are reflected in each other. We must check that we are not dreaming.

As we have seen, notes can best be identified in a melody, which, for all that, does not explain the notes. We will suppose that level 3 of complexity is the melodic object-structure. As a structure, it can be explained in terms of level 2 notes, but in its turn it will serve as an object to explain *a larger form*, phrase, or strophe, a movement from a work, *a piece of music*, as they say. For it must also be pointed out that the object *melody* is only noticed within the work by contrast like a figure against a background, or else it is articulated in it along with other melodies, accompaniment, or counterpoint: these melodies are analyzed within the work through *a musical sense* rather than bringing in *significations*.[1] When we say that

---

1. This expression suggests that at this level, and in a different way from language, music has a *meaning* rather than a signification.

the "theme" is recapitulated, reworked or merged with another, this type of *identi-fication* of level 3 melodies is really based on level 4, whereas the musicologist believes he has explained and described level 4 through the part played on that level by the components of level 3.

But our research is not aiming for these lofty heights of complexity. We have the intuition that the enigma of music, like matter, resides at the opposite extreme: in the smallest significant musical element, the one on which everything will be built from the very beginning.[2] Western musicians think it is the note. But what is a note? We can see that, because the question has never been properly put, there are no bases for any explanation.

Our argument could be turned upside down. Once we have managed to explain the note—that is, its structure and the objects on the level below—all we have done is pushed the explanation back. True. So our response will be that what counts is not so much to pry apart one more link in the chain but rather not to consider the note as a terminus. We must unblock the two blind alleys that obscure such an elementary concept: the blind alley of constituent criteria and the blind alley of the perceptual activity on which these are based. All of this goes back, infinitely more than we think, to our individual conditioning and our social conventions.

16.3. SIGNIFICANCE OF VALUES

The (supposed) resistance of some musicians to this sort of awareness is not spe-cific to them. It is shared by everyone who belongs to a *system* and is accustomed to experiencing it precisely as a *value system*, considering these values as *absolutes*, whereas in most cases they are no more than conventions. Hence the moral panic when the values table collapses or is smashed. How can these turnarounds, these breaks in the system, be explained? The meaning of music ultimately remains as impenetrable as the nature of its materials. Each one of us in this respect, and this is his secret, may have his own explanatory system or hypotheses about some way or other of using *the conventional signs of music theory* and will retain this rather than that, which has an effect on the interpretation of meaning.[3] This is true of the words in language and their relationship with ideas: one person knows what the spoken word means, another not at all. How much more true this is of music, because of its implicit nature, and its code, which is both impenetrable and inex-haustible.

We will take a less sensitive example. We can learn good manners from a book of etiquette, which is a music theory of the social code. This sort of book always

2. Just as the mystery of life is found at the cellular level.
3. As we cannot deal with all the levels at once, we will limit ourselves to mentioning the *meaning of music* for each, certainly infinitely less clear than the meaning of the language of words.

makes people laugh, why? Not only because it formalizes and fixes customs that are full of nuances but also because explaining these underlines how arbitrary they are. A code is not learned like this from books; no one would believe in it.

16.4. CODE AND LANGUAGE

The true code is unconscious. It is no less strict and remarkably detailed. Unconsciously, I bring my behavior into line with it, at the moment when it seems at its most spontaneous. Unconsciously, I apply it to my visitor's conduct. I don't say to myself, "He has failed to observe the code"; I say, "He's vulgar." I don't even say, "He's vulgar," but I see him *spontaneously* as vulgar.

How can there be something that is both ideal (since it is a group of conventions separate from the particular acts that conform to it, or any particular evaluations of it) and implicit? We may wish to clarify this. The clarification comes after the event. It is partial. It operates in the form of rules that are given as absolutes: "this is the done thing," and, above all, "that is not the done thing."

We may also come across the code by chance. The "new boy" joining a group learns this the hard way, not without playing a number of "wrong notes." But he assimilates the code directly, without really being aware of it. The one best placed to do this is the one who has experienced enough different environments to have learned about both the relativity of codes and their importance: knowing them to be variable, he will not confuse any of them with the Ten Commandments; knowing them to be binding, he will not attribute to individual traits of character what belongs to the general law.

Having at last observed and compared them, he may ask himself two sorts of questions: either he may wonder about their historical or psychological origins, and the factors that might change them; or else he may consider them at a given moment in time, independently of any value judgment or inquiry into causes, and wonder "how they are made." This is when we are likely to notice that they are *systems*, balanced wholes in which, as in perceived structures, changing one element necessitates amending the whole.

We find these various approaches clearly represented and differentiated in the sciences of language: grammar, normative, with its prescriptions and prohibitions; the separation, once this stage is past, between language systems[4] and speech, code and conduct, observed by Ferdinand de Saussure: on the one hand, the conventions

---

4. In his comparison between music and language Schaeffer uses the two words *langue* and *langage* in their Saussurian sense. As English does not make this distinction, we have translated *langue* as "language system" and *langage* as "language" throughout the book. Similarly where the linguistics distinction is made between *sens* and *signification*, we have used "meaning" for the first term and "signification" for the second.—Trans.

that enable us to understand one another, and on the other hand, the individual speech acts actually pronounced and heard that derive from them; the separation, in fact, of the study of language systems into two aspects: the study of their development (the historical, *diachronic* approach) and of their systems at a given moment in time (a *synchronic* approach).

16.5. LINGUISTIC STRUCTURES, MUSICAL STRUCTURES

We can now attempt to draw the parallel with linguistics. Apart from Danhauser's argument (?) ("music can be written and read as easily as we read and write the words we say"), we have other, perhaps better, reasons for doing this.

1. In no other domain will we see the problem of defining units in relation to structures, and hence in relation to the system and the main intention, presented with such clarity.

2. Like music, language is sound and takes place in time. It is interesting to compare the uses, structures, and perceptions that diverge from this shared basis. It is no less interesting to try to find a viewpoint, beyond these constructs, from which all these can be explored at the same time. We run little risk of getting it wrong if we assume that this viewpoint, if it exists, must be sought at the level of the sound object.

To be complete, our comparison should deal with the "meaning of music." The structures of language are obviously determined by its communicative function. A definition of musical communication, which immediately appears to be of another kind, would enable us better to understand musical structures through their functions.

Perfectly aware of this dependence, we have simply chosen to proceed from the other direction: the study of its structures, the problem of defining its units, may inform us about the meaning of music. And this indirect approach has the advantage of sparing us from aesthetic dissertations that lead nowhere.

16.6. THE LEVELS OF LANGUAGE: SIGNIFICATION AND DIFFERENTIATION

When we listen to speech, how and according to what criteria do we locate units?

At first sight the question appears otiose. The division of speech into sentences and words gives us no problem. Words are separated for us as easily when we listen as when we read, when they are separated by blank spaces. We are, however, happy to agree quite quickly that a foreigner who does not know our system of language would not separate them so easily. His ear will simply not allow him to know whether what he has just heard is two words or three. And we ourselves may hesitate if we do not have enough information about the meaning. "A Frenchman who hears a group such as *lavoir* will say immediately that it contains two syllables, but he needs to hear it in context to know whether it is two words or one: *lavoir* (a public washhouse) or *l'avoir* (to have it). A person who does not know French and who hears a group such as *je l'ai vu* (I saw it/him) will probably hear the number of syllables it has but will be utterly incapable of telling us the number of words as long as he does not understand the meaning."[5]

This, as Saussure observes, means that "language systems do not present as a set of signs delimited in advance, where all we have to do is study their significations and organization. It is an undifferentiated mass where only attentiveness and habit can enable us to distinguish particular components. The unit has no special phonic character, and the only definition that can be given of it is as follows: *a chunk of sound which, as distinct from what comes before and what follows it in the chain of speech, is the signifier of a certain concept.*"[6]

But, it seems, this amorphous mass is only so if we try through hearing alone to cut it up into units that are both sound units and meaningful. If we have not been told the significations, it is not surprising that we cannot do this.

Noting that the definition of units that appear so obvious to us, written into the sound itself, is relative to the meaning and our understanding of that meaning, we will continue our research. So what does a foreigner hear?

He hears syllables, as Malmberg has already told us (including, for reasons to be determined, a "probably"). We should add that syllables can be analyzed into phonemes (consonants and vowels). So we may suppose that a foreigner will hear phonemes? Absolutely not. If he applies himself, he will hear *sound objects* that are only phonemes to us. And if he does not apply himself, he will hear the phonemes of his own tongue, pronounced with a foreign accent.

16.7. PHONEMES: OR DISTINCTIVE FEATURES

Here again, we are misled by the written word. The same goes for English, German, Spanish, and French, although the language systems are different. We naturally assume that an *l* remains an *l* in every language system, that an *r* remains an *r*, simply admitting that they "are not pronounced in the same way." And we fall back into the illusion, already criticized by Saussure, that there are "signs defined in advance," which are organized later. The phoneme is not a reality in itself any

---

5. Bertil Malmberg, *La phonétique* (Paris: PUF, 1954). [Translated into English as *Phonetics* (New York: Dover, 1963).—Trans.]

6. Ferdinand de Saussure, *Cours de linguistique générale* (Paris: Payot, 1916). [Published in English as *Course in General Linguistics*, ed. Charles Bally and Albert Sechehaye, trans. Roy Harris (Chicago: Open Court, 1983).—Trans.]

more than the word. It is defined in relation to the language system of which it is part. Not only is the limited number of concrete sounds I hear as consonants and vowels, and which combine to form words, not identical from one language system to another, but they are infinitely varied within one single language system:

> We do not pronounce a vowel or a consonant in exactly the same way on any two occasions. What surrounds the sound varies every time. The accentuation, the speed of delivery, the register and the qualities of the voice vary from one occasion to another and from individual to individual. There are differences in pronunciation between individuals that can be explained by anatomical differences or individual quirks of speech. Spectrograms show significant differences between men's, women's, and children's vowels.[7]

Given all this, why and how do we identify these phonemes? Why do they stay *the same* despite their variations? How is it that we did not even perceive these variations, so much so that we have to use spectrograms to reveal them to us?

And why do we think we hear the same consonant in *qui* (who—kick) and *coup* (blow—coo), in *tas* (heap—tick) and *tot* (early—tock)?

> Spectrograms reveal acoustically different units in the various cases. Palatograms and X-rays show considerable differences in articulation. Why, finally, does a Parisian Frenchman, who pronounces his *r*s at the back of the throat, immediately identify a word such as *rire* (laugh) pronounced by a southerner, who rolls his *r*s? The answer is that the *k* before *i* and the *c* before *ou*, the masculine and the feminine *i*, the *a* after *s* and the *r* after *l*, the rolled and uvular *r*, are identical from the point of view of their *linguistic function*. Some features of the sounds in a language are important for identification, others are not. Every vowel and every consonant articulated in a context contains *distinctive* or *relevant* features together with a number of *nondistinctive* or *nonrelevant* features.[8]

In other words, the definition of the phoneme is relative to its function in the whole language system. It is "the smallest sound unit needed to discern one word from another."[9] Thus a Frenchman will identify the *l* in *tableau* (picture) with the *l* in *peuple* (people), whereas the *l* in *peuple* is more or less silent, and in *tableau* it is fully sounded. "For a Welshman, the sounded *l* and the silent *l* are two independent units that he will never think the same. The explanation for this is that the consonantal systems in Welsh and French are different. The Frenchman cannot change the meaning of a word by replacing the sounded *l* with a mute *l* or vice

---

7. Malmberg, *La phonétique*.
8. Ibid.
9. André Martinet, *Éléments de linguistique générale* (Paris: Armand Colin, 1960). [Published in English as *Elements of General Linguistics* (Chicago: University of Chicago Press, 1960).—Trans.]

versa. . . . The two *l*s are variants of the same phoneme. In Welsh, on the contrary, they are two different phonemes. The difference between the two is relevant."[10]

So, what seemed to us to be given immediately and even imperiously to perception is indeed given, but to a conditioned, trained perception, which has gradually become very adept at grasping relevant differences, while at the same time being *practically deaf* to those that are not. So much so that, when we learn a foreign language, we must unlearn to *articulate* and *hear French* while at the same time applying ourselves to a different training. This is why the acquisition of a foreign language is easier for a child, who still has the potential capacity to pronounce all phonemes, and a fresher, though as yet unskilled, ear.

16.8. FROM THE PHONEME TO THE MUSICAL NOTE

This description of the origin of language brings us back to our first chapter. In the sense we have just been describing, and without taking meaning into account, we have acknowledged the deafness of one musical civilization to another, the musical objects of one of them being heard by the citizens of another only as imperfect versions of their own phonemes.

In the same way, we have tried to describe the birth of unconscious musical systems, shaped simultaneously by practice and ear training, which makes the members of a musical civilization so skilled at recognizing features that are relevant (which play a part in the structure) and at the same time make them practically deaf to nonrelevant features—the former being at the cost of the latter. We can now measure more efficiently the power of this training and the whole process of learning needed to unlearn it and hear the music of others.[11]

As for music theory, we found it in more or less the same state as the grammars of the eighteenth century, codifying the structures that had arisen in the social unconscious after the event and confusing them with the norms of reason, like Lavignac identifying physics with music.

Finally, where the phoneme is concerned, we find the same ambivalence in the "musical note," which also, like consonants and vowels, is aided by a notation that misleads us, by making us think that, because it is fixed in advance on the score, it is a sign that existed before it was played. Its relevant features are, of course, pitch and duration, which have a functional role in musical structures. Jakobson, moreover, makes this connection explicit in *Fundamentals of Language.*

---

10. Malmberg, *La phonétique.*

11. Robert Francès, in his book *La perception de la musique* (Paris: Vrin, 1958), demonstrated the importance of this learning process in a great number of experiments, which lead him to say that "musical perception has little in common with hearing." Those who wish to have proof of this should refer to his work. [Published in English as *The Perception of Music* (Mahwah, NJ: Lawrence Erlbaum, 1988).—Trans.]

"Pitch-duration" values as relevant features have a radically different origin here from the one assigned to them in the previous book. Whereas previously these sound qualities resulted from a comparison of sound objects through *reduced listening*, with acoustic signals measured in time and frequency, these same qualities (or more precisely similar qualities with the same name) now come from comparisons made through musical listening in the context of a given language. We should not expect the three descriptive systems that are normally conflated—the third system being physics—to coincide nor, however, to be noticeably different. We will therefore keep in mind that the word *pitch* has different meanings according to whether it refers to physics (signal), *reduced listening* (sound object), or a cultural phenomenon (musical object).

Thus, listening to phonemes confirms the insensitivity to acoustic variations, sometimes considerable, which is ours. In music, similar experiments have highlighted the no less considerable variations in pitch that an opera singer is likely to produce (see Winckel and Francès). As for ignoring nonrelevant features, we need only to point to those clunks that the musician *does not hear* (the noise of the attack, for example, in a high piano note), whereas objectively (i.e., in reduced listening) they are louder than the tonic sound. This is, moreover, only one example among many. Noise, which is not remembered as a value, is present in all musical sounds, and its discreet presence, in suitable measure, is an indispensable element of sonority.

16.9. SOUND OBJECT AND PHONETICS

If, in the musical note, the constituent element of musical structures, we find the equivalent of the syllable, the constituent element of the speech chain, surely we will find a methodological precedent in phonetics? Perhaps phonetics could give us an example of a theory of verbal objects?

Yes and no. Our approach, at the level of concrete sounds, is indeed the same. The aims of our research, and hence the methods, are different.

(a) Yes, for the phonetician is, in fact, practicing that *reduced listening* that we are constantly urging our reader to try. The task of the phonologist, faced with a language system unknown to him, will be to locate the phonemes, while identifying their *variants:* either by consulting the *linguistic consciousness*—that is, defining units according to what the natives of the country count as the *same* in spite of variations—or through a general study of the structures of the language system (commutations method). Conversely, the phonetician will make himself listen to the sounds of his own language as if they were unknown to him and notice their variations.

This is, in fact, what we are doing when, making ourselves listen to a musical note with a fresh ear, we consider it as a *sound object* and in addition to its relevant features, which we call values, find in it many other characteristics (which could perhaps become values in other structures, as a phonetic variant becomes a distinct phoneme in another language system).

(b) No, for phonetics, which is subordinate to linguistics, is by the same token in an ambiguous situation. A natural, experimental science, it studies, using its own methods, objects that it does not define itself but receives already defined from phonology, which is itself a science concerned with relational and differential systems. All the phonetician has to do is record the differences between concrete sounds and phonemes. He is not concerned with the sound object independently of the use made of it by the various language systems. Therefore, to highlight these differences, all he has to do is give a physiological, articulatory description, equivalent to an instrumental and a physical, acoustic description.

Nothing illustrates the ambiguity of his situation more clearly than the way he traditionally classifies sounds, a classification that, according to Malmberg, amounts to a compromise between different principles: "We could say that the traditional classification of the sounds of language is physiological, modified by acoustic or functional considerations. The principle of an articulatory classification has never been fully pursued, and in any case would have led to obvious absurdities. Experienced phoneticians have let themselves be guided by their ear and their linguistic sense."[12]

At present, we are feeling the need for an acoustic, more rigorous, classification, but this has not yet been fully achieved. We could, however, object that a classification such as this is equally unwarranted: what is the point of spectrograms when they reveal differences that are eliminated in perception? It is quite obvious that they cannot in any case play a part in any language system. To identify those variations that are remembered in "linguistic listening," there is no other solution than the ear.

We have seen that the phonetician used and trained his ear even though he did not suggest this practice as an essential research tool. But we must also point out that the phonetician, concerned, like the linguist, with existing language systems and not the origins of possible languages, knows about it indirectly. If a particular variant, which will not fail to be shown up by the spectrogram, is used in another language system as a phoneme distinct from the first one, it is because this variant was also a clearly perceptible variation. Does he need to know more?

(c) The dependence of phonetics on linguistics has another consequence: the phonetician—except to note important individual variations in the articulation of a particular phoneme—is only really concerned with variations that are general enough to lead to modifications of the language system: those that are "combinatory," owing to the position of the phoneme in relation to the surrounding phonemes, and common

12. Malmberg, *La phonétique.*

to everyone; those that denote contrasting categories (men and women) or groups (regional accents), historical periods (changes in pronunciation, when they run counter to its oppositional system, leading to a transformation in the language system, which creates another system), or different language systems. Where laws are concerned, the level of generalization attained in linguistics is sought in phonetics in statistical regularities. There is no doubt that if linguists single-mindedly pursued that linguistics of *speech*[13] *(individual discourse)*, desired by Saussure, to complete their study of *language systems (a shared treasure)*, phonetics would feel the repercussions, take on a new importance, and perhaps change its methods.

16.10. DIRECTION OF RESEARCH

These references to the ideas of the pioneer of general linguistics, this rather brief summary of the major distinction between *language systems* and *speech*, is likely once again to antagonize two groups of readers. To some our parallels with linguistic disciplines in which they are specialists will appear cursory. To others they will seem esoteric, complicated, perhaps pointless. This is the abiding problem of interdisciplinary research: finding its material wherever it can but finding itself constantly at odds with different levels and types of expertise.

Our reasons for involving language were given in the preceding section and in section 16.5. The (musician) reader will not perhaps find the results very spectacular. What, all this fuss because a (distinctive, relevant) phoneme has the same (linguistic) function, despite its different (phonetic) variants? Is that all this discipline can contribute to music?

Important discoveries and meaningful comparisons cannot be measured by this yardstick. We know there are discrepancies, often very slight, between laws and measurements in physics, which leads to the questioning of a whole system, which then proves to be unsound at the outer limits. We believe this is what is happening here. We notice that the definition of musical values raises not only the strange question of anamorphoses, which we discussed in the last book, but also the question of social obfuscation and mass conditioning. As we said in section 16.8, we are dealing with three value systems: the values of a musical language system, physical measurement, and the laws of perception in reduced listening.

This means that by taking this detour we come back to *the three listening intentions, for the meaning, the event, and the sound object*, schematized in chapter 8 (fig. 2).

Two of these, as we know, go beyond the sound object, while using it as a vehicle for meanings or a bearer of indicators. So the sound object, ignored, becomes

13. Reminder: Speech as opposed to language systems. It is "language" that subsumes both language systems and speech.

the speaker's linguistic object, just like the musician's musical object, even if it has a natural origin or carries the marks of use and the secondary significations related to civilizations. The sound object, equally ignored for the sake of the event, becomes the horse, then the Native North American, the timbre of a beloved voice, or again the physical object. So there are many ways of using sound as a sign (language, Morse code, onomatopoeia, speech intonations). In addition we should not be surprised to find sound used in all manner of ways for analyzing some revealing property (it covers the whole gamut from primitive man to the scholar, from the ordinary user to the specialized practitioner).

Finally, there is *the sound object itself*, all the more ignored as it has been used to signify so many things or reveal so many others. The event that it is, the values it carries within itself, these are what our hearing intention ultimately targets. If the reader has figure 2 at hand, he will have recognized the plan of our three-part epilogue: at the top on the left the search for meanings (this word, used in a more general sense, includes the system of traditional musical values), at the top on the right the search for events, and, finally, at the bottom, with its two poles *reversing* the former line of questioning, and going back to the sound object, the apprehension of the object through *reduced listening*.

Since we have devoted a whole book to a comparison between the physical and the sound object, there should be no further need to spend time here on the boundaries between what comes from the physical event and what is perceived as sound, or music, or the spoken word. But underlying every sound object there is still an event (a musical instrument is being played, someone is playing a particular instrument, a particular language is being spoken, or someone is saying these words), which always stops us from ignoring this *natural* pole and this in all three possible cases: when all our attention is focused on the event, which is a particular musical or dramatic mode of listening (to the instrument or the performer), when all our attention is focused on the meaning (thus it happens that, with a language system, the speaker is ignored, how can this be possible?), or finally when our attention, focused on the object of *reduced listening*, uses what it knows of the event, and even the meaning, to reach a better understanding of how the object is made and what value it has. So this leads to a plan that should elucidate each of these three systems concerned with objects of hearing: the cultural system of words or notes, the system of natural sound events, and the system of *reduced listening*. We will, in fact, devote chapters 18, 19, and 20 to this. First, though, we must finish our comparative examination of linguistics and the musical. For we have not resolved a central enigma: how the science of language can restrict itself to a study of *language systems*, ignoring *speech;* and why, in music, a similar methodological bias would not be effective, except in exceptional circumstances when the *musicality* is minimal enough to do without *sonority?*

Comparative Structures

Music and Language

17.1. THE HIGHER LEVEL

Since this treatise is limited to the basics of the musical, it endeavors never to embark on musical signification, at least at the higher level of language. It cannot therefore be compared to linguistic research except where the latter deals with sounds, listening only to "what speaking does not mean." In other words, it remains at the level of phonetics and phonology.[1] We may in the first instance wonder if it is permissible to study different domains of language in this way, independently of each other. The answer is yes, and it comes from both the most traditional practices in music and the most modern approaches in linguistics. We can, and we do, in fact, separate theory and instrumental classes from classes in that grammar called harmony, which have very little to do with what we might call *composition* classes. Linguistics, for its part, willingly allows these types of distinction and takes them further: it distinguishes levels between phonetics or phonology (distinguishing level) and linguistics properly speaking (signifying level) and also between lexis and syntax, both domains giving rise to two areas of study: morphological, for their signifier aspect; semantics, for their signified aspect. Finally, lexis and syntax can be studied either in relation to their development in time (diachronic) or as a system at a given moment (synchronic) (see fig. 18). It is true that at the signifying level the different domains are blurred at the edges, and not all linguists agree with Ullmann's classification, which we have just summarized. Conversely, the separation between the two levels does not seem to cause them a problem: if

---

1. Furthermore, we must point out that these levels are much more essential for music than language systems.

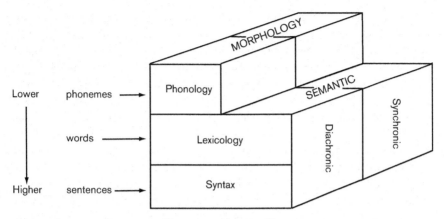

FIGURE 18. General illustration of linguistic studies, by Ullmann.

there are controversies, it is on the distinguishing level, about the relationship that phonetics and phonology have or do not have with each other.[2] Are they complementary, or is phonology, the science of differential sound units that aims to set up the system of phonemes, independent of a phonetics devoted to the study of "the physical and physiological nature of the distinctions observed"?

In music we are nowhere near having the benefit of such work on the classification of disciplines and domains. So we can only benefit from this precedent, provided that we do not settle for a comparison limited to the lower levels. So we must also carry out a very brief reconnaissance of the higher level. It is also from this level that we will be able to get an overview of the value of the comparison in general, a rather less intuitive evaluation of the axiom that music is a language. In any case, we will certainly not come to the end of a debate in which the best minds oppose each other in often contradictory statements.

17.2. LANGUAGE

This, says Jean Perrot, "is the association of the contents of thought with sounds produced by speech." Language is itself "one of the totality of signs that serve more or less conventionally to communicate significations that involve any of our senses."[3] But what, precisely, is a sign? Saussure helps us to answer this tricky

2. Here we return to the vexed question of the relationship between acoustics and an *acoulogy* at the same *distinctive* level. [*Acoulogy* is a term introduced by Schaeffer to designate the act of isolating and defining the musical characteristics of recorded sounds.—Trans.]

3. Jean Perrot, *La linguistique* (Paris: PUF, 1953). It would perhaps be better to say the totality of signs perceptible to any one of our senses and serving, more or less conventionally, to communicate meanings.

question to which any one of us is likely to give an answer that in fact misses the point: "The linguistic sign unites not a thing and a name, but a concept and an acoustic image. The latter is not material sound, which is purely physical, but the imprint of that sound in the mind, the representation our sensory experience gives of it. . . . We intend to keep the word *sign* to denote the whole process and to replace concept and acoustic image respectively with *signified* and *signifier*."[4] Such is the foundation of a budding science that generalizes the function of the sign: *semiology*.

These types of definitions, familiar to the linguist, will surprise the musician. He tends to imagine that language has very little to do with sound and that, essentially, it raises the problem of the arbitrary connection between the word and the idea. This is correct, as far as arbitrariness is concerned. Saussure explains: "The link between the signifier and the signified is arbitrary, or again, since by *sign* we understand all that results from their association, we may say: the linguistic sign is arbitrary." And immediately the musician replies: "You see." The musical sign, for its part, is not. Look at the fifth and the octave: they are simple relationships, inscribed in nature, which societies have not adopted arbitrarily but logically. Even if, personally, the author shares this opinion, it is not such a fashionable truth these days. We will not go into this but will move on to the joyfulness of the major, the sadness of the minor, the choice of scales or modes, the number of notes and the positioning of these notes, not to mention, obviously, the supposed rules of harmony or counterpoint, physicists' supposed consonance or dissonance, and the sound materials and the musical ideas directly inherited from instrument making, naturally historical and geographical and, consequently, social. . . . How can we not see in all this neither more nor less arbitrariness than in the formation of languages?

17.3. THE RULES OF LANGUAGE

"Speaking," according to Jakobson, "involves *selecting* certain linguistic units and *combining* them into more complex linguistic units. This is immediately evident at the lexical level: the speaker chooses words and combines them into sentences in accordance with the syntactical system of the language system he is using; these sentences, in turn, are combined into utterances. But the speaker is by no means an entirely free agent in the choice of words: the selection (with the exception of very rare cases of true neologisms) must be made from the lexical resources he and the recipient of the message have in common."[5] In Jakobson's account we should, it seems, identify the following:

4. Ferdinand de Saussure, *Cours de linguistique générale* (Paris: Payot, 1916).
5. Roman Jakobson, *Essais de linguistique générale* (Paris: Minuit, 1963).

1. General laws about two ways of arranging objects that are present at all levels of language.

2. A distinction between the following levels: phonological, dealing with the system of phonemes particular to a specific language system; lexical, dealing with vocabulary; syntactical, dealing with sentences; and finally, the level of utterance that relates to stereotypes.

3. A rising scale of freedom, going from one of these levels to another. In view of its importance we will again quote Jakobson's remark, already mentioned in our introductory remarks: "In combining distinctive features into phonemes, the individual speaker has no freedom at all; the code has already established all the possibilities that can be used in the language system in question. The freedom to combine phonemes into words is restricted; it is limited to the marginal situation where words are created. In forming sentences from words, the speaker is less constrained. Finally, when sentences are combined into utterances, the restrictive rules of syntax cease to operate and the individual speaker's freedom is substantially increased, although we must not underestimate the number of stereotyped utterances."[6]

What are these two fundamental laws at the different levels of language systems that we are likely to find feature by feature in a given musical language system? They are two processes that give every linguistic sign "two groups of interpretants" (Peirce)[7]—one related to the code, the other to the context, the sign being always referred to another group of signs: in the first case by a relationship of *substitution*, in the second by a relationship of *juxtaposition*.

To run through these two "modes of arrangement" once more:

1. *Selection.* "Choosing between alternative terms involves the possibility of substituting one of the terms for another, in one respect equivalent to the first and, in another, different. In fact, selection and substitution are the two facets of one process."

2. *Combination.* "Every sign is made up of constituent signs and/or appears in combination with other signs. This means that every linguistic unit is at one and the same time a context for simpler units and/or finds its own context in a more complex linguistic unit. Hence, it follows that every effective collection of linguistic units links them together in a higher unit: combination and contexture are therefore the two facets of one process."

"A given signifying unit can therefore be replaced by other more explicit signs belonging to the same code, by means of which its general signification is revealed

---

6. Ibid.

7. Charles Sanders Peirce (1839–1914) was an American philosopher, logician, and mathematician. He made significant contributions to semiotics, which he regarded as a branch of logic. Peirce is regarded as the founder of "pragmatism."—Trans.

(substitution point 1), whereas its contextual meaning is determined by its connection with other signs within the same sequence (juxtaposition, point 2)."

17.4. APPLICATION OF THE RULES OF
LANGUAGE TO MUSIC

We will plagiarize Jakobson's comments and apply them to music:

(a) Where *levels* are concerned, we could say: "Making music involves selecting certain musical units and combining them into units of a higher degree of complexity. This is immediately apparent on the instrumental level. The musician chooses his notes [from them] and combines them into phrases in accordance with the system of counterpoint and harmony of the [musical] language system he is using; the phrases in turn are combined into 'pieces of music.' But the musician is by no means a completely free agent in the choice of notes: the selection [with the rare exception of completely new instruments] must be made from the *musical code* he and the recipient of the message have in common."

Everything down to the last word can be applied to the musical.

(b) After this comparison of levels we will endeavor to plagiarize the *rules* as well, by placing ourselves at the *melodic* level, for example. Two "modes of arrangement" are suggested:

1. *Selection.* If I replace one instrumental note in the melody with the same note, played on another instrument, I will indeed have substituted one term for another, equivalent in one respect (the value pitch) and different in another (timbre).

2. *Combination.* The melody, which finds its own context in the piece of music, serves as the context for note units that themselves are the combination of values such as pitch, duration, and intensity.

We will continue transcribing the last sentence of section 17.3: "Every signifying unit (the note) can therefore be replaced with other more explicit signs belonging to the same code (violin or vocal note replaced by a more accurate piano or harmonium note but not a balaphone key or a gong, which do not belong to the same code), as a result of which its general meaning is revealed (alternation, point 1. It can also be demonstrated that piano and violin have synonymous notes that can give the same G), whereas its contextual meaning is determined by its connection with other signs in the same sequence (juxtaposition, point 2): the melody remains, with the G taking on all its value, to the point where, if we put F or A in its place, the new melody would have another meaning."

The plagiarism has once again succeeded, at least *if we restrict ourselves to* the most classical music, the music of the great Western era, consequently of the eighteenth century, where the system, at the height of its development, settles into a *synchronic* phase.

However much we may respect this apogee, it does no one any service to want to present other, particularly contemporary, musics as developments of or progress in the same system. We cannot supersede a system except by demolishing it. We seek another, through long and tortuous developments; we do not yet know to what these same, immutable, rules of language will be applied, to what code in the process of formation. Finally, even if we suppose that a new language system exists, we cannot describe it by referring to the same system of signs.

17.5. PERMANENCE AND VARIATION IN MUSICAL STRUCTURES

Taking our lead from Jakobson, we have described—on the modest but essential level of melody—the classic act of composition, through selection and combination. Now we will look at the result of that act: melody as a structure perceived by the listener.

We will start at the simplest level: a few piano notes are played. If they are a very long way apart (as Cage takes care to anticipate in some of his works), they appear as isolated events, standing out as objects. The composer may even endeavor to calculate the period of silence needed to avoid any sound's being too near to another. If this is the case, the object is heard in detail, and the listener can, at leisure, meditate on the strength of the attack, the brilliance of the Steinway, or the boredom of having to wait for the next sound.

Here there is no problem: the musical object whose qualities are being analyzed coincides perfectly with the sound object. There is no structure contextually speaking; the notes are far enough apart in duration for any modification of one of these components not to affect the whole. We are at the remotest frontier of music: if we are still there (which some of the audience at Cage's concerts seem to doubt), it could be for two reasons. One of them, anecdotal and therefore basically unacceptable, is the use of a piano, recognized socially as a musical instrument. The other, more essential, which would still be valid if a piece of sheet metal were used instead of a piano: on the one hand, this is music *by elimination* (if it is not musical, the event has no other interest and no other signification); on the other hand, even if no structure results from these objects, we are at least in the presence of a *collection* of comparable objects, with *shared characteristics*.

Now suppose that the sounds follow each other closely enough to form a melody. This time there is a split between musical listening to a structure, based on a particular dominant quality of the objects, which by definition we call *value* (pitch, but also duration and intensity if the musical phrase is articulated not only by means of melody but also through rhythm) and musicianly listening, which appreciates the sonority of the objects. Now we observe that with musical listening the structure comes to the fore. Play "Il pleut, bergère" to a child, to an uncultured listener (who belongs to our musical civilization; otherwise we cannot guarantee anything) on a piano, then on the violin, and there is every likelihood that he will say: "It's the same thing" before thinking of saying: "It's a piano, then a violin." It is only afterward that he will mention the difference of instruments. And even then he will mention the instrument, and not the characteristics of the objects.[8]

Why does structure predominate? Certainly not because of some mysterious preference our perception has for groups, but *because those qualities of objects that do not contribute to the structure through differentiation seem common* to those objects. Here we come back to the role of the instrument and the *permanence-variation dialectic* mentioned in chapter 1: the function of the piano or the violin is to produce objects having enough characteristics in common (timbre) for their value (pitch) to be differentiated.[9]

Now take a melody where every note is played on a different instrument: now timbre appears as a value that differentiates the objects. The latter straightaway become more noticeable at the expense of the musical structure, which stands out less imperiously. Its unity could be threatened through this lack of balance between permanence and variation if it were not already soundly established by the pitches.

The same melody, the same instruments, but all playing *staccato*. I cannot help noticing this *dominant character* of the objects. On occasions it even manages to mask the variations in timbre, their value diminishing and being replaced by this *invariant*. I go back to the example of the piano: the melodic structure is clearly strengthened by it, to the detriment of the *Klangfarbenmelodie*.

What precisely is a *Klangfarbenmelodie*?

For it to be absolutely *dominant*, nothing must mask the perception of *color*. As the perception of pitches unfailingly wins, as soon as they are used as values, we are obliged to use sounds of the same pitch (or complex sounds where pitch is not so clearly prominent: a register of diffuse sounds in the bass or midregister, unclear enough to be suitable). Now we will take this extreme example. A bassoon, a piano, a kettledrum, a cello, or a harp playing at the same pitch are supposed to create a *timbre-melody*. So this sequence, or structure, will be described by inverting the usual terms. In the previous examples, timbres generally appeared as characteristics and pitch as a value. Here, as all the sounds have the same *characteristic of pitch*, we must look elsewhere for values. But, when we attempt to do so, we will not necessarily find an obvious value in front of us; we may recognize *instruments* instead and not a true *Klangfarbenmelodie*. These timbres are either too much

---

8. These behaviors are highlighted *a contrario* in certain pathological states (auditory asymbolisms).

9. This rule, stated at the beginning of this work, is doubtless the musical equivalent of those stated by Jakobson for language.

COMPARATIVE STRUCTURES 239

in evidence, or too vague, to give rise to a clear value that would be apparent to our ear.

The attempt at *Klangfarbenmelodie* therefore comes up against two obstacles: either it remains masked by a dominant perception, pitch (and we must endeavor, by means of a new sound art, to *paint over* this perception by choosing ambivalent sounds), or else we must come to some agreement (by means of a new ear-training) that we are able to bring to the fore sounds that until now have been ignored or considered secondary: dark or bright sonority, matt or coarse grain, and so forth. *We are suggesting new conventions, requiring an accepted type of training.* Even if we managed to get rid of this dominant perception, in a very impoverished music, since it would be a series of tonic notes, there is no guarantee that *timbre* would be immediately perceived as a value. An inexperienced listener will go back to the instruments and will perceive a *structure of sound events* rather than a *musical structure.* Here again, we need an intention to hear musically, the result of a choice and a training process.

So we have the measure of the difficulties in extending music within its own system. While the gong threatens it with brutality, the *Klangfarbenmelodie* calls for unusual refinement. Faced with such a contradiction, the system collapses, and it is likely that *misunderstandings* dominate: some do not hear what others give them to hear. Nevertheless, there is an essential idea that should be remembered from this experiment: the permutation of values and characteristics (which seemed inconceivable in traditional music) appears accessible to experience. The system has been undermined: what was only *variant* can take on the value of *phoneme* in another system to come. It remains, of course, to test out these possible new relationships. But the questions are fundamental.

17.6. VALUES AND CHARACTERISTICS

So, from this series of examples we should remember this conclusion: within a musical structure *objects are differentiated in values through the similarity of their characteristics.* And it is solely these two functions, and not any difference in nature, that define these two terms in relation to each other. Values guarantee a differential structure; the similarity of characteristics also guarantees this, indirectly, by reducing the interest that may be shown in identifying objects that would otherwise present themselves as a series of heterogeneous, mutually independent events. This axiom seems to us to dominate traditional music. But, even more general than that, it could apply to other musics.[10]

We groped around in the dark for quite some time before getting to this point. We refused to give our opinion a priori on what absolutely *musical* values were, but how could we resign ourselves to leaving in doubt what might be the essence of music?

10. See chap. 21.

What should an absolutely musical value be? It should, it seems, meet the following definition: "a quality of perception shared by different objects *said to be musical* from a collection of *sound objects* (which do not all possess this quality), enabling these objects to be compared, ordered, and (possibly) calibrated, despite the disparity of other perceptual aspects."

Of course, having followed this approach, we will find a value: pitch. It is (almost) the only one that survives in the motley collection of other sound values or characteristics. A meager success, except that it reminds us, if this were necessary, that pitch, here considered as a characteristic, will always be a dominant characteristic to our ear.

As soon as we attack other traditionally recognized values, such as intensity or duration, we meet with nothing but confusion. If rhythm stands firm, it is, we should not forget, because of the *spacing of objects* much more than their duration.

Finally, a calibration of intensity can only be established between objects with the same properties of timbre, form, and so forth, and through correlating it with the calibration of pitch. We cannot compare the intensity of a piano note and a violin pizzicato or a flute or bassoon sound. Voltmeter readings would only lead us astray here. We have to give up, not only on account of how qualitative, and nuanced (they say "nuance" in music, and for good reason), our evaluation may be but also because of the structures in which the form of the sounds plays a part.

17.7. DIVERGENCES

So we end with an admission of failure. Our rules apply too well. If the only value is pitch, if we are reduced to the too-narrow and far-too-classical vocabulary of degrees, all we can really do is refine on serial permutations and construct diagrams that please the eye, playing with computers. We could even make the game more complicated by adding durations and intensities. As we have just pointed out, this is too much rigor with too much laxity. Traditional notes, while quite accurate in pitch, are not at all so in duration or intensity. Finally, the timbre of the notes themselves in their instrumental register links these three values closely together. Under these conditions it can be no more than cheating or naivety to speak of rigorously calculated structures.

How will we get out of an impasse so familiar, so real, that it condemns a whole generation to deny the evidence with the energy of despair? By making a very simple remark: we have laid so much emphasis on the parallels between language systems and music only to bring out their divergence. In this chapter, focused on music-language parallels, we have for the most part quoted norms, rules of *language systems;* we have abandoned *speech,* the other half of language. Keeping only to these comparisons, we have considered only the abstract aspect of music, notatable, encoded, even permutatable (as long as the code allows this). And even if it is true that we can account for all the structures of a certain kind of *musicality* in this way, it is by cutting music off from the inexhaustible resources of *sonority*.

Let me make myself clear. At what point, in what we have said until now, have we mentioned the study of speakers' *timbres*, their *intonations?* (And we do not mean individual timbre, style, this or that interpretation, that is, individual *words*, an aspect which we should prefer to ignore in order to make this demonstration really strike home.) All this is absent (at least in certain families of language systems, including ours in the West) from their *system of signs*.[11] The *Klangfarbenmelodie* experiment thus ingenuously demonstrates an attempt to remedy the situation by aiming to turn timbres into values. Electronic music has in the same way sought to reclaim other values, called *spectral*, which depend on a second, but unfortunately ambiguous and ill-justified, connotation of the word *timbre*.

Such are the efforts of musicians, often in the wake of scientific and linguistic theory, instead of being inspired by the proposition we have already put forward: that musical signs *are made to be heard in a different way from linguistic signs*.

17.8. LANGUAGE SYSTEMS AND SPEECH

"The vocal organs," writes Saussure, "are as external to language systems as the electrical devices that transcribe the alphabet into Morse code are unfamiliar with that alphabet; and phonation, that is, the execution of acoustic images, does not affect the system itself in the slightest. In this respect we could compare language systems to a symphony, the reality of which is independent of how it is played; the mistakes that musicians may make do not compromise that reality in any way."

Saussure thus turns to music much as we are attempting to turn to language, and if he were not, generally speaking, right, we might quibble over details. For the symphony to remain, first it is important that not too many musicians play out of tune. Then, if a musician plays a solo passage out of tune, a particular melody is no longer recognized, or, and this amounts to the same thing, they say he is playing out of tune because, as they have that melody in their head or can reconstruct it from a standard version, any part of it that he plays reveals at the same time what he is lacking. And so we come back to the processes described in section 17.4.

But we can follow Saussure in his analysis with three reservations:

(a) that it, in fact, applies to a symphony from the past, in the best-encoded system;

(b) that we clearly understand the *level* on which this recognition of meaning operates, which is an advanced level of exposition and not the level of the signs themselves;

11. This is not the case, for example, in the Chinese language.

(c) the last point is the more important and concerns the ambiguity of the word signal: signals in Morse code are, in one sense, as arbitrary as the linguistic sign; but if I listen to the Morse code device musically, ignoring the letters it produces, I will hear other signs, coming from the same signal now considered from a physicist's point of view. I cannot now say that these rhythmic signs, these Morse melodies, are so very alien to the timbre of this machine. Nor can I say that their meaning is in the physical signal; I must take delivery of the specific, musical sign.

"Perhaps," Saussure continues, "people will present as an argument against the separation of phonation and language systems the sound-distortions that occur in speech, and so profoundly influence the fate of the language system itself. Are we really justified in claiming the latter exists independently of these phenomena? Yes, because they affect only the material substance of words. If they attack a language system insofar as it is a system of signs, it is only indirectly, through the resultant change of interpretation; now, this phenomenon is not remotely phonetic."

Can we introduce such a firm distinction into music? Can we say that the sound distortions in *musical speech*, in the field of instrument making, for example, only affect the material substance of musical words?

A distinction like this is only possible, in language systems, because of Saussure's earlier analysis on the arbitrariness of the linguistic sign. Why should the sound signifier and the conceptual signified not, in fact, have two parallel systems and patterns of development? Saussure can therefore conclude with all rigor: "There are two parts to the study of language: the first, essential, concentrates on language systems, which are essentially social and independent of the individual; this study is entirely psychological; the other, secondary, concentrates on the part of language to do with the individual, that is, speech, including phonation; it is psychophysical."

We have some reason to be perplexed. On the one hand, our comparisons with language have been fruitful, allowing us to benefit from very significant analyses and a useful methodological precedent. On the other hand, we discover profound differences between music and language. Danhauser tells us that "music is as easy to read and write as a text." But we have experienced the contrary. Finally, common sense whispers that everybody is right. How do we get out of this?

17.9. THE TWO EXCLUSIVES IN LANGUAGE SYSTEMS

We may initially discover these differences through quite a crude approach, arising from the *four listening modes* identified in chapter 7. We said, fairly naively: we listen to someone, we perceive concrete sounds aurally, we hear distinctive features, and we understand what he is saying. Language systems could therefore be opposed to music, because one of these four listening modes is excluded in each system:

D. I understand (the word)   A. I listen (to someone speaking)

C. I hear (phonemes)   ⎡B. I forget (the sound)⎤

LANGUAGE SYSTEM - Section B is ignored, passed over.

⎡D. I have nothing to understand⎤   A. I listen (to an instrument)

C. I hear (values)   B. I perceive aurally (a sonority)

MUSIC - Section D is not reached
          since the value is targeted in section C

This is how we can explain *grosso modo* the obvious difference, so often pointed out, between language and music—one concerned with understanding arbitrary signs, the other with recognizing signs that are necessarily linked to the object. In one case all that is remembered of the object (ignored at B) is distinctive features (C) referring back to a signified (D). In the other the object is not superseded but is heard for itself (B), and a meaning (C) is drawn out from it.

And, changing tack a little, we have these two diagrams. Reduced in this way, each has three quadrants:

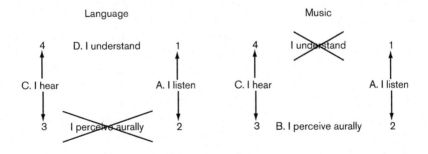

These two diagrams have the advantage of crudely summing up the situation while, however, remaining completely unable to account for them properly. For them to be entirely valid, we would, in fact, have to suppose that we could deal with language when deaf (and it is true that a deaf person can read) and also that there is nothing to understand in music.

In fact, there have been divisions and choices in language, in the *I listen* as in the *I hear*. And in the same way, for the musical, there has been a rejection of a certain part of the *I listen* and the *I hear* in a system of concepts. We will look at both of these.

Whatever the language, we must admit that human phonetic materials are universal, except that I must make a distinction:

(a) between the individual phonations of each person, which are different from his neighbor, and

(b) a phonology linked to that language system.

Everything, however, rests on the universal constitution of the mouth and the palate, the teeth and the nose, which enables us to generalize, extrapolate, symbolize a "normal," although entirely theoretical or purely statistical, phonation by making a distinction between dentals, labials, sibilants, and so forth. This is how it is possible to transcribe into international phonetic notation, a sort of abstract tape recorder, phonetic entities that are, however, completely detached from any particular utterance of them. And it can be seen that this dichotomy between language systems and speech applies just as much to the phonetic aspect of "speaking" as to the phonological aspect of hearing. In fact, in language systems it is accepted,

(a) on the one hand, that the sound features that contribute to the meaning of words are carefully separated from those that helped to color them: inflections, intonations, and so forth, and,

(b) on the other hand, that individual speakers and their way of playing words are discounted, including Saussure's "wrong notes," saved by the context. The only anonymous speaker capable of that frigid norm is the "Vocoder" voice synthesizer, which "speaks like a book": on the one hand, it has been given a normal, statistically based phonation, and, on the other hand, the intonations that color and interpret speech have been removed (see fig. 19a).

The same division can be found in music, except that the musician must listen to something very different from sibilants and labials: scrapings, breathing, beating on various utensils. Every musical civilization finally develops an increasingly well-established collection of instruments. Like language systems, music aims with all its might to detach these instruments from individual examples, played by individual performers, and also to retain only a particular distinctive feature of their sound objects, a compromise between a natural and a social acoulogy (fig. 19b). Such is the ideal program for pure music. What is pure music?

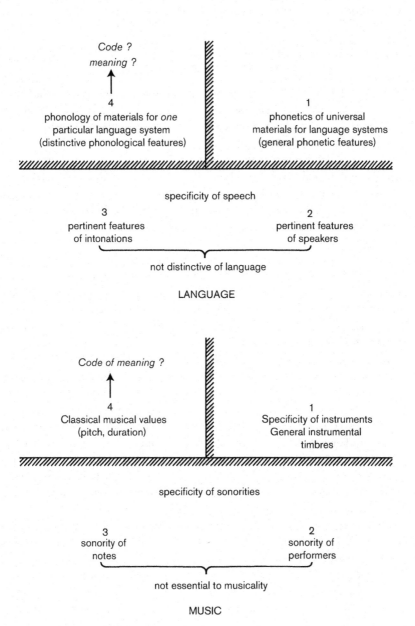

FIGURES 19a and 19b. Comparison of the materials of language and music.

17.10. A POSSIBLE MUSICAL LANGUAGE SYSTEM: PURE MUSIC, MUSICAL WRITING

We must first locate the point where music and language are most alike and where they give clear proofs of this. This will enable us to pick out their essential differences from the point of greatest proximity. Then we will be in a position to consider less clear, or more divergent, situations.

Since Danhauser refers us to writing, and Saussure to the symphony, and everyone is right, we will try first of all to find out on what grounds such valuable help is based. They give us a visible, and an additional, proof: so music and language can both be written down; the text is admissible evidence. We will accept this new testimony of similarity but immediately wonder whether it conceals some new difficulty.

Concerning where the written sign comes from, in both cases, we may recall, on the one hand, musical *homo faber* and, on the other, the words of Merleau-Ponty: "If there had not been a man with organs of phonation and articulation, and a breathing apparatus, or at least a body and the capacity to move about by himself, there would have been neither speech nor ideas," words which find their equivalent in Saussure: "historically, the fact of speech always precedes . . ."

The divisions we have been talking about are most fully realized in a language system and also in our Western musical system at the height of its development. If we limit ourselves to considering these two systems as they are, without paying any attention to their origins or development, our attention immediately turns away from the two (lower level) illustrative diagrams and toward the question of signification for language and meaning for music. We must make ourselves clearer.

In the same way that language systems have rejected what we might call the *musicality of the word*, as irrelevant to its aim (the specificity of intonations and speakers), so music has rejected as secondary the *sonority of its notes and ways of being played*. This is what makes us forget the sound object.

Here we are speaking of *pure music*, in the precise and, *in truth, exceptional meaning* of *The Art of the Fugue*, an *extreme* case, where the orchestration is left free and considered to be of no importance, or again the *Two- or Three-Part Inventions for Keyboard*, where the permanence of the timbre is analogous to the sameness of the human throat. Here the parallel is striking: music and language systems occupy sector 4 exclusively, and their phonological development is similar in method in every respect. It differs, of course, in the choice of signs. This similarity of methods, which is the same as "structuring," does not in the slightest, as we may suspect, involve a similarity of the consequent perceptions.

So what is the fundamental difference between these two sets of signs, so clearly coming from the same medium?

In one of these cases, language systems, there is now a disjunction between the signifying sound medium and the signified concept. It is only from the level above that codes exist, as much on the morphological as the semantic level.

In the other case, if we still speak of signs, it is no longer in the Saussurian sense of the term, as an arbitrary link, referring to something else, unless we bend over backward to support the thesis that musical values are unpredictable and exclusively social. This is an unlikely hypothesis, for the objects must serve some purpose. Diverting sound objects from their proper nature in this way to make them into vehicles for ideas does, indeed, give credit to human intelligence. But where will we find the meaning of musical objects if they have no intrinsic value? Why would societies remember unlikely passing fancies that nothing would justify for very long to other ears? Hence the impasse of a music in itself, which would only play with these objects, and an acoulogy as devoid of meaning as a phonology. Clearly, it is also at the higher level that music, like language systems, takes on all its meaning, in the combination of *objects of value*, as it were. And this is the whole debate about the meaning of music, which is at its purest at the level of pure music. The combinations of these objects (and, in pure music, only two main values are retained) clearly argue a collective musical consciousness. The more or less necessary relationships between combinations of objects and the properties of a perceptual musical field proper to man now appear as the essential problem of music.

17.11. INSTRUMENTAL MUSIC

It is when the score has no signs in words that it most resembles the text of a language system. As soon as there are directions such as "violin" or "clarinet" added to the sharps or flats, *the impurity* of music, or at least the complexity of its code, becomes apparent. There is, in fact, a major difference, from the point of view of the essence of music, between an invention for four voices for a single instrument (or a quartet or, at a pinch, a large proportion of so-called classical chamber musical works) and orchestral music. As long as instruments count for so little or nothing, and *voices* are identified by the coherence of the counterpoint, we can say that the language system dominates, with the reservation that the musical language system is *polyphonic* and even and in its purest state, above all, has this difference from the spoken chain, which is linear. But when instrumental sonority is included in the note values, when we have to read the score doubly symbolically, for the signs of notation and for instrumental concepts—voice, clarinet, drum, and such—we must admit that we have moved out of a pure system of twelve sounds and are in another richer but less pure system. The sector 1 code comes into the picture and intervenes, recombines with the sector 4 code. The vocabulary, from being restrained and combinative, becomes abundant and qualitative in another way. Another dimension—

and what a dimension, it has several dimensions itself . . .—opens up. At first sight the system defies analysis and, in any case, its written form becomes fragile and very soon misleading. In fact, as long as we stay with pure music, we are in the same situation as a language system in relation to its texts. There is a triangular relationship among the written sign, the sound value it represents, and the meaning. Whether I write the word *meaning*, or whether I say it, everyone agrees that these visual or sound signs are equivalent and refer me to the same concept. Whether I write a G quarter note or hear a G quarter note (however it is played), everyone agrees that I am referred back to the same meaning, that is, that this note, combined with a C half note (however it is played), will give the same higher level configuration that has meaning in a particular music. From the moment I read G on the violin or clarinet, I bring in other values, of another type, and I am obliged to imagine the music in two ways. Either, deliberately ignoring this detail, all I retain from the score is the skeleton (which I called pure music earlier), or else I imagine the authentic objects, but without being obliged to make the sound of a specific clarinet or violin: I color a particular note with a particular generic timbre in my thoughts. I must then take on board a plural music, a code with multiple, and very soon unpredictable, combinations. For a while, indeed, the score can be reduced like this, but we soon come back to that association of two terms that links the message and its speaker, the meaning and the event. Music will be twofold: on the one hand, the score, a series of musical signs in the classical sense, and, on the other hand, orchestration, a series of musical events, with a more and more active, evolving, impact. It is not that music is becoming more concrete; the word would be deceptive. We are dealing with two sorts of abstractions of the concrete—one concerned with a quality of sound objects, which gives them a *shared meaning*, the other concerned with a certain characteristic of the objects, which refers them back to a *shared origin*. So we can no longer say that music consists only in its *language system;* we must give it back its *speech.*

18

The Conventional Musical System

Musicality and Sonority

18.1. A DELIGHTFUL ASSORTMENT

So, off with the masks: let the traditional system say what it has to declare. It names four things.

Pitch, duration: we shouldn't ask too much of them. The manuscript papers are checked. Seven keys, that's a lot, what a large bunch for twelve notes.... A half note is worth two quarter notes? A quarter note three eighth notes when they're triplets? Maybe, as long as we don't look too closely. After book 3 there's an amnesty. We'll write that down in the register of values, which will, of course, have the number 4 on it. We will remark that those pitches are pretty approximate and are often different from the nominal value, as are a phoneme's irrelevant variants. We have already observed, more seriously, that half notes and quarter notes mark out spacing much more than actual durations: they give rhythm to silences, or at least breaks in silence, rather than to the presence of sounds. There will be no perceptible relationship of duration except within an instrumental structure or between instruments that make comparable objects (short-lived or sustained). Because we do not play in durations, we will accept the cruder value rhythm (at least in the traditional system, for there is no question of stopping there in a better researched music).

What begins to look pretty bad in the values filing cabinet is this intensity, elsewhere jealously measured in "amplitude," here visibly abandoned to the charming imprecision of an Italianate notation, where a double superlative is sometimes needed to bail it out from its depreciation: "pianississimo." Now, all this works admirably well, provided that we are not more demanding than the maestro himself

and are not made to take nuances for decibels. . . . The musician, of course, appreciates nuances for their acoustic content (decibels), the audiological transmission
(phons), and the absolutely unpredictable *weight* of complex sounds,[1] but he appreciates them much more for the *melody of weight* that these sounds create with their
neighbors (which is a consequence of the perception of structures). The disparity of
complex sounds is such, dynamically, that a musician can only hear them through
reference to their source, a pedigree that is always available to back up judgment in
the same way the candidate's youth or the weakness of his muscles is taken into
account when his performance is being evaluated. Never has a drumbeat prevented
us from hearing fortissimo a tiny piccolo sound. Never has a trumpet pianissimo
been confused with a violin fortissimo, which is, however, a meager acoustic presence compared to the other. There remains the fourth partner, the too notorious
musical timbre. This one, as we saw in the last chapter, cannot be confused with the
others.

18.2. A DANGEROUS INTERSECTION

We, who had believed we could put the abstract on the left, the concrete on the
right, just as we had placed the meaning on one side, the event on the other in our
diagrams in book 2, what are we to think of this irruption of the concrete into the
abstract, since every musical value, if we consider it rigorously, implies an instrumental quality? In the contrast we have drawn between language systems and
speech, just as valid for language as for music, do we not have the impression that
ultimately it is the abstract that rises to the higher sections in our illustrations,
having decanted concrete sound to the bottom? And now in musical composition
we are adding the generic syllables of sector 1 to the values in sector 4.

We inevitably come to the point of wondering what the abstract is, having
thought it so firmly in our grasp when it appeared in the reassuring form of written signs or musical symbols. We turn once more to Lalande's vocabulary for help:
"Abstract is said of every concept of quality or relationship considered from a more
or less general standpoint independently of any representation of it. Conversely,
full representation, as it is or can be given, is called concrete." We can see that the
end result is two sorts of musical abstractions: one leading to values, a quality recognized in a collection of objects; the other leading to instrumental timbre, the
mark of the instrument on other collections of objects. This process of abstraction
is very similar to the mechanism that allows us to identify the object in the structure, except that it summarizes experience. It is "an activity of the mind giving
separate consideration to one element—a quality or relationship—in a representation or a concept, giving it special attention and ignoring the rest."

---

1. See chap. 31.

Thus the term *violin*, in the direction "a G on the violin," is no less abstract than the value indicated by the symbol G. Ignoring the rest, we have retained what could be common to all possible violins.

In short, our schema is compromised. We have, in fact, tended to make it a one-way street, at least in conventional systems where the sound object is forgotten in favor of the meaning. But we cannot extricate ourselves like this without ignoring reality. The two diagrams in the last chapter, which depict a single schema of perceptual structures, have already shown this.

Thus, in every and any case we will have to make two in some way *perpendicular* phenomena *intersect*. One of them has been described many times: it is the way every sound object moves toward the two poles of the event and the meaning, the source that produced it and the message it delivers. The other is a relationship going from the general to the particular:

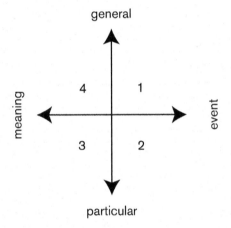

What can we abstract from a mass of particular experiences, going toward either pole? Where sources are concerned, it may be that instead of being overwhelmed by a profusion of disparate events, we manage to extract some general ideas that enable us to organize them, not only by sources (violin, voice, etc.) but by phonation. This is how the phonetician draws up a list of *phonetic material* (sibilants, dentals, etc.), which may be compared to the list of instrumental factures (friction, pizzicati, etc.) applied to various types of sound bodies.

Where sound effects or qualities are concerned, we know that they are only *retained* in structures of meaning. It will be even easier, once a way of using sounds is established by custom, to abstract these qualities: phonemes in language, values in music.

Thus, starting from a concrete experience, a story, or natural as well as cultural phenomena, we arrive at two concepts that can be encoded, notated, written down: these are the contents of sectors 1 and 4.

Indeed, but there is still the question of hearing. So we hear in two ways: either in reality, therefore specifically, or *in the mind*. If we *can read*, we can, by means of a text or a score, hear it in implicit or *imaginary* reality, which can only exist through the (spoken or sound) materials supplied by our memory. The exercise undeniably "works" better for language systems than music, and the reasons for this are immediately obvious. One is owing to the fact that in language the sound object is *superseded* (this is justified by the arbitrariness of the codes that allows signifiers to be easily permutated); the other is to do with the content itself of the written or musical symbols: with language systems, in any case, writing is much more reliable than in music.[2] The articulatory, causal event is entirely forgotten. It should never be the same with music, where the diversity of timbres (instruments and instrumentalists) *is part of the language itself.* So we observe a strange disproportion between the contents of sectors 1 and 4, since 4 summarizes the very meager residue of shared formal values; in 1 a multiplicity of instruments; and for each instrument a multiplicity, not only of notes, but also of factures. This is the divergence, already mentioned, between pure and instrumental music.

This helps to explain two tendencies in music: a tendency to orchestrate, inasmuch as this allows reference to events and the active presence of instruments; a tendency to *Klangfarbenmelodie*, in which, out of nostalgia for pure music, there is a tendency to reincorporate timbre (here not of the instruments but the notes) into sector 4 and make them into a value, as we explained in chapter 16.

18.3. MUSICALITY AND (TRADITIONAL) SONORITY

Finally we will tackle the work in its two forms, abstract and concrete: its score where it appears in a general, virtual state, in the form of signs, and the gramophone record where one of its particular performances is engraved. Can we give a clear account of such an everyday parallel?

Not very easily. All the ex-concrete from sector 1, all the ex-abstract from sector 4, are notatable and appear on the score. Like a literary text, which potentially contains a language system and speech, even if it is only read with the eyes and memorized in silence, the "work" is in principle given, once it comes off the publisher's press, and its unobtrusiveness would make us believe it is what it is not: a text.

---

2. All this is still schematic. The system of written signs can also develop more autonomously, float free from the word: ideograms, orthography in language systems and in music, theoretical scores playing the written sign rather than its sound equivalent.

This text, virtually but authentically sound, has, however, one particular qual-ity: it brings together an infinite number of potential performances, which will all have the "musicality" of the score in common, while each has an "individual sonority."[3] . . . We can think of no better definition of these two terms.

We will now look at all the notes used in the traditional system and take stock of them. First, the normal orchestra and its usual instruments, playing in accord-ance with the rules of music. It is with these *materials* that the composer will com-pose his work. We will simply present him with this material in somewhat better order than usual, and, remaining at the lexical level, we will not even mention the grammars or syntaxes he will have to obey or flout. Now we can sum up our results like this, and present them in four boxes (fig. 20), which should correspond to our definitions, otherwise so vague and ambiguous, of *musicality* and *sonority:*

·   *In the domain of musicality* we include everything that is *made explicit through symbols,*[4] everything therefore that can appear on a score, everything, short of performance, that enables a work to be constructed. We will take care to separate the values of "pitch" and "duration" on the left and instrumental timbres on the right, sidestepping nuances or, more precisely, bringing them into play in both diagrams.

·   *In the domain of sonority* we will hear . . . everything else. Opposite sector 4 with its values that can be symbolized, we must also mention the sonority ordinarily attached to all instrumental notes, which, one by one, take on color in their own way. This is assuming that in this *left-hand* part we only put (in our minds) what is general, what can be *abstracted* from the particularity of every performance. For example, we will know that a string sound, independ-ently of the violin or the violinist (or the viola, or the cello) will definitely have *complementary values* of sonority (resonances, harmonics, fluctuations, profiles, etc.) and that some bass sounds (piano, bassoon, double bass) will have a grain, or a value of thickness, that contrasts them with different parts of the register and has practically nothing to do with particular instruments or performers. The composer knows this, and, as he orchestrates, he anticipates and uses this knowledge in advance.

Finally, in sector 2 there is a *contingent residue,* the only individual, ultimately the only concrete elements, that cannot be determined on the score, even by using

3. This is proved by the fact that reading a score *never entirely* elucidates a work, even if the score *informs* the listener. The composer himself only really wants it to be performed in order to hear *what it's like.*

4. We use this term (the *symbols* of music theory) rather than *sign* because of the disparity between musical writing and the musical sign carried by the real-world sound object. The musical sign becomes synonymous with the musical object once this distinction has been made.

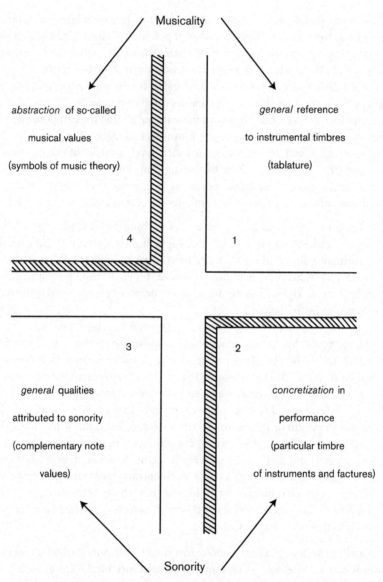

Musicality

abstraction of so-called

musical values

(symbols of music theory)

general reference

to instrumental timbres

(tablature)

4

1

3

2

general qualities

attributed to sonority

(complementary note

values)

concretization in

performance

(particular timbre

of instruments and factures)

Sonority

FIGURE 20. Musical-sonority summary (traditional system).

all that its symbols contain and everything they imply. This is the margin of freedom reserved for the performance. As we have placed ourselves under the austere conditions of considering only the material, *we will not even explore* the virtuoso's style, only his technique. By technique he produces notes in his own way, linked, of course, to his personal instrument; it is their particular sonorities that will appear in sector 2, to nuance, personalize, *put their signature on* the complementary values in sector 3.

18.4. INSTRUMENTAL OVERVIEW

This way of grouping is not easy, but it provides a *framework*, which until now had been completely lacking, for anyone wishing to draw up an inventory of the intrinsic characteristics of an instrumental domain, as much for use in composition as for its resources or performance margins.

How can we analyze the *musical domain* of every principal instrument? How can we assess, rather less vaguely than usual, and in ordinary words, what is called their *musicality* and their *sonority*, while still strictly limiting ourselves to the traditional system and its conditioning?

We will imagine that we are comparing a dozen of them in the following four ways, corresponding to the four sectors in our illustration:

Sector 4: *available values, quality, and quantity*. Extent and accuracy of the register, ability to deliver sounds within the code of pitch, duration, and intensity.

Sector 3: *sonority of notes*. Margin of coloration of the above values, additional enrichment, presence of sound values over and above nominal values.

Sector 1: *instrumental timbre*. General musical interest of the instrumental timbre: originality and richness of this. Permanence. Emergence of this timbre in ensembles.

Sector 2: *sonority of timbres*. Same relationship between 1 and 2 as above between 3 and 4. Particular coloration of individual instruments. Leeway left to the performer for personalization, enrichment, nuances.

Within the traditional system, musicians—whether amateurs, performers, or composers—have vast experience of this musicality, as well as this sonority that we have just mentioned. Teachers, like their pupils, know even better how to embark on the conquest of each of these instrumental domains—that is, what impersonal and rigorous foundations must first be laid (note values and a consistent timbre), and then what must be mastered in terms of register, color, and personality.

So many and such subtle judgments have—and for good reason—never been reliant on a clear description, and even less on a comparative diagram of the musicality-sonority complex. For it to be possible, in fact, to answer the questions we will ask, they must be perfectly well-founded and perfectly understood. In other words, we need a clear frame of reference on which the questioner and the questioned unhesitatingly agree. Developing this would demand of the author, as well as the reader, work that may well be pointless. In the absence of precision, all we can suggest is a sort of *parlor game*, which will be sufficiently instructive if it allows us to quantify the extraordinary complexity of the cultural references to which each one of us spontaneously relates.

18.5. WHAT IS YOUR FAVORITE INSTRUMENT, AND WHY?

Thinking about the use of instruments, not in experimental music but in the most strictly traditional music system as it is taught in the conservatories and put into practice in Sunday concerts, we will ask four questions in relation to ten instruments: six traditional instruments (1: piano, 2: violin, 3: flute, 4: harmonium, 5: trumpet, 6: voice), to which we will add a newcomer (7: ondes martenot), and three gatecrashers that have only one note in their entire vocabulary and are not therefore instruments but isolated sound objects (8: a gut-wrenching grating noise, 9: a complex electronic sound, 10: a gong sound).

The first question concerns the emergence of timbre: classify these ten instruments—or isolated sounds—according to their ability to stand out clearly in an orchestral ensemble, to be distinguished from the others both by differentiation and the originality of their own timbre.

The second question concerns the emergence of interpretation: classify these ten instruments—or isolated sounds—according to the opportunities they give for the instrumentalist to express his personality (or in other words, according to what the facture of the objects they come from can reveal about the talent and sensitivity of the instrumentalist).

The third question, not to be confused with the previous one, concerns the emergence of the sonorities that, as we have just seen, we consider to be independent of the interpreter's playing, his particular instrument, and values properly speaking. (The gong, for example, will have no register of values and will give hardly any margin for play. Conversely, its sonority will be indubitably richer than a piano note, beyond any musical notation in sector 4.) So classify the instruments according to their sonority, depending on whether this adds to the nominal values.

The fourth question is the most classical, and question 3 is related to it: classify these instruments according to the accuracy, the clarity and the refinement of their register, with reference to the nominal values of the traditional system.

This is all about assessing the instrumental qualities we have learned to identify: in the first and fourth question, those that give a guarantee to the composer; in the second and the third, those that provide reciprocal pleasure for the listener who enjoys virtuosi and the virtuoso who enjoys instrumental techniques.

In suggesting an exercise such as this to a group of people, we will stir up a lot of arguments and often come up against hesitation to the point of refusal to reply. For what it is worth, here is our personal contribution, which will at least shed light on the meaning of the questions.

First question: First, very obviously, come the grating noise and the electronic sound, which are far too recognizable. Then the ondes martenot because of its novelty in the orchestra rather than its intrinsic originality. Then the gong, this time for its originality. Then, in order, we would place the voice, the piano, the violin, and only after these the trumpet and the flute. Last by a long way, the harmonium, which has little chance of standing out in an ensemble.

Second question: Clearly, the voice and the violin give the musician the most leeway, followed by the flute, the piano, and the trumpet. The ondes martenot gives fewer opportunities for personalizing the sound, the harmonium and the gong hardly any at all. The two fixed sounds (grating noise and electronic sound), of course, give none at all.

Third question: The grating noise and the gong add most to the values recognized by the system and are therefore likely to "unbalance" it: the disproportion between this *added value*, sonority, and the nominal value is huge. The complex electronic sound, about which we are told very little, is doubtless not far behind. Then the ondes martenot and the voice, which we know can *give a very different timbre to* every note they make (we are talking about something quite different from general timbre, which refers back to the instrument). The violin comes immediately afterward. With the piano, the trumpet, and the flute the margin for coloration, which is there, is clearly more limited than in the previous cases; finally, for the harmonium, it is close to zero.

Fourth question: At the top is the ondes martenot, the grand champion of values of all types, continuous or discontinuous, chromatic or tempered, in the most extensive register, capable of guaranteeing durations, as well as nuances, with incomparable accuracy. Far behind, with less formal reliability and breadth (but also with the resources for chromatics, sounds sustained in duration, and subtlety in pianississimi), comes the violin. Then, the instruments tuned to a temperament, to the discontinuous and sounds that are sometimes short-lived: among these the piano comes first, because of its reliable and extensive register, with which the flute and the trumpet bear no comparison. Only then, the voice. Having made much of it elsewhere, here we must recognize its weak points: a restricted register and unreliability in relation to values. We will give low marks to the gong and the electronic sound, as very poor pupils, but with more or less indulgence depending on whether they are locatable in terms of the tonic or only in terms of color. No marks for the grating noise (or 1 at a pinch if, like its fellows, it places itself in an area of the register, with a minimum of discipline). In these last three cases the classification makes hardly any sense, given that we are no longer assessing registers but isolated objects. We will see that the latter may either approximate—roughly—to a note or—more probably—merge with other bass or high notes, which certainly achieves nothing in the "system."

In figure 21 we played around with transferring this classification of the ten above-mentioned instruments, based on each of the four questions, on to the four diagonal lines in the figure. By joining up the resultant dots, we obtain a sort of contour for each instrument. Quite well balanced for the piano, which has a very honorable ranking throughout, this contour takes on the appearance of an irregular quadrilateral with the highest point at personalization for the voice, or objective performance (in relation to nominal values) for the ondes martenot or the harmonium. The violin covers a large and well-balanced area, whereas the other instruments only cover smaller ones. Finally, as may be expected, we find the invalids (in relation to the traditional system), which hardly go beyond the timbre-sonority diagonal.

18.6. IDENTIFICATION AND DESCRIPTION

Even if the complementariness of musicality-sonority is obvious in music, we have just described it *from the outside* based on the de facto situation of the score and the performance. We can go back over these ideas, which we will now place on a higher level in order to explain them more fully and link them more clearly to the fundamental phenomenon of structuring.

We have already described in section 17.5 the various ways in which the object may appear: an isolated sound object, heard as an event (as in a piano work by John Cage), or for its particular meaning, grouped objects forming a structure, and so forth.

To come to firm conclusions within the traditional musical system, we must take another look at the processes we have described. As soon as we hear the notes of a melody, our conditioning *makes us name them*, and *all the more so if we are musicians*. Otherwise, if we were more amateur—or uncultured—we would be completely unable to name them, or we would perhaps hear differently. And better? No, not better: with an ear that is less accurate, less refined, less "intelligent," as sound engineers say, but perhaps more naive, more sensitive to what would be a novelty for it, which it would start by "tasting," as it would not be able to understand. For the musician, in his system, every act of melodic listening is not to describe the notes but to *identify* them. This done, he will ask for them to be played again, more slowly ("Stop on A-flat," says the teacher), to "taste" the object this time, to hear it outside the structure that identified it but did not allow it to be described. Hearing this note again, he can, all over again, *identify its component elements*, pick out the attack, the continuation, the decay, the vibrato, and so forth. This time he will only *perceive* them, name them—not describe them. It is by

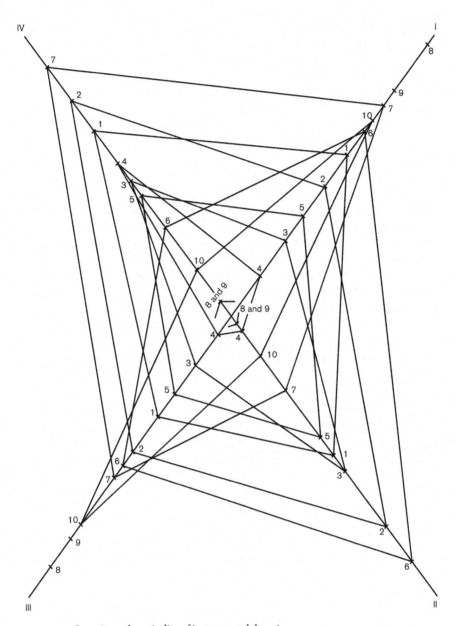

FIGURE 21. Sonority and musicality of instrumental domains.

isolating this fragment of object (this *feature*,[5] as linguists say), repeating it, reexamining it, that he will seek to describe it and naturally as a structure, doubtless the smallest he can isolate. All instrumental teaching is familiar with, or at least practices, this type of analysis.

Conversely, we go up the descriptive chain. This *feature* describes the note. The notes describe the melody, and so on.

Now we move on to timbres. In an orchestra the various instruments contrast with and differ from each other: instruments have left traces in the memory, and this is how we can identify *one of them*, among the others, or on its own. To describe it, we have to compare different examples of the instrument and form a structure of the same timbre, which will reveal *the timbre of the timbre*. These (what we have called sector 2) comparisons must not be confused with the note-by-note comparisons in sector 3. In 2, various pianos are compared. In 3, various notes from any piano are compared. This is irrelevant. The latter piano is concrete, the overall sonority of a particular piano compared to others. Comparing piano notes in general amounts to abstracting from all pianos a value added to all of their notes. The proof of this is that the notes from various pianos in general all obey the laws of the invariant described in book 3. So we can more easily see what the sectors are for. Earlier, they simply seemed to be a convenient set of drawers to evaluate the musicality-sonority pair. Here we see that they are part of the effective working of the "system." We identify, nominally, in sectors 1 and 4. Then we qualify in 2 and 3, either to complete the description of particular sonorities in 2 or to discover more general criteria of sonority 3. Once sector 3 has been explained, new musical values emerge (in 4). Thus analyzing sonority *would*, if possible, *use up* the contents of timbre (1) and *values that elude formal musicality*. If the analysis could be taken to its limits, only what is abstract in music and what is concrete in sound would remain, in the pair in the two sectors 4 and 2 alone.

18.7. *DIABOLUS IN MUSICA*

Systems, just like civilizations, develop, live, and slowly die while undergoing change. We should say straightaway that it appears particularly futile to claim to pull one system out of our hat and that this is not our intention. We know, however, that no radical change can take place without questioning the *whole* system, not revising it. Besides, every development makes its impact, focuses on a certain level of language, and stays there as long as this level is capable of dealing with reorganizations and extensions. The first to be attacked are the higher levels, more

---

5. *Feature* in the phonological sense is rather unfortunate in music, where the word generally denotes a particularly difficult phrase involving, precisely, virtuosity.

accommodating, where the aesthetic quarrels of ancients and moderns are finally settled to the satisfaction of all. That is what used to be done in our music.

One does not have to be a great scholar to diagnose the present situation: the crisis is much too serious, calling the very foundations of the system into question. We are not here to complain about this or rejoice in it, and doubtless it is in no one's power to hasten or slow down the course of events. It is, however, very pretentious and quite absurd to jump on the bandwagon of innovative, exclusive, self-assured systems when we are in a period of change and when, desperate to escape from an ancient system, people daily use its material, its notions, its methods, and, above all, an antiquated symbolism that conceals whether the value of signs is immutable or can be changed.

The crack, in any case, is clearly visible, and the fissure cannot escape anyone at the frontiers of the musical and sound. Contemporaries often make sectors 2 and 3 on virtuoso playing and eccentric sounds carry the burden of their innovations. Without good virtuosi using their instruments in unusual ways, providing effects way beyond the directions on the score, without the competition, this time creative, between players and their conductor, the work is worse than badly played; it *does not exist*, by which I mean it is not realized. The audience, often disappointed with so much "speech," looks for "a language system" that is absent. So what is going on? The frame of reference 1–4 has been superseded, it is no longer note values and timbre that count; the score is no longer an analytical score that gives an account of the work but an empirical score, entirely performance-based.

We will take some more specific, simpler examples and bring the ondes martenot into the orchestra. While paying tribute to this excellent invention, we cannot but acknowledge that it undermines the "system"; it muddies the waters in an apparently benign way but is indicative of catastrophes to come. In vain do we wonder about its nature. The papers are in order—an extensive, accurate, and nuanced register: timbres, which can at will be made meek or rebellious, concealing themselves turn and turn about through mimicry, yet remain ready to give a "helping hand" where colleagues fall short for lack of breath or register. It is too good to be true. Those cunning craftsmen who have been polishing up their tools for centuries, humble servants of a grand duchy fastidious about correctness, see it coming in its great clogs, the electrical device that can do anything, the vanguard of electronic or concrete hordes. . . . Is this too far-fetched a sketch?

The ondes had, however, done everything it could to seek inclusion and forgiveness. Consider the gong, infinitely more brutal. And the cencerros, comical and loose-living. These are, strangely, looked upon more kindly, and people allow themselves to be intimidated, corrupted by what laughs in their face. Doubtless, they were expecting the gong to be rarely used, that it would settle for playing the final cymbal clashes in a symphony, more gravely, more piously perhaps (wasn't it brought up in temples?). Here there are several of them. And each one acts on its own behalf. Who would believe in a keyboard of gongs? Messiaen, at Chartres,[6] for a moment makes as if he believes in one. Stockhausen does open-heart surgery.[7] . . . We must endeavor to make the roll call of our defensive sectors. In fact, it is not enough to say that each gong is located in sector 1 and its sounds in sector 3: we can see that the system is in disarray in two ways. We are no longer dealing with systems of structures but the perception of an isolated structure-object. As an instrument, it is off-key in sector 1. As an object it holds sway in sector 3 without bothering about values, and all we are left with is its presence (is it in 2?), without our being able to attach its sonority to a formal or complementary value. The system, if not completely destroyed, is at the least threatened by a foreign body.

The gong only disrupts the system so seriously because it suggests another system, whereas we might have thought it was simply an ambiguous case, an exception to the rule.

Other instruments could make us hear intercalated "wrong" notes or badly tempered keyboards. They would still remain within the concept of instrument; they would have a generic name in sector 1, and it is difficult to know what is most to be feared: sector 3 upsetting the balance of sector 4 because of the strangeness of the sonorities, or sector 4 being disrupted by unusual calibrations. Such systems may therefore oppose each other, be superimposed on each other, or fight each other; but they are still the same type of system, like two related civilizations, two homologous types of writing or language. But it is difficult to compare a population to a family, a language system to a cry, a city to a standing stone. In short, the gong, even if it is compared in the mind or the memory to other gongs, tears the orchestral system apart, and we need the amiable hospitality of contemporary laxity to enjoy this bombshell, this huge spelling mistake, and immediately bedeck this idol with garlands. . . . This gong comes to us from elsewhere. It stands out, a solitary sound object. You can hear nothing else apart from it. We try very hard to make it fit in with what is around it; it forms a musical structure only when it pleases—that is, if it pleases to sing along with it. This gong is not in a situation of its own: it is the situation of every more or less suitable sound object that is invited to make music within the system. It does not work.

When sound precedes the musical, the stakes are down. The system is turned on its head. Rather than ducking the issue, cheating, composing, we must resolutely look to the sound. To our very great surprise, instead of what we thought were formless noises, we find a system—antagonistic, no doubt, but perfectly constituted. That really is something.

6. Olivier Messiaen, *Et expecto resurrectionem mortuorum* . . . [Orchestral piece composed in 1964.—Trans.]

7. Karlheinz Stockhausen, *Mikrophonie 1.* [Piece for live electronics, with tam-tam, amplification, microphones, and filters, composed in 1964.—Trans.]

Natural Sound Structures

Musicianly Listening

19.1. THE UNIVERSAL SYMPHONY

It is there for everyone; it is within his reach, unless he turns *a deaf ear*.

We, in fact, find it quite natural, in an immense hubbub, to hear one thing rather than another. But this implies two preconditions: that we can *identify* a particular sound source, by attributing various sound effects to it, and that we can *isolate* it, by putting other sounds aside. This natural listening is the least passive possible; it is one of the most highly evolved activities of the human ear and the main activity onto which the various expert, specialized listening modes are grafted.

We will endeavor to understand the way this admirable calculating machine works: instead of obeying our *reflexes*, we will adopt a *contemplative* stance; instead of selecting one of the sources from a multitude of disparate perceptions, we will endeavor—and this is already a step toward *reduced listening*—to hear everything at the same time, if possible. A step backward toward passivity? Not at all. It will be an active *musicianly mode of listening*, as if we were listening to an orchestra and trying to focus on all the sources at once. Weary of hearing music passively, or the tune asininely played by the first violins, we will decide to open our ears, to grasp the whole of the orchestra's activity, which is what the conductor does supremely. There is already reduction: the focus on external objects, causes and sources, is no longer in order *to follow the events* they suggest, each one for itself, but rather to appreciate their working together—how, in their coming together, they are still distinct. This is the dialectic of the orchestra itself, the etymology of *symphony*, a unity that is constantly plural. Even if the listening mode we are describing is not *reduced* at the level of the sound object, we could say that it tends in that direction at the orchestral level or the din we have taken as our experimental field. It constantly mobilizes and also constantly eludes our attention through its richness and diversity. Even good professionals similarly lose their way in the orchestral mass.

We already know the results of such a simple experiment, and we know that, *except for music*, our parallel is valid. The same type of activity, the same perceptual structures (this time to do with sound, outside any musical system) prevail both in this sort of symphonic attention and in extraordinary opportunities to grasp the way various languages are articulated and to identify speakers. We also know that this is nothing to do with *referring* disorganized noise perceived in this way to *scores* notated in pitch, duration, and intensity; the mechanisms of listening to the orchestra cannot be explained any better by the existence of a score and a notation.

What happens spontaneously and often with extreme accuracy is that we *decode* with consummate skill. Now, far from congratulating ourselves on this and admiring our abilities, we are ashamed, and readily despise our marvelous autonomic systems, doubtless out of irritation because we cannot understand them.

So, to verify this, we will again imagine ourselves in the tumult of an amusement park, in a fairground or a packed meeting, chattering near a flight of birds beside the sea, amid the rustling of the trees in the wind. Our ear, much more *musicianly* than we would dare to think, does much more than identify these sound objects, which it names "twittering of birds," "my neighbor speaking," "sound of waves," or "barrel-organ music" as separate units. It does not mix them up with each other, as even the latest IBM machine would. In its own way, and in the etymological and not the symbolic sense, it makes a true *score*: creating each instrument's part and giving it its *continuum*.

Now we will suppose that the conversation is taking place in a language system unknown to the listener. To isolate each speaker and give him the right sound continuum, the listener must make an effort. But he will cope nevertheless, although the meaning (which of course would help him) is lacking in this conversation. In spy novels the hero similarly listens to two or three secret agents speaking in languages he does not know, and concern for his safety makes him adopt an acousmatic mode of listening: he cannot see them from his hiding place. He can clearly distinguish what he hears, however, and, boldly summoning sonorities or musicalities, true or false, to his aid, he *identifies* and *describes*: one has a deep voice, a throaty *r*; the other speaks jerkily, and so forth.

Now look more closely at these last few lines: we have given ourselves a spontaneous description of how our listening works. Each time we have used two terms: "twittering of birds," "sounds of waves or trees," "my neighbor speaking," "barrel-organ music." This analysis gives us not the key to this amazing, although spontaneous, decoding but its two poles: one of these words refers back to the source, the other to the content. However approximate the words in our description, it has covered the essentials. Though not understanding everything, we identified everything: on each occasion an essential permanence enabled us to analyze the identity of the cause; and notwithstanding the countless variety of those words, that barrel-organ music, those noises, we find it quite natural to take possession of those variations through which we can establish something permanent. For it is time, we believe, to realize that blind, or hidden behind Pythagoras's screen or the tape recorder, it is *through the diversity of the sounds* that we *inferred distinct causes* that we might readily give, logically, as an explanation. *Now, it is through their effects, of course, that we can go back to them!*

These universal sound structures, which we postulated tentatively and considered crude, are not hypothetical. They dictate everyday practice in the most incontrovertible way possible. Talking about indicators or significations, we too often forget the sound perception from which they came and which reduced listening, finally focusing on the sound object itself, will allow us to become aware of. And this sealed-off, subtle, unstable perception of the sound object, the vehicle, but brought to a halt, of all the other perceptions, is dominated by structures that, before being linguistic or acoustic, dramatic or prosaic, detective or medical, or, finally, strictly musical, are the structures of sonority.

19.2. THE REPERTOIRE OF CAUSALITIES

Already fruitless is the acoustician's attempt to get to grips with timbre. We ourselves have managed only with great difficulty to establish correlations between our manner of perceiving and the physical makeup of a few elementary sounds. This scarcely puts us on the road to an overall process.

Watch the acoustician at work. Just like his colleague teaching Monsieur Jourdain,[1] he carefully studies each causality, one by one: the phonatory instrument, the position of the tongue against the teeth, the resonators. "What a wonderful thing an A is," remarks Monsieur Jourdain, with good reason. But Nicole hears As just as well as her master, without knowing anything about them. *Perceptual structures do very well without technical expertise,* as much at the instrumental level as with the signal.

Now, we have emphasized the natural-cultural pair of opposites, postulating a human ear, universal, full of potential, precultural. Is this the ear that has that astonishing power of identification since it can identify speakers through speech it does not understand?

So what is the *natural?* When we think about it, it is not the opposite of the cultural but, more accurately, of the conventional: instead of focusing on concepts, joined to sounds by arbitrary links, and which only a prior knowledge of the code enables it to identify, "natural" listening gives a meaning to what it takes in, without going through any conventions but relying on already very highly evolved

---

1. This is a reference to Molière's comedy *Le Bourgeois gentilhomme* (1670). M. Jourdain is the middle-class master of the house, and Nicole is his maidservant.

previous experience, which could be called the acquisition of a personal repertoire, shared nevertheless with contemporaries. Just like learning a language system, this is the result of *an individual learning process in a group environment:* we mean the repertoire of *noises.*

Would these noises, which we readily consider *natural* (because we identify them with events: engine noises for contemporary civilizations, animal noises for pastoral civilizations) be understood without the help of a type of experience in which civilization adds to nature? When I hear an unfamiliar noise, with no prior reference point, it is then that I hear it as a sound object, since I immediately have to look for its cause; there are noises like this whose sonority I could best evaluate if they were not so surprising, and if I did not immediately attempt to compare them with other, known, noises with a view to explaining them—that is, *identifying and describing* them.

So the fact that noises seem *natural* is all very well: from our earliest childhood we spell out, we learn this *language of things* with the same diligence as a human language system. We are scarcely capable of imagining a world where noises were different or belonged to a repertoire different from the repertoire of this *planet.* Pathology provides proofs for our debate. In tactile or visual asymbolia, people are neither blind nor paralyzed, but the patient no longer recognizes what he sees or what he touches. What is this pencil? The patient replies: it's long, thin, pointed (as can be seen, he expresses himself in *values*): he has forgotten the repertoire. Thus, he might not recognize an object he feels with his right hand but recognize it with his left if his deficiency is unilateral.

19.3. THE LANGUAGE OF THINGS

So what seemed to be a metaphor becomes, ultimately, a statement of reality. Earlier attempts to find an explanation for our sound object identification structures still came from a sort of lack of realism, implicitly positing that the physical cause comes before the perceived effect. If we use language in its broadest sense, as we have learned to do in music, it seems reasonable to allow that *the language of things* can also be learned. We refer it back to its source using the register of its interactions because this is our experience and our training. If there are birds on Mars, or highly developed machines on a planet somewhere near Sirius, there is nothing to tell us about their general shapes and the variations of the sounds they make. Our familiarity with identifying so easily both their sources and the various sounds they make hides this learning process from us.

A horse has a *timbre* that is very easy to locate. We should note that it consists of various neighing sounds, as well as the noise of hoofs. A car enthusiast recognizes simultaneously the way the engine runs and the make of car: this is precisely the timbre-value, permanence-variation pair mentioned above. It is the result of a

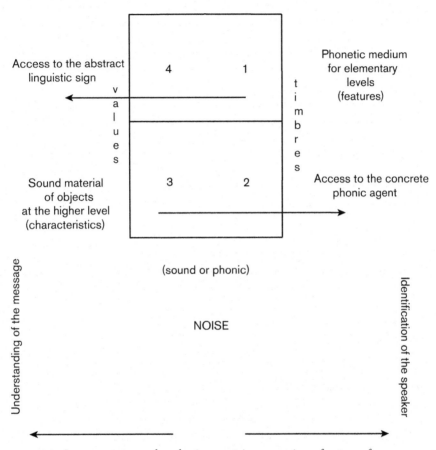

FIGURE 22. Language system code and noise repertoire: comparison of systems of conventional (and musical) language codes and the noise repertoire (sound events).

whole listening experience. We have slandered natural listening by calling it non-specialized. But it is specialized, at a basic level, in many domains.

So what is the difference between learning the repertoire of noises and the codes of language systems? We could say that it develops in the opposite direction (fig. 22). Linguistics does more than ignore the "speakers"; it only studies sound objects insofar as they are the bearers of abstract concepts. It uses the permanence-variation pair *a contrario*. Variations of intonation do not matter; the structure that commands perception is meaning. In the language of things (and for us things include the noise of conversations, the commotion of animals, etc.), some of the meanings do not matter or are impenetrable to us; but some indicators are clear and inform us, not about what the individual wishes to say to us but what we want to know about him. These modulations, which have no linguistic significance but are *obvious* noises, lead us to an identification of their common source, how they are produced and a description of his activity: as indicators, they have *pertinent characteristics*, just as in a language system the features that lead to the identification of a signified are pertinent.

It is often in the same way as that type of language that we understand—or fail to understand—music. Why, then, should we not add the decoding of what naturally emits sound to any approach to cultural music?

Besides, we cannot continue this decoding of sound objects if we limit ourselves to *natural listening*, at least if we want to use it to discover a musicality. It is precisely by putting aside spontaneous reference to sound sources, demonstrating *the processes behind identifying and describing* objects perceived across a whole variety of sound samples, that we might have some chance of progress. We are therefore *moving in the opposite direction from making lists of instruments* or from describing the *particular properties* of the samples they produce.

In book 5 we will endeavor to find such a method, one that can take into account articulation and intonation, the common bases for identifying any type of sound object.

But as we have said, we will not pursue such a general study for too long. Aware now of the disparity among sound objects, in relation to both their innumerable sources and their capricious modulations, we feel that it would be good to limit ourselves to the simplest, least indicative, least anecdotal objects, which carry a more spontaneous, although sparser, musicality. We will, however, take care to identify those *suitable* sound objects that lend themselves to *musicianly invention just as do the most universal sound objects. We cannot apply any musical perceptual structure to them a priori.* We will find out through practical work if this is possible.

19.4. THE CHILD WITH THE GRASS

Homo faber, grown old, no longer plays on anything but Stradivarius. So we must use a younger setting. We are going to listen to a child who has picked a suitable blade of grass, held it stretched between his thumbs, and is now blowing on the grass while the hollow of his hands serves as a resonator.

First we note that this child is giving us the right exercise in musicianship for our situation: we no longer want to hear the Stradivarius's *sound quality*, which is *too musical*, but *listen in a musicianly way* to the crudest of *sound objects*, and we will discover this mode of listening by doing it.

What is more, from the sound sources, he has chosen for himself one of those that seemed most *suitable* for what he is doing. In fact, this child is trying out his sounds one after the other, and the problem he presents is more his manner of making them than identifying them. Moreover, his intention is visibly musicianly. Even if the result does not seem musical to his exasperated audience, we cannot deny an aesthetic intention, or at least an artistic activity, on the part of the composer. He does not demand or use an implement. His aim is disinterested, if not disarming; it is even, we must admit, musical. Indeed, not content with fabricating sounds, he plays them, compares them, judges them, and finds them more or less successful, their sequence more or less satisfactory. As we said about Neanderthal man, if this child is not making music, what is he doing?

Our example is already outstripping our purpose. In the sounds of the grass there is more than sonorities. We will nevertheless continue. Suppose he is making "experimental music." What is heard by the listener, even casual, reticent, or hostile? For once, and this is not the norm, sound objects. In fact, scarcely has he identified the causality, grass, before the series of efforts by the virtuoso teach him nothing more, either about a grass anecdote or an unlikely piece of grass music: there will be no further "message," any more than event. Our listener will have to suffer a collection of objects devoid of *musical meaning*, and he will hear them all the better for this: one hoarser, another more strident; some short, others interminable; some trumpet-like, others rasping. The best of it is that, in fact, this (non-musician) listener will be doing the best *musicianly listening* possible. Constrained to listen, as the objects are so hostile, he will implicitly make value judgments. He would go so far as to mutter (provided he did not—wrongly—despise his unconscious activity): "That one's a bit better than the others."

In fact, he is practicing the two modes of listening: *musical*, which makes him locate a higher, a deeper, a short or a long sound, and so forth, albeit crudely; and another type of listening, *musicianly*, much more refined. He cannot stop himself identifying with the child, blowing along with him, succeeding or failing: the grass cracks, balloons out, straightens, bursts; it is as if he were playing it himself. The breaths are short, long, good, rushed; again it is the listener in agony, out of breath. What better confirmation of what we said in chapter 15: we are not listening to the sound for the event any more but to the sound event itself?

19.5. THE MUSICAL IN EMBRYO

And so we discover what might structure the perception of sound objects. We can see that these structures, the foundation of all sonorities, would also provide an initial approach to the musical, tending to describe (prematurely) certain formal aspects of the sound object. But we know that this was quite different from describing the object by means of a *crude musicality* (sector 4: bass, forte, piano . . .); we are dealing with a *refined sonority*, as much for sound effects (sector 3) as for details of performance (sector 2).

Where will we turn to make progress? Certainly not toward musical listening, which is conventional by definition, and certainly not toward an extension of existing musical conventions, to accommodate this new domain of sound. The man listening to the grass is only such a good musician because he has not won the Prix de Rome.

What are we asking of the experimental listener (at the tape recorder, for example) in *musicianly listening* to any type of sound over which he has no control? We are putting him into the acousmatic situation, forbidding him to ask questions about the origin of the sound, and also into a deconditioning situation, refusing him reference to any traditional music theory so that he listens with a fresh ear, which is curious to discern ways of describing sounds that are at present not in his "system" but that can be clearly heard and demand to be included in some other system, through *lateral generalization.*

Would we ask this listener to be as passive as his music theory is supposedly active? No. He listens to sound as if he were making it; he tries various experiments, approaches the object by listening to it several times over, just as the child with the grass made several attempts to perfect his motif, his *theme*. Though less apparent, his activity is just as real as the instrumentalist's.

Here there is symmetry in terms of *translation*. Since the recorded tape indisputably gives the same *physical signal* each time it is played, the listener can perceive the same sound object. Then his repeated listening acts as a series of rough sketches. He *is working on his ear* as the instrumentalist *worked at his instrument.*

Moreover, musicians, even without tape recorders, corroborate what we are saying: for an instrumentalist it is indeed the ear that counts. However difficult the technique, the positioning of a bow or the placing of a voice, the teacher advises the pupil to *learn to hear himself.* With a gifted pupil, they say he has *an ear*, before saying he has fingers or a voice.

19.6. THE CHILD WITH THE VIOLIN

Here, if I may, I should like to mention some personal memories. Throughout my childhood, listening to my father's violin lessons from the next room, I would hear his perpetual refrain: "*One* to get ready," he would say, "*two* to play." The poor children who, tearful or resigned, had to undergo this regime put up with this asceticism as best they could. A long moment of hesitation prolonged the silence: "Your bow like this; your fingers like that! Press with your fingertips, raise your wrist," and so on. I could sense a laborious positioning process. Then, at the number *two* the liberated bow ran across the string. The rosined pressure gave the sound a sometimes painful mordent; then the whole forearm at full stretch swept the air, usually vouchsafing a hoarse scraping noise, the brief and pitiful result of so much effort. When, fascinated by this nevertheless familiar listening process, I was drawn into following the twists and turns of the drama, I would, to my great surprise, hear my father reprimanding or praising the child, often, it seemed, the wrong way round. When for once he had played in tune and not made too many squeaking noises, he told him off. For other dreadful sounds, clearly out of tune, the gruff voice would encourage him. Perhaps, I thought later, it was because his stance was good, with his bow held well and a bold *extension* for an augmented second, which it was better to have wanted too accurate and risk being wrong than to get right sloppily or by chance. In this way my father seemed to inculcate in the young musician a separation into two stages of *making* and *hearing*, knowing that once he was a virtuoso, it would not be at the moment when the note was released that he could put it right.

When I started listening to sound objects, I remembered those lessons. With sounds in which I had nothing musical to hear (no traditional values), I could first of all endeavor to sense a facture, to listen a second, a third time, as if I were responsible for describing something behind the unknown or overlooked phenomenon. And so, I *worked on my ear*, and I learned to imagine the potential values concealed in badly articulated sounds, just as eventual qualities were developing in the scraping sounds of the beginner.

We will take this moral as far as it will go. My father could have been methodical, rewarding effort or intention more than success or result. This would be to underestimate the lesson. In the *two stages*, preparation and execution, he was making an instinctive dichotomy that went beyond the scope of teaching. The first stage was facture, entirely focused on results; the second stage was meaning, permeated with the facture.

The schema of musical communication itself was clearly visible in this, and, of course, it applied both ways, to the violinist as much as the listener, in the sense of prose composition as well as translation.

However reduced our listening to the sound object or to the sound event for itself may be, the two sides of this listening, and the links it still has with the two aims that usually go beyond the object cannot be separated: "What's happening?" and "What does it mean?" In chapter 8 we did try to "pry away" the sound object from its two neighbors, the event and the meaning, the cause and the aim: but our listening is structured by this same looped circuit, which harks back to the object: *musicianly listening to factures* by the instrumentalist, *musical listening to values* in the traditional system, and *invention* by the researcher trying to discover unknown—that is, previously unheard—structures, outside the musical code and musical manners.

19.7. OVERVIEW OF "SONORITY"

Through the example of the grass sounds, and also the violin lesson, we have gained important insights. We will continue with the same line of inquiry:

(a) Every object perceived through sound is only so because of our listening intention. Nothing can prevent a listener from destabilizing this, going unconsciously from one system to another or else from *reduced* listening to one that *is not.* We should perhaps even congratulate ourselves on this. It is through such swirling intentions that links are established, information exchanged. The essential is to be aware of some final goal, toward which the other perceptual activities are working, and to define the project that formally sanctions the sound object: reduced listening.

Thus, when we listen to a grass sound, we may unthinkingly focus on a traditional value (pitch), which masks listening to the structures of the grass (as sound or as music), which are rich in other ways.

But the troublesome question remains: which of these sound (grass) structures are common to all sound objects? Which, on the contrary, describe the sound object coming from the grass as if it virtually belonged to some particular domain? This question is far from idle. Above and beyond its theoretical importance, here is the experimental proof: sometimes the grass sounds like a trumpet; sometimes it moans like a child; sometimes it might, almost, give out a vowel, so . . .

(b) By comparing the (musicianly) activities of these two children—one using grass, the other the bow—we can prove that sound can indeed be more general than the musical.[2] It is by getting rid of the pertinent features in the various languages that we can discover, by subtraction, the essential sound structures that we have said are linked to "factures"; this is the shared comparative domain of all sound objects.

Later, we will retain only very few criteria for sonority, just enough to provide a basis for identifying and classifying musical objects (as sound objects). We should not conclude from this that this idea is simple, very much to the contrary. It is the extreme difficulty of making any general statements about the "common stock" of sound objects (which are described later on) that makes us so cautious.

(c) So we move inevitably from sound to the musical. We have generalized the specific study of the "sound structures of musical objects," in the traditional sense of the professional language, in the formula "musicianly listening to sound objects," and we have limited it initially to a selection of suitable objects.

It remains for us to clarify what "musicianly invention" is, that gives itself sound objects not yet described as musical but that lend themselves to this.

(d) We always dread begging the question, which we know is a danger for us. Although this is a very real danger at the beginning of a piece of research, which is

---

2. As in so-called symphonic listening.

always permeated with our conditionings or notions, it recedes as everything becomes clearer, and, better still, it becomes less daunting. The choice of the child with the grass shows, moreover, what meaning (inspired by him) we give to musicianly invention. It should reassure some and frighten others.

(e) As for "musicianly listening," we have just seen it at work. It is first of all listening to factures, in the manner of *homo faber*, whom we imagine ourselves to be. But it is also listening to effects, all the contents of sonority. In fact, it is the first step toward reduced listening, listening to sound at this point, but already striving to find identification criteria. We must make ourselves a little clearer.

19.8. RELATIONSHIP BETWEEN MUSICIANLY AND NATURAL LISTENING

1. *Musicianly listening is renewed by natural listening.*[3]

Musicianly listening takes musical intention beyond the conditioning of custom; it must therefore move away from traditional listening and refuse to limit itself to the objects of a culture.

But since it has a tendency to "go back to sources," to more inquisitive listening, it is in danger of turning back into natural listening, focusing not on the sound object but on the event. It must resist this just as much.

This *detachment* of cause from effect, this *reversal* of curiosity, may seem delicate and fragile. In fact it is *an exercise in power;* the distinction it creates, infinitely productive, is the secret of reduced listening. It amounts to *transferring traditional responsibilities from the composer to the object.*

2. *Musicians often practice natural listening.*

There are not two categories of listener, those who are entirely musicians and those who are not musicians at all. In a musical civilization a whole series of conditionings and skills creates different levels of listening and ways of accounting for them socially. Between the statement "I can hear a violin playing a tune" and this one: "When I switched on the radio, I happened to recognize Untel playing such and such a piece; he seemed in very good form," there is all the difference that separates a philistine from a skilled amateur or an experienced professional. But we observe that, even if the former has practiced ordinary, and the latter expert, listening, in each case they have drawn conclusions and paid little attention to musicality.

3. *The natural ear sometimes does musical listening.*

As musical language belongs to a civilization, musical characteristics and values are used independently of those who practice music to describe sound objects or objects that are targeted through sound. The doctor will speak of an arrhythmic

3. As in chapter 7.

heart, whistling breath, a fine death rattle. The mechanic will talk about his engine in musical terms. . . . It may be that he is focusing on the sound itself at the time, but only temporarily, to get some clues. To describe these clues, there is no reason why he should not use traditional vocabulary or refer to conventional musical values.

19.9. TOWARD A MUSICIANLY CLASSIFICATION OF SOUND OBJECTS

To what sort of classification of sound objects can musicianly listening lead us?

As long as the simple examples of traditional music are in our minds, we expect to obtain a classification of sound objects that is rather like instrumental classification. Since energetic events are the common basis of sound objects, surely instruments will enlighten us? In fact, we will see that musical instruments have very wisely minimized these events. In their development they have all followed the same rule: discretion. They are all busy trying to be forgotten and to load the sound object only very *sparingly* with musicality. A classification of sound objects would actually be ill-served by such highly developed examples: for example, piano notes, which have a particular predetermined calibration of values and a particular specialized facture.

But a general classification of sound objects still seems to be out of our reach and, in addition, to lack the effectiveness necessary for our purposes. We, who are still musicians, do not have the motivation, purely for the sake of knowledge, that would bring about such a classification. So in book 5 we will reach a compromise, a classification of sound objects that does not exclude *musical choices* in the *sound criteria*. We hope, however, once we have an adequate range of objects, to open the way for other researchers, who might follow the same pathway for other systems. One interesting direction would be research into the language of animals.

19.10. FROM SOUND TO THE MUSICAL

It was essential to go back to the sources of sound before moving on to the distinctions below, which will mark a new approach to objects and define the activities that target them, in a different way from the "conventional system."

(a) General nature of sound objects.

A moment's thought shows that the distinction sound object—musical object, as far as a difference of nature goes—collapses as soon as the sound object is defined theoretically: everything that can be heard in reduced listening. The former contains the latter. Musical objects, phonetic objects, industrial sounds, birdsong, and so on are sound objects. The common stock of these objects has as many branches as the categories these terms cover. How can we separate what belongs to the common stock and what comes from the descriptions of them?

(b) In listening to sound objects, therefore, we have to distinguish between two aspects: one to do with identifying, the other with describing, these objects. Where identification is concerned, very general rules have been suggested, which would enable objects to be *articulated* in the sound universe *independently of the pertinent characteristics of each source*. If such a general, even if not precise, approach to sound objects is successful, it will be applicable to the musical object in particular.

(c) We will abandon, however, our thoughts of an overall study of the ways sound objects can be described. Not that this is not interesting in theory. But it would be truly presumptuous to attempt such a study, mixing up so many objects whose qualities are, precisely, developed and differentiated by their use.

This is what made us say, conversely, supposing the question to be resolved, that a fully elucidated musicality could in its turn be applied to the problem of sonorities (at least if the axioms of musicality, both at the level of description and at the level before, have not already marked out an exclusively musical domain). The complementariness of what we are saying can be explained as follows: the laws for *identifying sound objects* give new material to musical research, free of the most narrow-minded musical prejudice; at the same time, a musicality explored for fairly universal musical objects could lead to methods that, if not parallel, at least come from *lateral generalization*, for a particular field of sonorities, arising from the various domains of facture or use.

(d) It is true, in fact, that we have introduced a further restriction, which is not of the same nature as the earlier ones, by speaking of *musicianly invention*: this should create sound objects varied enough to extend the study of sonorities while limiting their varieties so that, later, they can be found *suitable* for a musicality yet to be defined. It remains to be shown that this bias does not vitiate all our research and that it does not, right from the start, posit an implicit musical convention without defining it.

(e) All of this finally pins down the term *musicianly listening*, which has been becoming gradually clearer: it is doubly restricted, then, on the one hand, because it is not asked to explain all the sound structures of the object, but only *the structures that identify it* (point *b*); on the other hand, because, informed by it, we choose *suitable objects* (point *d*) for it. It is through these two restrictions that it makes "reduced" listening into a "specialty."

Points *a* and *c* may well come from logic, and point *e* from a particular terminology, but we still had to prove the validity of points *b* and *c*; this is the purpose of the examples given in this chapter and the argument in the next chapters.

The Reduced Listening System

Musical Dualism

20.1. DILEMMA OR DUALISM

Our mind is made in such a way that we will never have the last word on anything: scarcely had we escaped from the traditionally "musical," the conditioning of civilized musical man, to discover the reservoir of musical potential in the sound object, than we had to allow not only musically trained listening to this object but, furthermore, equally musicianly invention of objects suitable for the musical. In this to-ing and fro-ing from the conventionally musical to still *untamed* sound, we should nevertheless note that we are becoming richer, freer at every stage: the question raised by the sound object and the ways of listening to it make us reflect on what we call the musical. Reapplying this purified, liberated musical intention to the sound object, we discover potentialities there that, even if they are not easy to use, are nevertheless consonant with activity that is both *musicianly* and *musical*, and through which music was and is still being invented.

Now, all our listening exercises have led us to distance ourselves from two things: the present musical system, which restricted our ears to conventional "values," and natural listening, which referred back to indicators or sound anecdotes. We have gained from these acrobatics. In fact, we have continuously oscillated between *two ways of using sounds*, mostly mutually exclusive: their use as indicators, focused solely on the event, and their use as signs, entirely subjugated to the code. A piece of musical research can only avoid choosing between these two poles by taking them both on board. The essence of the phenomenon of music may well be in this dividedness, this ambivalence.

We must now draw out the consequences of these two sorts of statements:

- The musical message, contrary to the message of codes, is not used up in a series of signified-signifier relationships, any more than the element of music is reduced to a sign defined exclusively by its role in the context.
- Moreover, far from specializing his *phonations*, the nature and the ways of using sources and sounds, the musician combines them, as it were, at will: cowbells, drums, strings and wind, human and electronic sounds, the old and the new, the barbaric and the refined.

We cannot but ask, yet again, the same two questions:

1. Alone among other "speakers," the musician has not managed to define the musical object. Does he not know his own code? Or is it only partly a code, in other respects obeying natural laws?

2. Alone among so many users of sound, the musician uses disparate sources. Does he therefore, implicitly and approximately, possess the key to sound objects?

20.2. ARGUMENT FOR A GENERAL MUSICOLOGY

We will try, hypothetically, to see what research based on one of the two hypotheses would be like: the hypothesis that sees the essence of the phenomenon of music in the sign, defined by its function in a conventional system, and not the one that considers the essential to be the sound object, recognized as a unit in perceived structures.

What we have learned from linguists helps us no longer to confuse the sign with a physically preexisting reality: even if the definition of pertinent features, or values, appears to be relevant in a given musical system, we will stop trying to interpret other systems in terms of the pertinent features of our own. There is no doubt that in contemporary musics, even orchestral, a study of this kind gives us other constituent objects in addition to those indicated by a no longer adequate notation—provided that this study of structures is done after the event and is not confused with the a priori schemas of composers.

We would stop here if, as is the case with linguists, our subject were simply based on observation. All we would then have to do to give an account of the *nature* of musical objects as opposed to their *function* would be to describe the instrumental conditions for their realization and their acoustic properties. Where perception is concerned, only the various conditioned musical perceptions would be of interest to us. We would gain access to the generally musical by comparing systems; it would simply be their shared structural laws. It would be superfluous to go back to the musical object.

This approach is convenient. We cannot do without it. We cannot know the results until it has been attempted. We must not forget, however, that it will only inform us about *musical language systems:* it would remain to be proved that language systems are the most important thing in music. We have seen that this is only true at the limits, with so-called pure musics—that is, musics genuinely represented by their symbols. Above all, it would only tell us about musics that have already been made.[1] Now, our subject, we must not forget, deals with musics that are possible just as much as and even more than these. So our study must be seen not as *a posteriori* but as a beginning: at this stage we cannot tell what our choice of objects or their relationships will be or how they will be defined.

20.3. ARGUMENT FOR SOUND AS GIVEN

We will now move on to the opposite argument. This time, we are not dealing with a system that can be analyzed into meaningful elements since we are starting out from sound as given. How will we go about it?

If we were a philosopher, or rather a pure mathematician, we should be tempted to treat this problem in the absolute, from *sound objects in general*, of which there is no prior definition, except this: "everything that is audible." And then? With a little thought we can quite soon see that, however infinite the diversity of these objects, we can quite easily list some of their "infinities." For these objects are not abstractions. They must have a source somewhere and come from an energetic agent that gives them life. The question we must therefore ask ourselves is this, surprising in its simplicity: "What can produce sound in this world in which we live?" Not so very many categories of things or beings. The elements to begin with. Then living things. Among these, humankind. Among human noises, those that are used to communicate. Among these, those that have a musical intention. Thus, in six concentric circles we have, with disarming ease, enclosed five "infinities" of sound production, but it will be very difficult to go on listing them. We will not even try, satisfied that we have so quickly obtained a result that is rudimentary but undisputed.

This general schema of natural listening, opposite the summary of listening modes in our earlier chapters, explains how it works. The elements, by definition, have no intentions toward us, at least since mythology went out of fashion. Those who communicate, including animals, obviously have. The concentric circles above were only concentric through logical listing, an anthropomorphic focusing. We already find ourselves obliged to differentiate between, first, sounds without intention (including living beings *making a noise*) and, second, intentional sounds, made with the aim of communicating (and here we would certainly include animal cries, human speech, and Morse code or tom-tom signals).

1. Clearly, this historical approach might have taken priority if the circumstances had been right. Unfortunately, there is now a conflict between conditioned Western musicologists and musicians of non-Western music, now rare, and who have also taken on Western conditioning. So the other approach must be adopted as more effective and perhaps as a prerequisite.

And what about those who have the intention of making musical sounds? Where do they fit in?

Apparently at the junction of that strange pair, the musical agent and the message: the intention to *make music* consists in taking *sounds from the first category* (unspecialized in languages) and making them into *second category* communication (but which has no desire to say anything). And here we are, once again, caught between sound object and musical structure, between sonority and musicality.

20.4. MUSICAL ACTIVITY

In chapter 18 we analyzed the persistent dualism of musicality and sonority at the heart of the traditional system. We find it underlying the most tried and tested musical activity. We are therefore justified in going back to this experience, with a view to generalizing it. We will look at how we introduce a new element, a present-day invention, in fact, into a somewhat fossilized musical heritage that is, however, nothing other than the summation of successive inventions, going back through history, a whole evolution of musical concepts, always related to the means available to music.

Now, mostly, we only think of music in its static state. We are recipients of it, as it is, and the musician only has to play it in accordance with the notes he has been taught and the instruments he has been given. He receives these notes and those instruments from society, and the musical is thus reduced to a passive adherence to the state of affairs. People listen to music; they no longer invent it. The musician is himself no more than a listener.

What is musical listening? The meaning that this word has taken on in our musical civilization is this: refined but fossilized listening. We could set against this the term *musicianly listening*, which would denote the renewal of listening, investigating the sound object for its potential.

It could be said, and it would be more than a play on words, *that traditional musical listening is listening to sound in stereotyped musical objects, whereas musicianly listening is musical listening to new sound objects produced for use in music.*

By *listening to sound* we mean here the sum of the sonority of objects that have *ordinary* musicality, which we investigated above. And in this way we account, with great accuracy, not only for the meanings of the terms but also for the very common ways of speaking and thinking among professionals.

At this point we must clarify what we called an activity going against the flow, a counteroffensive that aims to reverse the current of ideas. As long as we stay with stereotyped objects, in fact, we are sure to find, opposite them, the intentions on which they are based. Now, we cannot cheat with these systems. It has been said that they must be approached tangentially. But what is this tangent, if there is no cheating?

This is a new subject: no longer an intention but an *invention*, and the tangent is reduced listening, applied to the sound object. The only thing, in fact, that *homo faber* can do for us is to give us objects that are not too demanding and that lend themselves to this difficult exercise, both shocking and sufficiently pared down to awaken a new ear. So these *suitable objects* will constitute a creative, and doubly creative, activity. Through musicianly invention, inherited from ancestral ways, we will endeavor to create sound objects that lend themselves to a new form of music. And once we have them, we will further endeavor, through *decontextualized* musical listening, to hear them as conveyors of intelligible elements into new systems yet to be deciphered.

So we must no longer consider these new intentions (to invent) to be opposed to the natural or conventional, sound or musical, object. It is already an original activity, whose perceptual structures develop little by little *as circumstances and training allow*. The intentions we are talking about involve *the inventiveness of the musician and the invention of the musical*. They are action structures: the renewal of sources to create objects and of connections to create structures. We will go back to a whole body of work against culture and against nature, coming from the depths and overturning the traditional way, moving from sound to the musical, and no longer from the musical to sound.

20.5. TWO PITFALLS

As we will see, it is all about invention, both musical and musicianly, without which we cannot help but fall back into classical ways of structuring, even well "intentioned."

(a) We are trying to *familiarize ourselves with sound*. And so, with an inquisitive, attentive ear we listen to the creaking of doors and the singing of birds. We do, indeed, discover what we said: an easy structuring that enables sources to be identified. One door can be told from another, and the chaffinch from the warbler. So we find something familiar to the musical: a timbre and melodies. In fact, we have already gone beyond *sound*. We suddenly find ourselves at the *highest level* of structure and meaning, which seems *natural* to us. Even if the languages of the birds are incomprehensible to us, we hear them, by and large, as we would hear a foreign language system. In any case there is no reason why we should not make a study of their throats and the sounds they make, with the aid of the Sonagraph, which would introduce us to a phonetics of bird modulations but with a code that would probably remain impenetrable to us, for if bird language has meaning, it is, clearly, on another level.[2]

---

2. We should add to these the whistling languages (there are still some traces left in the Canaries and the Pyrenees) studied by René Guy Busnel. [Busnel was a French anthropologist who collaborated with Schaeffer.—Trans.]

Where the door is concerned, it is quite another matter. Unlike the birds, it is not trying to communicate (the wind is moving it, not a speaker who might be using it as part of a code). Its activity, nevertheless, has a meaning, here focused on the event, and its "language," metaphorically speaking, comes from the wind playing with the door. If a composer comes forward and substitutes himself for the wind, our interest *changes direction*. His agency may make a whole door solo or a dialogue between a door and a sigh *meaningful or expressive*.[3] Is this music yet?

Let us say that here we have a *study in instrumental modes of play* and (musical) instinct, a very interesting experiment. Limited in this way to a domain of objects defined by their common source, the experimenter, here a composer, explores *the entire range of expression* possible for these objects, resulting from the *variety* of playing modes available to the instrument. There can be no better way of demonstrating the existence of meaning in the ordering of objects, even if we refuse them the status of musical objects. Thus experimental composition reveals the potential for undreamed-of ways of listening and some parallel system to be elucidated. This is not our aim, for, however odd it may seem, it concerns the higher level of composition and not the theory of *objects suitable* for research, which is our subject.

(b) One could even, in most cases, say that experimentation such as this in an instrumental domain is the main pitfall in research. We are only too tempted, in fact, at the beginning of a piece of research, to turn to instruments, to put sheet metal with sheet metal, ondes with ondes, membranes with membranes, and so forth, just as our ancestors put strings with strings, wind instruments with wind instruments, woodwinds with woodwinds to confuse sound bodies with the sound objects they produce.

We may also too facilely, and often conveniently, put sheet metal into scales[4] or make bow-sticks into a keyboard. We disregard complex sounds and ruin our ear when we try to describe the originality of the former through the easy route of the latter. At the very most, such registers may be used for labels, manufacturing techniques, or means of identifying not the object but its instrumental formula. Tinkering with the keyboards of sound bodies like this is to reject forms of instrument making that sometimes took several years to produce balanced instruments. All this for aesthetic reasons. But as for logic, how can we not see in this approach an ambition to rediscover only what we already know, the determinist nature of the system itself?

So we can see that the two ways of inventing the musical *(a)* and the musician *(b)* are not so easy.

3. See the work by Pierre Henry, *Variations pour une porte et un soupir* (Variations on a door and a sigh).

4. Baschet instruments, which deserve better than this, are nevertheless registered in scales. [This is a reference to the brothers Bernard and François Baschet, who invented several new instruments and sound sculptures in the 1950s.—Trans.]

20.6. MUSICIANLY INVENTION

We know all about the two pitfalls mentioned above: they threaten just as much those who want to hear as those who want to make something different. We might ask which of the two will get the credit for being the first to get out. Will it be the listener, filling his ears with a mass of sounds, *decontextualized* enough to structure them in a different way? This would be to underestimate *the prime of place* of both *conditioning* and *making*, as soon as we want to break with them. So we turn once again to *homo faber*. However ingenious he may be, is he not himself his own listener? So is he not in the same boat? Is he not also, and especially, the prisoner of timbres?

We have already seen them in action, those children with their grass or their violins; and the inventor who, according to the Gospels, will not enter into this kingdom unless he becomes like one of them, would do well to be inspired by them. Although the latter is destined for the traditional and the former for an experimental system, they are both groping in the dark, and the important thing is to recognize what they have in common: both are making the sound object for aesthetic reasons, and both are using it to achieve certain values, explicit or otherwise. So let us repeat that *homo faber*, conditioned just like the listener, has only one advantage over him: he links the sender and the receiver of every sound object, making while listening and listening while making, and this is what leads his listening on to reduced listening, if he wants to free himself from habit.

When he first starts out, however, we will see him obstinately endeavoring to find new timbres. He will strive to repeat traditional values that his experiment, if it is innovative, will deny him with the same obstinacy, whereas it would give him others if only he knew how to draw them out and integrate them.

What will happen if he becomes bolder and familiarizes himself with his own research? He will not immediately be able to discover the (new) sonorities of (old) musical objects but the (new and not so easily found) musicality of objects that are incontrovertibly sound objects (but perhaps ill chosen, unsuitable, which he does not yet know how to listen to, i.e., identify and describe). Obvious examples of these are those sound objects that were so interesting, though as yet apparently so unsuitable: the grass sounds and the creaking door.

So it is with the creator of sound objects that we can find in embryo both the musicianly and the musical invention that is our aim and that can only come into its own gradually and by dint of great patience. Even if, in the next chapter, we describe this *more general system* using a logic peculiar to it, we cannot overemphasize the trial and error that have accompanied its coming into being. The objects provided by experience are, in fact, already in groups (through causality or intention), and a certain amount of arbitrariness is required to *decontextualize* them, just as a certain amount of imagination is needed to regroup them naturally or conventionally.

20.7. MUSICAL INVENTION

Our *homo faber* would not get by without that aim that makes him look for a meaning in what he is doing. We are not talking here about primitive man with his calabashes, or the violin maker from Cremona, or the electronics engineer from Cologne. All of these were musicians passionate about music as an immediate objective. As researchers, they applied themselves to an art; they did what might be called *applied research*. If our *homo faber* is a *researcher into fundamentals*, his immediate aim is not the result—that is, material immediately appropriate for making music. His research is into the musical itself, the musical concealed in sound. He knows he is a prisoner of *established values;* he also gradually discovers (and this is much more important because it is much more unexpected) that he is a prisoner of the *natural timbres* of the groups of objects linked to instrumental sources. What is to be done, then, except to *ungroup* them and compare object with object, each from different sources? Is this not the first act toward releasing structures that are natural and, this time, belonging to sound as well as the musical? Thus he notices that a metal sheet, when struck, may resemble a bass note or chord on the piano and that the same metal sheet, stimulated with a bow, will be like a double bass. This directs him toward new values, still quite unclear but already attached to the properties of the object and no longer those of instruments. In addition, as we suggested to him in book 3, he will have compared the pizzicati of various instruments, sustained sounds, profiled sounds, and in this way he will have learned to compare *morphologies* belonging essentially to the object and not the instrument.

What may have seemed curious in the earlier books is that, although concerned with a more general range of sound than the musical, we have so often taken our examples and our demonstrations from the most traditional domain. But there is nothing odd in this. How should we learn about sound if not from the musical? If we admit, as we must at present, that the musical is no more than suitable sound—that is, purified, simplified, graded in order not to be too complex—how should we not classify sound as a musical differently understood and analyzed?

So we come back to one of our earlier formulae. If good (traditional) musicians have worked at *hearing the sonority of* (conventional) *musical objects*, we have inherited that ear from them, even if it means taking on research that they have not done. So we are tackling musical objects in general or, at least, those objects that seem to us to be *suitable*. This means that we will *listen to sound objects with a musical ear*, give ourselves suitable sound objects, and, consequently, shape them and take them from their natural context: this is the *musicianly invention* that comes from *artistic creation*. Focusing on hitherto unnoticed qualities in them, naming these, using them to describe the objects—this can only be done by making links that are both unusual and adequate: this is the *musical invention* that comes from *research strategies*.

In other words, we take an experience of sonority from traditional music and transfer it into a more general field of sound. This is the technique of successive approximations practiced in the experimental sciences. We will see how far the new system we are aiming for complements the first and runs parallel to it. It is developed through a *reversal* of the processes of structuring. Identification of the musical and description of sound exchange their fields of operation and their priorities.

21

—————

Musical Research

21.1. FUNDAMENTAL RESEARCH

In this section we are not going to try to redefine research into music. This whole work leads in this direction by endeavoring to demonstrate a practice rather than a theory and to limit rather than extend objectives. We think, however, that we should justify the *fundamental* phase in a piece of musical research.

We know that in science this term, apart from any direct application, denotes the exploration of basic principles, the possible revision of premises and the clarification of methods. In suggesting that the study of musical objects should come before the study of the way they are used (writing music, composing), we are likely to surprise some and discourage others. For the former this type of research is ultimately only justified at the level of language, and the most serious researchers may doubt that we can stop halfway, as it were. For the others, notably composers, this type of research goes against their instincts, which are to work directly toward music, any intervening theories (nowadays so frequent) being for the most part only aesthetic pretexts, trompe-l'oreilles, and hardly ever going right down to the level of the fundamental or the elementary. In both cases we must ask these preliminary questions: What materials is music made of? How much of these materials do we perceive? What part does our conditioning play in what we do perceive? What, beyond this conditioning, is the potential of sound, in relation to both the physical properties of the objects and the properties of perceptual structures, which man, naturally gifted, can seek to develop?

This is fundamental research, which we said should be inseparable from *musical experiments* at the level of language, and *experimental works*, which we should prefer to call *studies*, "experiments just to see." We do not think the necessity of this fundamental research can be denied, any more than a traditional musician would reject music theory or would claim immediate access to composition without it.

The aim of the present chapter is to give a general outline of the program for this fundamental research. So it forms a conclusion to the preceding chapters, which are its premises; it is an introduction to the last two books, which put into practice the theories defined in the proposals for a generalized theory of music. We must repeat that this work represents an initial approach and outlines a research program for the future rather than being a summary of definitive results.

21.2. INTERWOVENNESS OF LEVELS OF COMPLEXITY AND SECTORS OF ACTIVITY

Nothing appears so simple as the concepts of timbre, melody, and value, deduced from current experience. Nothing is so tricky as attempting to establish their foundations, as we wish to do, by trying to distinguish what may be natural or conventional in musical activity.

Gestalt psychologists discovered their theory precisely by emphasizing the permanence of melody across its instrumental or transposed variants. What is natural or cultural in such a simple experience? Do we need a piano to demonstrate this? Is it common to East and West, civilized and primitive man? This elementary problem can be extremely challenging: it conceals several other embedded problems.

The division into "sectors" has already shown us how to separate out what comes from the four cardinal points of musical or sound activity. But this "diagram," already loaded, comes into play at every level of complexity in a sound or musical chain. We have applied it (chapter 18) at the level of musical *notes*. This is already a highly expert usage. As for the listener, he instinctively applies it at the level of musical phrases or virtuoso passages in the course of listening. Later, if he tries to remember, his memory will doubtless function at a higher level of complexity: the work as a whole, the performer's style . . .

We will endeavor to sum up the parallels between various levels of spoken and musical discourse mentioned above.

Limiting ourselves to a reflexive analysis "from the meaning" starting from the higher levels of complexity (the easiest for ordinary listening), we find the following:

utterances in language	pieces of music
phrases in language	musical phrases
words from the lexis	melodic or rhythmic intervals, chords, motifs, etc.
phonemes (distinctive features)	values (pitch, intensity, timbre, duration)

But we know all this requires training. This way of proceeding does not in the slightest help us to make a reverse analysis—that is, a synthesis building up from the elementary levels. This should be the aim of fundamental research.

So we will complete this list with other links in the chain, from research activities or comparisons that are completely absent from the parallels above. First, between words and phonemes we will insert the syllable, the phonic object (in our sense, but which has so little sense in language that it is not even considered). Similarly, between intervals (or motifs) and values we will insert the sound (or musical) object: for we must recognize the existence of an object that carries these values. Finally, we will add two lines that, in any case, are of a level of complexity no different from phonemes:

L1 utterances in language	pieces of music
L2 phrases in language	musical phrases
L3 words from the lexis	musical motifs (chords, intervals)
L4 syllables (phonic object)	sound objects or musical object (instrumental note, for example)
L5 phonemes (pertinent or distinctive features)	(music theory) values
L6 phonetic features	sound criteria
L7 acoustic parameters	acoustic parameters

We should again emphasize that the last three lines are not in decreasing order of complexity but represent the selection of elements of equal complexity coming from different intentions, with a view to building up the higher-level structures.

21.3. PREPARATORY EXERCISES

We have already applied the experimental method to the conventional system; in effect sectors II and III (see illustrations below in sections 21.4 and 21.5) raised their own problems. In sector II we focused on factures; we practiced comparing pizzicati, bow strokes, and blowing, independently of the violins or metal sheets, trumpets or harps to which they belonged. We did not go very deeply into this study, which at the more advanced levels leads on to the characteristic features of a way of playing, an interpretation, a virtuoso. Of course, this very complex sector II would deserve a treatise of its own. We must keep in mind that we compared objects at quite an elementary level to see the emergence of new pertinent features, which are nothing to do with musical identification. Not that a well-executed bow stroke, tonguing, or vibrato are not important in music, but they serve to qualify the sonority and are not the basis of the musicality. These comparisons have been made implicitly (but it would be better, in future, to recreate the circumstances in which they were made, even from memory), by grouping together objects *that no longer have anything in common, neither timbre nor values*. In comparing only bow strokes, thuds, attacks, we were studying what might be called *the criterion for instrumental factures:* the *gestural typology* that governs the vibratory processes of sound bodies. This means that we substituted a new sector 2 for the old sector II, to accommodate different forms of structuring and grouping.

As for sector III we tackled it head-on when studying the notes of the piano keyboard. This time, we were going down to the most basic levels, neglected in musical listening, to values and timbres, but not to the sonorities of these values or timbres. We were making new comparisons between levels L4 and L6, with a collection of sounds marked out by a register L5 but examined differently; for from that point we refused to consider timbre, as it emerges crudely at the higher levels of causality, as an instrumental constant. Comparing one piano note with another accelerated or slowed down until it reached the same pitch, we discovered, this time, *the criteria for the note*, features ignored because they are not properly identified, though perfectly well perceived. In other words, we were undertaking a musical description of the note now considered a structure and elucidated by means of the elements on the lower level L6: the morphological criteria.

Without these preparatory exercises, we should be ill-equipped to tackle the systematic generalization that is our aim. First we will draw on them to discover the rules for identifying the object at the level of *sonority*.

21.4. HOW THE EXPERIMENTAL SYSTEM WORKS

How do we identify sound objects? We have already given the answer: the *most naturally* in the world, through a mechanism absolutely identical to the one mentioned above, which is the basis of sector I. At the more advanced levels of languages, it seems to us quite natural (although, as we have pointed out, this naturalness has to be learned), to identify the bird by its trills, the wave by its breaking, the engine by its throbbing, and so forth. This is far from being an analysis of *logatoms*,[1] and it is certainly not a general way into sound: it is the recognition of a superimposition of parallel sound chains, which, of course, include those of speech, which themselves, in every language system in the world and all possible codes, rest on the same phonatory material, which can be written in international phonetic script but not without considerably muddling the meaning of the text.

These are indeed the two extremes whose influence we should dread: the two extreme levels, one too advanced, Level 2–Level 3, enabling speakers to be recognized by their natural or conventional languages, the other too elementary, Level

---

1. An expression used in telecommunications and exactly comparable to the phonic object, the spoken equivalent to the syllable, the "atom of speech."

5–Level 6, applicable only to an even more specific domain of sound than the domain of music, such as the sonority of speech (phonic objects).

We must place ourselves at an intermediate level, where the meanings of languages are forgotten and instrumental domains, including the phonetic, are not yet specialized. But the latter can serve as an example, or at least point to a method. It is at this (syllabic) level L4 that we placed the instrumental note in the traditional system, and where we now place the elementary sound object, into which eventually the most complex sound chain will be resolved, just as words resolve into logatoms, not now for linguists but for telephonists.[2]

We have already noticed that the sound universe appears to obey the same laws of articulation and stress, provided we stick to generalities and interpret these criteria very broadly.

Here our experiments with the former sectors I and II will be of use. The factures of a *gestural typology*, in the new sector 2, could be a first criterion for *identification* and therefore also for *classification* of all sound objects. As for what we learned from sector III, we can conjecture that, beyond timbres or short of musical values, there is doubtless a fairly general *morphological* criterion characterizing *the stress of sounds* in the new sector 3.

We can see that here, also, generalizing musical experience leads us to a very different system. We replace the timbre-pitch pair in the old sectors I and IV, used to identify musical objects, with an *articulation-stress* pair in the new sectors 2 and 3, a first step toward a typomorphology that should enable us not only to identify but also to classify, and hence select, sound objects. What we lose in rigor, nuance, and musicality, we will gain in amplitude and sound dominants in general.

Thus, in future we will not accept objects from specific instruments, carrying sector I timbres (which we also forbid ourselves to describe, prematurely, with conventional sector IV values), and we also refuse to accept them already grouped according to their natural sources. Faced with so many disparate objects, totally without grouping, without their conventions or their natural patrimony, a *classification*, even approximate, is essential, a sort of "grid" completely replacing instrumental tablature or the natural repertoire of noises. For how can we study an infinity of sounds that are not identified in any way? We will therefore use "sound identification criteria." They will give us the means to isolate sound objects from each other, since we refuse to do this through the usual sound or musical structures. In addition, they will lead us to a practical classification of sound objects, an obvious prerequisite for any further musical regrouping.

2. See section 16.6 or, for Raymond Queneau, "If you think, little girl, s'OK, s'OK, s'OK . . ." [This is a quotation from the poem by Raymond Queneau in *L'instant fatal* (Paris: Gallimard, 1948). The words "que ça va" (that it's OK) are spelled as they are heard, "xa va."—Trans.]

Finally, we must recognize that this search for criteria for identifying sound is not without musical bias.[3] More precisely, since we do not wish to make premature judgments about music in general, we admit to a deliberate but specific intention, as musicianly as it is musical. What are these two so simple and, doubtless, so obvious decisions that we have taken years to make? We will not make the reader wait until he has read the next books, where they will be dealt with at length, before arming him with these two lamps to lighten the way: the *(syllabic) articulation* of sounds seems to us to relate fairly well to the *character of their sustainment;* the *(vocalic)* criterion of *(vocalic) stress* appears to be fairly well linked to intonation, to the fact that sound is *fixed or variable in pitch,* or that this pitch is *complex or harmonic.* In other words, by combining the typology of factures and the morphology of stresses, and retaining some of their criteria on both sides at the two poles of the object, we obtain an indispensable key to sonority, not at all sophisticated but with a bias in favor of music, as limited and as justified as possible.

Of course, we must not confuse sectors 2 and 3 on the origin of sound in a more general system with sections II and III in the earlier traditional system: the contents and the comparisons are no longer concerned with the same material. Figure 23 illustrates the definitive and comparative summary of the two systems.

21.5. CONTENTS OF THE TRADITIONAL SYSTEM

Although we have already given a rough idea of this several times, this time we will explore it more fully, to make a definitive comparison between it and the experimental system. Its contents are in the four corners of our summary illustration (fig. 24).

Sector I. Identifying timbres (concrete aspects of instrumental sounds in general).

Two questions arise from the conventional instrumentarium.

I. Identifying one (instrumental) timbre from other (instrumental) timbres.

Ia. Identifying various notes in the same timbre.

Sector II. Describing the sonority of particular timbres (specificity of the concrete aspects of performance).

II. Describing one instrumental timbre among other examples from the same instrument.

IIa. Describing various (identical) notes from the same instrument in other performances (performance timbre).

Sector IV. Identifying values (the abstract in general).

IV. Identifying the value of one (identical) note in various timbres: pitch, duration (?), intensity (??).

3. See section 19.10*(d).*

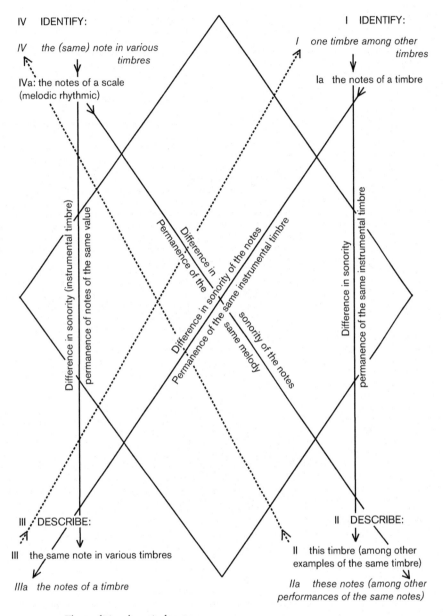

IV   IDENTIFY:

IV   the (same) note in various
                        timbres

IVa: the notes of a scale
(melodic rhythmic)

I   IDENTIFY:

I   one timbre among other
                        timbres

Ia   the notes of a timbre

Difference in sonority (instrumental timbre)

permanence of notes of the same value

Permanence of the

Difference in

Difference in sonority of the notes

Permanence of the same instrumental timbre

same melody

sonority of the notes

Difference in sonority

permanence of the same instrumental timbre

III   DESCRIBE:

III   the same note in various timbres

IIIa   the notes of a timbre

II   DESCRIBE:

II   this timbre (among other
examples of the same timbre)

IIa   these notes (among other
performances of the same notes)

FIGURE 23. The traditional musical system.

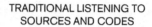

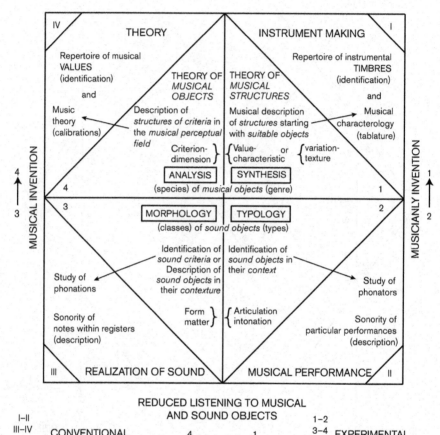

FIGURE 24. Program of musical research.

IVa. Identifying the values of different notes through reference to calibrations (melodic, rhythmic, dynamic).

Sector III. Describing the sonorities of instrumental notes (the concrete aspects of notes in general).

III. Describing the sonorities of the (same) note in various timbres (in general instrumental).

IIIa. Describing the various notes in the same timbre (in general instrumental). *Remarks.*

These questions make four pairs that, on the figure, match four relationships of *permanence-variation* or, again, *similarity-difference.*

We find:

I and II: That the same instrumental timbre is musically identical with the timbres of other instruments and that instrumental examples of the same timbre are different (in sonority).

IV and III: That notes of various (instrumental) timbres are (musically) identical in value, and various (instrumental) notes of the same value are different (in sonority).

These two pairs, going from the top down (musicality to sonority), describe respectively the sonority of *the* timbre identified among *timbres,* and *the* note among *notes* of the same value.

We also find:

Ia and IIIa: That the timbre of notes from one instrument is (musically) identical, and the timbre of each of these notes is different (in sonority).

IVa and IIa: That a structure of values is (musically) the same while their various performances are different (in sonority).

These two pairs, diagonally (musicality to sonority), describe the sonority of *the* notes identified by having the same timbre or *the* same structure of values respectively.

It can be seen that the identification-description relationships systematically refer back from the explicitly musical to an ill-defined sound material. It can also be seen that the traditional system, however simple and rational it may appear, raises eight interrelated questions that are, moreover, entirely to do with means of performing.

21.6. ORIGINS OF THE EXPERIMENTAL SYSTEM

How can we simplify these eight questions, on the one hand, and find greater independence between the musical and its instrumental means, on the other?

First of all, we can see that these eight questions are to do with the fact that the traditional system complicates itself by grouping notes at the level of the instrument. Along with its investigations into general values, it pursues investigations into timbre, which always have a double meaning: we never know whether we are dealing with the timbre of the note, which involves an additional description of value, or the timbre of the instrument, which involves a particular grouping of notes or a manner of performing them.

Is it possible to do without the specificity of the instrument? Yes, provided we no longer expect to find notes nicely grouped by (instrumental) timbre. But if

294   OBJECTS AND STRUCTURES

there is no longer an instrument, there are no longer any notes either. It would be simpleminded to imagine that, in losing the instrument, we do not also lose notes—that is, the registers of values that it enabled us to identify, in addition to its timbre. Conclusion: if we abandon traditional musical identification, we must find another system in the free-for-all of sound because we are no longer guaranteed anything: neither timbres nor values.

If we do then manage to identify objects in sound, we will have to analyze them musically—that is, describe them.

We will imagine the problem is resolved, and reexamine the four pairs of questions we have just put together. Using a degree of wordplay, we will imagine that the word *timbre*, by extension, refers to the most concrete aspect of each object, its properties as a whole, the fact that it is itself: its character, a more precise term than *timbre*. And that the word *note* refers to what is most general in objects, their shared properties as a whole: a criterion, a more general term than *value*. If the problem has been resolved, this could only have come about through a series of approaches, since our starting point is the generality of sound objects. Could the four pairs of questions above be taken up again to illustrate the passage from sound to the musical in four phases? As we are going from back to front, we should start with the last pair.

Questions IVa and IIa. Here we are comparing what is most disparate: a particular performance and a note value. Now the question is to find the starting point for a principle for identifying objects. Is it reasonable to ask the seemingly most sensitive question (and the most delicate: the facture of the performance), just when we are embroiled in the universe of disparate objects? Indeed it is: it is from the concrete that we must now start, but on condition that all we want to do, at this stage, is sort through it very approximately. The requirement is reversed. Instead of a delicate judgment about facture, we will retain only elementary criteria, common to all sound factures in the world. Instead of quibbling over values, we will be content with rudiments: whether the sound, for example, is fixed or varied, complex or harmonic. These questions, intersecting on an elementary diagram, give us a grid with two criteria, which will lead us to a typology: a means of grading, from which sound material will emerge labeled according to (musical) types of (sound) objects.

Questions Ia and IIIa. If we turn for a moment from the sound body and its specific timbre and focus solely on the difference in sonority of the "timbre of each individual note," we are comparing the sonority of these notes (as we did with the piano, taking no notice of values, which are now only numbers for ordering objects in a collection that is being studied for something else). A study of the sound forms or formal qualities of the objects examined in this way, without any premature consideration of calibrations of values, is a morphology. From it emerge criteria, distinctive features of the form of the objects (their identification underpinned by the morphology), some of which are described as musical, if we judge them suitable for the musical, or at least interesting enough for us to pursue a procedure for describing them. We will suppose that in this way we did find rules for identifying types of sounds and criteria for the perception of sound. We have still done no more than apply a musicianly ear to the totality of sound objects. We still need to *describe* these objects *musically*.

The pairs of *questions above (I* and *II, IV* and *III)* are no longer relevant, as they are based on particular instrumental groups. We may have to revise the way the questions intersect, giving the word *timbre* the generalized connotation we have adopted. In this case we must transpose a little.

Pair II-IV, which should read like this: do these timbres (these sound objects) produce the same type of note—that is, do they give a structure belonging to the same criterion? Is this criterion (which has scarcely any chance of standing out as a value in the disparate mass of timbres) perceptible to musical awareness and how? This is a form of musical analysis that aims first to describe a certain criterion and then to see if it can be incorporated in a calibration.

Pair III-I. If various timbres produce the same note, it is because, on this occasion, the fundamental timbre-value relationship has been achieved. We have described musical structures, from objects we know how to describe, then produce, and which then emerge as values. We have achieved the most general syntheses of the musical.

21.7. INVARIANTS IN THE EXPERIMENTAL SYSTEM

Figure 24 will practically govern the plan of all the rest of the work. The reader will therefore need to refer back to it. Like all syntheses, this one will only be useful once some of the many relationships it regroups have been tested out.

The basic axiom is still the same: a collection of objects displays certain similarities and certain differences. Whether we are dealing with the formulations of linguists (Jakobson's rules) or the first discoveries of a particular musical invariant (the latter varies in the collection, provided that the former remains constant), we always come back to the same somewhat paradoxical stumbling block,[4] which may, if we are not careful, sometimes be expressed as follows: "What varies is what is constant." Thus, the timbre of an instrument seems constant to us, but this is only if we find other timbres and observe that these timbres, in fact, vary from one instrument to another. Similarly, pitch appears as a constant value in a particular note in the melody but only if other notes also have a pitch and serve as a foil. Now, immediately, we can see that timbre is dispersed into notes (of the same timbre),

4. The difficulty is approaching it from the concrete angle. In the abstract field of ideas (and not perceptions), modern algebra and geometry constantly give examples of this (group theories, etc.).

each of which has therefore not only a pitch but also a timbre. In the same way that criteria including harmonic timbre, dynamic profile, and so forth are dispersed from a single note with a pitch, similarly, what was previously identified (that is, perceived as fixed and linear in a varying context) now appears as described; that is, its earlier fixedness and how it was identified (as a value) are no longer of interest to us, but the problem now is its complexity, which is revealed through new processes of identification, at lower levels, of the elements of which it is itself composed. Here, of course, we recognize the object-structure chain, and the two successive processes of identification (on the higher level) and description (on the lower). Was it necessary to say this yet again? Perhaps, for as often happens in mathematics, as well, a very simple axiom conceals many implications, which we will develop in detail in the next seven sections.

21.8. SUITABLE OBJECTS

This caricature of a formula, "What varies is what is fixed," elicits the usual shrug of the shoulders. A pitch structure reveals the value pitch. The tautology is only apparent.[5] The word *pitch* is used here in two senses. One is the *characteristic* attached to the object. The (harmonic) notes that are (implicitly) supposed to form the melody are very specific musical objects, and their *essential property* is, in fact, to present a pitch. As a result they can be put together to reveal a *pitch structure* in a second meaning of the term, as a *value* and, indeed, after this, a calibration of pitches, in a third meaning. This value of the object, now forgotten as such, becomes only a quality with a structure that allows of abstraction. This is the only quality of objects in a structure that we will retain. We will imagine three situations by way of illustration, then a fourth. We have a cymbal, a triangle, a piano, a gong, a violin, and a trumpet. Some of the sounds produced by these instruments have the characteristic of pitch; others do not. They are not *suitable* for the experiment. They cannot form a pitch structure. Second experiment: piano, violin, and trumpet notes. Despite the disparate nature of the objects, they share the *characteristic of pitch*. The experiment works, but attention may be divided. This is not how we would proceed with a child, a beginner, or a primitive man to make a value appear. Third experiment: we take notes exclusively from the piano or the violin. It seems now that only *the pitch changes*, thanks to a constant timbre. We know what to think of this timbre, so inconstant, which itself requires identification and description. We also know that each note possesses *its timbre* and that it is not only the value pitch that changes from one note to another. But there is indubitably a

5. This statement of the obvious in reality masks the indeterminateness of the relationship between the observer and the observed expressed in the standard vocabulary by this confusion about the same term.

reinforcement of perception. This collection is the most *suitable*. It is clear to the child, the beginner, and even the outsider from another musical civilization. The fourth experiment, altogether different, and which, beyond traditional theories, is at the basis of musical theories, is *calibrations*. So we have three levels of comparison between objects, simply for a value to emerge: unsuitable objects, because they do not have this characteristic; objects that are just about suitable, because they have this characteristic, but among a totally disparate mass of other characteristics; and, finally, very suitable objects (for music, let us not forget, therefore *musical*), because of the not necessarily simple reinforcement of the perception of a value through the nature of the other characteristics, which make this one appear special, *dominant*. And above all, we must be sure to separate this phase of identifying a value from any description of the same value using *intervallic relationships* related to *calibrations*.

21.9. PERCEPTUAL FIELD

In effect, in the above experiments we were, it seems, working only with the properties of objects, revealed by their structures, and we scarcely went beyond the descriptive. In fact, we could divide *the melodic experiment* in two, as we did with questions IV and IV*a*. This is where the play on words "What varies is what is fixed" is resolved. We determine *what is constant*, that is, *the perceived property* that enables us to identify this characteristic through a more limited, but more convincing, experiment: unisons in several timbres. Then, once we have found out about this, we focus on something else: the relationship between values this characteristic can assume, the interval these values give, and whether this relationship has *a meaning*. So these particularly suitable objects lead to a new experiment, quite different from the three earlier ones, concerned with *describing this relationship*, even *evaluating it relatively*, even *evaluating it numerically through a calibration in degrees*. This description can therefore be either all-embracing and instinctive (by *analogy* with other, not necessarily musical, perceptions: we do in fact say grainy, velvety, hollow, bright, etc.), or else we can *order them* (putting them roughly into a *series*), or, and this is the best, locate them in a *calibration* with relationships that are cardinal, not just ordinal, and even arranged in *their field* in the form of *vectors*.

21.10. OBJECT AND STRUCTURES

Until now we seem to have made no *hierarchical* distinction between these two related perceptions of the same object, except to note the paradox that if the object is identified at the higher structural level to which it belongs, we remember only one of its properties. It is only when it has been extracted from this structure that its true self appears; but, immediately, if we want to understand it, we must *explore this unit*, break it down in turn into components that explain it on the lower level, and describe it, components that the *object, now taken as a structure*, enables us to identify.

By dint of being moved back and forth from its function in the higher-level structure (where it is changed into a value) to its resolution at the lower level (where it is analyzed into criteria), the object seems finally to be *spirited away* and *reduced to the purely formal series of movements between one level and the other*. It is time to stop confusing the scaffolding with the monument. This commonsense remark can be backed up as follows.

The object, if we now intend to stay on its level, leads to two sorts of problems. One of these is *analytical*. The same object can in fact be transferred from one structure to another on the same level. If it is identified in one of them, how will it appear elsewhere? It will, we know, take on different roles, which emerge as various other values. And so melodic, rhythmic, or dynamic structures will bring out the values of the same note: pitch, duration, or nuance. Conversely, at its own level, the same object can be seen as carrying several different structures. As structures of duration, it will be broken down into slices of time, and attention will be given selectively, depending on its movement through time, to either its dynamic or its melodic criteria. As a whole, in its duration, memorized in time or perceived at a given moment, we could just as well consider this object a harmonic structure and endeavor to identify criteria, this time *vertical* and no longer to do with form in duration.

It can be seen that we still have to return to the *synthesis of the object*. Each of the earlier procedures in reality cancelled out the object on the level under consideration, in favor of a structuring process on both levels. But the object *is* all this; it is the sum of all these properties. It possesses all these characteristics. Any further, and we should forget its existence, its coherence, and think only about its functions. It does not have to be either in or out of a structure. We can isolate, contemplate, penetrate it. All this, explored, worked on by analysis, can be reassembled in an infinitely greater richness of perception, underpinned by our intention, if we wish. But do we?

21.11. MEANING AND SIGNIFICATION

Not always. And it is doubtless this that explains, more fundamentally than anything else, our two reservations regarding not only physicists but also linguists. We must once and for all determine the rules of the game between these two partners and the musician, who is a third.

The diagram in chapter 8, in fact, deals only with these three practitioners. One is concerned with the *natural* content of sound objects and, through the indicators it contains, seeks to control the event or demonstrate its workings. And this is where, as we have often pointed out, the scholar and the Native American are on the same side. The main thing is the focus on the event. The fact that it is natural—that is, common to man and animals, or referenced to meanings—[6]to more or less abstract systems is secondary, but it is understood that the focus is not on the object, that all that is retained from it is information about the event and not concepts, to which it would only be linked by virtue of convention. The linguist, in contrast, interested in sounds only insofar as they are signifiers conveying signified concepts, eliminates everything else from his study—that is, the properties of sound that have no function in this approach.

When we were dealing with music, we avoided using the term *signification*, too strongly suggestive of a code, or the purely arbitrary signified-signifier relationship, which, for sound, refers to the concept. Conversely, we can hardly deny that music has a *meaning*; that it is a communication between a composer and a listener, in spite of its essential difference from language (the sound no longer being the arbitrary medium of an idea, easily replaced by another); that a given music does not come, ultimately, from a system that, like a language system, is learned through two types of training, intellectual and auditory. It is this body of remarks that justifies us in saying that it is a language. Similarly, when we allow ourselves to talk about a "sign," we mean all the values or pertinent features that underpin the function of a particular sound object in a musical structure, leaving aside its other nonpertinent properties.

To try to find this meaning in an abstract relationship analogous to the linguistic sign is to deny the evidence. At the very least, part of the musical lexis and musical syntax are inscribed in nature. We will try to rediscover their origins in four axioms.

21.12. CONSTITUENT ACTIVITIES: THE FOUR AXIOMS OF MUSIC

At the beginning of chapter 16 we mentioned two perpendicular structural chains. Until then, the horizontal object-structure chain seemed a foregone conclusion. Indeed. It functions from the very beginning in accordance with preconceived ideas, with a given material. If I listen to a singer, I know that, on the one hand, I am listening to a speech chain, which follows a verbal material, a code, and so forth, and with an intention to understand a language system; on the other hand,

---

6. This is why the word *sign* is instinctively used in the sense of what refers to something else. Sign of rain, sign of flight, says the Native American. The acoustician talks about the electric *signal* not only because this informs him about the phenomenon but because he translates acoustic events (movements, mechanical energy) into electrical events (currents, electrical energy).

I also know (and can easily identify this if the singer hums without words) that I must operate in a quite different fashion, in accordance with a musical material and code, and with an intention to hear music.

The same "sound phenomenon" (for the singer has split into a speaking and humming singer only to convince us of this) can thus be broken down in different ways, depending on different *constituent intentions.*

We should not therefore be surprised that it is not enough to put ourselves in the presence of collections of putatively musical sound objects for something to happen. We must, here as well, examine the perpendicular chain and discover a *founding mechanism of the musical.*

The very great difference, then, between the conventional and the experimental approach is that the former can still seek inspiration in the linguistic approach, starting from a given material, in some way a scientific object, whereas the other starts from the other direction, backward, as we have already said. This, moreover, explains why, with the same numbers and in boxes as close together as the square and the diamond in our illustration, the contents are so profoundly different, perhaps more than we should like to admit on first reading.

The traditional situation is a de facto situation, and it does not much matter whether the facts are natural or cultural. They have developed so slowly, they have matured for so long, they have become so full of meaning, that we cannot but benefit from their being reorganized, even if these reorganizations seem at first sight artificial. For it is art we are dealing with, and in a moment we will prove that we have to return to this as the ultimate research objective. For instruments are given, registers are given, as are all manner of relationships between values (melodies, harmonies, rhythms), and also characteristics, since man first came into being and worked at his instruments. We can tear up all these collections of sounds grouped in this way, restructure or unstructure them. Let us take a pickaxe to this system: we are bound to find meaning in it; it contains a hidden treasure.

If we do indeed overthrow the lot, compare object with object, in the totally disparate mass of sound and the most uncertain intuition about the musical, how can we imagine this enterprise without formulating working hypotheses, without becoming aware of a choice of musical axioms that are tantamount to *new constituent activities?*

This is the main raison d'être for the *four major relationships* that appear in the four sections of the diamond.

It is indeed a matter of choosing four axioms for the musical. These choices are as follows. The *articulation-stress* pair underpins the choice of *types.* The *form-matter* pair determines *sound morphology.* The *criterion-dimension* pair is the one that ultimately gives *a meaning to the analysis of objects:* the meaning of its *musical proportions.*

This leaves the choice for the last section, where we find the well-known pair *value-characteristic* and a variant of it, which we will not deal with until book 6: variation-texture.

21.13. SYNTHESIS OF MUSICAL STRUCTURES OR THE INVENTION OF MUSICS

Whereas in the conventional system every structure was *given* (and, in theory, full of meaning owing to the suitability of the objects), in this one we start from the various structures of sound, which are immediately broken up and artificially restructured in accordance with the rules for identification and typological classification in sector 2. So we compare these objects in order to bring out the perceptual criteria suitable for the musical. There is nothing that is not classical about these two successive analyses, each time leaving the higher-level object in order to concentrate on the lower-level elements. So in sections 2 and 3 of figure 24 we have covered three levels, which from now on we will call *sound structures, sound objects,* and *sound criteria*.

Everything changes meaning and becomes expedience, artificial in the higher sections. Unlike a scientific or linguistic investigation, starting from natural or cultural facts, we intend to go the other way—to *put sound objects into a structure and see what this gives*. We must not forget, in fact, that every structuralist approach applies to *preexisting structures*, already given, for example, in languages. Thus the object-structure chain, like our grandmothers' knitting, unravels *in one direction*. It is impossible to knit it up again so easily, by going from preexisting objects to automatic structures. Thus the chemist is never sure of achieving a synthesis, which cannot be safely deduced from analyses.

So we try out groups of objects; we feel our way instinctively, until *the collection begins to say something to us*. This shows we are approaching, or can hope for, an authentic structure, that is, one that is perceived in reality, where, precisely, these objects could be *exploited as a value*. So the principle behind sectors 4 and 1 can be seen much more clearly from this new (and adventurous) perspective. In 4, we form collections of objects in which we identify a certain sound criterion, and we see whether these objects, in spite of the disparity of their other criteria, will reveal relationships within the criterion under consideration that are meaningful, that is, can be described, ordered, or located in our musical perceptual field. Then we know we are working in the worst of conditions. Our morphological experiment has indeed revealed this criterion (as was the case with pitch in our experiments in section 21.8); but at best, all we have is (various) pitches given by (various) timbres. We know this experiment was already less convincing for the most robust value in music. How fragile will be those in which, in the disparate mass of characteristics, we endeavor to postulate the structures of an unknown criterion, necessarily less secure than pitch. . . . This is *musical invention*.

Now we can grasp the complementary need for the *musicianly invention* in sector 1. We need to go back to collections of the third type, analogous to piano or violin notes leading to registers. Registers such as these, while having all sorts of equally variable criteria in terms of pitch, did not disturb that perception and sometimes reinforced it. Is this possible? We could say yes, technically. We might refuse to give such a prompt reply in respect of artistic value, that is, the potential development of musics based on fundamental relationships such as these. We have already demonstrated this mechanism with the *Klangfarbenmelodie*. By fixing a value for pitch, it is possible to make a structure of timbres, provided we remove any allusion to instruments. We know how to do this better than our predecessors, without, for all that, maintaining that it is a very joyous finding for music. We will go further. We will imagine sounds with a less salient pitch (e.g., nonharmonic sounds). A register of sounds like this, where the characteristic of pitch does not dominate, will offer the potential for another structure, color, or thickness, provided we are not concerned with a suitable harmonization of the characteristic shared by the objects in the collection. Now we imagine a series of melodic glissandi or dynamic grains. These are criteria that could become dominant characteristics. They are not necessarily desired by the ear: but such glissandi, such grains, demonstrate the possibility of structuring objects that have a strong, inherent characteristic between which value-relationships can then be established.

We thought of illustrating these ideas in figure 25. The first line shows a collection of completely disparate objects. It is only because of the artificial arrangement on paper or the comparison with other lines that we are tempted to arrange them in order of "height."

The second line shows the opposite extreme. A single object is cut into slices. This is the physicist's approach, taking no account of the form of the object and taking it to pieces from the top down, all other things being equal.

Line 3 introduces the neutrality of graphics; these objects, although formless, can nevertheless be arranged better in order of height.

Then there are two examples of a structure that is successful because of the permanence of its characteristics. In the last, there is reinforcement through concomitant variation in another dimension. In the penultimate figure, one dimension remains fixed, but the object retains its character. We must think back to the piano. We will represent the pitch of the note by the height of the X in our illustration and the brightness of its timbre by the width of its base. In a total transposition of a piano note, its specific timbre remained fixed, and only the pitch changed: this is what happens in the fourth line. In the case of the real piano the timbre becomes more bulky (the figure becomes wider) as the note becomes deeper (the height decreases): there is reinforcement and an equilibrium of proportion, visible here in plastic terms.

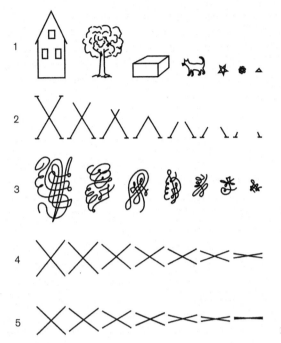

FIGURE 25. Objects and structures.

21.14. PROPERTIES OF THE
PERCEPTUAL MUSICAL FIELD

We can see that, ultimately, the study of musical objects leads to the study of the properties of musical sensibility. We might have suspected this. In a situation not lacking in humor, and to which we have already drawn attention, it is scientists who would happily study our (musical) sensibility, whereas composers, true workaholics, would only delight in arranging "structured" objects, as they say, without the slightest regard for our perceptual properties or for psychoacoustic curves. Without doubt, the criterion and the perceptual field make up that relationship of indeterminacy that so upsets our usual vocabulary. For us to retain a sound criterion, it must also, on the one hand, be suitable and have musical interest and, on the other hand, allow for evaluation in our sensibility, with everything depending constantly on the objects presented and their own contexture.

We will also have to *disconnect* what musical habit has taught us to link together so strongly, because of the *triple reinforcement* of the value pitch, dominant first as a characteristic, then also as an *ordinal* relationship, then finally exceptional for its *cardinal* evaluation and its "vectorial" tensions, the only value out of all his perceptions that *is given like this* naturally to man.

In other words, an initial faculty of the perceptual field is the capacity to compare two objects, finding the same property in them. A second is the ability to order these values. A third is the ability to establish, more or less precisely, degrees for this calibration. Thus, we can equate colors with great precision but without being able to serialize them, and even less, find relationships of octaves or fifths between them, and with good reason.

21.15. CONTENTS OF THE EXPERIMENTAL SYSTEM

It sums up everything we have just said and ultimately does nothing other than apply the rules of structuring four times over. We will look anew at this description of the experimental system without deducing it, this time, from the conventional system. In this way we will come back to the findings in section 21.6, previously deduced by extrapolation.

(a) In the experimental system, then, we do not at first know what a timbre, or even a value, is. We start from sound chains. We cut these chains into pieces using the identification criteria "articulations and stresses." And how will we sort these objects? By using the *sustainment-intonation* pair; we call this process *typology*. Identifying sound objects in this way, classifying and referring to them by a *nomenclature of types*, sums up the procedures in the *new sector 2*, the first sector of the experimental system.

(b) These objects, once identified, have *contextures*. To compare them is both to describe them (insofar as they are sound objects) and to identify the elementary perceptions to which they give rise. This is the *morphology* sector, which, in describing sound objects, will identify the perceptual criteria. How will we discover these? By analyzing the contextures using the fundamental *form-matter* relationship (which will be discussed in the next chapter, the first of book 5).

This concludes the *analysis of sound* decoded through what we have called a "musicianly" approach.

(c) But the comparison of sound objects has not yet involved the musical ear, in which, in theory, we expect to find a field of qualitative, even graded, appreciation. We are not going to claim to have rediscovered this entirely. We have practiced in it for a long time and are readying ourselves to refine or develop this field rather than limit it to what convention would give it to hear.

How are collections of objects, brought together to test out a particular criterion, structured in the natural field of the ear, refined, of course, by expert training? Here we find, by force of circumstance, the relationship of indeterminacy between the criterion presented to the ear and the perceptual field the ear can offer. We must not be premature in discussing this particularly delicate aspect of experience, always in the balance between the natural and the cultural, between innate gifts and the sometimes surprising potential of training: it is dealt with in *musical invention* in sector 4.

This relationship between the site of the criterion (or its caliber) and the perceptual field (or the dimensions of its musical calibrations) is the subject of sector 4, absolutely "analytical," more to do with the senses than the sensibility, more scientific than musical, at least more experimental than artistic.

How can we draw practical conclusions for music from all this? How will we attain a generalized but perceptible musical, without conventions that are more artificial and maybe more arbitrary than the previous ones?

(d) We do so by renewing, through synthesis, the fundamental relationships between possible musical structures and by identifying objects, now justifiably described as musical, which are also, of course, made up of "bundles of criteria" (character) that, when put together, can, through the permanence of their criteria, produce an easily perceptible structure of values and have musical interest.

That is just about all for this chapter, which from all the traditional and experimental systems has compared only one state of musical structures: the discontinuous state, where the objects are distinct from each other. But what if the musical structure is continuous, because the objects are variants and ultimately linked? This subject will be discussed in chapter 33. It adds to the earlier relationship that governs the discontinuous in music a complementary relationship that links variation to texture, a law of the continuous in music. Our illustration of musical syntheses would be incomplete without this addition, to which we will return at the end of this work.

These are the aims of sector 1, now final, the aims of *musicianly*, here as much as *musical, invention* in the experimental system.

BOOK FIVE

Morphology and Typology
of Sound Objects

22
———

Morphology of Sound Objects

22.1. THEORY AND PRACTICE

Discussed both in the last book and in those to come, theory and practice readily turn their backs on each other: logic and chronology do not sit so easily side by side.

We recall that Oppenheimer condemned nearly all types of teaching. "Precisely everything that constitutes the substance of scientific education," he writes,

> feeling one's way toward the right experiment, or the appropriate words to express subtle, complex phenomena, is almost inevitably reduced to nothing by teaching. . . . In fact, it may seem that only those who have had some experience of new knowledge, in the field of any discipline, have the capacity really to appreciate the greatness of the science of the past. We have the impression that only they can measure the greatness of what has been accomplished, by comparing past knowledge with their own efforts with a view to advancing a few millimeters further into the darkness that surrounds them.[1]

Our laborious journey does not threaten the reader with any such teaching; rather, he may complain about being signed up, willy-nilly, for some obscure ramble. This does not make it any less true that reflecting on what has been discovered after the event is in itself a form of research, different in approach from what led to these discoveries, and which we should be quite wrong to consider superfluous.

The experimenter, however, cannot expect to find himself immediately in this position. We must admit that like any other observer, he works for a long time in

---

1. Julius Robert Oppenheimer, *L'esprit libéral* (Paris: Gallimard, 1957). [Original English title: *The Open Mind* (New York: Simon and Schuster, 1955).—Trans.]

a particular instinctive or conditioned relationship with his field of operation. It is only gradually that he can take a particular stance, itself deduced from a group of findings in which at some time each one seemed vital and is now no more than one detail among others.

Everyone knows from experience what meanderings a line on a graph can follow apparently illogically in roundabout ways such as these, while the line of our dreams, completely straight, is impracticable, unreal. Then everything seems easy, seen from afar and above, but we can see immediately that a general topological explanation is not necessarily indispensable to a specific topographical route. It may be useful without being necessary, in the same way that the route actually covered may only give confirmation that is of secondary importance to the topologist.

So we have been very reluctant to bring the two points of view together in this one treatise, finding it sometimes even more difficult to create a synthesis than to mark out a route. We think it would be useful, in any case, if we are not to deserve Oppenheimer's criticism, not to link the above theoretical discussion too strictly with the practical chapters that follow. In this transitional chapter, which concerns the morphology of sounds, we will endeavor to forge the link, to show the connections between theory and practice, synthesis and findings, logical presentation and chronological exposition.

22.2. PROSE COMPOSITION AND TRANSLATION IN SOUND

We approached the route leading to sound in two ways, and we only differentiated between them after the event: translation and prose composition. First, using the closed groove in the early stages of our work with the gramophone (without the closed groove our method would doubtless have never come into being), we made ourselves extract "something" out of the most disparate sound continuum. Thus this surrealist violation, so far removed from the earnestness of our colleagues in electronic music, obliged us to cut up sound and face up to what was most ill-assorted, most resistant to organization. Could there be rules for listening that applied to all these cut-out pieces? And so the pieces taken from the gramophone led to exercises in translation. Isolated from the midst of speech, noise, song, and symphony, and from recorded sounds in the studio, the closed groove sounds had neither head nor tail, owing their existence merely to the chance moment when the cutter was lowered. Nevertheless, these fragments, repeated over and over, had potential.

Torn from their context, both deprived and yet full of meaning, they imprisoned us within their closed, captivating and absurd universe. Probably all deconditioning processes must go through this: violation, destruction, meaninglessness. For whatever our will to succeed, it has to be admitted that it was unlikely that we would discover a fragment of speech or symphony as a pure sound event, but this failed translation urged us toward prose composition.

This, conversely, consisted in the willed creation of sound objects and took us to the other extreme: using any sound at all, and in the greatest possible number of ways. But we had to unlearn the interaction of registers: sheet metal arranged according to size, calibrated wooden slats, and even the fruitless comparisons between what we wrongly used to call "sound matter" when they were only sound bodies—wood, iron, liquids, solids, and so forth. And here the closed-groove experiment helped. As far as our research was concerned, it, in fact, gave us the idea of isolating "spare parts" of sound, freed at last from the registers and instruments that by dint of serving sounds had ended up by putting them in servitude.

We could also add this, which tells us a lot about the philosophy of roundabout ways: the idea of the sound object did not come to us from book 4 but from two contradictory experiments. The closed groove did, indeed, give an object in the sense of *a thing*, hidden away, as it were, by destroying another object. We have just observed that this involves not so much an objective discovery as putting the participant in a different situation. What does he see now that he had not seen by similarly breaking up an elementary object, such as the sound of a bell, for example? Breaking it up informs him about the object, which he has—momentarily—destroyed only to hear it better. But if we bring the two experiments together, the closed groove and the cut bell, artificial, strange, antimusical objects, and if we open our ears, we begin to hear whatever it is, sound or musical, differently, thanks to *reduced listening*, an experience that these two exercises in disruption taught us.

Another example of disparity and mismatch between theory and practice. How in practice do we arrive at suitable objects? We reject objects that are both too musical and those that are too near to raw sound to find those that are *particularly* suitable, which creates not a dualism but a third category. Once these objects (which, prosaically, come under the adjective *suitable*) have been tried out, the idea of suitability appears to refer to no more than two ways of looking at the same object, for both its sound and musical content.

Furthermore, this happens in two ways, the implications of which are important to our frame of mind. With prose composition we make, and are in a good position to describe, sound objects for a *morphology*. With translation we listen, and we feel a clearer need to identify and classify, in short to imagine a *typology*.

22.3. PROSE COMPOSITION

We began collecting sounds by trying out various formulae. It seemed to us that it should be possible to approach traditional instrumental sounds themselves in a new way, once our education in noises was under way. But we collected the latter with some circumspection: interesting sounds, we observed, did not necessarily come from the most highly developed sound bodies; the opposite was very often true: anything that reminded us of the traditional instrument disrupted our quest, as did noises that were too characteristic. Most of our sound bodies and what they produced were discrete: small objects, vibrating coil-springs, marbles bouncing or rolling in cups, sand running over membranes, paper being torn or bird-scarers shaken (that metallic paper used to frighten birds away). Birds, as well, were often a temptation in the early stages. Less skillful than Messiaen in notating their song, and mistrustful of the very idea of notation, we settled for playing with instruments that mimicked them: birdcalls.

Between the two extremes of the orchestra and junk, sounds reputed to be musical and those called noises, there were fortunately two transitional areas: non-Western sounds, which civilizations other than our own considered musical, and vocal sounds, polyvalent, dangerously adaptable. Finally, there was a fifth partner: electronic engineers' synthetic sound.

By dint of manipulating such disparate sounds we achieved two results. On the one hand, we discovered that we would have to abandon any premature musical classification and, even more, the notation that everyone was urging us to find, without which, they said, our research would lead nowhere. On the other hand, and because we had no musical criteria, we would have to compare sounds using that mundane characteristic that, generally speaking, they all possessed: they had a beginning, a middle, and an end. Some of them completed this journey harmoniously, others less so. And so the idea of a comparative morphology came into being. But once we had done this analysis into three parts—attack, continuation, and decay—there was not a lot more to say about most sounds; so it was important to separate them into distinct types; without an initial screening we should only be able to describe morphologies in such a crude way that it would be of hardly any interest. But we could only do this screening by using morphological differences. So for many long years we hesitated between a scarcely formulated morphology and an ill-defined typology.

In the vague understanding that the most important thing was to get nearer to what lay at the origin of the *forms* of sounds in the most general sense, we began to compare *factures*. This was possible as soon as we accepted that it would take place independently of music theory or any causality directly linked to the nature of the sound body, and consequently as soon as we had resolved to ignore the creeds of instrument makers and acousticians respectively, and therefore, without really knowing it, to practice *reduced listening*.

22.4. TRANSLATION

So if I listen to a *sound environment*, such as we may come across in the countryside, where the sound of a mill is accompanied by some sort of local music—the hurdy-gurdy, now rare, or more likely a transistor—I can, with a small effort of my attention, discern sound sources that are natural (toad, waterfall), mechanical (the mill's paddle wheel, the creaking of an axle, the turning of a sawmill next to it), human or animal languages (people's conversations, cheeping from the farmyard), and finally the conventionally musical sounds coming from the transistor, to which might be added, for its remarkable purity, some toady F-sharp.

Now, ignoring origins and meanings, if I concentrate only on the sounds themselves, I can think of a more general way of classifying them.

I can apply an initial, crudely musical criterion to them; their greater or lesser fixedness in the tessitura, whether or not they are pure sounds or noises. The waterfall, the thuds of the paddle wheel, and the toad are heard in a certain position in the register that does not vary, although whether I can assign a precise reference to it is of little importance here. Conversely, the saw has in common with the spoken voice, the clucking of the hens, the creaking of the axle, the hurdy-gurdy, or the pickup arm that it varies in the tessitura.

Applying a second criterion, phonetic in inspiration, I may also say that some sounds such as the voice are articulated, others less so or not at all. The waterfall is unarticulated, as is the saw after it has attacked the tree trunk, and the sustainment of the hurdy-gurdy in the bass; whereas the toad's notes, the thuds of the paddle wheel, the regular creaking of the axle, and the saw biting into the trunk are articulated, as the syllables of language articulate vowels by means of consonants.

We were used to practicing this type of articulation in a particular specialized sound domain, where the permanence of the source and especially of intentions maintained a clear continuity through variations in words, noises, or musical objects. In addition we observed that then we identified not sound structures, properly speaking, but structures of meaning (linguistic, musical, etc.) or indicators (phonetic or instrumental identification, etc.). In the exercise of *translating anything at all from sound*, the heterogeneity is much greater. However, we have indicated how it is possible to make comparisons. As we can see, they are influenced by some of the criteria from certain specialized domains.

22.5. EXAMPLE OF A CLASSIFICATION

To clarify our ideas we will expand on the above suggestion about the articulation of sounds. The articulation of spoken language, as we have seen, is achieved through breaks followed by stresses. For all time the grammars of all language systems have made a distinction between consonants and vowels; both can be understood as indicators (for they are nothing more than events occurring in the vocal apparatus) just as much as meanings (since a particular language system retains from this material only what suits it, one making distinctions where another tolerates conflation). For our purposes, when we suggest the pair articulation-stress, the intention is not to study their phonatory circumstances. We forget that these articulations are due to the glottis, the teeth, or the tongue; nor do we attach any importance to the fact that a particular resonator influences the color of a particular vowel with its formants; we retain no more from phonetics and phonology than an overall piece of information, very crude but precious in that it seems capable of being generalized, "biased" as it were, to apply to all sound objects.

First, to recapitulate how linguistic material is classified. Various articulations can be associated with a given stress *a: pa, sa, ma*, and so on. Conversely, various stresses can be associated with a given articulation *b: ba, be, bu*, and so on. We therefore have a grid in which the two criteria can be combined: one in columns, the attacks or forms responsible for the emission and the nature of the sounds; the other in rows, the stresses relatively independent of the former. This gives the following schematic:

consonants: b d f g k l m etc.
vowels: a . . . .
               e . . . .
               i . . . .
               o . . . .
               u . . . .

This example is deliberately simplified as far as language is concerned; it is there simply as a model. Finally, we should observe that if there are phonetic objects requiring a more subtle classification, there are also "deponent"[2] ones: these are vocalic objects consisting, on the one hand, of isolated stresses without consonants (*a, e*, etc.) and, on the other hand, of unvoiced consonants, that is, without coloration, giving only attacks without stress (dentals, sibilants, etc.).

This breaking of the sound continuum into separate successive energetic events, into *logatoms*, came near to being used in music: this is how we would have distinguished *percussive* and *held* sounds.

But we know that music has not used these ideas. Instead of concentrating on its energetic aspects such as impulse or sustainment, it referred explicitly to the instrumental source and the distinction between sounds of well-defined pitch (*tonic* sounds) and sounds *of no defined pitch*, while as a general rule linking the latter with the idea of percussion and the former with sustained sound. Despite the piano (tonic notes obtained through percussion) or the quivering cymbals (sustained although not tonic), the percussion-sustainment contrast maintains this dreadful ambiguity, suggesting a wrong direction that is often found in musical analyses. This is why phonetics seemed more accurate to us.

---

2. Here we are using the adjective *deponent* figuratively, to denote (phonetic or sound) objects with one of their morphological components missing.

But with the mill concert we were able to apply a crudely musical yet general criterion, simply saying about any sound at all whether or not it was stable in a tessitura. Thus a turbine produces a held note of complex sounds, so vague that we cannot break it down into separate tonics, but this collection of sounds can remain perfectly fixed in the tessitura. In our view this is a stress criterion perceptible to our ear. The sound of the sawmill, just like a violin glissando, evolves in the tessitura. It is more important, and in our opinion more generally applicable, to observe and understand this aspect of the morphology of sound than to try and describe it prematurely through the intermediary of a notation in sharps and flats.

So now all sorts of classifications suggest themselves, all with different aims. Phonetic classification was hardly at all concerned with *intonation*: a drawling, reedy, tonic, or hoarse voice, fixed or sliding in the tessitura. It was more important to distinguish the coloration of the *a*, the *o*, or the *i*. Of course, we incline toward a parallel approach, directed toward music. For we have already said that our classification of sound will necessarily favor the musical. However much of an interdisciplinary specialist one may be, it is impossible to make progress without an *intention*.

22.6. MORPHOLOGY AND TYPOLOGY

We will now make our approach from "both ends": morphologies in the sense of prose composition, typologies in the sense of translation.

Morphologies were more apparent to us in the sense of prose composition, through the situation of the man who creates sounds one by one and examines their factures and effects at leisure. The difficulty in generalizing from this comes from the fact that when we make a sound or sounds in this way, we are operating in a particular domain, on arbitrarily chosen sound bodies, and if we try to characterize the sounds we have produced, it is very difficult for us to detach ourselves from the registers they suggest, echoing traditional values and analyses.

The need for a typology, on the contrary, arose from comparing and contrasting collections of sounds and, for the purpose of identifying them, retaining only their most general characteristics, notably articulation followed by stress. The difficulty here is arriving at criteria that are general enough without being indistinct.

These two complementary approaches come from the fact that morphology tends toward describing sound, whereas typology fulfills the need to identify objects. Morphology receives from typology fragments taken haphazardly from the sound continuum, for the purpose of evaluating and describing them. So we come back to the two functions shared by musicality and sonority, responsible respectively for identifying musical objects and describing their contents in the conventional system.

When we set about comparing all objects in this way, we start referring to what is "least musical," following the crude criteria of a "cut and slash" typology. Then these badly finished chunks, whose general similarity depends precisely on the few requirements we have of them at the moment, will have to be compared with each other through more and more careful, more and more refined, sorting and finally tested in the field of perception, which, in man, seems to be the source of musicality.

It is important to understand the scope of such a change in our musical customs. We would note:

1. That having abandoned any reference either to instruments or to accepted values, all we have is collections of disparate sound objects. All we can do is compare them with each other, in all sorts of ways, in their contexture or their texture. This activity is sound morphology.

2. We are already assuming that part of the problem has been resolved, since we say we have collections of sound objects. Even allowing (we have to start somewhere) that musicianly invention has provided a good number of disparate objects in the material sense, we still had to separate them from the continuums where they occurred and also classify them in relation to each other. If we took isolated objects, it comes down to the same thing: we are implicitly obeying rules of sound identification. What are they? They, too, can only be in response to an initial morphological approach. Typology, or the art of separating sound objects, identifying them, and if possible carrying out an initial crude screening, can only be based on morphological features.

3. We have said that we rejected the musical at the outset, just as if, having to unload a truck full of disparate articles or tidy our loft, we wanted to have the most generally applicable and practical classification schedule and not the most specific or refined. This is very true, but to stop there would lead to the very worst misunderstanding. We must add this paradoxical but very heartfelt comment: our selection criteria, where sound is concerned, are *the most musical* possible; they are, as we have said, biased; this bias toward musical invention now focuses on *extension*, whereas with traditional criteria it aimed for *specificity*.

4. Where does our inspiration find its direction? In the continuation of our earlier musical training. Our research really does not want to see itself cut off from tradition. Innovation is never so good as when it is inspired by the work of predecessors, and this is perhaps our greatest ambition (together with the wonder Oppenheimer referred to). Now, retaining what was most memorable, most subtle in our musical training does not necessarily mean limiting oneself to what one has learned. We are behaving no differently from the geometer who thinks up other geometries but only because of the one he knows, which has already structured space for him, and which he will return to as a particular, but central, example in his generalization.

This is why we postulate a *musical perceptual field* that we will verify later. It could also be said that this idea of field has an important advantage over classical musicality: instead of being based on a property of objects (naively conceived of as external to consciousness), and therefore completely attached to the specificity of these objects, it is based on those glimpsed capacities for synthesis, that ability to describe objects that is quite specific to man and to the most secret workings of his musical sensibility.

5. So, ultimately, morphology is based on this generalized *musical intention* when dealing with disparate sound objects. We give it this name to show clearly that it is an add-on; it introduces a tension, a tendency to move on to the musical tangentially. It is, in fact, a bias, an oblique tension, since everything culturally, normally, or naturally musical that we may find in our intention would lead us back inevitably to the conventional system.

22.7. THE FORM-MATTER PAIR

We need to anchor morphology somewhere—that is, make up our minds to compare sound objects in some way. So we thought of a typology that would be both a generalization and a specialization of the articulation-stress pair, considered as the most general law governing sound chains of any sort. In the mill concert, we chose, with evident ease, two criteria, one of articulation (sound production), the other of stress (intonation). Surely this is already tantamount to doing a rudimentary morphology? We have already seen that it was impossible to stop at a typology without defining a morphology. We will therefore have to move by a series of approximations from one to the other. So we also need the beginnings of a morphology.

This is, fortunately, where perception of duration comes in, which is so natural to us that we hardly thought of mentioning it, and which applies just as well to sound objects as to musical objects. Imagine that we can "stop" a sound to hear what it is like, at a given moment in our listening: what we can grasp now is what we will call its *matter*, complex, fixed in the tessitura and in subtle relationships with the sound contexture. Now listen to the history of the sound: we become aware of the evolution in duration of what had for an instant been fixed, a *journey in time that shapes this matter*.

It should be noted that it is the contexture of an object considered in isolation that we are breaking down into form and matter here, in the knowledge that later we will attempt to go on to analyze its form, the detail of its history in duration, and the makeup of its matter at a given moment. Once we have established a method and a terminology with the help of this procedure, it will be easier to compare one object with another. We will then discover forms that are similar but for their matter, and matters that are comparable but for their form. We are back to the most normal procedure in morphological investigation.

22.8. OBJECTS WITH FIXED FORM: CRITERION OF MATTER

We will now compare objects *without form:* in these objects, by definition, *matter* persists as constantly identical to itself. This is where we begin to break new ground in relation to music and phonetics. Music used to classify the matter of sounds according to pitch, phonetics according to the color of the vowels. Putting forward a *fixed-matter* criterion means taking quite another approach. Is a note, tonic or otherwise, fixed in the tessitura, or does it vary? Whether the vowel is *a* or *i*, is the stress the same, or is it colored differently? The mill turbine that *grosso modo* produced a prolonged held note, always the same, is classified just like a fixed held note on a violin or in a vowel in the *permanent matter* box.

As we can see, this box will contain many disparate objects; other criteria will appear later for various types of the same *fixed matter* criterion. Then we will be able to distinguish the proportion of noise that accompanies a harmonic content (grain), the bulk in the tessitura (thickness), the complexity of the timbre, and so forth. Most important, we will retain the distinction that involves the most robust musical perception: the perception of melody. What is immediately obvious is whether a fixed matter is complex or tonic. We will apply the term *mass* to this criterion of matter, which in contrast to others (e.g., grain or allure)[3] denotes *the occupation of the pitch field by the sound.* Tonic sound, in particular, is an example of a situation in which the tessitura is occupied at one single point (for perception, not for acoustics). Then the criterion of mass will diversify: we will talk about *thick* or *thin, channeled* or *blurred, colored* sound or *white* noise, whatever their other aspects (grain, allure, etc.).

22.9. OBJECTS WITH FIXED MATTER: CRITERION OF FORM

The absence of form facilitated the above screening process, which highlights mass as the dominant characteristic of the matter of a sound. However varied sounds with fixed mass may be, all these sounds nevertheless share a common definition that indicates that they remain unchanged through duration: they are, in a word, *homogeneous.* We can say of them that they present the phenomenon of sound in an atemporal state since their development contributes nothing over and above their immediate content. However unrewarding they may be from the aesthetic

---

3. The term *allure* given by Schaeffer to the way sounds behave through time is, indeed, one of the most controversial terms when translating his works. Its basic meaning is "way of going," and it is variously translated as way of walking, pace, gait, speed, rate, appearance, look. No English word truly represents the sense of the word; this is why it has been kept in its original French form. See section 32.8 for a fuller account of Schaeffer's use of *allure.*—Trans.

point of view, these sounds are of great interest to musical research in that they lend themselves to an investigation of matter without the difficulties arising from perceptions of form.

So now we will move on to an examination of forms. This new stage will initially concern only sounds with fixed matter, thus comparing objects of disparate mass (tonic, thick, etc.), which nevertheless have obvious similarities of form. For example, a *delta* form (a crescendo followed by a decrescendo) constitutes a *profile* that can be recognized equally well in both a pure sinusoidal sound and the thickest noise. In the same way we can compare their attacks, those singular features of form that are particularly noticeable in a great number of sounds. Evaluating the perceptions resulting from all the comparisons made in this way should lead to a *catalogue of forms*.[4] Our first hope from this theory of forms would be a typological criterion, after which we can return to a more detailed morphology.

Finally, very prosaically, we observe that all sounds are the result of a particular energetic process: this is *sustainment*, showing *how the sound persists in duration:* if it is only short-lived, we have an *impulse;* if it persists in a continuous manner, we will call it a *sustained sound;* if it continues through repeated impulses, we have a third way of occupying duration: *iterative sustainment.* Thus we close the triptych of this most rudimentary, but most general, of classifications.

22.10. EVOLVING SOUNDS: THE NORM

We will leave the developments of typology, which finds its foundations here, until the next chapter. But we cannot close a brief overview of morphology without considering the norm, *evolving sounds.*

Clarifying the morphology of these sounds, we should say immediately, would be tantamount to achieving a complete science of sound objects. An *evolving* sound can indeed be one of the most complex, presenting in its texture a summation of articulations and stresses varying both in matter and in form. Any fragment of spoken language, human or animal, of instrumental modulation or natural noise, can thus be described as an evolving sound.

Logically, to analyze it, our first step should be to "disarticulate" it, using its breaks and stresses until we come to elementary sound objects. Depending on the tempo of these components, and the always-arbitrary level of cutting, these stresses will be more or less complex and their articulations more or less clear. In any case, generally speaking, the profile of these objects will be of both form and matter; moreover, we suspect that the two extreme cases of fixed form and fixed matter will not give combinatory data and will be of little help under these circumstances.

---

4. Here Schaeffer refers to Plato's *Theory of Forms*, which asserts that forms, and not sensations, possess the highest kind of reality.—Trans.

And this is certainly why, in general, we do not have the words to analyze our perceptions, even when they present themselves to our ear with undeniable coherence. We must therefore go back to a tried-and-tested formula: leave sound quite soon, without going too soon into the musical: which is what a *typology* of sound objects, more or less "suitable" for music, is supposed to do.

Before embarking on these chapters we should say something about the ways and means of experimenting on sound. We must not forget that, if we have mastered the traditionally musical, it is thanks to its tools: musical instruments. It would be amazing if we could make an inventory of sound with the "naked" ear.

At the beginning of this chapter we were eager to give things their due importance in the development of ideas. This was only a historical, indeed a teaching, hors-d'œuvre. Research into sound cannot stop at gramophone techniques or votive tributes to the closed groove. The approach to and then the ordering of sound presupposed a very specific type of laboratory, not electronic but electroacoustic, microphonic, tape recordic: spectacles for the ear and cuts in sounds.

23

The Laboratory

23.1. ELECTROACOUSTIC PREREQUISITES

It is good to define the "musical system," to analyze its contents, and to understand the way it is structured. But we must have the tools to do this; without an electroacoustic laboratory the above analysis would have been impossible. When an artistic investigation becomes analytical, it may need equipment, not just to measure objects but also to display them in a different light, to "play them," as it were. The laboratory we are, in fact, going to describe, although based on an electroacoustic technology, will be little more than a musical instrument or, more precisely, the instrument of our *experimentation on musical perceptions*.

So the reader may be reassured: what we are going to say about this is no more than what a user should know about his car or a violinist about his violin, except that now we are not talking about playing in a concert but manipulating sounds.

It may seem surprising that several of the sound examples quoted until now were not taken from the electroacoustic context. In fact, if we have chosen our examples from the traditional domain, it is so that the reader knows what we are talking about and can benefit from the analyses involving such sounds, in particular the correlations in book 3.

Now it is quite obvious that without the electroacoustic system this work would have been impossible and even unthinkable, since we would have remained at the stage of the cultural conditioning described in book 4 without having any opportunity to become aware of it; we would have been going round in circles over aesthetic considerations (as is often the case with contemporary music: a prisoner of the system yet bewildered by its development). Only by overstepping the "boundaries of the blueprint," by tackling obstinately eccentric objects, can the researcher become disorientated enough to be forced to rethink everything. But we need both unusual objects and new ways of treating them. In this chapter we will discuss these new ways of making and hearing, already implicit in book 3.

In reality we should need a whole work. The first chapters have already introduced the idea of this electronic transformation (*Umwandlung*, to use an expression dear to Hermann Scherchen)[1] into music. We will limit ourselves to giving the framework of a development that we will doubtless need to add as a supplement to this treatise, which will only deal with the fundamentals of the research. Besides, adding more technical details unwisely or prematurely runs the risk of putting off the readers for whom it is written, who would think it is intended only for technicians.

The essential understanding, which everyone should make his own, is not about electronic sound synthesis, which we have criticized: through the deceptive facilities it provides, it encourages musicians to use electronics in the spirit of the old system and to work with frequencies, tempos, and levels as if they were using real musical values or elementary perception criteria. On the contrary, it is all about discovering that the electroacoustic system, where any sound at all is concerned, is an extraordinary piece of investigative equipment, which brings about the desired deconditioning and is also the instrument for the musical and sound analysis we lacked.

23.2. THE ELECTROACOUSTIC SYSTEM

We intend to describe the electroacoustic system briefly without going into detail about the equipment itself—although it is necessary to understand its basic functions—but recognizing the opportunities it gives at its different levels for sound intervention and manipulation (see fig. 26).

We will identify nine stages or links in this chain, going from natural or artificial sound events to sound projection with loudspeakers at the final stage, through a number of electric or sound modifications with extremely wide-ranging possibilities and repertoires.

1. *Sound domains*

As any sound can be recorded, coming from nature, from human or animal language, from raw or refined, willed or involuntary, elementary or complex sound

---

1. Hermann Scherchen (1891–1996) was a German conductor who strongly promoted twentieth-century music. He was very interested in Schaeffer's experiments and work, and he followed the activities of the GRMC very closely. In 1954, with the help of UNESCO, he created the Gravesano Studio in Switzerland, which became an important center for new music.—Trans.

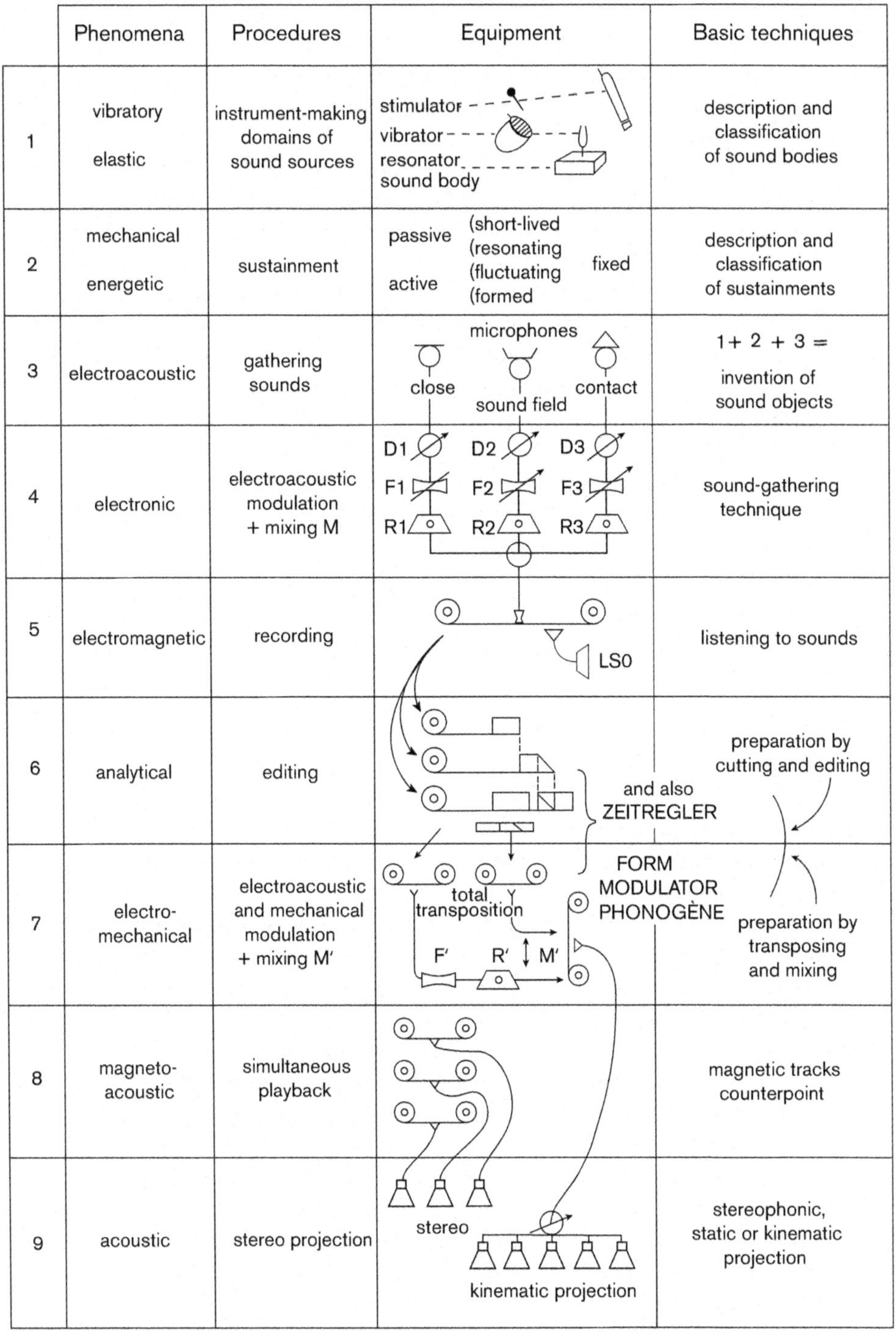

	Phenomena	Procedures	Equipment	Basic techniques
1	vibratory elastic	instrument-making domains of sound sources	stimulator vibrator resonator sound body	description and classification of sound bodies
2	mechanical energetic	sustainment	passive (short-lived (resonating active (fluctuating fixed (formed	description and classification of sustainments
3	electroacoustic	gathering sounds	microphones close contact sound field	1 + 2 + 3 = invention of sound objects
4	electronic	electroacoustic modulation + mixing M	D1 D2 D3 F1 F2 F3 R1 R2 R3	sound-gathering technique
5	electromagnetic	recording	LS0	listening to sounds
6	analytical	editing	and also ZEITREGLER	preparation by cutting and editing
7	electro- mechanical	electroacoustic and mechanical modulation + mixing M′	total transposition F′ R′ M′ FORM MODULATOR PHONOGÈNE	preparation by transposing and mixing
8	magneto- acoustic	simultaneous playback		magnetic tracks counterpoint
9	acoustic	stereo projection	stereo kinematic projection	stereophonic, static or kinematic projection

FIGURE 26. The electroacoustic system.

events, at various stages of artistic or social development, we are virtually in possession of an immense wealth of experimental *sound material.*

2. *Sound factures*

These, which are generally implicit in natural sounds, must be made explicit as soon as we are dealing with deliberate manipulations. We could suggest analyzing them as follows: into (1) sound bodies and (2) ways of using them, making them vibrate or maintaining those vibrations.

We can see that traditional musical instruments are a combination of (1) and (2), plus something else: a registration, which we will not permit ourselves to assume in sound in general. Electronic sounds, as well, are involved with sources (1) and ways of using them (2), through a particular system of multidimensional registration.

3. *Microphone recording*

This may involve one or several microphones, their positioning in relation to the source, and the conductive medium that links them to the sound body (air, water, contact, intermediary device).

4. *Electroacoustic modulation*

Each microphone delivers an electric current that faithfully reproduces the elastic vibrations it has recorded from the source; moreover, it can be used together with:

- an attenuator or amplifier, D_1, D_2, D_3 . . .
- a set of filters or corrector, F_1, F_2, F_3 . . .
- a reverberation device, R_1, R_2, R_3 . . .

In addition, the various microphones are linked together by a mixing device M, which controls the modulations from each one and provides a resultant modulation.

5. *Recording*

Whether this is done by mechanical, magnetic, or optical engraving, it gives a practically faithful "sound image" (except for corrections in engraving and playback) from M (see the reservations made in chapter 3), as we can verify by listening to a control loudspeaker LS_0.

6. *Manipulating the recording by editing and mixing (transformations)*

This is the possibility of intervening either in the succession or the superimposition in time of the sound segments, including the possibility of shaping the dynamic profiles of a given segment or adjusting the levels of two simultaneous or successive segments. In this box we will only put manipulations that do not affect the integrity of the *matter* of the sounds and only interfere with their *form.* Only scissors and the copying or mixing potentiometer are used. Finally, we obtain a sound object that combines segments taken from one or several component objects, having perhaps modified their dynamics.

7. Manipulating by modifying the recording (transmutation)

This is what we have just excluded: it involves not only the repetition of the last two manipulations, electroacoustic modulations F′ and R′ (described in 4), but in addition speeding up and slowing down or *total transposition*, where the time and spectrum of the frequencies are linked by an inverse multiplication or demultiplication coefficient. These manipulations, of course, give rise to new possibilities for mixing M′.

8. Synchronous playback

This is a parallel technique to multiple-microphone sound recording, followed by blending; we can either blend two or three magnetic or optical tracks, making sure they are in synch, or reproduce each of these tracks on a separate loudspeaker channel (still in synch) through multitrack playback, in which each channel may in addition be undergoing some of the electroacoustic modulations mentioned above. Nevertheless, for the sake of simplicity, we will assume that the latter are merely corrective—that is, that they are intended simply to get rid of possible faults in transmission to the loudspeakers of the signals on the recording medium, or to improve their output in high fidelity.

9. Spatial projection

We must be careful to distinguish between this last stage and the previous one. Not that it is not implicit in it: there is no multitrack playback without the beginnings of spatialization. But further levels of freedom come from the positioning of the loudspeakers, whether they are linked together or spread out in the field of sound reproduction, and the possible movements of sounds from one loudspeaker to another (*spatial kinematics* of sound projection).

The essential aim of spatialization, which is often confused with some strange myth of "spatial music," is to improve the definition of objects through their distribution in space, since it so happens that the ear distinguishes two simultaneous sounds better if one comes from the right and the other from the left. We are not dealing here with a luxury added on to our hearing but something to facilitate it. Before even mentioning space and sound architecture, we should talk about the identification of objects and their coexistence. Where they are is of little consequence; it is what this enables that is important: an incomparably *clearer, richer, more subtle perception of their contents.* In the same way, binocular vision gives the third dimension and by putting things in perspective with each other allows us to judge their properties and relationships better.

Finally, we should note the difference between *stereophony*, which consists in reproducing real *sources* in space, and *spatialization*, which consists in dispersing recorded *objects* (hence tracks) on loudspeakers judiciously situated in the three dimensions of space.

23.3. REPERCUSSIONS OF THE SYSTEM ON
FUNDAMENTAL RESEARCH

As we have said, these nine points are so many chapter headings for a possible "treatise on the use of electroacoustic resources in music" and include developments in applied music just as much as in fundamental sound research. At this point we will set aside everything that is not necessary to the latter, that is:

1. We will enter domains of sound only to take samples from them. We will not investigate them any further. We will, however, briefly describe the general workings of the way the sound body is used in music.

2. We will endeavor to discover the general rules that the facture of sound objects should obey—that is, the essential rules for identifying, choosing, and classifying them.

3. We will not go any further into sound recording except to suggest, as we have already done, that there is a difference between the "shot" of the object it is able to give and live listening (a phenomenon analogous to viewing angles, enlargement of images, visual salience, planes, and lighting).

4. Generally speaking, we will not allow ourselves to use electroacoustic manipulations other than regulating the level with the potentiometer, for several reasons, the main one being as follows: we observe that they merely muddle the characteristic features of the objects, without radically transforming or changing them, and that we perceive them in themselves as *the trace of the sound*, and therefore as *transformation*; in general, then, they distance us from effective understanding of the objects. But as laboratory manipulations we will use them for the purpose of analysis or when appropriate as correctives.

5. Ultimately, it is the most faithful recording that will be of most use to us—faithful, of course, to the object and the recording "angle." Faithful recording, without transformations, will not dispense with the need to go back to sound recording, combined with skilled, inventive manipulation of the sound body; rather the contrary—in the same way the photographer is keen not to use film gimmickry, and wants the photograph to examine faces or visual objects as frankly, as eloquently, as possible, simply using the ways the camera has of reinforcing the real as it is seen by the eye. So we reject electroacoustic sound cosmetics but claim complete liberty to approach and define a "type of sound" (theoretically perceptible to the ear) radically changed in its proportions by microphones.

6 and 7. The same attitude guides our preferences in the matter of using manipulations either by editing or filtering. Editing retains the *matter* of the object (6), filtering its *form* (7); we value these two manipulations because through them we can lay the emphasis alternately on each of these two fundamental aspects of the morphology of objects.

8 and 9. These techniques mainly concern applied experimental music. Of course, they also enable us to study other properties of listening. For example, in chapter 3 we saw the impact of the visual (section 3.7) in sound impressions. We should never forget that objects dispersed in space do not have remotely the same effect as the same objects, just as synchronous, coming from a single loudspeaker.

It remains for us to develop the following points:

· how a sound body functions when it is used in music;
· the opportunities for inventing sound objects by means of factures that use the combined resources of sound bodies and sound recording;
· the techniques for preparing the object from the recording of it;
· more advanced and recent techniques after critical examination of the earlier ones, it being clearly understood that, reserving the work of defining *research approaches* and *experimental disciplines* for a later analysis, we will limit ourselves here to a description of *ways of using the equipment* available.

23.4. DESCRIPTION AND USE OF SOUND BODIES

A good technological description of sound bodies should enable us to generalize the concept of musical instrument and lead us to the beginnings of a deconditioning from traditional practices, through analyzing what belongs to sound in general and to the musical in particular in each of them. We will borrow the Baschet brothers' analysis, the most classical possible, yet it led them to brilliant innovations in instrument making, particularly through the use of vibrating rods and wands suspended in the air by ingenious systems of their own devising. We could comment along with them that there are only two essential elements in a sound body: what vibrates and what causes vibration. A child playing with a rubber band is like the child with the grass. Each of them possesses the minimum—a vibrator: rubber band or grass; a stimulator: a finger using pizzicato or breath that sustains the sound. Here, too, we can see the two basic types of sustainment: one short-lived and "passive," the other permanent and "active."

The third element, dispensable but frequently added to a sound body intended for music, is a resonator. Yet we must point out that the term is ambiguous and masks two functions, which must be differentiated from each other and which could lead on to two distinct devices. The function of a resonator, properly speaking, is to characterize or transform timbre through the addition of formants (commonly occurring zones of frequency in the spectrum of a given sound) or acoustic filtering. Thus, the violin's belly colors the vibration of the string without imposing any particular formant on it, whereas the buccal and nasal cavities, used in various ways, give rise to specific formants that turn the sounds from the vocal cords into different vowels. Quite different from this is the "coupler" or "radiator," intended to adjust the sound body's "acoustic impedance" to the surrounding conditions: this, for example, is the role of the horn on trumpets or loudspeakers, which in Baschet instruments is taken on by antennae or metallic diffusion surfaces, which in fact improve acoustic output to an astonishing extent.

Finally, from a viewpoint this time frankly favoring the musical (and no longer only the musicianly), we find a registration, that is, a modulation device that in most cases is nominal pitches (percussive keyboards or holes in a bellows).

The interaction of the five elements—two (vibrator and stimulator) indispensable, two (resonator and coupler) desirable, then the fifth, both valuable and tendentious (register)—gives, as may be expected, innumerable combinations through which, provided we can produce them effectively, we could already to a great extent rethink "live" sound making. When we go on to consider the potential of linkage with surrounding conditions, of recording itself, of amplification and the various electroacoustic modifications, we are dumbfounded at the extent of the opportunities opened up to us; there is nothing to equal them except the ignorance of our contemporaries and their idleness as they wait for an electronic Father Christmas who will bring them a music machine, ready-made.

23.5. FACTURES: INVENTION OF SOUND OBJECTS AND SOUND RECORDING

Perhaps we have been using the word *facture* incorrectly, in a broader, more practical sense than the one that has been and will be used in typomorphology. In this latter connotation it will mean finding formal signs in the sound object of the way it was made. Here we will use it to refer to all the ingenuity (rarely revealed in acousmatic listening) that goes into the creation of varied, formed, willed sounds in an infinitely more extended register of matters and forms than either the musician conditioned to registers or the physicist obsessed with filters and frequencies could ever have imagined a priori. If, for example, I put a piece of sheet metal in front of the microphone, I seem to have neither varied sound elements nor parameters of freedom in the way of playing and hearing it. A traditional musician will immediately demand a set of metal sheets arranged in a register, and an electronics expert will rush to dissect this sound into slices of frequency or millimeters of duration. And so the evidence passes them by: all sorts of musicianly initiatives are possible, which have nothing to do with musical registration or acoustic measuring. From the studio point of view a host of sound bodies can be made to vibrate in all sorts of different ways. From the listening booth point of view, as we have seen, the sound recorder can make an original "take" of the sound object by adjusting the position and the setting of the microphones, just as the cinematographer or the "lighting" director in the cinema can choose the angle, the distance, the lighting for the object to be photographed. These apparent restrictions conceal immense potential.

So what can I do with this piece of sheet metal, put like this in front of active "phonography"? Like the young violinist, remember the teacher's advice: *one* to be ready, *two* to play, making sure this is one movement. Playing the violin linked muscle and bow, a kinesthetic reflex and a mechanical sense. I rediscover all this, much more crudely, in this sheet metal, which I scratch, hit, stroke in all sorts of ways, overcoming the human sense of dignity that would make this situation ridiculous. Finally, depending on the position of the microphone (or microphones), the setting of the potentiometer, the filters (sometimes in real time), I obtain surfaces, a detail, enlargements, a new coloration of every variant I draw out of the same gesture, which does not astonish merely the uninitiated; the professional, trained in a technique of fidelity, hardly ever knows what he holds at his fingertips, that often unimaginable extension of a technique that is all unobtrusiveness.

Now we will go back to our sheet metal and count the degrees of freedom I can combine in order to obtain so many and such varied objects from this one body that the acousmatician will not believe his ears. All sorts of percussive or sustainment factures, using many a stimulator, are possible: various drumsticks, used in all sorts of ways, from simple percussion to a continuous roll; scratching, also going from the mellow to a screech, through staccatos where the material of the stick comes into play: wood, metal, rubber, and so forth. Moreover, all the interesting places on the sheet metal can be explored: the surface, the edge, and practically all the points where it is fixed or suspended; we can use various tensions, degrees of flexing, and, finally, perhaps, coupling it to other resonators.

From the point of view of the microphone there are all these different approaches, involving the surroundings right to the point of contact, and the opportunities given by positioning them in responsive places in the acoustic field. But we could also imagine a temporal intervention in the facture on the part of the operator. If we wait until after the attack to turn up the potentiometer, we obtain a sound that will be astonishing in its originality as much as its authenticity: it is both a sound we know well and one we do not recognize. Where fairly long objects are concerned, therefore, a skillfully handled potentiometer can be as effective and subtle as the violinist's bow.

We can, finally, combine the sound of this sheet of metal with other types of percussion, such as the bass register of the piano, which is so similar to it. Thus we compose a sound object from two combined sources; we can make a hundred attempts before retaining the one that is preferred for the profile of its form, its scintillating matter. A technique such as this rapidly enters the zone of rhythmic articulations and melodic modulations, in short, live composition through juxtaposition and superimposition. We can see here the favored procedures in concrete music, in direct contact with the stuff of sound, like the sculptor with his clay.

23.6. PREPARING THE OBJECT

We have already mentioned the theoretical dissection of the object along the lines of its dimensions in physics. If we situate the physical object in its reference trihedron of ox, y, z (see fig. 27), taking time as the abscissas (x-axis), intensity as ordinates (y-axis) (oz vertically), and oy as end axis, the frequencies, the normal "cutting planes" at ox, y, and z are cutting at a given moment, cutting at a given frequency, and cutting at a given level. Cutting in accordance with time is not only the easiest (all that is needed is a pair of scissors) but also the most reversible: it works just as well for analysis as for synthesis. Cutting according to level is of no particular interest and in addition is very difficult to do electronically. Finally, cutting according to frequencies, by means of a set of bandpass filters, presents the pitfalls we all know about: it rarely isolates a real band of frequencies, due to the demanding technical norms it requires; moreover, the "form" of the object victoriously resists this dismemberment. As for the three-dimensional representation of the physical object, it is little more than a curio. Once we have had the satisfaction of seeing the perfect chord or the beating of a gong in the form of abstract sculpture, we can only regret this costly waste of time. The author, who has spent time on this in the past,[2] cannot warn the reader too strongly against this amusing piece of physics, which can be of no use whatsoever to music. We will return to the recording booth: what manipulations have we to hand?

We have already mentioned the first: intervening in duration, with scissors and editing.

The second is with the potentiometer: it consists in raising or lowering the overall levels of the object, or intervening in its profile.

The third, rather than "filtering," consists in total transposition by speeding up or slowing down, transposing both the spectrum and the rhythm of the object at the same time. In this way the form is dilated or condensed, depending respectively on whether the sound matter is transferred into the bass or the high register.

The above interventions are techniques belonging to physics. Our only originality is in making them solely for the purposes of musical evaluation while drawing a clear distinction between these two aspects of our experimental activity.

Suppose, in fact, that our experimenter is endeavoring to differentiate form and matter in objects, finding it difficult to evaluate both at once: he might decide, in his experiments, to emphasize form at the expense of matter or vice versa. Suppose, then, that the form, too complex and in a rich harmonic resonance, makes it difficult to listen to one moment of the sound. How can this instant be isolated to allow the ear to hear it comfortably?

2. See Pierre Schaeffer, *A la recherche d'une musique concrète* (Paris: Seuil, 1952). [Translated into English by Christine North and John Dack as *In Search of a Concrete Music* (Berkeley: University of California Press, 2012).—Trans.]

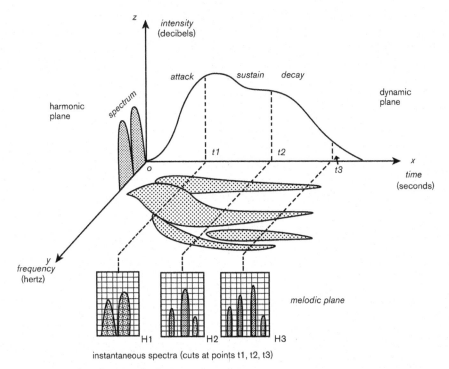

instantaneous spectra (cuts at points t1, t2, t3)

FIGURE 27. The reference trihedron.

Phonogènes are intended to provide an answer to this question, much more than to perform harmonic noise marches.[3] When we only had the *total transposition* they made possible, we discovered this additional use, which resolved the problem after a fashion: we slowed the sound right down and located the zone of interest. We cut a piece of sound out of this zone, appropriately dilated, and "looped" it. Once it was speeded up again, it found its tessitura and played itself over and over again. Of course, the samples retained a certain dynamic, and it was difficult to "homogenize" a loop like this properly (i.e., cancel out its form). Nevertheless, we must say that despite these imperfections, it enabled the experimenter to take hold of a slice of listening and a temporal element of its form.

Here is an example of the importance of such crude manipulations, taken from the beginning of our research. It would never have occurred to anyone to compare a bell and a wind instrument. Now since 1948 our first and crudest experiments

3. Phonogènes are variable-speed tape recorders.

with the "cut bell" have led us on to this new way of looking at sounds and establishing connections between them, which neither acoustics nor traditional instruments would ever have suggested. The "bell loop," in truth, was at that time no more than a closed groove from a bell taken at a carefully chosen moment of its resonance, and it made a sound like a flute. Hence our initial idea that the concept of instrumental timbre, hardly at all linked, as was claimed, to the presence of a characteristic spectrum, had to be completely rethought.

Therefore, to pursue these studies on timbres, we had to isolate the component matter and the component form, which now appeared as two criteria of musical listening, independent of elementary acoustic parameters. The systematic variations of these two components in relation to each other clearly indicated the most interesting direction for experimentation.

23.7. THE TRANSPOSITIONS OF THE OBJECT

The above techniques, in their crudeness, are like irreversible biological incisions. The combination of scissors and glue, the potentiometer and the phonogène, did allow us some syntheses, as well, but at the cost of what damage! But this is how our research progressed: successive copies, fragments dilated then condensed, levels raised then lowered, nothing that had much chance of appearing pleasing to a musical user.

That heroic period was set to be superseded by a happier, better equipped, phase, benefiting directly from its trials and errors. The important thing, as we have suggested, was to bring into prominence notions such as sound form and matter, without which there is no point in thinking about the device we will describe now and which, precisely, allows us to grasp these independently.

Springer's *Zeitregler* initially very modestly addressed a need felt in broadcasting studios, which are obliged to observe strict time schedules.[4] How could a symphony that lasted twenty minutes be made to fit into a slot of nineteen minutes? This was the mundane question addressed by the device invented by Springer, which for our own part we consider worthy of nobler application. In effect, in some way it resolves the problem of infinitesimal cutting, which haunted a number of composers such as Stockhausen when he visited our studio in 1952. Despite our rebukes, he insisted on cutting a tape into millimeter segments in order to be able to stick them together again in a different way. The "thousand-piece loop" was famous for the obstinacy and the trials and tribulations it represented. In practice, cutting taken to this extreme goes beyond the capabilities of the experimenter, as of the tape recorder, for reasons of output and sound quality. Now, Springer's device resolves the general question, which is very close to the one raised by Stockhausen's endeavor, of condensing or dilating a sound object that remains the same with regard to form or matter. Sup-

4. On the *Zeitregler* see Appendix A.

pose, in fact, that cutting and gluing together infinitesimal pieces of magnetic tape is possible. For example, suppose we cut the tape of a sound one second in duration (therefore 380 mm long)[5] into segments 1 mm long. We then number these millimeters 1 to 380. We try out the two following edits: in one we stick 1, 3, 5, 7 . . . together (i.e., all the odd numbers) or else 2, 4, 6, 8 . . . (i.e., all the even numbers); in the other, assuming we have a second tape identical to the first and cut in the same way, we stick 1 followed by 1 from the other tape, then 2 followed by 2, and so on. In the first we obtain a sound half the length, in the second twice the length. What will happen if we play these two edited fragments at the initial speed of 38 cm per second? As they are being played at the right speed, the components of the *matter* of these sounds (pitch, harmonic content) will probably be the same as in the initial sound, although one tiny fraction out of two is absent, or every fraction is repeated twice. But one of these sounds will be half, the other twice, as long—that is, its *form* will have been condensed or dilated: thus this first procedure acts on the form without affecting the matter of the sound. If, however, we play the short tape at half speed and the long tape at double speed, we transpose the entire sound spectrum an octave lower in the first case and an octave higher in the second. So here we return to the initial duration and therefore the form of the sound, but we have transposed its matter. In this way the *Zeitregler* enables us to dissociate sound form and matter to a greater extent than could be done through the use of the phonogène.

23.8. TRANSMUTATIONS OF THE OBJECT

While the above technique resolves major problems in both fundamental research (morphological examination of the different moments of the object) and applied music (independence of the rhythm—or durations—and tessitura of the objects), it does not yet give the means for that sound alchemy that is every experimenter's dream: a radical separation between the form and matter of sounds. We indeed imagined a bow stroke that could be applied to matter other than the violin, or a piano note with the sonority of the violin as its matter. If this were possible, would it not be the source of astonishing transmutations, here and in both fundamental and applied research? Even the best known musical instruments would be revolutionized.

Very recently, Francis Coupigny from the Research Service of the ORTF built an initial prototype that granted this wish: the form modulator, in fact, enables us to *mold the matter of a sound* homogenized earlier *to the form* of another sound (using the procedures mentioned above).[6]

---

5. The standard tape speed of a professional tape recorder is 38 cm/second. [15 ips.—Trans.]

6. On the form modulator see Appendix B. [Francis Coupigny was a French engineer who was a close collaborator of Schaeffer's in the Service de la Recherche of the ORTF; in charge of technical developments, he built the Phonogène Universel and the synthesizer that is named in his honor.—Trans.]

Over and above the first experiments "just to see," we can think of other applications for this: the composer-performer would use it to ensure the formal shaping of objects, the sound matter of which would be judiciously chosen. Once more, as can be seen, this is a "concrete" technique, in direct contact with sound.

23.9. ELECTRONIC GENERATORS

Experimental music cannot ignore electronic sources. The sounds they provide, although not audible until played through a loudspeaker, are part of the domain of sound. They are *previously unheard* by definition, since they are absent from nature. And this is why their appearance in a group of sounds is always accompanied by certain difficulties about their use: our conditioning to such sounds is still fragile. Even if they do not bring about the easy synthesis of all other sounds, as was initially believed, they nonetheless provide matters and forms we have certainly not yet exploited to the full. Another reason for taking an interest in them is the extreme ease with which they can be manipulated, which gives great flexibility to sound and musical experimentation.

We will give a rapid overview of the resources generally used in the electronic production of sounds.[7] On the one hand, there are generators that produce various types of electric signals; on the other hand, there are means for modifying or combining electric signals; finally, we will indicate briefly how these devices are used.

1. Generators

Generally speaking, an electronic music studio will have the following sources:

- Sine wave generators, either registered (e.g., in the tempered scale) or of continuously variable pitch. There are often relatively large numbers of the latter, to allow several frequencies to be added (e.g., the components of a given spectrum).
- Short impulse generators (clacking noise) of variable length and frequency of repetition.
- Square or triangle wave generators.
- Noise generators (sounds in which the spectrum contains all frequencies) with adjustable bandwidth.

2. Devices for modifying or combining sound. Their function is to superimpose the signals from the generators on or make them interact with each other. In general they are as follows:

---

7. See, e.g., Werner Meyer-Eppler, *Elektronische Musik*, in *Klangstruktur der Musik* (Berlin: TU Berlin, 1955).

- Addition: one signal is added to another.
- Attenuation, amplification, frequency filtering: these procedures are self-explanatory.
- Multiplication: a signal continuously produced by two given signals is obtained. The applications of this procedure are as follows:

(a) Frequency modulation: a frequency variation, regular or otherwise, is superimposed on a sound of fixed frequency, initially giving a tremolo effect.

(b) Form modulation: the (sine wave, noise) signal is given an envelope chosen in advance: square or triangular, for example. This procedure in particular gives profiles with predetermined attack, development, and decay.

(c) Frequency translation: a given signal is transposed by a given value. For example, the sum of two sine waves of 100 and 200 Hz (one octave apart), shifted 30 Hz, will give sounds of 130 and 230 Hz, which are no longer one octave apart. Special effects can be obtained with this procedure, even the inversion of spectra.

3. The electroacoustic procedures already described, in particular:

- Reverberation: an artificial echo (obtained mechanically or electronically) is added to the sound.
- Magnetic tape interventions: either the playback speed can be modified, thus obtaining total transpositions, or pieces of tape can be cut out, stuck together, and edited.

4. Performance devices to facilitate the exploitation of these various techniques:

- Keyboards, for instruments with registered or registrable sounds (from the Trautonium and similar instruments for manipulating new sounds to the ondes martenot for using new timbres in a classical manner).
- Manual adjustments with continuous variation: knobs, faders, triggers, ribbons. We should point out that keyboards have been constructed with keys that can be pressed down to various depths for adjusting the intensity, or with lateral movement to start and regulate frequency modulation (tremolo).
- Desks for switching on/off, selecting and mixing.

5. Various devices for encoding and recording procedures that enable a particular sequence of sounds to be prepared in advance, for example in the form of a series of perforations in a paper tape, which then start up the necessary equipment and combinations in the order and at the times required. Under this last heading we could also include automatic composition procedures using electronic calculators (ILLIAC experiments in the United States, P. Barbaud's recent experiments in Paris). We should point out, nevertheless, that these latter experiments are peripheral to our study, inasmuch as they postulate a fixed structure for musical language (e.g., the rules of traditional harmony or serial music): for us, obviously, the

discovery of the properties of sound objects and musical structures must come first in the logical order of priorities.

23.10. THE BARE ESSENTIALS

Since the simultaneous launching, just a few years apart, of musique concrète in Paris in 1948 and electronic music in Cologne in 1950, several studios have been fitted out worldwide.[8] What historian, what sociologist who is both philosopher and technician, will learn the lesson from these bold yet speculative experiments?

We will limit ourselves to two observations, not to defend our position come what may but to enable other researchers to work with greater peace of mind. We would suggest that musical research is not necessarily bound up with the implementation of some costly piece of technical equipment requiring specialized skills. Music that is called electronic today often has more acoustic than electronic sounds and in relation to the electroacoustic system uses the manipulations we have described, as well as electronic synthesis. A second observation is about the principles themselves, the intellectual rather than the material investment. An electronic studio is, in fact, usually set up by groups who see it as a technical project—installing a certain number of pieces of equipment. Now, we would point out that the essential does not lie here; it lies in the ear and its largely unexplored musical qualities. A few specialized studios may pursue technological research in this way, and others will benefit from it one day. But the common run of researchers, the innumerable musicians, especially the youngest, who are wondering about this new approach to the domain of music, should know that the essential is within their reach and almost their financial means. To carry out appropriate experiments, they doubtless need a good professional recording studio, not really specialized; but for their training and their "studies" all they need is an amateur tape recorder and microphone, which initially cost no more than a traditional musical instrument.

It is not enough, however, to possess this instrument; they also have to learn to use it. First, they must have a minimum of technique, which, whatever anyone may say, does not require any specific notions from mathematics or physics but, on the contrary, an operator's abilities: the sound engineer's. Then there is learning to make and hear at the level of the object, which is what this book is all about. This fundamental point is nearly always passed over in silence: the silence of ignorance or human self-assurance, a flight into the technical, a faith in machines that will take on the responsibility for a music for man without man's having to learn it? Doubtless all of this. Whatever others may say about a time when technical mar-

---

8. See *Répertoire international des musiques electroacoustiques.* [The book was compiled by Hugh Davies and published by the Service de la recherche of the ORTF in 1962. A free English copy is available at https://archive.org/stream/InternationalElectronicMusicCatalog/EMR2_3_djvu.txt.—Trans.]

vels are a must, we for our part claim that it is possible to have a musical situation where technique is reduced to a rightly subordinate role. We would ask the researcher, however, to submit to an essential personal and group discipline, to follow a simple training process, to take ownership of his technique in order to work at both his instrument and his ear.

Appendix A

(Cf. section 23.7)

THE TIME REGULATOR

The pitch and duration of a sound recorded on magnetic tape are proportional to the speed and duration of playback, respectively, which are, of course, in inverse proportion to each other when an ordinary tape recorder is used. If we change the speed at which the tape passes across the playback head, we will, in effect, have what we have called a "total transposition" of the sound under experiment, which becomes lower the slower (and therefore the longer) the playback and, inversely, higher the faster (i.e., the shorter) the playback.

The device thought up by Springer for his *Zeitregler*, and that forms the basis of the "universal phonogène" constructed and used by the Groupe de recherches musicales, enables the speed of playback to be separated from the time of playback—that is, the pitch of the sound from its duration. This is how it is done: four playback heads are placed around a small cylinder which turns one way or the other at an adjustable speed on a tape recorder, where the speed at which the tape passes through is also adjustable. The tape adheres to the "playback head" cylinder at an angle of 90 degrees; there is therefore always one head out of four, and one head only, in contact with the tape. The device works in three principal ways:

(a) As an ordinary tape recorder: the heads are motionless, one of them is working, and the tape passes through at standard speed;

(b) To transpose the pitch of a sound only: the speed at which the tape passes through remains standard; thus, the duration of playback is unchanged. But the playback head cylinder is rotated. If this is in the opposite direction from the direction the tape is passing through, the playback is, in effect, at a greater than normal speed (thus, the sound is transposed up); however, the four heads coming one after the other into contact with the tape has the effect that each one replays a part of what the previous one has already played: through these partial repetitions of the sound it is possible to make a sound played back at greater than normal speed last for a normal length of time.

A similar compensatory mechanism comes into play when the playback head cylinder is turned in the same direction as the tape, which reduces the actual speed of playback: in effect, only noncontiguous fragments of tape are played back, and it is by juxtaposing pieces that are only part of the sound that we can manage to make a sound played back at less than normal speed "keep" to its normal duration.

(c) To vary the duration only: the speed at which the tape passes through, and therefore the duration of playback, is changed. Then we rotate the playback head cylinder in such a way that the relative speed at which the tape passes through in relation to the playback heads equals the standard speed—hence the pitch is unchanged. The compensatory mechanisms that here enable us to lengthen or shorten a sound without the pitch being transposed are the same as those described above.

In practice, with a device like this we can obtain the following results: as pitch shifter, several octaves lower, and about a fifth higher; as duration shifter, we can change the normal duration of a sound by (plus or minus) 25 percent. Of course, these results depend on the sound being experimented on (held sound, word, music, etc.).

It is clearly possible to carry out the full range of adjustments between pitch shifter and duration variator and thus obtain modifications of pitch and duration at the same time, which leaves the experimental musician a great deal of freedom of innovation . . . but is occasionally likely to bring some confusion into his manipulations!

Bibliography for Springer's Zeitregler

Springer, *Gravesaner Blätter*, no. 1 (1955): 32–37.
Springer, *Gravesaner Blätter*, no. 11/12 (1958): 3–9.
Springer, *Gravesaner Blätter*, no. 13 (1959): 80–82.

Appendix B

(Cf. section 23.8)

THE FORM MODULATOR

We have seen that we could act on the dynamic of a sound by simply adjusting the potentiometer, but the precision and speed of this procedure are limited. This is why we turned to electronics to improve it. In a way the "form modulator" is an electronically controlled potentiometer. More precisely, it is a variable-gain amplifier: the relationship between the input/output signal is not constant, as in an ordinary amplifier, but depends on a special voltage brought in at the additional input point, called the "form" point. Thus, the signal entering the machine is "modulated" at its output by the "form" signal. In particular, if the input level is constant, the dynamic of the output signal is the same as the "form" signal.

The "form" signal is an electrical voltage that varies in time, according to a law that the experimenter should be able to choose or determine in the course of hearing. To obtain a form of some sort, Francis Coupigny has created the following devices:

(a) The optical reader: a 70 mm wide band of paper on which a continuous line in the desired form has been drawn passes in front of an optical analyzer system; the electrical voltage delivered by the system is always proportional to the length of the line on the band of paper.

(b) The demodulator: this receives the electrical signal given by an acoustic vibration (coming from a microphone or the playing back of a sound recorded on tape) and at its output delivers a "form" voltage, which may be either directly or inversely proportional to the envelope of the entry signal—that is, the dynamic of the sound it represents.

(c) All other devices that give an appropriately varying electrical voltage can be used as a source of a "form" signal (e.g., a generator of square or triangular signals, etc.).

The general law governing the workings of the device is as follows:

Output dynamic = (original dynamic) multiplied by the
(dynamic of the "form" signal)

If we use the same signal at the main and "form" input points, we obtain this:

output dynamic = (original dynamic)

We can also, with enough connections, obtain the following laws:

output dynamic = exponential function of the original dynamic

(which is, in fact, a violent expansion of the latter); or again:

output dynamic = constant

In the latter case the original sound has become a homogeneous sound.

We should finally point out the possibility of only allowing the "form" voltage to intervene in the modulation process at a particular level of the input signal.

Typology of Musical Objects (I)

Classification Criteria

24.1. THE PARABLE OF THE ATTIC

When we decided to study a sound morphology, we had to choose a specimen object: a typical object. As soon as we want to construct a typology, we have to involve morphological characteristics. To fully understand this link, we need to demonstrate the difficulty of categorizing material objects.

The best teaching aid, though the worst for the teacher, is to go up to the attic: everything lying around in piles surely fits the concept of object? No one would dream of denying that everything that comes to hand here deserves a good tidying up, unless, at the end of our tether and tiring of the effort, we give up altogether (which, incidentally, justifies the existence of attics).

Some of these objects, morphologically simple, would be easy to classify—for example, planks of various thicknesses, widths, and lengths. Also bottles with various capacities. If these examples come to mind spontaneously, it is because, to make the ordeal of the attic easier, I immediately think of the simple and the measurable: as can be seen, these are objects that, in fact, are to do with solids or capacities—that is, that fit in with the notion of physical object. But how do these planks relate to old clothes, wood shavings, a stuffed bird?

Shall I measure my bird and put it among the planks? Shall I squeeze in a deciliter of wood shavings among my phials? We can see that physics is of no help to me, quite the opposite. Someone suggests that I sort the clothes into sizes: this gives me no chance of sorting them in relation to the bird or the bottle. And can I possibly put a breastplate, a tailcoat, and a swimming costume, all three of them under the same heading, in sizes, or else according to the money the secondhand dealer would pay me for them? Although I can bring out various value criteria in the objects, these are of no use to me in the preliminary categorization that a typology ought to be.

We should therefore be tempted to give up and remark, moreover, that categorizing a jumble of objects is not only impossible but also perhaps even, at bottom, pointless. In fact, we feel that planks belong to the carpenter, clothes to the tailor, phials to the chemist; now, it is not the same with sounds. All sounds belong to the musician; and if the musician refuses some of them, he ought to know why: because, precisely, they are outside his *typology*. But he cannot pronounce on this unless he has examined a large enough range of sounds to know the norms that determine whether he retains or rejects them. If, for example, he only considers physically definable sounds, he is like the housewife who only keeps in her loft what she can measure on the scales or with a ruler.

We will continue the parable, as we have not yet come to the end of what it can teach us. Someone suggests classifying the objects according to what they are made of? Those made of wood go together, as do those made of cloth or metal, and so forth. This is already a more realistic suggestion than measurements, but it doesn't get us very far: should I put the wire with the forks? a violin among the logs? So should we instead classify according to what they are intended for? Or should we make a distinction between manufactured and natural objects? These are better suggestions because they are already linked to the way the object is used, its situation among other objects, and the two intentions that come together here: the maker's and the user's.

24.2. THE SEARCH FOR TYPOLOGICAL CRITERIA

Choosing these criteria is perhaps the most difficult thing of all in the approach we are attempting. In fact, we have spent many years on it and have changed systems many times. We should say straightaway that what we have chosen here cannot but be arbitrary and produce only one typology among many. There are, indeed, many ways of tidying the attic. None is absolutely excellent; none is absolutely right. Some are useful. Among the useful ones there is doubtless one that can be rationally justified better than others. Let us hope it is the one we have arrived at and that we are about to present.

In our attic, after giving up on classifying according to measurements, causalities, and so forth, we considered a variety of solutions: classifying with regard to use, or into the more or less natural, the more or less worked-on. We will find ideas like this with sounds. We will leave the parable, which would only lead us astray now, for the sound object clearly depends on different perceptions and has different uses from the objects in the attic.

What did we instinctively do when we sketched out morphologies of objects that were of necessity specific, simplified, and therefore typical? We took objects

342   MORPHOLOGY AND TYPOLOGY

with little variation in matter and with a form that could be easily perceived. Or again, we took formless objects but where the variation of their matter could be easily perceived. Thus, in a violin or vocal sound we can easily identify the various forms of pizzicato, held sound, swelled sound with crescendo or decrescendo. This is possible because the matter of these sounds does not vary too much.

By way of comparison we will take a succession of notes on the harmonium, turn the knobs of a heterodyne generator, or listen to a fire alarm: the (dynamic) form is markedly (musically) fixed, but we clearly perceive the development of the harmonic or melodic content, which constitutes the matter of the sound. This distinction between a matter and a form is a valuable indication, but it is also a treacherous pitfall. A typology intermingling matter and form would, in fact, prejudice its potential, tend to go too fast, and in reality could only classify objects that are too simple or of too limited a variety. For our examples were specious: in most cases development of form goes along with development of matter. The two essential criteria for describing objects do not hold the key to classifying them; they are too logical, too radical, to be open to the "rag, tag, and bobtail" of sounds, in the same way that shape and color do not hold the key to a biological classification. We should rather look toward more general criteria—that is, less frankly descriptive and not focusing on the morphological aspect of the object but linking it to its use or origin, as we suggested above.

In the first place we want to use sounds to make music. So we should look for an essentially musical criterion. What do we immediately find? Pitch, of course. Surely we will come up against the criticism we have already made about arranging planks according to size? Yes and no. We should be guilty of the fault we have already condemned if we took pitch itself as a criterion. But if we are content to speak of the possibility of an object's being heard in pitch, whether it is fixed and defined, or variable, or multiple and more or less locatable, it will be as if we said of material objects that they have one or several fixed or elastic spatial dimensions. With this approach we will not yet be claiming to categorize objects into values but only to estimate whether or not they have more or less clear, more or less "multiple," suitability for this value. And so in relation to the *sound mass* we can set up a typological criterion of fixedness, simple or complex variation, and, if the sound is fixed, for possible precise or vague evaluation.

Having thus retained a first criterion dealing with the (musical) *use* of sounds, we will return to an essentially musicianly fact, *facture*, in order to find our second criterion: the way energy is communicated and appears in duration, closely linked to sustainment.

With mass and facture, however general these may be, are we choosing independent variables, as all good classification systems demand? No. We are not dealing here with simple variables but with already very complex perceptions; as they relate to two intentions, two different ways of making and hearing, there is nothing to say to what extent these perceptions are linked. If, in fact, the energetic history is simple, there is a good chance that the matter will not be affected by very complicated variations. If the opposite is true, it may happen that the matter follows the fluctuations in energy. Initially, therefore, the reader is unsure whether he will find what he instinctively expects from a double-entry table, based on independent variables. But that is not all.

24.3. DURATION AND VARIATION

In choosing two disparate criteria for the musical and sound, the first dominant in musical and the other in musicianly listening, we have not retained the *duration* of the object, which is by no means negligible to the ear. Should we not, in fact, separate large and small objects in our attic? Surely the concept of macrosounds and microsounds should have a prominent place in our search for a classification system? Indeed, it would seem so.

Moreover, we have spoken about variations in form and matter. But what is a variation if not something that changes in accordance with time? We find *duration a second time*, not now in the overall bulk of the sound object but in a *relationship* that is like a velocity, the quotient of a difference (what changes) over the duration of the change. We should recognize that, in fact, a typology cannot ignore these two factors, which it will endeavor not to treat as values, limiting itself to mentioning them only as qualities linked to our first criteria: we will take account of the durations or the variations of objects by relating them to criteria of mass or facture.

24.4. OBJECTS IN SHEAVES

Before going any further, and in order to forewarn the reader about what we are looking for in a typological categorization, we will turn to a new image taken from material objects. We have abandoned the idea of a physical classification based on independent variables. We prefer a categorization that is both "psychological" and pragmatic, based on more subtle ideas directly involved with musical or musicianly perception. Now we are suggesting a second abandonment: of the hope of classifying every object once and for all in a specific box in our diagram of the future. We think, in fact, that the principle behind our classification system allows us to assign various boxes to the same object, depending on the listening intention. The search for an "absolute" typology is an illusion. We are trying to spare both the reader and research groups much wasted time and pointless discussion.

If I suggest a sheaf of corn as a material object, my intention may indeed be to "summarize," simplify, or, on the contrary, analyze or break it down. At a given moment it will seem to me to be the right object, that is, the right "middle term" between what would break it down and what would make it into a whole: it is at the right distance from my eye or within easy reach of my intention. If people insist or the person next to me quibbles over it, I will have to admit that it is a collection of objects: ears of corn. Furthermore, these ears of corn are themselves structures of grains. But on the contrary, perhaps this sheaf is part of a shock, or I have picked it out from a structure of rows of sheaves, or as a detail in a surface studded with similar points, a simple granulation in the midst of vast harvested fields? Here we have the two infinities, of both Pascal[1] and the structuralists, which must not be forgotten when we are setting up a typology. As soon as we focus on an object (and this is arbitrary), we have no choice but to accept that it will break down into components and be part of a whole. As long as we safeguard its coherence, its oneness, it will belong in one box in the diagram. If we happen to pick out its microstructure, it will change place, and very likely end up in a box for less-simple objects. If it forms part of a macrostructure, then it is no longer the isolated object of the earlier classification, and in relation to that macrostructure it becomes a simpler component: its individuality is dissolved; it is the macrostructure that tends to impose itself as the object to be classified.

We will now give our diagram a musical application: a bowed staccato, itself made up of little impulses from the bouncing of the bow, is like the sheaf of corn. As it is, it will take its place in a particular box in the classification. But if we decide to pay attention to the impulses of which it is made, from this standpoint the object will appear to require a new classification. In the same way, if many bows play the same or random staccatos, at roughly the same time, typology should also enable us to classify the more complex objects of which these macrostructures are composed.

24.5. BALANCE AND ORIGINALITY

We gave ourselves criteria for typological classification: mass and facture. Then we pointed out that we had to bring in the dimension of time, in two forms: duration and variation. Finally, we referred once more to the ambiguous situation of the object between two structures, giving it the status of a compromise between two complementary complex situations. But we have not yet found the main thread. How will we set about the classification—that is, basically: what ultimate purpose underlies it?

Since our purpose is to make music, our typology should essentially be open to objects that present to musical listening as compromises that can be easily manipulated, identified, and memorized (in the figurative as well as in the literal sense of this term). What are the characteristics of these compromises?

We can see two of them. The first is that the objects *central to* our classification are, as in the example of the sheaf of corn, good perceptual rungs of the ladder:

---

1. Pascal's two infinities are the infinitely great and the infinitely small. See Pascal, *Pensées*, 1670.

neither too elementary nor too structured. If too elementary, they would tend to merge spontaneously into structures more worth remembering. Conversely, if too structured they would be likely to break down into more elementary objects. We can see that duration will intervene in determining our *central* objects: the adjective *memorable*, while indicating a *form full of meaning*, also implies a suitable duration, neither too short nor too long, about the optimal duration for hearing objects. But the main difficulty in this research is that the elementary does not necessarily coincide with the short, or the complex with the long. If short objects tend to appear elementary and long objects seem likely to contain complexity, the contrary can also be true: a short object can be very complicated and a long object very simple. Therefore, if we were not careful to group together converging though more or less independent concepts on each line or column of the classification, we would rapidly end up with classification systems with a prohibitive number of inextricable dimensions. We will limit ourselves here to pointing out that we will describe objects as *balanced* or *unbalanced* according to whether they appear to be a good compromise between the too structured and the too simple or whether they are similar to structures that from a perceptual point of view fall short, either by default (too elementary) or by excess (too complex).

A second compromise criterion will be *the originality of the object.* This concept, like duration, is somewhat linked to the above characteristic of balance, for a complex structure is necessarily more *original* than an elementary one. It differs from it, however, when we consider two equally balanced objects in the same way as in the section above. Imagine a field of shocks of corn where some are real shocks but others only cardboard cones or pyramids, or bundles of twigs; or again, some of them are misshapen, stubby, or hybrid, made of the aforementioned materials: cornstalks, twigs, or rectilinear elements. We should have before us various degrees of originality, as of balance. The cardboard pyramid would be said to be "redundant," as it can be reconstructed mentally from just one small part of it. This is not true of the real sheaf, unless we ignore the irregularities made by the ears. By and large what surprises us is the degree of originality. A violin vibrato, similar in originality to a real sheaf of corn, will be more original than a plain electronic sound but less original than the same electronic sound given an unexpected profile.

24.6. SUMMARY OF TYPOLOGICAL CRITERIA

We have just reviewed three pairs of criteria that are very different in nature, which, logically speaking, would lead us to a six-dimensional classification system. The first pair is morphological: we focus, on the one hand, on the facture of the object and, on the other hand, on its mass. The second pair is temporal: we consider, on the one hand, the duration and, on the other hand, variations within the duration of the object in the light of the above criteria. The third pair is structural:

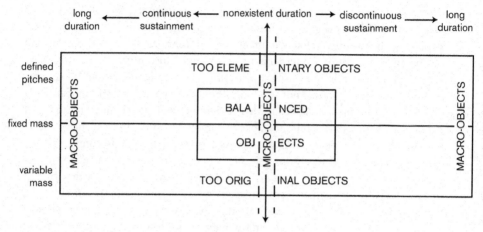

FIGURE 28. Recapitulation of typological criteria.

we consider the balance of the object, chosen from possible structures, and at this chosen structural level, the greater or lesser degree of originality.

Now we do not want to have anything to do with a six-dimensional classification system, which would be impracticable: we want to be able to formulate it on a two-dimensional illustration: a sheet of paper divided into four should allow us to help musicians in trouble without unnecessary complications. We must therefore suggest, on the one hand, ideas for simplifying the process and, on the other hand, an overall framework for drawing up the illustration.

First we will conflate the first two pairs by arbitrarily simplifying their relationships with each other.

With factures—that is, the qualitative perception of the energetic sustainment of objects—we will bring temporal variations into our classification so that horizontally we essentially have the two criteria of qualitative sustainment and duration (fig. 28). So we will produce the horizontal axis from a midpoint that by definition will be short durations. To left and right will be temporally more extensive factures. Thus, in the center we will have all the "impulse" types of objects where the energy is communicated in one short instant. On the left, for example, we will put sounds with continuous sustainment, and on the right sounds with discontinuous, repeated sustainment. Of course, this is just an approximate arrangement to encapsulate various phenomena. There are resonant sounds of significant duration but where the energy is sporadic. Our diagram will therefore have to allow for these, even though it does not explicitly cater to them.

Linking mass and variation in the same way, we will produce the vertical axis from a midpoint of "fixed" masses. As these are more common than defined pitches, this point conveniently accommodates a general group of musically interesting sounds, halfway between sounds of easily locatable pitch (on the vertical axis above this point) and sounds with variable mass (below).

The two axes, thus positioned, divide our diagram into four quadrants. So our classification has a center. Does this center have any significance in relation to our aim, which is to order objects in relation to the balance-originality pair? We may hope so, if this classification system manages to establish as central types those objects that have good balance and neither too much nor too little originality. In fact, and more precisely, we should expect to find a "vanishing line" (microobjects) in the middle of the diagram, but a zone of balance all around the center, and at the edges of the diagram, on the perimeter, a broad zone of objects that are not well balanced.

In the center there is both fixed mass, thus acceptable balance, and enough originality within the criterion of matter but a shorter and shorter duration: we are moving toward micro-objects, for which we must provide a vertical strip in the middle of our diagram, where we will put temporally unbalanced sounds, which appear elementary in structure, although their details, if they were spread out in time, could have turned out to be very complex (the ear cannot grasp these when the duration is too short). We will come across excess of originality linked with micro-objects again when there is an accumulation of microsounds in a memorable temporal duration (cell).

Vertically, originality will obviously increase from top to bottom. The more minimal, of determined pitch and at the limit of electronic purity, the sound is, the less original will it be. The more variable its mass, the greater will be its originality, but it will be all the more likely to be unbalanced (toward the bottom) because of the complexity of its structure and also its unpredictability.

24.7. A STUDY OF THE DIAGRAM COLUMN BY COLUMN

The horizontal boxes are distributed according to both facture and duration.[2] In the middle, as we are dealing with energy communicated briefly (pizzicato, pulse, glottal stop, etc.), the facture is doubtless marked, but it is not really perceptible as such. All around this zone we have well-formed, well-balanced factures, with enough originality, such as the bowed sound or the swelled note. To right and left, form thins out in time; were it to remain regular, whether in a continuously sustained sound or the repetition of an impulse with no history, we would be moving toward "nonexistent" facture. But we must not limit our suppositions to this. At the two ends of this axis we must also include among long durations factures that are continuous by reiteration (and not by simply being stretched out). On the side

2. In section 24.9, figure 30.

with continuous sounds, starting from a well-formed facture, such as a bowed sound, well-balanced in duration, we could just as well move toward *homogeneous* sound with nonexistent facture (a synthetic sound imitating an indefinite bowed sound or a continuous note on a hurdy-gurdy) as toward the *sample* with unpredictable facture (i.e., a bowed sound being repeated irregularly, linking one sound to another as if at random), giving rise to an object that has unity only because the causal permanence is perceptible through all the whims and fancies. On the side with discontinuous sounds, a well-formed staccato can also be "thinned out in time" in some fashion. Because the facture is impoverished, it may become mechanical, totally iterative, similar to the homogeneous sound. Or, on the contrary, we may end up with a more or less random and confused reiteration of the same sort of causality (and not the same cause continuing its action), giving a number of short objects with related factures; thus, a series of pizzicatos irregularly distributed in time or bowed impulses from a group of unsynchronized violins will form a multiform iterative, which, like the sample, will be a long, unpredictable, too-original object. Here the unity does not, as with the sample, come from a transparent causal permanence but from a certain family likeness that links the innumerable factures of the details. We will call an object like this an *accumulation*, a reiteration brimful of short, more or less similar, elements.

In this way we can put seven fairly clear zones along the horizontal axis where facture and duration are involved in a relationship that is specific to each, and which have different degrees of originality or redundancy, as is shown in the schema by a curve of originality, the ordinates of which go from zero (redundancy) to infinity (total unpredictability) (see fig. 29).

24.8. A STUDY OF THE DIAGRAM ROW BY ROW

The midpoint being arbitrarily chosen as situating masses fixed in the tessitura, above it we have masses of determined pitch (tonic sounds) and right at the top, if we want to refine this, the absolutely fixed pitches of electronic sounds.[3] The sound of a gong, cymbal, or bell, although complex, and although its pitch is not clear nor its composition harmonic, has a fixed mass and for us represents average originality, acceptable balance between the simplest (sounds with harmonic pitch) and the least simple (sounds with mass developing in pitch).

Below this median type, things are less clear. What is a sound of variable mass? What is the nature of this variation? Besides, does it not involve speed, and therefore again the duration of the object, which very much despite ourselves we should also include all the way down this vertical axis?

As soon as we move away from the type with balanced mass, we will very quickly come across unclassifiable sounds or, in any case, sounds with such rapidly

---

3. In section 24.9, figure 30.

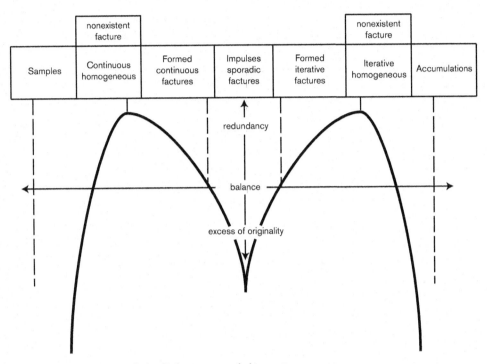

| Samples | Continuous homogeneous | Formed continuous factures | Impulses sporadic factures | Formed iterative factures | Iterative homogeneous | Accumulations |

FIGURE 29. Excess or lack of balance in sound objects.

increasing originality that very soon they no longer conform to the notion of object; for example, they will appear as structures or variations of pitch, the purpose of which will elude the listener and at the outer limit will be chock-full of totally unpredictable events. Two processes may, however, help toward maintaining the unity of objects for these sounds. Either, by randomly carving out a slice, or "cell," from this teeming mass, we cut out "something to be heard," with a short duration that could help the ear to memorize a content (thus giving it an artificial coherence, so that it can be included and classified as an object); or else, despite the variations, to make sense of the object we will have to depend on the ear to perceive the causality, which links the successive moments to each other. Thus, when the plumbing begins to make a noise, the whole hotel is treated to a symphony of sounds that, if the residents wish, they can listen to as a piece of "hydraulic" music but that doubtless asserts itself much more as a unique object emanating from a clearly determined aquatic episode, one with a beginning, a middle, and an end. We will call sounds such as these "large notes." So we have cell and large note, the extremes of typology, the limits of our exploration into possible examples arising thus far from a characterization that we hope is not entirely subjective.

So we should expect the next step to be to assign the two lower horizontal lines of the typology to objects that cannot be compared with the higher boxes, or even with those in the middle zone. These will be very original or very unbalanced objects. As they are likely to present variations in both facture and mass, possibly interconnected, we will reserve a final chapter for them, after we have discussed the most balanced and the most redundant objects in the next chapter. Before moving on, we will conclude our initial reflections with a summary diagram showing the various possible combinations of our criteria (fig. 30). It may be useful to keep in mind that this way of presenting things, however logical it may appear, is not deduced from a theory: it is a diagram of results that has been formulated only gradually, over several rough drafts, taken back many a time to the drawing board.

24.9. FOUNDATIONAL SCHEMA OF THE TYPOLOGY OF SOUND OBJECTS

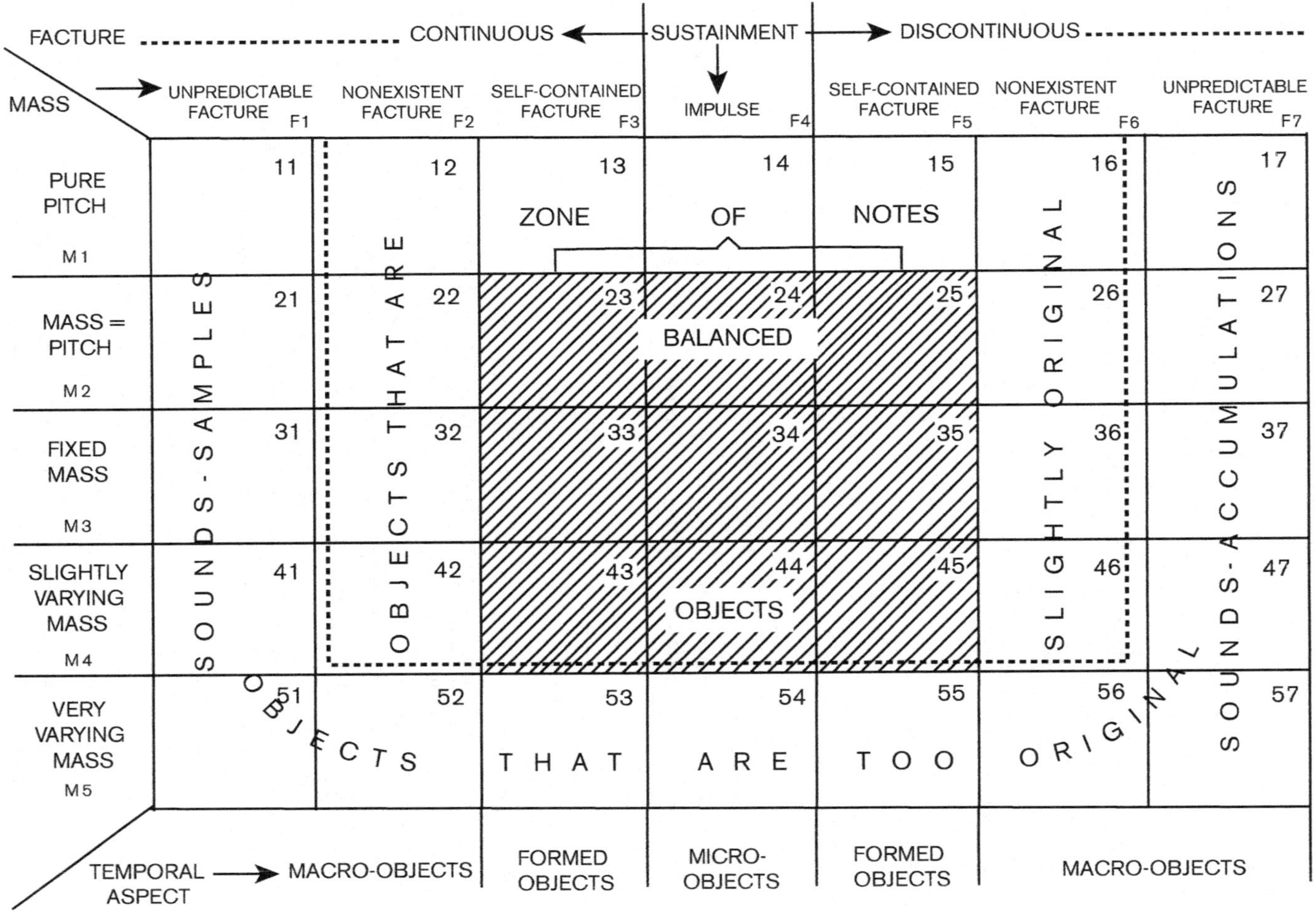

FIGURE 30. Foundational schema of the typology of sound objects.

Typology of Musical Objects (II)

Balanced and Redundant Objects

25.1. BALANCED OBJECTS

It is likely that the most suitable sound objects for the musical will be those that conform to the criteria set out in the nine central boxes in figure 30, numbered:

23, 24, 25

33, 34, 35

43, 44, 45

These objects have in common that they have a good form; that is, they are held together by an undeniable unity of facture, with an optimal time for memorization by the ear, with the exception of the middle column (brief objects right down to the micro-object).

As for masses, these are what the orchestra takes as its usual material: fixed percussion masses, determined pitches of sounds notatable on the staff, or again sliding glissandi on the strings, the drums, and so forth.

So here we come back to describing balanced objects according to the two criteria of mass and facture, at greater length than in the preceding chapter, the purpose of which was simply to give an overall methodological view.

25.2. ANALYSIS BASED ON THE CRITERION OF FACTURE

With the aim of clarifying our perception of factures we will first of all adopt a mechanic's approach, pointing out that it is possible to identify three characteristic ways of sustaining the vibration of a sound body: none at all (percussion), continuously (active sustainment), and repeated percussions (iterations).

Although traditional music, centered on pitch, has neglected this important and easily perceptible aspect of the sound object in formulating a theory, we can nevertheless pick up a distinction rather similar to our own in the form of performance directions, mainly for stringed instruments but also for woodwinds and even the piano:

—	•	"pizz."	"stac."	"trem."
(held sound)	(plucked sound)	(pizzicato)	(staccato)	(tremolo)

This notation really relates to sustainment, since with varying degrees of imperiousness it lays down a way of making sound, with a view to its effects. But the notation also indicates considerations that are not exclusively to do with energy. A system of classification by sustainment alone would not be enough to link together or efficiently separate out the types of objects we meet all the time in traditional music alone: a brief violin sound (arco) is in fact sustained, whereas a bass piano note is not, but it is clear that the difference in sustainment, although perceptible, is not the only thing that characterizes the differences between the perceived factures. So, using what is suggested by traditional directions, but taking into account the sustainment criterion given above, we will have to define original *facture* criteria more fully.

In some cases the gesture will be perceptible; the form given to the sound will depend on the movement of the forearm or the breath; it will respond to a living dynamic: there will be a crescendo and a diminuendo that will shape the note, even if they are scarcely perceptible. The facture may disappear through excess or insufficiency: through excess if it is prolonged, through insufficiency if it does not have the time to make itself heard. If sustainment is prolonged, the sound will no longer be perceived as a measured form; only the mode of sustainment will be perceptible in its regularity or its fluctuations. On the contrary, in brief "plucked" sounds the only thing perceptible will be an all-or-nothing impulse. Of course, we will come across hybrids: a staccato, well executed from one end of the bow to the other, is as well formed an object as a bowed note "on the string": the individual form of each impulse disappears into the general form. Finally, we should observe that our criterion of facture, linked with sustainment, will also bring into play the listener's capacities for memorization.

By bringing these various elements together, we get the following main types of facture, which, for the sake of simplicity, we will apply here to musical notes that are common but can easily be generalized. First of all, the note with no particular sign: N will be a well-formed sound, situated between the sustained sound $\overline{N}$ and brief sounds; among the latter we must distinguish between brief but sustained sounds, which we will notate N' (e.g., a plucked violin note), and those that are similar to the pizzicato (i.e., a brief nonsustained sound), which we will notate Ṅ. (Here we must point out that in choosing these, we are deliberately diverging from the traditional practice of notation, in which Ṅ, and not N', most clearly refers to a plucked violin sound.)

Furthermore, whether the sound is tonic or complex, we will generally keep the prime sign (') for brief sustained sounds and the full stop (.) for percussion sounds. But then we must distinguish between a woodblock and a piano percussion sound, given the great morphological difference between the two corresponding sound objects. We will use the fermata for the piano to signify that the resonance of the note ⌢ follows the percussion (.) while the use of (.) alone will indicate the contrary (the absence of any resonance); this is the sign for the impulse or the microobject.

Finally, we will use the double-prime sign (") for iterative notes—that is, those formed of repeated brief sounds, staccato or drum roll, for example. As brief sounds, as we have seen, may be of type Ṅ or N', we will have two types of formed iterative notes: (N')" and (Ṅ)", that is, the bowed staccato and the drumroll on a sound body without resonance.

So eventually we have the following series for noniterative notes, ordered approximately according to the duration of the note's continuation (whether this results from resonance or active sustainment):

$$\dot{N} \qquad N' \qquad N \qquad \overset{\frown}{N} \qquad \overline{N}$$

and for iterative notes two pairs of variants of N and N̄ respectively

$$(\dot{N})'' \qquad\qquad (N')'' \qquad \text{and} \qquad \overline{(\dot{N})''} \qquad\qquad \overline{(N')''}$$

formed roll   formed staccato   prolonged roll   prolonged staccato

But such distinctions, which we will necessarily return to when we embark on an analysis of values and characteristics in book 6, are too refined for the stage we have reached at present. For the moment we will leave out prolonged sounds and consider only well-formed, sustained, or iterative notes—that is, N and N": it will be simpler to place only one brief type between these two; we will not go into detail about sustainment. Therefore, ignoring the distinction between N' and Ṅ, we will notate all brief sounds N' and call them "impulses." For the sake of similar simplification, the two types of iteratives (N')" and (Ṅ)" arising from the previous ones will all be notated N". Furthermore, we can bring the piano and the bow together if we take into account that both have a characteristic, profiled, memorable form; the nature of their sustainment thus taking second place, we will conflate N̄ with N.

Ultimately we will retain only three central types: held sounds or formed resonances, impulses, and formed iterations, notated respectively: N, N', and N".

Criteria of facture

Ordinary note	N	N′	N″
Complex note	X	X′	X″
Varied note	Y	Y′	Y″

Criteria of mass

FIGURE 31. Typology of balanced objects.

25.3. ANALYSIS BASED ON THE CRITERION OF MASS

Either one or the other:

· either the mass of the sound is heard as condensed into one point of the tessitura—that is, it has a pitch that meets the *traditional definition* of the *musical note*—and we notate it N; or, without being able to be clearly located, the mass appears fixed in the tessitura (even if, as with the gong or the cymbal, it displays large variations in timbre), and then we have a fixed *complex note*, which we will indicate with an X;
· or the mass of the sound evolves in the tessitura in the course of its duration. We find few examples of objects like this in the sounds of the traditional orchestra; the Hawaiian guitar is the most obvious in the variety orchestra; but modern music makes very great use of glissandi produced in all sorts of ways.

Moreover, most natural sounds, perhaps because of the various causes that give rise to them, have masses that evolve in the tessitura. All notes like this, described as *reasonably varied*, will be indicated with a Y.

By combining the criteria of facture and mass, we finally obtain a figure with nine boxes of so-called balanced objects (see fig. 31).

We will now endeavor to classify a few simple sounds according to this figure. We have already given examples for the first line. Going on to the second, we can only name a very few traditional musical objects that in theory come under the notation X, although low organ, piano, bassoon, and double-bass sounds are, in fact, heard as complex notes just as much as, and even more than, tonic notes. Conversely, experimental instruments, electronic or concrete (among the latter we could mention rods or sheet metal played with a bow) produce a great range of X as well as Y sounds.

A cymbal with a metallic brush drawn across it will give us an example of X. The same cymbal, struck and immediately muted, will give an X' and, with a tremolo from ordinary or bass drumsticks, X" sounds. A very slurred tremolo where the pulsations are indistinct will go back to being an X. The same is true of the drum. So we may have to go from one box to another: depending on how much we concentrate on sustainment, the context created by other objects and the conditions under which they are used, we will need to emphasize different typological characteristics. A system of classification based on perception offers precisely the advantage of highlighting and justifying this sort of flexibility, in keeping with the context and the intention of hearing objects at different levels of complexity or according to different criteria.

We will use Y to notate every glissando that in our judgment should be highlighted, and not just the most obvious, such as glissandi on the Hawaiian guitar; if, however, singers use these discreetly in order to ensure their voices are accurately placed, we can still use Y to notate what is clearly included in a well-defined N. Asiatic music, on the contrary, deliberately seeks out these Y or Y' sounds, which bowed or wind instruments play slowly between two degrees on the scale, or strings and membranes produce when, violently plucked or struck, they begin to vibrate at a higher pitch than their final resonance. Finally, the slide-drum, dear to our avant-garde composers for its tremolo-glissando, gives us a surfeit of Y" sounds.

25.4. REDUNDANT OR NOT VERY ORIGINAL OBJECTS

Going back to figure 30, we can see that we have not shunned the lack of originality or the redundancy of objects with either fixed or slightly varying mass: so it is facture that appears as the first criterion of redundancy in our discussion. To obtain redundant sounds, all we need to do is start from balanced objects as described in the last section and extend their duration until all dynamic form disappears. As above, we will have two types:

(a) *Fixed mass:*

The balance of an N or an X (or an N" or an X") will be upset through lack of originality when sustainment is prolonged indefinitely, whether a mechanical device creates the continuity or whether the instrumentalist deliberately intends this extension in time and absence of salience. In the latter case, where slight dynamic variations can still clearly be identified, we will have the sustained notes $\overline{N}$ or $\overline{X}$, or the unformed iterations (prolonged beyond the duration threshold of the ear) $\overline{N''}$

or $\overline{X}''$. If the sustainment is mechanical, we can indicate the higher degree of regularity by using another sign to indicate homogeneity: the corresponding "homogeneous" sounds would be Hn, Hx, and the impeccable iterations Zn and Zx. However, as the transition between an Hn and an $\overline{N}$ may be imperceptible, our use of two notations does not justify using two different boxes.

Finally we should note that in general the redundant prolonged sounds Hn and Hx, Zn and Zx are of no interest when they occur in isolation; the more or less homogeneous sounds used in practice by the experimental musician are *wefts* T, harmonic packages or complexes of elementary N or X sounds put into "sheaves," which we will discuss later.

(b) *Variable mass:*

How can we reconcile the idea of a redundant object with the idea of variation? In other words, how can a varied note such as a Y become redundant? Because when it spreads out in time, the variation, which is reasonable at the level of Y sounds, becomes, if not entirely predictable, at least unsurprising. So it is a question of relative redundancy.

We will begin with sounds with continuous sustainment. When it is formed and limited in time, note Y contrasts very clearly with notes N or X, and we can easily distinguish a melodic (Yn) or a complex (Yx) glissando. As soon as note Y distends, this latter difference, at least as far as sounds that hold the experimenter's attention are concerned, will diminish. The prototype of $\overline{Y}$ is of little interest: it is the slow siren, both varying and redundant, more obtrusive than a homogeneous sound but wearisome in the monotony of the variation itself. Musically, the most interesting types are less ordinary either because they show slow variations of melodic-harmonic structures, interweaving held N notes, or because they have complex X timbres superimposed in a variable or slowly evolving manner. The word *note* in *varied note* no longer applies here for superimpositions of such rich sounds, heard nevertheless as groups, for they are not made to be constantly analyzed and can thus meet the concept of object. These fusions of slowly evolving sounds are called *wefts* in our vocabulary, and they will be notated Tn or Tx, depending on whether their structure is formed mainly of N or X sounds.

What will happen with iterative Y sounds? There are two very distinct types here, the first being less engaging than the second: it is still the siren, going on endlessly, but this time staccato. Beside this irritating specimen, which could still be notated $\overline{Y}''$ if need be, we have the lively varied note Y' constantly reiterated, like the interminable tweet-tweet of a bird or the regular creaking of a mill wheel. We are dealing with a sustained iterative of Y, which will be notated Zy. We are also happy to call this sound an "ostinato," by analogy with this type of piano or orchestral accompaniment. We will soon find ostinati in the same column, but for the reiteration of more complicated objects than Y or Y' sounds, and should prefer to reserve the letter P for this purpose and keep the notation Zy here for this particular example.

25.5. PURE SOUNDS

If, in the great final diagram in the previous chapter (fig. 30), we assigned the first line to pure sounds, it was in the interests of symmetry, in order to contrast this line 1 with an eventual line 5 and thus keep a center to our classification. Besides, as we have seen, this symmetry is more to do with the layout of the schema than its contents: the simplicity of the objects in the upper half does not in fact really balance with the huge diversity of those in the lower half. Moreover, differentiating between defined sounds with a recognizable instrumental timbre and electronically pure (sine wave) sounds, even assuming this were possible in every case, actually depends on a fine distinction that the general typology of sound objects could not accommodate. We therefore propose purely and simply to get rid of the first line as superfluous. It is true that sounds with weak facture will be more redundant there than elsewhere, stripped of any harmonic fluctuation, developing in a completely straight line. Since we locate these sounds in pitch, it will do to put them in the second line, which then becomes the first in the definitive figure.

25.6. SUMMARY DIAGRAM OF REDUNDANT OR NOT VERY ORIGINAL SOUNDS

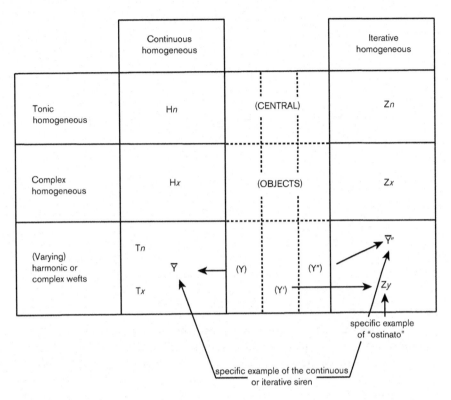

	Continuous homogeneous				Iterative homogeneous
Tonic homogeneous	H*n*		(CENTRAL)		Z*n*
Complex homogeneous	H*x*		(OBJECTS)		Z*x*
(Varying) harmonic or complex wefts	T*n* Ȳ T*x*	(Y) ←		(Y″) (Y′) →	Ȳ″ Z*y*

specific example
of "ostinato"

specific example of the continuous
or iterative siren

FIGURE 32

Typology of Musical Objects (III)

Eccentric Sounds

26.1. ECCENTRIC SOUNDS

Having looked at *balanced* sounds and those where the balance is upset by *banality*, we will devote this chapter to sounds where the balance is upset by an excess of *originality*. These are the "eccentric" types, both on figure 30 and for perception: our classification reserves a peripheral area for them, thus placing them at the outer edges of the musical domain. If, in fact, one of these sounds happens to figure in a work, it is likely to grab the listener's attention, for, too structured, too unpredictable, and generally too bulky, but always striking, it imposes itself at the risk of destroying any "form" other than its own: it becomes the central pivot of the structure in which it appears, rather than remaining simply as one element among many.

We have already examined the possible causes of this excess of originality: an excess of facture more or less linked to an excess of variations of mass; the dynamic and melodic profiles will be tortuous, confused. The excess of information generally makes people say of these sounds that they are "formless." More precisely, their form is not good, for far from being nonexistent, as is the case with homogeneous sounds, it drowns perception through its complexity and unpredictability. What is their form? Generally speaking, the narrative of the sustainment and its consequences, always dynamic, often melodic and harmonic; at least this is what is grasped by the ear when it has enough time to appreciate what the maker of such sounds himself took the time to put into them. In what follows we restrict ourselves to examples where a certain unity can be perceived in the sound, which therefore still comes across as a sound object.

26.2. SAMPLES

With continuous sounds it is the permanence of a cause, the persistence of one agent in pursuing its efforts, that welds the different phases of the sound event together across the incoherence of their detail. A child lightly touching a violin string with his finger while his bow wanders clumsily all over the place gives us a sound as incongruous as it is interminable but in which the unity of intention and the mode of realization impose themselves with unpleasant insistence; moreover, as this sound, which the word *sample* seems to us to describe very accurately, is not modulated, articulated, or organized to enable us to hear a structure or a fragment of musical language, we are justified in giving it the status of object despite its complexity.

26.3. ACCUMULATIONS

Now we will take the example on the other side, discontinuous sustainment. A shower of pebbles pours out of a truck, or a flight of birds twitters, or Xenakis's orchestra, even arranged according to the Poisson system or the bell-curve, makes "clouds" of pizzicati or glissandi: we should be very embarrassed if our typological classification did not allow for these vagaries of fortune; the most modern orchestra, here taking us back to nature at its most naturally disorganized, in effect, forces us up against undeniable sound entities, which require us to take them on board. We must look at them more closely. Instead of dealing with sounds endlessly deriving from each other, as in the last section, we have before us sounds with "short impulse" form, thrown together higgledy-piggledy. What order through all the disorder gives these sounds the unity that suggests something of the object in them? In the flight of birds, as in the avant-garde concert hall, the similarity of facture between elements of the sound texture brings the objects together for the ear and unifies perception. Each twitter recalls the others; the noise of each pebble falling on to the slowly forming pile belongs to the same sound family as the previous and following ones; each string glissando is a new instance of a unique causal process: as they pile up, "disorganized" more or less through art, more or less through nature, the ear can rely on their similarity and weld their diversity together into a characteristic object: the accumulation.

The two types we have contrasted, at least in our discussion—samples (persistence of the cause) and accumulations (similarity of a number of causes)—are not as far apart as one might at first think. In fact, it depends on our will whether we hear the sound of pebbles being poured out as coming from one cause (the truck tipping up) or as made up of short impulses coming from a multiplicity of similar causes (each pebble falling on the previous ones). It is quite clear that a number of sounds can be classified just as well from either viewpoint: it will be, as it were, a matter of taste. Thus, in the outer columns of figure 30 extremes meet.

26.4. CELLS, OSTINATI, AND FRAGMENTS

We will now move on to an artificial object for which nature has not really pre-pared us but with which electroacoustic equipment overwhelms us: the object arbitrarily determined by closing a groove in on itself or by cutting out a piece of magnetic tape at random. It is right and proper to acknowledge what we owe to the closed groove: the concept of the sound object. Even if it has led us to this funda-mental idea, however, we must also acknowledge that, generally speaking, this waif and stray is the one that can least easily find a place amid natural objects in our classification. Since, in fact, we cut it out of the magnetic tape, it is our scissors alone that will determine both a center of interest and a duration. Now suppose, on the one hand, that this duration is chosen from the zone of suitable, memorable durations (which will then, by construction, give us a sound with temporal unity) and, on the other hand, that we took our piece of sound from the middle of an avalanche of disorganized microsounds: helped by its temporal unity, the more originality its texture displays, bursting with both facture and variations in mass, the more easily will the sound isolated in this way tend to organize itself into an object and thus without any difficulty satisfy our intention to hear something. We call an object like this a "cell" and notate it K. Because of its roughly iterative and in any case cumulative structure we will classify it in the column for formed itera-tive sounds and also in a line below Y notes for *lively* variations in mass, which are called *irrational*.

Now we will repeat this cell, letting the closed groove go round and round: this time we obtain an "ostinato," which is a generalization of the iterative Zy already studied in section 25.4; whereas Zy was limited to having the same sound causality put into action endlessly and very obviously, with the cell ostinato we have a gen-eral example of what could be called a *cyclic* sound effect.

Finally, what happens if we cut into a tape containing a well formed N, X, or Y note, thus isolating a "fragment" φ? The distinguishing features of *edits* like these from violin or piano notes, a *cut bell* or a *cut cymbal*, are not necessarily their short duration: this may be perfectly memorable and even comparable to the duration of the initial object; the most characteristic finding from the cut is not that the sounds have been shortened but that their history has been disturbed, introducing an unexpected end or distancing it from its energetic origin, which in some cases is the only thing that accounts for the overall dynamic of the sound. So in most cases these fragments will at least be original, if not altogether eccentric, objects. To take into account their origin and their different nature from the cell, and also because of their importance for the experimenter, we will place them in the central column of our classification, thus reminding ourselves that we are dealing with sounds that are generally but not necessarily short. So it is no more justified to put the cell in with formed iterative notes (because of the suitable temporal module formed by the cut and a certain similarity of structure) than to include the fragment with the impulse because of a certain abrupt manner of presentation.

26.5. LARGE NOTES AND WEFTS

In the line of "unbalanced" notes in the lower part of figure 34 there are still two empty boxes, below formed held sounds and homogeneous sounds. Having examined iterative sounds and found cells and ostinati, we will try similar generalizations with continuous sounds.

In the column for formed held sounds, which object is the generalization of the varied Y note, an object that is both limited in duration and presents an "irrational" variation of mass, that is, one that is impossible to predict or follow in its details or complexity? We should not forget that this extrapolation of Y should by definition, like the glissando, not vary too intensely in tessitura; otherwise, it would be similar to a Y′ or even an accumulation of lively Y′ notes, which would bring us back to the examples above. The contents of the box in question are thus characterized by a fairly slow variation, though with many elements, within a coherent facture. With rapid variations and an incoherent facture we should accumulate microsounds and obtain a cell. Here, on the contrary, the object extends into multiform variations, branching out into a tracery of motifs that are still linked together in a logical way: this is a large note W.[1] It is not only the hotel plumbing, already mentioned in section 24.8, but the interminable gong, the bell with its succession of partials, new objects, as well, from electroacoustics, where the complex melodic-harmonic development visibly obeys a mechanical determinism. If this is not the case, if the technical device does not bind the object together logically, the large note loses its unity and tends rapidly to become a sample. Thus it is situated between a reasonably varied note of normal duration, whose structure it complicates by dilation, and the sample, whose disorder it simplifies.

This rather too original unity has not only the merit of providing a box for classifying a number of new, otherwise unclassifiable, sounds; it also reminds us that some musical motifs notated on the score are not in reality heard in isolation but are merged into a large note: for instance the notes added by Bach to a bass fundamental in figure 33.

We will place these large notes W in the column for formed held sounds below Y, as they are its giant variety.

---

1. In French the term is *grosse note*, literally "fat note," used to define a note where the attack, the continuation, or the decay have significant durations.—Trans.

FIGURE 33

Now we must generalize the concept of the weft,[2] starting from the specific wefts Tn and Tx. For these, in effect, we presumed a continuity of sustainment that eliminated any dynamic accident. Through fade-in-fade-out with homogeneous sounds the above wefts seemed to be generalizations of these: gradually evolving packages of N or X. From this we could easily imagine that sounds such as these, even evolving slowly, might present irregularities in dynamics or mass, or that a more or less clean rhythmic structure might slowly develop of itself within a regularity determined by a particular development. What will be the musical effect of such an object? Rather than the accumulation of rhythms, we will be aware of the "developmental permanence" of the object. In a melodic-harmonic or harmonic-dynamic weft it is the continuity that wins out. Comparable in originality to the cell ostinato, where the elements, taken in isolation, are totally unpredictable but where, by and large, repetition gives absolutely no information, the mixed weft, with its slowly evolving complex contents and a facture that is not necessarily regular, is relatively predictable, although the information it gives is not negligible. So logically it takes its place in the column for homogeneous sounds, extending the definition of these in the direction of originality.

Wefts like these are common in traditional symphonic music, when our observation point is a good distance away. In scored music they can of course be analyzed and appear as the result of the combination of a great number of well-defined N, X, or Y objects. But we think it of interest to characterize them as "group objects," both because for us they prefigure those natural macro-objects that no score can accommodate and because they are probably not meant to be as percep-

2. In French the term is *trame*, used to define a slowly developing sound with some variation, much as the weft of a material pursues a continuous line across the warp but may have some slight irregularities.—Trans.

tually distinct as the detail of the notation suggests; rather, it seems to us, the composer wants them to provide living continuity, a neutral harmonic and melodic base, and also a foil for the development of the significant events in the discourse. In the same way, the weft of a piece of material does not interfere with the pattern on it by being inappropriately original.

26.6. UNISONS

A particular case, very frequent in music, seems to have eluded our typology: unisons. Should we, in fact, consider a unison as simply a held sound arising, it is true, from several similar sound sources that can sometimes be separated out by the trained ear, or should we include it with accumulations, precisely by focusing on the fact that a number of distinct causes can be perceived in the object? We suspect that the answer depends as much on the quality of the unison, the facture of our object, as on the intention of the listener. If, indeed, our unison is well-executed, and the will to hear it as one note tends to unify it even more, then it will be a simple object, an N for example for violins or voices, even though a more subtle analysis can detect its multiplicity. If its component elements do not match, and if our listening intention is focused on this disparity, we will tend to perceive an accumulation, although we know full well that the performers are playing or singing badly the simple N note written for them by the composer. Conversely, if an orchestra is tuning up, giving As in different dynamic forms, in different octaves, and adorned with slight glissandi because the instrumentalists are turning the pegs of their violins, we will have a true accumulation of N and Y sounds rather than a unison.

26.7. SUMMARY DIAGRAM OF TYPOLOGY

(See next page.)

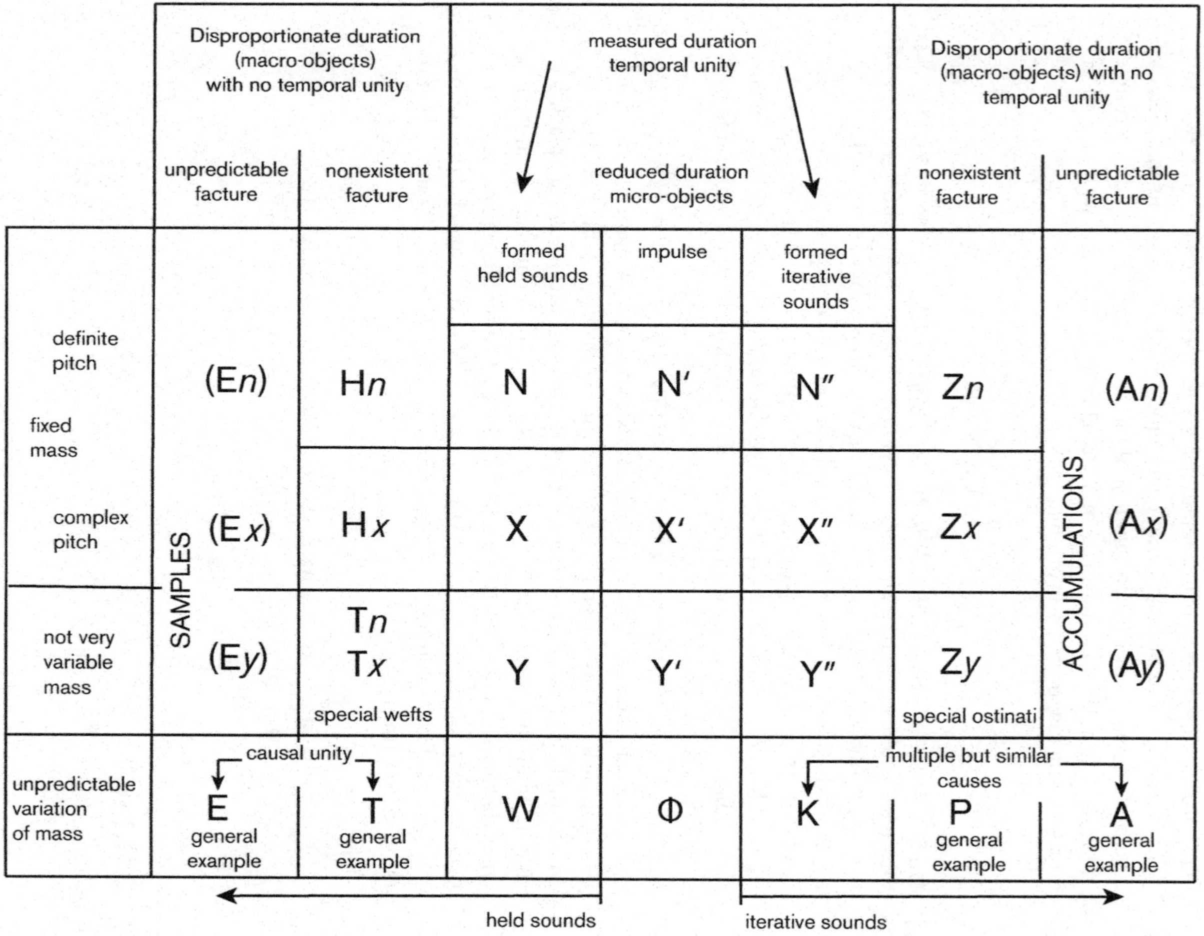

	Disproportionate duration (macro-objects) with no temporal unity — SAMPLES		measured duration / temporal unity — reduced duration micro-objects			Disproportionate duration (macro-objects) with no temporal unity — ACCUMULATIONS	
	unpredictable facture	nonexistent facture	formed held sounds	impulse	formed iterative sounds	nonexistent facture	unpredictable facture
definite pitch / fixed mass	(En)	Hn	N	N'	N"	Zn	(An)
complex pitch	(Ex)	Hx	X	X'	X"	Zx	(Ax)
not very variable mass	(Ey)	Tn / Tx — special wefts	Y	Y'	Y"	Zy — special ostinati	(Ay)
unpredictable variation of mass	E — general example (causal unity)	T — general example	W	Φ	K (multiple but similar causes)	P — general example	A — general example

held sounds · iterative sounds

FIGURE 34. Summary diagram of typology.

27

Working at Our Instrument

27.1. SOUND REELS

The researcher who wants to "work at his instrument" (creating sounds) and his ear at the same time will quite naturally have to go back to his instrumental and musicianship classes. This now consists in making, not scales, but what has taken their place: sound reels, in the usual language of the studio, and dictation—that is, descriptions (and not notation) of sounds.

This is the experimental approach, very different from the compositional approach, whether concrete or electronic. The "concrete" musician, in too much of a hurry to compose, goes straight to editing. The electronic composer, over-equipped, sits down at his keyboard of frequencies or formants, or constructs a blueprint with parameters. We would yet again advise both of them not to jump straight from ignorance to inspiration, from archaic concepts to modern techniques.

What is this sound-homework like? We must be careful to distinguish between the two possible pathways: either translation, a sort of dictation where we are taught to describe the sounds on a reel given to us, or prose composition, where we have to create sounds starting from the schema of their structure. By way of example, we will take a reel and go down the first pathway.

27.2. MAKEUP OF A TRANSLATION REEL

"Translation" consists in listening to a given object in order to describe its specific contents and organization, its *internal morphology*, as explicitly as possible.

Systematic training in translation will be aided by the creation of *translation reels*, containing a series of sounds with as wide a range as possible of origins and factures. Generally speaking, there is a number of sources to make these sounds:

- natural sources: trombone, flute, trumpet, piano, vibraphone, marimba, suspended cymbal, gong, sheet metal with bow or bass drumstick, for example;
- electronic sources: a sine-wave generator; a filter for accentuating or lessening the "timbre" of the pure sounds delivered by the aforementioned generator; a white-noise generator with filter for "cutting out" slices of sound of various thicknesses.

To create our objects we can stimulate these sound bodies in different ways: use the bow or the bass drumstick for the sheet metal, manipulate the electronic sources in various ways (any frequency for the sine-wave generator, more or less provided with "timbre" by the filter).

We can also position microphones at various distances from the sound sources, in different places and in varying numbers; finally, as we make the recording we can modify the "forms" of the sounds with the potentiometer, filter them, use the echo chamber, and so forth.

Thus we will be making our objects by playing an "instrument" that on each occasion will be the ensemble of sound source and means of recording. So we can make the following sounds, for example:

1. A tonic sound formed with the sinusoidal sound generator, "given timbre" by the filter amplitude, with its form provided by the potentiometer;
2. A tonic sound with vibrato formed with the same generator, with a frequency modulation to create the vibrato, and its form, as above, provided by the potentiometer;
3. A complex sound with a profile pianissimo—forte—pianissimo obtained from the filtered white-noise generator (only 1/3 of an octave remains), its profile also made with the potentiometer;
4. A complex impulse with resonance (an impulse of white noise plus echo chamber);
5. A flute sound with progressive attack, normal duration, then decay;
6. A trumpet sound with a sforzando at the beginning;
7. A trumpet sound with an ascending gruppetto right at the end;
8. A piano sound recorded on one microphone, imperceptibly merging (fade-in-fade-out) into a flute sound of the same pitch from a second microphone (making the output levels from the two microphones vary in reverse order at the time of recording);
9. A trombone sound with the following profile: pp < ff > pp < ff;

10. A gong sound, damped in the middle of the resonance;
11. A cymbal sound, damped just after the attack;
12. A thud from a wooden bass drumstick on the sounding board of a piano, with the resonance;
13. A large W note on a metal sheet recorded on two microphones, the first recording a complex bass resonance, the second locating a high tonic partial (the intensity of the sound is kept constant by raising the level on the potentiometer for about half the duration of the resonance);
14. A very complex channeled X sound (beating a metal sheet, a piano, gong, vibraphone, marimba).

27.3. STUDY OF INTERNAL MORPHOLOGY

We will now try to ignore how these sounds are made, which we explained to the reader in order to illustrate our point but which must of course be unknown to the listener trying his hand at musical dictation, since he is practicing acousmatic listening to sound for its own sake, *reduced listening*.

So this listener will notice

- balanced notes in which the three temporal phases appear clearly: attack, continuation, decay: flute sound (no. 5) and electronic sound (no. 1);
- balanced notes with conspicuous attack: sforzando attack: trumpet (no. 6); piano percussion-attack in the piano-flute fade-in-fade-out (no. 8);
- balanced notes with conspicuous decay: trumpet with ascending gruppetto at the end (no. 7), gong damped near the middle (no. 10);
- finally, balanced notes with a conspicuous continuation: the harmonic development of the metal sheet where we witness a slow transformation in the color of the sound (no. 13); and the electronic sound vibrato (sound no. 2).

It is nevertheless quite rare to find balanced notes—that is, notes where the three temporal phases (attack, continuation, decay) are clearly perceptible; most of the time two of these phases or even all three are merged into one. We will call these deponent notes.

- Either we find an attack followed by a decay (the usual case in percussion-resonances): in the very complex X (no. 14), the thud on the piano sounding board (no. 12) or the white-noise impulse with artificial resonance from the echo chamber (no. 4);
- Or the temporal phases are not distinct from each other and we go imperceptibly from the attack to the continuation, then to the decay, and it becomes difficult to demarcate these different phases: electronic sound (no. 3) and trombone sound (no. 9);

- Or else at the limit we find only an attack, so short is the sound: cymbal damped immediately after the attack (no. 11), and the electronic impulse no. 4 without echo chamber.

Reading our summary we notice that in truth, even if typology and morphology give some means of describing and notating and a certain sense of preparedness for experimentation, the description of sound, as far as dictation is concerned, is still short of terminology and a logical method of analysis. To carry out accurate dictation, we will have to return to this mode of listening once we are in possession of the ideas in book 6.

27.4. EXTERNAL MORPHOLOGY

Many sounds nevertheless seem to require an analysis of their *external morphology* first. What, in effect, stands out most of all when we listen to them is that they are made up of distinct elements, with forms that are separate from each other. This occurs very frequently. Moreover, some sounds have "impurities," elements that are not heard as an integral part of the object. We will make a distinction between these two typical examples of observable external morphology, which could be compared respectively to *compounds* (pure entities) and *mixtures* (impure entities) in chemistry:

(a) In the first example acousmatic listening can entirely contradict the specification sheet. The skilled reel-maker can take in his public by creating a coherent object in which different sound sources are superimposed or linked together; he can also play a single source yet give the sound several phases, to the point that it could be broken down into as many distinct objects. The sounds in question are *compound* objects made of several simultaneous elements or *composite* objects formed of several elements in succession. There are also dubious cases, unstable compounds, where the analysis depends to some extent on the listener's conditioning.

A high-register piano sound is, objectively speaking, a double sound. It can be considered as compound if through habit it is perceived as a single sound to which the striking of the hammer simply adds a particular color, or it can be considered as composite if through a different type of conditioning the ear is accustomed to hearing the striking of the hammer and the resonance of the string one after the other.

(b) Some examples do not fit into this situation where combined objects coexist. What happens, for example, if at the end of a long vibration (string, cymbal, etc.) another element is added, embroidering its own particular anecdote on to the sound? We are confused because the unity of the first sound wins out. Rather than

refer to compound or composite sounds we will say that a sound such as this is *accidental*. We will call the added sound the accident of the first.

An *incident* can just as well happen during the course of a sound. This is what we will call interference caused by some technical fault that is added to the sound and is neither wanted nor heard as a property of the sound. This type of impurity may be excessive background noise, a poor adhesive, a copying error, distortion, and so forth.

27.5. RELATIVITY OF ANALYSES

By linking a metal sheet and the bass piano through superimposition and fade-in-fade-out we can, as may easily be imagined, obtain an extremely varied collection of compound or composite objects. Some will be noticeably coherent and unique; others will display two distinct phases. Generally, the box they are classified in will ultimately depend on the listening context and intention.

Even when they are well linked, the two sounds (metal sheet and bass piano) will present marked differences of harmonic mass: so we really must make a distinction between two *musical* objects (according to the criteria that will be explained in book 6); but if the dynamic profiles match and complement each other to the point that they simulate true unity of facture, we will only hear one *sound* object. We can see from this example to what extent the application of the major distinctions in our typomorphology will depend in practice on particular applications and the listening criteria at the time. Besides, the role of our classification system is not, as we have seen, to put permanent labels on sounds but to open up the ear to the richness of the contents of sound; it is not a question of giving the composer of the future a stupidly inflexible code but of making him attentive to the way the object can fulfill a variety of sound *functions*.

So, generally speaking, we could say:

1. From a morphological point of view we can never be quite sure that the object is definitively split up into its "isotopes." A so-called thick sound may perhaps, after several months or years of training, appear to be reducible into constituent sounds. Other, composite, sounds will acquire unity when used in a particular way. Morphology, unsurprisingly, thus depends just as much on other surrounding sounds as on the listener's conditioning. What is important is to agree on a quick way of naming objects, describing them and still leaving a way open for breaking them down or building them up again.

2. From a typological point of view we are tempted to say this sound is a sample, a cell, a homogeneous weft. Nothing is as simple as the paradigm in an academic paper. Indeed, a disorganized scraping of the bow, a short sound bursting with values, a sustained bass note are by and large amenable to this type of classification, but here also context plays a part.

27.6. TYPOLOGICAL FORMULAE

(a) First we will try to communicate the interdependence of a group-object and its constituent parts, whether they are simultaneous (compound, like a piano chord) or in succession (composite, like a drumroll). In our notation we will indicate the difference between these two levels of analysis (group and elements) by using upper- or lowercase letters.

Thus in a complex X bell sound we can discern several sounds that are themselves complex $x_1, x_2, x_3 \ldots$ or even partials $n_1, n_2, n_3 \ldots$

We will notate the whole sound: X $(x_1, x_2, x_3, n_1, n_2, n_3 \ldots)$.

But it may be that I also wish to examine one of these elements separately x_1 or x_2, n_1 or n_2, but without ignoring the fact that it is part of X and is influenced by it. This time I will write: x_1 (X) or n_2 (X).

In these different formulae, then, the first term unambiguously indicates the object that is the focus of my interest: notated in uppercase letters, it contains the objects notated in lowercase letters in parentheses after it, or, notated in lowercase letters, it is itself contained in the group notated in uppercase letters in parentheses.

(b) But these symbols only mention the link between the group-object and its components, and vice versa; they do not take into account the relationships between the component objects. We have, in fact, separated the letters representing these component objects with commas, without prejudging their relationships of simultaneity or succession as a consequence. The double-high-register piano sound, for example (or any other percussion instrument where the noise of the percussion is heard at the same time as the resonance), is an extreme example of a compound sound: the two elements coexist in duration and are closely linked by their causality. To denote this type of link inside a *tonic* note in conventional listening, we will use the two juxtaposed symbols N *(x.n)*. But we could also highlight the typologically double nature of a sound such as this by ignoring conventional listening and then simply write *x.n*, a formula that represents a listening mode where equal attention is given to both aspects of the sound.

On the contrary, if the elements succeed each other in duration, we will use the addition sign to indicate that we are dealing with a composite object. This is the case with the drumroll notated X $(x+x+x+x\ldots)$. The same sign will be used for a juxtaposition of two parts inside an object, such as can be obtained through editing. A bowed staccato continuing with a held note gives us another example of composite sound: it has unity, but it also follows on from a note N″ and a note N. It could be considered their sum, and notated N″ + N. The staccato itself, analyzed separately, would have the following formula:

$$N'' \; (n' + n' + n' \ldots).$$

The above indications are not enough if we happen to have a fade-in-fade-out type of development: the squeaking of a metal sheet followed by its resonance gives an example of two very different, though not independent, types of sustainment. The resonance is already there during the rubbing, but it is masked; when it comes into the foreground, the squeaking noise has disappeared but remains present indirectly because of the partials it has released. Thus, the two elements are too closely linked for the addition sign to be used but not simultaneous enough for the multiplication sign; so in this case we will use a forward slash, representing the fade-in-fade-out: X'/X. Which introduces a time element and distinguishes this *composite* sound from the *compound* sound $X'.X$.

(c) We can generalize this system of notation by combining these various possibilities; for example, a trill in the high register of the piano could be notated this way:

$$\Sigma \left(x.n_1 + x.n_2\right).$$

It may be useful to explain that in compound sounds, X.N for example, the order in which the component elements are juxtaposed does not necessarily determine their arrangement; this notation is simply an attempt to take into account the simultaneity of a number of different elements, any of which may be called on to dominate depending on the context.

27.7. PROSE COMPOSITION: THE STUDY OF SUSTAINED SOUNDS

It would be good, first, to place the neophyte in a setting for acousmatic listening, the most favorable to the deconditioning necessary for a full understanding of the analytical side of musical research, by keeping him away from any reference points and also from preoccupations about how things are made.

But it would not be good teaching to keep him for too long simply practicing hearing: soon we must give him the opportunity to close the loop, to experiment all by himself on the concept of the facture of a sound. In short, we must give him sounds to *make*.

The obvious route is to discover the phenomenon of sustainment and its corollaries: allure and grain. Through sustainment, morphology becomes clear and typology justified. So by bringing together what conditioning had so completely separated—a violin, piano, or cymbal pizzicato, on the one hand, and their "held" notes, on the other—we get to the idea of the object and are freed from concentrating on specific instruments. The various methods—rubbing, breath, or resonance—that produce the same grain effects, the vibratos—with the fingers, a reed, or the glottis—that produce similar allures very quickly lead to a sense of facture and facilitate the discovery of *reduced listening:* too many different causes produce the same effects for us to go on trying to discover the explanation of sound objects in these causes alone.

The beginner will then endeavor to apply these notions to make sounds for himself by working on sustainments that give him different morphologies and also different types of sounds. The important thing is to take care over the diversity of sources, the guarantee of a proper exercise in both making and hearing, enabling him to learn to ignore the criteria usually thought to be the only important ones but that obscure most listening. Thus, whatever the sound body, the tessitura, the means of sustainment, the nature of the sound itself (tonic, complex, or variable), the experimenter will find himself forced to draw out only the elements that present themselves to the diligence of his gesture as of his listening: factures or sustainment criteria.

Below, by way of example, is the plan for a "reel of sustained sounds" as an exercise in making or hearing in the sense of "prose composition."

27.8. GENERAL PLAN FOR A REEL OF SUSTAINED SOUNDS

Reminder of the definition: the sustainment of a sound object is what maintains it in duration. Sustainment is therefore different from causality (especially the initial causality, on which the attack depends); it determines the continuation of the object, an essential element in duration.

(A) *Categories of sustainment*

Sustainment conforms to different "laws" or categories of its own causality:

1. No cause of duration: nonexistent or short-lived sustainment (e.g., whip, woodblock).

2. The environment may prolong or color the sound after the attack: sustainment through resonance (e.g., piano, guitar).

3. Regular prolongation of the sound by a renewed input of energy caused by a single law: sustained reed, more or less regular rubbing of a bow, electronic oscillation, and so forth. In this category we will distinguish among:

(*a*) fixed sustainment: a strictly constant supply of energy;

(*b*) modulated sustainment (predetermined dynamic): electronic sound for example; and

(*c*) active sustainment directly from the performer (wind or bowed instruments; ondes martenot).

4. The sustainment is not regular, although there is a single causal law; in this case it will be:

(*a*) irregular fluctuating (rubbing cymbals, maracas . . .);

(*b*) disordered (clumsy bowing, drumroll . . .).

5. The energetic input no longer has a single law, but:

(a) a series of willed or chance inputs (cascade of objects, rapid incessant manipulation of a potentiometer);

(b) the repetition of one identical fragment (staccato, tremolo, beating, etc.).

6. Finally, two or several categories of sustainment may coexist in one sound; then we will use the terms:

(a) compound sustainment if they are juxtaposed;

(b) composite sustainment if they follow each other.

The part of the reel with this exercise on it will have to have between six and twelve examples of each type of sustainment, if possible from each of the three domains: traditional, concrete, and electronic music—that is, in total eleven series (1, 2, 3a, b, and c, 4a and b, 5a and b, 6a and b).

(B) *Transition between categories of sustained sounds*

The point here is to show that there are no fixed barriers between these various categories:

1. Continuity between short-lived sounds, which always have a little resonance, and resonant sounds.

2. Continuity between resonant and sustained sounds, particularly with electric forms of sustainment.

3. Sustained sounds: subtle transition from fixed to active sustainment.

4. Register, clearly continuous, of all more or less fluctuating active fixed sounds (thus a good singer or violinist is distinguished from a bad singer or violinist).

5. Allure of prolonged sounds. The characteristic allure of a fluctuating sound (vibrato) will lead to a prolonged cyclic sound, while an irregular fluctuating sound will rapidly lead to a disordered sample.

6. Finally, prolonged types of sustainment, cyclic or irregular, rapidly destroy the coherence of a single object by producing either cells, samples, motifs, or sequences.

In fact, the idea and the perception of sustainment presupposes a certain morphological coherence that establishes the object; otherwise, we come back to a typological problem.

27.9. COMMENTS ON
THE EXPERIMENTAL TECHNIQUE

The firmness of this instruction will have been noted. In some respects it seems to go against classical instrumental teaching. The latter, in effect, concentrates on a specific instrument, from which an increasingly skilled technique draws objects that conform more and more to a given musical code and a certain aesthetics of sonority. But the training we advocate uses many instruments, some of them with age-old pedigrees, while others are unnamable or have to be thrown on the scrap heap after a single trial. If we want to be free of systems and generalize the use of sound bodies, we must bring all possible types of sonority into play regardless of the hierarchy. Moreover, we give our beginner no external model for making sound; it is enough for us if he learns to handle the bow and the bass drumstick, the microphone and the potentiometer judiciously and not without skill. To make what? Certainly not sounds that are valid according to particular musical criteria (which, in any case, it would be very difficult to define at this stage of research) but simply sounds as "decontextualized" as possible from the context of the traditional musical system and, at the same time, as successful as possible in terms of interest, originality, and subtlety, in other words, in their form and content, evaluated by *reduced listening*.

Such work, we must admit, involves a certain aesthetic sense. We should note, however, that an aesthetics like this is still instinctive, irrational, sensual almost. Its demands are not, for all that, any less urgently felt than elsewhere. Thus, the experimental musician will say quickly and decisively that a certain sound is "very good," another "suitable," and yet another "of no interest." What is certain is that the ill-defined freedom given to the performer of "any sound at all" cannot be fully exploited unless that performer submits to two disciplines: one involves the learning of new instruments, leading to practical virtuosities in making and recording sound; the other consists in rediscovering, through an imagination freed from known sonorities (which, in any case, does not stop him from using them), a way of reinventing sound. Is it necessary to add that without diligent practice, together with original gifts, we will never attain a standard high enough to inspire a generally accepted aesthetics?

BOOK SIX

Theory of Musical Objects

28

Musical Experience

28.1. MOVING TOWARD THE MUSICAL

As we have seen, it is the instrumental gesture that guides our rediscovery of sound form. In the course of our prehistoric meanderings we have already highlighted the crucial links between making and hearing, gesture and word, which other researchers, for their part, are rediscovering in the field of the relationship between auditory functions and motor activities. We also observed in chapter 19 that we use two words to name a sound: violin notes, dog's bark, nightingale's song, human speech, electron or IBM music. The verb is absent every time. On the right the meaning, on the left the agent, and at the end? The verb that refers to the activity of the individual, to *reduced listening*, or the *sound object* is absent.

And, in fact, very often in the course of our research we have felt as if we were crying in the wilderness. So many people are interested only in tools and schemata! Suggesting to them that we must also pay attention to the perceptual field seems to be an offense, a crime of score treachery, and immediately leads to accusations of naturalism, of considering nothing but the material, of confusing the musical and sound.

We will try to make ourselves very clear. The whole approach to sound, both typology and morphology, outlined above is only a preliminary to the musical. Certainly we needed time to establish a bit of order. But we must emphasize yet again: the most important part remains to be done, to move from the sound object to the musical object or, again, to find out from suitable sound objects what the repertoire of possible musical signals is. Olivier Alain's words make a lot of sense:

The composer's function today has practically nothing to do with where earlier composers started out, that is, assimilating a particular state of the musical language of his age at a time when, precisely, the language was developing in a continuous way (for tradition is synonymous with continuity). Perhaps we are embarking on a short and provisional period when there are no composers in the usual sense because there is no musical language in the usual sense either, that is, no material vehicle for a commonly perceived meaning. Does today's composer always know where he is going? And when he gets there, is it really the destination he had chosen?[1]

Only we are standing much farther back than a composer usually allows himself to do. This, in our opinion, is demanded by the present situation of music and the crisis provoked by the volume of new means he has to hand just as much as by a new state of mind. If our activities take the form of *research*, it is because they have a group discipline and reject individual whim. But we must not forget their ultimate aim: to lead to possible musics. At base, it amounts to *a new awareness and a deconditioning process with a view to creating something.*

28.2. THE SOCIOLOGICAL FACTOR IN MUSICAL EXPERIENCE

Why do we say this research involves group experience? Is it out of a desire to be social, a wish to teach, or to take into account the general conditions of advanced technology in our time? None of these reasons, all of which are valid, but none of which is absolutely right. On the contrary, art tends to appeal to solitary people, to exceptional talents and craftsmanship; if researchers do form a group, very rarely is it other than as assistants to a leader who remains very firmly alone in the face of responsibilities that are his. Teaching, furthermore, would seem very premature considering the still very approximate results and the lack of verification our findings have had to date.

The true reason for our statement lies in the nature of music itself, which like every language has a fundamental social dimension. Where there is already language, man often appears solitary; composer, author, performer, face-to-face with his music as the poet with his muse, his solitude is peopled with images of an already given world. But when he ventures into unknown territory, when, as we have dared to do, he stakes his all on the discovery of the materials of a language that is still to be spelled out word by word, man cannot do without others, not to help him, not as guinea pigs, which would not be enough, but as an essential interlocutor, a generator of experience. Faced with a collection of sounds, I may inspire my thinking, enrich my analysis with them; but nothing proves to me that this analysis is the same as other people's, that I am not dreaming. Of course, some-

---

1. Olivier Alain, *Nouveau Larousse musical* (Paris: Larousse, 1957), 2:380.

thing tells me that I am not deceived, that I am not enclosed in my own subjectivity. But in thinking this, I am already mentally involving other people; I am not listening only for myself. It would therefore be contradictory to think in this way in a studio, alone, refusing to verify through the actual presence of others what I was already positing. Besides, we know very well that even for the most reclusive composer, the most retiring writer or painter, the work has no meaning unless it is communicated. Even if he shuns the concert hall or the theater, even if he appears indifferent to success or failure (this happens), communication is a matter of principle to him, whether he has in mind a contemporary audience or ideal interlocutors in a culture or a time that is still to come. Moreover, if his research deals with communication using a new material, how much more necessary will group verification be!

We must not, however, confuse this essential social dimension of research with the actual, more or less anecdotal, existence of groups where they play at research as if it were a party game. It also happens that the experimental musician is in reality very solitary; but he is just as much subject to more or less indirect or chance communications; and in most cases it seems that the speed of his own learning is linked to those contacts, those reactions that filter through to him.

This will not come as a surprise. Psychologists who have studied learning processes, such as G. A. Miller, show that *abstractions*—that is, precisely what leads to music theories and to the evaluation of the qualities of objects—are for the most part products of society:

> A man living alone all his life would not react differently to different colors; nothing in his contact with the automatic *reinforcements* of the physical world would reward him for deducing the abstract concept of color. (Oddly, a solitary man would have no vocabulary to describe himself, for the notion of self is a social phenomenon.) Some primitive tribes have no nouns to describe the colors of the visible spectrum: they can see them, but the culture does not *reinforce* them in a differential way. Conversely, whatever is closely linked with everyday work and obtaining food is the object of meticulous distinctions; as such abstractions are *reinforced*. When culture and hunting had more importance for the average man, English distinguished between large and small livestock, flock, shoal, spat, herd, flight, swarm, and pack. These distinctions are now obsolete and can all be replaced by group. But modern English carefully distinguishes between terms closely linked to modern life; for example, the distinction between car, coupé, saloon, taxi, bus, open tourer, automobile, lorry, racing car, is perfectly clear.[2]

Until now our beginners have been lone men or men with a single technique or from a single culture. This is why their progress, focusing on establishing a new

---

2. George Armitage Miller, *Langage et communication* (Paris: PUF, 1956). [Original title in English: *Language and Communication* (New York: McGraw-Hill, 1963).—Trans.]

musical society, demands an initial dialogue to prepare for that society, the importance of which goes far beyond simple experimentation on perceptions: the promise of a language depends on this discipline.

28.3. DECONDITIONING EXERCISES

To recapitulate our rules for the use of sound:

(a) We do not refuse any type of sound object a priori. We do not debar anything to do with the sources or meanings of sounds, for we cannot see what would allow us to eliminate them before we have listened to them.

(b) We isolate them. We said there was no overall difference between object and structure, that it all depended on listening intention, and that given sound structures were always accessible to the intention to listen for the sake of hearing better, independently of events or meanings. In absolute terms this is right. In practice it is at the very least difficult: on the one hand, it is almost impossible to listen to a discourse uniquely for its sound organization; on the other hand, this is more accessible with an isolated, repeated fragment of discourse or familiar noise because the event and the meaning appear only partially here, and repetition dilutes them even more.

(c) We compare them. Doubtless the method is also practiced by musicians and physicists, but we transpose it into a zone that until now has been explored by neither: neither a work, nor a sequence of stimuli, an experimental musician's reel of sounds gives a succession of objects intended neither for the concert hall nor for comparative measurement. It has been said that it is like a reworked and generalized form of traditional musical dictation.

A well-composed reel of sounds, containing disparate sounds taken from the variety of sources indicated in section 27.2 (or perhaps, to start with, from a field not too far away from classical instrumental sounds in order to avoid too much disorientation) will say more than long speeches.

New researchers, who in an introductory session are invited to undergo a deconditioning process before entering a new society, will be asked to describe the sounds they hear in terms of their temporal evolution, if they lend themselves to this, or by comparison with neighboring sounds. They would do well to abandon immediately all specialized scientific or musical terminologies, which would soon become inadequate. It does not matter if the initial accounts are a mixture of confused morphology, elementary typology, or even insights already anticipating the theory that will follow. In any case, this simple experiment will have demonstrated that there is a lot to be said about sounds and that everyone hears them with quite remarkable accuracy, though no one has an adequate vocabulary to describe them.

28.4. RECONDITIONING EXERCISES

How can this group of progressively trained participants come to recognize new criteria for musical listening? Should we believe that these values are bound to emerge from collections of sound objects?

Things are not so simple. Even if the order in which we set them out is logical, educational, it cannot remotely reflect the chronology of our experimental approach.

We can say, however, that outside the safe traditional musical values to which we are already conditioned, certain criteria will gradually emerge from group observation of a fairly large number of sound objects. This always depends on the materials being experimented on, the working imagination and the inquisitiveness of the ear. If in the studio there are sound bodies that have been scratched or rubbed a lot, we could imagine a descriptive criterion that they might share, a very crude but very real musical criterion that, for example, could be called *grain*. In the same way, if we are working on vibratos, from the violinist's, which are willed, and the singer's, which are involuntary, right to the natural vibratos of bells, gongs, and such, we eventually draw out another criterion, which we will call *allure*, to avoid referring back to a too-specific way of operating. By comparing sound bodies that without giving tonic pitch produce dense sounds, rich in partials, compressed or spread out in the tessitura, the idea of the *thickness* of a sound, still quite vague, suggests itself to the researchers, guiding their shared *hearing intention*.

Now this description of experimental approaches, this emergence of concepts, these definitions of terms, all contributing to moving toward and then discovering those musical criteria we define more accurately later on, imply the application of the two rules of language (alternation and juxtaposition, described in chapter 18), which are used ingenuously, instinctively, with their workings only appearing later when everything has taken shape. But the discovery of these rules and the endless verification they presuppose would not be possible for the isolated researcher, any more than reels of sound with collections of sound objects carrying a specific criterion for experimentation would be intelligible to the layman. What will be the value of a *reel of sounds* like this to a professional musician invited to hear them without any other explanation? It will be nil. What can he deduce from a succession of sounds that in the first place he will obviously hear as low or high, loud or soft, coming from all manner of sources? What can he deduce if there is no structure that might directly or indirectly bring higher structures to mind. So, for the time being, what we have identified in common is a *criterion*, not *a value*. Without *the intention to hear grain, allure, or thickness*, this sequence of sound objects has no virtue and, lacking a demonstrative context, is prone to all sorts of misunderstandings. We therefore have, at the same time as the most cursory of preparations arising from the choice of objects, the beginnings of a convention positing an additional *form of communication*, in which hearing yields, or almost yields, to *understanding*. A *metalanguage* must now precede, clarify, and comment on the language being tried out; in simpler terms, participants must define their common listening intention.

28.5. TALKING ABOUT SOUNDS, OR THE "METALANGUAGE"

"Talking about sounds" appeared initially as an event of secondary importance. The embarrassment of the musician faced with an unfamiliar sound about which he can say nothing at all can be compared only with his confused terminology for describing a familiar sound about which he has too much to say.

We have observed that this silence could be linked to another musical infirmity: deafness. The discovery of a hearing intention in all musical phenomena inclines us to think that talking about sounds is not of such secondary importance. It is necessary first for revealing what went without saying: that we listened to traditional sounds in such and such a way, from the point of view of sonority as much as musicality. Then it is necessary to talk about it so that different listeners can agree on a shared listening intention. Thus, the idea of a metalanguage appears different from a teaching method or an explanatory critique: an organic need, linked to an art, to have an adequate terminology based on a realistic analysis of what is distinctive or perceptible in the objects it uses. The objects on the higher level do, indeed, form an original language, which can do without commentaries or can explain itself. This is not true two levels below, at the level of the components that make up the objects. Describing them, determining their functions, requires a vocabulary, at least at this level.

Then we may wonder whether this metalanguage verifies the existence of a three-way communication in the field of the musical. Currently, in fact, we assume two pairs of communicators: the composer, who *speaks* to his listener by means of sounds, and the listener (the author is also one of these), who in his innermost being communes with nature through this divine deceit. What a lot of literature on this! By comparing the two, we can see clearly that in the most solitary listening to sounds there is always a third: society.

Thus, when we listen to a "previously unheard" sound, detached from any preexisting language system, we may think that we are again alone in its presence. This would perhaps be true in a meditative state, where the sound would act as a drug or, to put it more respectfully, as a channel to a psychic state, where it would be not so much a matter of taking hold of it as being carried along by it toward another plane of activity. This is indeed a way of listening to sounds that is quite far removed from our Western ways but that itself would have to depend on a most refined system of knowledge. This previously unheard sound, striking in its novelty as much as by being listened to in a solitary state, still, in our opinion, implies the social. The listener, whether in fact he considers it as an object of art or science, gets ready to describe it, to give it a meaning and make use of it: all these activities presuppose the presence of others at every moment. Even better: as there cannot really be thought without verbal formulation, it is very unlikely that the listener thinks anything about this sound without recourse, implicitly, to words and ideas.

28.6. TWO SORTS OF MUSICAL EXPERIENCES

That participants can agree, relatively well and quickly, on what they have decided to hear in a sound object is undeniable and cuts right through the usual muddle: it proves that a little individual and group effort can establish a starting point as much in the selection of objects as in the definition of terms to describe them.

There is still, however, something annoying in this abstruseness, and we would like the visitor who had these reels of sound played to him to be convinced on listening to them, if not about the emergence of a particular value at least about the existence of a particular criterion. Is this possible? In other words, is it our technique that is at fault, or are we up against a fundamental problem?

Doubtless both.

Having acknowledged the cultural approach to music, we are practicing it *in embryonic form* through a vocabulary of musical neologisms and a completely fresh way of communicating group experiences: we have already detected this embryonic "musical" in the learning experiences with the grass or the bow. Now, even if our reels made progress technically, the fact is that a sound still contains all sorts of properties and an *obvious sound* should only have one, which is completely contrary to the laws of both acoustics and perception. We should have to use *a whole art* to camouflage the nonpertinent features so that the others would appear dominant to an inexperienced listener. Such a consummate art is no longer an experiment. The reels of sound would now no longer be rough drafts but would already be defining new rules of art: a strange discovery, which very clearly illustrates what happens when there are two objectives in the same laboratory—one analytic and scientific, the other synthetic and artistic.

This, expressed with all the naivety of our early years of research, is what we so often found frustrating: not being able to rely on communicating to listeners, who were nevertheless musicians, what experimenters, who were not always experienced musicians themselves, were now finding obvious.

We have just rediscovered experimentally an idea already discussed in section 21.13. Our experimenters, using a metalanguage, would define their listening intention, targeting a particular *sound criterion*. However ill-assorted, the collections of sounds made for this purpose enabled them to test their intention through *a particular sort of musical experience.*[3] On the contrary, when they played sequences of sounds to traditional musicians, the latter (even those who wanted to hear better and more than with ordinary traditional theory) could only perceive the emergence of the *values* of the traditional system; in fact, they heard *absolutely anything.* This expression, in no wise pejorative, means that everyone heard something, but in his own way, depending on his own implicit or explicit frame of reference. How, through *another sort of musical experiment,* can we obtain confirmation that would be more convincing? Obviously by going from the analytical sector 4 to the synthetic sector 1. In other words, experimenters, now able to take control of their criteria and recombine them into value-characteristic pairs that are at last convincing, would move on to a *sound art* providing musical structures to be perceived, structures that in their turn could demand some training.

We can well imagine that if such structures could easily be found outside the traditional pitch-timbre structure, we should at one and the same time have invented as many new foundations for music, or as many new musics, as there are fundamental structures. We are far, very far, from having found a single one that is convincing. This could be said to be the whole problem, everything that is at stake, in musical research.

28.7. INVENTING OBJECTS

It would be a serious omission not to mention the question of the provision of (suitable) and if possible musical sound objects for an experimental group, this being the central concern of its work and the condition for the productivity of its research. All the more so as, apart from a few short paragraphs for illustrative or demonstrative purposes, this book deliberately remains silent on a whole operational technique that would require a treatise on instrumentation for itself alone.

We will therefore limit ourselves to looking at the nature of this activity, its importance, and its impact on research.

We have already mentioned those periods, those fashions, those fads for a particular instrumental material, a particular realization or manipulation procedure, a particular discovery about sources or recording that cannot fail to appear in the history of a group. Thus, the group will be assailed in successive waves by materials that are too diverse or saturated with objects that are too alike. Of course, the experimenters themselves come into this, as much by their analytical input as by their contribution to sound gathering. So we find ourselves between two opposing types of excess. Some experimenters, lacking imagination, do not have a grasp of sound phenomena and obtain only unusable platitudes from them. Others, too gifted to probe into the material, make it into shapes and immediately obtain

3. To go back to the stages in chapter 21, this experiment targets level 6, and the other, level 5.

"composer's objects" from it. It reveals a style, a personality. Are these objects, too loaded with meaning, too clearly revealing an intention, still a product of music theory?

This question is all the more relevant as it also comes up in the context of the possible musical content the composer spontaneously gives the object when he intervenes in both the energetic elements he has chosen or overseen and the possible meanings he is aiming for or has in mind. This is why experimental musicians are not too willing to lend their sounds to each other, as they think these bear their mark; and a particular facture or a particular basic material often has such a recognizable character that the same object cannot be used several times in the same or different works without risking giving the impression of repetitiveness. We find here, in this new music, something rather like the painter's brushstroke or color, or the sculptor's "touch": there is a fusion of materials and composition, and the form of each component can take on meaning as well as the form of the whole.[4] The difference of levels between a piano note, which is an everyday occurrence, and a particular sound object of the same duration but original, like a composer's motif, is no longer classical. And so different musics are born, with their meanings attached to or beginning to emerge at one level or another.

In any case, at the music theory stage we must not try to decipher these meanings immediately but must carry on with our research independently of such preoccupations. Indeed, first we have to draw out the morphological criteria, even if on initial analysis it means putting aside as too specific objects that do not fit in with the definition of these: structures that are already too specific at the level of composition, and cannot be transformed into other structures without plagiarism, indeed, that are already *motifs*. These are no longer suitable sound objects, now through excess of musicality. Here also we come back to tradition: the musician instrument maker takes his material wherever he finds it, endeavors to retain what is ephemeral and to normalize what is too specific, and, rubbing strings, blowing air, striking membranes, strives to form universal materials, equally far removed from natural anecdote or the composer's whim.

We have not yet reached the point where there might be a question of a language system. It is therefore not the right moment, if we intend to decipher the whole of sound, to make distinctions of principle between intentional and nonintentional sound objects. The composer's intention, if it is visible, will be treated provisionally as an indication of origin. Even if it means keeping such objects for the exclusive use of their composer, we can still decipher the interaction of the criteria he has instinctively used, often without being aware of their workings himself.

Finally, we would ask the sound sculptor to produce enough samples to allow all of us to identify the possible rules for drawing out musical criteria from sound.

4. Once perceived, a microstructure has all the meaning of the level above on its own scale.

The experimenter will thus have to demonstrate not an individualism that would make listening to objects for themselves impracticable but an originality capable of revitalizing materials for composition compared to what is traditionally available. Researchers in a given experimental group will aim for this genuine originality, this golden mean between the too ordinary and the too original.

Supposing now that such *campaigns* in prose composition and translation have produced enough results—that is, in making and analyzing collections of objects—how can researchers finally give an account of them? In what form will they record their observations?

28.8. EXPERIMENTAL REELS

Starting from collections that have already been analyzed, research consists in assembling the sounds in a new way so that a particular *criterion* is highlighted in a particular collection. This work will take place in several stages.

(a) The first phase will still be tainted by working procedures. Depending on whether the studio has been invaded by a particular type of material, concentrates on acoustic or electronic sounds, carries out its manipulations in a particular fashion, or finally whether the researchers' taste is focused on one thing rather than another, the collections will not reveal the criteria in the same way. Some of them will stand out more strongly or emerge in a particular order. Generally speaking, a great deal of time is needed for a full enough overview to be obtained and for certain criteria, which were in the forefront, to be relegated to their rightful, sometimes modest, place.

(b) It is, and we should be in no doubt about this, the memory that will deliver the first syntheses, a musical memory together with much thought, shored up by research into correlations as shown in book 3. We may be surprised at how long it takes for a new understanding of sound to be developed: this slowness—assuming it was mainly a feature of our early endeavors—will doubtless be less of a threat to our successors.

Musical memory often operates through a relatively independent regrouping of the jumble of sounds in the studio. The important thing is that the sampling should highlight the main criteria strongly enough. But we cannot really count on sounds eloquently organizing themselves, revealing the *criteria* in *scale, classes,* and *genres.* The pursuit of criteria for the theory is so much an effort of will at this stage that it seems to run counter to the *rules of structuring.* The researcher's (and the composer's) temptation is then perfidious; to go to the opposite extreme: to ignore that the sounds in which he has learned to hear a particular criterion appear like this neither to ordinary nor even very easily to experimental listeners.

(c) So the next step will be to move on from *experimental* to *teaching reels.* This is the name given to reels that would no longer take their primary material from

the original sound gathering but keep strictly to the idea of "prose composition." Once we have discovered criteria, and provided that we know how to develop techniques for realizing them, we must take the trouble to *make sounds specifically to illustrate these criteria more clearly.*

So will we then have created the basic structures underlying particular musical relationships? Certainly not. We will have found a midpoint between the completely ill-assorted nature of the criteria and the value-characteristic equilibrium that can serve as a basis for a more confident musicality. Those teaching reels, giving suitable illustrations of criteria, will be able to highlight the *classes, genres,* or *species* of sounds without claiming, very prematurely, to be creating *scales* like those of the traditional system, which rest on the dominant timbre-pitch relationship.

In fact, it is probable that the quest for what might be called the philosopher's stone of new musics will not succeed with this analytical method. We believe the present treatise aims to go as far as possible in this matter but that it would be unwise, and doubtless unrealistic, to hope to arrive immediately at authentically musical structures by this route. On the one hand, there are too many possible combinations of criteria organized in too many different ways; on the other hand, our registers of sensitivity are not well enough understood for us to be able to work so logically.

The theory is not yet music.

28.9. STUDIES ON OBJECTS

The *studies in composition* we are advocating do not immediately claim to be music. Starting from a given, suitably *limited* sound material, they are intended to produce authentic structures that would demonstrate to others the criteria that the composer, using his own schema, has endeavored to "present to the ear." This method of discovery has no equal. Nevertheless we come up against two obstacles:

(a) It is extremely difficult to expect a composer, once he is involved in the activity of composing, to keep to a strictly experimental approach. However much he wishes to do so, he always runs the risk of going offtrack and using objects for the purpose of personal expression rather than for finding out about them through a systematic exploration of their functions. Here we have to choose between Czerny and Chopin.

(b) Finally, in the most scrupulous *study with objects* the perception of structures immediately dominates the perception of objects, with the result that experiments such as these often give results far removed from what was expected at the level of the object itself. It is very annoying to see these structures highlight other, often unexpected, criteria and other functions of the object rather than the ones we had wanted them to take on (a positive finding as well, if this is the case). We have no illusions about the limitations of such studies on one particular type of

interaction of criteria. Through the ages well-intentioned composers have written studies like these, from those *for the left hand* to *Mode de valeurs* and *Timbres-Durées*, but rarely does a study scrupulously observe what the title says; and this can only have happened once, with *The Well-Tempered Clavier*. Besides, the higher levels cannot but interfere at the level of objects: syntactical structures and musical ideas themselves. In classical music studies, lexis and syntax were generally fixed. In an experimental domain, how many unknowns, all at the same time! . . . We should need the genius of both a composer and an experimenter, capable of setting himself limitations well enough chosen to highlight a particular process related to one of the three operational levels: the identification of the criteria or contexture of the objects, the function of the objects in the structure, and the function of the structures in the work.

This is perhaps the price of musical progress: perhaps the goal of an intelligent composer should no longer be a dubious shortcut leading directly to the work. He should choose for himself the restricted, forever overflowing, framework of a preparatory exercise.

In any case, faced with too many possibilities and too much freedom (which is negated by creating compensatory systems), we would propose a different approach. We would suggest that the experimental approach, a prerequisite for authentic and realistic musical inspiration, should take place at the level of music theory.

29

Generalizing Music Theory

29.1. TRADITIONAL MUSIC THEORY

If music theory as it is practiced in traditional music is indeed the means of notating musical ideas as much as translating these ideas into sounds, oral training reveals the basic direction of this discipline: to obtain from an instrument sounds that correspond to symbols, in the sense of *prose composition*. The most deeply rooted way of doing this, the instrument that belongs to everyone, is the voice. It seems natural to think that the limits of the sol-fa are those of the sight reader's voice, the voice being the only instrument common to all musical civilizations, even if each civilization uses it differently and develops or ignores certain aspects of its potential.

If we take into account humming and gestures just as much as the harmonium or the manuscript paper of theory classes, we will reach a better understanding of the origins of a musical tradition and of a fundamental deconditioning process. A wonderful music, which in the space of a few centuries leads to such a paring down, to twelve notes that are finally tempered, to time signatures and a space where the beginner's fist and the teacher's finger prefigure the conductor's baton— all to the rhythm of a few basic pulsations: two-time, three-time, and several tempos: marching, the heartbeat, breathing, dancing.

Where the felicitous expansion of the musical domain, the progressive selection of sources, and progress in performance are concerned, the combinatory power of a reliable notation has been surprisingly efficient, beyond even what might have been expected from the extremely dry and ultimately incomplete analysis of elementary musical criteria it provides. If we compare classical and contemporary works, we observe that, for the former, theory enables an analytical representation of the work, which gives an account of it while leaving a certain degree of latitude for performance; for the latter the notations belonging to the same theory express less and less what is essential to music and tend to be valid exclusively on the operative level, which is itself more and more overloaded and persnickety. But as long as we keep to *"prose composition"* for the most modern musics and rely on traditional instruments, hardly anyone feels the need to change their habits: instruments being what they are, the notes on a staff faithfully transmit orders to the instrumentalist. The interpreters' training guarantees the precision of this. With this state of affairs—that is, as long as we keep to prose composition—a working score that avoids any misunderstanding is obviously better than a possible analytical score that would give a better account of a content, but where the symbols, all still to be discovered and systematized, would give no guarantee in performance.

But the need for musical signs that would communicate the real function of objects more directly is becoming urgent for composers. Given the growing importance of sounds that are more, less, or something other than notes, we now lack a link between musical thought and its realization. So composers improvise more or less adequate and communicable personal systems, which are intermediaries between the out-of-date symbols of traditional notation and the real content of music: exactly what a *generalized music theory* is looking for.

29.2. THE TWO SCORES

This critique of traditional notation, already outlined in section 28.5, links up with what we have already observed in relation to some needs of present-day music: if the composer is, in fact, working with "concrete" or electronic sounds, he has a choice between an intentions score based on the objects or structures he intends to bring to listeners' ears and a performance score representing the acoustic or electronic operations that are the means to achieve this. Now, whereas the old notation ensures that there is an adequate correlation between the symbol and the musical sign, it is impossible to say as much for most of the new procedures; these relationships are only roughly sketched out and are often crude. The gap between making and listening remains considerable, much more than it ever was in the musical tradition. Therefore, until such a new experience can crystallize, we cannot escape the need to consider the possibility of two scores without risking falling into the most serious ambiguities: one score, essential, for musical description and the other, operational, for performance.

As this work is a treatise neither on instrumentation nor electronic or acoustic composition, but first and foremost an attempt to describe the most general musical object possible, it will come as no surprise if we turn our attention to a theory of music in which the concepts must, above all, take into consideration general functions rather than the individual performance of objects.

29.3. SIGNS AND MUSICAL THOUGHT

So music theory, entrusting all the meaning to the *symbols of notation* and leaving the responsibility for reading them and transforming them into sound objects to the orchestra, necessarily obliges the composer to think in terms of these symbols. The composer is in the same position as the writer. He has an idea in his head, just as a proposition obsesses the philosopher or a situation tempts the novelist, and he can only *take hold* of this idea, as his colleagues can of theirs, once it is down in black and white: notated. How many of these thoughts have vanished or been totally transformed in the process of expression? And to what extent have the means of notation reworked themes, often giving them an almost unrecognizable structure, so different from the one imagined?

Hence the obstinate demand of musicians faced with any new source of sounds or any new way of modeling or assembling them: where is the notation? A naive question. There is no notation, and for the time being, there *should not* be any: any premature notation is not only impossible but disastrous. We will illustrate these two important points.

Impossible: the history of music shows that notation is not a starting point but an end point. It is not because for several centuries music has been learned through the shortcut of theory that we can hope for new musics devised a priori (as an extension or at the margin of tradition). If these musics are radically different from the *music based only on pitches* because they turn to other fundamental relationships, first we must discover these relationships, and a great deal of time will go by before a notation can emerge from such experiments, which are all, or nearly all, yet to be done.

Moreover, the disastrous aspect of any notation (including traditional notation) is that it prejudges relationships between musical objects: it is *tendentious*. If we use traditional notation, we *express our ideas* in terms of stereotypes. As this notation is the notation of pitch, when we use it, we are bound to bring everything back to, and try to explain everything in terms of, that dimension.

Nor let us go back over the use of the parameter score, even worse than the traditional score. A score such as this evades musicality for two reasons, one of which alone would be enough: it is stripped of its instrumental structures, the guardians of a permanence of *characteristics* and the perception of *values*. Everything is ultimately naively brought back to a persnickety pitch, notated in frequency, which no longer bears any relationship to what is heard. Finding one's way from a map that is wrong is the same as being lost.

29.4. OBJECTIVE OF A MUSIC THEORY

If the composer came to ask himself what precisely the structure of the work he wishes to compose is based on, most of the time he would be very hard put to find an answer. Over and above school formulae, on the one hand, and skill in manipulating the Western orchestra, on the other, he is, generally speaking, attempting an *experiment just to hear*. Furthermore, we must clarify the meaning of the expression *structure of the work*. Normally it denotes the relationships between the parts and the schema for the general layout. We have said again and again that we did not wish to tackle the problem of music at this level while the problem of the object had not been discussed.

In effect, every macrostructure implies a choice of basic materials and structures, that is, the functions of these objects. In traditional music these materials are the notes of the orchestra; their values, already categorized, guarantee their functions in *more highly organized* structures. These structures are themselves conditioned by reference structures. Not so long ago this was the scale and its tonal interactions. In atonal music it is the atonal series with its directions for use. In a music that is no longer atonal, that itself rejects the permutation of the twelve sounds, what is it? Various suggestions are put forward: repetitions, series, if it is still a logical music. If it is an aleatoric music, it will be distributions: clouds of notes, velocities of glissandi, and so forth. So in all this must we infer *pitches*, which our composers happily combine with precisely determined durations and intensities?

The question this raises is very disturbing. Are those pitches, those durations and those intensities we see notated on the score, structural elements or simply reference points? Are the suggested arrangements of them manufacturing techniques or structures perceived or perceptible in reality? Do we, as in the past, group orchestral notes in sequences or in separate chords? Or do we assemble them and weld them into macrostructures, which are new objects and must be heard as units? Finally, if it is the case that pitches are still perceived, what precisely is their role? If they are no longer perceived because they are so convoluted or so close together, or because of their accumulation or their variations, and so forth, what do we perceive? What is this music made of, and through what do we ultimately hear it? This is the aim of the music theory, before any notation.

29.5. SOUND ARCHITECTURE

The wildest, as well as the most calculated, works of contemporary music ultimately raise the same question as the one we are discussing with regard to the generality of musical objects, and the two approaches are two sides of the same coin. It would be just as much a mistake to believe that we can discover music by simply analyzing collections of sounds as it would be to believe that we can go on composing with an inadequate music theory. Describing materials and then experimenting on ways of assembling them in *studies with objects* must come before the discovery of new forms of music.

For those who are not convinced of this, we have only to look for a moment at the adventure of modern architecture. Architecture, just as much as language, could have been our model. Here we are not talking about some "slab of sensation," a piece of sound cut out of its three dimensions of time, frequencies, and amplitude.[1] It is a far cry from an object in space, with three homogeneous dimensions, an object of our vision, to an object with three heterogeneous dimensions, an object of our hearing. What is more likely to justify the instinctive parallel that we are tempted to draw between architecture and music is the very powerful and probably reasonable feeling that in architecture as in music there is *an appropriateness of the material to the way it is organized*—in other words, that the microstructure informs the macrostructure.

It is not so much a question of the physical makeup of construction materials. It is already more to do with their function in an assemblage, their formal role. Indeed, the architect must certainly continue with his own struggles between the visual forms he provides and the network of forces to which they owe their existence. Everyone has his own problems at this level: phonetic materials for the linguist, sound materials for the musician; everyone comes up against the resistance of the material, and it is here that drawing parallels, so often attempted, so often tempting, is ultimately so deceptive. If we recall the apparently theoretical distinction between the *perception of structures* and *perceptual structures*, we will hold the key to these comparisons: it is pointless to compare the objects of perception themselves, such different, always original, human ways of taking hold of various aspects of the world; but where the parallel remains valid is where we compare man's methods of classifying, assembling, giving meaning to these objects.

Thus, when we admire the fact that brick leads on to brickwork, dressed stone to intrados, and prestressed concrete makes possible the towering heights of paraboloids, we are admiring two things at once and rediscovering the subtle and often irritating point of intersection between what we usually call matter and spirit. If we operate with the same ease in this field of objects for seeing, constructing, and hearing, it is because our inner workings are the same. Everything—words, bricks, notes—then takes on structure, following the same chain of relationships discussed in chapter 16. We should therefore not be surprised by the connections that can be

---

1. We must caution the reader against this pretension: "every definable temporal stage (in the development of sound matter) representing a 'symbol' analogous to a phoneme in language." Abraham Moles, *Théorie de l'information et perception esthétique* (Paris: Flammarion, 1958), 116. [Translated into English as *Information Theory and Esthetic Perception* (Urbana: University of Illinois Press, 1968), 110.—Trans.]

made quite naturally among these domains. We sum these up by saying that a work of architecture is *informed* by its material just as a piece of music is. But the diversity of architectural materials has brought this phenomenon much more to the forefront. Music, which is also language, ultimately endeavors to conceal the disparity of its own materials. This is probably where the interest of comparison lies, in establishing this gradation: language rejects its material once it has been used; architecture lives in it; music forgets some of it, retains some. It is *speaking architecture.*

29.6. THE FOUR MUSICIANSHIP PROCEDURES

This comparison with music's two neighbors is therefore only fruitful in relation to the activities of the individual and not the properties of the materials. This is what corroborates our method of approach to a music theory.

Contrary to the precepts of the good Danhauser,[2] we have no intention of basing it on a particular physical property of sound, any more than a particular physical property of the ear. We have to be realistic (i.e., indeterminist) from the point of view of both the object to be heard and the structures through which it will be heard. Without going back over the reasoning in book 4, we will simply apply the conclusions of its final chapter—we will therefore refer to figure 24 in chapter 21—bringing a new descriptive approach to them.

Since, as we have said, figure 24 sums up four structuring procedures going step by step from the most general sound to what is most universally musical, we will of course find there the *four musicianship procedures* with a preliminary stage and a conclusion.

We will summarize them in turn before discussing them in the sections below.

(a) Preliminary stage (sectors I and II). We experiment on very diverse sounding bodies to discover many different factures. We record them and (except for the label, which is very useful later) we *forget all about* the origins of these sounds.

(b) First procedure: typology (sector 2). We *identify sound objects* in any sound context, and independently of their sources, using the *articulation-stress* rule. In addition, owing to the presence of criteria that are already morphological, we *sort through* the objects, enabling us to determine their *type.*

(c) Second procedure: morphology (sector 3). Once the sound objects are identified and classified through typology, we compare their *contexture.* This amounts to both identifying *component sound criteria* and *describing the sound objects as structures of these criteria.* The perceptual rule used is the *form-matter pair.* It allows us to determine the *class* of the object in relation to any one of its morphological criteria.

---

2. Adolphe Danhauser, *Théorie de la musique,* reviewed and corrected by Henri Rabaud (Paris: Lemoine, 1929).

(d) Third procedure: characterology (sectors I and II, again). Before going on to the scope of the criteria, we should point out that in reality no sound comes from just one of them. In order not to cover up this important aspect of the experiment and to make clear both the ill-assorted nature of other criteria and the combinations formed by groups of some of them, we have to go back to the *specific nature of the sounds* on which we are experimenting. This return to the concrete aspect of sound tells us the *genre of the sound* we are dealing with in relation to the sound bodies in sector I and the factures in sector II. But whereas in traditional music these references were causal, here they are only indicative, labeling the causality of the sounds whose *character we are about to analyze.*

(e) Fourth procedure: musical analysis (sector 4). In the knowledge that the experiment will always be clogged up with disparate, undesirable criteria, we must go on to compare and contrast *criteria-bearing* objects with the aim of using these to explore the *properties of the perceptual field.* As in theory these objects have been identified at the morphological stage, this will involve evaluating the site and caliber of a particular criterion—that is, the structures in the perceptual field that could lend themselves to ordinal or cardinal calibrations.

(f) Epilogue—Synthesis of musical structures: Music theory and instrumentarium in sector I. We will now compare these last two procedures: on the one hand, we know the *character of the sounds* and *what sources produce them;* on the other hand, we have deciphered the perceptual structures for the criteria despite the disparity of the other criteria. So all that remains to be done is to make syntheses, the aim of which is consistently to draw out a particular music from a particular instrumentarium or, again, to link *a theory of musical structures to a practice in timbres and registers.* Here we are no longer dealing with instrumental variations in the traditional orchestra, which all more or less conform to the timbre-pitch relationship; the question is to make a particular sort of music based on a fundamental relationship correlate with a particular sort of instrumental means (tablature). Our desire to mix everything together, different means and disparate musics, comes from a wish to aim for a generalized, *polymorphic* music.

We do not have the ambition to take the reader all the way. Just as we have been reserved about the preliminary stages, so we will be about the epilogue. It is already important that we have caught a glimpse of it. We do not at present have enough results to be sure about anything concerning possible or desirable syntheses.

We should say finally that even if this treatise seems to be borne out by experimental results where sound is concerned, what it is attempting to achieve musically is still only a rough draft. In other words, even if the conclusions of the first two procedures can be presented with confidence, the aims of the next two are presented much more at the stage of working hypotheses. We do not think we need to apologize for this. It will take decades or centuries. . . . The important thing for other researchers is to have the benefit of a method.

29.7. TYPOLOGICAL RECAPITULATION (SECTOR 2)

We notice that we have transformed the *most concrete section*, where there were only specific sounds, into *an extremely abstract* classification system. In fact, except for the two typological classification criteria we do not need to know anything else about these sounds. The only pertinent or distinctive identification features at this level are *sustainment* and *intonation*.

We did, however, go a little further. At the level of typology we not only separated objects out, but we categorized them using a method of classification for which we retained important, already *morphological*, criteria. So it will be no surprise that when describing objects we must state their *type*.

29.8. MORPHOLOGICAL CRITERIA (SECTOR 3)

These were briefly mentioned in chapter 22, insofar as these concepts were already going to play a part in typology: criteria of matter (section 22.8), form and sustainment (section 22.9), and development (section 22.10). In the last section we pointed out the difficulty of studying evolving sounds, which do not at all lend themselves to an analysis based on matter and form and which, in any case, it would be wishful thinking to try to describe using the combination of criteria that emerge from a study of deponent sounds.

This difficulty will continue to weigh on the whole of the music theory, just as it has influenced the evolution of all music; thus, the traditional system manifestly tends to eliminate these criteria, which resist all classification. How can we who reject such convenient solutions classify them without falling back into the error of the mathematicians of music, who with no compunction lump together now elementary stimuli, now formal values?

The reader will allow that our position is more subtle:

- By taking deponent examples chosen from a sufficiently large range of sounds, we are already considerably extending a mode of description that until now was reduced to identifying physical parameters or the three values recognized by the conservatories.
- While mentally recombining certain fundamental criteria, we keep constantly in mind that this synthesis will be valid only after it has been verified. This is probably the case with the slowly evolving sounds mentioned in chapter 14.
- Then, considering the criteria either as they have been recombined into characteristics or through testing them in the perceptual field against disparate criteria, we consistently call on *a specific musical and sound experience*, which alone will have the last word.

Finally, by keeping the aim to create syntheses as an "epilogue," we are showing that nothing in the absolute can be deduced from the analytical approach; it merely gives the elements for a prognosis.

With these reservations made and kept in mind, the way is now clear for us to draw out the main morphological criteria for a music theory of extreme examples.

29.9. MUSIC THEORY OF EXTREME EXAMPLES: DEPONENT SOUND OBJECTS

(a) Criterion of matter: mass.

Formless sounds, which remain the same from one end of their duration to the other, have no *dynamics* and no *variation of matter* (X or Hx sounds on fig. 34). Clearly, for the study of such sounds, which exclude all sorts of other musical values or characteristics, we will refer to the *criteria of mass* (and grain).

(b) Criterion of form.

As soon as we move on to sounds that have a form in duration, we are immediately dealing with a far greater number of objects. We could initially limit ourselves to the *forms of the masses* that remain *relatively fixed in the tessitura*—that is, a study of the criterion of *dynamic forms* (including the study of allure).

(c) Criterion of sustainment.

Sustainment links form and matter at every moment. It gives the object original features: grain and allure, which could just as well be perceived as criteria of matter and form respectively.

(d) Criterion of variation.

Overall, musical objects may *present variations of the above criteria*, in particular a variation of mass in the tessitura, most often in association with a dynamic form.

The next step, therefore, in light of these essential morphological criteria, is to attempt the following sequence, which prefigures the sequence in the next chapters:

(a) Theory of *homogeneous sounds*, analyzed through the criterion of *mass* (chap. 30).

(b) Theory of sounds with *fixed mass*, but which have a form that comes under a *dynamic* criterion (chap. 31).

(c) Theory of *sustainment*, that is, the features that link form and matter: criterion of *grain* and *allure* (chap. 32).

(d) Theory of sounds that do not fit into the preceding simplified categories *(a)* and *(b)*, through a specific study of the criteria of *variation* (chap. 33).

(e) Recapitulation of findings and examination of criteria applicable to the analysis of the musical object in its *most general form* (chap. 34).

29.10. MUSICAL ANALYSIS OF THE
CRITERIA (SECTOR 4)

We still need to clarify our definition of *criterion*, since until now we have relied on examples and comparisons to explain this term.

We should start by making clear that these criteria are properties of the perceived sound object, the correlate of *reduced listening*, and not measurable properties of physical sound. Our experiments on the perception of pitch compared to frequencies, duration compared to time, and intensities in contrast with levels are enough to remind us that these two domains must not be confused.[3]

It should also be noted that some of the criteria we have defined do not correspond to any simple acoustic parameter: this is the case with grain, thickness, volume, and allure, which, however, it is easy to isolate and bring to the attention of a listener. We must give these a place in the theory: an *acoulogy*, which must not be confused with the study of the physical object or of the pertinent features of conventional musical structures.

We will now focus on this latter distinction between criterion and value.

Values, as we have seen, are immediately obvious to the musical mind, to the point of appearing as absolute properties of objects. In reality they only appear as such if certain conditions are fulfilled, that is, if the objects are part of a musical structure, which itself presupposes permanence of characteristics between comparable objects, as well as differentiation of values. Conversely, criteria seem to be apparent only after a whole labor of abstraction and when attention is deliberately turned toward a particular quality of the object that would otherwise not have been immediately obvious to perception. The mind and the memory are therefore necessary to identify the same property in very different contexts.

---

3. Acousticians themselves agree on this. We could point out that the two *additional* qualities (apart from level and pitch) attributed to simple sounds by Stevens (*volume* and *density*) essentially depend on the *sound structure* in use; indeed, it is in their work that we find the beginnings of what they call the *psychological dimensions* of sound in the same way as with sight, where experimenters were deeply disturbed by the fact that a piece of coal under a very bright light still appeared darker than a sheet of white paper under a weak light, which caused Woodworth to say, "It is almost impossible for a normal man in possession of all his faculties to see the image his eyes present to him. . . . On removing from the perception of colors the illusory appearances of the objects that carry them, we still find three *dimensions* of sensation (shade, brightness, and saturation), whereas a homogeneous light is perfectly well defined by the two physical dimensions of intensity and frequency." Robert S. Woodworth, *Psychologie expérimentale* (Paris: PUF, 1949). [Original title in English is *Experimental Psychology* (Oxford: Holt, 1939).—Trans.]

Finally, we should note how much more advanced the psychology of light perception is than sound perception and to what extent "intriguing problems" have been acknowledged in this field. The confusions between music and acoustics are very unlikely to pose a threat to the visual domain, which is infinitely better perceived, if not understood.

Is this contrast clear-cut, however? Surely the fact that a criterion can be identified in different sound contexts implies a permanence-variation dialectic comparable to the one that gives rise to values? Our sample of grains goes from the coarse to the velvety; our sounds are more or less thick, our allures more or less close together. And more naturally still, surely it is the variation of a criterion occurring in the duration of a single object that guides us in our perception of it? Will grain dominate from one end of a sound to the other? Will that allure be maintained, or will it relax? That thickness become wider or narrower?

At this point we come back to a mode of perception that is still analytical but just as spontaneous as in classical structures. This is hardly surprising: we have already pointed out that an isolated object can be analyzed in *contexture*. Then it forms a microstructure, which has its own unity, its own continuity, and its own time envelope, and it is in relation to this structure that criteria are then identified, just as values were earlier in relation to the context of a group of objects.

Even if these criteria, which vary in the course of the duration of an object, rarely appear in traditional music, they are just as much part of it.

In what space do they vary? Within the dimensions of a perceptual field, the seat of the musical mind, which we have mentioned several times and which it is now time to explain.

29.11. THE THREE DIMENSIONS OF THE MUSICAL PERCEPTUAL FIELD

We return to the paradox of the invariant mentioned in section 21.7. Listen to an object as classical as a fairly slow violin glissando. What is the dominant criterion at every moment of the sound? Pitch. What varies? Pitch again. Within what space does it vary? In the pitch field. These are the two meanings defined in section 21.14: pitch as the criterion that describes a sound and pitch as a dimension of the sound field. Surely this example would be disturbing only if it were the only one. In that case people would thank us for sparing them a concept, rather than complicating things. But the same is true of a profile and for the rhythm of the pulsations in a grain or an allure. The loudness of a sound, the criterion of intensity, evolves in the dynamic field, just as a grain or an allure, which are modulations of duration, can evolve in duration. So here we have three *uncouplings* of the qualities of sound, depending on whether they are present as an *identification criterion* or a *dimension of the variation of the sound*. But there are more complex criteria where the distinction will stand out even more. A *thick sound* does, indeed, present a distinct criterion—that is, the perception of an original quality so independent of the criterion of *pitch* that it is precisely the criterion of thickness that prevents the sound being heard as tonic. But then if we manage to describe the thickness (which is by no means certain), surely it will be referred back to the pitch field? If the thickness becomes wider or narrower in duration, or if it remains the same and evolves toward the low or high register, surely we will still be obliged to situate its variation in the pitch field?

So we can see two ways of comparing and contrasting criteria, depending on whether the experiment will be done in the *discontinuity of a context* or the *continuity of a contexture*—that is, whether the criteria are artificially *put into a structure* or naturally *form a structure*.

(a) Structure of calibrations of criteria in the field of discrete sound objects

Comparing the different states of the same criterion in various objects, we try to make "experimental reels" that may lead to calibrations. We would then be tempted to say that we are returning to the values-characteristics formula, where the criterion does, indeed, play the part of shared characteristic and where its different modules illustrate the values it takes on. We have just seen the difference. It is in one sense a musical structure, but it is one that is no longer spontaneously perceived; this structure is observed deliberately for the purposes of analysis, valid for an *acoulogy* but not transferable into music as it stands. The "module-criterion" relationship is therefore infinitely more fragile and unstable than the value-characteristic formula. Conversely, values, like characteristics, are not "acoulogically" simple: they are musically balanced "bundles of criteria."

(b) Perception of a criterion varying in the contexture of a single object

This involves a listening mode that is less artificial, although still part of an analytical description. But it is only valid for varying criteria. If this is not the case, the comparison of different states of a criterion can only be made as above.

In conclusion, it seems to us to be possible, ultimately, to link together the two sorts of results. Then we discover seven main criteria that differ in their variants of class and type. Opposite them, giving them a field of variation, it seems to us that there are only three musical dimensions, which once more must not be confused with acoustic parameters. We cannot, however, deny the very strong correlation between the perceptual field and the physical dimensions of sound, in other words, the objective powers of the ear. Yet we must repeat that the perceptual dimensions, even if they are reduced to the three types of evaluation—pitch, duration, and intensity—do not coincide either fundamentally or numerically with the reference trihedron of acoustics: frequency, time, and level. Finally, we cannot prejudge musical effect by recombining criteria. Music, in its largely unpredictable structures, is ultimately an art of perceiving.

29.12. FINAL DIAGRAM FOR THE THEORY:
TYPES, CLASSES, GENRES, SPECIES OF SOUNDS

In our eagerness to investigate the sound field, which ultimately brings together all the potentialities of music, we have neglected one of the four procedures involved in the theory defined in section 29.6. We had said, however, that before conducting these two sorts of experiments—perception of a structure of criteria in the discontinuity of a collection of objects and perception of the variations of a criterion in the continuity of a single object—we would first need to know what *genre* of sound we were dealing with. For the analysis of this field, the field of sector 4, to be carried out under the best conditions, we would, in fact, need a better understanding of what bundles, in real sounds, form the criteria to which the criterion under study belongs; in other words, we would need to know the *characterology* of the real sounds (sector I). This is far from being the case. The contents of the higher sectors can only develop through a series of approximations. So we can only refer to our practical knowledge of sound bodies (sector I) and factures (sector II) to give a crude description of the links between criteria through what we know about morphologies; thus, an attack, and a continuous sustainment on a particular sound body with known acoustic properties, will unfailingly link the mass of the sound to its sustainment, the dynamic to the melodic profiles, and so forth. Without these reference points our analysis would be unrealistic, as our attempts at abstraction need to rest on a well-stocked *sound bank*.

After deciding the *type* and *class* of the sound with which we are dealing, the theory will therefore concentrate on determining the *genre of the sound* from the main examples of combined criteria in sound and musical reality. It is only once this third theoretical procedure has been completed that we can move on to evaluating individual species.

With regard to this analysis, in sector 4 we come across the same two questions that were raised in the traditional sector IV about describing values musically. Situating a criterion is one thing, calibrating it quite another.

We have already pointed out the difference between these two sorts of evaluation, one precise, the other vague, rather like the perception of color. The very complex diagram in chapter 34 will summarize these four ways of classifying sounds, by type, class, genre, and species.[4]

29.13. ANALOGICAL CRITERIA

We could indeed find this method austere and ultimately very empirical, since we have already admitted that the sound references we will give illustrate not only *genres of sound* but also types of factures, classes of criteria, and the way they occur in or can be calibrated into particular species. Yes, but at least we will not be going outside the domain of music as we pursue a more and more rigorous strategy of comparing and contrasting, a structural discipline.

---

4. This diagram (fig. 41), in section 34.3, which is called the "Summary Diagram of the Theory of Musical Objects," will be quoted frequently in the following chapters, under the shortened name of "general diagram" or "section 34.3." The boxes in this diagram have two numbers: the first indicates the row (criterion), the second the column (type, class, genre, species).

Might there be other, less laborious, more straightforward, ways of tackling the description of sound and the musical? By using analogy, for example, as we do every day to talk about sounds. What do we say, for example, about a voice? That it is "clipped," "piercing," "harsh," "shrill," "dull," "drab," "caustic," "strained," "flat," "metallic." . . . The adjectives referring to a "vocal color" are a little less trivial: "colorful," "clear," "dark," "monotonous." . . . Then there are the tautologies: "with tone," "without tone" . . ., the metaphors: "piping," "ringing," "incisive" . . ., images from physics: "warm," "cold" . . ., from dimensions: "large," "small," "tiny," "thin," and so on.

In reality, going back to analogy is a sign of defeat. It simply shows our basic inability to describe an object *in itself*, separate from any structure. If we refuse to refer this sound or that voice to other sound objects, the only solution is to go and find references elsewhere, in other domains of perception or thought: sight, the kinesthetic sense, thought, and so forth. We will not entirely reject this vocabulary, although it is irremediably imprecise. But it is important for us to point out the alternatives: *talking indirectly about the sound* (analogy); talking about the *sound* itself, through comparison (collections, structures, calibrations).

We should note in passing that the physicist uses analogy as well. He is quick to talk about the "form," the "amplitude," the "height," the "volume," the "density" of a sound, ideas that he nevertheless intends to isolate from the object as absolute qualities or quantities. Then he also compares sounds with one another: when he draws curves, when he makes measurements, he also is doing nothing other than forming analytical structures for the purpose of calibrating a perception that has been as simplified as possible. . . . It was perhaps not pointless to remind the reader of this role played by all vocabularies, including the vocabulary of physics: they are simply men of straw.

Finally, in the verbal fireworks display of artistic or scientific analogical words, we can recognize three of our four procedural pathways:

1. We do not, of course, find typological terms, which involve a quite artificial abstraction of sound. But we have ourselves chosen analogical terms for abstract concepts: *cell, sample, accumulation*, and so forth.

2. *Round, sharp, large, small, tiny, thin* are all morphological terms, as are *tense* and *flat*. They denote forms just as much as "factures," specified as incisive, stressed, piercing, and so on.

3. *Metallic, ringing, shrill*, like the tautology "tone-toneless," suggest genres of sound, emphasizing the allusion to instruments.

4. *Light* and *dark*, like *warm* and *cold*, are of course analogies that, as in sector 4, find an equivalent to musical dimensions in the registers of color or temperature. In the same way, physicists' *height* and *level* are also spatial analogies; *intensity* and *strength* kinesthetic analogies.

The difficulties we have in agreeing on a metalanguage are not confined to us. They apparently occur in all fundamental research. Therefore, the words we choose will not be more important than the symbols of traditional theory: what counts is not so much the contents of each word as the experiential field it delineates in relation to other words. This vocabulary is a mode of classification, and its only aim is to guide particular types of comparisons between musical objects, possibly to give rise to others. Its relevance will not be judged through reading or ideological dissension but through listening. The words in every theory are checks, which only our experience of sounds can fund.

30

Theory of Homogeneous Sounds

Criterion of Mass

30.1. EXPERIMENTAL MATERIAL

The most well-defined, most rigorous, and most easily analyzed typology of homogeneous sounds is often the most difficult to find materials for in practice: we need sounds that remain the same through time. They have no form, contribute no new information in the course of their duration. We accept sounds of this type from any origin, traditionally musical or not. So we will find sounds that are or are not tonic but, generally speaking, no noises (which in most cases are certainly not without form). The most ordinary, least-interesting example is electronic white noise, with which everyone is familiar: this is what in the studio or in electronic technology is called "hiss." It is, indeed, a homogeneous sound, the exact opposite of tonic sound (as it occupies the whole tessitura): for statistical reasons every moment of listening is the same as the one before. These circumstances are to some extent reproduced in applause, water falling, or pebbles being poured out—indeed, in any agglomeration of sounds provided they are varied enough and their distribution in the tessitura and time follows the laws of chance. The accumulation of all the sounds in the world would doubtless be a white noise, which explains our distaste for this perfect disorder.

If we only had the scale of traditional sounds and the vagueness of white or similar noise (even when they are cut into "slices" of so-called colored white noise by filters) to explain the concept of mass, we should not get very far. This doubtless explains why mass is so underrepresented as a sound criterion. What is so poorly perceived, however, is glaringly obvious. Despite their nominal pitch, some of the most traditional sounds, such as tonic sounds, incontrovertibly present masses that are not perceived as occurring at discrete points. The low notes of an organ, for example, or a sustained double bass or bassoon note compared to middle-register or high notes on the same instruments, or other instruments on the same tonic, already suggest the term *mass* rather than *pitch*.

A tonic sounds on the note but is a bulk in the tessitura: physicists' frame of reference for the spectrum cannot tell us whether our ear can detect a certain *thickness* in the sound, apart from its nominal frequency. Suppose we play three or four adjacent notes in the medium or high register of the piano: does this package have a greater or smaller mass than a single low sound? Even if the answer is inconclusive, the question still has meaning: mass is a perceptual criterion.

Then we could think up some comparisons. Since we are able to cut out slices of white noise through filtering, could we not compare the above sounds with these thickness samples? Such an experiment, seductive in its simplicity, nearly always comes up against differences of genre: we perceive here a fundamental, crowned, as we say, with a *thick* timbre, there a package of frequencies without timbre. In fact, comparisons like these amount to asking ourselves to compare an invertebrate with a vertebrate. So there are several *classes*, or *genres*, of massive sounds.

In the sense of prose composition we could think of constructing thick sounds on a predetermined model. Thus, Luc Ferrari built up superimposed layers of sustained violin sounds that formed perfectly homogeneous wefts. Why "wefts"? people will ask. Aren't they chords? We must be very clear about the word. We can use the term *chord* as long as there is a possible resolution—even a difficult one—into constituent musical objects. As soon as resolution is impossible, it is because a new perceptual criterion has appeared. Contemporary music is full of these false chords, these packages of notes written on the score with the greatest care but that in the overwhelming majority of cases the ear clearly cannot resolve. The works we are thinking of are therefore not based on the nominal pitches of these notes but on the mass of the sound objects created in this way. It is better to acknowledge this state of affairs and use the term *mass* than to pretend to hear what no one can any longer perceive. But how?

By way of introduction to and illustration of our discussion, we will examine how far and with what vocabulary musicians and physicists deal with sound qualities that do not come directly from classical scales or measurements.

30.2. ANALOGICAL CRITERIA FROM TRADITIONAL MUSICAL EXPERIENCE

When evaluating tonic sounds, musicians habitually describe them using the following analogies:

1. Their *volume*. Generally speaking, a high sound will seem less extensive than a low sound. But, again, a clarinet sound will appear "narrower" than a flute sound of the same pitch. Here we come back to the dimension of amplitude,

independently of the tonic quality, which gives us to understand that all tonic sounds are discrete.

2. Their timbre, which will be *dark* or *light*. *Timbre* here denotes a quality of the notes and does not refer to the instrument; thus, a violin or a voice can sound light or dark. We would say that here timbre is understood as a value and not a characteristic. We can say, however, that the bassoon is generally dark, while the oboe is light.

3. A musician will also say of a sound that it is *rich* or *poor*. These qualifiers will be applied equally to the timbre, with the same ambiguity as above. A singer can produce sounds that are hollow or full, with or without timbre. The flute has a poorer timbre than the clarinet. What does this mean, except that we can perceive a greater or lesser complexity, a fuller or less-full texture?

4. It may happen that even a *rich* timbre does not *come across*, is *muffled*, has no radiance, no *brilliance*. And so we say that a violin or a voice *comes across* to a greater or lesser extent, probably depending on whether the partials reinforce each other when the sound is produced or whether it strikes the ear that receives it in the registers where it is most sensitive.

30.3. SCIENTIFIC CRITERIA: ADDITIONAL PROPERTIES OF PURE SOUNDS

We intend to "reclaim" some work done by physicists on sensations, which seems to have been totally forgotten by even the most acoustics-obsessed musicians, set on retaining only the three perceptual dimensions of frequency, level, and time in pure sound. If they had done their homework, they would know that experimenters such as Rich, Stumpf, James, Koehler, and, more recently, Gundlach and Bentley, Zoll, Halverson, Dimminck, and finally Stevens, have kept up a continuous inquiry into properties of pure sounds other than pitch, intensity, and duration. These authors acknowledge the existence of additional qualities because of the fact that the properties of perception depend as much on the characteristics of the receiving system as the stimulus: so we are indeed dealing with objective properties, but they are highly likely to elude experimentation, owing to the imprecision of analogies and the conditioning that the listeners we consult about them cannot avoid undergoing. It is not so much the quantitative results of this research that interest us here but the curiosity that motivated physicists, without being explicitly aware of it, to take an approach similar to experimental music, though still applied to the least suitable material: pure sound.

The work to which we allude, summarized by Woodworth, concludes that, putting aside duration, simple (sine wave) sounds have the following qualities:

1. Sound strength (intensity) increasing with the level (decibels or phons), and at equal level varying in a complex manner with the frequency (Fletcher's curves);

2. Pitch, rising with the frequency, and perceptibly, although to a lesser degree, affected by the level;

3. Volume, increasing with the level, and at equal level diminishing with the frequency;

4. Density, increasing with both the frequency and the level.

More precisely, where pitches are concerned, physicists distinguish two sorts of calibration, depending on whether the evaluation is *harmonic*, by comparing simultaneous tonics, or *melodic*, when the sounds are heard successively and outside the harmonic context (we then obtain the calibration in *mels*). In the first case the main reference points (octaves) are repeated over increasing frequencies as powers of 2; in the second (mels) octaves are ignored and the sound spectrum is considered in its entirety as a sort of fabric more or less stretched out from the lowest to the highest register. In practice these two types of evaluation almost coincide in the medium register and diverge in the low and high: from the point of view of mels, the high octave of the piano is worth only "half" a medium octave; this proportion becomes even smaller in the very highest register (see section 10.7).

We find, however, that with increases judged to be equal, the qualities of volume and density are linked to inverse variations of frequency (see fig. 35): at equal intensity the participant finds a low sound "more voluminous, less dense" than a high sound; for him to judge them to be of equal density, the low sound must have a greater intensity than the high sound; finally, these sounds do not seem to him to have the same volume until the high sound is louder than the low sound.

What are we to make of these observations? First we note that they are all expressed in a vocabulary of analogies that finds its origin in references that are only "notionally" auditory. Here, however, we can distinguish two situations: in the first the analogical terms continue an established tradition, terms such as *pitch* and *intensity*. We can hardly reproach an experimenter for using abstract terminology so widely employed in so many other fields of sensory or kinesthetic activity. In the second situation the analogy is far-fetched, and we may question its real value and effectiveness: what characterizes the concept of volume compared to density, and how can we so easily separate these perceptions from the notion of intensity? Surely these qualities are much more linked to a mode of operation? This would not be at all surprising, as we know that structural relationships depend on the order and frame of reference of the comparisons.

To clarify our thoughts, it may be useful to compare them with a remark by Stevens on the results we have mentioned above:

> So we are faced with four types of different responses, the result of the interaction between a two-dimensional acoustic stimulus and a multidimensional neuroperceptual system. The method used in these experiments gives the participant a role rather like a measuring device detecting zero: the instructions given to him at the start of

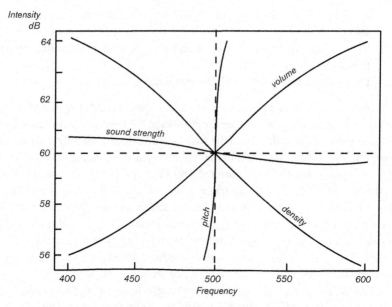

FIGURE 35. Densities and volumes of pure sounds. Relationships between volume, sound strength, density, and pitch at different frequencies, this being compensated for by a difference in the intensity of the stimulus. The rectangular framework represents the physical dimensions of intensity and frequency, the curves indicating the relationships when the volume, density, etc. are equal. With the curve labeled volume, read, for example, that according to the average from several participants the following stimuli gave sounds of equal volume: 400 cycles at 56 dB; 450 cycles at 58 dB; 500 cycles at 60 dB; 550 cycles at 62 dB, or thereabouts; 600 cycles at 63.5 dB, approx. Same reading for the other curves. Thus a sound of about 508 cycles at 64 dB is considered the same pitch as the standard 500 cycles at 60 dB. (Adapted from Stanley Smith Stevens, "The Attributes of Tones," *Proceedings of the National Academy of Sciences of the United States of America* 20, no. 7 [1934].)

the experiment "tune" and "condition" him to detect differences in a particular field of his domain; then he adjusts the stimulus until the difference disappears. What we must point out is that the participant can respond in four different ways. The fact that each type of instruction may lead to a response that is a function of the two physical variables of the stimuli may make us think of a two-dimensional type of experiment; but the fact that there are four different responses shows that we should be able to find at least four characteristic pathways in the nervous system at the exit from the cochlea.[1]

1. Stanley Smith Stevens, "The Attributes of Tones," *Proceedings of the National Academy of Sciences of the United States of America* 20, no. 7 (1934): 459.

In our eyes, however, these experiments and the results obtained have the advantage of using objective methods to underline ways of perceiving sound that are mostly or totally ignored by those who wish to find "scientific" support for a particular aesthetic theory; and so, it seems to us, they open up a point of contact with the interests of the experimental musician.

30.4. METHOD OF APPROACH

It was perhaps necessary to refer back to the problems raised by musicians and physicists, and the specific terms used in their inquiries, in order to put our approach more fully into context.

Far from refining instrumental timbres, or the somewhat uncommon subtleties of the perception of pure frequencies, we are extending our field of investigation into sounds in general, and we intend to cover the groundwork on what we call the *criterion of mass in homogeneous sounds* by making a large number of comparisons, as we have already stated several times:

1. By comparing all possible sounds we have defined general *types* of sound masses (cf. Typology).

2. How do these perceptions divide into musical *classes* when we examine homogeneous sounds in general?

3. How do they most frequently group together to form musical *characteristics* of mass, which we will assign to different *genres* of homogeneous sounds?

4. How, where *species* are concerned, can these criteria of mass be *situated* or *calibrated* in relation to the scales of the musical field?

30.5. HARMONIC TIMBRE AND MASS

There are two extreme examples, as we saw at the beginning of this chapter: the tonic sound of musicians and the white noise or colored sound from electronic generators. We have called what continues throughout duration *matter*, in tonic sound as well as white noise, and obviously in all intermediate cases (cymbals and sustained notes, packages of indistinguishable notes, etc.).

At the end of numerous experiments on sounds we propose that listening to sound matter should be conducted with these criteria: a mass criterion properly speaking, a *harmonic timbre* criterion (as distinct from timbre in the sense of instrumental source),[2] and, finally, a grain criterion subsuming sustainment. We will look at this last point in chapter 32.

---

2. Throughout this chapter the word *timbre* will always be used in the sense of "harmonic timbre."

We will use the term *mass* for the quality through which sound installs itself (in a somewhat a priori fashion) in the pitch field, and *timbre* for the more or less diffuse halo and more generally the secondary qualities that seem to be associated with mass and enable us to describe it. This is an approximate, entirely empirical, distinction that, as we will see, allows for all sorts of osmoses. Our aim is precisely to proceed by a series of approximations, not by setting up dogmatic categories. How, then, do we apply these concepts?

- with traditional tonic sounds we quite naturally distinguish between pitch and timbre: so we return fleetingly to tradition;
- with pure sounds the analogies chosen to indicate the associated qualities mentioned above, volume and density, are linked to their mass;
- in most cases, nontonic sounds, mass is less easy to perceive, but *what we do not locate* as an integral part of mass is still a timbre, and this is so whatever the listener's training or the sound context. In effect, depending on his level of skill, his attentiveness, and also the environment of the object presented to him, the listener can distinguish between mass and timbre in a whole variety of ways. For example, a bell will be situated at a different pitch (evaluation of mass) depending on the tonic with which it is compared; or again, it will seem to be composed of tonic or complex sounds (of indeterminate pitch) depending on the listener's aptitude for unraveling clusters of sound. Similarly a metal sheet giving a homogeneous sound can seem to be a confused mass or, on the contrary, a superimposition of tonic or vague components, with the whole perhaps surmounted by a high-register harmonic with its own particular timbre.

Consequently we intend to use the two criteria of *mass* and *harmonic timbre* in conjunction with each other, considering them rather as connecting vessels, with the exception of certain specific examples where the attribution seems beyond doubt given the classical nature of the sounds and the strength of listening habits. (We know, however, that for Helmholtz timbre and mass actually did "communicate" if he could indeed resolve a tonic into its harmonic partials.)

30.6. CLASSES OF MASS IN HOMOGENEOUS SOUNDS

We will distinguish seven classes of homogeneous sounds (fig. 36; cf. fig. 41, box 12).[3] At the two extremes we will put sounds with pure frequency (class 1) and white noise (class 7): the sounds best and least suited to the perception of pitch. Roughly,

---

3. "Box 12" refers to Schaeffer's "Summary Diagram of the Theory of Musical Objects" in chapter 34.3. The first numeral in "box 12" refers to row 1 (Mass), and the second refers to column 2 (Classes). The box formed at the intersection of this row and column is "box 12" (i.e., box one-two). Schaeffer uses this system in his explanation of how figure 41 should be interpreted.—Trans.

Classes	MASS TEXTURE	HARMONIC TIMBRE TEXTURE	PITCH DIMENSIONS DEGREES
1	Pure sound	nonexistent	
2	Tonic sound	tonic	
3	tonic group	channeled or continuous tonic	
4	channeled	complex or continuous	
5	nodal group	complex or continuous	
6	nodal sound	complex or continuous	
7	white or colored noise	nonexistent	COLOR

FIGURE 36. Classes of textures of mass and harmonic timbre.

we could say that toward the top of the figure the listener's reactions will be in keeping with traditional musical conditioning (harmonic intervals, successive octaves) and toward the bottom, in accordance with the calibration in mels that we spoke about above (here, to refer to his perceptions, he will use analogies—for example the "white noise" image—since no term from traditional theory will help). We should point out that these two modes of perceiving pitch are *independent*, and we should not expect to find examples where perception follows an intermediate law; rather, in doubtful cases, we will obtain two sorts of *simultaneous* perceptions.

A cymbal clash gives a sound similar to white noise, centered on a particular zone of the tessitura: *nodal* sounds such as these will be situated above the box for white noise (6). Tonics on traditional instruments, less pure than sinusoidal sounds and colored with a characteristic timbre, will be placed symmetrically below the box for pure frequencies (2). Several simultaneous cymbal clashes centered on different zones of the tessitura will constitute a cluster with nodal elements that can be isolated: we will call this a *nodal group* and place it above nodal sounds (5), in the same way that we will situate *tonic groups* below isolated tonics, their traditional chords, which can be resolved into their constituent notes, being the simplest example (3). Finally, a central box will be reserved for ambiguous sounds—for example, gongs, bells, metal sheets, and so forth—which, depending on the sound context, are perceived either as nodal sounds or groups of nodal sounds, some of them so narrow that they sound like tonic notes or as more or less clear tonic groups surrounded by a complex halo. Such sounds deserve to be evaluated from the point of view of both traditional intervals and color analogies. We will call them *channeled* sounds.

30.7. CHARACTERISTIC OF MASS: TEXTURE OF A SOUND

We have just seen how to perceive sound in terms of mass: typologically according to whether the sound is fixed or variable, and morphologically according to whether it is tonic, nodal, or channeled. These various classes of mass seem very general as soon as we find ourselves in front of a real sound: they crudely summarize too many sound experiences. When we move up into the sections for the musical, we ask ourselves two questions: one is about describing the criterion of mass in relation to the properties of the perceptual field, and the other is about the possibility, if not of describing particular examples, at least of identifying the main *genres* of sounds in terms of their mass.

The popular expression "a bit like" expresses this idea of the *character* of a sound very well. For it does more than name the example: piano, metal sheet, bell, electronic sound, and so forth; it generalizes it; it states that a particular sound, over and above the specific example, can present itself as representative of a general structure. If I play packages of notes that give a thick mass on the piano, I will no longer hear the tonic sounds, no longer analyze the chord, but I will do more than appreciate a width of more or less vague thickness. Between the *chord* where I resolve the tonic sounds and the *thickness* that is an admission of vagueness, I pick out a texture, a certain organization of the mass, as, for example, in a bell sound. I can compare metal sheet and bass piano, saying that the *texture* that characterizes these two sounds, which are otherwise different (in tessitura, thickness, etc.), is formed of a thick underlay, surmounted by a bright fringe . . . (whereas in the bell I perceive various nodes I can more or less situate): it is possible to perceive relationships such as these between sounds belonging to the same *genre*.

30.8. SPECIES OF MASS

We saw in section 30.3 that depending on the listening conditions, the pitch field was covered from one octave to another across repeated harmonic intervals—which is the case with traditional music—or else in a continuous fashion, in a calibration where the degrees are melodic (calibration in mels). We suggest that if the tonic notes are far enough apart to be perceived in the traditional way, this is precisely because of the presence of harmonics (not perceived in isolation, although contributing to the timbre) that put a sort of grid in the pitch field and thus give a defined context for perception; but as soon as adjacent notes are piled on top of each other, these notes and their respective spectra occupy the pitch field in too confused a manner to impose any sort of order on the ear, and then we find ourselves in the perceptual conditions for the calibration in mels. Even if it does not explain the criterion of mass, this property of the field, explored by physicists with pure sounds, at least demonstrates why in certain cases the notion of thickness replaces the notion of interval. Between these two extreme examples, each one coming under one of the two reference points in the perceptual pitch field, are sounds of ambiguous pitch: depending on context or conditioning, in these cases we hesitate between describing them as colored mass or breaking them down into a number of tonic sounds.

Thus, when contemporary musicians accumulate tonic sounds, happily mingling them with nodal sounds (gongs, cymbals, bells) while still notating everything in discrete pitches, it is a safe bet that this notation lets them down in the way it indicates harmonic intervals. They are no longer dealing with traditional reference points in the pitch field. The other mode of perception intervenes, which only has thicknesses and colors in indeterminate relationship with the reference degrees or intervals.

The experience of electronic music leads to the same thoughts. Slices of white noise of perfectly homogeneous mass are calibrated into distinct intervals: now, the accuracy of the cutting produces nothing remarkable as far as perception is concerned; it is even impossible usually for a listener to calibrate such sounds on listening to them and to situate them any more than approximately in the tessitura unless he retrains his ear, a notion that, it seems, has not even entered the heads of the electronic school. The experience of concrete music, which uses all sorts of sounds, has brought to light numerous ambiguous examples where perception functions in two distinct registers, depending on whether the sounds appear tonic or thick. Generally speaking, suitably grouped tonic notes give not a chord but a mass satisfying a criterion of thickness (which we can attempt to calibrate, but with no great accuracy) and that is situated more or less clearly in the tessitura (which we can train ourselves to locate, not in degrees but in register).

This double evaluation, in the general run of things where sounds cannot be reduced to tonics, can be defined as a particular *species* of mass—in register and in thickness. Here we are not dealing with the extreme precision of a cardinal scale but the subtleties of an ordinal series. In ambivalent cases, depending on context, only one of the two reference modes will appear appropriate, either degrees and intervals or color and register. It should be noted that we have no specialist vocabulary to describe the perceptions belonging to the second mode; this is why here we use an exclusively analogical vocabulary to talk about species of mass.

30.9. THE TWO PITCH FIELDS

So what made us think there are two sorts of field, two ways of calibrating and evaluating pitch? Were it not for the presence of various masses—either tonic or thick—such an idea could not command attention since it runs counter to any simple generalization. Similarly, physicists only had this idea when, instead of pure sounds in a harmonic context, they presented a series of *long, drawn-out melodic sounds*. But where they saw only two calibrations, they should, in fact, have seen two sorts of object-structure relationships: one discontinuous, fitting in with the idea of harmonic context, the other continuous, fitting in with the idea of melodic texture. These two markers then lead to two sorts of relationships called value-to-characteristic relationships: one is the degree-tonic relationship, the other the color-thickness relationship. From the point of view of the objects (thick or thin), the question is to go further into *characteristics;* where the field and perceptual markers are concerned, it is to define *calibrations*. In the first case we encounter the problem of pitch calibrations, which are cardinal, in the other color calibrations, which are ordinal.

We do not intend to go any further into the former. Is there anything that has not been said, written, thought, dreamed up about pitch calibrations and all their baggage: tonality, modality! We will leave it to an abundant and scholarly body of literature to develop the associated questions; as for ourselves, we will concentrate on establishing their place in perceptual reality. In fact, this raises a fundamental question, one that is often tackled in musicologists' manuals: is the scale natural or artificial? Is it the product of historical usage, linked to a tradition (and how then can the origin of such a tradition be explained), or is it determined by the sound structure of objects, where the individual person and nature, physiology, and acoustics come together?

30.10. PITCH CALIBRATIONS

When a harmonic sound is perceived, we must imagine that it occupies the ear, not just with one degree but also with all the degrees of its partials, a structure that is precisely that type of perception where synthesis is carried out spontaneously. Should another sound present itself, we easily imagine that it enters all the better into the previous grid because it occupies one of those degrees itself or, more precisely, that its spectrum leads to a perception that relies in part on the structure perceived previously. Here we are referring to the so-called phenomenon of consonance, as well as the physical-acoustic correlation between the different sounds in the scales. We will take the risk of sticking our own little oar into everything that has been said and said again on this subject.

Physicists, we have seen, attempt to explain consonance by the absence of irritating beats. This is a very flimsy explanation because it is in the area of consonance—when, for example, two tuning forks are very near to being in tune—that beats are most clearly heard; now, in music there is never absolutely precise consonance in the physical sense of the term; moreover, if this were the case, temperament would be impossible. This apparent paradox has led many musicians to consider temperament as a dreadful compromise, indispensable but regrettable, a sort of original sin. These two attitudes seem neither realistic nor genuine. Consonance is explained intuitively by the partial superimposition of the spectra of the different sounds in a chord. And for this to be done statistically in the best possible way, a tempered scale has to be found—not sin, at all, but the salvation of the system!

In reality, if we run quickly through the famous names still associated if not with the invention at least with the defining of scales, we can see the same musical intention: to find, unsuccessfully as it happens in the case of Pythagoras and Zarlino, the square of the circle: temperament!

30.11. TEMPERAMENT

Convinced, intuitively and not without reason, that there is of necessity a relationship between the degrees of the scale and the successive partials, these ancestors of experimental music, as we know, are confronting a very simple but very insoluble arithmetical problem.[4] Pythagoras starts from the sequence of fifths and at the twelfth jump, after F, C, G, D, A, E, B, then the series of sharps, the last fifth (E-sharp) does not fall accurately as the seventh octave of the initial F: the scale does not resolve. Zarlino also starts from fifths and shrewdly places them at the two ends of the perfect chord (the third being obtained by lowering two octaves of the fifth harmonic, thus in the relationship 5/4 with the tonic). Two perfect chords attached in this way to C, E, G, one lower with C as the dominant, the other higher with G as the tonic, give seven notes, which are:

4. We would remind anyone who is doubtful about this explanation that it rests on that structural truism: there are no (harmonic) intervals except in a relationship of tonics (themselves harmonic). This little formula seems to us to give incontrovertible proof of the natural validity of simple relationships, by virtue of a reciprocal similarity between human psychophysiology and the acoustics of sound bodies.

	F	A	C	E	G	B	D
in relationship with C taken as a unit as follows:	2/3	5/6	1	5/4	3/2	15/8	9/4

arising from the same proportions (1, 5/4, 3/2) applied to the two other perfect chords; hence Zarlino's scale:

	C	D	E	F	G	A	B
corresponding to the relationships:	1	9/8	5/4	4/3	3/2	5/3	15/8.

We need to find the middle way. Is the A obtained in this way the same as the A in the fifth of D? The latter would be 3/2 of D (i.e., 27/16). Now compare this fraction with the 5/3 that establishes the A in Zarlino's scale; the fractions 27/16 and 5/3 are as 81/48 and 80/48, and this is the notorious comma of difference between the two As 1/81 away from each other. The only rational solution required a so-called irrational number, unknown to the Ancients: the twelfth root of 2—that is, the number that multiplied twelve times by itself gives 2—enables the octave to be restored.

If we compare this now practicable scale with Zarlino's, we can see that the tempered fifth is moved nearer by 1 savart (i.e., 1/300 of an octave or 1/25 of a semitone); the fourth is accurate; the third and the sixth are moved nearer by about 3 savarts (roughly 1/8 of a semitone).

We can easily understand that marking out the harmonic field does not follow a superstition, a myth of simple relationships. An approximation is just as good for this purpose, the twelfth root of 2, the generator of a system that is approximate but remarkably well-suited to instruments, as well as to the human ear.

An instrument tuned in this way has every chance of making its entire string system resonate, as does the piano, because of the latitude of sympathetic phenomena. For its part, the ear doubtless adapts perfectly well to the fact that from the very first fifth everything is approximate, provided that the other sounds fit comfortably into the same grid. This is doubtless what explains both the necessity of temperament and its success since Bach. We can also see how far other musics get it wrong in terms of excess or default—some through being too scrupulous with a too precisely harmonic system, which unsurprisingly deprives them of harmony (India), others through a lack of instrumental rigor that only achieves approximate and limited degrees in calibrations of pitch (Africa).

30.12. CRITERION OF HARMONIC TIMBRE: CLASSES AND CHARACTERISTICS

Because of the mutual interdependence of perceptions of mass and timbre we will find *classes* for harmonic timbres that *complement* classes of mass. For masses in class 1 and 7 (pure frequencies or bands of frequency): a nonexistent timbre. For tonic masses in class 2: a "tonic" timbre. For nodes (classes 6 and 5), the timbre, as we have said, constitutes the "rest" of the sound, what is not described in the mass, and is often the subject of a later analysis (complex timbre): it can thus conceal practically unperceived channelings, unless the node, perfectly fused together as in a cymbal, is inseparable from it: we could say that then the timbre is merged or "continuous." A sound that is itself channeled will be heard as timbre for the halo, which is not analyzed: this halo will present further channelings or a continuous timbre, depending on how far the analysis is taken or whether the masses are more or less well fused together. Finally, a group of tonic sounds can present a continuous, even harmonic, timbre depending on the texture of the chord and its instruments.

But in certain cases and within certain limits timbre remains independent of mass. If a violin plays a note, then two or three notes close together, it is the mass of the sound that will become thicker, without the timbre appearing to change, nor does the timbre appear to change if the violin plays with double stopping. Conversely, we only have to refer to the interplay of harmonics and unisons in stringed instruments to highlight all sorts of refined and clearly apparent interactions of timbres. Also, when we refer to differences in timbre between an open string, a vibrato, and a harmonic, we are clearly talking about the different characteristics of a violin's timbre. Here we need only quote those who have witnessed this.

Can we take the study of characteristics further by using acoustic correlations? Could we take up some work done by physicists for this? Certainly, at this precise point in our discussion, we can discuss the characterology of objects. The findings of some physicists might help to smooth over problems with the instrumentarium, but often too many variables are involved, it seems, for us ultimately not to prefer the judgment of the ear, which is so spontaneous, to laborious syntheses. Characterology dealing only with well-established timbres is only of secondary interest to music: it concerns phonetic, vocalic, or consonantal objects and, furthermore, the aim of the analysis and synthesis of their formants, which, we now understand, is to identify consonants and vowels, not to describe them. These have much more to do with the distinctive features of phonetic sounds than sonority or diction. They are only marginally relevant to musicality.

30.13. SPECIES OF TIMBRE

We defined the method for evaluating *different species of mass* above. Can we do the same for timbres, given the reciprocal link between these two aspects of perception? This is very unlikely. Timbres, in traditional music, do not have the fundamental structural role given to pitch; moreover, the perception of timbre has practically always been referred back to its causal origin and even studied as such, doubtless in order to explain polyphonies more clearly. If it happens that we can assign a fundamental role to it in contemporary music, this is because it seems possible to go against the tide in two ways: one against nature, by greatly refining our perceptions, the other against society, by renouncing our customs.

In any case, there is no classified index for perceptions of harmonic timbre. We could suggest using terms such as the *fullness* or *narrowness* of timbre, its *richness* or *poorness, brilliance* or *dullness*—all terms intended precisely to make up for what the specification of the corresponding masses lacks in terms of the perception of the matter under study. But, as with nontonic species of mass, in practice this vocabulary can only really be used if it drops vague analogies. We will give two examples of what might be an aural exercise to lead to a better appreciation of timbre and the choice of an appropriate qualifier.

Here is the first: the higher a sound, the clearer, generally speaking, it appears. We should have no difficulty in getting listeners who have had no specific training to agree on the fact that a high piano note appears clearer than a low note. Now, suppose we give these listeners a few lessons in musicianship with the tape recorder, giving them the benefit of our experiments on the piano and our comparisons between accelerated and slowed-down sounds. We already know that a low note contains high harmonics: it is both rich and brilliant; a high note, on the contrary, has hardly any harmonics: it is poor and dull. Our listeners, after these comparisons, will have to agree to revise their terminology: the low note is relatively clearer than the high note. This is because they have learned to separate the perception of the tonic, dark or light, from the harmonic halo, light or dark. A few weeks of training would lead our listeners on that offensive against both the natural and the cultural. Perhaps tomorrow's musical education will include such training.

A second example is highly traditional: a nonmusician will perceive a piano chord as a single sound object. He knows very well it is a chord, and he will recognize a certain texture of mass in it, but he will be incapable of analyzing it, which a beginner from his first years of theory classes will do very well: C, E, G, he will say. Now play him the same chord with its notes divided among various instruments, and his musical training will soon prove to be inadequate: perhaps he will be able to identify the notes, but he will not manage to recognize the timbres. Perhaps an excellent musician would not manage to do this either if the timbres have fused together, which, in any case, is desirable: so we will have to refer to the timbre of the chord. Such, as we can see, are the different levels of training at the very heart of traditional musical society. So we will be very careful about describing harmonic timbre in the pitch field. We could in fact suggest two characteristic pairs, for the thickness of the timbre, on the one hand, and its site, on the other. The fullness or narrowness of the timbre would reveal its extent in the tessitura, while we could deduce its color, dark or light, from its site. These terms can only be clarified after much research. We can also hope for some help from correlations between spectra and perceptions; we should at least see if these analogical terms are appropriate for both the physical phenomenon and the musical perception, which would shed light on the whole process.

We can finally turn to timbre in the field of intensities; here we would be dealing with the brilliance or the richness of the timbre relative to the intensity of the tonic. But we know that sounds without harmonics also have secondary qualities of volume and density: should we include these with mass, or say that they are a timbre—that is, the "rest of the perception"—even when there is no spectrum? So the complementary pair volume and density would then be the hostile pair of what is perceived in color and degree? We lose ourselves in speculation.

30.14. IMPORTANCE OF THE CRITERION OF MASS

To round off this chapter, we would like to highlight the particularly important role of the perception of mass and its criteria in experimental music. First of all, mass is remarkably permanent in music, the permanence of the matter of homogeneous sounds, and therefore lends itself to close and detailed study. But as we have seen, the concept of mass contains perceptions deriving from two modes of apprehending the pitch field—one traditional and codified, the other new and, until now, explored more or less in the dark. Finally, the concept of mass is a crossroads where ancient and modern musics can meet—the tonic and the thick sound, the chord and the "stuff" of sound (or "species of chords," in the words of Messiaen, who often sees music in color). We should note that the logic of our experiments leads us to generalize the notion of timbre and *on the perceptual level* make it into a complement of the mass of every musical object. We must go beyond the ancient method of referring timbre back to instruments. We can return to this when appropriate, the other way round: for analyzing genres of timbres, and for synthesizing instruments.

31

Theory of Fixed Masses

Dynamic Criterion

31.1. CONCEPT OF THE NOTE

We should say straightaway that we do not link the idea of the note with notation. The notes we are talking about and that we will use in our study of the dynamic criterion, the second basic aspect of sounds after mass, are no more notatable than the masses themselves. They are *formed* sounds with *fixed mass*, that is, where the matter conforms to the criterion of homogeneity if we omit their dynamic.[1] We will come on to variations of mass in a later chapter. In this chapter we will try to hear pure sounds, tonic or thick, vague or channeled, with the same ear, provided that their form is comparable. To concentrate our attention on this, we must avoid having to think about mass; so we will choose fixed masses.

Apart from pitch, what characterizes the note on the score, when it is played, is the duration and nuance specifically indicated on paper, a particular dynamic curve it traces in sound-space, with a beginning, a continuation, and a decay, an elementary morphology we have already described. In a traditional score the dynamic aspect is generally neglected; the idea of a note goes without saying. At the very most we find a few directions for performance: plucked, legato, and so forth, which are hints for the instrumentalist rather than formal elements of composition. But the score also contains a whole system of signs that establishes a network of dynamic directions or discourses between these notes: links including a series of successive notes, crescendo, and so forth. Moreover, there are overall

---

1. Here we should note the purely mental dichotomous workings between two modes of perception: we are, indeed, dealing with a new type of training in perceiving distinctive features that are usually conflated.

nuances (*pp, mf,* etc.), where the articulation sometimes requires specific precise dynamics (*sforzando, forte-piano,* etc.). Generally speaking, all these directions help to situate the appropriate nuance for each note in the context of an overall expressive dynamic; and ultimately, despite rather vague beginnings, every note in a traditional score is a *temporal form* that is by no means insignificant and that of itself should become part of the rest of the composition by contributing something quite specific to the overall musical effect. We are therefore justified in generalizing the concept of the note by applying it to every dynamic form that can be identified as such.

31.2. METHOD OF APPROACH

The problem of dynamics is relatively simpler than mass for various reasons. The first is that its main dimension is time and that temporal correlations between the physical object and the sound object have an irrefutable medium, magnetic tape, and also a relatively accessible means of describing them: the bathygram. Moreover, magnetic tape gives us opportunities for intervening we did not possess with mass, in particular for highlighting similarities just as much as differences (which we have described under the name of anamorphoses between physical time and perceived duration). For example, we are aware of what is probably not generally known: the localization of perception at the moment of attack, the importance of that attack in the perception of certain timbres, the conditioning of the ear to the density of information, the temporal dissymmetry that results from this, and so on.

To recapitulate the various analyses of duration and sustainment we have already made in chapters 12, 13, and 14 and in typology: in chapter 14 we distinguished three zones of sensitivity to duration in the ear: in the first, very short sounds are heard as impulses (and we saw that it is the "initial conditions" of the development of the sound that are important here, in particular the initial dynamic slope); in the third, conversely, the sound, which is very long, is followed like a sort of sound movement from moment to moment, as the ear tots up the progressive accumulation of information; finally, in the intermediate zone we situated sounds that have an optimal duration for memorization by the ear. In this latter area, unless we have a "coherent and interesting" form, with neither excess nor triteness, the sound will easily be grasped and will leave an imprint on the memory that demonstrates its value and readability, which does not happen in the other two cases.

So the next step would be to account for a general criterion of duration by distinguishing among anamorphosed sounds (where the attack predominates), sounds with a form (or profile), and long sounds with a weak form. Moreover, linked with these general data on the perception of duration, we have seen that typology roughly identified nonexistent factures (continuous or iterative homogeneous sounds), unpredictable factures (accumulations and samples), and, finally, "closed" forms. Our distribution of forms into *classes* will take all these considerations into account.

Elsewhere, in chapters 12 and 13, we discussed the relationships between instrumental timbre and attacks: in sounds where these are dominant (resonant sounds in particular), it seems they should constitute the basis for a classification of forms. We will see that, generally speaking, they will help us to define the *genre* of sounds in relation to their *dynamic timbre*.

Finally, we need to define *dynamic species* of sounds. For this we will suggest reference points for the intensity and depth of the *contours of the profiles*.

So far, the plan we are suggesting is similar to the plan we followed in the last chapter for studying masses. Here, however, we will start with the study of the criterion of attack[2] (genres) to take account of the fact that the profile given intentionally to the sound is in many cases itself dependent on the genre of sound available. In particular, for purely physical reasons the profile is often entirely predetermined by the attack itself (in all percussion-resonance sounds).

Moreover, we cannot leave aside double percussions, which occur when the initial onset does not have the same mass as the resonant sound: the vibraphone, the high register of the piano, for example. So here there is duality of mass at the same time as duality of form. Finally, we should note that during their attack even sustained sounds often have a mass that varies rapidly before attaining its equilibrium: the sound does not achieve its "timbre" instantly. Without anticipating the chapter on variations, we will have to discuss those cases where the establishment of certain forms is closely linked to secondary, yet perceptible, effects influencing both the form and the mass of the sound.

31.3. CRITERION OF ATTACK: GENRES OF FORMS

So now we will look more deeply into the criterion of attack, so much linked with the instrumental *genre* of the sound in traditional music. We will anticipate a classification in seven columns (see fig. 37), which is enough to mark out different attacks without going into too many subtleties. Going from the *harshest* to the most *nonexistent*, we will put so-called *abrupt* attacks (instruments with plectra, woodblocks, for example) in the first column in the classification and in the last column imperceptible attacks (sounds where the intensity is established very gradually).

In the middle, in column 4, we will put *flat* attacks such as the harmonium and, indeed, all homogeneous sounds; these are sounds that have their full intensity

2. More precisely, a criterion of *steepness of attack* since, as we will see, it does not involve the harmonic content—that is, the *color* of the attack—at all. Nevertheless, for the sake of simplicity we will use the term *criterion of attack* in the rest of the text.

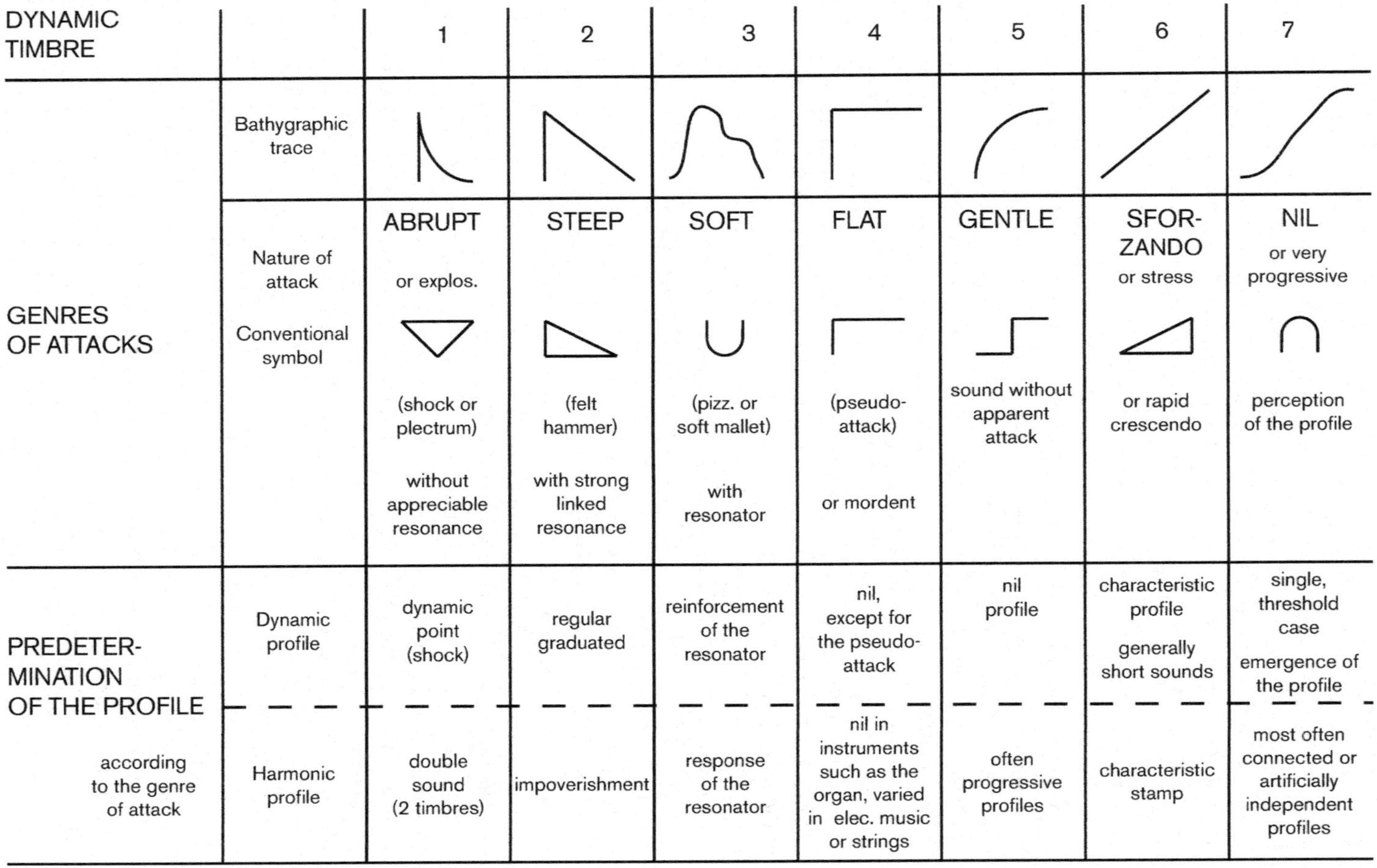

	1	2	3	4	5	6	7
DYNAMIC TIMBRE — Bathygraphic trace							
GENRES OF ATTACKS — Nature of attack	ABRUPT or explos.	STEEP	SOFT	FLAT	GENTLE	SFOR-ZANDO or stress	NIL or very progressive
Conventional symbol	(shock or plectrum) without appreciable resonance	(felt hammer) with strong linked resonance	(pizz. or soft mallet) with resonator	(pseudo-attack) or mordent	sound without apparent attack	or rapid crescendo	perception of the profile
PREDETERMINATION OF THE PROFILE — according to the genre of attack — Dynamic profile	dynamic point (shock)	regular graduated	reinforcement of the resonator	nil, except for the pseudo-attack	nil profile	characteristic profile generally short sounds	single, threshold case emergence of the profile
Harmonic profile	double sound (2 timbres)	impoverishment	response of the resonator	nil in instruments such as the organ, varied in elec. music or strings	often progressive profiles	characteristic stamp	most often connected or artificially independent profiles

FIGURE 37. Genres of attacks.

from the outset. We should note here, however, that as we saw in book 3, these sounds produce a *pseudo-attack* in the form of a very short white sound, as the energy suddenly rushes into the ear. As our classification is musical—that is, having to account for the effect and not the physical cause—we will put into the column for so-called flat attacks all the attacks that include slight mordents, whatever their origin: rosin on the bow, tonguing in wind instruments, as well as the pseudo-attack from the scissor cut.

In columns 2 and 6, balancing each other, we will put *steep* attacks, on the one hand, and *progressive* or *sforzando* attacks, on the other. We must not forget that we should not expect perceptions as "symmetrical" as our boxes, or even the printouts from the bathygram. On the one hand, we have sounds whose intensity is established quite quickly, but not instantly, and which are usually sustained sounds; this latter characteristic dominates the character of the attack, which therefore has a secondary role: our attention turns to the overall sound. On the other hand, a steep attack, the prototype of which is the piano, focuses listening on the beginning of the sound: in this case, as we have seen, we have temporal anamorphosis, and here the character of the attack is dominant in comparison with the character of the continuation of the sound.

We still have two columns to fill, on either side of the central column for pseudo-attacks. Between this and the sforzando attack we will put the attack that gives the impression of a musically softened sound, although it appears to establish itself immediately: in practice we obtain sounds like this by being careful about releasing the sound energy. Many sounds are discreetly placed between the mordent of the rosin and the sforzando, between the glottal attack and the rapid but progressive stress, with no clear profile but also with no interference or deliberate mordent. We will call these *gentle* attacks.

Column 3 is at first sight difficult to fill. We will use it for attacks that can be described as *soft*. As we will see in the next section, we could think of these as a combination of the first two attacks. A guitar string would normally give rise to a sudden attack like a mandolin, but apart from the fact that it is plucked more gently (fingertip rather than plectrum), the initial impulse is relayed by a strong resonance; the dynamic seems to gain new impetus, and its slope can be weaker than a piano's, so we will say that a guitar sound has a *soft* attack and, with it, all those supple pizzicati followed by reinforcements due to the resonance.

This very rough classification does not by any means give an accurate account of all instrumental examples. It will be a waymark. A drum, cymbal, or gong percussion sound, depending on the hardness of the beater and the relative strength of the resonance, will be classified in 3, 2, or 1: a woodblock percussive sound in 1, a guitar pizzicato in 3, and instruments where the impact and the resonance are perceptibly well-balanced in 2: harp, vibraphone, piano, for example. We should further note that repeated percussion sounds with felt beaters progressively stimulating sound bodies (cymbal and drum tremolos, etc.) will be classed with attacks on the right-hand side of our figure (cols. 5, 6, and 7).

31.4. CRITERION OF PROFILE: CLASSES OF FORMS

The above classification puts us in a situation to reach a better understanding of profiles. Depending on the genre of attack, in fact, the dynamic profile is either determined by that attack or else it frees itself from it because of the subsequent sustainment. With percussion-resonance sounds the resonance profile can really only be perceived in itself if we manage somehow or other to free it from what determines it. The second example applies to the majority of sustained sounds: here the attack and the continuation of the sound have relatively independent dynamics.

Besides, we have seen that some dynamic profiles were linked to a more or less weak, but perceptible, variation in mass. Indeed, and we have already discussed this in chapters 12 and 13, this is the case with the majority of percussion-resonance sounds, especially the sound of the piano in the middle and upper registers, where the harmonic content loses various components as the resonance decays. Here, in general, we will use the term *linked* harmonic and dynamic profiles. Conversely, these profiles may be relatively more *independent* where the continuation of the sound is shaped by the instrumentalist (or the experimental musician) to be more or less independent of the attack.

Taking all this into account, we will divide forms into two classes: (1) profiles determined by the attack and, in general, linked to a harmonic profile (especially in double attacks); and (2) profiles not determined by the attack and, in general, not linked to a harmonic profile.

1. *Profiles determined by the attack*

In practice this is the case with percussion-resonance sounds belonging to the attack genres 1, 2, and 3. Experience shows that in this case it is very rare for there to be a development of the harmonic content of the sound during the resonance that is not entirely under the control of the instrumentalist: whether it is striking a bell or a piano keyboard, touching the strings of a mandolin or a harpsichord with a plectrum, a violin pizzicato, or a percussion sound on a drum, there is only one way to go about it: the instrumentalist puts a greater or lesser amount of energy into striking, or stretches the string to a greater or lesser extent with the plectrum. These different sounds form the class of resonant attacks, or anamorphosed dynamics.

(a) The piano: simple attack

We saw in chapter 12 that however preoccupied pianists are with the weight of their forearms or the suppleness of their wrists, in the final analysis it is the strength of their percussion alone that determines the strength of the attack, and hence, on the one hand, the duration of the resonance and, on the other hand, the initial harmonic content and its development. We should not forget that in the bass register of the piano this initial harmonic content remains approximately the same throughout the duration of the note. So can we still refer to linked dynamic profiles and harmonics? Yes, insofar as it is still the strength of the percussion—hence of the attack—that will determine what that constant harmonic content of the note will be. If softer, the attack will give a poorer timbre; if vigorous, the timbre will be brilliant. This is why across the whole register of the piano, pianists, through the strength of their playing, have the power to determine the timbre of every note; even if their action has only *one degree of freedom*, they identify it in order to attain a *level of nuance, dynamic timbre, and harmonic timbre indissolubly linked* to every production of a note. It is therefore a complete illusion to believe that with the piano we can keep the same timbre while changing the nuance or vice versa. Conversely, for each note there is an extensive register of nuance-timbre pairs, in every case associated with a particular strength of attack. Finally, we should note that with the piano as with all instruments where it is possible to stop the resonance of the sound at any moment, the musician can have an effect on the decay of the note as well; but here it is the duration (and not the profile) that is no longer entirely determined by the attack.

(b) Most common example: double attack

Compared to what usually happens with percussive sounds, in fact, the piano has the peculiarity of balancing, and hence of not making us hear separately, on the one hand, the impact of the percussion and, on the other, the resonance, at least in the bass and midregisters.

This is precisely because the piano has been set up like this, except that it does not work in the high register, with the resonance becoming comparatively less and less significant. Now, this is what happens with most percussive sounds. When the surfaces in contact are hard, the impact gives an initial sound, a noise that is rapidly muted (sudden decay), the specific color and timbre of which depends on the surfaces in contact, as well as the strength of the blow. Meanwhile, the resonance moves in, and its timbre depends on both the nature of the resonator (piano soundboard, gong, membrane, tensed string, metal sheet) and the strength with which it has been stimulated. The whole impact-resonance gives a double sound, with each of its components having its own law of decay, timbre, and level. There are two harmonic and dynamic profiles.

We find three main examples:

a. The impact is more significant than the resonance profile. This is the case with the woodblock, typical of the sudden, dry attack with two timbres.

b. The attack is sudden, but gives no second timbre and in addition is quickly taken over by the resonance: this is the case with the pizzicato. Although the resonance is not more intense than the attack, it is nevertheless richer and the overall perception includes attack and resonance equally. The pizzicato has these two characteristics, and this is why traditional music adopted it long ago, to the extent that it eliminates the impact, an undesirable perception.

c. The impact is suitably cushioned, and the resonance, for its part, is very strong: this is the case with the mid- and bass registers of the piano, where the impact is practically masked by the resonance.

In vibraphone or high piano sounds the ear can easily distinguish between the impact and the resonance. So these sounds belong physically to type *b*, with an impact that is not present in the pizzicato. Now, what is of interest to musical perception is mainly, or perhaps exclusively, resonance: psychologically, we pass over the impact in *c*, since a particular listening intention obliterates it, just as a more objective listening intention restores it.

We can represent these different examples by superimposing two profiles, impact, always sudden, and resonance, disproportionate in the woodblock, but balanced in the pizzicato or the vibraphone, and apparently dominant—that is, drowning out the impact—in the bass register of the piano (see figure 38).

2. *Profiles not determined by the attack*

With the attack types 4, 5, 6, and 7, which imply a steady sustainment, the instrumentalist can dissociate the attack and the continuation of the sound. At a pinch they will be entirely independent of each other.

What happens here to harmonic development in relation to dynamic profile? We can accept that in most cases they are fairly interdependent, although the instrumentalist or singer endeavors to control the sound permanently in order to keep the same timbre through a crescendo or a decrescendo. In electronic music composers have made much use of the opportunity afforded by the electronic studio to create "sound stuff" with completely fixed mass and intensity that can vary from *pp* to the most deafening *ff*. We must say, however, that the latter often seems worse than strange or unpleasant; this is because in classical instruments it rarely happens that dynamic and harmonic profiles are so independent of each other; a singer *adds timbre* to her voice as the swelled note opens out, and the violinist does the same thing; and it is to this close association that the average listener is conditioned. He is therefore startled when he listens to electronic sounds that present the opposite: color becoming brighter while intensity decreases. Here the listener is shocked by what is unusual, not to say "against nature," in these sounds.

In any case, in sustained sounds the link between the two profiles, harmonic and dynamic, is the result of the habituation of the ear to musical practice, which is itself subject to the laws of sustainment of sound bodies; in sounds in which the profile is not determined by the attack, the instrumentalist remains relatively free to choose and shape both harmonic content and dynamic profile as he wishes. We will place the objects we are dealing with here in the *profiles* class if their dynamic form has some three-dimensionality and with *amorphous sounds* if the profile inclines toward the regularity of homogeneous sounds.

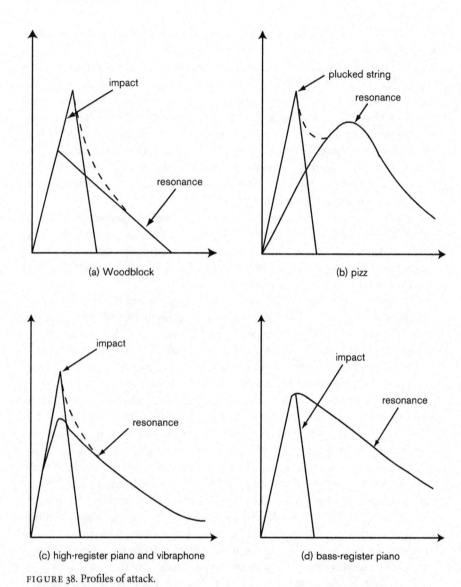

FIGURE 38. Profiles of attack.

31.5. MANIPULATIONS ON FORMS

We prefer to look at this from the standpoint of classical music notes, both because the reader has them in his ear and because it is interesting to apply our analysis to the most classical materials; most of the time these are linked and stereotyped dynamic and harmonic profiles. Thus, using sounds with such random factures as a rubbed string, cushioned or hard impacts, pizzicato, sustainment by breath, and so on, our music has reached this amazing achievement, almost totally erasing the dissimilarity of origins and forms, to the point where durations and nuances seem able to be fixed according to general norms and to be articulated in the notes flexibly enough to create very willed overall forms.

In contemporary music, especially electronic, the composer can work right from the start on the forms of objects; he is free to choose the profiles, dynamic as well as harmonic. Whether we are pro–electronic music or not, we cannot ignore the almost limitless scope that musicians now have to "play" profiles. Musique concrète, for its part, seeks a proper balance between natural and artificial forms.

(a) Manipulations on dynamic profile

The dynamic forms of sounds from traditional instruments can really only result from the more or less rapid extinction of a resonance or skillfully judged crescendos or decrescendos. We cannot recommend going against these forms by using back-to-front sound, contrary to nature. But there is no reason why we should not enrich a resonance artificially or shape a sustainment. In this way percussion loses its rigidity and does not necessarily impose the initial impact, which is not always desirable musically; the flat sound acquires salience. Thus, in addition to its "delta-shaped" classical form (< >), we can obtain a "hollow" form (> <) within the limits acceptable to the ear. Recording, manipulations with the potentiometer, the presence of several microphones judiciously turned on or off, enable us, generally speaking, to realize subtle interplays of form from a sound with a crude form. Enriching the resonance, especially, does not lead to manipulations that are complicated or destroy the texture of the sound: if enough acoustic energy is available, all we need to do is record the beginning at an appropriate level to allow for the required gradual reinforcement before the decay of the resonance.

(b) Manipulations on harmonic content

A natural link due to the nature of sound bodies generally associates a rich, high beginning with an impoverished, darker continuation and decay. This is the case with most sounds with *linked profiles*. The listener is so accustomed to this link that he no longer perceives the variation in the corresponding mass: it merges into the dynamic development. But in the studio there is nothing to stop us from modifying the usual features appearing at the beginning of a percussion sound and then sharing out the high harmonics to compensate for their disappearance in the unmodified sound. To do this, strategically positioned microphones can record different timbres from the same sound body at the right time and in the right place; filters can also be used, with care.

It should be noted here that by trying to keep the sound's initial characteristics of mass throughout its whole duration, we are simply imitating the traditional concerns of instrument makers, who always endeavored to obtain a better musical output from the sound bodies available to them. It should also be noted that there is a great divide between the subtle practices we are suggesting and certain crude electroacoustic manipulations that are carried out against all common sense and with no care for the nature of the objects.

(c) Modulations of form: separation of profiles

The usual link between dynamic and harmonic profile can be broken, as we have seen, but we could go further. The two families of forms come from percussive and sustained sounds. Could we overcome this natural division and produce, for example, a sound with the form of a piano note but the mass and timbre characteristics of a violin, or vice versa? Manipulations such as these are now possible thanks to the *form modulator* described in appendix B in chapter 23. Apart from its interesting technical performance, it offers a useful tool for both applied and basic research.

(d) Mixing, editing, and so forth

Less ambivalent in their principle, although perhaps more surprising to the ear, are mixing and editing using elements of recorded sound, enabling us to fashion original sounds by a more or less free association of different timbres and profiles. This is one of the most obvious opportunities for experimental music, but, as we can see, it often tries composers' patience. A technique such as this requires the same care as animation image by image, which is saying a lot. Less-patient musicians expect that electronics will soon give them a synthesizing or analyzing machine, or else they prefer to go back to the orchestra, entrusting it with the effects they have acquired in the studio. But the studio, in our opinion, is still far from having given up all its secrets.

31.6. THE DYNAMIC FIELD

We suggest that the reader consider what we call *dynamic field* as the counterpart in the perception of forms of the *pitch field* in the perception of masses. Fletcher was first to explore this field with pure frequencies in a steady state. For sounds with unremarkable mass and profile this dynamic field is *almost unknown*. Perceptions are only partially additive, even where there is permanence and with tonic masses, which is particularly apparent in the fact that sounds *mask* each other. As soon as a mass is profiled in time, however, the question of its overall intensity is raised, as well as its intensity in relation to the accidents of its profile. There are so many problems that need their researchers, researchers aware that there is probably no form of synthesis that would allow us to move from simplified examples to the level of the supposedly general, because every particular mass or profile structure gives rise to new perceptions. So we can only suggest an outline for study that will serve as an aid to memory and at the same time discourage any rash generalization of Fletcher's curves.

(a) Mass profile

We could already have discussed this in the context of the position of mass in the pitch field. The *mass profile* is made up of all the (perceived) intensities of the various components of the spectrum of a sound. It is a more or less overall or detailed perception of the components and consequently can only be very roughly deduced from the acoustic spectrum or Fletcher's curves. Wegel and Lane (1924), in fact, show that "prolonged sounds of sufficient intensity mask high notes over more than an octave above them, although they do not mask lower sounds at all."[3] The presence "of an intense pure sound of long duration," says Winckel, "with a frequency of 800 Hz (around G 5) raises the pitch of the neighboring notes by almost 7%, i.e. a semitone, across a fifth. The difference is still 6% for a 500 Hz sound (close to B 4)."[4] We should not forget, however, as Fletcher's curves show, that at equal level (decibels), sounds with different frequencies can have very different levels of loudness. The perception of the dynamic mass profile must therefore be the subject of specific experimentation with its waymarks within perception itself, intended to draw out characteristics of the *genre* of the sound, which are unpredictable from an a priori starting point.

(b) Weight of a mass

The idea of weight can be deduced from the above reflections if we notice that we cannot talk about the intensity of a mass, where there is no steady state, without referring to the context: we use the term *weight* for the intensity of a given sound in relation to one or several other sounds. We can find all sorts of comparisons here: comparisons that can be made between sounds belonging to the register of a single instrument, when we evaluate the respective weights of its notes, and in relation to a *yardstick sound* used as a reference for all possible sounds; so, then, we are in experimental conditions leading to a generalization of Fletcher's curves. Such comparisons, apart from their difficulty, are of practically no use in music, inasmuch as in traditional music we are always in the contexts of particular instruments, and in experimental music we ought only to compare dynamic structures formed of objects of the same *genre*.

---

3. R. L. Wegel and C. E. Lane, "The Auditory Masking of One Pure Tone by Another and Its Probable Relation to the Dynamics of the Inner Ear," *Phys. Rev.* 23 (Feb. 1924): 266.—Trans.

4. Fritz Winckel, *Vues nouvelles sur le monde des sons*, trans. Abraham Moles (Paris: Dunod, 1960). [Published in English as *Music, Sound and Sensation*, trans. Thomas Binkley (New York: Dover, 1967).—Trans.]

(c) Nuance field

It seems that the majority of nuances occur less in the loudness than the softness of sound. The subjective calibration of sonorities in terms of decibels, 5 for C, shows that half the nuances (from *ppp* to *mf*) have been covered as soon as the physical level (decibels) of the sound changes by a quarter of its value. More precisely, we could say that on either side of mezzo-forte two "laws" of nuance in relation to decibel level come together: one, linear, going toward strong nuances, and the other, more rapid, toward weak nuances. These findings will come as no surprise to musicians who know the subtlety and effectiveness of pianissimi in music, which is tantamount to saying that the ear is in the best conditions of receptivity and attentiveness with soft sounds. In any case it is important to remember that the scale of nuances remains, above all, a specifically musical mode of perception, the criteria for which depend on the context and particularize the overall indications of physical measurements but without going against their general meaning.

31.7. DYNAMIC SOUND SPECIES

We will continue waymarking these *terrae incognitae*, first of all discussing the balance between perceptions of mass and timbre:

(a) The salience of harmonic timbre

Here we must proceed with extreme caution. We have already tentatively sketched out a little four-box diagram contrasting the pairs *dark-light* (site) and *narrowness-amplitude* (extent) for a salient sound in the pitch field. The boundary between timbre and mass is vague, since we attribute to timbre in our sense what we do not know how to identify in the mass. A real analysis of mass profile would take everything into account, including harmonic timbre, but would ignore that musical custom of more or less separating the two perceptions. We will therefore, with a few question marks, place the property of *richness* in column 6 of the general diagram (section 34.3) as the counterpart of mass profile. As for the secondary qualities of the perception of pure sounds (density-volume), if we want to distinguish them from mass, we will have to compare them with the narrowness-amplitude pair of a subjective timbre.

(b) Weight of a mass in relation to its duration

The relative intensity (weight) of a permanent sound depends on its duration and its profile. At the two extremes, either the ear will not have analyzed how the energy appears and disappears (short sounds), or else it will have become tired (long sounds). Furthermore, loud sounds oblige the ear to adapt, or tire it, which is shown by an apparent reduction in intensity that also affects the subsequent sounds for some time. Von Bekesy has shown that a sound that followed a loud, prolonged sound at the same pitch was heard as less loud (by about 5 sones) after an interval of a second and a half. Independently of these phenomena, there is no doubt that dynamic profile introduces a perception of nuances different from the perception in a steady state. The intensity of a piano note or a pizzicato is evaluated differently from a held breath or bow sound. There is an anamorphosis in the perception of intensities, as in temporal localization.

(c) Impact of sounds

So in addition to the perception of *weight*, we must consider the fact that this perception is more or less anamorphosed or localized at a particular moment in duration—that is, the *impact* of sounds, corresponding less with their intensity than the nature and speed of their variations. We will give three examples of these effects, which we will group together under the name *impact*. The first is commonplace: in a high-intensity sound context, what we perceive best, provided the ear is not physiologically saturated, is what varies fast enough to bring about precisely what we call *impact*. For example, the meowing of a cat, with a weak level, will nevertheless stand out in a hubbub. So it is a question of the *three-dimensionality of the variation* in relation to duration. Second example: the acousmatic listener's surprise when he hears unexpected noises on the record, untimely coughing that he had not heard in live listening. We have already given a partial explanation of this fact when we said that he ignored this information when he was in the concert hall. But what interests us here is that these noises are all the more inopportune when they are made up of rapid forms. Third example: concert halls that become silent before the opening bars of a concert demonstrate the same phenomenon: the slightest creak of a chair, a string breaking, a dropped drumstick are disproportionately sensational sounds because of the tenseness of the silence: the reference level then is exceptionally low. So what we call *impact* gathers together everything that weight had omitted.

Finally, these psychological aspects are not the only consideration. Whereas we expected that prolonged sounds, which as we have seen tire the ear, would diminish its sensitivity, we notice that, while its overall sensitivity is indeed affected (the intensity of sounds seem to decrease), its differential sensitivity increases: von Bekesy's work has shown that after listening to a prolonged sound, we perceive subtle variations in intensity (and also pitch) better. Is the ear better adapted, or more receptive, to a new "piece of information"? It does not really matter; the fact is there, and this differential sensitivity increases with duration to attain a permanent maximum after one minute. Impact is therefore not only linked to the density of a variation in profile but also to tiny breaks in unvarying sounds. So no dynamic can be calculated rationally either through the laws of physics or the writing on a score. While the interplay of pitches conforms reasonably well to our predictions, the same is not true of the plastic forms of the structures of objects produced by each individual act of assembly and molded in different ways by each individual act of listening.

32

Theory of Sustainment

32.1. CONCRETE CRITERIA

We have noticed that a collection of objects could be explored for other things than the forms it suggests. This is what happens when, for example, we say of a number of figures that some are printed, others drawn by hand, or with a ruler and a hard or soft pencil, with a saw-edged roller, or a paintbrush. This is nothing to do with the interaction of forms in these figures. What holds our attention is the diversity of factures or, more precisely, the variations in the "sustainment" of the line in different drawings. We can easily transpose this example to the domain of hearing.

We have already discussed sustainment as a morphological criterion, which allowed us to identify objects and underpinned their unity: nonexistent, continuous, or iterative sustainment. It was the crudest, most general thing we could say. Here we are dealing much more with the characteristics of sustainment, its "manner," involving the manner of the energetic agent.

The reader may find it surprising that the analyses above did not bring in the "manner" of sustainment. Surely we were studying sustained sounds, which therefore came under the corresponding criteria? And, indeed, the criteria for grain, which apply to the perception of the matter of sound, could have been studied in homogeneous sounds, and the criteria for allure, which primarily concern small variations in dynamic profile, would logically have come into the picture when we studied formed notes. We preferred, however, to keep the theory of allure and grain for a chapter of their own, thinking that if mass and dynamic profile come from the *abstract* pole of the object—that is, its effects—then grain and allure on the contrary are perceptions that reveal the *concrete* pole of objects, closely linked to the energetic history that relates the origin of *every moment of the sound.*

More precisely, since sustainment criteria are obviously themselves abstracted from the data given by a specific act of listening, we should say that the perceptions of allure and grain readily come to mind as bringing together two extreme examples of dynamic and mass perceptions, at the junction of the criteria for form and matter. It is this special situation that made us decide to study them separately.

32.2. SUSTAINMENT CRITERIA

(a) Grain

A homogeneous sound may include a microstructure, generally due to sustainment from a bow, a reed, or even a drum roll. This property of *sound matter* reminds us of the *grain* of a textile or a mineral.

If we observe the movement of a bow filmed in slow motion, we do, in fact, notice that in the most limpid note the best "held" bow in reality produces a series of attacks in which the jolts are more or less far apart, more or less regular. Similarly, a bassoon reed emits as many "noises" as beats, and then we find ourselves in a zone where two sensations from the same phenomenon merge: the perception of pitch from the beats, and the perception of beats from differentiation of the impacts. Finally, a quivering cymbal, even when left alone, "teems" with sounds, and the resulting impression is also similar to grain.

Here we can measure the importance of a type of musical analysis that groups three such physically different phenomena under the same perceptual heading; purely dynamic, or purely harmonic, with nothing in common between the grain of the bow and the cymbal where causes are concerned; conversely, the grain of a bassoon is one of the two simultaneous qualitatively different perceptions of the same periodic phenomenon, the other being pitch. The idea of grain, with its disparate physical origin, sums up all these aspects of a single type of perception.

(b) Allure

We know that the dynamic profile of an object is the envelope of the dynamic variations of the sound in the course of its duration as it could be represented as a curve. We can easily observe that, while some profiles are characteristic of the instrument (piano, guitar, pizzicato, etc.), other profiles are characteristic of the sustainment and even the style of sustainment of the instrumentalist: violin vibratos, which are deliberate, and singers' vibratos, which are more or less involuntary. Therefore the overall profile, often typical of the sound body, may also have an *allure*, a vibrato for example, typical of sustainment.

How is allure distinct from dynamic *profile?* In that the latter characterizes the *object* while ignoring sustainment. Does a sound come to a sudden end, does it have a steep attack, or does its energetic development make it a swelled sound?

Morphology identifies this profile in an initial perception of energy. But sustainment is also revealed in irregularities by a *law of sustainment* that characterizes the object only secondarily.

Allures, as we can see, are more like dynamic than mass criteria. Nevertheless, allure is not only a dynamic criterion; the more or less regular oscillations that are its hallmark also cause variations in pitch (vibrato in stringed instruments, singers, etc.) and harmonic timbre. We could say that allure is made up of many factors (in varying proportion depending on the type of sustainment), the most important of which are associated with the dynamic and pitch of sounds.

Allure, therefore, gives one of several pieces of information about the history of the energy in the course of duration, which ultimately we perceive in three ways:

(a) *first-order* information, concerning overall forms: the *intensity site* that musicians allude to when talking about *nuances* and the *contour* that we call the *dynamic profile*.

(b) information that could be thought of as *second order*, inasmuch as we perceive the *details of the profile* as oscillations occurring, for example, at a rate of several per second: this is the *allure* of the sound.

(c) finally, *third-order* information, which appears as perceptions of *matter* (even though sometimes they are dynamic microstructures) incorporated in the form of *grain*, which is therefore a mutation of perceptions of allure when it becomes tighter.

32.3. THE SIGNATURE OF FACTURE

We have found several types of grain, corresponding to the most general modes of sustainment: it was more a matter of refining typology than distinguishing different classes. The *genres* of grain will, on the contrary, be illustrated by concrete examples: a particular facture applied to a particular sound body. A process of analysis centered on sector 4 (see chap. 21, fig. 24) will be needed to find calibrations and define *species* of grain in relation to each other in grains where type and genre are close enough together.

Allures would lend themselves better to morphological classification as embellishments of profiles or details of forms. Surely they are only transition criteria? With a limited definition such as this, allure would not deserve to be retained as a criterion. The dynamic aspects of a violin vibrato, the natural vibrato of a voice, or the random events in a fluctuating sound from a sound body moving in space would merit only a passing comment: but this is not the main thing about allure. Just as grain "leaves its signature" on matter, allure, in our sense, "reveals" the energetic agent's way of being and, very broadly, whether this agent is living or not: life, in fact, is revealed through a typical fluctuation. Thus, such signs of facture, sometimes tiny, will appear much more important than obvious dynamic embroiderings. In other words, as with grain, we will look for types in sector 2, while we will examine genres in sector 1 and species in sector 4.

Finally, it may be noted that when we speak of sustainment, we find words more easily than when we look for words to describe the abstract in music; saying that an allure is living consists in stating a fact and discerning a very common type of causality. Obviously, we would still have to see what demonstrates life in allure.

As for grains, the criterion is so concrete that we immediately think of analogies that seem justified. When we speak of a rough or matt, velvety or limpid sound we are comparing sound to a stone, skin, velvet, or running water. Analogy with microstructures seems much more justified, although applied to perceptions that have no tactile or visual links. There must be a reason why these comparisons are made in everyday speech, spontaneously and convincingly: it is because here it is not the objects of sight or hearing themselves that count but the way they are ordered. At this level it is the structural facet of the object that is perceived: it does not matter whether it is sound or image since we perceive the same ordering process underlying the two forms.

32.4. TYPES OF GRAIN

We have, it will be remembered, distinguished three main types of sustainment: the impulse with nonexistent sustainment, continuous, and iterative sustainment. It is very likely that they will give rise to three types of grain, which the ear will identify as different in nature before organizing them into calibrations.

First we will turn to the most ordinary musical experience. As examples of nonexistent sustainment we could take a string pizzicato, a piano note, or a gong or cymbal sound. The pizzicato has no perceptible grain. In the bass piano notes, on the contrary, we can perceive a scintillation that with some pianos suggests an iridescent dust. As for the cymbal sound, apart from its harmonic mass and timbre we can clearly hear a sort of rapid tingling. Close to the harmonic timbre, therefore, and one of its generic characteristics, these are *resonance grains* or scintillations.

To classify the grains associated with the other two modes of sustainment—continuous and iterative—we will have to interfere somewhat with instrumental distinctions. In fact, for us who listen there is no great difference in sustainment between the beating of a bassoon reed in the bass notes and the roll of hard drumsticks on a bongo. But neither of these sounds is at all like the sound of a bow, which, lightly brushing the string, imprints a completely random microdynamic on it.

So there we find two types of grain, depending on whether the sustainment is really iterative (and relatively regular) or, from rubbing, much more continuous and tight (and, in fact, irregular, its apparent regularity being only because it obeys the laws of statistics).

Thus, wind instruments can be divided into two categories, according to their type of sustainment: a flute sound, for example, has a very perceptible rubbing grain owing to air, which could be compared with the rubbing of the bow. As for reeds, they vibrate, "crenellating" the dynamic. Similarly a voice in the lowest bass notes gives not a rubbing grain but a succession of breaks in and intakes of air: so the glottis can be compared to a vibrating reed, and its grain, crenellated, to a bassoon in the bass register.

32.5. GENRES OF GRAIN

Our division into three types is therefore based on three characteristics specifically linked to the mode of sustainment. Resonance, rubbing, and iteration will produce *pure* types: *harmonic, compact,* and *discontinuous* grains respectively. But in practice these types of sustainment are superimposed and combined. What are the main combinations that will constitute *genres* of grain? Where, for example, will we classify the grain that results from rubbing a rough surface? The iteration of micronoises from the rough edges is mingled with the perception of the rubbing itself. We are inclined to suggest an illustration of the main mixed genres, combining the earlier types in pairs; we could take the analysis further by identifying the contribution and proportion of the three typical components in the most complex examples (see fig. 39).

How can we classify the noise of a cart on paving stones, for example? The wheels creak (rubbing), hit rough bits (striking), and these impacts resound (resonance) on the cart. A buzzing noise is explained by its consonants: a rubbing sound "zz" and a plosive "b." A marble rolling in a gong has all three grain types mingled together: rubbing, micronoises, all wrapped in a scintillation from the resonance. The terminology of this figure is reminiscent of the Italian "noise" men, the precursors of that rather too anecdotal part of music theory.[1] Although preoccupied with the dramatic effects of noise, as we can see, they must instinctively have attempted the act of generalization that properly belongs to music.

Reducing grain to six main genres does not, of course, exhaust the ear's capacity for discernment; we could make distinctions within each genre; thus, we can find scintillations that are regular (as in a bass piano note) or random (as in a cymbal sound). Other sounds may present a progressive or varying scintillation. We will make a distinction between rubbing through friction and "aeolians" (wind, breath). With vibrations we will have to distinguish those that are regular or random, rhythmed or progressive, or those that develop, become tighter or open

---

1. Here Schaeffer refers to the "Bruitiste" movement initiated by Luigi Russolo (1885–1947) based on his manifesto *L'arte dei rumori* (The art of noises). The movement developed noise-generating devices brought together into a noise orchestra. His manifesto was very influential among artists and musicians.—Trans.

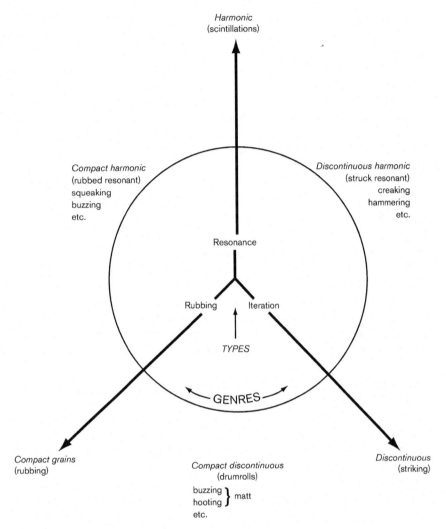

FIGURE 39. Types and genres of grain.

out, causing both their relative weight and their module to vary (boxes 66 and 69 in fig. 41).

32.6. SPECIES OF GRAIN

With *species* we expect to find the various ways of describing the emergence of grain in the musical field. But how does this hybrid criterion between matter and form present itself in this field? Does a grain have its own sort of mass and intensity? How does it relate to duration? We will make a brief exploration of this virgin territory.

The most elementary description concerns the *dynamic texture* of grain: this can be more or less *tight*. In contrast, though, we could say that, if grain is understood as distinct from mass, this raises the question of its *weight* in a relationship between mass and "background noise." This relationship is very marked in high notes on the violin, for example, which have a veritable corona of white sound, the aesthetic or nonaesthetic nature of which depends less on the level than the quality of the grain. We must admit, however, that this example is somewhat dubious, for a grain can only exist "in" a sound, since it is a property of the sound matter itself; when we have objects where the grain seems to "detach itself" from the continuation of the sound, we are justified in taking the analysis further by breaking down the sound into two distinct objects. This is what is done by the listener who hears the grain as noise in a musical note (for example, the high notes of a violin and the rubbing of the bow). In extreme cases this breakdown leads us to describe grain as a mass, as shown in boxes 64 and 65, 66 and 67 in figure 41 (section 34.3).

When the listener is faced with mixed grains, he similarly separates out the objects that carry these grains; these then become distinctive criteria, even where the objects are inextricably entangled in the pitch field; this analysis applies to the example of the marble rolling in a gong, where a clear distinction is made between the marble (discontinuous grain) and the gong (resonance grain); it is the same type of analysis that allows us to find distinct musical notes in the miscellany of harmonic instrumental sounds.

When we are dealing with much more complex sounds, this sort of phenomenon often facilitates the analysis of contexture; in fact, some of these nodal sounds will be discerned by their grain. Thus, grain is the signature of the sound, the sometimes crude, sometimes subtle sign that leads to its identification. Helmholtz had remarked on this without using the word. On this subject we should note that instrument makers have constantly striven to obtain grains that are subtly and closely linked to mass. The success of stringed instruments is significant in this respect.

Accustomed as we are to the *smoothness*, the *softness*, the *purity* of the sounds a good violinist draws from a good violin, cinematographic slow motion, as we have said, has some surprises in store: what the camera reveals is a continuous starting and stopping of the string in an unexpected, highly instructive state of agitation. This is an excellent lesson, indeed, which should prevent our confusing our descriptions with the physical or instrumental event: a *soft* grain, a *pure* sound, are, fortunately for our ear, living, perpetually disturbed, subtly changing realities.

32.7. ANALOGICAL CRITERIA: CLASSES OF GRAIN

Seeing yet again how little the physical nature of sounds accounts for the actual perception of them, it seems better not to take the earlier theoretical descriptions of species of grain too far and to prefer the empirical classification obtained by describing the "aspects" of sound matter (as we would say: the aspect of the surface of a material object). From this new standpoint, nearer to morphology, we will be able to reintroduce the earlier gradation. In effect, to say that a grain is rough or matt is also to say that it is more or less tight, but in addition it involves referring to a quality linked to sound matter, differentiating one mass from another.

We will therefore place a grid for further evaluations of grain in box 62 of the general diagram, putting comparable grains in analogical relationships. Rather than comparing a resonance and a rubbing grain, it is better, with grains of the same type, to evaluate how they progress from *quivering* to *limpid* via *tingling*, from *rough* to *smooth* via *matt*, or from *quavering* to *fine* via *dense*. This is the best approach for spontaneous description and suitable terminology.

32.8. ALLURES

The quality of grain attached to sound matter suggested the surface of a material object and the sense of touch. Similarly, the criterion of allure, attached to the form, suggests the dynamism of the agent and the kinesthetic sense; it enables us to appreciate the vivacity and energy specific to the object. The example of the violin is particularly convincing in this regard. Our ear judges the action of the right hand, the hand that manipulates the bow, by its results: whether the resultant sound will be described as beautiful, full, shrill, or insipid depends on the grain. Conversely, the action of the left hand, the finger vibrating on the fingerboard, the vibrato, reveals the sentient presence through an *allure* that can in turn be described independently of profile or mass: it will be *broad, dense, ample, tiny*, or again, *generous, brilliant*, never *irregular* or *mechanical*. If it should be missing, we would listen more attentively to the right hand and recognize the violinist all over again by the inevitable fluctuations in the sound in another sort of allure (besides, surely vibrato is made precisely to compensate for and move beyond the mechanical uncertainty of the performer in life's fluctuations?). On the contrary, if a barrel organ plays its naive tremolos, the ear will identify its allure before any musical description: it is a machine.

This is a very common question asked by man about any object, musical or otherwise: "natural or artificial? craftsman or machine? wood or plastic?" With the musical object it is allure that gives the answer. In allure, perception focuses on everything that can reveal the presence of the differentiated, the living.

What seemed only to be a second-order dynamic aspect of sound is therefore linked to a fundamental question. We immediately distinguish a very regular vibrato played by a violinist from another produced by a machine: where form is concerned, the difference between the two is not great. However minimal it is, it is immediately seized on and interpreted by a faculty of perception that seeks to know if the event, dependent on natural laws, is totally predictable, if it is the product of human will or merely of chance. We must not think for one moment that this endeavor is beyond the capacities of the ear: in the domains into which the ear is led by ancestral training in decoding clues, it is capable of grasping second- or third-order information very easily and shows extraordinary skill in deducing from the smallest fragment of sound whether its origin is human or mechanical, its character predictable or random.[2]

The allure that gives equilibrium to a tangle of small events, the *fluctuation* characteristic of a living agent, is a central class or type in all modes of sustainment. On the two sides we will put predictable mechanical *order* on the right, and the unpredictability of chance, *disorder*, on the left.

What professional sound effects engineers (on the radio, in the theater, etc.) are trying to do is precisely to deceive the listener about origins. Thus, they imitate the howling of the wind in the trees, a railway engine, footsteps on gravel. Without an accurate intuitive understanding of allure on the part of the sound effects man the stratagem fails; so we recognize nature, man, or the machine by allure, just as much as or even more than by the contents of the sound chains they produce.

According to our definition, allure, which affects not only profile but also, indirectly, matter through very slight oscillations in every characteristic, is thus a powerful means of identification. Here we are not talking about recognizing an anecdotal causality—"Who or what in particular produced this sound?"—any more than for grain, but we are trying to find the answer to a more general question, which places allure in a range going from redundancy to disorder.

32.9. TYPOMORPHOLOGY OF ALLURES

So this leads us to classify allure just as much from the deductions we make when we perceive them (the allure of the agent) as from the study of their effect (the allure of the form).

For this classification we suggest a nine-box diagram (fig. 40), where "normal" allures are placed along the diagonal; normally a *mechanical* sustainment is regular, a *living* sustainment is fluctuating, and a *natural* sustainment disordered. The boxes on either side of the diagonal contain the other allures, such as those that

2. This considerably reduces the interest of a stochastic view of music, which deprives us of one of the most essential motives for aesthetic curiosity.

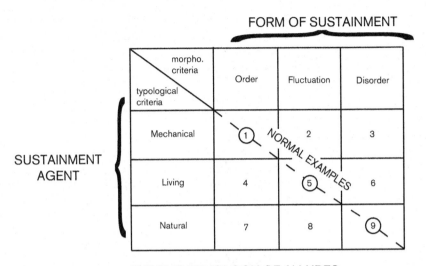

FORM OF SUSTAINMENT

morpho. criteria / typological criteria	Order	Fluctuation	Disorder
Mechanical	① NORMAL EXAMPLES	2	3
Living	4	⑤	6
Natural	7	8	⑨

SUSTAINMENT AGENT

TYPOMORPHOLOGY OF ALLURES

FIGURE 40. Typomorphology of allures.

would enable us to identify the action of man or machines in a disordered phenomenon. Thus we strive to obliterate any difference between real and stage thun-
der; we are trying to characterize the allure of the metal sheet being shaken in the
wings, stripping it of anything that could indicate human or mechanical intervention, in order to create the illusion of natural disorder.

We will concentrate here only on what directly concerns our subject: music
being communication, the listener naturally expects the message to come to him
from another person, but he accepts that within certain limits this partner may use
machines. People do not really like electronic sound, but the piano is a machine,
as is the organ; the violin is more sensitive. By mutual consent we put up with a
noise and fluctuations in sound from the violin that would make any other instrument intolerable. Custom alone is the judge between innovation and conditioning.
This divide is debatable and mobile.

The typomorphology we have just been discussing will figure in columns 1 and
2 of the summary diagram (section 34.3): it is highly abstract. In reality, sustainment can be both ordered and fluctuating, or it can bring together a mechanism
and a living presence. Although vibrato, as we have said, basically indicates this
living presence, it nevertheless comes under mechanical causalities; thus, it can be
regular, symmetrical, obey a "pendular" law, or be dissymmetrical and come from
a relaxation oscillation or, finally, an iteration. The term *allure* is therefore a way of
looking at sounds from a point of view that takes in many causalities in a different
way, in very different examples: percussive accumulations, variations in the pitch

and intensity of a vibrato, cyclic repetitions of a loop. In all these examples we evaluate the law of sustainment in the same way, immediately describing its regularity or irregularity, its progression, itself regular or irregular depending on whether the pulsations are closer together or farther apart, accompanied by the variations in their regimen.

We can also speak of the particular allure of an object, as well as the characteristic allure of a collection of objects, such as a set of bells or a vibraphone keyboard. If a collection of sounds has an incident in its sustainment, this particular moment will also characterize the allure. Thus, particular circumstances in sustainment, the "bonds" it imposes on every value, sometimes call for the term *allure* prior to any more abstract analysis. But this would be to go back to pure causality; first we must complete the first-order bonds of the dynamic profile discussed in the last chapter.

32.10. SPECIES OF ALLURE

Although it is everyday parlance to use the term *allure* in a very general sense for a sound, in the final analysis we will not retain such a broad connotation. We should be able to distinguish this dynamic differential from dynamics itself even more easily than grain from matter. We can also calibrate allure as the differential of the average pitch of the sound (amplitude of the vibrato in the tessitura). Allure, thus limited, affects pitch and intensity criteria with its oscillations; it also emerges in duration, either by its module (the number of pulsations in duration) or by the variations in its regimen.

In these three cases we will limit ourselves to a brief analysis. No pitch or intensity site for allure, since it is only a differential, with its salience in columns 5 and 7 on the summary diagram in chapter 34, where it is simply shown in three calibers: weak, medium, or strong; these calibers evaluate the "dip" in the height or the intensity at the edges in relation to the pitch or weight of the sound. Of course, we link columns 5 and 7 to the last duration column to find the common module for frequency of pulsations.

If the allure varies, we compare the extent of the variation with its speed of development in a small nine-box diagram in columns 8 and 9 (which we will see repeated in the next chapter for all sorts of variations): three degrees of caliber intersect with three degrees of module, enabling us very roughly to show the degrees of a development in three numbered points of reference with, for example, the three following phases—initial: medium and tight (4); median: strong and well adjusted (8); final: weak and slack (3).

33
———

Theory of Variations

33.1. MUSICAL VARIATION

So back to the Flood: we discovered music, in the beginning, in the kitchen. Now we must tell the story of another, more poetic, origin. We cannot confirm that it happened like this across the ages. But the same history happened to us once upon a time.

In the confusion of a chaos of natural sounds, we imagine our early man for a moment less attentive to signs. Why should this be so, when he is usually so vigilant? Because one of these noises, still from the same cause, varies in its effects without there being any cause for alarm: the wind moaning more strongly or loudly, the wave battering the shore with more vigorous regularity, the sound of a pebble bouncing away, its echo reverberating farther and farther into the distance. If this development of sound signs were a source of information, he would listen for this. This is not the case, for the wind is always the wind, the sea goes on forever, and the distant falling of pebbles is neither here nor there; he is listening for something else: this residue is music. When effects vary and the cause is cancelled out, then the sound object comes into being, poised in readiness to be musical.

When, much later, within a settled musical civilization where music is in place and the ear conditioned, a new early man places the chaos of recorded sounds on the turntable, he has all too many reasons to decipher its contents, the natural and the cultural, in terms of one of the codes at his disposal. Whether the turntable goes round at about average speed or changes gradually or in "chromatic" leaps, there is our man, rediscovering ancient (though still highly conventional) experience; even if he is exasperated by the "wow," or the harmonic progression the

447

phonogène plays over anything recorded, the phenomenon deserves his attention, for it is the springboard for music: a variation that causes the contents to be forgotten.

It is important to understand that this new input into the musical gives a sort of symmetry to the first chapters of this book. We had imagined *homo faber* moving from the utensilar to the instrumental by a process in many ways analogous but where the emphasis was on the discovery of sound bodies, each one providing an object immediately related to structures. Such were musicianly invention and musical intention, both spontaneous. Here the birth of the musical is different: no longer from a discontinuous structure created by distinct bodies that enable objects to be easily identified but from a continuous movement coming from the object itself, revealing a form and bringing this form face-to-face with the "dimensions" of the perceptual field.

33.2. PERCEPTION OF VARIATIONS

Prosaically we rediscover the basic axiom "every structure depends on a variation," but we are brought to this discovery through two very different experiential journeys. One discovers structure in a discontinuous configuration, a *series* of "musical" objects; the other sees it in the continuity of *one single* object.

So we should be tempted to study a glissando, for example, in terms of traditional pitch and thus to relate its value to a discontinuous calibration: it would occupy an interval of a fifth, for example. But this is a physicist's approach. A glissando occupies pitch in a strange way: it is an original perception that has very little to do with the interval shown on the score: the glissando is the criterion or a *new* musical *object*, different in every way from the nominal interval it occupies in the symbols of traditional theory.

But the scale, the melody, the harmonic relationships seem to be indisputable referential facts. We thus need to understand how these various facts can be reconciled: the scalar structures of musical objects, on the one hand, and musical variations within objects—that is, continuous musical structures—on the other. It is commonly believed that we can relate the perception of the continuous to the discontinuous: this is a mistake often made by musicians; physicists, who sometimes also make it, have, however, identified the first two scales of sensitivity, structured differently according to whether discontinuous harmonic pitches (calibration in intervals) or continuous portions of sound (calibration in mels) (see chapter 30) were played.

An even more striking example of disparity was given in book 3, with anamorphoses: the dynamic variation in the sound of a piano note is not perceived as a variation in level but as another sound quality: an attack. An even more convincing example: if I vary the spacing of successive impacts, what physical law will enable me to predict what will happen? I simply expect a variation that conforms to a criterion of rhythm, from slow to fast. But soon the extrapolation ceases to be valid. The rhythm, now fast, changes meaning for perception: it is perceived as allure or grain. Then there comes a zone where once again we perceive a variation of the criterion of grain, from wide to dense. When the grain becomes "velvety," this is yet another perception (which we have grouped together with grain to avoid spreading our analysis too thinly). Meanwhile, another perception has appeared concurrently, which no theory of rhythm could have foreseen and with no connection to the preceding one: pitch. We have already quoted the example of the bassoon to highlight not only this movement from one perception to another when the same physical parameter varies (frequency of a movement) but also their coexistence: this same causal parameter is perceived in two different ways at once, under two distinct criteria of the discontinuous and the continuous, grain and pitch.

33.3. VARIATION AND STRUCTURE

This section should be an important crossroads for the reader, both for bringing together the various approaches attempted in this work and for carrying out the essential synthesis of the two concepts.

This fundamental, ultimately very simple, musical truth is not particularly easy to see for two main reasons. The first, as we have said often enough, is that tenacious belief in parameters and physical laws. We must get rid of this prejudice once and for all. While an unequivocal physical law may well link a particular parameter to a resultant effect (or a number can unequivocally mark out a magnitude such as frequency or dynamic), the faculties of our ear have complete freedom to make us hear this or that as we please (we humans), and not as the logic of the particular parameter, for example its continuity, would dictate.

The other difficulty in reaching a proper understanding of music resides in the fact that, as we have just seen, it presents in two ways: through experience of the discontinuous, mentioned in the first chapters; and of the continuous, of variation, which we are about to discuss. Between the two, we have spoken at length about structure. How can we put all this into words?

We will return to the previous examples. As we have often said, physicists, perhaps without making the fundamental distinction between the *criteria for the object* and the structures within which it presents itself for their study, have nevertheless the merit of being the first to demonstrate the existence of two perceptual fields, one with *simultaneous harmonic sounds* they call harmonic, and the other melodic (an ill-chosen term) when, using quite special measures, they produce successive *melodic gaps*. Thus a fifth in the high register (A6–E7) would have the same "melodic magnitude" as a third in the medium register (C3–E3) on condition that they are successive notes, that there is no "tonal context," and that (if we may be so bold) the musician who consents to take part in this experiment is happy no longer to act as a musician. This history of the mel at odds with the octave has long intrigued us, and the only explanation we can see is in a structural context. Physicists are wrong to emphasize simultaneity (harmonic) and succession (melodic). Their experience is apparently totally determined by their conditioning. But it is likely that mels (we have not had time to support these ideas with systematic experiments) are much more like continuous gaps (which disconcert the best musicians) than well-articulated melodic intervals.[1]

In any case, we can summarize these various experiments by placing the perceptual qualities related to the discontinuous and the continuous in two columns:

MUSICAL PERCEPTIONS OF THE CONTINUOUS AND THE DISCONTINUOUS IN SOUND

	DISCONTINUOUS	CONTINUOUS
Frequencies	(a) harmonic spectrum, heard as tonic (pitch)	(a) complex spectrum or spectrum of bands, heard as color (thickness)
	(b) between two tonics: intervallic relationship (harmonic)	(b) movement in tessitura (glissandi): melodic relationship (mels)
Level	(a) constant (homogeneous sounds), heard as nuances (intensity)	(a) slow or lively dynamic movements: profiles or anamorphoses
	(b) between two homogeneous sounds: dynamic gap (weight)	(b) between two formed sounds: dynamic relationship (impact)
Time	(a) spacings of attacks (rhythm) intersecting with...	(a) ... regular repetition of impulses (from several tenths per second): sensation of pitch
	(b) rapid pulsations: allure. linking up with...	(b) ... more rapid pulsations (beyond the resolving power): grain

Such is the disparity of the main musical perceptions compared to what most strikes our contemporaries: the (mathematical) possibility of reducing everything to three parameters: frequency, level, and time.

1. See figure 3 (section 10.7) and chapter 35.

How is our discontinuous sound made? From the continuity of the fragments it is composed of the continuity of rafts of frequency, dynamics, and pulsations. We can only perceive the discontinuous through the cohesion of its elements: the sensation of pitch from an A, and not the identification of 440 rhythmic pulsations; the velvetiness of a grain, and not the perception of a bow tearing off the rosin; the impact of an attack, and not the detail of the sound diminishing. The continuous is therefore the obverse of the discontinuous: it ensures it is perceived. The perceptions of these elements are therefore *necessarily, naturally* all *different* (otherwise there would be neither sound nor music).

Now we will look at what we have called the other gateway into music: through varying objects. We fundamentally change the *orders of magnitude* so well devised by nature. Instead of hearing sound the right way round, we examine it "back to front." There are two ways of doing this: either, in the laboratory, with the aid of equipment unaffected by orders of magnitude, we receive revelations on what happens physically; our ear, sufficiently informed, can endeavor to hear what was masked in natural listening. Or else we transpose forms *into a higher level of duration.* The attack, anamorphosed, spreads out in profile. The frequency, too low, begins to float and beat right down to a sixteenth note. The glissando spreads out, different from a scale, or like a scale spun out to the point where its degrees are joined together. Now we find *other perceptions,* of the same order as those that underlay the objects of our listening to the discontinuous. We find them, *for the same reasons, different.*

So how is variation related to structure? At a certain level the (isolated, coherent) object was a structure of continuous elements welded together, not perceived individually. It was not itself perceived as a structure but as an object forming part of a higher-level structure: discontinuous. What if this object happens to be expanded (or joined to others) at a level such that now this (continuous) structure itself appears within the framework of normal perceptual durations? The whole previous (masked, unconscious) lower register of perceptions comes into play; the higher-level perceptions disappear, dissolve for lack of structure: the object is its own perceptual structure. If it happens to be composed of discontinuous elements itself, it is these, in turn, that will gradually take on the register of the previous perceptions.

33.4. TYPOLOGY OF VARIATIONS

If the musical domain of continuous, more or less fixed sounds is already extensive, the domain of combined variations is intractably complex. We will therefore proceed step-by-step and endeavor to establish similarities between perceptions that are all too strange, too previously unheard.

We have therefore chosen to make our entry into musical analysis through the study of the simplest deponent examples. Homogeneous sounds gave us access to the study of fixed masses; then these same fixed masses, this time formed in duration, introduced us to the theory of dynamic forms. But already, in order to take the latest experimental data into account, we have had to associate simple variations of harmonic timbre (linked profiles) with the dynamic profile itself, while still remaining within the framework of the theory of formed sounds with fixed mass. We can easily imagine that once variations are taken into account, this framework will sooner or later be destroyed, because the ear will stop perceiving the fixedness of a mass or the general profile of a form as primary data. This is where the "fortified zone" of the theory of variations begins.

We have already besieged it from afar in chapter 14, with musical duration. As what matters to us now is no longer musical duration itself but the criterion of variation, itself affecting a particular sound criterion, our initial idea will be a variation rate, something like a *speed* or a "density of information." More precisely, to repeat the observations already made in the first chapter on typology, we could say that variations will come to our ears in three ways: either they will be slow enough for us to be able to link our perceptions to fixed discontinuous values (variation of a preceding criterion), or they will be comparatively rapid and will give us an original variation criterion in a "characteristic form," or, finally, they will be too rapid to be followed, and their form, decipherable on the bathygram, for example, will be anamorphosed. This is what these *perceptual mutations* may be: *variation criteria*. Thus a female singer's held note has a practically nonexistent profile, but her slight inflexions of nuance will be perfectly perceived, although without these variations distorting the practically homogeneous character of the sound. A bow stroke on the violin may present a clear variation in intensity perceived as an "envelope": this is the median example of dynamic forms; finally, at the extreme, a piano sound, given the rapidity of its (dynamic) variation, gives a new type of perception: percussion-resonance anamorphosed sounds.

So density of information is the first criterion in our typology of variations. In the first example we will use the term slow *progression* of sound in a given dimension—mass or intensity, for example; in the second, medium variations, we will have *profiles* (the prototype being the dynamic profile mentioned in the theory of forms); finally, in the third, rapid variations, we will simply use the term *anamorphoses* (the perception of percussion-resonance is the model for dynamic variations; the very rapid glissando, heard as the crack of a whip, is another example of anamorphosis).

But this initial analysis needs to be completed. Speed of variation is, in fact, too broad a criterion for us to be able to refer to it effectively, even in a typological classification.

Besides, it would be a mistake to dig our heels in over numerical values: the information we are talking about is tainted by subjective curiosity linked to deciphering the event, and it may be that this is all the stronger with subtle variations (the singer) than large dynamic shifts (piano). The former belong to the suspense of the tightrope walker; the latter come from *clear predictability*.

We can also see that the median example (the formed bow stroke) floats between two clearer extremes. In one case we pay attention to the sound all the time, and so we know what we have "our ear on" (we do say of something moving that we have "our eye on it"); in the other case we received the impact of the sound right from the beginning. These median examples are situated between the two and borrow from both. We suspect that in the first example we will find fused perceptions that will bind together the criteria for the discontinuous in a temporal unity, whereas in the extreme example other criteria are perceived. We can only find this out from experimental material. The first example, therefore, raises the question of a morphology of profiles, the latter of a temporal anamorphosis of perceptions.

So we have just found a first criterion for the typology of variations: density of information. We need another to provide a rather better explanation of the character of what varies. We do have three modules for density of information, but information about what? As we have been plunged into the abstract, it is time to go over to the concrete side: the making of a variation.

Here also we can make three completely general distinctions. We may have a variation that is felt only as an imperfection in a desired stability; we have already mentioned this type of *fluctuation*. It may be a progressive *development*. Finally, it may be a *modulation*—that is, a development in stages—already sketching out a scalar structure.

So our typology of variations can be summarized as follows:

Density of information	Types of factures		
	Fluctuation	Evolution	Modulation
weak (progression) ...	1	2	3
medium (profiles) ...	4	5	6
strong (anamorphoses)	7	8	9

33.5. VARIATION CRITERIA

Since we have already isolated the dynamic criterion, having studied it in sounds with fixed mass, it only remains to study the variation of mass criteria like the variation of sustainment criteria. It would obviously be convenient to proceed in

454   THEORY OF MUSICAL OBJECTS

stages: studying sounds that apparently have no dynamic profile, where the mass can be considered as fixed. Then we would study selectively the movements of this mass in the pitch field: melodic progressions, profiles, or anamorphoses. Then, taking sounds with neither dynamic nor melodic variation, we would take those that have variations of mass. This is possible in certain specific cases. Now, it is very clear that as soon as we approach varying sounds, everything is given all at once, that melodic variations are linked to dynamic variations, and that it is extremely difficult to isolate mass variations that do not have a melodic profile. Finally, a study such as this, based on deponent examples, might seem to give results, but on a very limited scale since they cannot be extrapolated without the risk of making mistakes.

It is therefore without great conviction, rather as an exercise in method and a plan for research, that we will embark on the presentation of typical variations, since we cannot take on everything at once. So we will hypothetically separate the "representative examples," if not of the "purity" of an isolated variation of one of these criteria, at least of its "dominance." Then we will use this main type to shed light on other examples, always expecting surprises both in the recombination of textures and the reaction of the contexts.

Before going on to the four main examples—melodic and mass variations, allure and grain variations—we will see how this will bring us back to the comparisons of type, class, genre, and species.

Our general typology of variations will obviously apply to each of these four examples. First we will have to clarify the last two lines of the typology briefly outlined in chapter 24. Morphology will cover variations where the progressions and profiles are not disrupted by too great a density of information. Apart from these we will discover new perceptions experimentally through the "genres of sounds" that make them up. As long as our extrapolation of the discontinuous retains a value, we can talk in terms of melodic or mass profiles. As soon as we hear differently and something different, we have to name the new objects given to us by the experiment. This is precisely where, closely linked, we find variation criteria forming original configurations. As for examples of species, which are already difficult to situate or calibrate in the simplest of sounds, they will obviously become all the more so. For a variation criterion can also vary. This is even the norm. A melodic or mass profile can speed up, slow down, fluctuate, or modulate in the course of its duration. These variations (in the square. . .) could then be evaluated for their importance in the same perception through a second-order analysis, inevitably leading us back to density of information again: the large, medium, or small gap (in relation to the property under consideration) linked to a slow, moderate, or fast variation duration. We will apply these general principles one after the other to mass or sustainment variation criteria, in the knowledge that they have already been mentioned in earlier chapters.

33.6. TYPOLOGY OF MELODIC VARIATIONS

The involvement of densities of information explains the difficulties we were in to classify varied sounds, which may be fast or slow, simple or compound. The three types $\bar{Y}$, Y, and Y′ clearly correspond to the three "states" of information: slow, moderate, or fast. With the simplest example, which serves as a schema for many other developments in melodic evolution, the glissando, we will say that in the first form ($\bar{Y}$) it is not perceived as such, but as a continuous gradation of pitches; in the second (Y) it is a form in the tessitura, a suitably assembled and memorized movement; in the third (Y′) it is an anamorphosis that transforms the perception into a snapping sound, the crack of a whip (the tweeting of a bird, for example). Next to the note Y, supposedly simple, occupied by the variation of a single (thick or tonic) mass in the tessitura, we will place derivative types related to much more complex amalgamations, which we want to put together for various reasons, such as the way they are made (single causality) or used (overall function). Thus we find:

	Fluctuation	Evolution	Modulation
Progression $\bar{Y}$ ..	Tz	Ty	Tx (slow)
Profile Y		W	M
Impulse Y′			K (fast)

The large note W, even when long, brings together linked profiles; the cell K groups together disparate and necessarily scalar impulses; the motif M, homologous with the large note, exhibits an artificial organization. We cannot take these unpredictable morphologies any further. We will be coming back, however, to note Y, which has a "reasonable" profile, to remind ourselves that it had already been considered in traditional music.

Meanwhile, we must add some finishing touches to the typology in chapter 26, which only dealt with fixed masses or a simple development of mass (Y row) and relegated run-of-the-mill variations to a fourth row. What were this simple and these run-of-the-mill variations? On the one hand, surely our "fixed masses" already allowed for some fluctuation? On the other hand, our variable masses only suggested generally coherent developments resulting from the determinism of a causality, going from the very simple sound object Y to the large note W. Now we must take into account a "modulation" type, hence scalar, variation, the result more often of the will of a composer than an instrumental causality. We said rather hastily in section 28.7 that our theory of the object must be as free as possible from authorial intentions, since it is a study of material. The time has come to say that this is not always so easy for two reasons or in two cases. The first, which we find in classical music, produces visibly modulated objects, easy to break down but whose overall structure we may wish to consider. We therefore need a term to describe them: they are *groups* of notes. The second occurs in new musics, beyond the concept of the note. As long as there are notes, and instrumental notes, we know what we are talking about. As soon as there are new sound objects, more or less distinct or more or less fused together, merging into each other, we no longer know what to say. It does not matter whether they are composer's objects, fashioned deliberately or chosen from a wide sample; they are already too specific to constitute a general material: we have said that we will call them *motifs*. This could well be condemned as a system in which every object would be so original that no commonality would be possible. What happens is different. Instead, we have a new style of musical perception, continuous now, that fuses the criteria formerly dispersed in notes into one object. So there is no reason to be alarmed if such objects present themselves as too original for typology. This means that they are already musical motifs, whether an object has been made like this or modulated intentionally, or whether a naturally occurring development or modulation has been chosen for its originality.

To sum up: the development-modulation pair can be applied in two contexts— the purely morphological context of a transition between continuous and discontinuous, and the context, this time musical, of the perception of an intention, the recognition of originality, whether in a natural development (large note W) or an artificial modulation (motif M).

So from these various approaches in our brief establishment of order, to complete the panoply of classification terms, we will retain the new definitions of the group G and the motif M. We will also keep in mind that the *weft* T denotes the slow development of scarcely differentiated structures, whereas the *ostinato* P can give rise to the development, also slow, of structures organized as groups.

We will then find a typological regrouping that may be summarized thus:

Forms of variation: Speed of variation:	Progression slow		Profile moderate		Anamorphosis fast	
Facture of variation:	1	2	3	4	5	6
(a) Fluctuation	N̄	X̄	N	X	N′	X′
(b) Evolution	Ȳ	T	Y	W	Y′	W′
(c) Modulation	Ḡ	P	G	M	G′	K

(At the intersection of lines a and c and columns 1, 3, 5, are the materials of traditional music. The rest of the diagram refers to the most general music.)

33.7. MUSICAL TRADITION OF MELODIC
VARIATIONS: NEUMES

If it is true, as Armand Machabey writes, that neumes are "simply an aid to memory referring only to the movements of the voice, to the exclusion of the value of intervals and the absolute pitch of sounds and their duration," if they "perhaps correspond to chironomic gestures . . . when the melody included melismas of two, three or four notes on the same syllable,"[2] then we may conclude that for several centuries *the musical unit* was *the varied musical object* and not its breakdown into notes, an object that finds its equilibrium in music and text chanted syllable by syllable in this way.

Thus the aim of musical symbols was initially to express the movement and continuity of figures rather than the discontinuity of values. Soon condemned as superfluous, replaced more effectively by the notation of the *result* to be obtained, this type of figuring nevertheless reveals spontaneous musical intuition: the equilibrium of a gestural and a perceptual structure. So, for a very long time we have looked to letters (or other signs) to indicate values and to neumes to represent objects: when writing in neumes, which was linear, gave way to a notation in degrees on the staff, "tied notes remained," and these continued to emphasize pitch relationships (intervals) and typological units simultaneously. Hence, for example, the *clivis* (descending interval) and the *podatus* (ascending interval); so we expect a symmetrical notation: now, the *clivis* is notated by a displacement, with the *podatus* superimposed on it; the former is feminine, the latter masculine; finally, the variation in tessitura doubtless also linked to the accent and the rhythm. Neumes thus brought features together and created figures full of meaning, the product of a highly evolved morphology.

Here there is a profound conflict between two ways of representing objects but also of thinking about music; there would be much to say on this subject. Ultimately, one of them had to win, not because it was right in essence but because it was practical, accurate, and it worked. On this utensilar level the other could not compete, but it alone holds the secret of Gregorian plainsong. It alone might have safeguarded the essential key, otherwise lost, to grasping hold of music directly, at the level of the object. Music has of course progressed, thanks to the precision of its notation and a necessary separation of the abstract and the concrete. But at the same time it has lost a certain sensitivity to the real and a certain inspiration linked to the direct involvement of the senses in the symbols of notation.

---

2. Armand Machabey, *La notation musicale* (Paris: PUF, 1958).

33.8. CLASSES, GENRES, AND SPECIES
OF MELODIC VARIATIONS

Neumes, although intended to represent variations in a specific source (the voice), can provide us with a model. The notation (in relation to progressions and simple melodic and developing profiles of Y and $\overline{Y}$) is general enough for us to draw out our main *classes* of variations from it: *podatus, clivis, torculus,* and *porrectus.* We still have to move on to genres and think of a way to calibrate examples of species.

In music of the Western tradition melodic variation is usually inopportune: portamento is in dubious taste, as is the Hawaiian guitar—at least to our ears. In fact, it is in primitive or non-Western musics that we find this type of sounds, deliberately varied in tessitura: drawn-out sounds due to slack strings, giving rise to sounds where the continuation is consistently lower than the attack; the progressive rise in pitch of Japanese instrumental groups (Noh psalmodies); the "come hither" of Indian musics, which play with pitch in an orgy of erotico-mystic approaches and invitations. We will not go any further in our evaluation of possible *genres* of melodic variations.

We will be no less careful in our attempt to define *species* of melodic variations. We simply suggest adopting as definitive the rough pointers we have used before, which consist in evaluating the module of the variation in relation to its speed:

Speed of variation

	Slow	Moderate	Fast
Weak	1	2	3
Medium	4	5	6
Strong	7	8	9

Melodic gap

Different combinations of these numbers enable us to present the melodic profile, which may occupy the whole or only part of the duration of the sound, in diagrammatic form.

33.9. MASS VARIATIONS

The above domain was already more or less unexplored; this one is even less so. Electronic music thought it could approach it a priori, while it was done empirically by electroacoustic musics. We cannot really draw any conclusions from this, given the confusion that prevails in both the concepts and the applications. We can, however, understand the interest of such a study, which probably has greater potential than the study of melodic variations.

We have already touched on the subject in chapter 31, while examining certain variations in harmonic timbre. How does the mass profile differ from this? Neither more nor less than mass itself from its harmonic timbre. We have seen how much better we can distinguish a mass from its timbre as the ear is trained and also how we can act on each selectively, depending on the objects and using new procedures. We have already given examples of inversion of the harmonic profile: we know how to enrich it whereas normally it becomes poorer in the course of the sound. But these easy interventions, made with the potentiometer and filters, tend only to "sculpt" into the mass itself as a secondary process, either electronically or by electroacoustic manipulation.

Examples: a tonic sound can evolve into a thick sound, or vice versa: a resonant sound very loaded with harmonics or partials and relatively thick is gradually reduced into a tonic. We should again note that, conditioned by traditional listening, we are likely to hear only developments in timbre here; a more experienced ear will perceive the development of mass, independently of or linked to the development of timbre.

Here the distinction between development and modulation is also valid. The progressive organ arpeggio already mentioned is, in fact, a varying aggregate of low thick sounds to the unpracticed ear. In a typological context it is similar to a large note, but its scalar variation organizes its structure, and what we finally perceive is a variation of mass forming a motif. Many figures in modern music that use this type of mass effect (blocks of piano or other instrumental sounds) warrant the same analysis, which we introduced in sections 21.12 and 21.15: *the fundamental variation-texture relationship*.

33.10. SUSTAINMENT VARIATIONS

The violinist who allows his instrument to resonate after bowing it produces a sound that is initially sustained by rubbing and has a perceptible allure, then is prolonged by resonance: it is a type of sound to which we are so accustomed that we find both the change of grain and the change of allure quite natural. We are more taken aback by less familiar or more complicated sounds. Suppose we listen to the prolonged creaking of a door. Apart from the dynamic, melodic, or mass profiles, we have, of course, various grains one after the other: rough at the beginning of the sound, then smooth if the movement is more rapid, they may, if the door opener is skilled enough in his final deceleration, go all the way back down the scale of calibrations until at the end they are heard as iterations or separate impacts. The reader to whom this trivial example may seem very far removed from music will recall that it is no different in the orchestra, when the long final chords of a symphony are played by the brass section: the cymbal's tremolo does not just give a dynamic crescendo but also a more and more violent scintillation—that is, the strongest variation of grain.

What do grain variations consist of? According to the examples, in going from rubbing to iteration or resonance; a typical variation of allure, going from a living to a mechanical or disordered sustainment. As for genres of grain or allure variations, we touched on these in the previous chapter and summarized them in boxes 63 and 73 in the general diagram.

Variations in amplitude and module in both grain and allure in the course of the duration of the object have already been shown (boxes 68, 69, 78, 79) in a schema similar to the diagram in section 33.8.

33.11. STRUCTURES OF VARIATIONS

If we reflect on sounds in general, we are obliged to think of situations with sound that cannot be contained in the above schemas, even if every effort has been made to include a first then a second degree of variations in them. In a cell of short, chance sounds, just as in an ordinary "sample" coming from the clumsy scraping of a bow, there are more sounds, more objects than we can describe. Hence two approaches intended to get rid of troublesome sounds: one is not to consider them at all, the other to go into great analytical detail and to spend more time on these sounds than would be needed to compose a study.

How can we keep the theory in a compromise that is neither simplistic nor excessively complex? Is the musical helped by the possession of such complex objects? Surely originality should be sought elsewhere?

Here we are reminded of the old gestaltist precept: a strong form takes its virtue from the clarity of its elements (and vice versa). As long as harmonic pitches are clearly perceived, pitch structures are strong. As soon as harmony mingles degrees and timbres, the distinctness of the pitches weakens, along with the structures. Serial structures, which often rest on playing around with musical writing and are not certain to be perceived, hang together by a thread. This thread is easily broken, and we come back to aggregates of notes, those "varying schemas" (Boulez) that appear as macro-objects or continuous structures and thus belong to a new type of musical analysis, a new theory, since we are dealing with new perceptions no longer taken into account by traditional notation.

What are these variation structures, of varied objects, in the real world? Quite simply structures of glissandi, variable masses, variously accentuated profiles. What is the mistake not to be made? The mistake of believing that we can tell from a first-order variation, at the level of the varied criterion, what the organization of the structure on the higher level will be. It is probably rather the opposite, and this is, indeed, the final stage of our approach. The making of varied objects must be considered experimental, and the approximations to "deponent" variations attempted under this name, which we know do not recombine automatically, are of little importance. In fact, ultimately the perceptual sanction will be brought in at the higher level of structures (not conventional, certainly, but also not premeditated, not calculated), which will be formed by assembling objects experimentally. Not only will we hear if such structures have meaning, but it is they that in their turn will draw out the dominant value of their constituent objects. Previously, they were simply materials whose characteristics had been analyzed, a bundle of sound criteria, of variations in particular. At this point the attention we gave them determined whether any of them seemed interesting, potentially musical. But should an otherwise disparate collection of them *take on a structure* by chance, this is where the musical appears, in accordance with the notorious permanence-variation relationship, on which rests the musicality of the structure linked to the musicality of its component objects. What will this element of permanence (of the object) that varies (in structure) be? In this chapter it is the variation criterion itself that ensures this permanence.

This concept is perhaps difficult to understand or give an account of, but it is very apparent to the ear. A structure of glissandi reveals the criterion "glissando" as permanent and gives its (musical) meaning to a variation of these glissandi: a variation of a variation. We can see that it is the mathematical formulation that leads us astray by its complexity, for, although rationally precise, it does not tally with the simplicity of musical experience. A glissando is no more complex to the ear than a frequency—probably less so. A piano note does not have varying characteristics, even though it is principally a dynamic form evolving in duration.

This said, theory stops here. Music begins. In fact, the movement from object to structure, and the meaning structure gives to the object, is the true birth of music. In traditional music this is called the Theory of Music, basically the theory of scales. We have said that we cannot go as far as this.

34

Analysis of the Musical Object as It Generally Appears

34.1. THE TROUBLESOME EXAMPLE

This is the usual situation: in his quest for sounds, the researcher is like a collector who never has the right label to pin on to his butterfly. Every sound, once it is freed from tradition and shows its personality, appears unclassifiable: this is because then it presents a good balance between interest and coherence, originality, and banality; this is a good sign but, for all that, not easy.

The fact is that every sound brings together—the more coherent it is, the more closely and the more interest it has, the more originally—those criteria we have already identified in simple examples or by abstract thinking, which uses intellectual schemas rather than authentic and sufficiently varied experiences. What we find in practice are *genres* of sound, resulting from certain techniques and often having very obvious characteristics, which are not at all easy to describe or analyze using a bundle of criteria. If we do manage to make this analysis, it will often be hybrid: musicianly here, scientific there, musical if it so happens. So we will not be surprised at having to grope around in the dark. An analysis or a classification that might have been done at one time by a particular experimental group will have been made out of date or invalidated later by the same group or others. The most important thing is to situate the analysis, to date it, to attribute it to a particular group experiment and to leave it to the passage of time, which alone can bring such a long process to maturity. We should not lose sight of the fact that each individual has a "background," a particular sum of experiences, a particular memory, a particular ear, depending on the type, character, and morphology of the objects he has been working on until now, and that he will to a greater or lesser extent have modified his frame of reference. To the uncertainties of the researchers must be added those of the rules of perception: we can no more break down an object with certainty using independent criteria than we can build it up again a priori within the hoped-for structures: every isolated object is, in fact, potentially a value in a possible language (since its normal situation is to be expressed in a meaningful context), but this language is precisely what we are looking for.

34.2. ANALYTICAL DIAGRAM

Even if it is destined to be only an outline of a method and a grid of "deponent" examples, a music theory should end with practical conclusions, in the form of an analytical diagram that enables the musician both to classify a sound appropriately and to list its *dominant properties*, properties, as we have just said, that will only reveal themselves in a particular context. The difficulty and the interest of our theory are precisely to exclude contexts sufficiently for us to make an inventory based on the object itself and its intrinsic potential for appearing here or there in different guises in the various relationships that may be imagined for later use. Right from the beginning, therefore, our analytical schema contains the two contradictions of claiming to *analyze* and *decontextualize* a musical object, whereas ultimately there is no musical value outside a context. But we are held to this contradiction because we want to *talk* about the musical object as it generally appears.

These two contradictions would be insurmountable if we wanted to squeeze the description of the most general object into a diagram that claimed to be definitive. Our analytical schema is more a questionnaire, where a particular object cannot be asked all the questions at once. Some questions are about the interobject relationships that form the basis of *perceptual types* and *classes*, that is, describe and diversify the *criteria* for the object. Others are about the relationships it may have with the musical structures of the perceptual field *(species)*, in the knowledge that we are dealing with, if not an entirely specific object, then a *genre of object*, with characteristics comparable with examples taken from the real world.

As with typology, this will not be an absolutely logical classification based on mathematical or physicists' definitions, which are exclusive of each other. This overview of perceptions, presented in as practical a manner as possible, is intended to resolve particular examples. It endeavors to bring together the maximum of information, including information from the main regroupings of criteria. The aim, in fact, is to bring out the essential and not the elementary, since ultimately musical meaning arises from complex perceptions. A physicist's diagram would make much of elementary criteria, as few as possible, then their combinations and variations. There are still, we must confess, some vestiges of this method, to simplify what would otherwise have been impossibly complicated. The reader should keep this in mind.

34.3. SUMMARY DIAGRAM

		1	2	3
	Description (2–3) / Evaluation (4–9) of CRITERIA of musical perception	**TYPES** typomorphological recapitulation	**CLASSES** musical morphology	**GENRES** musical characterology
1	MASS	TONIC type N COMPLEX X VARIABLE Y OTHERS W, K, T	1. PURE SOUND 2. TONIC 3. TONIC GROUP 4. CHANNELED 5. NODAL GROUP 6. NODE 7. WHITE NOISE	characteristic TEXTURES of mass

2	DYNAMIC	homogeneous H
		 nil:
		     iteratif Z
		 weak: web N, X, T
		 formed: note N, X, N″, X″
		 impulse N′, X′
		 cyclic Zk
		 reiterated E
		 accumulated A
			SHOCKS V
			 Anamorph:
			 RESONANCE ∩
			 profiles cresc. ＜
			    decresc. ＞
			    delta ＜＞
			    hollow ＞＜
			    mordent ∧⌐
			 Lifeless:
			    flat ⌐
				ATTACKS (dynam. / timbre)
				 1. abrupt ▽
				 2. solid ◁
				 3. soft ⌐ pseudo
				 4. flat ∧ mordent
				 5. gentle ⌐
				 6. stressed ◿
				 7. nil ∩

3	HARMONIC TIMBRE	either: GLOBAL TIMBRE
		
		 or: secondary timbre of
		   masses masses
		   M1 ht1
		   M2 ht2
		   M3 ht3
		   ... ...
			(conneced to masses)
			
			 NIL 1–7
			 TONIC 2
			 COMPLEX 6
			 CONTINUOUS 3–4
			 CHANNELED 4–5
				CHARACTERISTIC OF THE SOUND BODY
				
				 hollow-full
				 round-pointed etc.
				 bright-matt

FIGURE 41. Summary diagram of the theory of musical objects.

4	5	6	7	8	9
SPECIES (site and caliber of the dimensions of the musical field)					
PITCH		INTENSITY		DURATION of the variations of emergence	
SITE TESSITURA	CALIBER WIDTH	SITE WEIGHT	CALIBER SALIENCE	IMPACT	MODULE
7 oct. x 12 = 84 deg. — HARMONIC COLOUR — REGISTERS: ex low -1, very low 0, low 1, med. low 2, diapason 3, med. h. 4, high 5, very high 6, ex. high 7	HARMONIC INTERVAL — COLOR THICKNESS	WEIGHT OF A HOMO-GENEOUS MASS	1 ppp, 2 pp, 3 p, 4 mf, 5 ff, 6 ff, 7 fff — PROFILE of the texture of mass		(threshold of recognition of the masses for short sounds)
		WEIGHT OF A PROFILED MASS according to its module — 1 ppp, 2 pp, 3 p, 4 mf, 5 f, 6 ff, 7 fff	MODULE OF THE PROFILE	VARIATION OF THE PROFILE	SHORT SOUNDS

Lower intensity sub-table (columns 7 & 8)

	slow	moderate	lively
weak	1	2	3
medium	4	5	6
strong	7	8	9

(column 9: MEASURED SOUNDS / LONG SOUNDS)

4	5		6	7		8	9
COLOR	FULLNESS		RICHNESS			variation: of fullness, of color, of richness no. 1 to 9	(threshold of recognition of the timbres for short sounds)
	narrow	ample		dens.?	vol.?		
dark	1	2	poor timbre	1	2		
light	3	4	rich timbre	3	4		

		1	2	3
	Description (2–3) Evaluation (4–9) of / **CRITERIA** of musical perception	**TYPES** typomorphological recapitulation	**CLASSES** musical morphology	**GENRES** musical characterology
4 (VARIATIONS)	**MELODIC PROFILE**	*(Progress / Profile / Anam.)* Fluc. N̄, X̄ | N, X | N', X' — Dev. Ȳ, T | Y, W | Y' — Mod. Ḡ, P | G, M | K	(Only Y notes) podatus, torculus, clivis, porrectus	characteristic of the profile: pizz, melodic, dragging, etc.
5 (VARIATIONS)	**MASS PROFILE**	Typological development — Fluc. N/X or X/N — Dev. Y/W or W/Y — Mod. G/W or W/G	(Only thickness) swelled, delta, thinned, hollow	Characteristic development of mass, of harm. timbre
6 (SUSTAINMENT)	**GRAIN**	Pure or mixed of [resonance, friction, iteration]	Quiv. Shim. Limpid / rough matt smooth / coarse net fine	harmonic / compact-harmonic / compact / compact-discontinuous / discontinuous / discontinuous-harmonic
7 (SUSTAINMENT)	**ALLURE**	Pure or mixed [mechanical, living, natural]	order fluct. disord. / 1 2 3 / 4 5 6 / 7 8 9	regular cyclic / vibrato / progressive / irregular / abrupt decay, muffled / incident

4	5	6	7	8	9

SPECIES (site and caliber of the dimensions of the musical field)

PITCH		*INTENSITY*		*DURATION*	
				of the variations of emergence	
SITE TESSITURA	CALIBER WIDTH	SITE WEIGHT	CALIBER SALIENCE	IMPACT	MODULE

or site of the profile	melodic width.	linking of the melodic profile		slow mod. lively	Partial see col. 3 ⌈onset cont. term.⌋
	⌈weak	————————————→		1 2 3	
	medium	————————————→		4 5 6	
(see mass)	strong⌋	to the dynamic profile		7 8 9	or total

incidence on the tessitura or color (mass and harmonic timbre)	width of interval or thickness	linking of the profile of mass		slow mod. lively	Partial see col. 3 ⌈onset cont. term.⌋
	⌈weak	————————————→		1 2 3	
	medium	————————————→		4 5 6	
	strong⌋	to the dynamic profile		7 8 9	or total

GRAIN APPRECIATED THROUGH MASS OR TIMBRE		Relative weight GRAIN-MASS LINKED	Dynamic texture of the grain ⌈weak medium strong⌋	variation of grain fullness/speed no. 1 to 9	tight med. slack 1 2 3 / 4 5 6 / 7 8 9
color of the grain	thickness of the grain				

	pitch width of allure ⌈weak medium strong⌋	Relative weight allure/dynamic	dyn. salience of allure ⌈weak medium strong⌋	variation of allure fullness/speed no. 1 to 9	1 2 3 / 4 5 6 / 7 8 9 tight med. slack

34.4. LAYOUT OF THE DIAGRAM

Ultimately, we are summarizing seven criteria, one per horizontal row, numbered 1 to 7. Two of these, analyzed in chapter 30, are mass (row 1) and harmonic timbre (row 3), which group together the distinctive features of homogeneous sounds. If we can unambiguously identify the timbre of the mass in a sound with tonic mass, the timbre crowning it can be analyzed in turn as soon as the mass becomes more complicated, and the difference between the two is less clear-cut. Now, our document must be practical: in less simple instances we will say that what constitutes the main part of the sound—that is, what it seems must emerge or, in fact, emerges in a structure—comes under the criterion of mass per se. Additional masses (not meaningful in the structure) and the harmonic halo are deemed to come under the criterion of harmonic timbre. Finally, we will include the details of textures in the column for sound characteristics, by describing the genre of sound with which we are dealing.

Then we have the three variation criteria: first, the dynamic criterion (row 2), studied with formed notes in chapter 31, and which in some cases led us to discuss the harmonic profile associated with the dynamic profile at the same time, the analysis of this development being situated on the appropriate lines, then the melodic and mass variations studied in the last chapter (rows 4 and 5).

Finally, we have the two sustainment criteria, grain and allure (rows 6 and 7)

These seven rows intersect a number of columns. The first is a typological recapitulation; the second (classes of criteria, column 2) clarifies the nature of the musical perceptions brought about by the object; the third describes the ways in which they combine in the character of the object (genre, column 3); and, finally, returning to the abstract, the last ones attempt to complete the description of the object with reference to the perceptual system for musical dimensions (columns 4 to 9). The reader will recognize in these various specifications the result of the four music theory procedures set out in section 29.6: after typological (sector 2) and morphological (sector 3),[1] twenty-five comparisons, the determining of the particular genre (sectors I and II), and, finally, the evaluation of the particular object in the musical field (sector 4).

Here we will briefly recapitulate the methods defined in chapters 21 and 24: typology makes an initial comparison between a sustainment criterion (the continuous or discontinuous) and a morphological criterion (the fixity or variation of mass). This initial procedure enables sound objects to be regrouped in the context of a musicianly intention already freed from anecdotal or instrumental causalities but without any description of content or selection of perceptions. Continuing with the comparisons in sector 1, we see seven criteria emerge, through studying

---

1. Sectors 1, 2, 3, and 4 of the experimental system are set out in chapter 21.

deponent examples it is true, but far-reaching enough for us to be able to consider them as classes of sound in general. The term *genre* sheds light on the analysis by reference to the concrete character of the object we intend to analyze: compared to a particular sound specimen produced by a particular sound body determined by a particular facture, we know that this object will link the criteria in some characteristic way.

34.5. EVALUATION OF CRITERIA IN THE PERCEPTUAL FIELD

The purpose of the last six columns is to situate and calibrate the criteria, that is, to evaluate them for their average or differential value within the dimensions of the perceptual field.

(a) *Pitch field*

Box 14. Depending on whether the sound is tonic or has a complex mass, it can be represented by a measurement in (harmonic) degrees or in colors of the register.

Box 15. Differential relationships flow from this: either evaluated in (harmonic) intervals for harmonic sounds or in thickness.

Box 34. The site of the timbre in the tessitura could (with the reservations already made) be evaluated after appropriate training, using the descriptive pair light-dark.

Box 35. We would then put the complementary amplitude pair with this, depending on how far it is possible to evaluate the extent of the timbre, other than from its site in general.

Box 44. The site of a melodic profile is no longer very meaningful except to give it an approximate zone in the register.

Box 45. The melodic profile's small, medium, or large gap will have to be compared with its duration: this will be the melodic profile module, assumed for the time being to be regular. These three cursory indications of the importance of melodic gap will therefore be intersected with two other duration types (slow, moderate, fast), which will be found in column 8, to provide the nine-box reference points we have already described several times.

Box 54. We have said that a mass profile could also be perceived in the tessitura or in harmonic timbre.

Box 55. The mass profile, where the gaps are very much vaguer than in the melodic profile, may nevertheless present thickness modules in accordance with duration and give rise to the nine-box layout intersecting the information in columns 5 and 8.

Boxes 64 and 65. Depending on how the grain emerges in the mass, it can be evaluated for its color or even its thickness. We know that a grain can just about be heard as a distinct object, which would justify our applying the same analysis to it as to mass.

Box 75. Allure is a differential crenellation that can affect pitches, and its temporal module is clearly the same as for the dynamic crenellation in column 7, but it is not necessarily linked to the same interaction of gaps. It is normal for a strong dynamic vibrato to be melodically strong as well, but these two qualities may be independent of each other: all they have in common are the pulsations. The grid of modules intersecting columns 5 and 9 may therefore be independent of the grid intersecting columns 7 and 9.

(b) *Field of intensities*

Boxes 16 and 17. These deal with the weight and impact of a homogeneous mass—either its average weight, compared to the weight of other masses, or the harmonic impact, that is, the relative weights of its various textural elements. This is to do with the sensitive perception of the spectrum (and not the physical spectrum itself). So we would compare the weights of the different slices that could be cut out from the mass. But this would be to destroy it. So we need perception to reflect on itself to evaluate where, in a channeled mass, for example, the center of gravity can be found, or what the relative importance of the nodes is. This evaluation is related to those in columns 4 and 5.

Boxes 26 and 27. These deal with the weight of a mass, a function of its profile, completed by the effect of the impact. The weight is different, depending on whether we are dealing with short, moderate, or long sounds (column 9), as it is affected by the extent to which the intensity is integrated into the duration. In addition, the perception of dynamic variation, which goes from anamorphosis to differential sensitivity to nuances (including the phenomenon of saturation), plays a distinct part in the differential emergence of objects. This impact, as we have said, may cause a heavier sound to be masked by a sound of lesser weight: this is an original perception as distinct as an interval is from a degree or thickness from color.

Box 36. The third and last pair of timbre values, in the always fragile hope of evaluating it: it deals with the weight of the timbre in relation to the weight of the mass, richness, and poorness.

Boxes 46, 47, 56, 57. Melodic and mass profiles also have an effect on dynamics. Apart from the fact that they are usually linked to the dynamic, they influence the weight but even more the impact because of the density of information they carry.

Boxes 67, 69, 77, 79. These involve counting the grains or undulations in the allure and comparing their number and caliber in duration. They are the modules in column 9 we have already discussed.

Boxes 66, 76. For the record, the possible influence of grain and allure(?) in the emergence of the object. We still have no proofs of such hypotheses.

(c) *Field of durations*

This has already been mentioned under variations. We still have to deal with:

Boxes 19 and 39. For the record, the thresholds for the recognition of masses and timbres.

Box 29. Clearly the ordinary notion: general module or classical duration value.

Column 8. Overview of the variations of the seven criteria in duration.

So we are adopting three general types of notation. If the variation is nonexistent, this is because the criterion is regular, possesses a *fixed value* (including the so-called variation criteria themselves) defined in a diagram of *modules* numbered 1 to 9. A melodic profile, for example (boxes 45 and 48), will have the module 6 if it is of average gap in a fast tempo. If it has *irregularities*, these will affect its *impact*. Finally we will call it *composite* if it *changes module*, going, for example, from module 6 to module 2: this profile decelerates while reducing its gap. Variations of mass profile are treated in the same way (boxes 55 and 58). Finally, a dynamic profile can also be regular, irregular, or composite; but the diagram of "examples," the suggested expedient (boxes 27 and 28), is too cursory here: we have more accurate ideas about attacks and slopes that enable us to characterize a composite profile (box 23).

This leaves grain and allure variations (boxes 68 and 78). This is perhaps where the diagram of modules is at its most satisfactory for showing, for example, that an allure goes from tight and weak (module 1) to well adapted and average (module 5). But for grain we may prefer the more evocative analogical diagram in box 62 to these somewhat crude quantitative modules. Although classes and species of grains have in common that they are marked out in duration, they differ profoundly in their ability to intersect, which in box 62 is no longer a blind quantitative evaluation but an indication of origin clarifying the characteristic of grain and not only its weight as in box 66. The two sets of information are relatively complementary (boxes 62 and 69), rather as the two independent modules intersecting boxes 75 and 77 with the number of pulsations in column 9 were for allure.

34.6. MUSICAL SCALES

It is not one of the smallest paradoxes in the musical to find oneself between two sorts of perceptions. Some, based in nature, have, moreover, been the object of a long process of social, and above all professional, conditioning; the others, more subtle and often masked, are not cultivated, as if they were thought to be without value. Now, we know that the latter sort of perceptions (we are thinking here of timbres, for example), far from being without value, contain, in fact, the most refined ways of describing musical *sonority*. This example of the contrast between pitches and timbres merits closer examination. If we roughly count the number of scalar degrees a musician with some training can name, we multiply the twelve notes of the tempered scale by at least seven octaves and find eighty-four degrees, which are so many reference points available to the Western ear. An Indian ear could find many more. But now if we endeavor to evaluate timbres, we will have great difficulty in getting listeners to agree on the single pair light-dark. What will trouble us here, much more than the randomness of a calibration of sound "colors," is our relative lack of experience in separating the distinctive qualities of timbre from the characteristics of the instrument, whereas we perceive the latter perfectly well if we are to judge by the subtlety we can show in distinguishing between the sonorities from two instruments alike in principle or even between two notes from the same instrument.

So ultimately we should like to be able to set up a finely differentiated calibration for timbres in the same way as for pitches, by bringing order into evaluations, determining vocabulary, and training individuals. It remains to be seen if this is possible and within what limits.

Given these well-known difficulties, it may appear odd that we have fairly systematically included numbers referring to registers or pairs of descriptions in our synoptic illustration. The Westerner cannot at present evaluate a melodic variation except by indicating the chromatic interval it covers, but a glissando resists such analysis, which is inadequate to describe its variation. So we would have a second way of evaluating the perception in question, but we do not know how to do it. It may be neglected in the West, but the interplay of melodic variations is infinitely diverse in China and Japan and presumes a subtlety that the schemas of traditional music theory are completely incapable of taking into account. In the same way rhythms, even if they are not notated in sixty-fourth notes, speak differently to the African ear than to our own; instead of being in conformity with the modules in column 9, they tend to be autonomous rhythmical structures introducing relative values that do not figure in that stage of music theory. Other musics than ours, therefore, presuppose an ear training different from ours and, consequently, calibrations we do not have or structures we have not developed.

However, lacking the knowledge and, most of all, the experience, we are not in a position to put forward calibrations other than our own. Specialists themselves are, in general, too affected by their conditioning to grasp references or structures that give non-Western musics their meaning; our music theory can only distort their originality and take away all their savor.

34.7. NUMBERS AND NUANCES

The reader will also probably wonder about the number of nuances (or degrees, or boxes) chosen for the various specific examples. We will give a brief explanation here.

Two intersected pairs of qualities form the most elementary four-box square. Introducing a median point into each of the dimensions for evaluation gives a nine-box diagram. We should not attach more value to these divisions than they have: we present them to the reader simply as working hypotheses.

Besides, our seven-degree calibrations do not come from any mystico-symbolic inspiration, as will be seen. Two opposing states (for example, forte and piano), separated by a midpoint *(mf)*, then extended through the inclusion of doubling *(pp* and *ff)*, then tripling *(ppp* and *fff)*, naturally lead to a series of five, then seven, distinctions, as the logical development of a basic triad. We should note that the validity of these scalar gradations is confirmed in a statement by George A. Miller: according to this psychologist it is scarcely within our power, generally speaking, to discern more than seven degrees or distinctions in a single perceptual dimension,[2] excluding, of course, for trained individuals, the absolutely exceptional case of the pitch field, which contains several hundreds of degrees. But as soon as we move away from tonic sounds, there ceases to be a chromatic calibration, and appropriate experimentation would doubtless show that there is a number of "colors" near to seven, from the extremely low to the extremely high. This registration in colors is probably just as good for complex masses as for continuous melodic trajectories.

In the dimension of durations, as we have seen, the fundamental triad of the three characteristic modules makes its appearance: the short (and anamorphosed) sound, the moderate (and memorized) sound, and the long sound (which is therefore followed in the course of its duration).

The seven classes of mass, like the seven nuances of weight, track the development of a fundamental contrast with an equivocal midpoint, the ambiguous channeled sound that comes under different pitch calibrations, depending on context and listening intention. In the same way our numbering of attacks in seven degrees tracks a contrast between sounds with dominant attack (sudden attack) and those with no attack (nonexistent attack), with the midpoint the usual situation of flat attack (with a slight mordent due to the sudden onset of the sound).

Finally, our typology itself, as will be realized, allows several fundamental binary or ternary divisions that were discussed in the introductory chapter to typology (fixed and varying sounds, balanced and eccentric sounds, redundant sounds, etc.).

34.8. OBJECT IDENTIFICATION CHART

The summary illustration in section 34.3 is both an aid to memory for the music theory and the model for an *analytical* chart for the musical object in general. It

2. George Armitage Miller, "The Magical Number Seven," *Psychological Review* 63, no. 2 (1956): 81–97.

does not, however, give any information at all about the origin of this object, how it is made, and so forth. We will briefly demonstrate here how to set up the identity-card for a sound, for example in the form of figure 42. This *identification* document contains four main types of information, concerning, respectively, the instrumentarium, recording, studio manipulations, and various other technical details.

34.9. MEANING OF THE ANALYTICAL DIAGRAM AND HOW TO USE IT

At the beginning of this chapter we warned against the surprises that await the decoder of sounds. In our typological classification we had already pointed out the latitude he had in classifying a particular object in a particular box, depending on whether he intended to focus on a particular level of complexity in relation to the context or the contexture under analysis. Now we come across another sort of difficulty. Whatever the object, our diagram always seems to fall short by being both too precise and not precise enough. For one particular object it will ask a series of questions that seem superfluous or out of place, but it will not ask the questions that are really relevant to it with enough detail or even clarity. This is because the analytical diagram is synoptic and at the same time pursues the dream, which we know is utopian, of describing or comparing all musical objects. How can one chart, even with sixty-three boxes, hold every single one of them? Even if the combinations of these boxes and their various subdivisions or distinctions provide a fairly complete introductory structure for all possible musical objects, we will not, in practice, be anywhere near the efficiency, limited though it may be, of traditional music theory. Ultimately, it is not so much a theory of music as a preparatory stage for screening sounds and the perceptions to which they give rise, an inventory setting out the *main questions to be asked in musicality*. No object, as we have said, will really have to answer them all. The following remarks could be made on this subject:

(a) Columns 1 and 2 give information about the *perceptual domain* brought into play. We could say that they indicate the *class* of music that object may belong to, the musical domain it is part of.

(b) The last six columns suggest possible evaluations of relationships between criteria within a particular dominant musical dimension but have no significance outside the contexts where a particular *species* of music is possible.

(c) Column 3 gives information about the nature of perceptions through reference to sources and factures that produce objects of the same genre: it involves a concern for the instrumentarium and for the concrete choice of the characteristic material inseparable from the aims of a music of a particular *genre*.

So in general a given object, once it is morphologically locatable, presents well-defined potentialities that in theory assign it to a particular class of music within the framework of one dominant perception. But outside a context it is freed from

INSTRUMENTARIUM	RECORDING	STUDIO MANIPULATIONS	TECHNICAL OBSERVATIONS
(a) *electronic source:* generator: - of sine waves - of impulses - of rectangular signals - of sawtooth waves - of white noise - etc. - electronic instrument (b) *musical instruments:* - classical - exotic - various (c) *concrete source:* nature and number of sources	(a) studio: - normal recording - special recording - number and types of microphones - positioning of microphones (b) booth: manipulations while recording: - correction - potentiometer - reverberation - filtering - rerecording - various	- editing - direction (forward or backward) - looping - potentiometer - reverberation - filtering - reinjection - mixing - total transposition toward the high register toward the low register interval - transposition harmonic interval temporal relationship - repetition - linking - various	(a) number of tracks: - mono - stereo - two track - multitrack (b) original or copy (c) faults: - in the live sound - interference - distortion - others (d) general information: - composer - sound engineer - date made - studio (e) various: (device, special equipment, etc.)

FIGURE 42. Sample object identification chart.

this fate in the sense that its indeterminateness would lead the researcher who is trying to use it to compare it with all possible stereotypes; so we can only make progress if there is a defined context—a context that is not necessarily active, not yet realized, but must at least be expected or imagined, "intentioned," and in theory may be so from the moment two previously indeterminate objects are put together. More precisely, we can identify three types of context, depending on the aim in view.

1. The first is the experimental study. It comes under the prose composition approach. Just when the researcher is most overwhelmed with objects and variables, he must choose a criterion and restrict himself to a few types of structuring; then he checks the interaction between dominant perceptions, criteria that contribute to them, and sensitized areas of the perceptual field.

2. The second comes under translation, musical dictation, and training. If it is the case that the reel of sounds has not been prepared by a master of music theory, which will doubtless be the case, it is very unlikely that it will give natural structures of perception directly. The listening mode will thus necessarily be deliberate, conscious, willed, rigorously following the analytical instructions of music theory. We will nevertheless avoid taking this exercise too far, as it will become utopian as soon as the real capacities of analytical perception are exceeded.

3. The third will be the trial composition and the attempt to find a musical class, linked to an instrumentarium that provides a *genre* of sounds. This is the context of the discovery, in the disparate welter of sound, of objects that have characteristics in common. It is the most ambitious, the most rigorous, the most creative stance; it requires a composer's inspiration (and thus an intuition for relationships), an analyst's ear (recreating various contexts through imagination alone) and finally the hearing of a violin maker mastering an instrument that has too many degrees of freedom.

Do we need to add that very often it is this latter trap that ensnares the experimental composer, intoxicated by too many possibilities, ill-informed about the real problems, and forgetful, in this time of all-conquering mechanization, of the fact that in music at least we must continue to "think with our hands" and write music (if I may put it this way) with our ears.

BOOK SEVEN

Music as a Discipline

35

Implementation

35.1. HOW SHOULD WE MAKE AND WHAT SHOULD WE LISTEN FOR?

Having so clearly marked out the limits of our study, it would seem that we were generalizing without crying, "Beware."[1]

Moving on in this way from objects to their implementation is surely tantamount to going beyond the limits we had determined for ourselves? Since we thought we should, and could, make a clear distinction between composition and the discipline of music theory, why change our minds? Are we going to add to the question about the use of objects another question, even more unwise, and particularly presumptuous at the level of materials, the question of ultimate meaning? In other words, having written about the musical object without being willing to write a single note, are we going to tackle music itself, its beginnings and its ultimate purpose?

We are indeed going to do this, immediately making clear the limits of our ambition but also accepting responsibility for what we do.

First, it would be difficult to see how a piece of research of such importance could be put forward without instructions for use. We have said often enough that

---

1. In the title for this section Schaeffer is referring to the aspect of music that, together with *entendre* (listening), he considered most important. "Le faire" (making or doing; see our translators' introduction) involves not only the whole process of music-making—for example, music itself, instruments, pseudo-instruments—but also all the activity, the "doing," that goes into the production of music. We have therefore used *make* intransitively here, first, to emphasize this aspect of music and, second, because its connotations are so broad.—Trans.

479

the study of material was indispensable only because of its involvement in musical organization. As for the choices that emerge thereafter, we will not take sides.

At least we should say clearly what these might be. We think, moreover, that these choices determine which, of all possible musics, we intend to make and play, its performance potential, its communicative qualities; these choices, in turn, depend on the intrinsic properties of the material, which determine the particular relationships and functions it can take on. This is the subject of this chapter.

So we must allow the theory to go thus far. If, in the next (and last) chapter, the author happens to go a little further and exceed the limits he has set for himself here, this is a matter of temperament and vocation. After such an arduous scrutiny, it is tempting to give a few opinions: to recommend reasonable aims, identify contradictions and dead ends. This can be done without embarking on a pointless and often harmful aesthetic debate: it is a question of indicating not preferences but possible musics.

35.2. ON THE RIGHT USE OF A MUSIC THEORY

If in this book we have never used the symbols of traditional theory, it is not because we despise them. Assuming that everything they represent was already well known and had nothing more to teach the reader, our intention was not only to describe what these symbols do not show but precisely to put him on guard against this particular symbolism. We should not forget, for example, that mathematics has often preceded, prepared the way for, made possible, the discoveries of physics. Its role is not limited to putting a phenomenon into an equation; it suggests new experiments to researchers, provides a medium for their imagination. Notation plays a similar part in music. We can see this tendency in action in the propensity musicians have at present to rely on it to calculate their scores, and we cannot be angry with them for seeking to predict music with a little more method and "rigor" than their ancestors did in their absolute devotion to their inspiration. But the tools must work properly, and the figures must not be rigged. In any case, a careful examination of the bases of the calculations themselves cannot be wrong.

In sketching out a "generalized" music theory, going way beyond the immediate needs of present-day composers, we had two applications in mind: one concerns musics that are "different" from our own (ancient or non-Western), where it is our contention that the present way of deciphering them is poor, crude, and inaccurate as long as we apply the Western frame of reference to them; the other concerns musics yet to be invented, which clearly preoccupy musicians of our time. The moment has come to test these out.

First we will see how this new way of looking at music might enable us to explore musical civilizations. Then we will see how present-day developments can be explained by it and how it reveals a number of methodological errors; so we hope that, by broadening their vision, we may be able to free composers' imaginations.

Before going any further, we should immediately point out a contradiction that usually remains latent in contemporary musical thought. The latter, in fact, looks at music in two alternative ways. It is supposedly an expressly *cultural* language, which finds its meaning only in use: so in contemporary developments we see an extension of the traditional system, which involves an attachment to these signs. But people also refer to acoustics, physiology, parameters, the response curves of the ear; that is, they postulate a *natural* explanation for music, which they seek in organizational formulae (mathematics) or the properties of sound. This means that we come back to the central problem of the essence of music: is it natural or cultural? From the very beginning we have recognized this dualism, and in every concrete instance we have found its mark. The serious thing here is that most composers do not even seem to be aware of the problem and dwell in ambiguity. In short, when it suits them, they do not hesitate to go without any warning from one side to the other.

35.3. ATTEMPT AT AN EXPLORATION OF TRADITIONAL MUSICS

Rather than go backward to the past, starting from the most highly developed Western system, we propose to discover the musics of the various civilizations through their origins. We can imagine that they develop from the resources available to *homo faber*, always precisely situated in time and space. Yet, instead of excavating his remains with the same care that archaeologists show for fragile pottery, perishable varnishes, and unstable glazes, we turn the field over with a bulldozer, which is nothing other than our piano (forte), steel-clad and rosewood-finished. So strong is the faith in our own musical signs that it seems impossible to approach other civilizations, which are, in fact, often unreadable, in any other way than through these signs, which then leads us to describe their development in terms of tetrachords. But tetrachords can only apply to civilizations whose offshoots we are and that in their time made the choices that are ours. There may be others. The story of music should be related in ages: bamboo or skin age, fiber string age, bronze and cowbell age. We may imagine that then the struggle between sounds of determined pitch and complex sounds was not so unequal and that consequently musique concrète is not such a bad route back to the sources. Eventually, we discover that *the* music we so improperly call "traditional" is practically contemporary with the modern, technological period, preceding the electronic age by only a few centuries.

We, on the contrary, intend to take a more universal approach to musics. An authentic analysis of these should rest on the type of comparison of sounds we have suggested, by classes, genres, and species, first raising the question of the historical choice of a *class* of dominant perceptions when a *genre* of sounds is being played. Here we discover "in embryo" one or several interactions of *values* when a particular *characteristic* of sound delivers them. So it is very easy to explain how primitive civilizations—unable to develop harmonically and having no well-determined registers, which depend on refined instrument making—should have turned not only to rhythm but also to evolving and complex sounds, in short to all the objects described in our typology.

The exploration of non-Western musics also reveals two main "states" of objects or at least the fact that some of these musics turned to the *continuous* as well as the *discontinuous*. Here Asia gets its revenge; in these musics it is very difficult for us to appreciate both sounds that vary from one degree to another and also intermediate notes that in our mother tongue are wrong (even if exquisitely so) and that Asian people must surely hear with a different ear. Our notation of this language (in discontinuous degrees and duration) will thus miss the essential, seeing as important what is not, and vice versa. The question is not how to transcribe these languages into our alphabet but how to discover the functions of their own musical objects and the original organization these bring about. It goes without saying that this must involve varying criteria, trajectories, and a particular dialectic of the perceptual field for this purpose, developing a particular natural relationship culturally among practitioners of this music.

Finally, and only then, comes the question of calibrations, always stupidly presented as essential and prerequisite. They are, as might be expected in our vocabulary, only *examples of species*. We will probably find that they, too, have a balance between the natural and the cultural.

35.4. CALIBRATIONS OF VALUES

We had promised not to discuss calibrations of values, because in a treatise that deals only with the description of the object, we were not in a position to do so. In fact, we find ourselves in a very one-sided situation between the attention given to some values, the central theme of impassioned discussions, and our neglect of the others (since some values are not even acknowledged and the relationships the perceptual field allows them even less so). So we fall between two schools: the excessive competence of Western musicians in the so-called chromatic calibration and our incompetence in those we can only glimpse. The important thing, however, is to point out the plurality of calibrations and to condemn the tendency to bring them into line with the calibration in degrees, as if this were the model, both natural and cultural, for all the others. This tendency is all the more absurd as it coincides, historically, with the rejection of diatonicism.

In this chapter we will at least endeavor to clear a terrain cluttered with very different problems, which have usually been conflated. We will distinguish between

- the natural phenomenon of the main harmonic degrees,
- the cultural phenomenon of the scales based on these,
- the frame of reference formed by these scales,
- leaving out of our discussion the exploration of harmonic rules, which themselves can be deduced from the above.

A program such as this is very similar to those that have been expounded by more competent researchers than us.[2] We have absolutely no intention of discussing this question all over again but only to attempt a brief foray into the natural foundations of music, limiting its scope to musics "of tonic pitch." Moreover, we will be happy simply to explore the possible origin of the diatonic scale. We cannot but be surprised, in fact, at the ever-greater divide between musicians of equal good faith but firmly lodged, it seems, in one or other of the warring camps where the problem of consonance is concerned.[3]

Pythagoras, according to Jacques Chailley, did not "make it his aim to determine the intervals produced by preestablished relationships, but he was struck by the coincidence between previously known intervals and relationships between string lengths."[4] So here we have an experimental finding and not an a priori construct. "Of course he does not know the principle of harmonics, discovered only in the seventeenth century, and sees only string lengths, therefore *relationships between consecutive sounds*, which he transforms into simultaneous consonances only by means of an *a posteriori* thought experiment." How can a string be divided? Into two halves of course, but then? The simplest fractions after this are two-thirds and three-quarters. And so we obtain the fifth and the fourth, and we notice, with Chailley, that tone is not defined "as the relationship between harmonics 8 and 9, but as the difference (relationship) between the 2/3 fifth and the 3/4 fourth." The string length relationship corresponding to the tone is indeed: $2/3:3/4 = 8/9$. For Chailley, the mastery of degrees happens progressively. "By ending direct observation at the number 4, Pythagoras is simply conforming to the state of consonance of the primitive ear at the first stage of its progress from level to level. . . . Thus the framework of a Pythagorean melody cannot be the perfect chord C E G C. It is

2. See, perhaps most notably, Jacques Chailley, *Formation et transformation du langage musical* (Paris: PUF, 1961).

3. Only a few researchers are endeavoring to bridge this abyss; see, e.g., Edmond Costère, *Mort et transfiguration de l'harmonie* (Paris: PUF, 1962). While not sharing the ideas or the conclusions of this author, we must acknowledge that the general direction of his research is very much needed.

4. From earliest antiquity: Egypt, etc. See Chailley, *Formation et transformation*.

usually C F G C, and to the very end of the Middle Ages every Western melody is Pythagorean."[5]

35.5. SIMPLE RELATIONSHIPS

The debate generally gets off to a bad start because people seem to put forward "simple relationships" as a sort of metaphysical justification. We need to take a closer look.

Two experimental facts establish what we called in book 3 "correlations" between the physical phenomenon and musical perception. It seems that no one has ever properly identified that the two facts are different or that they are correlative rather than explanatory. The first "fact," the Pythagorean experiment, can be verified by pupils in the string classes in our conservatories. When a cellist goes up the scale on the C string, he divides the string successively into fractions respectively equal to 8/9, 5/6, 3/4, 2/3, 3/5, in order to play D, E, F, G, A after C on the open string (and we wisely stop there, before the "leading" note, and for good reason).

What Pythagoras had neither seen nor heard was discovered in the seventeenth century, and Helmholtz worked out the theory of it a hundred years ago; it is something completely different: the same string (and not the strings next to it on the lute or the fractions of the C string divided up by the cellist's finger) vibrates like a spindle for the fundamental, but also in two, three, four, five, and so on spindles, revealing the existence in the same "tonic" sound of a series of harmonics, whose comparative frequencies are like successive whole numbers.

The two phenomena (the old and the new) are so different that they can be isolated. "Pure" electronic sounds with no harmonics show only the first correlation between frequency and degree if we make them go up the scale.

Now, even though the way these two distinct correlations tally appears remarkable to the physicist, it is only convincing musically through a general consensus. If we want to rewrite history, we deny this consensus. And so these days we observe two contradictory (and largely uncompared) attitudes on the part of physicists and musicians: the former continuing to attach the greatest importance to consonance, the latter not caring a damn.

The discussions about all this are therefore far from achieving unanimity, even among scientists, because of the prevailing uncertainty about the perception of harmonics. Some ask, What role can they play, since we can't hear them? Others remark that, as harmonics are different from one timbre to another, consonances must be subject to change. Helmholtz's classification is challenged by another, related it is true, based on the (subjective) perception of additional or differential sounds N_1+N_2, N_1-N_2, and so forth.

5. See *Proceedings of the Colloque international d'acoustique musicale de Marseille* (Paris: CNRS, 1958).

It is in Professor Winckel's[6] writings that we find the most positive contribution.[7] "Helmholtz," he says,

> had already drawn attention to the similarity of harmonics in consonant chords. The notion of residual sound enables us to see that there is also a degree of similarity in the residual fundamental; that is, we can find identical components coming from two different intervals. . . . The view that sinusoidal sounds would give the same sensation of consonance has now been invalidated after a series of experimental demonstrations. Natural sounds show a coincidence between residual harmonics and hence a greater degree of similarity. The effect of consonance is therefore proportional to the number of harmonics, that is, the *richness of the timbre*. So this effect is weaker for chords on the flute than on the trumpet.[8]

This remark corroborates what we have said: consonance is not a relationship in itself but depends on the objects present and, since they are assumed to be tonic, on the structure of their timbre. The perception of intervals does, indeed, rest on facts and classifies them in a certain *natural order*.[9]

Even if the fact is confirmed in this way, the explanation itself is not always given. This is because, misled by the schoolboy axiom—an error expounded again and again—that we hear tonics through the fundamental, we cannot really understand the purpose of these harmonics we cannot hear, or that we hear in the form of timbre, in the reasons given to explain consonance. Now, we demonstrated in book 3 that as a general rule the perception of tonics involved the whole of the spectrum, and we were surprised that this observation, which we were not the first to make, had so little impact. So it is otiose to ask whether we hear harmonics or not;[10] it is harmonics, their series, perceived as a whole (a musical object precisely) that reveal the tonic to us. From this starting point the explanation becomes convincing: when we compare two sounds, we are not comparing two numbers (their simple relationships would not necessarily explain a law of perception) but two "structures," which have a greater or lesser number of "shared" as well as "different" features. The permanence-variation law thus applies to the most basic phenomenon in

6. Fritz Winckel, *Vues nouvelles sur le monde des sons*, trans. Abraham Moles (Paris: Dunod, 1960). [Published in English as *Music, Sound and Sensation*, trans. Thomas Binkley (New York: Dover, 1967).—Trans.]

7. See *Proceedings of the Colloque international* (cited above).

8. Helmholtz classified intervals in this way, according to their degree of consonance, basing his findings on the number and proximity of their shared harmonics: octave (2/1), twelfth (3/1), perfect fifth (3/2), perfect fourth (4/3), major sixth (5/3), major third (5/4), minor third (6/5), minor sixth (8/5).

9. This whole discussion about "consonance," to our mind, concerns only intervallic functions and not the justification of the rules of harmony, which raise a completely different problem.

10. A new proof of musical theorizing, taking into account only the value or the (physical) magnitude, and ignoring the object: priority should be given to perception.

music: the intervallic relationship. The more points two of these structures have in common, the more apparent is their consonance (melodically at first, then harmonically). The fewer they have, the less natural is their relationship (these harmonic structure relationships are represented visually in figure 46).

So we can now understand more clearly why the theory of scales has remained so elusive. One of the reasons for the ambiguity is that so-well-taught error that tonics are perceived through their fundamental; the other is too much naturalism: theoreticians would like to base the Western scale entirely on the natural phenomenon of consonance. Because they cannot, they sell the whole thing down the river. He who wishes to prove too much . . .

35.6. REFERENCE STRUCTURES

It is beyond our remit to look any further into the origin of scales and to decide for good and all whether the seventh degree is a convention. We know enough about it to say that this is highly unlikely and to state that musical civilizations will diverge profoundly from here, perhaps attaching the most intense significance to this one degree of freedom: so the leading note is well named. From the above facts we can also identify the origin of the diatonic scale in three perfect superimposed chords or, again, the so-called Pythagorean scale in the sequences of fifths; all very logical but constructed as a complement to natural data. Finally, once these degrees are given, the freedom to take one rather than another as the tonic for a mode is just a question of choice, tradition, and conditioning. So we go from a few fundamental natural elements to a quite different order of facts, obviously cultural, developed through the most rigorous learning processes.

So we have two categories of very different problems, depending on whether they involve natural or conventional reference structures. This difference is not generally perceived, and for good reason, since the idea of a fundamental dualism does not even cross people's minds. The examples we are about to give will endeavor to explain each type of problem in turn.

First we will look at the problem of the change in cultural references at a high level of development and formulation. Atonalism, just like the Chinese scale, rejects diatonicism. But these three systems also have some degrees in common (used in different ways, it is true), apparently arising from that minimum of natural bases that we have just been discussing. How does this serve them, or does it limit their freedom?

We will start with *atonalism*.

The term indicates that it rejects tonal reference. Better still, the rules for the use of the twelve sounds without omission or repetition guarantee this. Here we have a conventional level of complexity, where it is certainly difficult to alter spontaneous reference but where earlier developments in tonality had prepared the way through successive transgressions. There are still degrees, however, that are harmonic in the atonal scale, and it is difficult to deny their effectiveness, which—in our view—is of natural origin.

The recourse to the value of intervals is, moreover, implicit in atonal music—for example, in the creation of series by inversion. Also there are two ways open to atonalism. One consists in reincorporating intervallic functions outside diatonicism,[11] the other in getting rid of them and going imperceptibly and, as it were, unconsciously from distinct, tonic pitches to "blocks of sound," which come under our definition of "complex mass" and no longer allow chromatic relationships to be heard. Between the two, there are short-lived musics, and ambiguities between the intervallic relationships and gradations (not the degrees) of a pitch register, presenting the same type of *nuances* as the register of intensities.

We can give a striking example of the ambivalence or contradiction between using and simultaneously rejecting the harmonic register. From the standpoint of a generalized atonalism, people go so far as to reject the octave relationship and contemplate calibrations of sounds, from low to high, based on a choice of proportions independent of any traditional interval. This is technically possible in instrumental music and even more easily so in electronic music. So there is every chance—the tonal or consonant context being absent and also thrown into disorder by the complexity of the blocks of sound or the rapidity of the features—that the listener will no longer listen harmonically but according to the calibration of mels: the true (perceived) intervallic relationships between high and low are not now those from inverting or transposing, still in favor in serial music, but those determined by working out intervals in mels. Thus, Paul Pedersen gives as the equivalent of motif (a) in the midregister, not the same notes transposed into the bass register (b) but the equivalent motif in mels (c), a group perceptually nearer to the initial motif (a).[12] The composer is probably right on this point, but then it is the writing down that is likely to mislead. For, continuing to read in the key of G or F on a harmonic staff, we always attribute a (harmonic) value to these notes. They no longer have one; they are merely signs for performance, like piano keys or instrumental fingering. They are no longer simply inadequate symbols that mask additional contents but signs that have lost all value. Worse than an illusory sense of security, they give false ideas and misinformation about the merchandise. Just as the physicist refuses point-blank to write decimals when he only knows the approximate value of their magnitude, so the musician should reject as false

11. "Does the disappearance of diatonicism mark the end of that imbuing of minds by the natural affinities of the octave, the fifth, the fourth? Not at all, and it is easy to demonstrate this: the most revolutionary of musicians are so inculcated by them that they conduct their musics as if they had imposed its law upon themselves." Costère, *Mort et transfiguration de l'harmonie*, 68; see also examples from Stockhausen, Boulez, et al.

12. Paul Pedersen, "The Mel Scale," *Journal of Music Theory* 9, no. 2 (1965): 295–308.

FIGURE 43

currency signs that no longer correspond either to what we hear or even to the relationships he is claiming to determine. Thus, even if we have decided to get rid of a conventional structure such as tonality, we continue, in fact, to return to the calibrations involved, and this on the two levels of making and hearing. We continue to produce harmonic sounds and notate them on a staff, and we pretend to hear them (or we endeavor, with the help of the score, to find them), without noticing that this may be either impossible, because of new contexts, or unjustified, because of new choices (see fig. 43).

This duality of planes does not occur in our second example, where harmonic perception, instead of being blurred (or negated), is reinforced. The Chinese scale (according to the most scholarly description of it) is also constructed on a series of fifths but limited to the first five. All its degrees are identical to ours and its intervals simplified. So they will not present any problem for natural perception: on the contrary their calibration, too obvious, will appear as follows:

C   G   D   A   E

which gives the scale:

C   D   E   G   A

or this other mode:

A   C   D   E   G

This last structure is remarkably symmetrical: two minor thirds frame two tones and form the following group of perfect fourths and fifths:

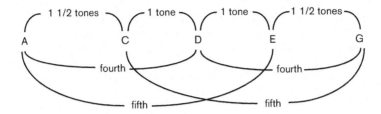

The strength, the "meaningfulness" of such a structure is very evident to Western ears. Instead of finding a neutral scale or a reference structure like the Chinese, we hear a motif. Also all Chinese melodies, for us who are differently conditioned, are only variations on a theme, insistent and repetitive, the *pentatonic theme* related to our own scale. The *musical meaning* in a traditional system therefore rests on the perception of *differential structures*.

This all-too-brief and very sketchy incursion into the domain of scales, in the penultimate chapter of this treatise, clearly demonstrates that it is ending precisely at the point where the debate most often begins. We hope it will at last inspire the reader to generalize the idea of the musical and also to set a boundary stone. At the basic level where we have chosen to be, the question of scales does not, in fact, yet arise: music theory defines the basics of musical perception, and so stops at the criteria for this and the interaction of the potential relationships among these criteria. Musical theories, which underpin particular musics, affirm the taste of civilizations: the choice, out of all possible structures, of those that will serve as their frame of reference.

35.7. LISTENING TO CONTEMPORARY MUSICS

Now we will count time not in millennia but in decades. In our day we are witnessing the confrontation between two tribes. The first is composers who construct musics *a priori* on precisely calculated scores. As these composers sometimes possess an overtrained ear (and here we must acknowledge the progress of the Western ear, at least in a specialized sense of making and hearing), they have some chance of hearing their music as they have written it. The other tribe is (uninitiated) amateurs or (experienced) enthusiasts who both have nothing but their ears. Scandalized or interested, they generally hear something different from what the composer intended for them—the same thing that arouses their repulsion or their interest. Then come the elect (this is us, reader), in the minority but enlightened by a modest revelation: we also only believe our ears but ears trained over several years in the practice of the types, classes, genres, and species in the generalized theory of music. Here, independently of any organizational analysis (and of any aesthetic allegiances or dislikes), we practice musical dictation: we are capable of deciphering these, and other non-Western, musics. We even occasionally observe strange similarities between the former and the latter (which, from our point of view, is by no means a criticism). We feel uneasy, however: our reasons for appreciating these so-well-calculated compositions are not the same as their composers' reasons: we can see a divorce between what they intended to write and what we were able to hear.

This is where, in our opinion, the debate should take place; the communication between composer and listener and their shared interpretation of what is "given to hear" could be made very much clearer if this were so.

Several of us have in fact practiced careful listening to contemporary works, whether orchestral, electronic, or electroacoustic. We have applied our typological rules for identification to them, our division into classes, genres, and species, which, moreover, these "dictations" from experience have led us to revise constantly, bringing them to their—still quite rudimentary—state in the present study. We can say that this analysis is fruitful and, in any case, gives an account of reality in a better though other way than a symbolism that is both inadequate and persnickety. Even if we have been reluctant to elevate such analyses prematurely to the level of composition, we are convinced that they are possible, indispensable even, and certainly very different from the working schemas of performance scores.

To recapitulate the methods and the findings of these exercises in "musical translation":

(a) We identify objects in the works, and we carefully observe whether they emerge in the classical way through traditional values or if they form new aggregates because of the complexity of the perceptual criteria involved or the continuity of their variations. Generally speaking, this is how *musical objects* define themselves in relation to the continuity or the discontinuity of the musical fabric.

(b) We also recognize the *types of objects* the composer chooses in a particular work, and this, of course, stems from the way he uses the orchestra or instruments. In general, these do not play note by note any more, and it takes only a moment to discern the composer's preference for webs, iterative sounds, rapid varying objects, cells, and so on.

(c) Independently of this typology, often characteristic of a composer's "style," we will have identified the *genre of sounds* he favors and the main permanence-variation relationships he uses. Of course, this is where the listener's agitation is the greatest, an agitation shared, let us be in no doubt, by the composer himself. The latter may very well have worked everything out on paper, but where the results are concerned, he is usually in a state of uncertainty unless, fanatically obsessed with his own ideas, he is resolved to hear only what is on the performance schema he has finally learned by heart. We are sorry for him. We can only advise him to go back to the classical gesture of the painter, who stands back to see the *effect*.

(d) So, then, the listener will always turn to his natural reference structures, developed by his own conditioning. The contents of his listening then become very personalized. He hears in detail or in "bulk." He may refer to what is too well known or be taken aback by too much strangeness.

(e) We are talking here about listening *from beginning to end* in memorizable sequences that do not necessarily coincide with phrases. What is certainly important is that the work should communicate a *meaning* that will be examined at greater depth on further listening, which is always essential. But what is this meaning (or these possible meanings) at the level of the overall form?

We can see that we have just gone round the cycle of "quadrants": identification of the state of objects or types in *(a)* and *(b)*, perception of the *genre of* fundamental *relationships* in *(c)*, measured against *reference structures* in *(d)*; finally, in *(e)* we come to the question of *meaning*—that is, of the work as an overall structure, which rests on the whole preceding framework.

35.8. A PRIORI MUSICS

Unfortunately, analyses such as these are not at all convincing to anyone who is not trained in *reduced listening* and has not attempted to use this training to decipher works. We would wager, however, that when a sophisticated public, or at least an experienced composer, listens to a modern work—without being party to the score—they do hear roughly what we have just more clearly outlined: dynamic or harmonic forms, the stuff of which sound is made, developments of matter or color, dust clouds or traceries of sound, profiles, and webs. The difference between the two approaches is that the one we are recommending, made at the level of perception, does not aim to be anything other than a description of the objects perceived (and not a justification of their organization), whereas note-by-note analysis, based on the score, generally claims to do both things simultaneously: to *describe* what the listener is perceiving, while at the same time *justifying* the validity of the work. The debate that for years has pitted serial music against experimental music certainly reflects this difference in perspective.

We will look a little more closely at the two typical variants of a music justified a priori in this way—the score and the blueprint—leaving to theoreticians the task of upholding their theses.

We will begin with an analysis of a passage from opus 31 by Webern, as presented by Michel Fano:

> Four different blocks of sound: six initial and six final sounds in similar and contrary series with their homeomorphism seen in pairs, I and II, III and IV:

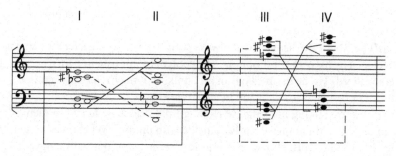

FIGURE 44

as is the permanence of the variant (in dotted lines) for the two pairs. Furthermore, on each of the four blocks, a transformation—timbre, register, intensity, duration—an example of which on block IV is shown below:

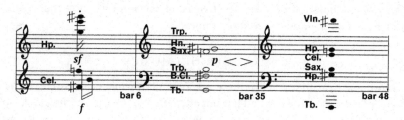

FIGURE 45

In the latter example (Bar 48), block IV being only a component of a 12-tone complex.

Fano continues:

> Where we observe the persistence of certain *invariants*—not necessarily affecting the same parameters—the result is successive distortions of an identical sound block, a homeomorphic character i.e. a bi-univocal and bi-continuous transformation of its components.
>
> Even if a whole *collection* of blocks that are themselves homeomorphic gives a similar number of different sounds, we will nonetheless be dealing with a single figure.
>
> Moreover, if we isolate the transformation *variants* in the various blocks we will identify a *group* of operations (in the group theory sense) which, freed from their individual sound blocks, will have an influence on other organizational planes, thus creating an isomorphism of structures whose series will turn out to be the *law of composition*.
>
> All we need to add is that only a *diagonal* intermingling of structures (and not a juxtaposition or a superimposition) will lead to a torsion of the *entirety* at any par-

ticular moment by bringing about the essential interactions that will affect all the groups, without which any formal attempt is likely to remain fruitless.[13]

It is not we who have done the italicizing but the author, and we are grateful to him for it: there could not be a better opportunity to explain the similarities and differences between this method of analysis and our own. First, the *permanence-variation* axiom, although couched in highly abstract terms, will have been recognized; the "single figure" refers to permanence, and the "different sounds" are the possible variants of this. As for the "block of sound" that is being worked on (a term not defined in any other way), it doubtless refers to something more general than a chord since it is given another name: why not what we call "musical object"? But even if we notice the transfer of block IV on to other timbres, we are told nothing about the nature of this transformation; as for the "diagonal intermingling" that ensures the perception of the "entirety," how does it work? In other words, Fano's explanation seems to us to be extremely accurate as far as musical writing is concerned, but it stops there and takes hardly any account of what is "given to hear." Now this is where our investigation starts; what, with this judicious organizational formula, are the justifications, the perceptible effects, as much on the level of this group of "blocks of sound" as of the development of the *entirety?*

35.9. SERIAL GENETICS IN ELECTRONIC MUSIC

Before continuing the discussion, we will examine the other way serial music operates: Stockhausen's method in his 1953 *Electronic Study No. 1.* We admire many other works by Stockhausen, where the instinctive inspiration is, in our opinion, infinitely better than the explanatory systems he recommends. We are less impressed by the text we are about to discuss now. We should, however, give him credit for having shed light on the assumptions behind a *theoretically* conceived electronic music. Finally, we should make it clear that the experiment described in this text deserves closer technical examination on account of its serious nature.[14]

We do not want to quibble with the author over his use of sinusoidal sounds, or of any particular procedural detail; all that concerns us here is his overall attitude toward the musical:

> Starting from the optimum auditory field, the fact that sounds will tend to move toward a nonexistent frequency on the one hand and an infinite frequency on the other will be felt proportionately as these sounds tend toward either infinitely small

13. Michel Fano, "Pouvoirs transmis," in "La musique et ses problèmes contemporains, 1953–1963," *Cahiers Renaud-Barrault,* no. 41 (1963): 50–51. [Michel Fano (b. 1929) is a composer, musicologist, and teacher who collaborated with the GRM in the 1960s.—Trans.]

14. Our reader may refer to Karlheinz Stockhausen's whole article, "Une expérience électronique," in "La musique et ses problèmes contemporains, 1953–1963," *Cahiers Renaud-Barrault,* no. 41 (1963): 91–105.

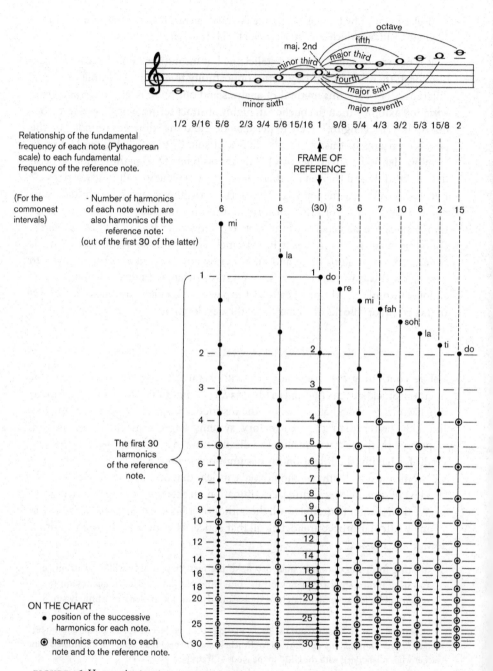

FIGURE 46. Harmonic structures.

FIGURE 47   FIGURE 48

amplitudes or infinitely short durations. In other words, taking into account the physiological conditions of listening in the low and high registers, the perception of the shortest duration and also thresholds of intensity (pain and audibility thresholds), we have acknowledged that there is a frontier, nevertheless quite relative, beyond which the tendency toward a soundless, timeless absolute is implicit. Could this one day be made perceptible? Thus serial structure will suggest a rotating sound world, with no possible development: the essential, the tendency to move toward thresholds, will be implied in the creation of each series: concepts suggesting tension, such as "beginning," "development," "end," "middle," or "final" will be abolished; past, present, and future will be one and the same.

We can see several initial assumptions here, as well as a reference to Fletcher's curves (which give the frontiers of the absolute). The composer could just as well have tried to compensate for the deterioration of sound sensation at the limits of the audible; on the contrary, he has chosen to accentuate this fading away. Thus he postulates a "rotating" (we would say "rounded") domain, where the usual tensions, particularly those between pitches, tend to disappear and where as a result time, it is hoped, will be abolished (?). Furthermore, superimpositions of pitch will create timbres: "by using simple intervallic proportions (harmonic proportions), timbre will simply be the result of their combinations."

So everything depends on the series of the chosen proportions. This is where we must pause in contemplation; this is the Elevation, the moment of pure performative authority, of supreme freedom: it is decided that the series will be as follows:[15]

$$\frac{12}{5} \quad \frac{4}{5} \quad \frac{8}{5} \quad \frac{5}{12} \quad \frac{5}{4}$$

The implacable law will now apply to the entire creation of the work: the general illustration of the frequencies used, the grouping of sound complexes, the variant of these groupings by "modulo-permutation"; for the latter, it is true,[16] a second sovereign act occurs in the form of an organizational series, chosen

15. To give a clear idea of these proportions, they can be written down like this (fig. 47).

16. This is the tempered approximation, which gives an idea of the sonority of these complexes (fig. 48).

"because it is asymmetrical and determined by the overall formal concept." This magic formula is:

4   2   3   5   6   1

One more detail: as it is necessary to "make a clear distinction between the individual timbres of each complex by means of dynamic degrees," complexes of frequencies will be made by means of the following dynamics, corresponding to each number:

1: flat profile;	2: flat and resonance;
3: crescendo;	4: crescendo-resonance;
5: decrescendo;	6: decrescendo-resonance.

However arbitrary these various choices may be, we can rely on Stockhausen to have reduced his authorial interventions to a minimum. The idea is, in fact, clearly asserted: "When a series of sound complexes were used in my two latest works, a contradiction emerged between the use of preestablished spectra (instruments) and the application of the serial structure to the timbres. A solution to this problem can be found by working with sinusoidal sounds, for the timbre will be defined by the number of sinusoidal sounds that make a vertical complex and by the intervallic proportions between these sounds and their respective amplitudes. Composing with complexes defined in this way amounts to integrating timbre into polyphony by the very fact of bringing them into play."

There is certainly something fascinating (like self-harm) or absorbing (like totalitarianism) in this ferocious quest for the compulsory link, for integration at all costs, for the development of the whole from an initial cell that could be—and soon will be for others—taken from chance itself. Unfortunately, all the facts of perception we have discussed in this treatise run against such a concept of musical genetics. Furthermore, if Stockhausen, as he admits, has conceived "a real aversion to the dead-end experiments with 'sound objects' made by the musique concrète group," we should in turn acknowledge—in all friendliness, why not—our no less real aversion to the sort of experiment we have just been discussing. We should at the very least take note that these are two implacably opposed attitudes toward the musical.

We could interpret Stockhausen's position as a salutary reaction against worn-out ideologies, an essential return to concrete principles. Even then we ought to retain aspects of the scientific spirit, adherence to the real, mistrust of hypotheses, instead of giving in to a mimicry of numbering and measuring. Now a physics of musical listening based solely on Fletcher's curves, which ignores the most elementary facts of perception, even those acknowledged by other physicists, can only lead to formulae for manufacturing instructions. It is our turn now to denounce a self-satisfied and deceitful aspect of the most blinkered amateurism.

Michel Fano's analysis of Webern's "sound blocks" is, in our opinion, just as obsolete. We have acknowledged the idea, already familiar to us, of a balancing act between permanence and variation. But, whereas we take our information only from listening, Fano confidently deduces a law of composition from a formula, basing his analysis on the score alone. Certainly, this varying element in unvarying structures has a good chance of being perceptible. If we set out to verify it, we find a—highly interesting—experimenter's hypothesis. If this is imposed as a law justifying composition, it is through blind obstinacy and the confusion of three levels: *elementary perception, referentiality*, and *meaning*. Using the pretext of the nominal permutation of a note or the transferral of the block to other instrumental timbres, they want to make us say at one and the same time:

(a) that we can perceive this formula,

(b) that it is has a frame of reference, and

(c) that with further perceptions of its variants it can form the basis of the structure of the work.

This is too much for such a narrow base. It is unfortunately often possible to observe in contemporary thought a refusal to see this upward movement and a taste, as it were, to keep to lower level determinist systems. We really must try to understand why. This is what will lead us, in the next chapter, to raise the level of debate.

35.10. OUTSIDE THE SERIES

Let us go back to language.[17] The phonological level is the only one that does not refer directly to meaning, except to give access to the signifying levels of lexis and syntax. Lexis and syntax make up a code, with which every speaker must comply under pain of not being understood.

But as soon as this speaker combines words following the rules, *he says something*, which knowledge of the code alone would never allow us to expect. Once the thing is said, we check that the utterance conforms to the code and actually respects the linguistic rules. But the content of the message and its literary, poetic, philosophical, or scientific value belong to the writer, the poet, the philosopher, the scientist, in short to the users of the language, speakers or listeners, who concentrate on the meaning while forgetting the rules that allow this meaning to be transmitted.

Whether music is a language or not, it appears impossible not to recognize these three levels. The most everyday musical analysis, even the most inaccurate

---

17. The word *series* in this section's title is a reference to serial music, a concept against which Schaeffer fought, as being predetermined composing not based on listening. Here "hors série" is also a play on words, as the expression (referring to music other than serial, and most probably to "musique concrète") also means "out of the ordinary," "special," "exceptional."—Trans.

literature on music, distinguishes at least implicitly between theory, syntax, and the work, which has a meaning. We need to know whether this distinction still exists in contemporary musical thought. Are we the only ones who think this way?

"Grammar is not language," Luciano Berio writes, "but only one of its dimensions. In a language continuity such as our own, we could not possibly have a single grammar, but many ideas and possible levels of 'grammaticality,' independent of any idea of semantic signification. The word comes later. . . . That is why I consider the concept of serial music as something linguistically indefinable—the opposite of a complete language. This concept may perhaps be useful to give a generic description of a tendency toward grammatical plurality and multiplicity, or to designate part of the chronology of the most important musical events of this century."[18]

This sentiment is echoed by Pierre Boulez, who first of all sheds some light on those notorious "sound blocks" discussed by Fano (chords or objects?):

> In reality, there is a great deal of ambiguity in the use of these chords, which are "sound blocks" and can become "whole" objects, the timbre and intensity then being an integral part of this combination: this is where we would call for the creation of a hyper-instrument whose sounds would be a function of the work itself. This links up with the present concerns of electronic music, where this goal is pursued with pure sinusoidal sounds; however, in most cases until now, a timbre that appears as such is very rarely achieved by superimposing sinusoidal sounds: we are more likely to obtain refined harmonic effects. The aim of research should be to try to analyze under what conditions, whether with electronic sinusoidal sounds or this hyper-instrument, a combination of existing instruments, the ear can really perceive a timbre that results from these, and is not a simple add-on.[19]

Point made. So we come to recognize a unit of perception until now given the all-purpose name "sound block," which would be a "whole" object indissolubly linking together pitches, timbres, and intensities.

"The misunderstanding that dogs us and that we must be terribly wary of," Boulez continues,

> is confusing composition and organization. A coherent system is, in fact, a prerequisite for any composition. . . . But the web of possibilities made available by this system must not be simply set out (on the page) and considered to be enough in itself for the requirements of composition. Indeed it seems that, out of a "religious" respect for the magic power of number and the desire for an "objective" work depending on

---

18. Review of *Preuves*, no. 180 (Feb. 1966): 31, Luciano Berio's contribution, "Façon de parler," to André Boucourechliev's survey *La musique sérielle aujourd'hui* (Paris: Preuves, 1965–66).

19. Pierre Boulez, "Auprès et au loin," *Cahiers Renaud-Barrault*, no. 3 (1954). [The article can be found in English as "Near and Far," in *Stocktakings from an Apprenticeship*, trans. Stephen Walsh (Oxford: Clarendon, 1991).—Trans.]

a much less uncertain criterion than the composer's free will, and out of some thought still about a contemplative mode of hearing, we are abandoning the task of composing to organizational systems.

We ought, on the contrary, to see the work as a series of rejections in the midst of so many probabilities; we must make a choice, and herein lies the difficulty so well sidestepped by the express desire for objectivity. It is precisely choice that constitutes the work, repeated at every moment of composition: it will never be possible to reduce the act of composing to the fact of juxtaposing these nascent connections in one immense set of statistics. We must safeguard this inalienable freedom: the constantly hoped-for good fortune from an irrational dimension.

These are important lines. They should enable us to distinguish between personal inspiration, which we do not share, and methodological conclusions identical to our own.

That from an aesthetic point of view Boulez bases his choices on "rejection," whereas we base ours on "expectations"; that the word *contemplation* is pejorative for him, whereas, if there is still any trace of a preestablished harmony in the series, that it should be contemplated is precisely what we would ask; that, finally, he sees what is inalienable in our freedom as "the irrational," whereas for us freedom is reason—all this is of little importance in our present discussion. In fact, from the methodological point of view the idea that there is a distinction between sonority and musicality, between the experience of the ear and of the mind, and between the planes of the perception and use of objects, which we have argued time and again, is acknowledged here (although vaguely, and as it were secondarily).

We could simply shrug our shoulders at all this: what is the point of these arguments over method? Provided a musician has talent, he will get by; the main thing is that he makes music. True, but must we then go back to the cult of personality, after castigating the libertarians for this for so long?

35.11. THE THREE TIERS

The details of the discussion on new bases for music about to take place here, although very ancient and fundamental, are, in fact, very poorly understood. Certainly, we share the opinions we have just quoted, but we are scarcely any further on. If we accept that there are "several levels of grammaticality," then we must conclude that these days we have no fundamental rule for music, or at least no generally accepted musical rule base that would constitute what was, for several centuries, the "common fund" of the musical language system. First of all, therefore, there is confusion between the levels linguists call phonology and morphology. If new frames of reference are in the process of being formed, then it is amid the most impossible tangle of stereotypes and neologisms. If, moreover, we need to distinguish between organization of materials and composition, this is because there is a higher level of meaning, to which organization itself is subordinate. Now, in the traditional system, we could clearly see these three tiers of musical language. At an "acoulogical" stage, which was so well integrated that it seemed as if it were immutable, with no possible variants, was a certain number of sounds made by a limited instrumentarium defining a "musical" completely purged of "sound." Then there were the structures of music theory; and over and above these were the structures of scales whose hybrid origins we have briefly mentioned, the whole melodic-harmonic code that we have put aside as being beyond the remit of a music theory, but which very clearly constitutes practically the whole traditional frame of reference. Finally, there were the works with their internal regime guaranteeing the meaning, like the meaning of a text, about which we said that it did, indeed, depend on the language system but in its essence eluded it. What is left of all this today, and who is openly asking questions about it?

This is why we have deviated from present-day problems, which seemed to us to be wrongly presented, and have analyzed the traditional system. We have made a distinction here, and we still attach great importance to it—because it is unusual—between the theory of harmonic sounds and the theory of scales with its various consequences. And above all, we have certainly not deduced from what is above what we vainly expected from it: a more rational harmony or rules for new languages. Similarly, when we suggest parametrical relationships, and—ultimately in a true spirit of empiricism—link together various arbitrarily chosen values, it is simply an instinct (which should be tested experimentally) that justifies the new choice and ordering of objects; there is nothing to prove that this is getting us any nearer to the final level of meaning or even that we can be reassured about musical perceptions at the elementary level of objects. We were able to work at the strictly linguistic level to devise new codes or syntaxes, but we still need to see whether they will be perceived and to test out what contribution these new utterances make. In other words, we should be able to test out every new, relatively arbitrary, musical system at its two extremes: materials, for the *structures actually perceived*, and ultimate meaning, where *perceptual structures*, always rather general, come into play. These reflections show the futility of a single frame of reference or a unitary generic schema: what is below can neither give rise to what is above nor account for it.

35.12. MUSICS

This plural has often been used in the course of this work. The reader will have understood that it refers to the variants presented by musical civilizations. But they were implicitly referred back to "Music," thus arguing a common ancestry for all these musics, as once we argued an original language system, the common ancestor of all language systems (an idea now abandoned for language systems but certainly not for music, owing to the importance of natural data in the phenomenon of music). So it remains, it seems, to clarify from the variants what this common ancestry is. This whole treatise has endeavored to answer that question. At least it has finally recognized two shared features of all traditional music: a fundamental, more or less developed, harmonic relationship between pitch and timbre and a staging over three successive levels (objects, frames of reference, and meaning).

A quite different aspect, a quite different plural, now appears. It is the common ancestry itself that is in jeopardy in two ways. We have already mentioned the first, which consists in introducing relationships other than harmonic between objects, which is masked by present-day notation. But more important still is the abandonment of any shared reference system, and this, indeed, seems to be the result of the development of serial musics latterly. Our entire critique of a priori systems has, in fact, been made with a view to finding justifications for the musical both below and above serial schemas. Below, it would be verification from authentic perceptions, confirmed by an experimental approach or an artistic practice. Above all, it would be verification through a dialectic resulting from differential structures, in accordance with "implied" reference structures.

Even if we still hold to our criticisms attacking the absence of perceptual bases for most serial formulae set up a priori, we do not think that every music is absolutely required to have conventional reference structures similar to the traditional melodic-harmonic code. But then this music must *renounce* the *status* of our usual musics. Polemics aside, this is what we would suggest to clarify the idea of "variant schemas" suggested by Boulez. In effect, from the moment when the relationships between the distinctive features of sound are perceptible, and set up as musical criteria through an artistic decision gradually adopted by society, why should we not arrange objects *directly* in structures, going straight from the "acoulogical" level to the level of overall organization, as a building is constructed according to the logic of the materials, and not a discourse arising from a code? There is no objection to this, but we must be aware of what we are abandoning. Saussure's essential idea for defining language systems is differentiation ("in a language system there are only differences");[20] similarly, the traditional musical language system is only a language system because we have forgotten sound, almost as much as in the language of words. It is by reference to tonality and modality that musics are listened to. And the proof of this is given by the extraordinarily different meanings attached by an Indian, a European, an African, or a Chinese

20. Ferdinand de Saussure, *Course in General Linguistics*, ed. Charles Bally and Albert Sechehaye, trans. Roy Harris (Chicago: Open Court, 1983).—Trans.

person to a particular melodic structure (e.g., Indian morning and evening modes; major allegro for us, not for the Greeks). In this context we find a remark taken from linguistics by Theodor Adorno: "the material of composition is as different from the composition itself as spoken language is from the sounds at its disposal," and this is what makes him also say that "the psychology of music is problematic."[21]

Now, when we abandon the melodic-harmonic code and put forward "variant schemas," it is because meaning is no longer being sought through differential structures: meaning must be found in the work itself, its internal proportions, as with a building. This is where Adorno's statement is most unfortunate. We have never had more need than at this time to understand the object as material whose psychological properties are becoming essential, since we no longer have a code to assimilate and go beyond its immediate meaning toward a conventional significa-tion. Adorno's is a crucial remark, therefore, the importance of which will not escape those who recommend a music based on "variant schemas": no one has more need than they for a music theory that is realistic and completely restruc-tured from new experience.

But this is not all. Suppose now that the middle tier between the two outer tiers of meaning and fundamental perceptual structures has disappeared, at least as far as its strictest and best-known conventions are concerned. We must then look for meaning in the assemblage itself, in a completely new coherence between forms and material. Compared with the former music, a music such as this brings with it two simplifications: its perceptual registers are less refined but more "natural" (dynamic or color perceptions, much more apparent to the ordinary ear, are asso-ciated with harmonic perception); in addition, the disappearance of the conven-tional tier makes these musics more universal (as may be the case with a building, which is always more comprehensible to a foreigner, even if only more or less, than the native language system). So it is important to agree about terms, about what we call "music": we should, in fact, have two words or else take the plural "musics" to refer not only to relative differences in the code but to a divergence that is now radical on the level of both elementary materials and meaning.

But it is not enough to mention these differences in nature; we must also iden-tify differences in means. The image of a building substituted for a language is an opportune reminder. While it has always been possible to hum traditional music, it seems that the shape of contemporary music relies much more on

---

21. Theodor W. Adorno, *Philosophie de la nouvelle musique* (1948), trans. Hans Hildenbrand and Alex Lindenberg (Paris: Gallimard, 1962). Published in English as *Philosophy of New Music*, trans. and ed. Robert Hullot-Kentor (1949; Minneapolis: University of Minnesota Press, 2006).—Trans.

gesture.[22] What are these instrumentaria, very different daughters of the voice and hand?

35.13. TABLATURES

Here we return to origins of a sort, not a primitive stage used as an allegory but the perfectly clear origins of the present situation. Primitive man must have spelled out his sounds by any means at his disposal; we, who have all of them, must adopt a similar stance: to decipher those relationships between sounds that lead to one music rather than another. For it is not from a new instrument that we must now expect music; on the contrary, it is our quest for a music we desire that will make us invent instruments appropriate for it. It is no longer a question of scrambling an ill-matched orchestra together but of defining a *tablature*. We are using this old word in the absence of anything better to describe the development of an instrumentarium that would be more than instrumental technology developed at random and subject to every whim. The definition of *tablature* given by Machabey, "the representation of musical sounds specific to a particular instrument or category of instruments,"[23] refers, in fact, to something different from a technology of means; it is almost an analysis of contents. More broadly, tablature should describe the value relationships available to the sounds from a particular group of instruments. A "representation of musical sounds" such as this would, in the final analysis, be nothing other than an analysis of "*genres* of sounds," which we spoke about in earlier books.

It will not do to have experienced the extraordinary discovery of the universe of sound if we end up getting lost in it. As anything is possible at present, through analysis or synthesis, now is the moment to vigorously gather together chosen ways and means with a specific end in view. But what will we choose out of such abundance? Our aim is, precisely, to establish a little order and to reach a conclusion.

Ultimately, there are two extreme types of tablature: a "harmonic" type, where all the sounds have tonic pitch, and a "complex" type, where there are only nonharmonic mixtures of natural or artificial frequencies. Making a bold guess about what may happen in the future, we could say that every new sound instrument will more or less borrow from one of these systems and will strike the ear in one of these registers (or both at once, if the instrument is mixed).

22. Michel Butor, in an enthusiastic article, tells us about this truly exceptional feat: he hums Stockhausen. [See Michel Butor, *La musique, art réaliste* (Paris: Minuit, 1964).—Trans.]

23. Armand Machabey, *La notation musicale* (Paris: PUF, 1958).

35.14. MUSIC AND MACHINES

In the quest for means, what is the role of electronic machines, whether for composing scores or synthesizing sounds? We should make a distinction between synthesizers, devices for making sounds out of encoded electronic data, and calculating machines, which can process musical information in the same way as any other information. In both cases we may well expect to have to make preliminary choices, since we must give the machine a set of instructions. We will leave aside the question of machines used in automatic composition, which are suitable for research dealing with a completely encoded musical language. It is at the elementary level that we, who are focused on the material, are seeking to use machines—synthesizers as much as calculating machines in association with them.

Synthesizers are very flexible instruments for dealing with the combinatory initiative of a composer, but, as we know, they start from first principles that are quite different from those of musical experience. So it is lack of experience in knowing the right set of combinations to give the machine that has led experimenters to the failures we have discussed. Not that the machines themselves have no limitations of their own (perhaps they will never have the subtlety and sensitivity of a crafted sound), but electronic synthesis has suffered mainly from the simplistic ideas held by musicians about sound and the crude or arbitrary models they devised. Hence the need to undertake a thorough study of natural sounds, which are still very poorly understood and to stop reducing them to combinations of parameters.

How, under these conditions, can we use an instrument made specifically to combine parameters for the purposes of music? This is where the calculating machine may well outstrip the synthesizer. We think we need to give the synthesizer not a few crude and raw data, as Stockhausen used to do, but a very large quantity of data, and certainly instantaneous parametric data, to form each sound. Synthesis would then appear not as the gratuitous act of an inventor, or a composer's whim for "rigor," but as the equivalent of preliminary analyses, as has always been the case with technologies. The analysis we have recommended in this work consists in observing natural sounds or, if they are artificial or have never been heard before, observing *perceptual criteria*, which can be combined in innumerable *original* ways. The natural sounds would then be *models* with properties that could be reproduced or developed by the machine, capable of continuously "nourishing the sound" in the same way as the performer himself. This seems to us to be what is not only possible but also desirable, even if not profitable.[24]

---

24. We may also ask why go to so much trouble, if musical craftsmanship is still not only more subtle but above all more economical?

There is little likelihood, however, that this direction will be taken because of the two tendencies to be oblivious to the psychology of perceptions and to be too ready to hand over to machines the problem of choices and the quest for values, which is ultimately only the concern of the musical consciousness in the context of a personal and group experience. We will certainly need several decades more of furious research into machines before researchers, brought to their senses by the rebuffs of determinism, consent to go back to their own resources and, as we have suggested, admit to the necessity of a preexisting music theory.

35.15. THE TWO MUSICS

In the light of the two types of tablature defined in section 35.13, we find two "main" musics, which divide the common stock into two main branches. One, based on harmonic pitch relationships, has all sorts of cultural variants, each with "three degrees" of complexity: they are the musical languages known to date. The other, based on nonharmonic relationships, brings elementary perceptual structures and the overall form into direct contact with each other through "variant schemas." This branch leads to a music that (for the moment) has only two levels of complexity and is more like a building.

Of course, we are talking here about extreme examples (pure musics). We are more likely to come across transitional types, with a mixture of reference structures and variant schemas, chromatic notation and no authentic notation at all, in the most perfect ignorance of the distinctive features of sound and the musical registers perceived in practice.

In fact, depending on which of the two tablatures it is dealing with (or it may be a mixed type), the ear relies on one or the other perceptual pitch field (or both at once), which are marked out differently, orientated differently—one precise and the other not, one cultured and the other not. So we have two musical registers: one structured, the other amorphous; one repetitive, logarithmical, calibrated, the other only linear, approximate, nuanced.

In the same way, we can find two contrasting pairs of structures on the plane of intensity: structures that are uncompromisingly rhythmical, with fixed *spacing*, and dynamic structures that indicate the *presence* of sounds. We should add that sounds will have to be arranged in two large groups: homogeneous (or perceptibly homogeneous) sounds where the downbeats match the upbeats of the silences, and formed sounds where perception is different—the rhythm of the spacing, marked by impacts, no longer conforms to the laws of their internal duration, and the perception of this is anamorphosed.

So if we leave aside the question of timbres for a moment and concentrate, as in pure music, only on the dimensions of pitch and intensity in relation to duration, the two variants of music will share four relationships in the perceptual field, two by two. We have already identified a "harmonic field," chromatic in classical terms, where the location of tonic objects takes place, and a "colored field"[25] (by analogy with the visual appreciation of colors), to denote that other way of situating *non-harmonic sounds* (thick or complex) by means of approximate nuances going from the low to the high register. We will also give the name *rhythmic field* to the field of perception of *spacing* and the name *dynamic field* to the field that integrates *profiles*. The four relationships on which pure musics are based are thus as follows:

- harmonic field, with tonic objects,
- colored field, with complex objects,
- rhythmic field, with spacing or homogeneous sounds,
- dynamic field, with the impact of formed sounds.

35.16. THE CONTINUOUS AND THE DISCONTINUOUS

These four relationships assume the use of discontinuous objects described by means of pure, unambiguous criteria: tonic pitch or complex mass, homogeneous duration or impact. The theory of traditional music has always considered sounds as fixed, determined by the instrumentarium, unvarying through time; this is still the case here, except for objects that come under the last criterion, where the fluidity is masked (at least in traditional music) by a reassuring keyboard (piano) or a completely evanescent sound (string pizzicato). Now suppose we have fluid objects where these four criteria evolve in continuous variation. What will happen? Can we perceive new relationships? Doubtless, but we must look at them more closely. Our initial observation is that a glissando of pure pitch will not appear as anything other than a sound of complex mass evolving in pitch; conversely, a sound of complex mass going up the harmonic degrees in a scalar fashion creates intervals in conformity with the harmonic calibration. Moreover, an intensity evolving in duration, no longer anamorphosed as in an attack, but clearly perceived as in a swelled sound, is nothing other than a generalized dynamic profile of the object, now perceived as a dynamic trajectory. Consequently, although the perceptual criteria for these various objects are very different (a fixed complex mass is very different from a glissando, an attack very different from a willed dynamic profile), we can see that once more we come back to the two perceptual fields, colored and dynamic, *as a general mode of perceiving*. All this can be summed up in a diagram

25. The etymological identity of this term is amusing: there are two types of "chromaticism"—one has several hundreds of degrees; the other can be counted on the fingers of one hand. Therefore, we prefer to avoid the term *chromaticism*, which is too ambiguous to make a clear contrast between *harmonic* and *colored*.

describing six sorts of fundamental relationships between the objects presented to our ear and perceptual registers, in the knowledge that, depending on the speed of development, relationships in the continuous oscillate between the memory of old and the originality of new perceptions:

Objects presented to the ear:	Discontinuous harmonic sounds (fixed tonics)	Discontinuous nonharmonic sounds (fixed complex masses)	Glissando sounds (tonic or complex)
Properties of the perceptual field for scales of pitch:	Logarithmic, repetitive structure of pitch intervals: *degrees*	Linear continuum of nuances in the register: *color*	Evaluation of *melodic trajectories,* referred back to the registers of intervals or colors depending on their speed of development
Objects presented to the ear:	Homogeneous sounds	Sounds with attack	Sounds with sustained profile
Properties of the perceptual field for temporal *scales:*	Repetitive, arithmetic structure of *duration* intervals	Anamorphosis and location of an impact: *rhythm* of spacing	Evaluation of *dynamic trajectories,* referred back to the values of duration or to the rhythm of the spacing, depending on their speed of development

Objects presented to the ear.

This comparison gives two important results; it encourages us,

(*a*) on the one hand, in our ordering of objects, never to confuse the opportunities to employ either the repetitive register, eminently suited to the abstractness of formulae and figures, or the linear register, much less "musical" but very similar to a plastic register (visual, kinesthetic). We can see the enormous confusion on scores as soon as notations valid for the second column are applied to objects in the last two columns;

(*b*) on the other hand, to understand how to go from one music to the other by changing types of objects or, what amounts to the same thing, by changing duration modules, as described in chapter 14.

On this last point we will go into more detail. We will start with the most classical music. At the level of notes, which are the basis for optimal memorization, a
discontinuous material is used. On the contrary, on the level above, phrases, the
continuous is brought in: the linking of instrumental features, the development of
nuances, melodic development. As we have paid due attention to *ear time* and bulk
in the field, we are assured of good memorization, and the perception of the most
precise relationships, in short, the best "yield" from the perceptual field suitably
occupied by distinct aggregations.[26]

Imagine, on the contrary, that we have a music that uses continuous or complex
sounds. On the one hand, it has glissandi or masses that are neither situated nor
calibrated in the harmonic perceptual field. On the other hand, it gives melodic or
dynamic trajectories that did not exist before. This music has therefore chosen
both other objects and other perceptual qualities, which we call "plastic." It could
even be insinuated that it seeks its meaning where the previous music evaded it.
Suppose, in fact, that a classical type of music is hugely slowed down: phrases will
vanish over the horizon of memory, and discontinuous sounds will expand and
give rise to attack profiles that turn into dynamic trajectories, drawn-out sounds,
otherwise imperceptible, and so forth.

In a way these two musics are focusing on two different uses of the duration of
the object; "plastic" music adopts the level below the other music as its distinctive
level, after expanding it into a normal memorization module. At the higher level,
on the contrary, this new music made of elements in continuous variation, where
timbres and values are fused together, finally forms macro-objects, not phrases. At
the level of expression we come back to the discontinuous: a series of objects that
should find its meaning in an interobject relationship and not in relation to the
classical reference structures for the discontinuous, which at this level of complexity are completely lost from view.

35.17. POLYPHONY AND POLYMORPHY

Obviously, we have greatly simplified the fundamental relationships in the perceptual field, studying them in only a few types of objects (in general deponent, as the
reader will have noticed). But most objects figure in both fields, with more or less
prominent or nuanced dominants. Hence the importance of tablature, and of where
its resources are directed. Depending on which tendency dominates, we will have a
more "musical" or a more "plastic" music. One of the musics chooses the most subtle
field but has to be careful about the suitability of its objects on pain of being unintel-
ligible; the other chooses the most instinctive field (since it organizes itself naturally

---

26. This analysis can be generalized beyond the tonal system: it does not involve a particular choice
of scale but only the provision of a context allowing harmonic intervals to be perceived.

in a similar way to our other sensory registers) and relies on a general sense of proportion related to the dynamics of gesture, movement, muscular tension, and so on.

But we have left out that embarrassing partner, timbre. How can we include it in this overview? We can do so by introducing a third pair of types, arising from the fact that musical chains are multifarious, and can give the very classical alternative of counterpoint and harmony,[27] which we will generalize in the expression "polyphony-polymorphy." In fact, either we want to emphasize the coexistence of discourses that are both distinct and connected, and separate the "voices" through the artifice of instrumental timbre (the distinct voices of the traditional orchestra) or the independence of the parts of the fugue (the counterpoint of a single timbre); or we want to bring the constituent elements more closely together, do away with these voices as isolated protagonists, and reintegrate what they contribute into the web of a general metamorphosis: first, we turn to harmony (and so to orchestration that fuses timbres together into general chords or phrases); then we fashion orchestral objects by cutting out (the pointillism of timbres within the same form); or, finally, we fuse them together, not now to form dynamic trajectories set with timbres but to obtain blocks, iridescent sound stuff (polymorphy).

A music that gradually fuses its "voices" thus moves little by little from one perceptual field to another: it becomes polymorphic, and it is very clear that the development of an increasingly loaded harmony, which gradually blurs intervallic and timbre relationships, has always been one of the tendencies of traditional music.

So it seems that we can distinguish four poles in the way music is implemented, cardinal points that could help us situate the various domains of musical organization through illustrations similar to those in chapter 18.

These main tendencies would then be:

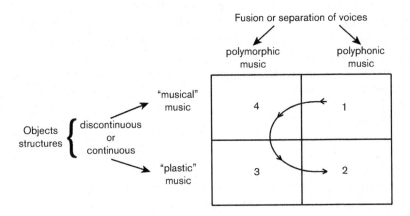

27. We are suggesting the schematic sense, of course: the juxtaposition of horizontal lines with a contrasting series of vertical slices.

It seems that Western development ran through the cycle in this way: if indeed a more and more harmonic music (4) has naturally succeeded the original polyphony (1), complicating and mingling contrapuntal relationships (1 → 4), we end up, also naturally, with a transitional music such as serial music (4 → 3), a music perceived as a series of objects linked together in the most logical way possible (3). But it may be that this logic is not convincing enough, while a polymorphic relationship between several chains of objects (2) would reestablish meaning, as in a building where a particular form has no meaning in itself but takes on meaning within the whole. We often speak about a new dimension in music (wrongly called "spatial"); this is nothing other than a polyphony of chains of objects that, in the absence of instrumental clues, can only be distinguished by their spatial localization.

35.18. MUSIC AND AESTHETICS

Thus, through questionable systems and despite errors of principle, music is developing in the direction we have indicated: new relationships between objects, new problems of form and, perhaps, a music that is radically different from traditional music.

Admitting this, however, amounts to a considerable change in attitude. First of all, we must let go of all exclusively natural or cultural prejudice about the foundations of music. This means ceasing to pull it in all directions, from scientific determinism to linguistic structuralism. It means allowing hybridization, the merging of disparate elements and hence an interdisciplinary approach. It also means identifying the different planes and the levels of complexity in musical organization, which are currently almost never perceived, and thus questioning many premature claims to success. We must also have the will and understand how to welcome the most divergent experiments, which all carry a share of the initial draft, and endeavor to be not conciliatory and eclectic but full of curiosity and willing to experiment. We must also follow our preferences: working out a method or going straight to the results.

We could then turn our attention to aesthetics, to which artistic requests, for the most part unfinished, are addressed with the comment "Return to sender." We are then relieved of responsibility and would end up turning a welter of ignorance and idleness into a sort of specialty. Similarly, when chemistry was in the doldrums, chemists came up with the idea of phlogiston, an unknown fluid that leaked out of bodies and that, it was believed, could be studied separately, independently of its material medium.

We have pinpointed two lines of research that, in fact, involve aesthetics, provided that aesthetics is understood from the outset as a crossroads between disciplines. One of the questions focuses on the most general structures common to all the arts; the other focuses specifically on music inasmuch as it explores the specific domain of sound perceptions.

So this is quite different from a friendly chat. We need to consult a whole body of knowledge to gather together the "bundle of criteria" for a reasonable study. Since we believe in science, why not adopt the rational approach to something that so clearly borrows from physics, linguistics, and mathematics? But, at the same time, how can we not ask questions about the particular development of the musical, which so mysteriously links the psychology of perceptions and the psychology of the depths of the human mind?

A refusal to do so would be difficult to explain logically. Nevertheless, we must say that an interdisciplinary perspective demands conditions and a working approach that run very much counter to circumstances.

35.19. MUSIC AND THE DISCIPLINES

An interdisciplinary project is always ambitious because of the areas of expertise that need to be brought together. Either a single researcher must take them all on board, in the knowledge that he will only be an amateur in each (this has always been the author's feeling and regret), or he must get them to come to him, which is possible in theory but like jumping through hoops in practice. Research organizations would have to adopt some original viewpoints very far removed from what justifies their activities at present. If we managed to do this, we should come across new difficulties. It is, in fact, at the limits of areas of specialization that we discover almost unexplored territory and find an interdisciplinary project. If we try to go that way, we find it is attitudes, much more than the contents of disciplines and the specificity of languages, that now diverge.

Specialists all have their own way of understanding things; they all have a system of reference and thought; finally, they all have their faith. It is not enough for one to take a few steps toward another—for the philosopher to become a bit of a physicist or the mathematician a linguist; we are talking about something quite different from versatility. It will rapidly appear necessary for researchers from different disciplines to decide on more than a shared *objective:* the shared *object* of their listening (since we are dealing with sounds) and their *thinking* (since we are dealing with meaning). We have shown the importance both of secondary disciplines for gathering musical data and of the choices that must be made as soon as the first tentative steps in typology are taken. It is possible for well-disposed individuals to get to this point under the leadership of a philosopher rather than any other mentor. We are thus unambiguously focused on the individual. We do not allow the object to be diverted from this encounter. In short, to go back to our schoolboy schemas, on the figure showing the three possible intentional directions (see section 8.9) the chosen direction is, at the bottom, gravity, self-examination, and, in a word, contemplation of the object.

But who contemplates the object, if not man! The above approach still involves an "individual": not altogether a man. It is still the external man, taken as an object in the world, and still the anatomy lesson: a wrapped-up mummy, a stuffed man, *homo sapiens*, who is as like a real man as a waxwork in the Grévin museum. The musical and that man will never live happily together. It is up to us to be filled with the feeling that dare not say its name, the respect for humanity that comes to us from the domains of ignorance and fear.

To pursue music without situating it, without taking into account the problems of the times, the ideas of the moment, the vocation of art in general, would be to believe in a music in itself. We have just examined it at its very beginnings, but its meaning is also to be found in the remotest distance, near the ultimate goals.

36

The Meaning of Music

36.1. ORPHEUS

The unhappiest man in the world is the hero of the feast. A hungry crowd exploits and delights in his cries of pain, his tears. Respected even by wild animals, he will have no such respect from the experts. Does he not already observe them with a tear-filled and hypocritical eye? Can true grief admit such affectations? Is it possible to weep for Eurydice and yet play the lute?

No one will make us believe that Orpheus can so easily be spirited away or that there is not something ritualistic lingering in latent form in our most disembodied concerts. As the accepted frontiers of belief are pushed back, the sacred deconsecrated, and myths demystified, other magicians, cunning and well-bred, will take their place, with the mien of distinguished colleagues or senior civil servants.

We had become accustomed to the fresco, however, now faded, of this beardless and yet more reasonable false Christ, who asked less of us. The man of Art, less fanatical, more controlled, was still vaguely inspired by folklore. Plunging into the depths of the Hell of the Unknowable, rather than telluric fire or archaic terrors, for want of a wife, he brought back a grief that inspires. What we could no longer describe as unbelievable, or suggest was undoable, could be entrusted to this go-between, this daughter of man: now divine mediator, now courtesan.

Given over to these two uses, we cannot say that music has not submitted; from the sacred to the profane, from the cantata to the ditty, from liturgy to the music hall, she has worn out her hands in prayer, her lips in kissing, her eyes in weeping: might we find her repellent now, grown old and ugly, given over to merchants and doctors?

There is now as great a distance between us and Orpheus as between that lyrical singer and Neanderthal man. How, then, should we rediscover, in the words of Francis Ponge, the "original onomatopoeia"?[1] Surely, to cry out, that man must have breathed in and out? These two halves of life, this fundamental alternating movement of all living creatures as of all spirituality, have always been propounded, have always been valid throughout time: how well is this two-stroke engine of inspiration and expression working today?

So here we come to the ultimate question, which, however, we had promised ourselves never to ask. Why should we indulge ourselves in wondering about the ultimate aims of music when we will doubtless have no more to say than anyone else? Is it simply to assert that this question should not be avoided? Certainly. Asking such questions about the inspiration and the goal of music is playing the agent provocateur. It means that we will probably be taken for a fool or an upstart. But we do not very much like the wisdom of the day, which consists in doing anything at all, provided no thought is given to what it is for. It seems to us that in these huge devices, these never-completed adventures into which our contemporaries so readily throw themselves, philosophy is in rather short supply.

The order may well have been final: there must be no turning back; to catch sight of Eurydice is to lose her. But we can ask ourselves about the meaning of the instructions and Orpheus's situation: much less alone than the play represents him. For even if Orpheus does not know where he is going, he must know who compels him and what inspires him.

36.2. MUSICAL CONSUMPTION

To change this demigod into a music dealer is a bit much all the same. And this is doubtless what we should have to do if we followed the trend and launched ourselves into a serious examination of music as historically determined, conditioned as is to be expected by socioeconomics ... (or perhaps the sociocultural grabs us?). We will leave this question to the academically competent. We have a shortcut to suggest. Indeed, the problems of dissemination are important, and they will always bring the guardians of Culture and the industrialists of Art into conflict with one another. However divisive the problem, and however real the pressure of dissemination on consumption, and thus in the long term on production and on the musical environment especially, we will not attempt to track the whole process. Rather we will look at what this musical environment is.

Otherwise, we would be caught between the frying pan and the fire: what is secretly brewing in our studios, and what is shouted from the rooftops. As far as the studio or laboratory is concerned, we must confess that we cannot bury our

1. Francis Ponge (1899–1988), French poet.—Trans.

research there. We may well involve all of sound, extract the object from it, summon witnesses to experiments for this purpose, and improvise with them a metalanguage for the initiated, but this is not the whole story. We must accept that many other considerations, apart from logical, physical, physiological, or psychological, preside over the creation of present-day music. A whole series of factors inspires its favorite techniques, its organizational trends, its vocation to become a particular kind of message. But there is a considerable distance between a select private circle and mass communication: it is between these two extremes, not necessarily precisely halfway, that we will find the true environment.

Now, in music everything happens as if, ultimately, the mass of present-day consumers were of no importance. In fact, we have only to think about two environments where the exchange between doing and listening takes place. One is that hypothetical and historical environment where we more or less placed the developments that over millennia, then centuries, enabled the musical object to be extracted from its gangue of sound. The other is the one that surrounds us and that the musician hardly ever mentions. He desires the opposite from it: that people mention him. So the situation could not be more confused. In many cases later generations have only retained from traditional heritage what its contemporaries had either hated or not understood—which motivates the innovator rashly to pursue his course and listeners who wish to be sophisticated to avoid making their ancestors' mistakes. Such is the starting point of these microenvironments that, these days, make or unmake reputations, will or will not hear musics, consent or refuse to play them.

Music is a very strange thing. Literature teaches, architecture is lived in, paintings furnish. In the most disinterested arts there is still something functional. Now the first performance of a work summons a society to a language it cannot understand and to an enjoyment that is very unlikely. This is not because society is not open or well informed but because this is the linguistic fact of the musical: we must first hear it without understanding it and gather together to do so. Isn't that interesting?

36.3. THE MUSICAL ENVIRONMENT

Now, there are always people responsible for music: they are two people in conversation, which must not be confused with the composer-public pair, in which we find only a secondary echo, a more or less loud "resonance" of a "criterion of attack," as it were: the patron-composer pair. These terms are not offensive. They are necessary for the development of a process we do not see could take place otherwise. The patron has doubtless been democratized. He is no longer the Enlightenment prince. But the patron community, ultimately, rests on a few promoters with private or administrative budgets. The patron's motive may have changed: it is no longer to do with small pleasures, perhaps hardly even "the pleasure of music." What else could it be?

We need to look around a bit. If it is true that music is a community language threatened with destruction, it has never defended itself so well, thanks to its dissemination through mass media. While the painter can always paint, the novelist is finally published, the architect eventually finds some chinks for new ideas in the welter of new developments, music, a treasure for popular consumption, has also "gone wholesale," no longer allowing the slightest degree of freedom. It is true that new musics were born in those very studios that broadcast a mass language: the fact is that a civilization, even an all-consuming one, contains the seeds of its own destruction. But this is a marginal and long-term problem, which does not in any way change the present-day problem of the musician involved in his linguistic revolution. Now, he needs means for performance, which he can only obtain from society itself: sixty players, a recognized conductor, illustrious concert halls, a budget requiring only popular success to be profitable, and more.

Where can we find a justification for this "music in itself," which does not fulfill any natural need, which, hypothetically, clashes with society? How can it in some way become functional again? Through an unexpected, though absolutely logical, turnaround. Giving offense to an entire people and foreign to the court, intolerable to the faithful themselves, it can only be performed and gather together its means and its audiences by becoming the sign of a new caste, the prerogative of a new elite. Not that snobbery is the only element in a certain measure of success or justifies what is being attempted now in music. But it would not be very scientific to deny its fundamental importance or even the way it confirms the nature of the musical as something into which we have to be initiated. Some people begin to grasp this; others pretend: no one has "stayed with it." Thanks be, then, to snobbery, the modern form of collective solitude, without which, doubtless, nothing decisive would be attempted in the development of music.

Theodor Adorno has shown this very clearly, in choicer terms than ours:

The possibility of being heard by many is at the very root of musical objectification, and where this does not take place this objectification is necessarily reduced to something fictitious, the arrogance of the aesthetic individual who says "we" when it is still only "I," and who nevertheless cannot say anything without also postulating a "we." ... His rigidity is the anguish of the work in the face of despair about its own truth. It tries convulsively to get away by losing itself in its own law, but by the same token its nontruth increases along with its substance. ... The rigor of its own logic increasingly petrifies the phenomenon of music; from being something that signifies it turns into something that is simply there, impenetrable to itself. ... What is still simply there by dint of heroic effort could also not be there. The suspicion previously formulated by Steuermann is plausible: the concept of serious music itself—now taken over by radical music—could belong to a specific moment in history, and in the era of ubiquitous gramophones and radios humanity may quite simply forget the experience of music. Purified into an end in itself, it suffers from its pointlessness no less than consumer goods suffer from being made to serve particular ends.[2]

36.4. MUSICIANS

This sociological approach is obviously much more attractive than a mass-consumption approach, which follows after an interval of several decades, if not centuries. Hence the particular responsibility our "microenvironments" have. It would not be enough to analyze them only insofar as they are in conflict with general consumption. And we should also include the psychology and sociology of the musician, some archetypes for which are found in Epinal prints.

These prints, of the solid and naive type, still quite recently represented the musician as misunderstood and miserable in his calling, giving pleasure to others largely posthumously. Several biographies, radio or television programs for the "general public," which smack more of the soap opera than music, bear witness to this. We have changed all that. The modern musician generally enjoys good health, is no more unhappy than the next man (or at least he carefully hides the fact), and in order to live, modestly it is true, but with dignity, displays exceptional gifts. The music he produces being practically unfit for human consumption, we may conjecture that this involves quite a lot of energy and some bitterness on his part.

A "true" composer, tied down to the contingencies of the profession, could hardly admit to this without betraying himself or his clan. For the circumstances of contemporary musical creation are very much like those of a totalitarian universe. You must do the same as everyone else or perish. Without that fierce energy, those tight calculations, the musician is lost, for he has become an outsider who speaks no known language and who, perhaps, admits to himself in secret that he does not even know what language he is speaking. A Hiroshima bomb has fallen on music. Until the Austrian serialists started mining their seam, there was still a musical language system, more or less taught, more or less practiced, more or less shared. The 1939–45 war and its upheavals, and the exchanges that followed, make the series compulsory, at least for the minority who wants to be active. Why? We may well wonder, so unpleasant is this music, "radically" contrary to ancestral musical practice.[3] There is only one answer to explain the involvement of certain people, their courage and their aggressiveness, their faith and their bad faith: because it is *new*. Is this the criterion for art, or our time, or the art of our time?

2. Theodor W. Adorno, *Philosophie der neuen Musik* (Tubingen: Mohr, 1949). [Published in English as *Philosophy of New Music*, trans. and ed. Robert Hullot-Kentor (1949; Minneapolis: University of Minnesota Press, 2006).—Trans.]

3. I do not, of course, exempt those involved in concrete music from this sociological analysis, but it is difficult to be both judge and judged.

36.5. THE INSPIRATION OF THE MOMENT

To have brought together so many "disconcerted" concert audiences, there must have been reasons over and above snobbery; snobbery itself must have needed reasons. Whether we are talking about real musical discoveries that will be validated by posterity, or false initiatives, bluffs, half-truths, untruths, or, in short, suchlike experiments, there must have been motives and possibly ideas. When music wants to put itself together again after falling apart, to be relearned in the midst of the cut-glass environment of dilettantes and connoisseurs, it needs attention-grabbing superstructures for its structures laboring to be born.

Now, just as we find Napoleon in Beethoven or Schoenberg, pegs on which to hang our cloudy thoughts in Wagner or Mahler, nymphs in Debussy and boleros in Ravel, we had to have the frills and furbelows of some fabulous inspiration, truly of our age, an age in which myths are statistics, playthings cybernetic, and painting an object. Rigorous, therefore, will be the music of a civilization armed to the teeth, which possesses the atom, which cries for the moon, on condition that we do not tamper with tribal taboo, that we never loosen the girdle of fortune, that we never look where we are going. "That objective rigor of musical thought itself, which alone confers dignity on great music," this is what a whole generation, with Adorno, is demanding. It is the most commonly found word in concert programs, the quality most generously recognized in musics that are the most insecure in their principles (but, it is true, the best calculated in their detail). "The development of a logic of musical rigor such as this, to the detriment of the passive perception of sounds for their sensory qualities, distinguishes art from below-stairs humor."[4] Strong words. So no more sensuality, and no more of what goes with it: no more *Amours du poète, Hymne à la joie, Ich weiss dass mein Erlöser lebt*. Thus denied, inspiration is still inspiration. Passion, fervor, and faith, spiced with ordinary biographical details, the whole lot now ultimately thrown into the purifying inquisitorial fire. The empty wineskins finally deflated, the bloody brotherhoods stripped of their face paint. Why, then, so much emotion? Icy rejections, distant silences . . . Rejections, simply.

36.6. FROM THE SCRIBE TO THE ACROBAT

Extremes meet. Objects in themselves as much as insensible objects, the pretension to objective rigor in the same way as "below-stairs humor," are the victims of the same contagion. On the one hand, to be a force for equilibrium, the arts must reject any usefulness, any function. On the other hand, the "inspiration of the moment"— while strictly refusing useful subjects or usable ideas—causes them to seek their fundamental structures in the same processes whose quasi-magical omnipotence—

---

4. Adorno, *Philosophy of New Music*, 22.

new idols, new beliefs—dispenses at one and the same time the economy of opulence, the ultimate weapon, and gadgets. So concentration on things is displaced: from the thing made to the thing usurped by what is being done with it. As for meaning, there always is some, whatever we do: art for art's sake meaning. But, out of politeness, we will call it hypermeaning or hypomeaning. Otherwise, it does not really matter whether we apply one or the other description to these two types of "artistic" expressions that rub shoulders daily and of which it may be said that each of them, in effect, aims both above and below itself: those that acrobats entertain us with and those given over to the pontifications of scribes.

So deny the work: it's action that counts. If breaking a piano becomes painting, crushing a keyboard with both forearms with all desirable compunction and 333 times in a row can contribute a most serious item to the concert, especially if it is based, and why not, on Zen philosophy. In this art galore, everything is permissible, except one unpardonable error: doing what might already have been done. Hence an enormous expenditure of energy and imagination to find something new, new and yet again new, and you have to take your hat off to it all: these children of the times never have more than two hands and two feet, two eyes and two ears, are 1 m 70 cm tall (increasing, it seems), have a few sensitive organs, among which a sex organ losing its oomph, which is also beginning to turn its back on consumption.[5] Of course, you can make naked girls straddle motorcycles, squash chicks with nostalgia for the black masses of yore (but no more religion, too bad, no more black masses!); you can crush a few cars (sculpture at last, cars have a soul!) or give a few roars in a theater between two happenings: it is difficult to rise to the demands of "what's in" on a daily basis and constantly merit the pass mark "it's different." All this, as the expression goes, has *gotta be done*. Truth comes out of the mouths of these babes. They've said everything. Action is clearly entertainment, commitment, emotion, and communication at one and the same time. They must have been pretty frustrated to get to this point!

Frustrated, they are indeed. The parents drink; the children chink glasses. Except for the leather jacket—but they had helmets, and with horns—the Valkyries "were doing it" here on horseback, there under the sea, shot straight from Valhalla, caving in the deep, these lasses did not have cold eyes, sang at full throttle, all of it truly in the flesh. With Wagner (he did it as well) our ancestors took pleasure in a very different way from us: the whole thing leading to two world wars and rising again, as best it could, from the world of the concentration camps. We can understand why the most serious people mistrust this music, which is far from being a civilizing influence. It is only too right that we should have become ashamed of our more ostentatious feelings, our repugnant aesthetic emotions, that we find old

5. The French term *consommation* used here also means "consummation" in the sexual sense. The pun could not be retained in English.—Trans.

songs disgusting, the systematic exploitation of the official symphony revolting. It is better for a music with nothing left but skin and bone that a wind, if not of purity, then of drought, should blow on it with all its locusts than that it should be satiated and paunchy. But the demon of lying doesn't mind a joke, and austerity befits him after feasting. Let us have the benefits of fasting but acknowledge that we haven't much left to get our teeth into. Let the scribes and Pharisees veil their faces and entwine themselves with phylacteries! It is always the original man, the ordinary man who will get the better of them.

36.7. THE EXPERTS

The gap between what Hegel calls "dilettantes" and "connoisseurs" has existed for all time. If we can ignore the middle-class dilettante, suspected of being a consumer of music for shameful reasons, what, these days, has become of the competent listener? Adorno himself frowns: "The connoisseur has turned into an expert, and his knowledge, which alone still gets to the heart of things, has become routine and pretentious information that is killing him. Everywhere where technique is no longer considered as an end in itself, we come up against a mixture of corporate intolerance and obtuse naiveté from him. . . . His gesture is reactionary: he monopolizes progress. But the more evolution makes the composer into an expert, the more the contributions of the expert, as the agent of a group that identifies with privilege, enter into the intrinsic composition of music."[6]

If this is the case, the musician is in good company. He is not the only one to possess "this mixture of corporate intolerance and obtuse naiveté." He is surrounded by numerous colleagues: the experts, just as distinguished, and contemporary techniques. Intolerant they certainly are, for the accumulation of knowledge, the speed of developments, the incalculable—or sometimes all too foreseeable—consequences of their actions give them every reason to be demanding, even if it only means sharing those skills and responsibilities with a more and more limited number of people. But the same process is repeated everywhere and for many others. Those gigantic forces, those radical transformations, those divergent powers no longer see eye to eye but overspill the boundaries of all reasonable information, all reasoned knowledge. Happy are those who are not at work on some venture openly devoted to cooking up some deadly weapon of which it is said (and this is where the obtuse naiveté comes in) that it will be supreme against what it is about to cause: war. There is at present such a gap between technical sophistication and common sense, collective responsibility and personal irresponsibility, that there is now no point in looking for a "decent man" in our midst. This expression, once full of meaning, is now nothing but a joke . . . of the "below-stairs" variety.

6. Adorno, *Philosophy of New Music*, 33.

THE MEANING OF MUSIC   521

Now it is difficult for a man to put up with this. As he cannot attack what oppresses him, or direct the purpose of the device he is helping to make with such great skill and scrupulous labor, he looks for excuses for himself precisely on both levels where his conscience is pricking him. He cannot fail to notice the explosion of knowledge and the way it is increasing. He will therefore make haste to absorb some concentrated measure of it, to add some foreign ingredient to his own concoction. But, still debarred from any end result and from values themselves, he will seek out some tiny corner in the most limited sphere to defend, some "motivation" for a joust condemned to take place in the closed field. Hence these general features, which can be found everywhere or in most people: a feeling of power all the more pronounced the more pathetic or sibylline the conquests are, an inverted moralizing that takes professional punctiliousness to the point of absurdity. And so we see the humanities colluding with the general madness, and, for example, the psychosociologist working with the merchant and the money lender to exacerbate perfectly fallacious needs, in order to sell off the overwhelming torrents of merchandise.

It is time to close this door, which for a moment stood ajar. Not to breathe in the atmosphere of the times would be to deprive ourselves of our daily inspiration. The excesses of *thingism* are a direct result of it. It would be pointless to object that music has nothing to do with it and in any case can do neither good nor ill. In the same way that we can neither impute the atomic threat solely to academics nor entirely absolve them, we cannot let artists off the hook, those loners, witnesses, and finally—sometimes without their knowing—heralds of their age.

36.8. THE ROLE OF ORPHEUS

Refusing to integrate music into Time is already to take a stance. It amounts to saying that musical activity takes place outside the real. It is also saying that music is all, and the rest is worthless or else that musicians are neither influenced nor influence. We only have to make these statements to see that they are false. But then where do we go? Why talk about what is better unsaid?

Because musicians are being pointed in two directions, and they are not the right ones. One is political commitment, justified by some theory about the function of art in the city. We know all too well that its being used for a purpose is no better than its being used in commerce. Hegel had already grumbled about this: "The composer concentrates only on the purely musical structure of his work and the ingenuity of its architectonics . . . often remaining all his life among the most unaware and insubstantial men."[7]

---

7. Georg Wilhelm Friedrich Hegel, *Esthétique*, trans. Serge Jankélévitch (Paris: Aubier, 1944). [Published in English as G. W. F. Hegel, *Æsthetics: Lectures on Fine Art*, trans. T. M. Knox (Oxford: Clarendon, 1975).—Trans.]

Another verdict that needs scarcely any explanation. Were all these helots to produce just one genius per generation, we should be overwhelmed! What a useful citizen. . . . But that musician is not the one described by Adorno either, trapped in a load of gobbledygook about truth and nontruth, draped in his primordial pointlessness. To contrast the nonconsumerism of Art with functional overconsumption, the abstruseness of an elite with mass communication, amounts to refusing to fight, accepting humanity exactly as we are making it, worshipping the idols of the day.

For we will end up turning to Magic when we run out of arguments. The new all-modern man is still Neanderthal man, who, in our opinion, could be thought to be exclusively devoted to concrete or electronic musics. But this man is also a diplomat and a general, the head of businesses and squadrons, a university professor, a bishop, and equally a motorist and a television watcher. He has—too bad for him—many other weapons at hand. All the same, we observe each other, poker-faced, in a cold panic, not without a shade of suspicion, and the winner is he who does not laugh last. Nobody dreams—we're not mad—of seriously challenging the idol; the boldest among us gestures with his fan, cuts off a cuticle, flicks a finger; out of the question to spit on it, he would be lynched.

It is in this circus that Orpheus appears, like an inverse Futuristic Figure: obsolete rites, lost from sight. We observe each other. Will he offer the sacrifice in the manner of the ancients? Will he swap the lyre for the guitar? Intone plainsong on three notes[8] (the text in French) as in *Parapluies de Cherbourg*? Or surrounding himself with architects, foremen, astrologers, will he build castles in the air and recite the logarithm table? Is he going to make films, stereo sound recordings, do card tricks? Summoned, nevertheless, to go down into the Underworld, will he mobilize steam shovels, bulldozers, and Bull machines to make excavations on a truly grand scale, announcing from time to time in a more and more inhuman voice, over the vocoder, the odds on the lowest point?

36.9. RESPECT FOR HUMANKIND

There is another, more plausible, way. Why jump on our high horses? People will say:

These problems arise, certainly, but what do you suggest? A new alchemy? As for your interdisciplinary teams, what elixir are you expecting them to find? It's all much more simple. The music you call radical or the research you call musical are only particular sections, important certainly, fundamental as you say, of an extensive domain, the functions of which are no mystery: all musics, from the most common to the most erudite, the most sensual to the most intellectual, are justified, each in its

8. As recommended by the Concilium.

own way. In truth, music acts on man in all sorts of ways, from emotion to dance, from meditation to conditioned reflex, from intelligence to sex, from nausea to frenzy. This is true of all musics in the world and across all ages, except that in this age musics have become specialized, and what you call "music" now only interests the few, and their thoughts about it seem to be quite disproportionate: some too lightweight, and others rather mad.

So we need to go on various information-gathering missions. Thus we would set out, our tape recorders under our arms, in pursuit of lost musics and their functional secrets. . . . We may go and steal the secrets of ragas and their action on the stomach, gamelans and their tonic virtues, erotico-maniacal tom-toms, gagakus that made the Samurai, guitars that unmade Hawaii. . . . Is this really what we want? . . . This colonial-helmeted musicology, this pharmacopeia in a bandolier is only equaled in ridiculousness by its Phrygian-capped colleague, aesthetoscope round his neck, a heart specialist. This face-pulling from both sides rightly reminds us of our emptiness, which will not be filled by either of the equally crude approaches via function or consumption. Here we are again with our backs to the wall.

If it has secrets to yield up, the past is well defended; other civilizations, as well, keep their lips sealed. Moreover, were we to find any Masters, they would not chatter about music; they would make us make it. Perhaps, then, they would focus on the precise point where we place our hyphens: matter-spirit, sentiment-sex. *For such phenomena cannot be studied; they are lived.*

We will therefore go so far as to say this. Throughout this work we have deferred to respect for humankind. We have never dared to take our idea of reduced listening as far as it would go. We have obeyed the implicit axiom of all Western knowledge, that it is merely of the intellect.

36.10. ORPHEUS IN THE UNDERWORLD

The underworld is not beneath the circus ring. All that can be done, terrestrially, has been or will be done, and everything will also be done to reach other Earths, without our having any reasonable hope of finding there the answers to the questions raised in this one. As, furthermore, the heavens are empty, it is difficult to see how Orpheus could go down into the Underworld except by going into himself.

This dialogue in the deeps, which can only connect him to others like him, is suggested to him by music, on the sole condition that he makes no deals with the enemy, that he does not refuse the mystery that he himself is operating. Can we not find some echo of this idea in contemporary thought?

Yes, occasionally, but muffled, as it were, tardy like repentance or some concession to a recalcitrant madman. For Adorno "the artist has become simply the one who carries out his own intentions, which present themselves to him as inexorable demands alien to him, springing from his works in progress."[9] Why "simply"? Did not that artist, in olden days superb, affirm himself through a nontruth that was about to change sign? Why foreign to him, these demands? What is this musician's music, which is so different? The mind, refusing the whole enterprise of music at this point, is about to contradict itself gratuitously.

Freud also had noted the foreignness of the creative act: "Unfortunately the creative power of an author does not always obey his will; the work takes shape as it can and often stands before its author like an independent, indeed alien, creation."[10]

Why describe this situation as unfortunate? If this work resists, stands, to the point of appearing independent, why not rejoice? What worse misfortune, for Orpheus, than to descend into himself and find only the void, no one to speak to? We are struck by the similarity of the reactions, and the words themselves, by a sort of disappointment coming after other ambitions; we should listen to Boulez:

> The outlook is scarcely pleasing, and we are all too much inclined to let ourselves be hypnotized by the mirage produced by the ambition for rigor; the inquisition moves in; we pacify it. . . . We have no other aim than to try to seal ourselves off ever more stringently from predecessors on whom we are completely reliant. The analytical "account," in fact, is neither valid nor disinterested: a certain number of procedures are highlighted, procedures that in the most plausible manner "account for" either the composition or the structure of a given work. Nevertheless, if we indulge in an exegesis of this sort, it is by no means only for the sake of the futile satisfaction of understanding "how" the composition works—a pleasure easily foregone—or to rid ourselves of curiosity. Great works, fortunately, never cease to yield a reward for their intransgressible night of perfection, if we are careful not to fall back on the humor of despair in the face of this mystery that spurns such an inquiry: a sort of act of faith that the trade will be passed down from generation to generation in this unique and irreplaceable way, although a second impossibility then arises: the work can never be entirely proportionate to us.[11]

36.11. A SPIRITUAL TECHNIQUE

When we get to this point, panic always sets in. At the outer limits of technology there are the closing words, the doffing of the hat, the two perilous leaps. Orpheus does not have faith.

We must be very clear about this word. We should like to rid it of all its tenants, its returned goods, its poor. We would go so far as to empty it of all content and

---

9. Adorno, *Philosophy of New Music*, 27.

10. Sigmund Freud, *Moïse et le monothéisme* (Paris: Gallimard, 1948). [Published in English as *Moses and Monotheism*, trans. Katherine Jones (London: Hogarth, 1939).—Trans.]

11. Pierre Boulez, "Auprès et au loin," *Cahiers Renaud-Barrault*, no. 3 (1954).

retain only its driving force, the general attitude it conveys: an intention to believe. For faith thus understood is ultimately simply an orientation of consciousness. Just as consciousness cannot be void of an aim, it cannot be void of this inspiration: consciousness is always magnetized.

Now, the attitude of the musician is radically different depending on whether he finds a means or an end in his technique. So we will not escape the question of trust. Besides, it does not really matter what inspires him, provided it is something other, that he does not make his technique an end in itself. Reciprocally, it is important that everything should depend on the latter, since technique is magic, if we are willing to take this word seriously.

So it is foolish to look for contents in musical inspiration, and it matters little whether we focus our opera glasses on Olympus or Valhalla. But confirmed atheism does not allow us to consort with dubious idols, either, or to betray man by substituting inferior mechanisms for him in the most stupid way imaginable. So in the name of this equally radical faith we condemn the two compensatory mechanisms adopted by a good many pious souls of our time. Converting shaky beliefs into mathematical bigotry, these fanatics of a digital catechism turn their parameter mill, going into trances at the slightest electronic laying on of hands. But they are easily consoled by this, demiurge apprentices, creators of swathes of sounds, brandishing Poisson's formula just like the lord his sparrow hawk or Jupiter, that electrician, his kilowatts.

But we must moderate our transports. It is the vexation at seeing so much talent going astray, so much time being wasted, so many shortcomings to be corrected and so many fatuous onlookers. It is also the horror of the void and that desire for nothingness that ultimately sickens and angers.

Sometimes our little Masters also ogle the great ones, spying out their procedures, remembering from those faces only nods and winks that may bode well for them. To hear Bach or Mozart in this way is to deride the world. It amounts to mistaking the route for the destination, the shell for the nut, wasting the unhoped for, almost unbelievable, lesson that was sometimes given. It does not matter that Bach was Christian and that his music found that visible source of inspiration. We do not insult his memory by suggesting that if his music is religious, it is not in any way confessional. We should be pouring scorn on inspiration if we defined it as a compulsory relationship between a technique and ideas: the cantor was not in direct contact with dogma when he made a play on the four letters of his name or put together some already recurrent series. Such alphabetic games must not be confused with the message. It is remarkable, however—and it does not matter whether we believe in historical determinism or the God of ancient times—that the high points of music, from the Middle Ages to our day, from East to West, are religious and, as the etymology of this word suggests, link together scattered, unnamed, ineffable elements in man (which he often throws out in a naive description of the divine). Here tolls the bell of condemnation, so different from that which, according to Dante, adorns the entrance into damnation—it is solitude. It is not a question of abandoning all hope but of believing without seeing, feeling oneself followed by someone or something. If looking at it is against the law, the symbol becomes vulgar as soon as we reduce it to the mechanics of the absurd, or an old wives' tale. If the partner could be looked at, it would be only a replica of ourselves. If it can direct us from behind and beneath, from below and above, it is because it is forever hidden from our overt investigations, which are perfectly inadequate in any case. The condition of this power is to be above knowledge. The expression of this power is music.

36.12. THE MEANING OF WORDS

In a recent interview, Francis Ponge was explaining his work. To hear him, an inattentive person could have thought that he was recommending solitary poetry; an unthinking person could also come to the same conclusion, on reading pages laboriously devoted to the description of a glass of water or a meadow. Denying that he is a poet, or "writes poetry," Ponge for his part demanded that we should cleanse language of its ideological associations and take it seriously, adopting (these were his very words) a phenomenological reductive approach. Refusing to use words to express some fortuitous idea, he would go so far as to keep the rough drafts of his writings to retrace their itinerary, in search of meaning. Thus he redefined poetry, of which it could be said that it is the inverse of utensilar language, as the musical object is the inverse of signs or indicators that go beyond the sound object. Nothing to do with poetry in itself, a pointless game of words or images. Analyzing his text, as the most fastidious professor of rhetoric might have done, delving into the substance of words, digging out the roots, Ponge discovered the meaning of what he was doing—and this does not exclude that exquisite form he occasionally cannot help using: not the work of an author who has something to say but work on words, which in the end say more than the author ever knew by moving toward meanings that he himself only perceives after the event. Nothing ersatz—sound alliteration or symbolic analogies—can henceforth satisfy our poetic hunger now that we have eaten of this bread.

These, then, are the two lessons he gives us. The first, it is true, derives from the semantic nature of language: "a palpable sign," Ponge says, quoting Jakobson. This fact, "the mind's salvation," links words together and us to them. The second lesson derives from the declared purpose of this research: to rediscover, through a careful and obedient use of the objects of language, full of modesty, the way of mankind. There is no more whimsicality of expression or that other self-indulgence that consists in making an engine of despair for oneself, a pretentious toy, something to offer to a snobbery of nonconsumerism out of the sterility of one's method. It all comes down to common sense: what things have to say to us has been buried away inside them by generation after generation, since the invention of language, since, as Ponge says, "the original onomatopoeia." Here also, and for better reasons, we could invoke Zen, in that watchful noninterventionism that, sometimes, illuminates.

36.13. THE LANGUAGE OF THINGS

It is possible to devote six hundred pages to not saying what one had to say. As long as we are working on the object itself, we scarcely have time to speak about it. And if we do speak, we do not speak well.

He who gives an account gives an account of himself. That light we wanted to shed on the object also treacherously puts us in the limelight and makes us wince. Was it worth narrating this adventure, very modest in any case, and still so far from any convincing applications? Instead of pursuing—as common sense would have suggested—additional experiments on "correlations" or "studies with objects," which are so necessary, here we are abandoning the experimental field to throw ourselves into the publication of what we dare to call a "treatise on the object." So what is going on? We must turn to language. There will be some surprises.

The language of words, as soon as we begin to make an inventory of it, investigate its connotations, dig it out of its ruts and remove it from its false dawns, gives us, as it were, everything; we have to agree: it is all there; it has all been said. But it must all be said again, discovered again. The mirrors of the past are tarnished, the effigies gone; the most precious treasures are devalued, and some people would rather have the glitter of false gold. But if we take the trouble to examine these treasures, what teachings they provide, what hubs of meaning!

Now, the ancient simplicity of the most frequently used terms—*form* and *matter, value* and *characteristic, indicator* and *meaning*—leads straight to interdisciplinary research. Scarcely, by going on to higher ground, have we found the outline of cities buried under the sand, than we also discover new levels, recognize that materials have been reused, sometimes stolen.

How, in effect, can we not want music to be as modern and also as ancient as possible? How can we not consider its historical stature? How can we not want to bring past and future together, an even more problematic relationship than the one we are endeavoring to build between present-day disciplines?

The search for words makes us open the dictionaries at the word *music*. When we compare the volumes of the *Littré* dictionary and those, too recent, of the *Robert* dictionary, it makes our heads spin. Whereas the most recent work gives us what could be a series of howlers, which it would be all too easy to pursue, its elder brother takes no time at all to show how, in a century, the course of music could have gone downhill. In *Robert, etymology* is nothing but a shameful memory, but in *Littré* the file is still open; we have not only the nine Muses to testify to this: the movement of the Heavenly Bodies, according to Pythagoras, comes under this art, while Plato wisely observes that we cannot make any changes to it without changing the State.

The search for ideas around the word *object*, then *structure*, projects us, furthermore, into the dizzying chasm of the mind observing itself, reflecting back its own image in a series of mirrors, its most modern endeavor being to take a grip on itself and on what it might apprehend. Now, knowing why music—if we take it seriously—might escape this type of reflection is not the question. The real question is knowing why, in fact, it seems to have done so, the interest taken in it being vaguely respectful, consisting of polite ignorance and negligent or neglected sentiments. Those who would speak hide away. What is the point of continuing the debate? It is simpler to put down a marker stone to leave a sign for whoever would like to aim higher or use the gift of second sight.

Believe us, music, indeed like all the arts, will soon have to change status or else become part of the debris of under- or overconsumption. In effect, once the arts of our time have worn themselves out in various contortions and used up the last resources of execrable Western exhibitionism, they will indeed have to beat a retreat or go in for religion, to use this word in its earlier connotation. And this is what attaches us to music, when we rediscover the essential in it—when it has this grace. It can all be summed up in a very ordinary expression: man does not live by bread alone. If art gives him food, there will be no poison: fakes or feces. Now, these types of menus are in fashion, and respect for humankind wrinkles its nose. Art retains its capital letter, provisionally: it is the ass loaded with relics.

We will hazard a dictum: Art is simply the sport of the inner man. All art that does not aim to be this is pointless and harmful. There is a technique of the spirit, as well as the body, and the two are linked. Those who do not accept this, on both sides, are simply going back to the old antiphon of the dichotomy between body and soul and are postulating a dubious metaphysics. For those who have no soul, sport is recommended, and for those who have one, spiritual exercises as well. In both cases we are not talking twaddle but music theory. Like sport, art means working on oneself: from sensory perception to spiritual perfection, from the five senses to the threefold consciousness: intellectual, affective, and active.

But this total exercise has, fortunately, nothing to do with aesthetic narcissism. Consciousness, thus developed, is a consciousness made of objects and the ordering of objects: we are not being invited to the pelican's feast. To measure ourselves in this way against objects and their ordering, to grasp other implications through them is ultimately to understand what we are. What we are offered, on the contrary, is a disintegration of the world: science on the one hand, art on the other, and between them, the approximations of aesthetics; this is not very cheering. So we look with envy on ancient simplicities, the intuitions of Greek thought, historic monuments covered with respect, dust, and finally condescension. But why should Pythagoras's thinking not still be relevant today? The entire harmonic scale, which replicates the series of whole numbers, still presents the same enigma. What unacknowledged motives would turn away a whole physics- and mathematics-obsessed age from this fundamental thinking? The musical object, the most disembodied, the most abstract of all objects it is given to us to perceive, has, in fact, the virtue of being both the most mathematical and the most sensory. Perhaps it is that dazzling relationship that people turn away from: they are afraid.

So the mystery of music and its dualism cannot, fortunately, be resolved: it is here that men who believe just as much and simultaneously in man and nature, in their contradictory and reciprocal order, are drawn together.

Provided, certainly, that we confront this partner whose objects are a strange exception. All other objects of consciousness speak to him about other things than consciousness: in the language of men they describe the world to him in accordance with the ideas he forms of it. Sound objects and musical structures, when they are authentic, have no informative mission: they turn away from the descriptive world with a sort of reticence in order to speak all the better about it to the senses, the heart and mind, to the whole being, ultimately about himself. This is how languages take on a sort of symmetry. They are man, described to man, in the language of things.

Penultimate Chapter

In Search of Music Itself

In matters of research it would be scarcely fitting to announce a final chapter. Ten years after the publication of the *Treatise on Musical Objects* the text that follows aims to guide a rereading, certainly from a more open-minded point of view.[1]

The main fault of this book is, in fact, that it is still the only one. More than six hundred pages devoted to objects weigh down one pan of the scale. To counterbalance it, the author should also have produced a *Treatise on Musical Organization* of equal weight.

I crave my critics' indulgence: I have had neither the time nor the genius to undertake such a work, particularly in a domain where everything still has to be done.

The *Treatise on Musical Objects* can therefore be interpreted in two ways: positively, as a bridgehead on the side of materials and the faculties of hearing;

This chapter was written by Pierre Schaeffer ten years after the publication of the *Traité des objets musicaux*. It was included in the 1977 edition published by Seuil.—Trans.

1. We would also recommend reading issue no. 2 of *Cahiers recherches/musique* on the *Traité des objets musicaux dix ans après* (Paris: INA-GRM, 1976). The article by the author in this issue published under the title "Music par exemple" has also been published in *Musique en jeu* (Paris: Seuil, 1976). The reader wanting an overview of *Les musiques électroacoustiques* may refer to the work of this name, by Michel Chion and Guy Reibel (Paris: INA-GRM/EDISUD, 1976). Finally, a *Lexique du traité des objets musicaux* by Michel Chion, assisted by Jack Vidal, will be published some time in 1977, in the *Cahiers recherche/musique*. [The book by Michel Chion was finally called *Guide des objets sonores: Pierre Schaeffer et la recherche musicale* (Paris: Buchet-Chastel, 1983). It has been translated into English by John Dack and Christine North as *Guide to Sound Objects: Pierre Schaeffer and Musical Research*, (Monoskop, 2009), https://monoskop.org/images/0/01/Chion_Michel_Guide_To_Sound_Objects_Pierre_Schaeffer_and_Musical_Research.pdf.

negatively, as having missed its target, since it seems to ignore the other side of the river, the combinations that give meaning to collections of objects. Between these two banks runs a deep river: reference structures, with that term, vague or precise depending on its use and its users, denoting the intermediary configurations by means of which the river can be crossed.

The work has, however, been reprinted as it is, without changing a single line. Some readjustments in its presentation could have been desirable for teaching purposes. But no basic amendments seemed really essential to correct mistakes or even a terminology that could, indeed, be improved, but that it is better to leave alone, given that it has already been to some extent used in practice.

Even so, it would be impossible for the author to overemphasize the shortcomings of the *Treatise*, often interpreted tendentiously as resulting from bias or carelessness. The research is not finished. The statement that there are lacunae is much more than an admission here: it is the recognition of the unexplored. In research, it is not enough to "tackle the unthought"; we must give it a chance as well!

So what is the musical "unthought" tackled as a matter of urgency in the *Treatise*? It is the incompatibility, often concealed, between two types of knowledge that keep on pointlessly referring to each other. Traditional musical knowledge rests on a solid tripod, the legs of which are known even to the uninitiated: a music theory for the ear, a practice for instruments, a score for works. Danhauser, in a few brief paragraphs, refers to acoustics to justify *the art of sounds* in their unspoiled natural state. Contemporary music may have turned its back on scales, but with electroacoustics it has seized on a second, apparently more rational, tripod, the "reference trihedron": pitches calibrated in frequencies, intensities calibrated in decibels, durations calibrated in seconds. As synthesizers make possible the most exquisite combinations of frequencies, decibels, and milliseconds, we have deduced from this that all possible music could be made in this way with appropriate combinatorial rules, on condition that the computer could be made to produce.

We will, however, merely comment that these two types of knowledge have come up against each other in complete mutual ignorance, that contemporary music, electronic at least, is forever seeking the values for its theory, the register for its instruments, and the code for its scores. There is something wrong somewhere.

This problem is the subject of the *Treatise*, which sets out from this historical situation, complicated by an earlier one: musique concrète. Oddly, that "feral" practice was the only one (I am still waiting for a rebuttal) to fill the gap in question. Even if, as its name suggests, the synthesizer was powerful in combinatorial terms, it gave the ear no procedure for analysis, and, worse still, it imposed its conditions. On the contrary, a simple turntable, with its "closed grooves," or magnetic tape, so easy to cut up, provided inadvertently, as it were, a mine of experiments that is still far from being exhausted.

Experiments on what? Listening, of course, at a time when the ear is not in fashion and composers are interested in a priori combinatory systems and sophisticated techniques. This is what explains the backwardness of musical research through a lack of motivated researchers and makes the *Treatise* a book that goes against the flow.

This postface should allow us to dissipate the most pernicious misunderstandings. It should also help the reader to grasp the essential more quickly. For the *Treatise* is not an educational work. It is the summation of a body of research presented as it developed, rather than a logical presentation of results and possible applications. Furthermore, it is about the materials of music, not music itself. Now, as these (musical) materials imply music, we are likely to find throughout the book an uneasiness linked to this implication. But we had to begin at one end or the other. What the author can do *in fine* is encourage the reader not to restrict himself simply to the contents, and even, in the absence of a supplementary treatise, to read this one "with a view to" musical organization, doubtless changing "object" but not method.

To guide this second edition I should like to make a distinction among what may be considered experimental knowledge (in particular the "anamorphoses" between music and acoustics), what may be defined as a methodology, and, finally, what can be set down as aural knowledge (through the theory and practice of the "four listening modes"). A middle section will endeavor to explain the misunderstandings arising over the last ten years by both positive and negative interpretations of the *Treatise*.

Having thus clarified what is and what is not in this work, I will try to say how it could inspire a set of questions about "music itself." This is the aim of the last parts of this text, which are a reprise, an octave higher, of the theme of the first three. What is the experimental situation of contemporary works? What could be the new subject for research? Do the results from the four listening modes ultimately apply to musical organization? Perhaps finally, beyond and short of music theory, we will have to say what its premises are and explain the historical resistance they cause at a time when contemporary music, to borrow a famous saying, seems to waver between "will and representation."

ANAMORPHOSES BETWEEN MUSIC AND ACOUSTICS

My interest was initially drawn to noises and their powers of suggestion, well known in radiophonic work. It was therefore very much despite myself that I was plunged into a musical adventure, then led to do experimental research. The nevertheless convincing results that I obtained then, by surprise and almost without difficulty, did not impress my contemporaries. Six more years and the help of computers were needed before the work of Risset at Bell Telephone (the analysis of spectral dynamics from *Music V* by Matthews) and Chowning at Stanford were to corroborate the results I had obtained during the 1950s.

I had no specialized equipment in my modest broadcasting studio: an oscilloscope, at the very most, in addition to microphones and recording machines. My godfathers were the same as everyone else's: Danhauser and the *Solfège des solfèges*, Helmholtz and his resonators, Fourier and his series; finally, and more up-to-date, Fletcher and his stimuli. (I am just restating here, more informally, what is explained at length in book 3). I therefore expected, along with Danhauser, that pitches would be frequencies and durations seconds. I expected, along with Fourier, to analyze complex sounds into packages of simple frequencies and, along with Fletcher and his calibrations, to recompose sine tones into audible effects. Finally, as a good rationalist, I did not for a moment think that a sound's attack could be anywhere but at its beginning. At the Telecommunications College, had not my elders taught me that certain "transient phenomena," in both the sound body and the ear, interfere with the initial phase of perception? So I installed an oscillograph to understand fully what I had been taught, especially the conformity of the signal to the timbre. I could see nothing to corroborate the teaching (in any case, I would have needed a computer to verify it). So I took a pair of scissors and started to cut out the sounds recorded on the tape into fragments, which I listened to separately. I played the recordings at different speeds, and occasionally I used filters to make other cuts, this time in the material in the tessitura. A deluge of discoveries followed. You can, reader, easily check these with your amateur's material, just as much in Mimi Pinson's[2] little room as at Bell Telephone.

(a) Importance of a hitherto unknown concept: *the dynamic form of sounds*, the "history of their energy." By cutting out the beginning of a sound from the tape, we should have eliminated all trace of the attack along with the transient processes. Now, after cuts of around one second from the beginning of a bass piano note, for example, the rest of the sound perceptibly reproduces the same sensation of attack.

So what is this initiatory phenomenon that cannot be located at the beginning of a sound? As other supplementary experiments have taught us, it conveys an overall perception of the dynamic envelope. With a bass piano note the energy diminishes in a regular slope (in a logarithmic scale), and the cuts do not change the general form. If, however, the slope is irregular, a cut in a dip is enough to make the sound unrecognizable. This is how, by a surprising instrumental transmutation, a medium-pitch piano note cut in this way will begin to resemble a flute.

(b) Timbre and instruments: If the absence of an anatomical detail (normally masked by the "roundness" of a well-established note) is enough to go from piano

---

2. A reference to the poem of the same title by the romantic poet, novelist, and dramatist Alfred de Musset (1810–57).—Trans.

to flute, from string percussion to a wind instrument, what becomes of instrumental classification?

The recognition of an instrument is linked to a group of permanent *characteristics*, whereas the register given by its keyboard enables the musical *values* to be varied. But we must point out that these characteristics are not so permanent, nor are these values so pure. Every note on the piano carries a particular *dynamic character*, every pitch a *harmonic timbre*. What makes the piano immediately recognizable is a *law of compensation* that can be expressed thus: the lower the notes, the more—harmonic—timbre they have; the higher they are, the steeper—dynamically—they become. This law results *naturally* from the mechanism of sound bodies, familiar to the ear over millennia. We must emphasize this adverb: registers have natural laws that we cannot break arbitrarily.

(c) The *musical values* we are accustomed to notating in pitch, duration, and intensity are, in reality, as complex as instrumental characteristics. Thus pitch, the dominant value, presents in two forms: with glissando sounds the ear discerns a *trajectory* in a more or less linear way; with sounds of *fixed* pitch it situates their "mass" in the tessitura—or in the case of harmonic sounds locates them as tonic sounds—in a logarithmic scale. The interval is thus not of the same nature when there are two fixed sounds or a sound sliding between the same reference points. Musical value does not therefore depend solely on degrees but on the form of the sound object, fixed or mobile in the tessitura. Even tonic sounds are perceived in two ways, according to whether they are high or low: the ear locates the fundamental of high sounds and discerns their harmonic timbre; but it reconstructs the fundamental of a bass sound mentally from its harmonics, even if, as very often happens, this fundamental is physically absent.

Last and shocking experiment: if we play a recording of a complex sound at double or half speed, we obviously expect it to be transposed by an octave: now, in many cases, the sound does not move an octave . . .

And all the rest is literature.

From this critique of so-called musical acoustics, from traditional music theory to serial practices, two fundamental conclusions should be kept in mind:

Musical perception is qualitative. The same (physical) causes do not have the same (musical) effects. Among many more detailed proofs, the following is an eloquent illustration of this fundamental principle: if we accelerate a series of impulses, initially perceived as distinct from each other, they will be heard when they are closer together as a vibrato (an "allure"), then as a characteristic "grain" of the sound matter. Up to twenty or thirty impulses per second, they are separate beats: a rhythm. Beyond this, we perceive pitch and harmonic timbre. This movement from one perceptual field to another is not discontinuous: there are intersecting zones where several ways of hearing interact. The bassoon is only such an outlandish instrument because it clearly displays this disparity across its whole register.

Corollary: there is not necessarily any similarity between a progression calibrated into parameters and a scale of musical values. Musical values themselves vary depending on the objects: they may give rise to a qualitative appraisal or a quantitative evaluation, in a sometimes linear, sometimes logarithmic calibration. Moreover, however carefully we listen to isolated and relatively simple objects, we cannot easily deduce what groups, or composite objects, would sound like. Finally, the density of information specific to each object, in accordance with time, models perception far beyond any elementary expectation.

RETURN TO THE OBJECT AND THE MUSICAL ENDEAVOR

The above observations alone would be enough to demonstrate the *musical* worth of going back to the sources of sound perception, upstream of aesthetic or scientific systems. But we should dispel the misunderstandings occasioned by the concepts of sound object and musical object.

Some of these misunderstandings have a historical origin: they come from the association between musique concrète and musical research. Others, due sometimes to the reader, sometimes the author, are to do with the interpretation of the *Treatise*. They all finally lead to the same undeserved criticisms—or praise: I have apparently minimized the importance of musical organization and worshipped the sound object for itself alone.

(a) *Music and noise*

Originating in 1948, the age of the supple disc, musique concrète by force of circumstance initially had only one "sampling unit": the closed groove.

Music could only be organized by repetition, juxtaposition, and superimposition of these sound fragments, using a technique comparable to the "montages" of the surrealists. It had nothing to do with an aesthetic stance but rather with a limitation from which—as the texts of that time bear witness—I did everything I could to liberate myself. Despite the radical break with traditional ways of composing these new procedures involved—or even because of it—I was endeavoring not to destroy music but to rediscover its general laws. Present-day musical expression may well still be at the stage of laboriously cultivating old surrealist challenges amid instrumental disarray, and the fascination for the *readymade* or the *happening*, but I have said often enough that this was not my ambition. Duchamp was never my mentor, and I never considered mentioning Russolo or Marinetti—in any case I did not know them in 1948—as founding fathers. Even Varèse was too fascinated by the dramatic and anecdotal aspects of sound for my liking. I have no academic reply to the question: "Object, what do you want of me?" I am only interested in results. Objects give you something back for the attention you are willing to give them. Objects are made to serve.

I have also been credited with a historical mission: to bring noise into music. Rather, I would boast of the contrary: of having discovered the amount of noise that musical sound contains and that people persisted in ignoring. The deconditioning of the ear, which I recommended to composers and audiences, tended to raise once again the question of the primary opposition between music and noise, by uncovering the potential musicality of sounds normally considered noises, as well as by pointing out the noise involved in supposedly pure sound: the grain of the violin or the voice, the impact on the soundboard in a piano note, the complex proliferation of sound in the cymbals, and so on. It should be remembered that these are not regrettable imperfections: these supposed impurities are an integral part of the musical given.

(b) *Sound object and musical structure*

Reference to the text of the *Treatise* shows it would be impossible to contend without malice that I reduce the problem of music to the problem of its materials; I gave many warnings to beginners, who are all too tempted to construct "object musics" or apply the criteria for analyzing sound to musical structures. The analysis of structures and works—as I have said and will say again—comes under another heading. This type of study complements the study of objects. It cannot be deduced from it.

I do, however, understand the reader's difficulty on one point: it is not always easy to pin down the distinction between sound object and musical object. At a pinch we could even say that the musical object in the singular does not exist, given the extent to which this adjective is linked to the emergence of relationships that come either from implicit references or the perception of a whole.

If, in fact, musicality rests on value relationships, these relationships form a structure. Either the recognition of this structure makes the perception of its constituent objects fade into the background (the classical example of the melody recognized as "the same" despite instrumental variations), or else careful listening discovers in one isolated object variations in values it can appreciate musically. But this is because, in the second case, the object is already considered as a "feral structure" and appreciated by an ear trained in this mode of listening.

We must explain the insidious transition from the notion of object to the notion of structure by describing an experiment anyone can do on a tape recorder: when separate notes are played on classical instruments, each note is indeed an object, and when these notes are strung together in a melody, it is this latter perception that is significant enough to cause the objects to be forgotten. Not only is the melody heard as a structure, but it also suggests *reference structures* (tonality, modality, series, etc.). Suppose, on the contrary, we were studying a rather voluminous sound object (a prolonged creaking noise, a cloud of impulses, etc.) with a similar duration to the above melody. We have said it would be heard as a "feral structure." To analyze it into its constituent objects (as if we were trying to find notes), we cut the tape into fragments separated by silences. We are very surprised: each fragment emerges as a separate object, and the "piece of music" is quite different. We have to join the objects up again *in our minds* to connect the two acts of listening. But this analytical (and ultimately intellectual) experiment will certainly help us to enrich our initial listening: thus reheard, clarified by this recent referencing, the structure will appear less "feral." Then, perhaps, we will repeat the analysis with one of the fragments, which itself can be cut into smaller pieces. Then we would say that we have changed levels, the previous fragmentary object now playing the part of the structure in relation to these smaller pieces. In any case we will learn the same lesson, with the same surprises.

The object-structure pair cannot therefore be dissociated, since it always refers to a relationship between component and compound, as much in natural sound and musical fact as by virtue of cultural or recently adopted references. It can be seen, moreover, that in absolute terms these words do not denote any specific level. The above example showed the interaction between the object-structure pair in detail. We can also find it on the global level in a sequence, a whole movement, an entire work. Ultimately, it consists in studying the relationship between a whole and its parts.

In traditional musicology this relationship obviously applies to the analysis of both "major forms" and key passages. So we will refer to motifs and themes, reprised, varied, or contrasted from one movement to another—in short, a logical examination, a "textual analysis." In addition, we will make a second analysis, morphological this time, at the level of theme and motif using our music-theory reference structures, still comparing them to syntax and grammar.

Every new music easily lends itself to textual analysis as far as the editing and articulation of its parts are concerned. There is no need to spend any more time on this. What we are persistently trying to do here is an internal analysis of the "passages" that may perhaps pertain to nascent reference structures.[3]

(c) *Material and the musical endeavor*

---

3. In so doing, we will have to leave the reader considerable latitude to judge which cases this type of analysis may apply to, or not. Otherwise, he would be perfectly justified in criticizing us for wanting to apply the traditional model at all costs by too rapidly postulating intervallic relationships or values between notes. In many contemporary musics the sounds are, in fact, dissociated in macroscopic developments that do not really lend themselves to such a subtle analysis. Works such as these should be approached through more general features: if not their phrasing or punctuation, then at least the rough outline of the interaction of fluxes of sound that become perceptual units. They do not give the density of information or the almost immediate intelligibility that ensure the effectiveness of traditional music. This, incidentally, is what explains the length of some of these works: the length is necessary for them to be understood. Hence also their insistent imposition of effects that are perceptible rather than intelligible. Whether he congratulates himself on this, or regrets it, the experimenter is obliged to take the works as they are. It is consequently up to him to choose the appropriate type of analysis in each case.

The object is made to be useful, I was saying. Useful for what? For making music. The whole question is how to go from sound to the musical.

Before making his choices, the musician cannot, any more than the architect, be ignorant about the properties of his material, and it is in his interest at this stage that his scrutiny of them should be as foresightful and impartial as possible. Since these materials cannot be reduced to physical measurements—we think we have demonstrated this very fully—we must submit them to the judgment of the ear, that is, treat them as sound objects. Finally, since it is impossible to prejudge the potential musical structures and values in the various objects immediately, the musician must first consider these sound objects in general. But, however disinterested it may appear, the attention he gives them is part of a plan: to locate those of them that are "suitable" for his purpose. And this purpose is not a phenomenology of sound, however fascinating this may be: his pausing over the object is a provisionally suspended musical intention.

One difficulty remains: how do we know that one object is better suited for the purposes of music than another? By trying to listen to it musically. How do we know the properties of musical perception? From the objects it chooses. We will take a mundane example: to diagnose shortsightedness, astigmatism, or color blindness, the optician routinely gives his patient visual objects made for this purpose. Nobody argues about whether the first thing to be looked at is vision or the large or small letters or numbers. It is obviously through experiment, through successive approximations, that the particular features of vision and the greater or lesser "suitability" of the objects for the optician's purposes are determined. Why is it so difficult for this method, which no one finds surprising when applied to vision (and diagnosis), to be accepted when dealing with hearing (and aesthetics)?

The *Treatise* defined the musical object more succinctly as "the object of musical listening." This is only apparently a vicious circle. Not all sound objects are equally suitable for musical listening. They must not, for example, be too full of anecdote or too directly suggestive of their instrumental cause. They must not, and this leaves a very wide margin, be too short or too long, in order to be within the ear's "time screen" without falling outside the frame. Of course, the continuous or discontinuous nature of the events that are traced on this screen is of prime importance. As for time, do we need to repeat that we are dealing with a subjective duration linked to the density of information specific to each object? Finally, objects are not necessarily particularly distinct from each other: they may be fused together in sequences, new perceptual units.

As we can see, the discovery of the object is at one and the same time an exploration of the faculties of the ear, its remarkable capacity for learning and its astonishing powers, and also of its demands. In what our tradition has bequeathed us, we can learn to discern the essential factors in historical contingency. We can gradually conquer new domains. We certainly cannot violate the laws of sound perception in general or musical suitability in particular. We should be ashamed of saying such obvious things, if they were not—and how arrogantly!—ignored by the ideology of the day.

THE FOUR LISTENING MODES

Thus, the *Treatise on Musical Objects* is first and foremost a treatise on listening. Is it so surprising that we should wish to recall what is always forgotten? The object implies the conscious subject; the activity of the conscious subject confronted by any object is the bedrock of the musical.

We can even anticipate the *Treatise on Musical Organization* that has not been written: without any doubt, on its very first pages it would have suggested applying the diagram of the four listening modes to short fragments of works, which are incontestably places where the musical phenomenon resides, as well as to new "musical objects" to be sampled, identified, described, classified. It is from the comparison of these fragments that further research should arise. It is significant, and even amusing, for us to be going back to the ordinary meaning of the age-old term, "a piece of music," to describe them.

But we must not run ahead of ourselves. Before embarking on this investigation at a higher level of complexity, it is essential to understand fully how the four listening modes interact and to separate this, as it were, from an exclusive focus on elementary objects. Ten years of teaching have shown me what contradictions were possible. This is what I would warn against:

- There is a common tendency to see the diagram of the four listening modes as a sort of *storage drawer* for material things, like a classification system for instruments, for example.
- On the contrary, it is an enumeration of the *activities of the conscious mind* (i.e., here, listening, or the ear, as you will); as all consciousness is "consciousness of something," these activities clearly have objects as their *correlate*.
- Just like the eye, which can run over objects and examine them in various ways, the ear can hear in several ways simultaneously. It so happens that these *simultaneous activities* are fairly well represented in the positioning of our four cardinal points.
- The same schema (divergent and simultaneous for each act of listening) applies just as well to *the most diverse situations* and to objects as different as an isolated sound, lyrics, a symphony, or the hubbub of a public place. On each occasion the diagram must be deciphered and read differently.
- It is only *by extension* that it can be used for recapitulating, defining listening disciplines or summarizing cultural aims.

- Finally, useful though it is for sound and for the musical, the diagram of the four listening modes could also be used to analyze *other types of perception*, especially *visual*.

This diagram is presented for the first time in chapter 6 of the *Treatise*, with a commentary focusing on "listening functions" and perception in general, with some use of the definitions in the *Littré* dictionary.

The horizontal line dividing the diagram in half contrasts, from bottom to top, a disinterested contemplation of the object (presupposing a distancing comparable to Husserl's *épochè*) and the activities that spontaneously focus beyond the object on the groups (natural events, deliberate structures) of which it is likely to become a part.

The vertical line contrasts on the right, origin and facture (*homo faber's* domain), on the left, meaning, cultural references, willed structures *(homo sapiens)*.

The four quadrants thus obtained define four hearing intentions. The two most spontaneous ones go immediately beyond the object to discover both its *origin* and the *meaning* it carries. We would say that the object is taken as an *indicator* or *sign*. Through it, the event or the message is targeted. Conversely, we have to make a special effort to put aside these ordinary aims in order to concentrate our attention on the sound object itself. This *reduced* listening seeks to appreciate its facture (the trace of the agent) and its contexture (the reservoir of potential values). Since we are removing the references (the repertoires of natural events, as well as cultural codes), why do we not find just one aim? Because the object, in order to be appreciated even for itself, still needs to be compared with something. We can really only compare it with other objects that carry comparable factures (typology) or have a similar contexture (morphology).

We would place particular emphasis on this point because we are talking about a fundamental activity of consciousness, the elucidation of which requires an effort of the mind associated with a particular practice. We would repeat that the same theory could be applied to sight and visual objects, a prospect that would greatly broaden the horizons for other research and would shed light on many other relationships between sound and the image.

Figure 2 in section 8.9 is therefore of fundamental importance. This *final summary of listening intentions* illustrates four pathways: two of them lead from the "raw theoretical object" (in other words a theoretical listener's object, when we have not yet determined his intention) to the deciphering of *indicators* or *signs;* two others go in search of the *sound object*, at the cost of striving, against both nature and culture, for disinterested contemplation and deconditioning. Again at this level we find two poles: the traces of an origin and the features of a contexture. The "theoretically" triangular schema will therefore almost immediately show, toward the bottom, the facture-values dichotomy.

Two of the possible listeners concern us in particular: the physicist and the musician. Will they be interested in the same sounds; will they listen in the same way? As their objectives and their pathways are different, what are the chances of their meeting up? Figure 1 (section 8.3) endeavors to answer this question, as delicate as it is decisive.

The physicist sets out from a generator of simple sounds, preferably pure frequencies calibrated in decibels. He measures the signal and uses it as a stimulus to measure the ear's *response* (which he calls the "sensation"), under conditions where he takes no account of the psychological impact. These are not sounds that are useful for music. To obtain them, he expects to recombine this table of simple correlations for complex sounds. Here, as we have shown, he is taking a wrong turn.

The musician is interested in rich sounds and clusters of even more complex sounds. He would like the physicist to analyze them and discover their formula. The physicist has not yet reached this point and persists in giving him the above findings. Thus we have a dialogue, not of the deaf, but between different intentions, in the absence of authentic correlations.

What can their meeting point possibly be? Over the medium, the magnetic tape where, now, sounds that are interesting and complex enough to be musical may be recorded. It is an irrefutable witness, which could be quoted time and again but is, for the moment, dumb. Is that sound, repeated on the recording, still a signal or a perception? It may, precisely, be the *sound object*, common ground finally for individuals trained in reduced listening in groups, away from repertoires and previous codes.

Once this stage is reached, the two practitioners may if need be exchange pathways. As we will see later, the composer could be helped in establishing his score, not by calculating parameters, impracticable or illusory, but by the *lines* on two devices that give the physical *readout* of the signal dynamically and harmonically: the bathygraph and the Sonagraph. Two different interpretations must still shed light on each other: the interpretation given, on the one hand, by the two machines and, on the other, by the human, especially the musical, ear.

We will come back to the four listening modes schema. We have said that sometimes our diagrams summarize hearing functions in general, sometimes the aims of a particular discipline. Thus figure 20 (section 18.3) gives a summary not of a listener's intentions but of traditional music considered as a system.

This type of recapitulation becomes frankly difficult by figure 24 (sections 21.5 and 21.6), where a second square is added inside the first.

This is because the traditional system, which goes *from top to bottom* (from theory and instrumentation to realization in sound and musical performance), and the program for musical research, which, in its quest for possible values and structures, must of necessity start from the sound object and reduced listening, from *bottom to top*, have been superimposed on the same illustration.

If all we had to do were to turn the page upside down depending on which approach we wanted to adopt, no great harm would be done. But why has the musical research square changed terminology? Could it have swung round into the first square? No, the North has not shifted! The references have changed, and the two spaces can no longer be superimposed. We only concertinaed them together to compare them better. In fact, the concrete aspects of sound can no longer be identified with instruments, and objects taken one by one now come just as much from the boxes at the top as at the bottom, depending on whether they take on musical values (pertinent features) or only come from a secondary sound. What we have at the bottom is the typomorphology of sound objects: what is posited at the top is a whole generalized music theory, a potential instrumentarium—that is, what would be acceptable to the ear and doable in new, fully worked-out systems. As this is not the case, our—distant—objective is to set up new reference points: this is the aim of the music theory described in the large diagrams in chapter 34 and the diagram of adequate registers of synthetic instruments.

Thus, the whole of sound as it is given is available to everything that can lend itself to musical abstraction. Two questions remain: *How should we hear? How should we make?* To hear objects, after an initial typological sorting out, it is relatively easy to imagine a morphology that would account for all the ways they could be described, including those that have not yet been defined. But how can we master "making," when today we make music with anything: instruments, sound objects manipulated in various ways, or instruments that are directly calibrated into values instead of guaranteeing, as before, permanence of characteristics? It would require a science of syntheses, which the *Treatise on Musical Objects* never claimed to embark upon, and which is not available even now.

BEYOND THE MARK, SHORT OF THE MARK

So we may come to the conclusion that there is a fundamental dualism between what can be heard (through the device of sound) and what it would be relevant to take on as musical (through the nature of the ear). It would be yet another way of understanding the opposition between creative chance, the *artifact*, and the laws of perception, a sort of scientific fact. This description is not altogether wrong, but the contrary is also true. Surely sound is the opposite of the musical as is the natural of the cultural? We will not go down these one-way streets: they always tend to favor art or science, nature or culture, "object" or "subject" (in the same way as the trivium).

The interest of musical experience lies, on the contrary, in the dialectic between natural and cultural and in the dialogue, personal for everyone, between what can be heard and what is perceived. The word *object* simply sums up the periphrasis:

object of my, your, our listening. The object must not be confused with what is seen (modulator, movement of the bow), or manipulated (sound body, potentiometer input), or stuck together by editing (fragment of tape, closed groove). Here we must talk in terms of generator, procedure, medium. As for the object, it is in my head. This is the stumbling block of all musical thought.

But in its quest for the musical object the *Treatise* does not give its reader adequate means to get out of the trap—if he has already fallen into it—of the *sound object*, by throwing him the other line: *structures of objects*.

The twofold approach we are about to discuss concerns components and groups, materials and works. Of course, the subject-object relationship operates on both of these levels: if the study of material requires simultaneous consideration of the hearing given and the perceptual field, knowledge of the work, faltering or brilliant, necessitates a similar dialectic between the given and the understood. Where does the *Treatise* stand in relation to these two complementary research objectives?

We will borrow a military metaphor. The aim of research makes us think of artillerymen who initially work at "getting the target in their sights." It is likely, since in reality we have two targets, that we will shoot short of the nearer, the material, and risk shooting beyond the more distant, the work.

(a) *Beyond the mark.*

We will start with the distant target. How is it possible, beyond works themselves, to predict the "sort of music" they would come under?

The *Treatise* says that music is *plural*, and this is not an empty form of words. We are quite clear that there are *musics* and that this is not simply a matter of differences between *genres* (such as lyrical or symphonic) but without any doubt of differences in *nature*. In the arts that mobilize the ear there could be a diversification like the diversification in the spatial arts. How this hypothesis can be explored remains to be seen.

In music, as elsewhere, organization is conditioned by the material. We cannot, it is true, deduce the style or function of the building from the properties of prestressed concrete. With freestone, glass, or steel, however, these properties offer specific opportunities for architectural inventiveness and impose specific limitations.

We can make a similar distinction between the continuous and discontinuous in music (especially with pitch) that will give rise to either more calibrated or more profiled musics. These will sometimes resemble a building in stone, sometimes the rods in concrete.

In another connection our musical habits incline us to attribute a "part" to an instrument, which facilitates its dialogue. If there are no identifiable instruments, how will the ear react? Either some process for generating sound will ensure the permanence of a source (if not an intelligible utterance), or else everything will be indissociable and, as it were, fused together. Hence our allusion to two sorts of music, polyphonic and polymorphic, which differ from each other in the same way as ballet and drama differ from sculpture or architecture.

(b) *Short of the mark.*

Beyond these doubtless vague, but indicative, conjectures, the *Treatise* had undertaken to list value relationships without omitting a single one: in other words, it aimed to study every type of interval (generalizing this concept), whether in pitch, timbre, or duration, in both the scalar and the continuous—a research program introduced at the end of book 6, vast indeed, and that remains not only unfinished but abandoned by researchers.

How can we explain this abandonment? Ought I to confess that my project was a mistake? Yes and no. It is possible to be right in theory and historically wrong. I believe, in fact, that one day we will have to come back to a much more careful exploration of all intervallic relationships (in the general sense in which I understand them). But the number of combinations is infinite, and in any case research such as this can no longer find its meaning and its driving force at the elementary level. To test out such a grid, to calibrate its gradations experimentally, we would need a whole army of researchers and years of work. We would need phenomenological physicists or multidisciplinary musicians, drawn to the laboratory even more than the concert hall. History has shown that these people do not exist, and we know that History is never wrong. So what more can I say?

I will say that my utopia—or the program I anticipated—made the error of being overzealous in that I wanted to reinvent a whole musical language system myself, by way of grammar, then syntax, as they wanted to do in Esperanto. For a synthesis of existing language systems, it was doable, and more! Why not in music? Because musics are untranslatable or unpredictable. One cannot be generalized by reference to another. Their creation, through trial and error, rests also on the response of the audience—not the immediate success of the concert, the instantaneous backing of fashion, but the consensus that, much later, will appear as convincing through a transformation of the imaginary of a few into the intelligible for the many. We must, sooner or later, leave objects behind and, even if it means coming back to the *Treatise* later, start to compose.

THE MUSICAL RELATIONSHIP

There is, therefore, between a theory, even generalized, and compositions in progress a gulf that the absence of frames of reference (grammar, syntax, etc.) makes unbridgeable at present. If we allow that the properties of the material have been sufficiently explored, how do the works we must tackle head-on under these conditions appear?

Where these are concerned, we will put the researcher back into the initial situation recommended by the *Treatise* where isolated sounds were concerned. We will impute the same, possibly overweening, ambition to him: to study the generality of (musical) works just as (sound) objects were studied. He will consequently have to give up practically all his previously acquired knowledge or, at least, avoid applying his particular cultural references inappropriately to the whole domain. The project would certainly be absurd if he did not have the support of experimental opportunities similar to those that guided earlier research.

Paradoxically, it was *the lack of two things* that guided us to the concept of the object. Acousmatics (listening without the aid of sight) helped us to turn our attention away from (visible) causes and focus on the form of the sound itself, independently of the instrument that had shaped it. Where effects were concerned, there was no traditional notation either: the amount and novelty of the material obliged us to reinvent music theory.

The same goes for works, as soon as they have been "uncoupled" from the production and representational systems in which we usually place them.

Most notes on contemporary works are only about their production. Where effects are concerned, people are much less eloquent, and with good reason! We will not escape this imbalance either. It will be much easier for us to sum up the conditions for production, and indeed communication, of contemporary musics that come in part, entirely, or by imitation from electroacoustics (even if they fall back on the traditional orchestra) than to describe their effects. Our only originality is in admitting our ignorance. We should like many more composers to have enough humility to accept this maxim, which could be the starting point for shared research: "I know how I did my music, but I don't know what it does for you."

The concert hall is, at least symbolically, the place where these questions occur. While the object already mobilized intersubjectivity in the intimacy of group listening, the work on the formal musical occasion (however aloof the loudspeakers or distant the radio) involves social relationships and carrying out some still not fully understood function of music.

First we will go back to the acousmatic mode to demonstrate that it is not tied to electroacoustic music. Traditional music heard on a record or tape is the same. Some music lovers already used to close their eyes to hear better. So the work is there in its entirety whatever the recording procedure, the groove on the record or tape or digital informatics, except for purely acoustic variations in duplication and reproduction.

We will dismiss hybrid examples: musics as an accompaniment (cinema, ballet) or those that try to reintroduce direct contact through the use of various artifices (the presence of a few traditional instruments or a live electronic performance). Whether successful or not, the counterpoint of several modes of expression, with or without figuration, raises other problems. They do not provide an answer to the essential question of the "meaning of music."

The listener's situation in this respect is essentially not unlike the composer's. We cannot even say that he is at a disadvantage compared with the latter. Having made his work, the composer is judge and judged: it is left to him to hear it in the same way as anyone else. Hence the saying: music is made to be heard. Classical music defers to this.

Before practicing this listening discipline, acousmatic in principle (and not necessarily in practice), we should, however, consider the trade secrets and the pitfalls presented by the electroacoustic instrument, as well as the new opportunities it offers.

Electronic machines and computer science guarantee hitherto unimaginable power, precision, and opportunities. But all sensory relationship between man and instrument has disappeared. From musical conception to musical production there is now nothing but causal relationships, which we must *understand* to control. Certainly, as Charles Sanders Peirce says, the workings of a machine are always comprehensible. Is this true of the workings of music?

As long as the virtuoso is one with his instrument, and his muscles and nerves act directly on it, a spontaneous cybernetics is established between them. But this cybernetics tends to become impoverished as soon as any mechanism comes between the quality of the gesture and the musical effect. The instrument may then offer new resources to the musician but in return imposes the fixed qualities for which it has been made. Once we move from the violin to the piano, the game is already up.

The traditional musical model allows us to distinguish easily between the instrument, music theory, and composing. These handy terms mask realities that are already more subtle: a register, a choice of values, a "program" linked to the production device. Tirelessly, contemporaries have returned to this schema in the hope of calibrating new sources and justifying new systems. What is lacking, apparently, is genuine interest in means of access and notation in the intermediate zone. It seems clear, however, that in the absence of a minimum of notation, it remains impossible to mobilize sources and organize groups.

That is not all. The problems of contemporary music still come under the three sectors of instrumentarium, values, and organization. But they no longer occur as groups of separate variables. In each of these domains we find a great mishmash of instrumental resources, value choices, and readymade musics.

Ambivalent relationships have grown up between the engineer and the musician, very different from those the latter used to have with the instrument maker. The instrument maker was happy to give him the tools. The engineer supplies devices and means of access that already make sequences and determine a system.

Suitably deployed, access to the instrument could be musical. But for the engineer to make a suitable recording, his partner, with the help of a relevant notation system, must have already determined the anticipated variations and values.

Alas, what can the musician do, except laboriously apply the rudiments of an outdated acoustics? After keyboards of pitches, the poor thing puts the blame on pure frequencies and their combinatorial rules, since he has been told that these are the source of timbre. So he leaves it to the engineer.

How do the teams working on so-called concrete or electronic music manage in this respect? The techniques are certainly different and seem opposed to each other: the former is nearer to "stop-motion" film; the second brings to mind the special effects, feedbacks, and cut-ins of video. But in both cases the musician does what he can with what he is given. At the present time it is just as impossible to master instrumental technique as to pin down the interactions of values in a notation. On an individual level everyone manages as best he can. But none of these methods is collectively acceptable or transmissible. This may be the explanation for a truly astonishing phenomenon, unique in the development of music: after a period of ultrarapid growth, a slowing down—a quarter of a century of stumbling around in an ever-increasing welter of productions and inventions.

At the same time, computing was coming on to the scene. For the future the computer looks likely to be a providential aid for the musician and the engineer as far as the instrumentarium and composition are concerned. This is on condition, however, that they are capable of making clear what they want. That is to say, the computer starts by sending us back to present-day problems: means of access and notation. With the tape recorder or the electronic keyboard we can still embark on manipulations without preconceived ideas. Faced with the computer, lack of foresight becomes powerlessness: a silly question gets a silly answer.[4]

At the moment, the means of access to the electronic instrument are like a power station or a calculating machine. With concrete music we are reminded more of work on minerals: extraction, purification, electroacoustic plating . . . not very attractive comparisons. To transform these technologies into musical procedures, we must make them part of ourselves, relax the procedure. We must also be capable of making them adapt to a program.

I would hesitate to mention a personal work in this text, were it not for the fact that the conditions under which it was made perfectly illustrate the uncertainties of today. In composing the *Trièdre fertile* in 1975, we might say I wanted to manipulate the synthesizer, if only once, at the end of my career. It was a way of proving that my personal dislike of electronic sounds had not distorted my analyses of "a priori music." The trihedron in question is the reference trihedron that enables the signal to be described in relation to the three parameters of frequency, time, and intensity. I think I had amply demonstrated that this physical description gives absolutely no insight into sound perception or musical intelligibility. How, then,

4. A double edition of the *Revue musicale* on the Stockholm meeting on music and technology specifically echoes these difficulties. See *Revue musicale*, no. 268–69 (1970).

can music be made with devices that only understand physics? This is the paradox alluded to in the title.

In any case the answer is simple: by using our ears. I was fortunate to be working with Bernard Durr, who is both an electronics engineer and a musician. I left composing the sequences to him, not only because of his skill but to make myself work directly on groups of sounds while shedding all initiative where materials were concerned. *Mutatis mutandis*, I rediscovered, more than twenty-five years later, the type of collaboration I had had with Pierre Henry, when I handed over entire voice or prepared piano sequences to his virtuosity in order to concentrate mainly on assemblage.

So I am not speaking metaphorically when I take the liberty of saying that the seven movements of the *Trièdre fertile* composed themselves, if not without my knowledge at least without my taking the decisions that are usually attributed to the composer. My fellow team member was at the controls of the machine, well acquainted with its functioning. It was by using my ear alone, feeling my way through trial and error, that I chose motifs or fragments and combined them through mixing or editing to draw out a structure, coherent if possible, and if possible, I readily admit, a degree of pleasure.

So I did not *produce* this music; I *heard* it first. Can I say I *understood* it? I made my choices instinctively, without being able in the slightest to justify or explain them. This is a fine example of what I will take the liberty of calling *back-to-front music*: music that we do not know how to make—since we do not know what we are doing—but that we know how to hear.

A second experience was even more enlightening. My account will be brief: I have spent more than three times longer on the analysis of the *Trièdre fertile* than on composing it, and I have not managed to give a satisfactory account of it.

BACK-TO-FRONT MUSIC

To parody Boileau, if we may be so bold: "Even if the sounds to say it come easily— What is clearly conceived of comes from the understanding."

It may well be so much more difficult at present to describe a work, even in broad outline, than to make it, but virtuosity lies less in making than hearing, in both senses of comprehending and perceiving (or more precisely comprehending what we perceive).

This phenomenon is both very classical and very modern. It is very classical in the contrast between overall perceptual evidence—a landscape or a face, for example— and the impossibility of analyzing it rationally. It is very classical also in that other contrast between the complexity of the instantaneous calculations made unconsciously by the painter, the musician, or the writer at the moment of composing and the poverty of the explanations or theories available to him to explain his choices.

It is very modern, on the contrary, in the increasingly talked-about man-machine relationship, the failure to recognize this fact: there is a superb machine, always forgotten, in man also. We would like to see only the rational in ourselves, always in tow behind the irrational, to which, stupidly, we give poor marks to reward the clumsy boy who is good at prose composition.

And so we forget that the human computer (in other words, the ear) is faster than the automaton, more demanding and more *powerful* than it. While schemas are blind, the best electronics engineer loses his way in operational combinatorial systems, and the best music theorist just as much in the problems of his notation, the instinctive ear—that is, the authentic calculator—easily dominates the achievements of even the most sophisticated machine, achievements that it occasionally finds incongruous and often monotonous.

So what is that faculty of appreciation, if not the gift for music, as irreducible as the gift for language? And this is where the composer reclaims that tiny margin for intervention that he still has: either to choose, or to assemble, or finally to decipher.

Then we discover that virtuosity is no longer in our fingers. It is in our heads. The ancient precept "Work at your instrument!" today becomes "Get your head working!" The violinist's and pianist's marvelous craftsmanlike relationship to the tool becomes the two relationships between the electronics engineer who is enough of a musician to plan his schemas, not like a score but a musical instrument, and the musician who is gifted enough to see and bring out the musical content.

From these remarks I can now clarify what has for so long put me at odds with a number of my contemporaries, and not the least important ones:

- Musicians of the postserialist generation hoped, with the help of electronics, to master a music in which the combinatorial rules would be guaranteed through *parametric calculation* with a precision and range not available from traditional instruments. Two distinct facts in the logic of the series run against this project. It is not enough to remind ourselves, as did the *Treatise*, that this type of calculation does not enable us to anticipate perception, which makes the combinatorial system unhearable, in the literal sense. This failure may only be temporary, until computing, better able to analyze natural sound models, provides more convincing syntheses. The second shortcoming to be overcome is by far the more serious: such a willed music cuts itself off from the resources of instinct. Set up a priori, it encloses listening in the predetermined schema the composer wants to put across at all costs, and which he will soon enforce with totalitarian aggressiveness, precisely because of its failure where sensibility is concerned. And soon we will come to assert the superiority of what is written down over what is heard in music.
- In this self-imprisonment of the musical will the obsession with systems will show itself in two ways. Musically, arbitrary structures will be declared

supreme, while instruments will be developed to extremes to serve this will for power. Under these conditions the gulf between musician and technician, their two specializations and their two mind-sets, can only grow wider and is therefore bound to be filled in chaotically with clandestine connivance or plagiarism, in a mutual enslavement that dare not even speak its name. In frankly admitting, as I did earlier, how the tasks were divided between Bernard Durr and myself in the composition of the *Trièdre fertile*, I wanted to show how invention itself could be shared between complementary temperaments without any more claim to dominance from either than in the relationship, let us say, between a pilot and a mechanic. Under these conditions it is no longer appropriate to talk about a singular work or an exclusive composer. It does not really matter, in any case, since it is through a series of trials and errors that music is developed *back-to-front*. This is why I once put forward the term *experimental music*, to break once and for all with the aesthetic pretensions of an art so easily satisfied with itself.

· My final axiom is *communication*, which demands to be explained and taken together with the saying I have already quoted: "Music is made to be heard." Does this mean that the composer says something to a listener who understands it? What precisely did Bach or Beethoven say that we "receive," it seems, so well? At the time of the greatest coherence in music, and for the greatest geniuses, what counted was that we could be almost sure of hearing their music as they themselves heard it. Their genius was in giving birth to music—not in a particularly explicit message but in a testimony truly bearing their hallmark: that things are just so, that the world is as it is, that we hear the same discourse, though ineffable, and share a similar emotion. This is what I call the *meaning* of music, and it clearly surpasses any musicology, any grammar, any syntax, although paradoxically resting on the structures of the system. This is the mystery of music, which people desperately want to reduce to the workings of the intellect, whereas I will doggedly defend its sensory dimension.

Recalling these eminent examples is not without relevance to what is happening today. Quite the contrary. If we put aside the stupid idea of musical progress, we can at least accept that music is being sought *in another way*, since we must cling to the hope of one day discovering other musical "languages." This is hardly the case at the moment. We sometimes ask ourselves this question, only to put it aside immediately by carefully dissociating the "poietic strategy" of the composer and the "esthesic strategy" of the listener.[5] In fact, how can we appreciate the suc-

---

5. As does Molino and, later, Jean-Jacques Nattiez in his *Fondements d'une sémiologie de la musique* (Paris: UGE, "10/18," 1975). [Translated into English as *Music and Discourse: Toward a Semiology of Music* (Princeton, NJ: Princeton University Press, 1990). (Jean Molino is a semiologist; he was Jean-Jacques Nattiez's professor, teaching today in the University of Lausanne.)—Trans.]

cess of the "poietic strategy" (and how does it happen?) except by observing that it has or has not succeeded in putting across, over and above the recognition of the causes, the appreciation of the effects ("it doesn't matter how it's done; the essential thing is what it does to us")?

On the notion of "what can be heard," the authenticity of which cannot be guaranteed and which can be interpreted in different ways, musical experience should come clean. We must rid ourselves once and for all of the mythology of an ineffable Art, almost beyond criticism. We must be systematically skeptical as we listen to works, while still retaining our curiosity and open-mindedness. Even if we lose the aesthetic pleasures—in any case compromised—to which we were accustomed, we will perhaps find others: anthropological, for example. Music is much more (and much less) than music. The activity of composers, like other activities, reflects the procedures, the tendencies, the methods of our technically minded humanity. In it, as elsewhere, strength and weakness, want and plenty are interwoven. Lacking language, since music is fortunately not explicit, this is where the collective unconscious satisfies its obsessions, realizes its fantasies, utters its cries.

The protagonists in this social adventure are the groups and the factions that give the composer his prestige, attract or repel him, admit or exclude him. But ultimately every composer, between the changing environment around him and the musical secret within him, finally delivers his "piece of music." Whatever his justificatory schemas may be, it falls to others to evaluate this product and, lacking its secret, to decipher this secretion. Then we realize once more that the style is the man, as recognizable as the timbre of an instrument. Just as noise is the indelible trace of a natural event, composition is the "composer's noise."

THE COMPOSER'S NOISE

We are not talking about *telegraphers'* noise (as in the too-famous *Information Theory*: interference in the transmission system, scrambling of the message). Physicists were the first to mess around with this term, and then the humanities got hold of it, until general confusion reigned. I use this word with the same meaning as in ordinary experience. That noise heard by the Native American on the lookout, the caver, the technician, is quite the opposite of disorder: it is the natural organization of sound coming from an event whose rationality is worked out backward from the clues. Contrary to the sign, which is intentional, contrary also to "background noise" or interference, noise is an indiscreet trace of what we would really like to hide. The composer would like to put his idea across. He is revealed through his noise.

Musicological misunderstanding comes essentially from the fact that we suppose the problem to be resolved. In new musics we should like to find a surprising discourse in a familiar language system. This is tantamount not only to guessing what the language model will be but to supposing that the language system is already formed. We might hope, more wisely, that the listener and the composer are in the same situation with regard to the work, considered as a meaningful object. But this is not automatically the case: there is nothing to say that in music, the nature of which is to invent and destroy itself in order to be reborn, the new work will be musically meaningful. Viewed like this, it may be meaningless or mad. We must look for its purpose elsewhere, since everything, it seems, is meaningful. . . . The concept of noise then becomes appropriate, without irony.

Perhaps, then, we will have to look even more closely. Sometimes we will examine fragments of works, applying the four listening modes to each of them as we did for elementary objects; at other times we will take a bird's-eye view of the whole of musical production in order to sketch out its typology: the four listening modes diagram will be able to provide classifications and a summary of overall trends, as was previously the case.

Once again, as we cannot get so rapidly to the heart of the matter, we are trying to bring our target into the frame by shooting either beyond or short of the mark.

TYPOLOGY OF CONTEMPORARY MUSICS

Shooting beyond the mark is the easier. The work, this new musical object, is only too easy to overshoot: we are aiming beyond it at a different object. Suppose we indulge this natural, but also cultural, inclination. It will take us to the outermost boxes at the top of the diagram on both sides, the agent (sector I) and the systems (sector 4). Because we have not examined the work for itself, we will happily place it in categories dealing with processes and procedures—that is, instruments and theories.

This is what we used to do, in the best of all possible worlds, with eighteenth-century music, for example. But then our mode of listening, harmoniously balanced between these cardinal points, became more particular about authorial styles, nuances of the system, and finally interactions of sonorities or values in the reduced listening in sectors 2 and 3. Failing to explain what happens at the bottom, we now take flight toward the top. Boxes 1 and 4 will all too conveniently reconcile wildly differing works in the making. In the closed field of musical affirmation we may expect to find conflicting, exclusive, eccentric pairs, as the top sectors can be when they are cacophonous.

(a) Historically, the first conflict is between *systematizers* and *empiricists*, inventors of schemas and instruments. Instruments (shown in sector 1) designate nascent musics by their type of manufacture (concrete, electronic), their medium *(music for tape)*, or their mode of transmission (acousmatic, live, mixed). The aesthetics follow, instinctive, premature: a collage of objects (in the trivial sense) or a sequential electronic synthesis. Then come the combination of techniques in elec-

troacoustics and the project of a computer program. The inventor, in direct contact with the machine, is helpless. . . . We have described his new learning processes and his unexpected regression into sound. The listener, outside the loop, is amazed, admires, hates, and asks how it's done, having failed to make his impressions clear.

However, by a historical synchrony from which two or three generations will suffer, systems strive to lock on to the most opportune technique, if possible, or even impose their own precedent on it. This was how electronic music started. We should go back further, however, to examine serial music as such in the light of the four listening modes. A defector from tradition, Schoenberg made the series, which in any case was invented by someone else,[6] into the ultimate weapon. For destroying the tonal system nothing, in fact, is more effective than to permutate the twelve sounds without omission or repetition. This precept is not positive but negative: it certainly forces listening to adopt a reference system other than major or minor. What, precisely? A dialectic of intervals? A cultural mode that immediately replaces centuries of natural intelligibility? That is asking a lot of the ear. It may be that it scarcely perceives the series but instead what it did not hear before: subtle discourses, graduated attacks, in short, *sonority* (from *dynamics* to the *Klangfarbenmelodie*), which I make bold to call *concrete* aspects. And so the sweetmeats of sound seemingly take the place of defunct musicality. Alban Berg's genius can cope with this, showing how much even an arbitrary system can be surpassed by its overall treatment and the ardor of the musical impulse. Webern, paradoxically, is very particular about objects. Somewhere, clandestinely, links are being reestablished with a tradition that has lost its brand. After the conjuring tricks performed by these experts, too bad for the followers: those who, lacking talent if not shrewdness, believed their music would be guaranteed by the formula. Thus it happens that sector 4 at the height of its aims quite simply takes us back to sector 1.

(b) Now we will move on to another conflict, which does not arise from an excess of dialectic but the doubtless legitimate desire to compensate for these frustrations: the performance/contemplation pair.

The musical field is now so deserted that it is advisable to desert it. People are looking elsewhere, further still. Either for want of an ear, the eye will be offered something to take in, or for want of meaning, there will be states of mind without any discourse, the work now repudiated. Occasionally these extremes meet. While Kagel, among others, makes much of *acting music*, and *repetitive music* claims to

---

6. Josef Matthias Hauer, the author of a *Traité de musique atonale*, published in Vienna in 1920, who called himself "the spiritual father of twelve-tone music, and, in spite of mediocre plagiarists, the only person who knows what to do with it." Cf. Arnold Schoenberg, *Le style et l'idée*, writings collected by Léonard Stein, translated from English by Christiane de Lisle (Paris: Buchet/Chastel, 1977); and *Style and Idea* (London: Faber and Faber, 1975).

smuggle in relaxation from India, Cage kills two birds with one stone. Opus no. X (if it has a number), by repeating the same notes on the piano, banged out three hundred times by an insistent forearm, gives its dumbfounded listeners food for both eyes and ears with ridiculous economy, which challenges snobbery in a way that cannot be ignored: if you are with it, you must go through with it. Another unforgettable work is those few minutes of silence, which bring to mind all those minutes of meditation on the memory of the departed—which, quite simply, make one think. What has just disappeared here is music, and this does take some thinking about. Luc Ferrari, less inhuman, fills this gap: he records, and with subtlety, anything and everything, sounds of the countryside, for example, and asks us to listen as attentively as he does. Thus, from provocation to extreme examples, we are forced to hear silence, or repetition, or anything at all, in which we now have to assume there is music, which, after all, is no worse than the opposite deviation: musical voyeurism, complete with erotic video and cello.

(c) Yet music, now so far off, must be brought back. Here we must return to the earnest, the respectable, which can sometimes be so tedious. As there is no musical necessity (no longer any system) or personal risk-taking (now condemned as authorial whim), both *chance and necessity* are needed, to quote the time-honored expression. Randomness, if we believe physicists, follows the laws of the cosmos, and also ensures the emancipation of the man in the street. Back to sector 1, specially designed for the ideas of participants. *Open works* are played from the rostrum where scores are interchanged, and from scores where sequences are interchanged. Failing one convincing work, we will have several. Drawing lots protects this type of cheating. At the opposite extreme, which perhaps amounts to the same thing, an algorithm will be chosen, a geometric figure, or perhaps a stochastic model, from which a rigorous work, immediately considered scientific, will be deduced. Credulous critics and ordinary people, easily pleased, always manage to hear something: the composer, a genius of course, also gets by, sometimes successfully.... And then, in the salons, how can we close our doors on the science that now inhabits music?

We will have a very great fall—oh, how great!—if we persist in looking in the lower quadrants for sound, become contemptible, or the musical, improbable.... The *époché*, even Husserl's, will be a sorry sight. Will we then be *reduced* to the musicianly condition?

AN UNDESIRABLE TEACHING METHOD

Going back to the lower levels of a listening mode stripped of all ideology is not just a matter of bias, which could still be a matter for discussion. We must also have the desire. Without the desire for a pure music, there would be no criticism of ideology. For the higher quadrants, as we have seen, have moments of sublimity.

What do the musical content and even the absence of (formerly) musical pleasure matter, if the music carries us toward action or contemplation, suggests science or revolution? See the orchestra freed from its conductor, that fascist, and delivered from its composer, that overlord. We will do better than they, in a collective where we share out the musical domain among ourselves, after agrarian reform: to each instrumentalist his genius and even the right, the recommendation, to use his instrument the wrong way round, to scrape the strings behind the bridge, to rattle his clarinet. Would we be blamed if we made concrete music ourselves? In the final analysis, why have professionals, since the public is talented and everyone is *creative*? If Society (always Society) would only lift its taboos! They are lifted. This type of liberation fits in nicely with industry, which manufactures musical automata with directions for use, providing more and more machines and talents at democratic prices. At school, as a consequence, the antiquated question of music theory and deadly dull lessons is resolved. That *do re mi fa so* is doubly outmoded: the last vestige of a dead music, the deviation of an ear bidden to many other types of concert.

For the author of the *Treatise* the situation took a turn that was devastating or comical, depending on his state of mind, when, doubtless carried along on the waves of '68, he found himself once more (associate) professor at the Conservatoire national de musique in Paris.

So here I teach music theory and the instrument, even generalized and even electroacoustic, in an incongruous respect for tradition, beneath the frowning face of my violinist father. And I consider myself doubly suspect. Certainly, I have called for another mode of listening in the face of the enormous resources of sound, advocated the approach through objects in the face of the unknown capacities of the ear. But I also identify with traditional practice, natural constraints, and also ever more training, as much in the new as the old. Now, the trend is for illusionism and facileness. The "allergy to work" finds its justification here.

Music theory, even generalized, is not electroacoustic; it belongs to the ear. These ideas are not so very new; they are prefigured either in our written Western tradition or in other unwritten traditions, sometimes more crudely, sometimes more subtly. Electroacoustic systems are powerful, but they are not musical instruments; they are sound machines. And before putting questions to the computer, we must know what we ourselves think.

This brings us back very prosaically to the lower portions of the plan, the reduced listening sectors, and the teacher's unwelcome lecture.

There is no reason either to be offended or to put out the flags just because student composers, after a few months of training, can obtain ingenious sequences, varying from the previously unheard to the hackneyed, from machines. This means that outmoded grammar and syntax and unwelcome work on an instrument, which required so much time to be a virtuoso, will not be scrapped so rapidly or without opposition. How can we make people understand this type of requirement, when everything seems so easy, given in advance and trendy? I will endeavor to give three pieces of advice for anyone who wants to hear them:

(a) The first piece of advice, logically speaking, will doubtless be the last to be followed, once real interdisciplinary research has been established. I have already said that it should begin with a far-reaching sampling of fragments of works, chosen from the most significant. It is pointless, in fact, to study the factures and values of an isolated fragment. It will not give up its secrets: no one can tell whether such factures are productive or the value-relationships pertinent. It is only with many more fragments, after attempts at classification, and comparing and contrasting through repeated listening, that this will one day become clear in a typology of musical registration and possible morphological reference points. As I said, this research, necessarily laborious, has hardly even begun. Meanwhile, what can be done?

(b) The second piece of advice concerns the instrument, which is misused in two ways, whether insolently exploited while blaming the procedure, or cunningly camouflaged, confusing the issue. Filtering and mixing, loops and insertions, accumulations, reverberations are to experimental music, as the pedal is to the piano: confusion in cahoots with inadequacy. It is time to be open about the procedure, without dressing it up, and to endeavor, if possible, to balance it out with an interplay of relationships that will give our "piece of music" some meaning. Too bad if this piece sounds more like Czerny than Chopin. Many a learner has finally acknowledged that these *compulsory studies* bore more fruit than *free composition*, which, in any case, is not prohibited.

(c) But how will we go about this type of exercise? Are two years of study to lead so soon to a lack of confidence in expression? We have insinuated that this is not so. What counts, *even for a composer*, is knowing how to hear musically and being capable of agreeing on the same passage with others in an adequate consensus. Why not go back, then, to that respectworthy exercise: *theme and variation?* Rather than freedom of expression, that pitfall, the beginner is given freedom of choice. From his predecessors' endeavors let him take as his theme the passage he particularly likes. We will be careful not to inquire into the reasons for his choice. At the very most we may help him to imagine his personal variation by questioning him about what he intends to keep and what he is trying to transform. Group listening with the teaching team will assess the success or failure of the exercise. Words are not important. We simply need to observe whether it "works" or "doesn't work." And so, uninterrupted by speech, the musical communication circuit is completed.

THE THREE LEVELS OF THE SCORE

It is perhaps disconcerting to see us, after so many warnings, recommending the use of the bathygraph and the Sonagraph to describe a piece of music. We have taken the precaution of pointing out in the third part of this work the usefulness and the limitations of this: while machines work in accordance with their scientific logic, the musician's activity is divided between sound and the musical. As soon as notation and, even more, the score come into the equation in electronic musics, these three levels of analysis are very clearly needed.

These score-writing exercises have given rise to many setbacks and many criticisms at the Conservatoire. They have been judged too easy, or too difficult, pointless or essential, premature or outdated. Directions about editing or planning can always be given in personal notes on the score. These more or less improvised outlines are not really like scores: who, in this busy world, would take on the monastic task of giving a completely exhaustive account of what has been done or what is being heard? Ligeti, it appears, made one of his students spend more than a year on a color representation of a work that lasted a few minutes. This precedent is more discouraging than convincing.

In fact, setting up a score should not be the object of individual or private study. It should sum up different approaches and be based on a consensus.

The traditional score, as we know, strikes a very good balance between making and hearing, in the higher quadrants of the diagram. An experimental score, made after the event for the purposes of research, can and should be considered differently. Why not from bottom to top—on the three levels of the physical, sound, and the musical—which would give three types of synchronous representation describing three different aspects of the course of the sound?

On the physical level the bathygraph and the Sonagraph give two graphs of the *signal* in *real time*: its projection on the dynamic and the harmonic plane. Of course, these lines are not very intelligible because perceptions of sound differ so much (by anamorphosis) from the signal on the printout. But for giving a rough organization of events these two printouts will save hundreds of hours of painstaking, often impossible and probably premature, work. It is a silent but precise temporal map.

The next interpretation focuses on sound. Some details of the dynamic graph can be ignored, despite their accuracy. Others show essential stresses. Similarly, in harmonic contents we will still have to decipher what is heard as tonic, mass, or trajectory in accordance with what the *Treatise* teaches us, and which the graph does not conform to. This level of sound, we should not forget, is objective: it is what is heard by ordinary people who are not deaf and who are paying attention.

Only the musical level, in third place, is problematic, since we have to decide from one sound to another, from one passage to another, if there is a fortuitous or essential relationship. Here interpretation is doubly open. Because there are no reference structures, there are no rules. And because there is no model, everyone hears the music in his own way. This is where authorial intention and the listener's interpretation come face-to-face, just like prose composition and translation; furthermore, there can be several versions among various "interpreters." If everyone agrees on a passage, it is a good sign, not of the excellence of its musical value but of the principles, good or bad, on which in the general view it rests.

MUSIC AS WILL OR REPRESENTATION

This allusion to Schopenhauer (taken from Wagner and Nietzsche) may seem superfluous. Well, yes it is an author's whim! I like the expression, and the atmosphere around it, the chiaroscuro of a philosophy of music where we will never have the last word. Allow me to appropriate it as a final comment, for nothing describes the situation better.

Here, on the one hand, are our musicians faced with the most difficult problems of the automaton and the calculator, very different from the subject of music itself. And, on the other hand, their social function is becoming obscured, pulled in two directions between elitism and demagogy, voluntarism and spontaneity. What they produce reflects the huge divorce between prodigious means and uncertain ends: so it is indeed a music of its time.

With music man is as he is elsewhere; and so his world is naively "set to music." Our innovations, apparently unobjectionable, are accompanied in this midcentury by two others: atomic explosions and space exploration. Will I make so bold as to compare the closed groove (that first splitting of sound) with atomic fission, and the synthesis of frequencies with atomic fusion?

These phenomena have no common measure except in the mind. The musical object was indivisible, sound limited to the range of the voice and the gesture. Now it bestrides electromagnetic waves, and conversely the electronic combinatorial system prefigures its course. And yet in one respect man remains the master of events, provided, of course, that he wishes to do so and does not pretend to be unaware that he possesses the machine par excellence, an inner calculator.

The ear can easily decipher the most complex sound sequence, whereas graphs are utterly baffling. And that does not satisfy it: sound is never complex enough to be interesting if it does not bear the unexpected, here very simple, mark of an intelligible intention (we do not know how, but we will know why). If need be, the ear will invent it. When two sound sequences of any sort interact, a dialogue is inevitably set up in the two temporal dimensions of simultaneity and succession. And just as the ear knew how to separate tracks technically, it prepares itself just as spontaneously to distinguish voices, at least if it is spoken to. Whether the speech is articulate or muddled, willed or fortuitous, it knows immediately whether it finds it interesting, pleasurable, or otherwise. So we must carefully reconsider that propensity toward fugue and counterpoint that seemed to be dictated by the logic of a particular time and to which we so spontaneously, involuntarily, return. Just as skilled in decoding noise as meaning, the ear is always looking for an interpretation. Not only is it capable of doing this, but it cannot do otherwise.

In traditional music the musical was given in advance, guaranteed by the score. The *added value*—if I may use this expression—was sound. In experiential music sound is heard as a matter of course, and the ear wonders about the musical. This is certainly not a reason for advocating chance or denying oneself any sort of purpose, but this purpose should aim toward verifying hypotheses, by systematically varying the experimental conditions while, most importantly, preferring the slightest proof to the most grandiose pretensions.

And this is how, finally, the function of music is revealed. The work in hand is exposed to hybrid, unstable types of listening, fluctuating between simultaneous goals. The essential thing is the response, more than the purpose. Hence the expression "back-to-front music" that I suggested. This music, which we do not know how to make but which we know how to hear, insults our will to power. We would do well, however, to learn to recognize our image all over again in this music, inverted in the mirror of sound. It is often said that immense resources of the human brain remain unknown or untapped. If we only make the music we can conceive of, we perpetuate banality. If we scale the heights of the absurd, we are sometimes rebuffed, and that is very fortunate for us. For it is our own indispensability that is revealed in our successes, sometimes aided by chance. Music can reveal this "of man" to us: only we must learn to allow ourselves to be guided by our divinations rather than our deliberations.

THE TARGET

This approach through understanding could apply to the whole of art. I will keep to music. In contrast to science, which gives us mastery over nature, music, complementarily, can enlighten us about ourselves. But the mode of understanding that it promises is not the same as anthropology, does not satisfy a purely—and coldly—intellectual curiosity. In fact, we are not so much interested in explaining our own workings as activating them, in short, living and no longer being alone in the world.

Music is "man described to man in the language of things." This expression, which concludes the *Treatise*, may seem sibylline and too literary. When we get to this point, we feel some reluctance to go further. But I have made up my mind, finally, to express my desire, even my will. Perhaps then my fears and my admonishments will be better understood.

In shooting short of the mark in my teaching and beyond the mark on contemporary works, considered from a typological point of view, I have certainly gone against the rules. But I very much fear I am not wrong in finding in present-day music not so much a will to create as the dull representation of the world we are making—its liking for results, its blind mechanization, its foolhardiness, its brazenness. Just like the solar system, which at the moment is closed to us, the musical

560 MUSIC AS A DISCIPLINE

domain remains a closed field. Almost our only choice is between accessible but uninhabitable planets and others, doubtless inhabitable but out of reach. It is the same with the musics we should like to emigrate to.

The will, under these conditions, feels aggrieved, abandons great projects, hunches over miserable trifles. Competition, from being superhuman, becomes petty, just like our concerts where people hesitate between magic unconditional freedom and submission to determinism. And so we are led back into the formulae and group drug-taking wilderness.

Science, which knows its way around where innovation is concerned, had nevertheless taught us its lesson, which we could not hear: it uses a vast array of devices principally to question categories of reasoning or to feed the imagination. Some of this equipment is put on standby, with the responsibility for verifying improbable ideas remotely—Einstein's, for example. For their part, mathematicians are trying to outdo physicists in extraordinary ideas, to bring into the world mathematical entities amazing enough to espouse the real or go before it. Such is authentic science as it is not taught, no more scientific, it seems, than Marx was Marxist, in a to-ing and fro-ing between the conceivable and the possible, very similar in music to the confrontation I have referred to again and again: between making and hearing.

We should not be misled by the term *confrontation*. Civilizations more skilled than ours in martial arts teach us that in combat the most important thing is not so much to have the upper hand, to put down the enemy, but to tackle him with an equal measure of strength. It is as an extra, and without expressly wishing it, that the archer hits his outward target: he was aiming at a different one, within himself. I have always thought, I have sometimes whispered, that in the matter of martial arts all we have left in the West is music. A violin, a voice, a work is a duel, a duo, judo. Knowing how to yield, outsmart the adversary, give him his own way in order to take a hold over him—this, in the great periods of history, was *playing* music.

March 1977

POSTSCRIPT

When it is a matter of thinking, the greater the work done—which does not coincide in the least with the number and extent of the writings—the richer, in this work, is the unthought, that is to say what through this work and by it alone, comes toward us as if never yet thought.

—Heidegger[1]

But if they want to follow a plan similar to mine, they do not need me to say anything more to them other than what I have already said in this discourse; for if they are able to go further than I have done, they will be so all the more to find by themselves everything that I think I have found . . . and they would have much less pleasure in learning it from me than from themselves: and furthermore the habit that they will acquire by first of all seeking out the easy things and passing gradually, by degrees, to others which are more difficult, will be more use to them than all my teachings could be.

—Descartes[2]

1. Martin Heidegger, *Le principe de raison* (Paris: Gallimard, 1962). Translated into English as *The Principle of Reason* (Bloomington: Indiana University Press, 1991).—Trans.

2. René Descartes, *Discours de la méthode* (Cambridge: Cambridge University Press, 1923), 29. Translated into English as *Discourse on Method and Meditations* (New York: Liberal Art Press, 1960).—Trans.

INDEX

abstract (adjective), 7, 8, 27, 31, 32, 35, 36, 41, 43, 82, 83, 85, 86, 87, 90, 96, 97, 112, 189, 195, 197, 248, 251, 252, 254, 260, 290, 381, 404, 436, 439, 453, 457, 468, 529, 542; definition of, 250; (verb) 7, 8, 79, 251, 253, 260, 437. *See also* concrete

accumulation, 347, 348, 361, 363, 365, 366, 404, 424, 445, 556. *See also* typology

acoulogy, 244, 247, 402; definition of, 233, 400

acousmatic, xxxiii, 15, 63, 187, 192, 195, 210, 211, 270, 329, 435, 546, 552; definition of, 65–69, 545; listening modes, 111, 113, 115, 264, 328, 369, 370, 373

acoustics, 65, 98, 332, 385, 417, 481; musical, 13, 101, 119–129, 165, 215, 532, 534; spatial, 54

Adorno, Theodor, 502, 516, 517, 518, 520, 522, 523, 524

aesthetics, 2, 4, 7, 8, 42, 100, 152, 269, 376, 535; music and, 510

Alain, O., 379, 380

allure, 373, 375, 383, 399, 400, 401, 436, 437–439, 443–449, 454, 459, 460, 468, 470, 471, 534; definition of, 318

amplitude, 65, 89, 91, 123, 124, 134, 175–177, 184–185, 395, 404, 407, 434, 446, 460, 496

analysis, 38, 57, 65, 97, 132, 135, 218, 322, 460, 462, 491, 493, 497, 532, 536, 537, 548; Fourier, 174; instrumental, 34, 41, 44, 45; language, 242, 248, 260, 286, 287; mathematical, 138, 151;

perception, 81, 86, 89, 91, 111, 156, 157, 158; in Programme of Musical Research, 292, 295, 300, 304, 352, 354, 355, 370, 372, 380, 397, 398, 400, 402, 403, 419, 431, 434, 437, 438, 440, 442, 446, 451, 454, 462–474, 503

anamorphosis, 435, 452, 455, 557; definition of, 163; functional, 187, 188; temporal, 194, 196, 198, 426, 453, 470

a priori, music, 5–7, 277, 393, 483, 489, 491, 501, 532, 547, 549; thinking, 59, 92, 239, 268, 382, 433, 459. *See also* serial music

articulation, 158, 187, 213, 226, 229, 246, 268, 290, 313, 314, 329, 423; stress, 289, 300, 304, 313, 315, 317, 319, 396

Art of the Fugue, 97, 152, 246

atonal, 4, 394, 486, 487

attack, 27, 38, 61, 125, 147, 151, 159, 161, 164, 165, 169–183, 187, 189, 193–199, 258, 228, 237, 288, 312, 314, 319, 329, 335, 363, 368–370, 374, 403, 423–430, 437, 448, 451, 471, 473, 506, 508, 515, 533, 553

Bach, J., 97, 363, 418, 525, 550

balance, 198, 199, 238, 355, 356, 358, 360, 363, 369, 402, 426, 429, 473; originality, 344–352

banality, 360, 462

Baschet brothers, 32, 281, 327, 328

Baudelaire, C., 74

Bayle, F., xl